NEW YORK AND LOS ANGELES

EDITED BY DAVID HALLE

New York & Los Angeles

Politics, Society, and Culture

A COMPARATIVE VIEW

The University of Chicago Press
CHICAGO AND LONDON

David Halle is professor of sociology and director of the LeRoy Neiman Center for the Study of American Society and Culture at the University of California, Los Angeles. He is also an adjunct professor at the City University of New York's Graduate Center and the author of *America's Working Man: Work, Home, and Politics among Blue-Collar Property Owners* and *Inside Culture: Art and Class in the American Home,* both published by the University of Chicago Press.

The University of Chicago Press, Chicago 60637
The University of Chicago Press, Ltd., London

Printed in the United States of America

12 11 10 09 08 07 06 05 04 03   1 2 3 4 5

ISBN: 0-226-31369-7 (cloth)
ISBN: 0-226-31370-0 (paper)

Library of Congress Cataloging-in-Publication Data

New York and Los Angeles : politics, society, and culture : a comparative view / edited by David Halle.
p. cm.
Includes bibliographical references and index.
ISBN 0-226-31369-7 (cloth) — ISBN 0-226-31370-0 (paper)
1. New York (N.Y.)—Politics and government—20th century. 2. Los Angeles (Calif.)—Politics and government—20th century. 3. New York (N.Y.)—Social conditions—20th century. 4. Los Angeles (Calif.)—Social conditions—20th century. 5. New York (N.Y.)—Civilization—20th century. 6. Los Angeles (Calif.)—Civilization—20th century. I. Halle, David.

JS1228 .N385 2003
307.76′09747′1—dc21

2002156524

♾ The paper used in this publication meets the minimum requirements of the American National Standard for Information Sciences—Permanence of Paper for Printed Library Materials, ANSI Z39.48-1992.

CONTENTS

ILLUSTRATIONS

FIGURES

TABLES

ACKNOWLEDGMENTS

Producing a book that considers the nation's two largest cities and surrounding regions is a vast enterprise that requires the best thinking and research of many people. My thanks to the distinguished authors of the volume's chapters who worked so hard on this task.

LeRoy Neiman created *Times Square* suitably Los Angelized for the book cover. Bennie Terry and Guillermo Gonzalez directed the multimedia materials. Camilo Vergara was principle photographer. Several of his insights, derived from a lifetime of exploring the cities of New York and Los Angeles, are included in the photo captions. He took all photos in the book except those otherwise credited and i.8, 2.4, 2.5, and 7.1, which were taken by me. Robert Gedeon was a superb editorial assistant. Gihong Yi was principle data analyst and helped to make this the first book on New York and Los Angeles to incorporate the results of the 2000 census. Kevin Rafter and Joshua Smith were principle cartographers. Andrew Beveridge's experience of making thematic maps for the *New York Times* over the past fifteen years was invaluable.

Many others contributed comments and suggestions. They include César Ayala, Michael Dear, Mitch Duneier, Herbert Gans, Carla and Malcolm Halle, Phil Kasinitz, Bill Kornblum, Barbara Lal, Ivan Light, Wilfredo Lugo, David McBride, Louise Mirrer, Philip Mirrer-Singer, Allen Scott, Edward Soja, Jill Stein, Eddie Telles, France Winddance Twine, Kathryn Wylde, Tim Yarger, and Sharon Zukin.

LeRoy and Janet Neiman's generous gift, which established the UCLA LeRoy Neiman Center for the Study of American Society and Culture, provided a wonderful base for a complex book of this kind.

The National Science Foundation (DUE-0088657), the Russell Sage Foundation, and the Haynes Foundation provided additional financial support. Any opinions, findings, and conclusions expressed here are those of the authors and do not necessarily reflect the views of these foundations.

INTRODUCTION

The New York and Los Angeles Schools

David Halle

This book compares and contrasts politics, society, and culture in Los Angeles and New York—the cities as well as their surrounding regions. New York, with 8 million residents in 2000, and Los Angeles, with 3.7 million, are America's two most populous cities. Los Angeles County is the nation's most populous county, with 9.5 million residents in 2000, while the 21.2 million people of the New York region (i.e., the New York consolidated metropolitan statistical area [CMSA], as defined by the Census Bureau) exceed that of any other region (see fig. i.1).

Los Angeles and New York symbolize the two major, but apparently contrasting, developments of the modern American megalopolis. In Los Angeles, no longer does a central urban core organize the hinterland. Instead, there are multiple clusters of economic and social activity dispersed around the region. "Los Angeles," in short, connotes sprawl and decentralization.

"New York," by contrast, has for the past three decades represented renewed interest in the central city as a place to work and to live, albeit punctuated by periods of economic recession, high crime, and now urban terrorism. It has symbolized the rediscovery of, and refocus on, the urban core, especially in this case Manhattan, but also inner sections of Brooklyn, Queens, and the Bronx.[1]

Thus Los Angeles and New York are ideal laboratories for studying the two most interesting developments in urban America: the vitality of urban peripheries and the return to the urban core, to the city. The essays in this volume capture much of what is new and exciting in urban and suburban studies.

The contrasts between the way the two cities and regions are often

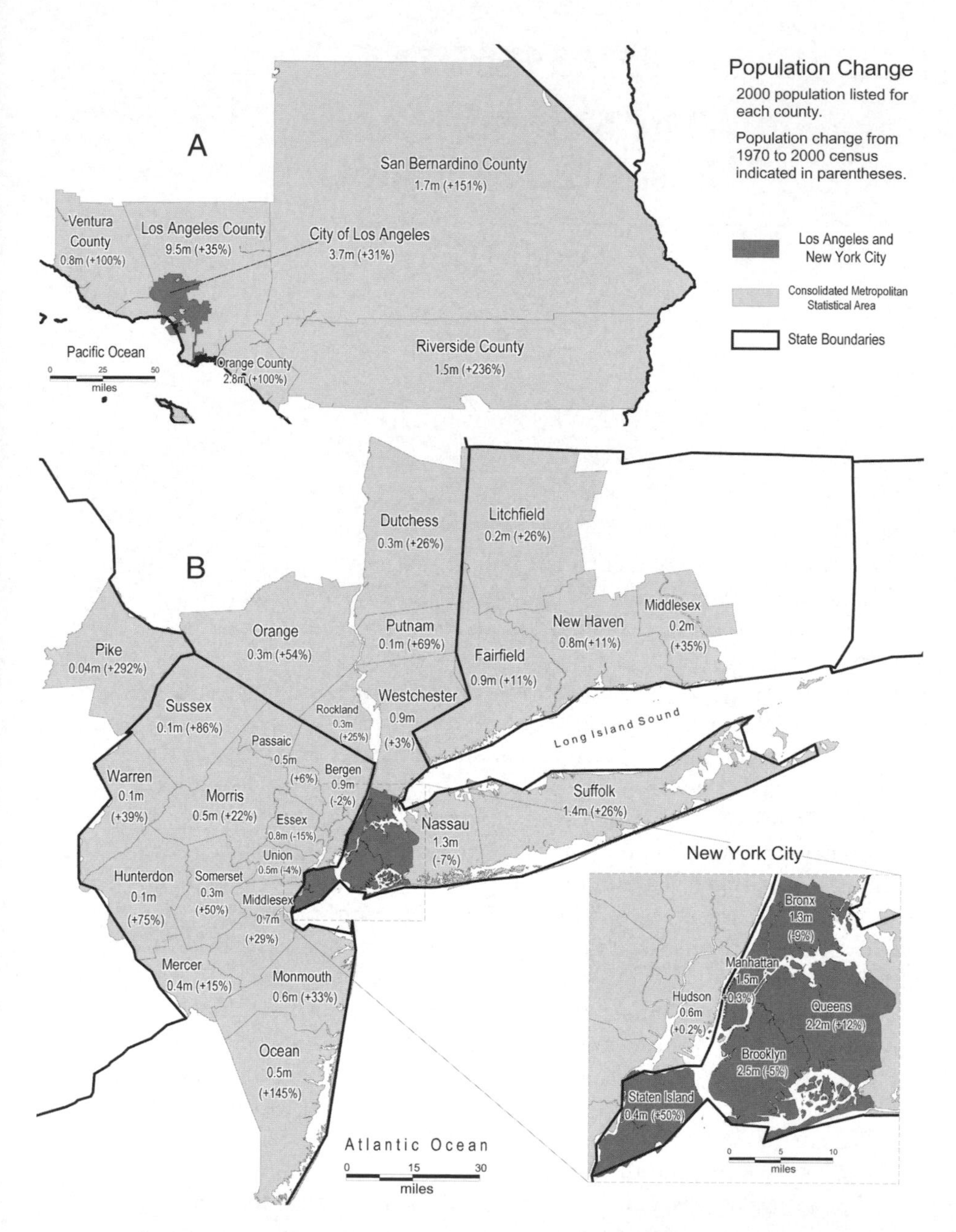

Figure i.1. *A,* City of Los Angeles and CMSA: Boundaries and Population Change, 1970–2000. *B,* New York City and CMSA: Boundaries and Population Change, 1970–2000

Figure i.2. Disney Hall under Construction, Bunker Hill Area of Downtown Los Angeles, February 2002. In 1992 Frank Gehry was picked to design the future home of the Los Angeles Philharmonic Orchestra, but because of cost overruns and leadership problems only the $116 million underground parking structure was built. Energized by the triumph of Gehry's Guggenheim Museum in Bilbao, work resumed on Disney Hall in 1999. A major concern is the limited street life in the area, especially on Grand Avenue "You have to bring life to that street," cautioned Gehry. "There ain't no there there."

viewed are partly based on real differences, but the differences should not be exaggerated. For example, the city of Los Angeles has long had a project to make the central city attractive to the wealthy and middle class. This has focused, for instance, on the construction of a series of major cultural centers downtown, of which the latest is the Disney Center designed by Frank Gehry and built as the home of the Los Angeles Philarmonic (fig. i.2). There is also an emerging urban parks movement, referred to as the "greening of Los Angeles," that seeks to develop forsaken and blighted inner-city areas into parks, bikeways, and nature preserves. The centerpiece of this movement is the restoration of the Los Angeles River (Mozingo 2000). Still, only 10 percent of the land within the city limits of Los Angeles is currently designated as open space, compared with 27 percent of the land in New York City. Also, it will be hard to convince locals that, in the semisecluded banks of the river (fig. i.3), they will not be easy crime targets. Further, the new cultural centers are

Figure i.3. The Los Angeles River, Downtown (Fourth Street). The Los Angeles River bank is typically desolate and viewed as too isolated for safe recreation. Also, the water is polluted and often used by local residents as a garbage repository. There is a citywide move to make the river bank a desirable recreation site. Perhaps the hardest part will be to ensure that, as people descend to the semisecluded riverbank, they feel safe from crime (along the lines of William Whyte's successful plan to open up Bryant Park in New York City [fig. i.10]).

beset by doubts as to whether audiences will wish to live nearby rather than just drive in and out of the cavernous parking entrances and exits that dominate Grand Avenue (Goldin 2002). Thus the project to make downtown Los Angeles an attractive place for residence by the well-to-do as well as the poor is fraught with difficulty. (For a detailed history of the redevelopment efforts in downtown Los Angeles, see Loukaitou-Sideris and Banerjee [1998].)

Likewise, the stereotype that "Los Angeles" is hyper spread out compared with New York (and other urban areas in America) is true only if stated carefully and with a distinction between geographic spread, where it is basically correct, and population density/housing size, where it is far less true. Considering geographic spread, the city of Los Angeles's 496 square miles exceeds but certainly does not dwarf New York City's 303 square miles. But Los Angeles County, which includes and surrounds the city of Los Angeles, contains 4,089 square miles, over twice as much as the combined land of New York City and the six New York/

New Jersey counties that surround New York City, which together constitute 1,746 square miles (see fig. i.1). Finally, at the level of the region, defined as the Census Bureau's consolidated metropolitan statistical area, the contrast sharpens further. The Los Angeles CMSA, which consists of Los Angeles County and the four counties that surround it, contains an enormous 34,040 square miles of land, while the New York CMSA, which includes New York City, Long Island, several New York counties north of New York City, a large part of New Jersey, parts of Connecticut, and Pike County, Pennsylvania, contains 11,670 square miles, only about a third of the square miles of the Los Angeles CMSA.

But if Los Angeles is so geographically spread out why do the approaches by air to the city of Los Angeles reveal residential areas as densely packed with single family housing as much of the single family housing in the New York region (fig. i.4)? The answer is that simple comparisons of square miles can be misleading when considering population density/housing size, for large parts of the five county Los Angeles CMSA are too hilly or mountainous for residential, commercial, and industrial purposes (see fig. i.5). About three-quarters of San Bernardino's 20,069 square miles are unusable for development, and San Bernardino County constitutes about two-thirds of the five-county Los Angeles CMSA. Substantial parts of the land in Riverside, Ventura, and Los Angeles Counties are also too hilly for development. There is no question that much of New York City is far more densely populated than anything in the Los Angeles region. Manhattan's fantastic 68,200 people per square mile contrasts with the city of Los Angeles's 7,027 persons per square mile and, together with Manhattan's other attractions, fully justify the popular image of this dense urban maelstrom. Still, even some sections of New York City are comparable here to Los Angeles. Staten Island's population density (7,043 persons per square mile) resembles that of the city of Los Angeles. Outside the two cities, the contrasts should be drawn more carefully still. Ventura, Riverside, and San Bernardino Counties in the Los Angeles CMSA have low population densities, even when adjustment is made for the fact that much of the land there is too mountainous for residential development.[2] But Orange County's population density of 3,410 persons per square mile is substantially higher than that of Westchester (1,948) and Suffolk Counties (1,427) in New York and not much lower than that of Nassau County (4,439). Indeed, much of the single family, detached tract housing in the Los Angeles region is as closely packed as the single family housing in the New York CMSA outside the borders of New York City, Newark, and other older cities.

Thus the central aims of this collection are to highlight, and to subject

Figure i.4. Overview of the City of Los Angeles, Looking Southeast from Mulholland Drive, with Downtown in Background (February 2002). Detached, single family houses in the city and region of Los Angeles are often as densely packed as in the New York region, for much of the land in the Los Angeles region is too hilly or mountainous for residential use.

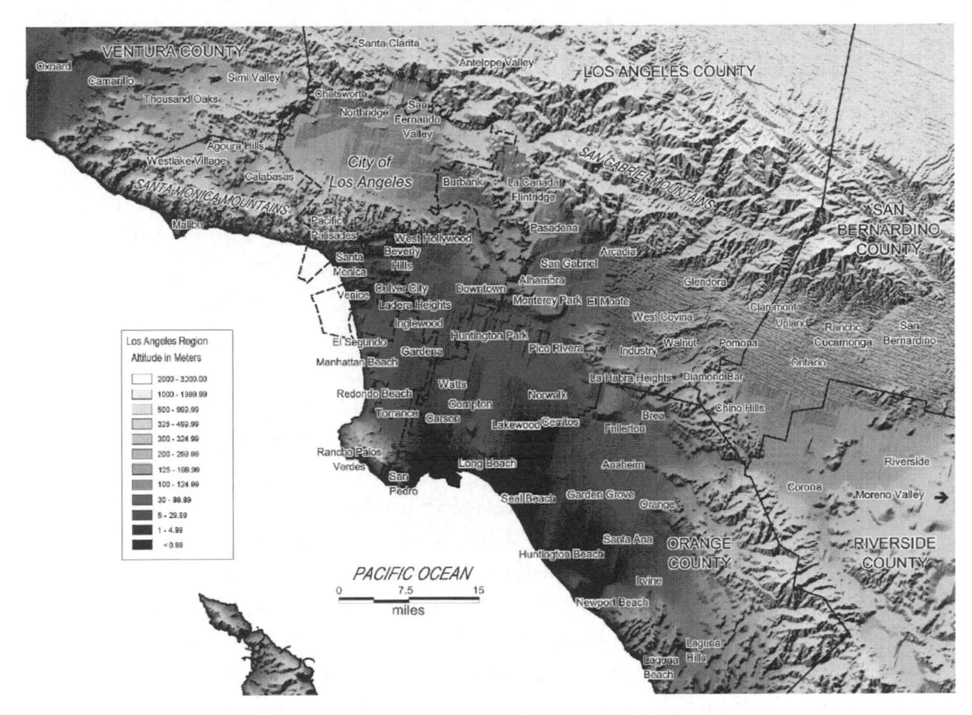

Figure i.5. Los Angeles CMSA in 3-D Relief, with Neighborhoods

to critical analysis, the stereotypes of the two cities and regions and to compare them along a set of central themes on which researchers in each region have long focused, and which I outline below.

THE "LOS ANGELES" AND THE "NEW YORK" SCHOOLS

In Los Angeles and New York, a cluster of researchers have, for many years, been analyzing what is occurring in a way that is, in each place, sufficiently distinctive to constitute a "school." The main, though by no means the only, focus of the Los Angeles school is the "sprawling, polycentric character of the urban, built environment" (Scott and Soja 1996, 6). The New York school, by contrast, is characterized by an interest in the central city. What is going on there, what should the central city be like? Can it be a place where the wealthy, the middle class, the working class, and the poor reside? And, after the World Trade Center attack, how can New York City, and other urban concentrations, be defended against terrorism? Thus the foci of some of the two region's most important researchers reproduce, to some degree, the popular distinction between Los Angeles, representing the decentered megalopolis, and New York, representing a focus on city, especially central-city, life.

The Los Angeles School

Although the term "Los Angeles school" is recent, the school's founding text is arguably Robert Fogelson's *The Fragmented Metropolis: Los Angeles, 1850–1930,* written in 1967.[3] Fogelson traces the evolution of Los Angeles from a "nondescript agricultural village" in 1850 to a large city of 1.2 million in 1920 and thence, already by 1930, to a dispersed and decentralized "metropolis": "More than any other American metropolis—and with remarkably few misgivings—Los Angeles succumbed to the disintegrative, though not altogether undesirable, forces of suburbanization and progressivism. And as a result it emerged by 1930 as the fragmented metropolis par excellence, the archetype for better or for worse of the contemporary American metropolis."

Fogelson thus lays out the central idea of the current Los Angeles school, among whose major representatives are Michael Dear, Jennifer Wolch, Allen Scott, Edward Soja, and Michael Davis. For example, in 1993 Wolch and Dear wrote that "the Los Angeles prototype—with its patterns of multicentered, dispersed, low-density growth—is perhaps a new paradigm of metropolitan growth." They contrasted this new urban paradigm with the formerly dominant "Chicago model," which analyzed urban development as a number of zones, concentric circles in their tidiest forms, radiating out from a perennially dominant core composed of the central business district (Wolch and Dear 1993).[4] In similar vein, Scott (1996, 276) pointed out how, by the end of the twentieth century, southern California and especially the Los Angeles region, is made up of a "multiplicity of discrete industrial districts (some of which are individually comparable to Silicon Valley in size and rapidity of growth) scattered over its entire geographic extent." Following the Los Angeles school's tendency to argue that a new vocabulary is required to capture what it is uncovering, Scott proposed the term "technopoles" for these dispersed, high-technology, industrial districts.

Joel Garreau's *Edge City,* a book often cited by the Los Angeles school, explores the way these industrial districts and other recent sources of employment combine with residential development to constitute new urban centers on the periphery of traditional cities. He defines edge cities (another neologism) as places that have substantial leasable office and retail space, have more "jobs than bedrooms," are perceived by their populations as a unitary place, and have appeared in the past thirty years.[5] Although Garreau writes about edge cities throughout America, he sees the Los Angeles region as the prototype.

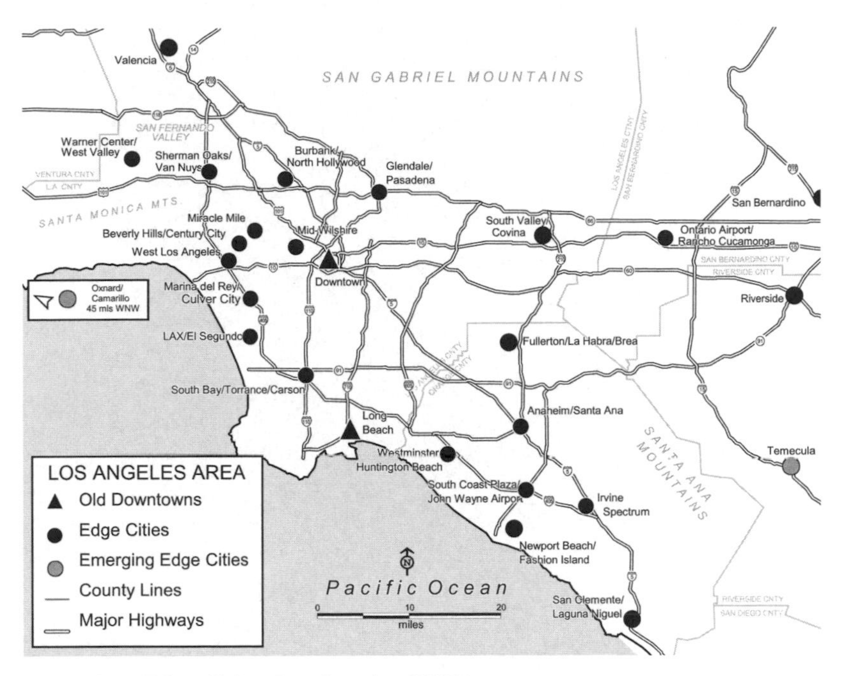

Figure i.6. Edge Cities, Los Angeles CMSA, 2002

His opening sentence proclaims that "every single American city that is growing, is growing in the fashion of Los Angeles, with multiple urban cores" (i.e., edge cities). In the last half century, Garreau says, Americans moved, first, their homes, then their marketplaces (shopping malls), and finally their jobs out of the traditional city. The resulting edge cities constitute the "biggest change in a hundred years in how [Americans] build cities" (Garreau 1988, 1–7). Figures i.6 and i.7 depict the edge cities in the Los Angeles and New York CMSAs, respectively, as of 2002.[6] There is now a small cottage industry that tracks edge cities, with an edge city newsletter.[7] However not everyone is enamored with the concept. In a review of the first edition of Garreau's book, Herbert Gans argued that these do not merit the term "cities" but are really shopping malls and office areas or, for short, "CONs, commercial-and-office nodes" (Gans 1991, 35).

Developing a related idea to Garreau's, Robert Fishman (1987) coined the term "techno-city" to refer to edge cities and "techno-burbs" to refer to the entire peripheral zones that have emerged beyond traditional cities and that, containing industrial parks, shopping malls, campus-like office complexes and a full range of housing types, are largely independent of the traditional city. He argues that the classic

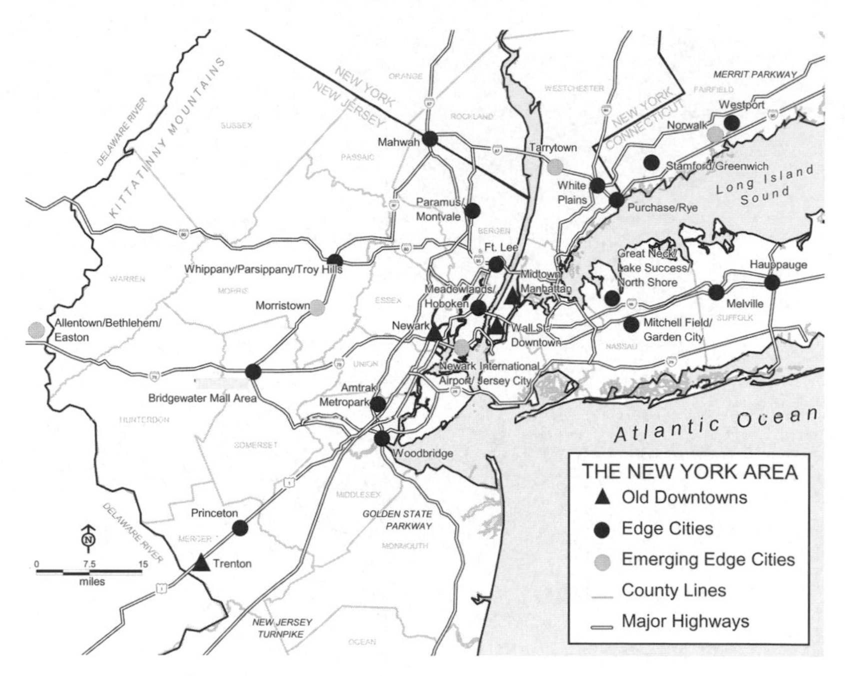

Figure i.7. Edge Cities, New York CMSA, 2002

suburb, defined as a serene bedroom community (a "bourgeois utopia," as he dubs it) from which people commuted long distances to jobs in the older city, is now almost obsolete. It can be recognized, in retrospect, to have been a transitional phenomenon paving the way to self-sufficient technoburbs on the periphery. This is why he titles his book *Bourgeois Utopias: The Rise and Fall of Suburbia*.[8] And this is why other members of the school argue that the region beyond the central core of the city of Los Angeles is not "suburban" but "postsuburban." (Kling et al. 1995; Soja 1996, 426–42).

The Los Angeles school is often uneasy about much of what it finds, especially the untrammeled growth. This unease at the dark or, to use the term its writers like to borrow from literary and film analysis, "noir" side of Los Angeles life is also a hallmark of its approach. Mike Davis, for example, patrols the periphery in dismay at the ecological effects of urban sprawl. Writing in 1990 about the development of the Antelope Valley (fig. i.8), a vast area of the Mojave Desert about 50 miles wide around the northeastern border of Los Angeles County, Davis comments: "The Antelope Valley has nearly doubled in population over the last decade, with another quarter million new arrivals expected by 2010. . . . The pattern of urbanization here is what design critic Peter

Plagens once called 'the ecology of evil.' The desert . . . has been prepared like a virgin bride for its eventual union with the Metropolis; hundreds of square miles of vacant space engridded to accept the future millions. . . . The region's major natural wonder, a Joshua tree forest with individual specimens often 30 feet high and older than the Doomsday Book, is being bulldozed into oblivion" (1990, 3).[9]

Along with the idea of a sprawling, multicentered urban environment, the Los Angeles school stresses the weakness and fragmentation of the political structures, both those of the city of Los Angeles and those of the areas beyond. In a book jointly edited with Michael Dear and G. Hise, Eric Schockman (1996) titles his essay on city government, "Is Los Angeles Governable?" The central point is the notoriously weak mayoralty system of Los Angeles, hedged around by a powerful set of city council members (dubbed by some people as "mini-mayors") and by quasi-independent groups of civil servants (boards/commissions) that control such crucial functions as transportation, harbor, airports, and police. During the 1992 Los Angeles riots, many people outside California discovered to their astonishment that mayor Tom Bradley could not fire his truculent police chief, Daryl Gates, since the latter had civil service protection. More recently, the federal government had to step in to deal with the city of Los Angeles's police scandal known as

Figure i.8. Antelope Valley—Development. Antelope Valley, at the northeastern edge of Los Angeles County, is about fifty miles from downtown Los Angeles. Here, construction of new housing in the desert is shown.

Rampart—among the worst scandals in the history of the U.S. police—on the grounds that the mayor either could not or would not deal with police corruption. (Rampart is discussed later in this introduction.) The mayor has also, for several years, been fighting a battle against the at-times powerful secession movement of the San Fernando Valley, which would deprive the city of 170 square miles, just over a third of its total area.

Further, the region around the city of Los Angeles is highly fragmented politically. Scott and Soja (1996, 11) point out that from 1970 to 1990 "over 30 new municipalities were incorporated, mostly in the regional periphery . . . these included the fastest growing small cities in the United States: Irvine, Mission Viejo, Lancaster, Moreno Valley, Santa Clarita." Here, too, the Los Angeles school is uneasy. The existing regional political structures are seen as too fragmented and weak to coordinate all the economic and social activities, especially those associated with rapid growth. For example, Wolch and Dear (1993, xxiii), writing about the acute problems faced by the homeless in the Los Angeles region (in 1984 the U.S. Department of Housing and Urban Development dubbed Los Angeles the "homelessness capital of the US"), complain that extreme political fragmentation impedes solutions: the region's "social heterogeneity, geographic sprawl, and economic vitality have encouraged an intense and effective localization of politics, work, personal life, and culture. One important consequence is the difficulty of formal urban governance. The region is split into many separate fiefdoms, their leaders in constant battle. As the urbanized area continues to expand geographically, local government becomes increasingly remote and less able to respond to grass-roots concerns."

Likewise, Scott and Soja (1996, 19–20)—after arguing for the urgency of reforms to take greater account of Latino, Asian, and African-American communities, to provide affordable housing, and to permit more regional planning, especially for public transport—complain that the political structures make such changes difficult: "Behind all these efforts looms the need to rethink and reorganize regional government and planning. None of the programs identified above is likely to succeed if the present, highly fragmented, government structure of the region remains intact. . . . The new metropolis is regional in scale, scope and functioning more than ever . . . some organizational structure for coordinating local economic development strategies and for seeking to build agreements between important local constituencies (e.g. banks, industrial associations, labor organizations, government agencies) is highly desirable."

Thus two motifs—the development of urban peripheries and the fragmentation of politics—are central to the "Los Angeles" school. Neither motif is new on the intellectual scene or unique to Los Angeles, but even when first stated by their original authors it was usually said that Los Angeles was in the vanguard and presented the traits in pronounced form.[10] Indeed, another characteristic of the Los Angeles school is to suggest that developments in Los Angeles may be the new model that other urban areas will follow. This claim is typically hedged. Perhaps the Los Angeles region is the harbinger of the future, if not already the present, of many of America's other major urban areas. On the other hand, it may be unique (both claims are often contested by observers outside the Los Angeles region). For example, Wolch and Dear (1993, xxiv) write: "It is already self-evident that southern California's emergent urbanism possesses more than local or regional significance. Given its implications as the prototype for future urban dynamics . . . Los Angeles is preeminently qualified to serve as a laboratory for our analysis. . . . Whether or not Los Angeles represents the model 21st century urban development is a question we shall leave to others."[11]

The claim that the Los Angeles region represents the future of America's major metropolises has certainly been disputed. For example, the geographer Jan Nijman (quoted in Miller 2000) and the urban historian Robert Schneider (Schneider 2000, 1672) argue that Los Angeles is too gargantuan to be typical of other American metropolises. Nijman suggests Miami exhibits many of the tendencies of Los Angeles but, being smaller, is more typical of the future of U.S. cities. Schneider suggests that Los Angeles, with its large population of homeless, may be more typical of contemporary First World cities such as Mexico City, Cairo, Calcutta, and São Paolo than of urban areas in the United States. Still, it is plausibly argued, the study of Los Angeles is important. Even if Los Angeles turns out to be unique rather than the future of other urban regions in the United States, its sheer size make developments there of great interest.

The Los Angeles school's tendency to propose new terms to understand these developments has already been mentioned. Going further than most here, Dear and Flusty (1998) have suggested an extended family of concepts including "global latifundia," "privatopia," "cybergeoisie," "protosurps," "holsteinization," "praedatorianism," and others to capture what is new about life in the Los Angeles region. The authors cheerfully acknowledge that some critics, upset at so many new categories, have accused them of "neologorrhea" (Dear and Flusty 1998, 68).[12]

Three other ideas, each with a long lineage in urban studies, are associated with, if not the hallmarks of, the Los Angeles school. These ideas are not especially closely related to the previous three motifs but they are closely related to each other. There is the idea of a "post-Fordist economy," the idea of a bifurcated labor force, and the stress on the impact of immigration on the economy and labor force.

Thus the Los Angeles school highlights the distinctiveness of the Los Angeles economy. It is post-Fordist in that it is based on high-tech and small-scale craft production, rather than on large-scale, mass production. Unlike the economies of paradigmatic American industrial metropolises such as Chicago, Detroit, and Pittsburgh, which were based on "Fordist," mass production industries churning out automobiles, steel, machinery, and domestic appliances, the economy of Los Angeles is composed of "enormously diverse, flexible production sectors, including financial and business services, high-technology industries, and various craft, fashion, and cultural product industries ranging from clothing and jewelry to motion pictures and music recording" (Scott and Soja 1996, vii).

Related to the idea that the economy of Los Angeles is based on the twin pillars of high-tech and small craft production is the idea of the bifurcated labor force. Thus Scott and Soja write that the social structure of Los Angeles is no longer characterizable in terms of a (numerically) dominant, unionized, and moderately well off blue-collar working class (the labor force associated with "Fordist" mass production). Instead, they argue, it is "deeply divided into two distinctive segments, as represented on the one side by an upper tier of highly paid managers, professionals, and technicians, and on the other side by a lower tier composed of low-skill, low-wage workers."[13]

Immigration is, of course, a central topic of the Los Angeles school (as it was of the classic Chicago school of urban sociology in the 1920s). Los Angeles's immigrants, predominantly from Latin America and Asia, are "part of an extraordinary global migration that has made Los Angeles one of the most culturally heterogeneous metropolises the world has ever seen." Immigration is related to the bifurcated labor force. For "the vast majority of the lower tier workers are immigrants, many undocumented" (Scott and Soja 1996, viii). (However an important proportion of immigrants also move straight into the upper tier of the labor force.)[14]

In sum, the Los Angeles school of research is characterized by a stress on the multicentered nature of the region, by a stress on the region's political fragmentation, by pessimism and, in some cases, a deep strain of "noir" about the possibility that serious problems can be reformed, and by a view that Los Angeles may be the prototype of the future urban development of America's cities. Secondary ideas associated with the Los Angeles school are the importance of immigration and the existence of an economy that is "post-Fordist," along with a labor market that is bifurcated into a prosperous managerial and professional elite and a struggling lower sector. None of these ideas is new, and all have been stated about other urban regions. Moreover there are, not surprisingly, numerous splits and disagreements among researchers associated with the Los Angeles school.[15] Still, the core notion of the need to explore urban regions in general (not just Los Angeles) as multicentered is, these days, associated with the Los Angeles school. It is a perfectly reasonable, and still largely unfulfilled, research goal, in part because the task is, by definition, huge.

The New York School

> To be frank, I like dense cities best, and care about them most.
> *Jane Jacobs* (1961, 16)

The New York school, by contrast, is characterized by an interest in the central city. What is going on there, what should the central city be like? Some of its key figures are Jane Jacobs, who is the doyen of the school, Sharon Zukin, Kenneth Jackson, Robert Stern, Richard Sennett, and William Whyte.[16] They share a fascination with contemporary New York City, especially with Manhattan, and a belief, in some cases passionate, in the superiority of city life over suburban life. They also often see New York City as a place for the middle class and the rich, not just the poor and working class.

The New York researchers have not, so far, been explicitly identified as a "school," partly because they do not tend to identify themselves explicitly in this way. But arguably their views are as distinctive as those of the Los Angeles school, and their history goes back at least as far. It is true that members of the Chicago school, which dominated urban studies in the 1920s and 1930s, shared with the later New York school a tendency to see city life as of great interest and value and were interested in reforming it. But they differed from the New York researchers in several ways. Above all, they often agreed with the value judgments of residents at the time, who saw the outer suburban zones as the preferred places to live. They did not envisage the central city as an especially desirable place for the residences of the middle class and, still less, of the rich. The inner city was a place for central business, new immigrants, vagrants and hobos, and the working class. Indeed, they were often alarmed about the potential for "social disorganization" in the central city associated with the new immigrants.[17]

The New York school, or at any rate Jane Jacobs, has won at least one major political victory, over the Lower Manhattan Expressway, which was finally defeated in 1969. This ten-lane highway, to have been lined with huge apartment towers, would have cut Manhattan in two from east to west and wiped out the entire neighborhood that later became known as Soho and, also, much of neighboring Little Italy and Chinatown. The battle against the expressway, which several of its opponents argued would "Los Angelize" New York City, lasted from 1959 to 1969. It was led by Jane Jacobs, whose preface to her 1961 seminal work, *The Death and Life of Great American Cities,* dedicates the book to New York City. The victory against the Lower Manhattan Expressway had national significance for American cities. It was one turning point against the urban renewal programs that, since the end of World War II, had enabled city governments, in collaboration with the federal government, to destroy so many downtown neighborhoods in American cities. These programs typically tore down older, often working-class, housing and replaced it with grand projects—high-rise corporate office buildings, entertainment centers for the well-to-do (such as Lincoln Center in Manhattan), and so on.[18] (A major reason why urban renewal programs faded was protest from those outer neighborhoods who were designated to receive the mostly poor people whom urban renewal displaced.) The defeat of the Lower Manhattan Expressway was also presented, with some exaggeration, by some as a grassroots victory over top-down, autocratic planning.

Soho was a one-time industrial district whose cast-iron buildings artists had moved into and converted to loft residential-work spaces. Demand for these buildings had been weakened first because industry was moving from New York City anyway and second because they were apparently doomed by the projected Lower Manhattan Expressway. After the defeat of the expressway, Soho became a prototype for neighborhood preservation and for the "recycling" of buildings both in New York City and nationwide. One study argued that the Soho syndrome had done more to retain the middle class in the cities and stimulate new economic innovations than any planning or government funded program (Gratz and Mintz 1998). Indeed a number of the numerous downtown districts that have developed in the last thirty years so as to resemble the Soho model in some way acquired names that stressed the link. "Soho" stands for south of Houston Street (in Manhattan). Examples of areas with names mimicking Soho include NoHo (north of Houston Street, in Manhattan), Dumbo (down under the Manhattan Bridge), LoDo (lower downtown, in Denver), SoMa (south of Main Street, in San Francisco), WeHo and NoHo (west and north Hollywood, in Los Angeles), and SoDo (south of downtown) in Seattle. The

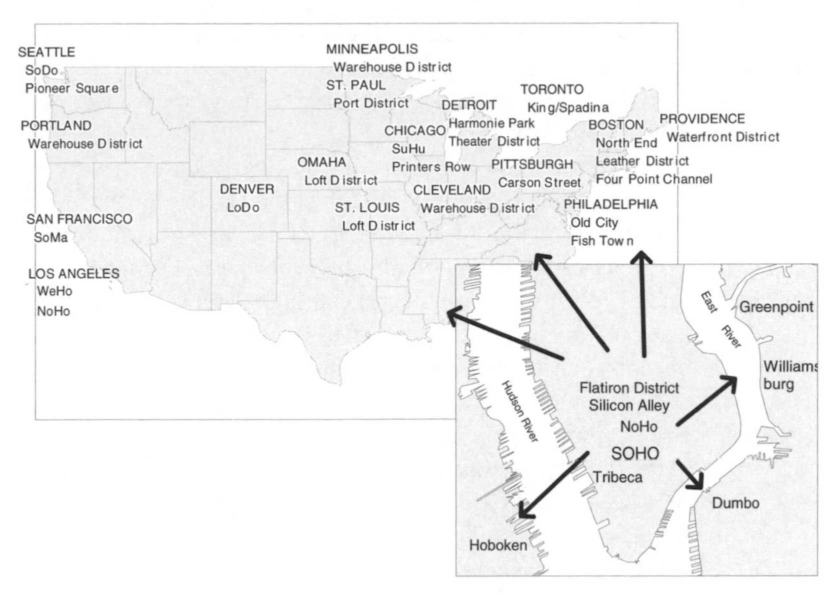

Figure i.9. Soho and Its Influence on Other North American Cities

influence and cachet of Soho has also spread abroad. By 1980, Paris building owners were advertising "les lofts" (Zukin 1982, 1). Figure i.9 sketches out the "Soho" syndrome for other North American cities.

In 1982 Sharon Zukin published her pioneering study of loft living in Soho. It was also one of the earliest accounts of urban "gentrification," for she situated the Soho loft movement in that context. Gentrification she defined as typically occurring when "a higher class of people moves into a neighborhood, makes improvements to property that cause market prices and tax assessments to rise, and so drives out the previous, lower-class residents" (5). A concern with those driven out gave Zukin's study a sharp, reformist edge. She was interested in countering the claim of the real estate industry, city officials, and the *New York Times* that loft living had social and economic benefits for all those involved. Instead, she pointed out that the gentrification process associated with loft living claimed specific victims. First, by raising rents it displaced the existing owners of the small, manufacturing businesses, who were often lower middle class, and it also displaced their employees. Later, as rents and the price of apartments continued to climb, the gentrification process devoured many of its early practitioners—artists, craft workers, performers, photographers—who had moved into Soho in the first wave before 1970 but could no longer afford to live there.

Zukin's study is one of the seminal texts of the New York school.

Reflecting their stubborn affection for the city in the face of the suburban alternative, then highly touted by many people, she dedicated her book on loft living to her parents "Who have never understood why I wanted to live in New York."[19]

Another doyen of the New York school is Kenneth Jackson, who has spent most of his academic life at Columbia University in New York City. His magnum opus *Crabgrass Frontier* is a history of the suburbanization of America from 1814 to the present (Jackson 1985). But a central "subtext" of the book is a regret-filled analysis of how policies of the federal government undermined the economic and social health of America's central cities and urban neighborhoods in the twentieth century, especially for about fifty years starting in the 1920s. Such policies, often acting under severe pressure from real estate and construction lobbies, for example, wrote public housing legislation that almost guaranteed it would be clustered in the central city rather than spread evenly through the region and followed mortgage policies that discriminated against central city neighborhoods, especially those with large concentrations of minorities, thus undermining the value of the housing there. Jackson also shows how twentieth-century suburbanites, acting through their state legislatures, which establish city boundaries, set about throttling older American cities by preventing them doing what they had done throughout the nineteenth century—namely, expanding their borders geographically to capture for the city the new economic and residential developments on the periphery.

Jackson, like Jane Jacobs, makes his preference for the city clear. In *Crabgrass Frontier* he writes: "A major casualty of America's drive-in culture is the weakened 'sense of community' which prevails in most metropolitan areas. I refer to a tendency for social life to become 'privatized', and to a reduced feeling of concern and responsibility among families for their neighbors and among suburbanites in particular for residents of the inner city. . . . The life of the sidewalk and front yard has largely disappeared. . . . There are few places as desolate and lonely as a suburban street on a hot afternoon" (1985, 272, 279–80).

In a later essay, Jackson criticizes that suburban icon, the shopping mall. He complains about how suburban malls are allowed to flourish freely in America, to the detriment of the economic health of the downtowns of older cities with which they compete. By contrast, in England and Germany, he points out, public policy has aimed to protect older cities by restricting the growth of suburban malls (England) or the hours at which shopping can occur (Germany). Jackson's dislike of the American suburban mall is open: "In my view, the shopping mall and the automobile culture that makes it possible waste time, energy, and land that the United States can ill afford" (1996,1121.) By contrast, Jackson's 1995 *Encyclopedia of New York City* pays homage to the city by assembling everything one would ever want to know about it.[20]

The famous architect Robert Stern is another member of the New York school. In a massive three-volume work he charts the architectural history of New York City. Volume 3, which deals with the period from the start of World War II to 1976, is a tour de force of almost 1,400 pages (Stern et al. [1960] 1997).[21] Although the book discusses New York City as part of an evolving, regional megalopolis, the heart of it is about Manhattan, New York City's undisputable core. The first 894 pages deal in exhaustive detail with Manhattan's neighborhoods, followed by just 131 pages on the other four boroughs, referred to as the "outer boroughs," and only thirty-three pages on the regional context. Stressing this focus, Stern writes: "Despite our opening up of the discussion to cover not only the outer boroughs but also the suburbs, our concentration on Manhattan seems justified. As the city planner Charles Abrams noted in 1961: 'What saves New York is Manhattan—the city's "downtown." It is a kind of national downtown, a crossroads of America'" (Stern et al. [1960] 1997, 10). Although Stern is here writing about how Manhattan was perceived in the early 1960s, and although his work and interests have ranged far beyond New York City, the lovingly detailed attention to the city in this volume assuredly makes him part of the New York school. So do his continuing interests. He was, for example, a central figure in the 1990s renovation of Times Square, a widely debated project that some people argued involved the "Disneyfication" or "Los Angelization" of Times Square and its conversion to a tame theme park along the lines of Universal City Walk in Los Angeles (see fig. 2.2). The sex shops peddling intercourse and peep shows were closed down. Every building that faced the square was required to display a large neon sign. Stern, a board member of the Walt Disney Company, was a key figure in getting Disney to purchase and restore Forty-second Street's grandest landmark theater, the New Amsterdam, and to open a Disney Store nearby.[22]

In 1969 William H. Whyte, already famous for his 1956 book *The Organization Man,* a critique of white-collar life in the new Chicago suburb of Park Forest, began studying the use of space in New York City. The City Planning Commission had asked him to help draft a somewhat unusual plan, to do with the growth and workability of the city and its government rather than with specific land-use projections and the kind of futuristic projects typical of city plans. There was a strong emphasis, too, on the use of incentive zoning to provide parks and plazas, an area in which New York City was doing pioneering work. Whyte set up a research project to study how these spaces were actually used by people in the city, with the goal of discovering how to draw people to them. In many cities at that time such public spaces were often avoided as dangerous. Whyte found that, ironically, the main culprit was the actions taken to keep away the "undesirables," that is, the people seen as making these spaces unattractive. Undesirables consisted of such groups as the homeless, derelicts, bag people, drug dealers, street vendors and musicians, and teenagers. The standard approach to containing them was to wall off the area and make it uninviting, providing few if any seats, placing spikes on low walls to prevent people resting there, closing down restrooms, and so on. This, Whyte argued, was exactly the wrong thing to do. It made the place inhospitable to the rest of the public too, turning it into just the kind of semideserted setting that encouraged the occurrence of the bad things that people feared. The solution was to do the opposite. "The best way to handle the problem of undesirables is to make a place attractive to everyone else" (Whyte 1988, 158). Whyte advocated opening up these spaces, making them visible, and providing comfortable facilities such as ample seating and bathrooms.

The successful redesign of Bryant Park, next to the magisterial New York Public Library (fig. i.10), showcased Whyte's ideas. In the 1970s Bryant Park was a haven for drug dealers who had the run of the place because most of the public tended to avoid it. The park was surrounded by a spiked iron fence and thick, overgrown shrubbery that blocked the view from outside of what was going on inside, thus making being inside hazardous. Whyte suggested some simple measures to open up the park and make it more friendly. The fences and shrubbery were taken down, replaced by grand, welcoming entrances. Inside were placed numerous chairs and tables, and open-air cafes were installed, which, Whyte argued, were the best security measures. These days Bryant Park during the day is a well-used facility for office workers, families, tourists, and homeless and poor people who coexist (Gratz and Mintz 1998, chap. 2). However, at night the homeless are often not permitted by the police to remain, and some critics have argued that the Bryant Park Restoration Corporation, a private organization that essentially runs the park, has inappropriately imposed a "middle-class" culture on a public space (e.g., Zukin, 1995, 29–34).

A central interest of Richard Sennett, another important member of the New York school, is charting the changing history of interpersonal life in the West since classical Greek times. Sennett argues that the quality of modern interpersonal life is markedly deficient in some ways. The

Figure i.10. Bryant Park, Sixth Avenue and Forty-second Street, with New York Public Library in Background. In the 1970s, the park became the site for open drug dealing and other lawlessness. Following the ideas of sociologist William Whyte, restoration in the late 1980s and the 1990s opened the park to full view and made it a hospitable place for the public, with numerous chairs and cafes. The park is now a congenial place for almost everyone.

problem, he maintains, is that Christianity has taught us to hide our private selves so that we are unable to interact in an emotionally engaged way with "strangers." He uses the case of New York City, which he argues has so much potential because of its diverse and dense population, to underline the difference between interpersonal life as it is and as it ought to be: "New York should be the ideal city of exposure to the outside. It grasps the imagination because it is a city of differences 'par excellence.' . . . By walking in the middle of New York one is immersed in the differences of this most diverse of cities. . . . [But] in New York City people are emotionally walled off from each, they conceal their private emotions" (Sennett 1990, 128).

Sennett does not think that interpersonal life is better anywhere else in America. On the contrary, life in the modern American suburbs, he believes, is far worse than urban life. New York City is his benchmark because of its wasted possibilities: "A New York street resembles the studio of a painter who has assembled in it all the paints, books of other artists, and sketches he will need for a grand triptych that will crown his career; then the painter has unaccountably left town" (Sennett 1990, 129).

To justify their choice of city to study, the New York school tends to use one of the same two opposite strategies as members of the Los Angeles school use to justify their study of Los Angeles. Some argue that what they uncover is typical of many other big cities and helps us to understand them. Jane Jacobs, for example, wrote: "In trying to explain the underlying order of cities, I use a preponderance of examples from New York, because that is where I live. But most of the basic ideas in this book come from things I first noticed or was told in other cities" (Jacobs 1961, 15). Others justify what they do on the grounds that New York City is unique or, at least, extremely unusual (Duneier 1999).[23] What makes it unique—for example, its size and cultural importance together with the economic power of Wall Street—tends to be what make it a crucial object of study.

In sum, the influential group of researchers whom I have called the New York school are distinctive in at least one, and usually more than one, of the following ways. Either they write more about New York City than about what is going on beyond the borders of the city. Or, when they examine contemporary life beyond the borders of New York City, they compare it unfavorably with life in the city or they complain about the favored treatment of suburban areas by comparison with New York City and with American cities in general. Further, they are often interested in New York City, and especially Manhattan, as a place for the middle class and rich as well as the poor and working class.

There are, of course, many important researchers in New York City and the region whose work scarcely, or only partly, fits this New York school model. An example is Herbert Gans, a towering force in urban sociology. In his 1962 ethnography of the West End of Boston, Gans took on urban renewal programs. He argued that many inner-city neighborhoods slated for demolition under such programs were not typically "slums" but supported a viable and dense working-class lifestyle and should not be bulldozed (Gans 1962b). In opposing urban renewal Gans sounds like his contemporary, Jane Jacobs.[24] But Gans was never against tall apartment buildings in the city. Furthermore, unlike Jacobs and several others, Gans has resolutely refused to agree that urban life is superior to that of the suburbs. In his classic 1967 account of Levittown, a large suburban tract development in New Jersey, Gans chastised those who denigrated the suburban lifestyle of its working- and middle-class inhabitants as dull, homogenized, or lonely. For most of those who lived there, Gans insisted, it was none of these (Gans 1967). Reviewing Jane Jacobs's *The Death and Life of Great American Cities,* Gans criticized her, too, for denigrating the suburbs. Further, he said her argument that urban life was intrinsically superior to suburban was elitist since the lack of space in the central cities means that only a minority can live there anyway, a point that many others have reiterated (Gans 1962a).[25]

EXAMINING THE MOTIFS OF THE LOS ANGELES AND NEW YORK SCHOOLS

Each chapter in this volume covers at least one, and often several, of the rich themes that have occupied the Los Angeles and New York schools over the last several decades.[26]

Demographic Dispersal and Decentralization

Taking up the topic of dispersal and decentralization, Andrew Beveridge and Susan Weber, in chapter 1 of this volume, examine the social geography of Los Angeles and New York from 1940 to 2000. They insist, in the manner of the Los Angeles school, on the importance of treating equally seriously, and in the same analysis, the urban core, the near-core, and the periphery. From this geographical stance they look at patterns of income distribution, where minorities lives, commuting patterns, and governance. Their conclusion is that the New York region now in many ways resembles the Los Angeles region, with large proportions of the higher-income groups, nonminorities, and non-foreign born living beyond the urban core. In this context, Beveridge and Weber argue that the "gentrification" of New York City in the past decade is more modest in scope than people sometimes think. Mapping the 2000 census data on income, they show vividly just how poor most of New York City is, with the important exceptions of much of Manhattan and small sections of Brooklyn, compared with many of the surrounding suburbs (fig. 1.6). Beveridge has, over the past decade, provided the data to support more than 100 *New York Times* articles on demographic trends in the city and region, which puts him in a strong position to challenge conventional wisdom on the city.[27]

Taking the time period 1940–2000, Beveridge and Weber also show that although the counties on the New York periphery grew by almost 3.5-fold during that time, the counties on the Los Angeles periphery grew almost fifteenfold. Indeed, if one factor validates and explains the fascination of the Los Angeles school with the periphery it is the statistics on population growth in the Los Angeles CMSA from 1970 to 2000 (see fig. i.1). The dynamism of the counties surrounding Los Angeles

County is startling. Orange and Ventura Counties each grew by 100 percent to 2.8 million and 0.75 million, respectively, San Bernardino County by 151 percent to 1.7 million and Riverside County by 236 percent to 1.5 million. Even the population of Los Angeles County grew continually, so that its 2000 population (9.5 million) is 35 percent higher than in 1970.

The contrast with New York City is sharp. Thus New York City's 1970 population was 7.97 million. By 1980 it had dropped steeply by 11.3 percent to 7.07 million. Thereafter it made a modest recovery, growing to 7.32 million in 1990 and 8.0 million in 2000, a milestone touted by city boosters, though it left the city merely a third of 1 percent above its 1970 level. Only in Staten Island did the population grow more or less continually, so that the 2000 total of 443,728 was 50 percent higher than in 1970. In the other four boroughs, population declines, sometimes enormous, from 1970 to 1980 (−21 percent in the Bronx, −17 percent in Brooklyn, −7 percent in Manhattan, −5 percent in Queens) were followed by small increases in 1980–90, ranging from 3 percent in the Bronx to 4 percent in Manhattan, and then mostly faster increases from 1990 to 2000: 14 percent in Queens, 11 percent in the Bronx, 7 percent in Brooklyn, and 3 percent in Manhattan (all still below the 17 percent in Staten Island). Yet by 2000 only one of these four boroughs, Queens, exceeded its 1970 population total by much (12 percent), while Brooklyn was below by 5 percent, and the Bronx was below by 9 percent.

As might be expected, some of the counties on the outskirts of the New York CMSA grew robustly, too, from 1970 to 2000. On the northwest fringe, Pike County, Pa., grew at a spectacular rate of 292 percent, but from a low base (2000 population is just 46,302). Ocean County, N.J., had both a spectacular growth rate of 145 percent and a substantial population base (510,916 in 2000). Indeed, Ocean County is the one county in the New York CMSA for which population growth, in terms of rate and absolute numbers, makes it definitely comparable to the four Los Angeles CMSA counties that ring Los Angeles County. In the New York CMSA, the population of Sussex County, N.J., grew at 86 percent with a respectable population base (2000 population is 144,166) and Hunterdon County to the south grew at 75 percent, also with a respectable base (2000 population is 121,989). Several other counties had population growth from 1970 to 2000 of from 33 to 70 percent, notably Putnam and Orange Counties, N.Y., and Somerset and Monmouth, N.J. Still, various other New York CMSA counties that were not in urban cores had modest growth rates of 20 percent or less. Overall, the growth rates of the New York CMSA cannot match the growth of the four counties surrounding Los Angeles County.

Data on job growth in the two cities and regions, as presented by Gladstone and Fainstein in chapter 2, reflect this pattern. From 1977 to 1997 employment grew in both cores—11.9 percent in New York City and 35.5 percent in Los Angeles County. In both peripheries, the rate of job growth was higher than in their respective cores, but far more so in Los Angeles than in New York. In Orange, Riverside, San Bernardino, and Ventura Counties, job growth exceeded 120 percent over the 1977–97 period. Job growth in the New York metropolitan area (as defined in table 2.6 and which excludes New York City) at 43.8 percent, though nearly four times that of New York City, could not match the growth of the counties surrounding Los Angeles county. All of this underpins the Los Angeles school's fascination with the periphery of the Los Angeles urban region.

Beveridge and Weber, using their broad geographic perspective, also deal with political fragmentation. Acknowledging New York City's strong mayoral system, they show that the region outside of New York City is in many ways as politically balkanized as the Los Angeles region and perhaps even more so since, for example, state jurisdiction is split into three—New Jersey, Connecticut, and New York.[28]

Political Fragmentation and Concentration

Sonenshein's chapter on the Los Angeles City Charter (chap. 10), approved by the voters in June 1999 and implemented in 2000, is concerned with dispersal and political fragmentation, while adding a dash of New York noir. He points out that this phase of charter reform was, in origin, intended to calm a strong secession drive on the part of the San Fernando Valley, as well as Hollywood and the harbor area. It aimed to do this by providing a more inclusive form of city government, with neighborhood councils and area planning commissions.

Additional aims quickly surfaced, including Mayor Riordan's push to address the problem of political fragmentation by strengthening the mayor's powers. Reflecting this fragmentation, the mayor and city council were unable even to agree on a single charter reform commission, so the city ended up with two, each legal. The city council created one, of which Sonenshein was appointed executive director, and the other, backed by the mayor, was elected by the voters. The pros and cons of the New York City mayoral model were vigorously discussed during the whole process. Key figures in the Los Angeles charter debate saw New York's strong, even overriding, mayoralty as "noir incarnate," giving the mayor the kinds of powers that facilitate corruption and venality and to be avoided at all costs. Using the twin specters of the recent Giuliani (fig. i.11) mayoralty in New York City and the venal Los Angeles mayor

Figure i.11. Mayor Giuliani, with Shaved Legs, High Heels, and Flesh-Colored Tights, Dancing with the Radio City Music Hall Rockettes, at the Inner Circle Dinner, March 4, 2001. The dinner is an annual event at which the press "roasts" the mayor and the mayor responds. Guliani, who made his reputation as a tough federal prosecutor, law-and-order mayor, and take-charge leader after the World Trade Center attacks, here shows his well-known penchant for dressing as a woman and displaying a feminine side. Photo by Joe DeMaria.

Frank Shaw, who was recalled in disgrace by the voters in 1938, opponents of a strong mayor largely prevailed. Ironically the proposals to implement neighborhood councils, which were adopted in the new Los Angeles City Charter as the main hope for undercutting succession by offering some local autonomy to neighborhoods, were copied, with little fuss, from the experiments adopted by New York City in its own charter reform of 1989. (The 2000 Los Angeles City Charter also adopted local planning commissions, with real implementation powers, which do not exist in New York City.) In a November 2002 ballot, the residents of the San Fernando Valley did, by a slight majority, vote to secede from the city of Los Angeles, but the secession proposition failed because a strong majority of residents of the rest of the city voted against it.

Immigration

Each city and region is a major magnet for immigrants. In the late 1990s New York City (plus Putnam, Rockland, and Westchester Counties) ranked first as the destination of entry for immigrants to the United States, receiving about 14 percent of all immigrants each year. Los Angeles County ranked second, receiving about 8 percent of all immigrants each year. The third most important entry place, Miami (Dade County), received about 6 percent each year. Georges Sabagh and Mehdi Bozorgmehr's chapter (chap. 3) compares the immigration streams in the New York and Los Angeles metropolitan regions. In doing so, they take up a Los Angeles noir theme. They contrast the hostility toward immigrants that has historically and until recently been shown by many native Angelenos with the far more receptive and welcoming attitude of native New Yorkers. Among the explanations they offer are New York's much longer history of immigration, which has created a political culture that is accustomed to accommodating newcomers. The 1965 Immigration Act rejuvenated immigration to New York, while in Los Angeles it basically started a new era of mass immigration. A second explanation focuses on a difference in the composition of the "white populations" in Los Angeles and New York. Many of Los Angeles's "white" population have consisted of transplanted internal migrants of, for example, Swedish and German descent but long settled in America and mostly from rural areas and small towns in the Midwest. They may bring with them the nativist's fear of everything foreign and are quick to blame immigrants for the problems of large cities. By contrast, many "white" New Yorkers are descendants of Jewish, Italian, Irish, and Greek immigrants, who are much less likely than the predominantly WASP Angelenos to be hostile to foreign newcomers. A third explanation that Sabagh and Bozorgmehr offer for the greater hostility to immigrants in Los Angeles is the large presence of Mexicans in the immigrant population there. Mexicans are more likely than many other immigrant groups to be undocumented and to lack education and, therefore, in the cultural climate of Los Angeles, to arouse resentment and feelings that they are a drain on social services. Their large numbers of undocumented have also made it harder for Mexicans, as a group, to defend themselves in the voting booth. Still, Sabagh and Bozorgmehr show that anti-immigrant sentiment in Los Angeles has lessened considerably in the past few years, in large part as Latinos become more likely to vote. However the authors also suggest that the large proportion of immigrants in the New York region from the Middle East and the even larger proportion of Middle East immigrants in the Los Angeles region may, after the World Trade Center, test Los Angeles's new and New York's traditional tolerance for immigrants.

In their chapter on Chinese in New York and Los Angeles (chap. 4), Min Zhou and Rebecca Kim address immigration though the lens of dispersal and deconcentration. They show how in both cities recent Chinese immigrants often skip the traditional immigrant period of living in the inner city and instead move straight to residences in the suburbs or at least the outer city. Using as case studies Monterey Park, just beyond the eastern border of the city of Los Angeles, and Flushing in the northeastern section of Queens County, New York City, they argue that associated with the current wave of immigration is a degree of instant suburbanization.

Zhou and Kim also note that Chinese in the suburbs do not necessarily assimilate there. They may, instead, inhabit heavily Chinese neighborhoods amid hostility from their non-Chinese neighbors. Here the authors join the classic immigration debate, namely, To what extent will immigrants and their children assimilate ("melt") into American society and culture? This debate has been given new life by the enormous increase in immigration into the United States in the past thirty-five years. Sabagh and Bozorgmehr's discussion of the differing extent to which immigrants are accepted, even welcomed, in the two regions also speaks to this integration motif.[29]

The case of Latinos in the suburbs of the Los Angeles region, especially in the eastern part of the five-county region, is of great interest here. (The terms "Hispanic" and "Latino" will be used interchangeably in this book, following the new guidelines adopted by the Office of Management and Budget and applied to the 2000 census [Office of Management and Budget 2000]). In the eastern part of Los Angeles County and in San Bernardino and Riverside Counties, Latinos often constitute 40–60 percent of the population of new suburbs, and their proportions are rising at about 10–20 percent a decade. This movement of a minority, and largely immigrant, group into new suburban developments in such proportions and at such a speed is unprecedented in the history of U.S. suburbanization. It suggests the need to rethink our image of residential separation and segregation since it is not clear how traditional categories that relate to residential tensions would apply here, as we (Halle, Gedeon, and Beveridge) suggest in chapter 5.

Art Galleries: Dispersal and Concentration

András Szántó's chapter on the sociology of art galleries and museums (chap. 14) also deals with decenteredness and concentration. He points to the extent to which the Los Angeles gallery scene, set in a car culture, is dispersed with no particular focal point or sense of place. New York's art world, by contrast, has for long revolved around the clear-cut and extremely concentrated neighborhoods of Manhattan (the upper East Side, Fifty-seventh Street, Soho, and now Chelsea), each connected to different phases in the history of the art world. Szántó concludes by arguing that sky-high real estate prices in the late 1990s caused the New York gallery world to more closely resemble that of Los Angeles as galleries scattered, in search of affordable space, to once peripheral areas such as Harlem, Long Island City in Queens, Williamsburg and Red Hook in Brooklyn, and Jersey City and Hoboken in New Jersey.

Urban Issues and Problems

GROWING LATINOS, DECLINING BLACKS, AND THE DEBATE OVER WHO ARE THE "WHITES"? Of the many aspects of recent immigration to New York and Los Angeles, the growing Latino presence is among the most consequential. By 2000, the city of Los Angeles was 47 percent Latino, up from 39 percent in 1990 (table 5.2). Latinos were 27 percent of New York City's population in 2000, up from 24 percent in 1990, and now the same proportion as the black population, making these the two largest minority groups. But while the Latino trajectory in New York City over the past decade is up, the black trajectory is down, by 2 percent, despite a sizable immigration from the Caribbean. The proportion of blacks has also fallen in the city of Los Angeles, by 3 percent from 1990 to 2000 to 11 percent. The total number of blacks in the city of Los Angeles is now less than a quarter of the total number of Latinos. In part this declining proportion of blacks is due to suburbanization, but in part it is a result of a movement in the period 1990–2000 for blacks in the West, Northeast, and Midwest to return to the South thus ending the century by going back to the region they spent much of the century leaving (Frey 2001).[30]

This rising Latino presence and declining proportion of blacks in both cities raises a host of new issues. First, the current wave of immigration has led to a Latinization of traditionally black ghettos. This phenomenon has been widely noticed in Los Angeles, where Latino immigrants from Mexico, El Salvador, and elsewhere have been encroaching on areas of the inner city that have for many years been predominantly black. In New York, when the city's Landmarks Preservation Commission declared sections of Harlem an official historic landmark in 2000, the commission pointedly refused to refer to Harlem as a "black historic district." In part, this reflected the fact that the black sections of Harlem are also shrinking, though not as rapidly as in Los Angeles, with Dominicans, Mexicans, and other Hispanics increasingly taking over sections to the north-northwest and also expanding east from traditional "Spanish Harlem" (Siegel 2000).

The rising Latino presence should also challenge a racial stereotype of the cities of New York and Los Angeles. It is common to argue that as the proportion of minorities in these cities has risen over the past few decades the proportion of whites has dwindled. But this image of "dwindling whites" and even "white flight" runs afoul of the fact that at least half of the Latinos in these cities classify themselves as white when asked about this by the census, which is inconvenient for some people's stereotypes of Latinos. It is, therefore, more accurate to argue that the composition of the white population of these cities is changing (e.g., more Latinos, fewer Irish and Italians and former Midwesterners) rather than dwindling. This is why chapter 5 (Halle, Gedeon, and Beveridge) suggests that we need to reconsider the deeply held nostrum that whites are a fading proportion of the country's two largest cities.

MAYORAL ELECTIONS Karen Kaufmann's analysis of the past three mayoral elections in New York and Los Angeles (chap. 11) shows the growing importance of Latinos. In 2001 a Latino mayoral candidate ran strongly, though in the end unsuccessfully, in both cities. In New York, Fernando Ferrer of Puerto Rican origin narrowly lost the Democratic primary to Mark Green, while in Los Angeles Mexican-American Antonio Villaraigosa lost the general election to James Hahn. Neither city produced a viable black candidate even in the primaries. Recent mayoral elections also show how questionable the assumption is that blacks and Latinos will typically form natural political allies, an assumption that would be more obviously questionable were it to be widely acknowledged that half the Latinos in each city classify themselves as whites when asked by the census. For example, in New York City the percentage of Latinos who voted for the Republican mayoral candidate rose

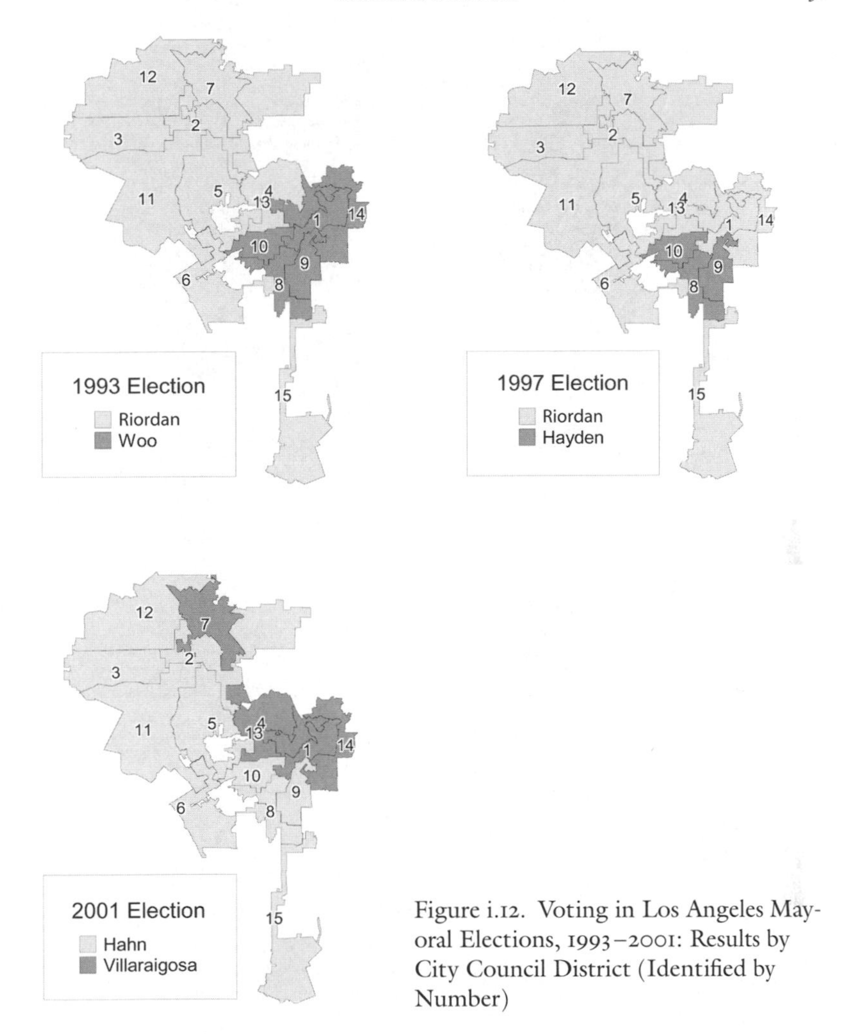

Figure i.12. Voting in Los Angeles Mayoral Elections, 1993–2001: Results by City Council District (Identified by Number)

steadily from 35 percent in 1989 to 37 percent in 1993, 43 percent in 1997, and 47 percent in 2001. By contrast, the Republican mayoral candidate never received more than 25 percent of the black vote during that time (table 11.1). Electoral maps (figs. i.12, i.13) show clearly how in both cities much of the Democratic opposition to Riordan and Giuliani in 1993 and 1997 was in areas with large concentrations of blacks. But 2001 also shows complexities, as in Los Angeles where while most Latinos voted for Villaraigosa, many blacks voted for Hahn, a liberal Republican whose politician father was seen as having done much to benefit blacks.

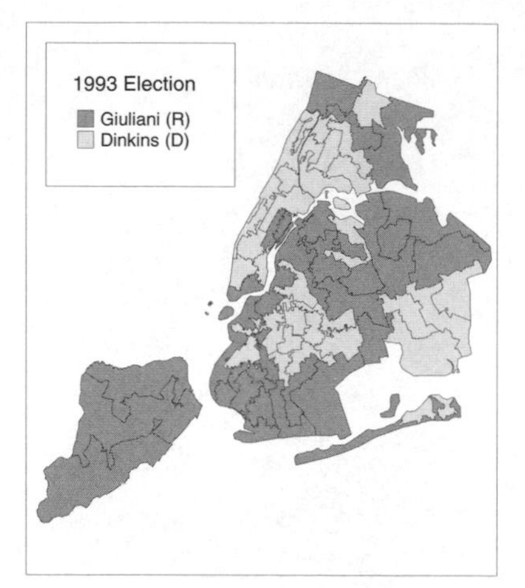

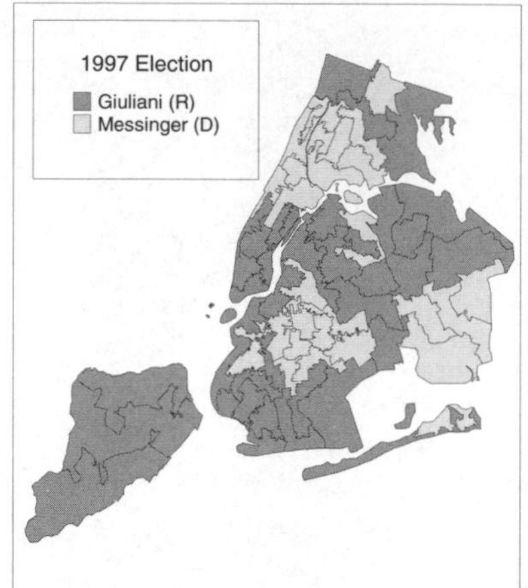

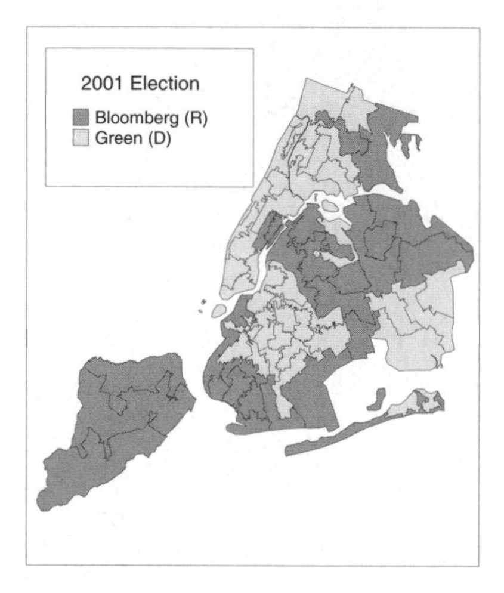

Figure i.13. Voting in New York City Mayoral Elections, 1993–2001: Results by State Assembly District

MAIN ISSUES ON VOTERS MINDS IN MAYORAL ELECTIONS

Beyond the issue of the growing Latino presence, both cities are key laboratories for studying some of the other central urban issues of our times including welfare, the economy, public schools, crime, race relations, and riots. The exit polls conducted as voters left the booths in the past three mayoral elections (1993–2001) asked voters what was the main issue determining their mayoral vote. The data, displayed in tables i.1 and i.2, show that in the city of Los Angeles the economy and education were the two main concerns in all three elections, with crime coming a constant third. In New York City, crime was of overriding concern in 1993 and important in 1997 but had faded as an issue by 2001. Race

Table i.1. Most Important Issues for Voters, Recent Los Angeles Mayoral Elections

	1993 (%)	1997 (%)	2001 (%)
Jobs/the economy	39	21	16
Education	21	38	47
Crime/gangs	15	12	11
Rebuilding Los Angeles	4	4	...
Environment	2	3	4
Illegal immigration	2	3	3
Race relations	3	2	3
Improving the Los Angeles Police Department	1	1	2
Taxes	0	1	1
Homelessnes/poverty	2	2	2
Growth/traffic (2001)	...	...	
Affordable housing (2001)	...	...	1

Sources. 1993 exit poll (3,402 respondents); 1997 exit poll (3,035 respondents), 2001 exit poll (3,422 respondents); all polls conducted by the *Los Angeles Times.*
Note. The survey question typically asked respondents which issues were most important to them in deciding how they would vote, and allowed them to check two issues. The data here present just the first issue mentioned by each respondent.

Table i.2. Most Important Issues for Voters, Recent New York Mayoral Elections

	1993 (%)	1997 (%)	2001 (%)
Crime (crime/drugs 1997)	39	32	11
Race relations	23	3	4
Quality of life (not offered as a possible response 2001)	15	24	...
Economy/jobs (jobs/unemployment/economy 1993)	12	10	43
Public schools (education 2001)	6	18	22
Police brutality (not offered as a possible response 1993 or 2001)	...	8	...
Drugs (only offered as a separate possible response 1993)	2	...	...
Taxes (only offered as a separate possible response 1997)	...	7	...
Rebuilding the financial district (2001)	...	...	8
Preventing future terrorist attacks (2001)	...	...	7
Housing (2001)	...	...	5

Sources. 1993 exit poll (1,788 respondents) conducted by Voter Research and Surveys (1993); 1997 exit poll (1,997 respondents) conducted by Voter News Service (1997); 2001 exit poll (1,608 respondents) conducted by Edison Media Research (2001).
Note. In some years (e.g., 1997), respondents were asked to select one issue only that was the most important to them in deciding how they voted for mayor, while in other years they were asked to select their first and second most important issues. The data in this table present only the first most important issue. Also, the columns may not sum to 100 percent because of rounding.

relations were a concern in 1993, doubtless reflecting the Crown Heights and Washington Heights riots of 1991–92, but faded after that. The "quality of life" (a favorite theme of Mayor Giuliani's) was a major concern in 1993 and 1997 but not in 2001, when the main issue by far was the economy, as the national recession that officially began in April 2001 was exacerbated by the economically catastrophic September 11 World Trade Center attack, just weeks before the mayoral election. The second main issue in New York City in 2001 was education. All of these topics are the subject of chapters here.

EDUCATION With 1.1 million students in New York City and 711,000 students in Los Angeles, New York and Los Angeles have the two largest public school systems in the country (the boundaries of the Los Angeles Unified School District [LAUSD] extend slightly beyond those of the city of Los Angeles, and the New York system's boundaries are those of the city). Each system is highly troubled and is perceived as such by many of their electorate. In January 2000 the new superintendent of the Los Angeles Unified School District wrote: "The LAUSD is in crisis." At the same time, New York's Mayor Giuliani described his city's public school system as "out of control" with a "bloated management." A few months later, both cities took the unprecedented step of hiring noneducators to head their school systems—Harold Levy in New York, a lawyer from the banking world, and Roy Romero in Los Angeles, a former Colorado governor. After only two years, Harold Levy was gone, as Mayor Bloomberg replaced him with another noneducator, attorney Joel Klein.

In chapter 7, Julia Wrigley highlights problems shared by the two systems. Both face overcrowding, low student achievement, and crumbling buildings. Both take in waves of immigrant students, often living in poverty and speaking limited English. Middle-class students have left each system in massive numbers heading to private schools and the suburbs. Figure i.14 shows how generally dismal is the performance of children in New York City school districts by comparison with those in the suburbs. Further, the worst performing school districts of New York State are almost all in New York City. Only in Manhattan below Ninety-sixth Street, in sections of northeast Queens, and in small sections of Brooklyn, were sixth-grade students performing at levels comparable to almost all the school districts in New York State outside the city. In much of Brooklyn, the Bronx, and northern Manhattan, a majority of students were reading at levels deemed seriously inadequate by the state. In Los Angeles as well as New York, the loss of middle-class students has

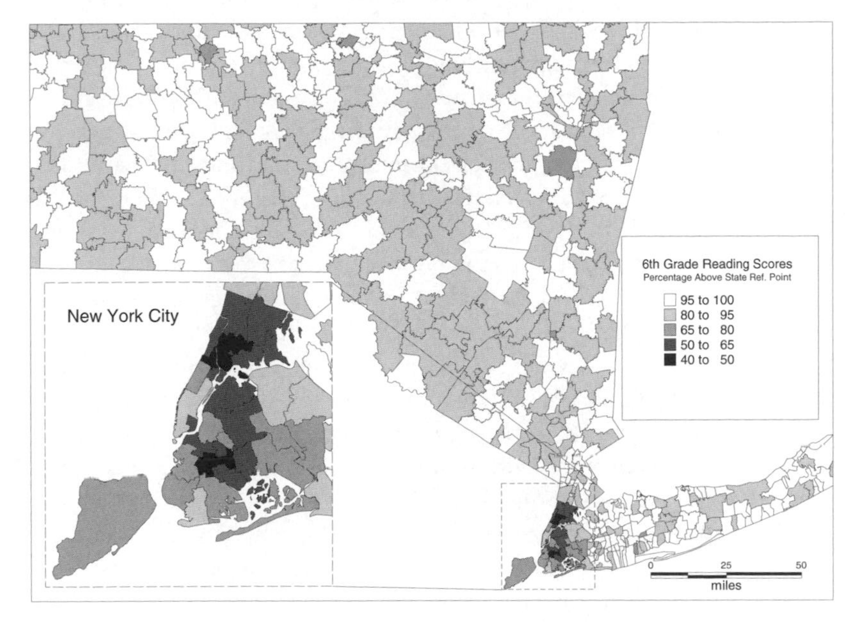

Figure i.14. 1998 New York Public Education Program Test Results—Reading

meant the loss of political clout. School boards serve as targets for their city's mayors, who assail them for ineptitude and the protection of hidebound bureaucracies. Intent on raising standards after years of social promotion, the leaders of both systems have embarked on a major refocusing of curriculum around standardized testing.

Wrigley's chapter also shows how, despite the similarities noted above, the two school districts differ in ways that reflect the familiar motifs of centralization /decentralization and political fragmentation. The New York City school bureaucracy is enormous and rigid and continually penetrates the school system down even to the classroom level. In Los Angeles, fragmentation, or the risk of it, has been a far larger issue than centralization. For the Los Angeles school district, the risk has been both physical, that the district would be dismembered, and political, in that it has operated in a chaotic political environment. Above all, it has operated in a political situation in which those it primarily serves —the children of immigrants—have had their futures controlled by non-Hispanic white voters at the state and city levels.

WELFARE REFORM The Welfare Reform Bill that President Clinton signed in August 1996 was one of the most radical pieces of legislation of the post–World War II period. It restricted all welfare recipients to five years of federal benefits in their lifetime, and it required that states enroll 30 percent of their recipients in work programs in 1998, rising to 50 percent by 2002. It cut off several key benefits from legal immigrants and from children whose parents, though poor, failed to meet the eligibility criteria for receiving welfare. In addition, the Welfare Reform Bill changed the mode of distributing welfare. It replaced federal responsibility for giving cash grants to the poor with a system of block grants to the states that allowed the latter to do almost anything they pleased so long as they kept within the restrictive criteria outlined above.

The chapters by Levitan (chap. 8) and DeVerteuil and colleagues (chap. 9) on the impact of welfare reform in New York City and Los Angeles County constitute some of the earliest reports of how this critical experiment is faring in two key places. (Local welfare programs in the United States are almost all administered by the county, which is why the Los Angeles chapter deals with data at the county level. But in New York City, welfare programs are administered by the city, so the New York welfare chapter operates at the city level.)

Long before welfare reform, both areas faced poverty rates well above the national average, partly no doubt because of their large immigrant populations. Los Angeles County's poverty rate for all residents in 1995 was 22.7 percent. compared to 16.5 percent for the state of California and 13.8 percent for the nation. New York City's poverty rate for families with children, which rose from 29.3 percent in the late 1980s to an astonishing 36.0 percent for 1993–95, and then declined to 29.5 percent in the late 1990s, was throughout this period almost twice the national average (fig. 8.1).

The results of welfare reform so far in both places suggest reasons for concern, especially given that almost the entire, short period of reform took place during an unprecedented economic expansion. By some Faustian chance, this boom ended in the first months of 2001, just about coinciding with the five-year lifetime benefits cap imposed in 1996. On the one hand, during the years of welfare reform each area drastically reduced the welfare rolls. They fell by 50,000–60,000 per year in New York City after 1996. In Los Angeles County, recipients of CalWORKS (California Work Opportunity and Responsibility to Kids: the California welfare-to-work program that replaced Aid to Families with Dependent Children after welfare reform) fell 20 percent from 1996 to 1998. This accelerated a decline in welfare rolls already long underway in Los Angeles County, as it continued to struggle with budgetary problems dating all the way back to Proposition 13, which froze property taxes in 1978.

But each area has had great difficulty in moving people from welfare into jobs that pay enough to get them out of poverty. In Los Angeles County, DeVerteuil and his colleagues report that nearly three-quarters of those, and their families, enrolled long term in the county's main welfare-to-work program were still below the poverty threshold by the late 1990s. In New York City, Mark Levitan notes a large growth from 1989 to 2000 in the percentage of "poverty families" in which at least one person was in paid employment (a "poverty family" is defined as a family with children at or below the poverty rate).[31] In the 1980s, only 29 percent of poverty families had someone who worked at any time during the year. By 1999, the figure had grown to 50 percent. This rise in the "working poor" suggests what other data support: that many of the jobs available to people who were once on the welfare rolls pay too little to keep them out of poverty.

The concerns of Levitan and DeVerteul about the growth of the working poor are supported by Gladstone and Fainstein's chapter on the economies of New York City and the city and county of Los Angeles (chap. 2). They point out that in New York City and in the city and county of Los Angeles the bifurcation of the occupational structure is growing, with a shrinking middle-income group sandwiched between a high-income sector and a vast, poorly paid working class. This growing low-wage working class is associated with the plentiful supply of immigrants, the decline of unionized jobs, and the broadening of the poorly paid service sector.

CRIME/MURDER Crime dropped dramatically in each city from the early 1990s until the end of the decade, with New York leading the way. The number of murders, a statistic laden with drama, highlights this trend (see fig. i.15). Murders tumbled from a peak of 2,245 in 1990 in New York to 629 in 1998, and then to a low of 575 in 2002, and from a peak of 1,092 in 1992 in Los Angeles to a low of 387 in 1999, even though the total population of each city was rising during this time. Figure i.16, which takes population changes into account, shows that in the city of New York the murder rate dropped from a 1990 high of 30.7 per 100,000 population to a 1999 low of 8.3, while the murder rate in the city of Los Angeles fell from a high of 30.3 in 1992 to a low of 10.5 in 1999. Recently, there has been a substantial and much noticed increase in the city of Los Angeles in some categories of crime including murders (between 1999 and 2001 the number of murders in the city of Los Angeles rose 52 percent from 387 to 587). But there is no indication of a return to the heights of the late 1980s and early 1990s.

The causes of the drop in crime have been among the most hotly

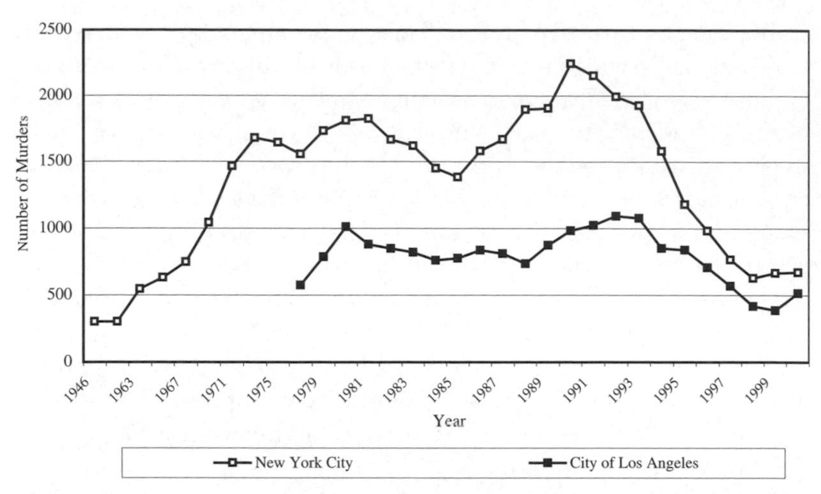

Figure i.15. Number of Murders in the Cities of New York and Los Angeles. Sources: U.S. Department of Justice, FBI (2001 and other annual reports) and New York City and city of Los Angeles Police Departments, e.g., New York City Police Department (2002) and Los Angeles Police Department (2001). Drawing on slightly different sources, Katz (chap. 6) has slightly different numbers (e.g., for New York City he reports 2,262 murders in 1990 rather than 2,245; 1,566 in 1994 rather than 1,582; and 638 in 1998 rather than 629). These minor differences, none of which affect the arguments presented in the text, reflect the fact that individual cases are reclassified over time and so on. We present both sets of figures rather than trying to impose a uniform "truth" on the data.

Figure i.16. Numbers of Murders per 100,000 Population, Cities of New York and Los Angeles. Sources: see figure i.15.

debated topics in contemporary America, with much of the debate focusing on New York City. The city's innovative and articulate police commissioner, William Bratton, credited new police tactics adopted while he was commissioner, from 1993 to 1995 (Bratton and Knobler 1998).[32] Critics replied that since the number of murders in New York City was falling for two years before Bratton became commissioner, if anyone in city government is to get credit it should be then Mayor David Dinkins and his police commissioner Raymond Kelly. But these critics also questioned whether police tactics had anything much to do with the drop in crime, which they pointed out occurred in other cities where the New York Police Department's tactics were not adopted (see references cited in chap. 6). They argued, instead, that demographics (especially a drop in the teenage population, which commit a disproportionate share of crime) and the decline of the crack epidemic were responsible for the decline in murders. Bratton and his supporters replied that the teenage population was not, in fact, declining in either city, and even if the number of murders was falling in New York City before Bratton became commissioner, it fell at a much faster rate after he took over. Others added that some of Bratton's reforms had, indeed, been introduced two years earlier by Raymond Kelly, which would explain why crime rates started to fall before Bratton began. The appointment of Bratton in November 2000 as chief of the LAPD, with a public mandate to repeat his New York City success and to reform the LAPD in the light of its Rampart scandal (see below), provides a fascinating test of Bratton's theory that police reforms introduced by an energetic leadership can make a major difference in crime rates and police culture. In truth, the complete causes of the decline have not been understood, which is why one of the recent studies of the topic was titled *New York Murder Mystery* (Karmen 2000).

At the same time as crime declined, notorious cases of police brutality toward minorities emerged, raising the question of the cost in each city of achieving lower crime rates. In New York there was the 1997 Abner Louima case followed by the Diallo case in February 1999 (both described in chap. 6), followed in March 2000 by the Patrick Dorismond case (described in chap. 13).

In Los Angeles there was the Rodney King beating in 1992. Then, toward the end of 1999, details of the Rampart scandal began to emerge, a scandal that was as bad as anything ever portrayed in any Los Angeles noir novel or movie. As many as seventy members of a Los Angeles Police Department (LAPD) antigang unit stationed in Rampart, west of downtown and one of the city of Los Angeles's toughest neighborhoods, had been robbing, murdering, and framing gang members for many years, thus exploiting the propensity in the city to attribute serious crime to gangs (Cannon 2000).

Jack Katz's chapter (chap. 6) enormously enhances our understanding of the cultural climate that allowed Rampart to happen. Katz writes about how Los Angeles has had, over the past three decades, a reputation as being ridden with gangs, who have then been blamed as a major cause of crime. By contrast, crime in New York City has, during the same period, been far less likely to be seen as caused by gangs and far more likely to be seen as the result of uncontrollable and chaotic, often random, forces. Katz argues that these two dominant ways of understanding the causes of crime are rooted in cultural myths that pervade each city rather than in statistical reality. Further, these myths are dangerous since they can contribute to violence and instability. For example, an important contributory cause of the 1992 riots was community anger at the LAPD's recent arrest of hundreds of gang members, arrests driven and justified by the gang theory of the origin of crime in the city. This "gang myth," as became clear several years later, was also quietly acting as a shelter for the Rampart scandal.

In an intellectual tour de force reminiscent of the work of the French analyst of social myths, Claude Lévi Strauss, and showing the potential of a comparison that relates the economic/material structure to cultural analysis, Katz argues that each city has, in recent years, had a mythical image of its police force that interacts dialectically with its mythical image of the causes of crime. In Los Angeles the police force has been seen as disorganized and incompetent, in contrast with the image of most crime as the result of organized gangs. In New York, the police force has been seen as largely organized and professional (an image Bratton both benefited from and helped bolster) in contrast with the disorganized and random nature of much of the crime. Here too, Katz argues, the reality is more complex than the image.

The saddest of the many examples that support Katz's insight is the World Trade Center attack of September 11, 2001. For about an hour-and-a half after the first and second planes struck, hundreds of people were trapped in floors above the flames, unable to descend by stairs, and calling for help on their cell phones. Although police helicopters were hovering nearby, there were no helicopter landing facilities on the top of either tower and the doors to the roof were securely locked, as always at that time, making it impossible for people to escape onto the roof from where they might have been rescued. Yet not until six weeks after the event did the first story appear asking why there was no New York Police Department (NYPD) helicopter rescue (*Wall Street Journal* 2001). It turned out that years of squabbling between the NYPD and the Fire

Department had allowed the Fire Department's view to prevail that during fires helicopter rescue attempts, the province of the NYPD, were pure grandstanding and should be discouraged at all costs. It also turned out that Los Angeles was the only major city in the United States that required all high-rises to have helicopter pads on their roofs and had elaborate plans and procedures, successfully implemented on several occasions, for rescuing people by helicopter from burning high-rise buildings. There is little doubt that if, in a similar tragedy in Los Angeles, it had emerged that the city had allowed its most prominent skyscrapers to lock people in so that they could not escape onto the roof and had made the roof inaccessible to rescue helicopters, there would have been an immediate torrent of criticism of the police and fire forces for allowing this.

If the World Trade Center attack underlined Katz's point about a tendency in New York City in recent years to place the police and fire forces on a pedestal, the 2002 unraveling of the Central Park wilding rape story of 1990 underlined his point about the tendency in New York City to see crime as chaotic and random. The most famous underpinning of this myth was the story of a group of roving youths who supposedly raped and beat almost to death a young female Wall Street professional who was jogging in Central Park. The youths were sent to jail, and the story, and its lessons, were much mulled over and entered popular culture as a classic case of an unpremeditated set of acts by rampaging and unorganized ("wild") kids. Yet thirteen years later, in a revelation that stunned analysts (e.g., Kassin 2002), DNA evidence from semen proved that the core of the "wilding" attack story was myth. It turned out that the assault had been committed by a single, older assailant, a serial rapist and murderer (i.e., an entirely predictable perpetrator for such a crime) who had never even been mentioned at the original trial.

Katz suggests some causes of these respective New York and Los Angeles myths. To explain the Los Angeles stress on gangs as the cause of crime, he points to the massive immigration into Los Angeles in recent decades, which has brought an unaccustomed (by contrast with New York City) influx of young people from backgrounds and places that are quite different from those of traditional Angelenos. These young people, from cultures often not well understood by other residents, afford a context for the dark conviction that a multitude of gangs of youngsters are out there planning crimes. To explain the contrasting images of the two police departments, Katz points to the fact that in New York City seven prosecution offices (a district attorney for each borough and two federal-level U.S. attorney offices) are available to go after police misbehavior and are ready to compete to do so, if necessary. Hence police misbehavior in New York City, when it surfaces, is likely to be prosecuted aggressively, which bolsters the view that the NYPD is held to high professional standards. By contrast, in Los Angeles, prosecuting police misbehavior is the job of a single (Los Angeles) county district attorney plus one U.S. attorney whose jurisdiction is all central California, making for lackadaisical oversight.

RACE RELATIONS AND RIOTS David Sears (chap. 13) constructs a balance sheet of black-white conflict in Los Angeles over the past forty years, which he then compares with New York City. On the one hand is a series of racially charged events, some specific to Los Angeles and some also statewide. They include Proposition 14 in California in 1964, which repealed the recently enacted Rumford Fair Housing Act (67 percent of the voters in the city of Los Angeles voted for repeal); the 1965 riot in Watts, the most destructive race riot to that point in post–World War II America; the formation of "Bustop" in the San Fernando Valley in 1978 to force the recall of LAUSD school board members who had voted for mandatory busing; the racially polarized 1978 debate throughout California over the passage of California's landmark tax revolt; Proposition 13, which capped property taxes and implicitly attacked spending on welfare, public schools, and public health; the 1992 Rodney King acquittal riots; and the 1996 passage of Proposition 209, which eliminated all state and local affirmative action programs for minorities and women. On the other hand, a liberal biracial coalition reelected Tom Bradley as mayor of Los Angeles for five consecutive terms from 1973 to 1989, making Los Angeles the only major American city with a small black population (which never exceeded 18 percent during this period) to have a black mayor serving even one term in the 1970s and 1980s.

Sears suggests that racial polarization in New York City during the same period has not necessarily been less severe. Although its proportion of blacks was often more than double that of the city of Los Angeles, it has managed only one black mayor, Dinkins (1987–93). And survey data indicate that public opinion in New York City was even more racially polarized over the killing of Amadou Diallo by the New York police than was public opinion in the city of Los Angeles over the beating of Rodney King.

My own essay with Kevin Rafter (chap. 12), which discusses riots, the ultimate breakdown of social order in the city, questions, like Sears, whether Los Angeles is really worse on this score than New York is. Because of the 1992 Rodney King verdict upheavals, which made Los Angeles the only city in America to have a mega riot in the 1990s comparable in scale to some of the biggest urban riots of the 1960s, the city of Los Angeles might appear more prone to major riots than is New York City or any other American city. Yet in the 1990s New York City had two major, albeit not mega, riots, one just before and one just after the Rodney King riots ("major" and "mega" are defined in chap. 12). The August 1991 riot between blacks and orthodox Jews in Crown Heights, Brooklyn, lasted four days and probably cost mayor Dinkins the 1993 election, and a July 1992 riot in Washington Heights in northern Manhattan, which was triggered by a police officer's fatal shooting of an unarmed Dominican resident, lasted six days, a day longer than the Rodney King riots in Los Angeles. Further, despite the tendency of many New Yorkers to believe that their city does not have mega riots, the blackout-related riots of July 13, 1977, were arguably just that. During the twenty-five hours the city was without lighting there was widespread looting—just over 1,600 stores—in every city borough, a total of thirty-one mostly poor neighborhoods. More stores were looted than in either of the two Los Angeles mega riots, Watts in 1965 and Rodney King in 1992. In short, a systematic comparison of riots in the two cities/regions since 1930 suggests that neither city has reason for complacency.

Both chapters speculate about the future. My and Rafter's chapter suggests that the cases of the cities of Los Angeles, New York, and Miami, which have seen many of the most serious riots of the past thirty years, may be harbingers of a return, in the context of recent heightened immigration, of the interethnic/racial riots (e.g. blacks/Latinos against Koreans in 1992 in Los Angeles, Jews vs. blacks in Crown Heights in 1991) that were the dominant type of riot throughout the nineteenth and early twentieth centuries but, since the 1960s, had appeared to have faded from the American scene. Sears argues that Asians and Latinos will in the long run assimilate into American society, but like Nathan Glazer (1997, 120–21), he predicts continued "black exceptionalism," whereby blacks will be markedly more separate, more subject to discrimination, and more prone to civil upheaval than any other group.

DEFINING THE BORDERS OF LOS ANGELES AND NEW YORK

The contributors to this collection have, quite appropriately, different geographic foci as they consider "New York" and "Los Angeles." For some, such as Sonenshein on city charters, Kaufmann on mayoral elections, and Katz on explanations of crime, the main discussion is limited to the borders of the two cities. Other contributors move somewhat beyond the city borders for either New York or Los Angeles or both, as with Szántó's discussion of the dispersed nature of art galleries in Los Angeles, Zhou and Kim's discussion of the suburbanization of Chinese in Monterey Park, and my discussion of the 1967 mega riot in Newark, New Jersey. Some contributors broaden the focus still further to include the entire region, the consolidated metropolitan statistical area. An example is Beveridge's discussion of patterns of population growth, income distribution, residential racial concentration, and commuting.

Monitoring the interplay between various geographic borders is enormously revealing. Indeed, many debates over differences between Los Angeles and New York turn on a confusion over which geographic unit is the point of comparison, in particular, whether the geographic unit is:

1. the two cities;
2. the two cities plus the counties that immediately surround them; or
3. the entire region as defined by the U.S. Census Bureau, the "consolidated metropolitan statistical area" or CMSA. (Beveridge in chap. 1 chronicles the Census Bureau's attempts, culminating in its introduction of the concept of a CMSA in 1970, to find geographical boundaries that are adequate to capture these sprawling metro areas.)

In this book, we take care to avoid using "Los Angeles" or "New York" without specifying a precise geographic referent. The main exception is Giovacchini's analysis of "Hollywood" (chap. 15), which, following the historian Carey McWilliams, Giovacchini refers to as a "a state of mind, not a geographical entity"(McWilliams [1946] 1983, 330). Giovacchini's study traces the way the reputation of Hollywood among intellectuals, especially those based in New York, has fluctuated from 1930 to the present. The least flattering image of Hollywood was that which prevailed midway in this period, from 1948 to 1960. Using the momentum of the House Committee on Un-American Activities' attacks in 1947, Hollywood was widely denigrated by New York intellectuals as a machine for the production of a mass culture, which the audiences then absorbed passively. New York, by contrast, was thought of as an island of independent, avant-garde, and creative filmmaking. The picture of Hollywood reflected by New York before 1948, and since 1960, is far more respectful and subtle. For example, in recent decades such successful contemporary New York–based filmmakers as Spike Lee and Martin Scorcese have absorbed Hollywood's narrative style without feeling the need to move or film there. As Giovacchini has said of this "new hybridized cinema," "by the mid seventies it was possible to 'go Hollywood linguistically' while maintaining a Manhattan address" (chap. 15, 444). New York films, New York actors, and especially New York streets are increasingly at the fore of American mass-market cinema. Indeed, movie audiences now display a growing interest, perhaps even at times obsession, with New York City. In only two consecutive years from 1968 to 1999 did New York City fail to figure prominently in a top-five grossing movie.[33]

THE BOOK'S SCOPE AND LIMITS AND THE COMPACT DISC/WEB SOLUTION

This collection is not intended as an encyclopedic account of the two cities/regions. Rather, it covers many of the central themes and interests of the Los Angeles and New York schools in an updated form that reflects today's issues. Comparing the cities that symbolically represent the two dominant, but very different, motifs of urban studies—the decentralized periphery and the revitalization of city centers—ensures that the topics studied will cover many of the central issues facing urban America. It also ensures that any claims to uniqueness on the part of one city or region will be subjected to scrutiny. This study could have gone beyond New York and Los Angeles to include detailed comparisons of other urban regions, and almost all the contributors quite properly make some reference to other cities. But to focus explicitly on more than these two mega cities/regions would have involved a loss of richness and detail. Anyway, other scholars will, for sure, continue to undertake comparisons of a variety of other key megalopolises.

Some excellent books have focused on Los Angeles or New York through a single lens or topic, but an axiom of this book is the need to consider a cluster of motifs.[34] For one thing, the various topics of this study clearly interact dynamically in the social and political life of the city and the region and can, thus, only be fully understood in relation to each other. This interdependence of topics and themes is why studies that focus on a single one of the topics dealt with in this book, or on what might seem like a master topic as in the "globalization" of such cities as New York, Paris and Miami, typically end up in fact covering a series of topics. So it seems appropriate to recognize these as separate but related topics from the start and consider them together in one study.[35]

There remain many issues to cover, and I hope this book will stimulate others to cover them. At the same time, one innovation of this book is that it comes with a CD, available from the UCLA LeRoy Neiman Center. This CD has several aims and advantages. It includes material that simply cannot be included in a book. Thus it contains Andrew Beveridge's software program Social Explorer, which allows the user to access easily census data and maps for the New York and Los Angeles CMSAs for every decade of the twentieth century. The CD also allows contributors to update their chapters with data and events that have occurred since the book's publication. And it includes material that could not be included in the book without making it too large to market at an affordable price. As an alternative, much of this material is also available on the UCLA LeRoy Neiman Center Web site.

PART I

OVERVIEW

CHAPTER ONE

Race and Class in the Developing New York and Los Angeles Metropolises

1940–2000

Andrew A. Beveridge and Susan Weber

Everyone has seen the Saul Steinberg poster, *The View from Ninth Avenue,* according to which New York is "Gotham," the center of the universe. There is little west of the Hudson, except Chicago, Kansas City, Las Vegas, Utah, Texas, and, of course, far distant Los Angeles and the Pacific Ocean. The contrary image of Los Angeles is of a "great big freeway." There is "no there, there," which, of course, was originally said of Oakland. According to the stereotype, the sprawl in southern California has no counterpart in New York, still considered a walking city where old ethnic neighborhoods thrive and people take taxicabs and subways and even walk from home to work. In Los Angeles, everyone drives, there is little public transportation, and, indeed, one can be stopped and even arrested for walking. Movies such as *LA Story* and *Bowfinger,* songs from such groups as the Beach Boys and Randy Newman's classic *We Love LA,* Raymond Chandler novels, and general perceptions drive these stereotypes home.

Yet, if one looks at the entire metropolis of New York and of Los Angeles, both sets of stereotypes begin to give way. New York City is part of a larger urban structure that spans four states and includes many affluent suburbs, along with other areas of urban density. The Bureau of the Census, starting as early as 1940, has formally recognized this development. As will be seen, the inner-city "core" of New York, with the exception of much of Manhattan, is becoming more and more a remnant from an earlier era. Furthermore, most recent development has occurred outside of the "city limits." The New Jersey Turnpike, for instance, is every bit as large and heavily traveled as many of the freeways in Los Angeles. A governor of New Jersey ran radio commercials touting the advantages to business of locating on one of the turnpike's many exits.

Local and state governments foster this outward development, even while some have decried it. This pattern has major and unsettling implications for the organization of many features of metropolitan life, including education, health care, employment, transportation, the arts, and shopping. The provision of government services by numerous local entities fosters inequality. Conflicting patterns of aid from each of the state governments and the fragmentation of authority furthers it even more. Nassau County, for instance, has some 3,000 separate tax rates for its residences, depending on which of the many taxing authorities applies to where one lives. There is even a taxing authority for an escalator to one of the Long Island Railroad Stations (Schemo 1994). The crazy quilt pattern of school districts, villages, cities, and towns also abets this fragmentation. New York City has one school district, for instance, and teaches about 43 percent (more than 1.1 million) of all of the children in New York State. Westchester County has forty-two districts, many of them with fewer than a thousand kids. School districts outside of the city do not necessarily follow municipal lines. Yet, often upward of 80 percent of property taxes flow to school districts.

This chapter will examine the extent to which there has been a convergence of urban patterns in these two important metropolises, tracing their development from 1940 through 2000. It will observe shifts in income and race and the extent to which New York City's and Los Angeles's hinterlands are integrated into their core areas.[1] We will see that the "LA-ification" of the New York metropolis is far advanced, though substantial differences remain. Also, to some extent a "New York–ification" of Los Angeles's inner core has been underway for some time, with conglomerations of neighborhoods of poor people alongside moves to enhance the city's parks and to make downtown attractive to the middle class.

WHAT CONSTITUTES THE NEW YORK AND LOS ANGELES METROPOLISES?

The exact limits of the New York metropolitan area, what we prefer to call the "New York metropolis," is subject to much discussion. The Regional Planning Association, for instance, a group that has believed for decades that New York City is really a region, defines an area of thirty-one counties. Many people use the area of seventy-five miles from Times Square. Other regional organizations and the media choose other definitions, all of which have some merit.

The Census Bureau, the Web site for which used to bill itself as "The Official Statistics," has been concerned to conceptualize the expanding boundaries of metropolitan areas for many decades.[2] It, along with the Office of Management and Budget, is responsible for defining metropolitan boundaries/areas of various sorts. Figure 1.1 presents the overlapping definitions of the New York City metropolitan area that the Census Bureau has used since 1940 when it first formally considered New York City to be part of a larger metropolitan district. The bureau's 1940 definition of a metropolitan district was based on collections of townships or so-called minor civil divisions, which are subcounty areas. In the East these are towns but can vary in size from about 720,000 (Hempstead on Long Island) to a few thousand. In 1950 and later, the bureau used counties throughout the United States to define metropolitan areas, except in New England, where towns were still used. The bureau expanded the New York metropolitan area to include such counties as Suffolk, Westchester, Somerset, and Morris. In 1970, recognizing the need for further expansion of these boundaries, the bureau first introduced its consolidated metropolitan statistical area (CMSA) concept. Figure 1.1 shows that by 1995 the New York CMSA consisted of twenty-nine counties and small parts of two others; it has within it some fifteen primary metropolitan areas. The only differences between the 1990 and 1995 CMSAs were the addition of the New Haven–Meriden and Waterbury metropolitan areas and the inclusion of rural Pike County, Pa. With all of the changes on the "borders" of the metropolitan area, the core point remains: New York City's five boroughs are now joined with well over twenty counties to form a large metropolitan area.

The Los Angeles metropolis now consists of the five counties delineated in figure 1.2. Even in 1940 the Los Angeles metropolitan district also included parts of Orange and San Bernardino Counties, though the city of Los Angeles was its core. For 1950 and 1960, the metropolitan district was expanded to include all of Orange County combined with all of Los Angeles County and was called the Los Angeles metropolitan statistical area. San Bernardino became its own metropolitan area. In 1970, Riverside was added to the San Bernardino metropolitan area, while Orange County became a metropolitan area of its own, as did Ventura County. Although the Census Bureau first introduced its consolidated metropolitan statistical area concept in 1970, only New York and Chicago, the first and second largest cities, qualified. The bureau did not yet recognize the unified metropolitan character of the Los Angeles region.

In 1980, the area that is now the Los Angeles consolidated metropolitan statistical area was finally designated. It is a huge area of five

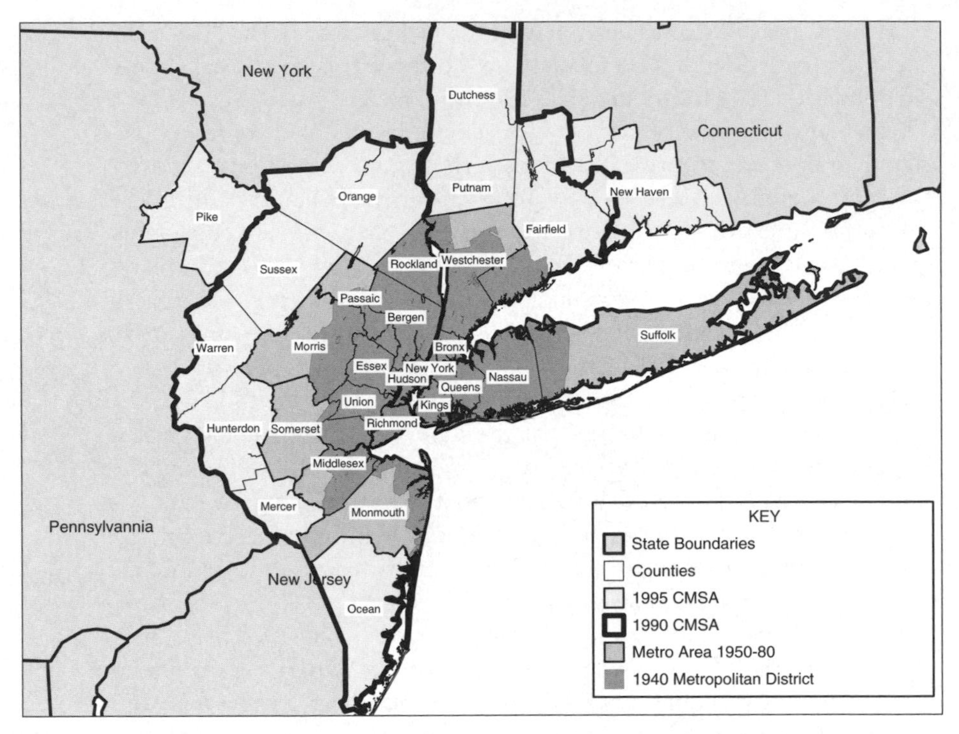

Figure 1.1. Changing Definitions of New York Metropolitan Area, 1940–2000: New York CMSA, 1990–95; Metro Area, 1950–80; and Metro District, 1940

counties: Los Angeles, Orange, San Bernardino, Riverside, and Ventura. The definition has remained constant since then. This is the area we will compare with the New York metropolis (CMSA).

CREATING METROPOLITAN DIFFERENCES: 1940–2000

What have been the directions of development of the New York and Los Angeles metropolises since World War II? For New York City, many of the social and political trends are well known. They include the following: movement of population to the suburbs; continuing migration of African-Americans from the South at least until about twenty years ago; a dip and then increase in the number of migrants from abroad; heavy migration of population out of the area to other parts of the United States. While large-scale suburbs were developing in New York, the Los Angeles area continued to settle and to sprawl. Though some people

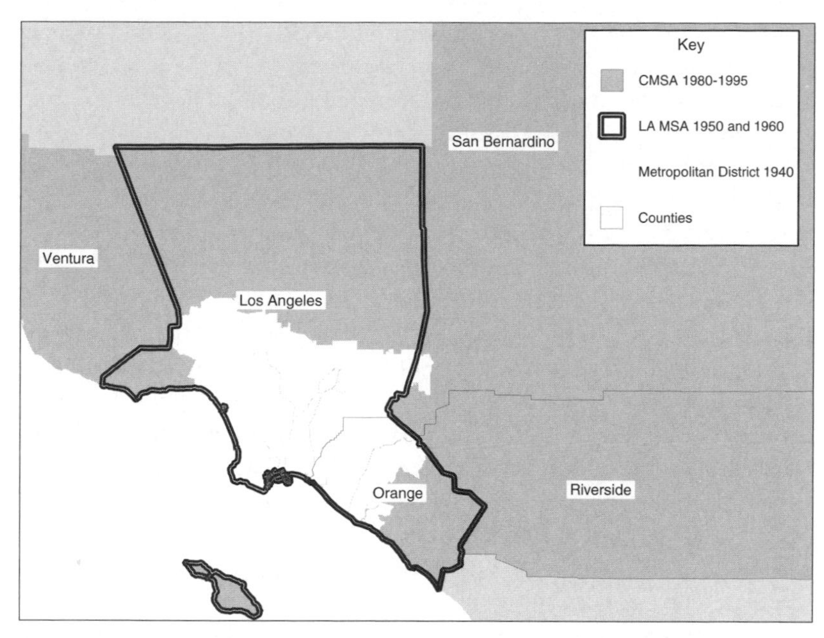

Figure 1.2. Changing Definitions of the Los Angeles Metropolitan Area: Los Angeles Standard Consolidated Statistical Area/Consolidated Metropolitan Statistical Area (SCSA/CMSA), 1980–95; Metro Statistical Area, 1950 and 1960; and Metro District, 1940

might have been leaving New York, California was one of the major destinations for emigrants. How have these patterns shaped the metropolises? Have they made the New York area, in part at least, much more like Los Angeles? Have they made Los Angeles more like New York?

To look at these questions, the current five-county Los Angeles CMSA and twenty-nine-county New York CMSA were used. For New York, the counties were classified as belonging to one of three different groups: core urban, near to the core, and periphery. The placement of counties requires some comment. The core consisted of four of the five boroughs of New York, with Staten Island excluded. The core also includes Hudson and Essex Counties in New Jersey. Staten Island was excluded because even today it is not strictly an urban area. Indeed, there was, in the early 1990s, a movement for Staten Island to secede from New York City, from most of which it is truly very different. Hudson and Essex Counties in New Jersey are included in the core because Hudson includes the older cities of Jersey City, Hoboken, and Bayonne, while Essex includes the city of Newark, one of the most highly concentrated urban environments in the country. This classification only points up the arbitrary nature of political boundaries and the fact that specific characteristics do not necessarily relate to such boundaries. The counties designated as near include Staten Island, Nassau, and Westchester in New York and Bergen, Passaic, and Union in New Jersey. Each of these counties is directly adjacent to a core county. The other seventeen counties are periphery.

The Los Angeles metropolis was divided in a similar manner. The Los Angeles core consisted of the Los Angeles minor civil division. This includes the city of Los Angeles and the embedded municipalities of Beverly Hills, West Hollywood, Culver City, Ladera Heights, Marina Del Ray, and View-Park Windsor Hills. The extent to which these municipalities shared services with Los Angeles has changed over time. Indeed, Ladera Heights and Marina Del Ray were only recently incorporated. As of 2000, these small municipalities had a combined population of about 170,000, roughly 4.3 percent of the 3.9 million total population of the Los Angeles minor civil division. The core also includes unincorporated East Los Angeles. Including all these areas with the city of Los Angeles makes it possible to assess the changes over time in a geographically homogenous region. The near area consists of the rest of Los Angeles County, while the periphery is the other four counties. One could argue that the division of the Los Angeles metropolis into these three areas is somewhat arbitrary. But since the object of this analysis is to compare Los Angeles and New York, it is important to divide both in roughly the same way. Furthermore, if the divisions are truly that arbitrary in Los Angeles, then no real pattern should emerge, which is not the case, as we show.

Figure 1.3 reveals that in New York the population of the core counties has barely increased since 1940 and, indeed, suffered a sharp drop from 1970 to 1980 from which it has only recently recovered.[3] The population of the near counties increased markedly from 1940 to 1970 but then ceased to grow. By contrast, the population of the counties in the periphery increased continually. They substantially surpassed the near suburbs by 1970 and would by now be approaching the total population of the core had not the latter started to grow again from 1990 on.

In 1940 the total population of the New York area (CMSA) was roughly 13 million, about 8.8 million or two-thirds of whom were in the core. By 2000, the New York area had a population of more than 21 million, but now only 42.5 percent of this in the core. New York moved from being a highly concentrated urban region to looking much more like a large metropolitan area.

The growth pattern of Los Angeles has both differences and similarities. Unlike New York, Los Angeles's core more than doubled from

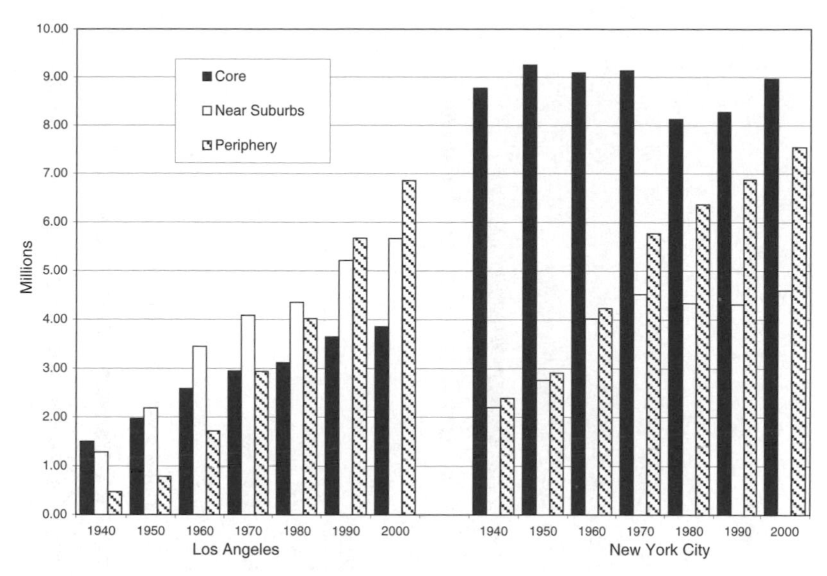

Figure 1.3. Population Composition of Los Angeles and New York City Metropolitan Areas, 1940–2000. (Source: table 1.A1.)

1940 to 2000. Like New York, in Los Angeles the near and periphery grew, but the rate of growth in Los Angeles was much faster. The near area more than quadrupled, while the periphery grew almost fifteenfold. At present, only modest growth is continuing to occur in the core and near areas, but the periphery is still growing rapidly. Considering the metropolis as a whole, the periphery now constitutes about 42 percent of Los Angeles, compared with about 36 percent for New York. Both metropolises now have a substantial fraction of their population well distant from the center. Plainly, New York is becoming more like Los Angeles.

The starkness of the change in both metropolises becomes even more obvious when the composition of the population is examined. Figure 1.4 presents data on the "nonwhite" population. The growth of nonwhite in the core is breathtaking. In 1940 the core of New York was 6.4 percent nonwhite, while the near and the periphery were 3.9 and 3.5 percent, respectively. By 1950, the core was about 10 percent nonwhite, while the near and periphery had barely changed. By 2000 the core was 56 percent nonwhite, compared with 26 percent in the near counties and 18 percent in the periphery. Some areas with large concentrations of nonwhites, such as Yonkers and Bridgeport, are not included in the definition of the core because they are located in the periphery though ecologically, as urban areas, they are really core. Were these areas to be

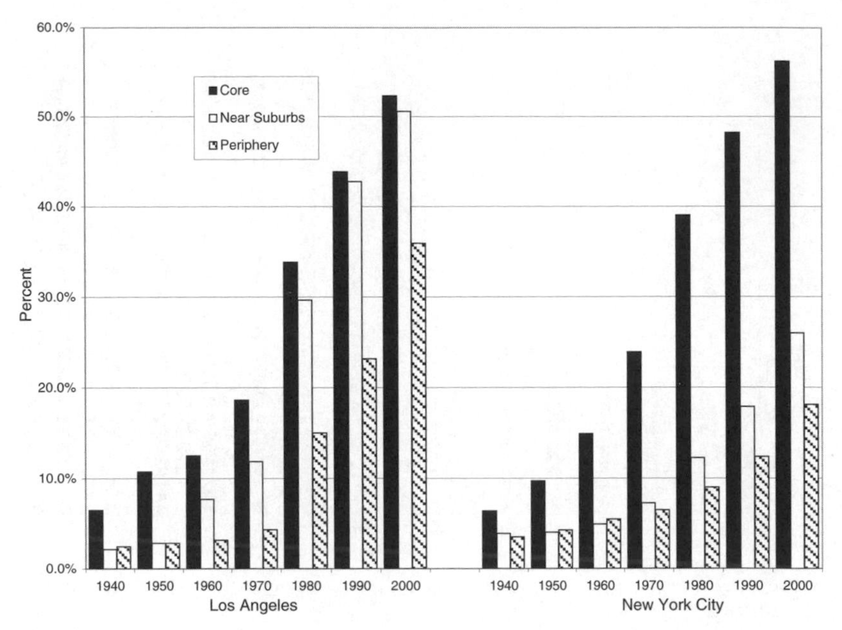

Figure 1.4. Percent Nonwhite, 1940–2000, in Los Angeles and New York City Metropolitan Areas. (Source: table 1.A2.)

included as core, the proportion of nonwhites in the suburban periphery would appear even smaller.

The pattern in Los Angeles for the core is similar. It went from 6.5 percent nonwhite in 1940 to 52 percent in 2000. But in Los Angeles the near and periphery are much more nonwhite than in New York. The near suburban area is about 51 percent nonwhite, and even the periphery is 36 percent nonwhite.

Notice that though the proportion of "whites" has declined markedly in both cores, it remains sizable at around half the total population. A common stereotype that suggests that the white proportion of each core has declined much further than this is based on the practice of excluding from the whites all Hispanics who classify themselves as "white" on the census, a practice that we (Halle, Gedeon, and Beveridge) discuss and criticize in chapter 5.

The pattern for median family income is shown in figure 1.5. The gap between core and near/periphery has grown in both New York and Los Angeles, but at a faster rate in New York. In 1950, the median family income in both New York and Los Angeles was a little higher in the near than in the periphery or core, but these differences were not marked. By 2000, the income gap between the core and the rest of the region is very

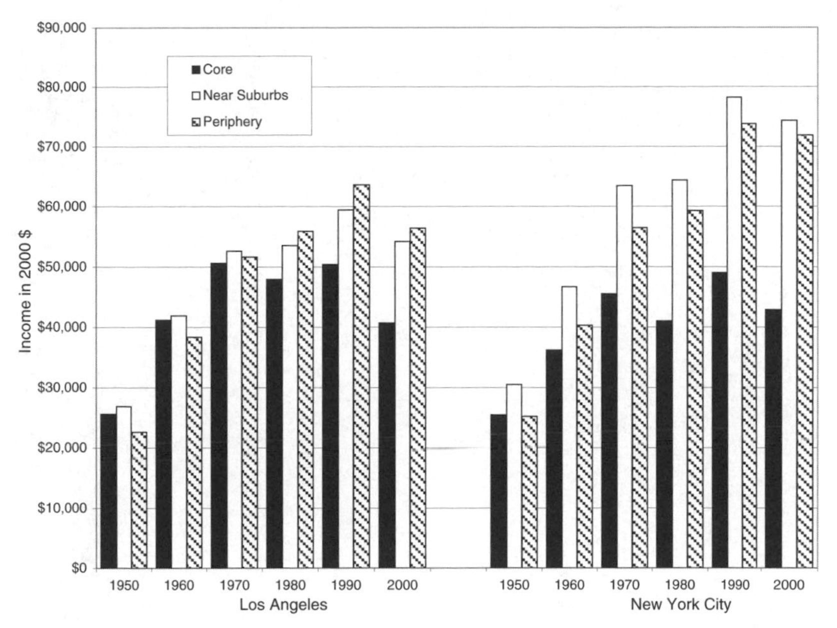

Figure 1.5. Median Family Income (2000 $) in Los Angeles and New York City Metropolitan Areas, 1940–2000. (Source: table 1.A3.)

large in New York. Median family income in the core is $42,900, but more than $74,000 and $71,000, respectively, for the near and periphery. In Los Angeles, a similar but less sizable difference between core and near/periphery is found in 2000, roughly $40,709 for the core, $54,207 for the near and $56,402 for the periphery.

In short, the 2000 census revealed that for both New York and Los Angeles, those who lived in the periphery, on balance, did better than those in either the near suburbs or in the core. Still, the comparison between 1990 and 2000 is revealing. There was a decline in median income in both regions in the core, near, and periphery, though the decline was far more marked in the core, especially in Los Angeles. Indeed, median income in the Los Angeles core was lower in 2000 than it was in 1960. Doubtless much of this decline was due to rapid immigration.

In New York City, the decline in income in the core did not, on the whole, occur in Manhattan, which is likely why median income in New York's core did not fall as far as that in the core of Los Angeles. Indeed, virtually every neighborhood in Manhattan, except for Chinatown, experienced an increase. The rapid growth of the financial sector fueled a boom that saw those living in the Wall Street area, in Tribeca, in Soho, in Morningside Heights, and in the Upper West Side with much higher

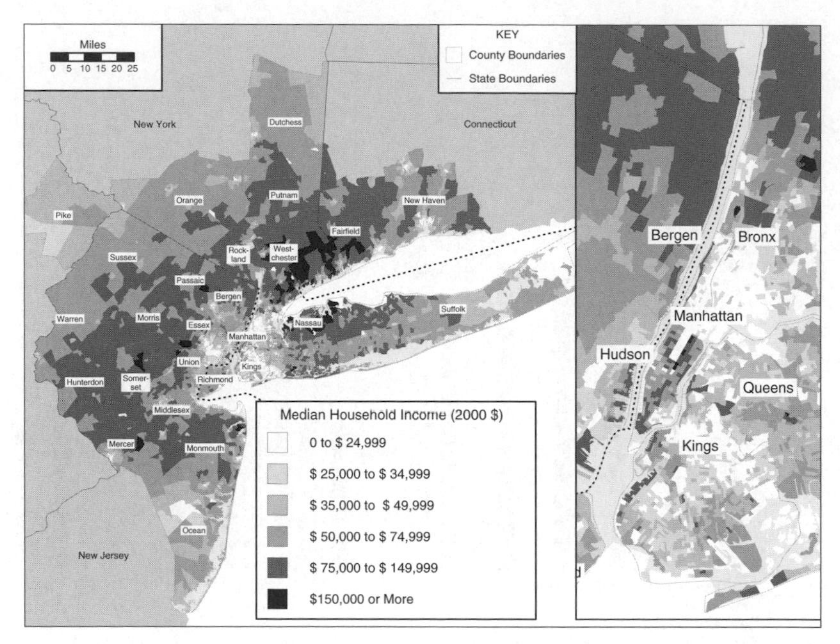

Figure 1.6. Income Distribution, New York Area, 2000, by Census Tract

median income in 2000 than in 1990. The boom spread to Harlem, East Harlem, and Washington Heights. Income grew, too, in certain well-known "hot neighborhoods" in Brooklyn—Boerum Hill, Brooklyn Heights, Carroll Gardens, Park Slope (including South Slope), Prospect Heights, and Williamsburg. New Yorkers did not have to be involved in finance to participate in Manhattan's boom. The stockbroker benefited his landlady in Carroll Gardens, restaurateurs could open new eateries in Williamsburg, real estate values could surge in "the Slope."

Even on the periphery of both regions, median income fell from 1990 to 2000, very slightly in New York, somewhat more in Los Angeles, which did not have the benefit of an expanding Wall Street sector to offset a sharp decline in well-paid jobs in aerospace there. Most of the new jobs created in that decade were not especially well-paying. The decline of income even on the periphery serves as a reminder of the heterogeneity of the suburbs and of the fact, now increasingly recognized (e.g., Krugman 2002), that many of the gains of the 1990s were highly concentrated in the upper 1–5 percent of households.

The distribution of income in New York and Los Angeles is shown in figures 1.6 and 1.7, respectively. The well-known pattern of higher income moving west from Los Angeles is shown graphically (Beverly

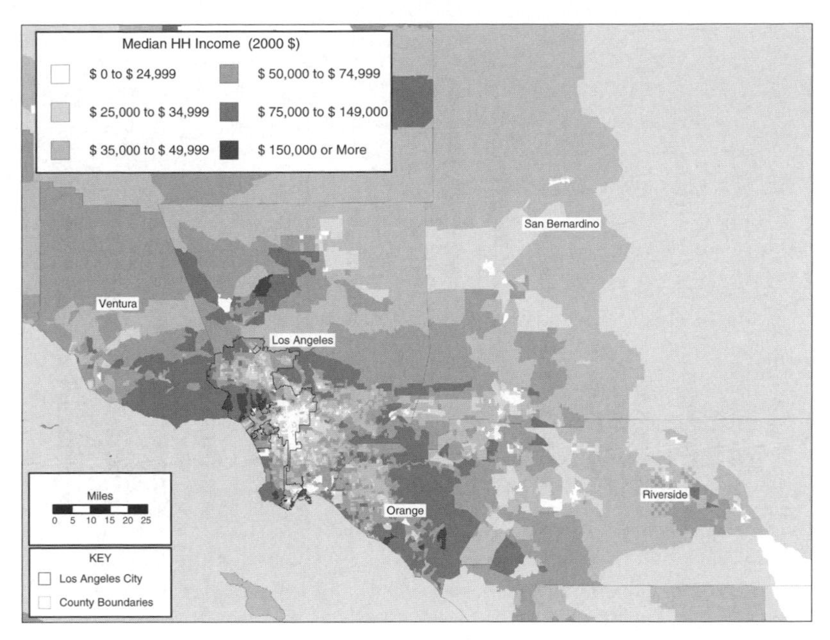

Figure 1.7. Income Distribution, Los Angeles Area, 2000, by Census Tract

Hills, Century City, etc). Other areas of high-income concentration appear near some beach areas and in some of the areas with hills. High income in Los Angeles, as in New York, seems to follow areas with low concentrations of African-American or Hispanic population and to cluster outside the core.

A careful look shows that there are only a few high-income areas left in New York City. These include the upper east and west sides (the latter at least up to the Eightieth Street), Brooklyn Heights, Battery Park, and some "gentrifying areas," such as Soho and Park Slope. Most affluent areas are out of the city in the near suburbs or even the periphery, in a band that goes on both sides of Long Island Sound, as well as in central New Jersey. Places like Greenwich, Conn., and Smoke Rise, N.J., are areas of concentrated wealth. While the New York core has become more and more African-American and Hispanic, those with high income in general live well outside the city.

The New York area has always been home to many immigrants. Migration from abroad continues to have a major impact on the area. In 1940, roughly 28 percent of the core population was foreign born, as figure 1.8 shows. The foreign-born population steadily declined through 1970 in all areas in the region. Since then it has grown markedly, espe-

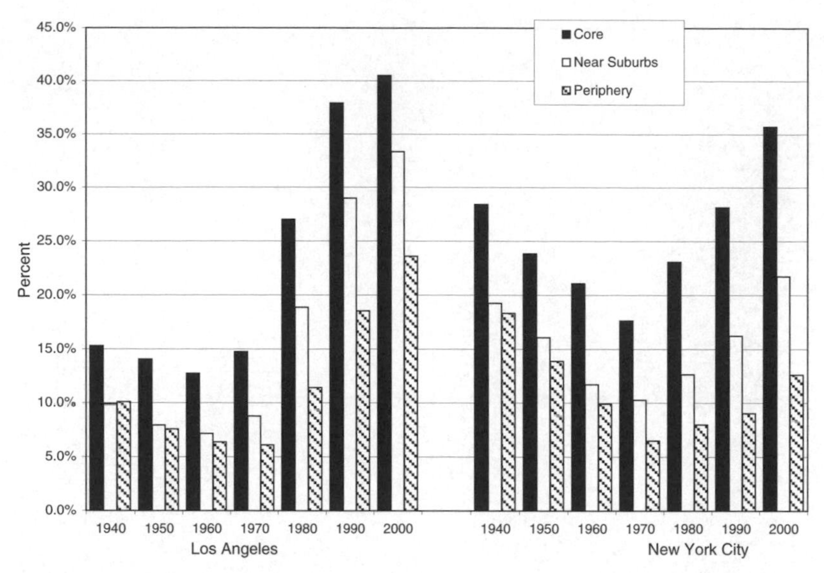

Figure 1.8. Percent Foreign Born, 1940–2000, in Los Angeles and New York City Metropolitan Areas

cially in the core, which by 2000 had a larger proportion of foreign-born population than in 1940. The near and peripheral counties have not rebounded to the same extent, so that the differences between the core and the rest of the area in terms of foreign-born population have grown. In 2000, the near was 22 percent foreign born, while the periphery was only 12.1 percent foreign born, about one-third the concentration found in the core.

In Los Angeles, the pattern of change is different since mass immigration is a relatively new phenomenon. Even by 1970, only a small proportion (about 10 percent) of the population in the Los Angeles metro region was foreign born, though the proportion was markedly higher in the core (about 15 percent) than in the near (about 9 percent) and periphery (about 6 percent). Since then, there has been a massive growth of the foreign-born population settling in Los Angeles. By 2000, the proportion of foreign born in the core (41 percent), near (33 percent), and periphery (24 percent) was substantially higher than for the corresponding areas of New York. So in both metropolises a substantial proportion of those from abroad settle in the core, but sizable proportions also settle in the near or periphery areas, though more so in Los Angeles than in New York. These points are further developed in chapters 3 and 4.

In 1980, the Census Bureau first began to collect detailed information about the Hispanic population in the United States. Figure 1.9 displays the overall growth of the Hispanic population in Los Angeles and New York from 1980 to 2000. The growth is marked in both areas, but more so in Los Angeles. The Hispanic proportion of the population of the Los Angeles region grew by about 71 percent during the 1980s, and by about 40 percent during the 1990s. In New York the Hispanic growth was 33 percent during the 1980s and 38 percent in the 1990s. In both areas the concentration of the Hispanic population is greatest in the core. But the differences between core and periphery are much greater in New York, where, in 2000, 28 percent of the core was Hispanic versus 9 percent of the periphery. In Los Angeles, 46 percent of the core was Hispanic, 44 percent of the near, and 34 percent of the periphery. Indeed, Los Angeles now has startlingly high concentrations of Hispanics in the suburbs (near and periphery), as figure 1.14 also shows. Some implications of this unique development for the topic of residential segregation are discussed in chapter five.

Figure 1.10 presents a breakdown of the components of the Hispanic population of both areas in 2000. As can be seen, more than four-fifths of the 6.6 million Hispanic population in the Los Angeles region are

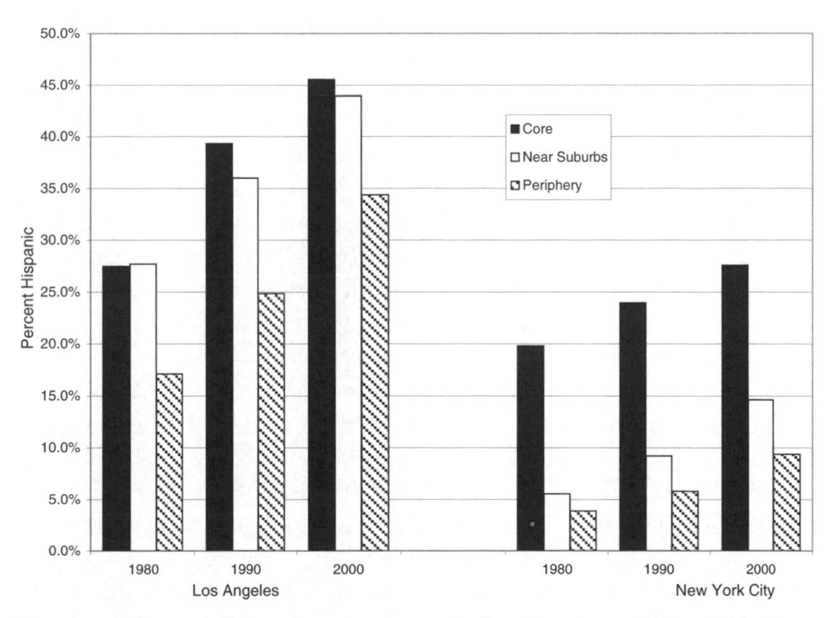

Figure 1.9. Percent Hispanic, 1980–2000, in Los Angeles and New York City Metropolitan Areas. (Source: table 1.A5.)

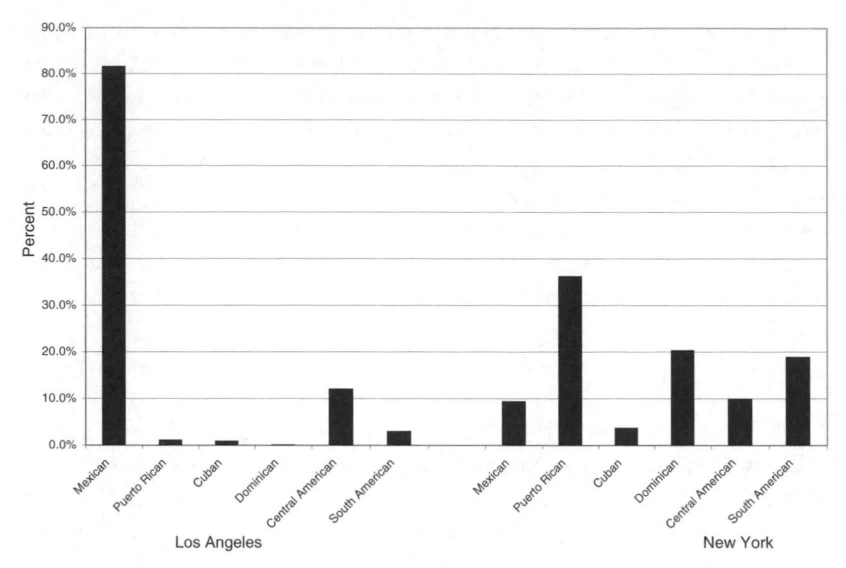

Figure 1.10. Origin Groups as a Percentage of the Total Hispanic Population in Los Angeles and New York City Metropolitan Areas, 2000. (Source: table 1.A6.)

Mexican. The largest group among New York's Hispanic population is Puerto Rican, which makes up about 36 percent of the total. The next largest group is Dominican, which makes up about 20 percent. Mexican increased by 250 percent from 1990 to 2000, and now number almost 360,000. Other groups with populations of more than 100,000 include Cuban, Columbian, Peruvian, Salvadoran, and Ecuadorian. For Los Angeles, only Guatemalan and Salvadoran populations number more than 100,000. In short, the Hispanic population in New York is much more varied than that in Los Angeles, where it is overwhelmingly Mexican with sizable Central American and moderate-sized South American populations. In New York, there are many different groups.

To summarize, in terms of race, economic position, and nativity, the core has become much different from the rest of the New York area as the latter has grown in population.[4] Immediately after World War II, the New York area core was not all that different from the region of which it was a part. Now it is much less white, more foreign, and, with the important exception of much of Manhattan and a few parts of Brooklyn, poorer than the noncore areas. The noncore areas are very suburban, very dependent on automobile travel, and much more like Los Angeles. The core area is in a way an urban remnant that has become increasingly inhabited by the poor, those from abroad, and nonwhite and Hispanic populations. The rest of the New York area—the near and the periphery—is becoming more and more the opposite.

In Los Angeles, several of the patterns of growth are very different, but the direction of change plainly is making the core of the Los Angeles region more and more like the core of the New York region. The core is poorer, less white, more foreign, and a little more Hispanic than the rest of the region, though the differences are not as marked as in New York.

RACIAL SEPARATION IN THE NEW YORK AND LOS ANGELES METROPOLISES

Chapter 5 discusses residential racial segregation in detail. But a few overview remarks are appropriate here. New York City is hypersegregated.[5] For example, using the primary metropolitan area (New York City, plus Westchester, Rockland, and Putnam Counties), New York was the third most segregated metropolitan area with respect to African-Americans in 1990 (Ong 2001) Further, unlike many metropolitan areas, the pattern of segregation in New York City did not decrease between 1980 and 2000.

Figure 1.11 shows, at the tract level, the distribution of the non-

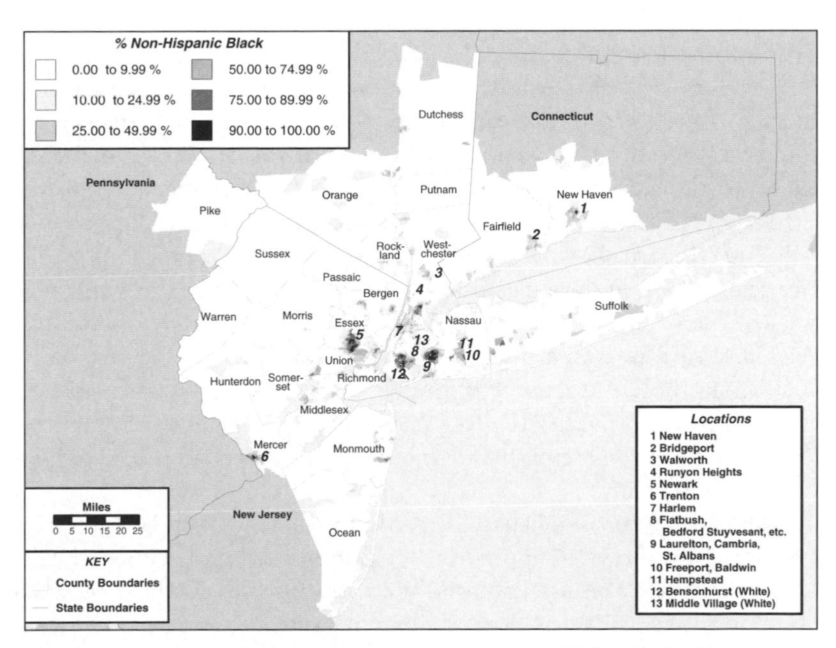

Figure 1.11. New York Metro Area: Percentage Non-Hispanic Black, 2000, by Census Tract

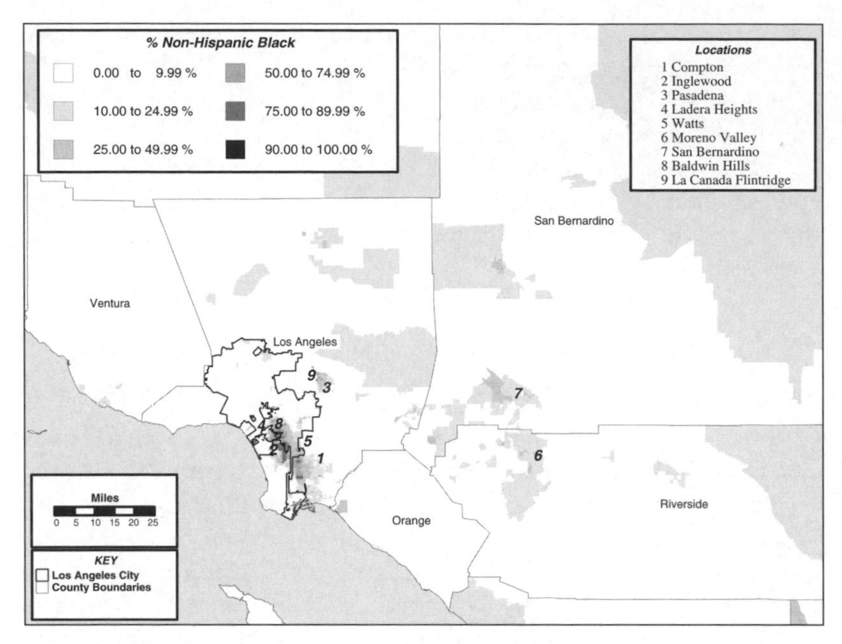

Figure 1.12. Los Angeles Metro Area: Percentage Non-Hispanic Black, 2000, by Census Tract

Hispanic black population in the New York CMSA for 2000. There are large concentrations of African-Americans in a few areas in the core and in a few other areas in the near suburbs. There are also some pockets of minority concentration beyond the core and near areas, but many of these are in the downtown or inner-city areas of places such as Yonkers, Bridgeport or New Haven, Conn., or in the areas close by. The Los Angeles area pattern shown in figure 1.12 also reveals concentrations of African-Americans in the area around South Central and to the south and west of there, as well as in northwest Pasadena. But levels of concentration of African-Americans in these areas are, on the whole, markedly lower than those in the areas of the New York region just mentioned. At the same time, in both the New York and Los Angeles CMSAs, there are also sections where blacks are more dispersed and suburbanized, as chapter 5 discusses.

The concentration of Hispanic settlement in the New York metropolitan area is shown in figure 1.13. Though not as highly concentrated as African-Americans in New York, the pattern seems similar. Hispanic concentrations tend to be close or adjacent to areas of African-American population. In Los Angeles, figure 1.14 reveals a different pattern. There are numerous areas with a high concentration of Hispanics, and while

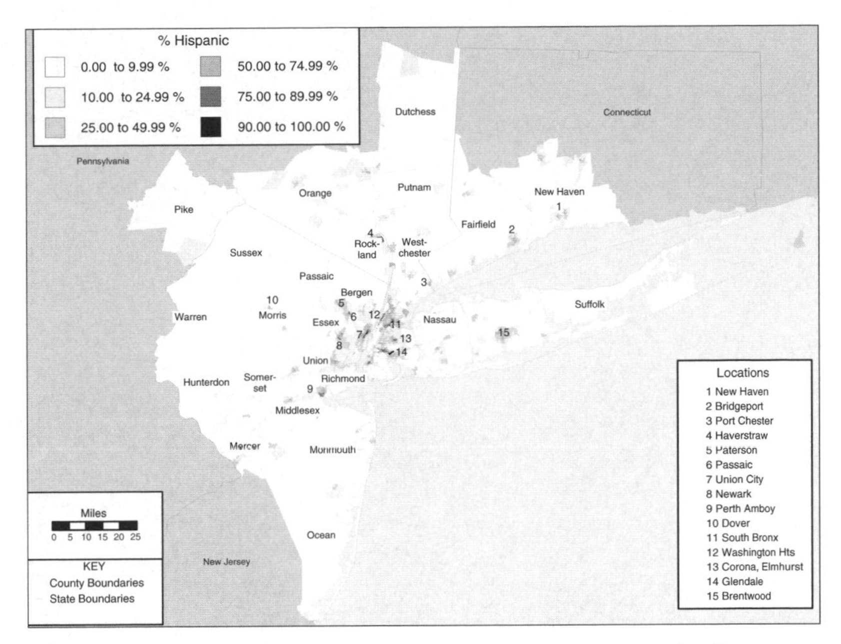

Figure 1.13. New York Metro Area: Percentage Hispanic, 2000, by Census Tract

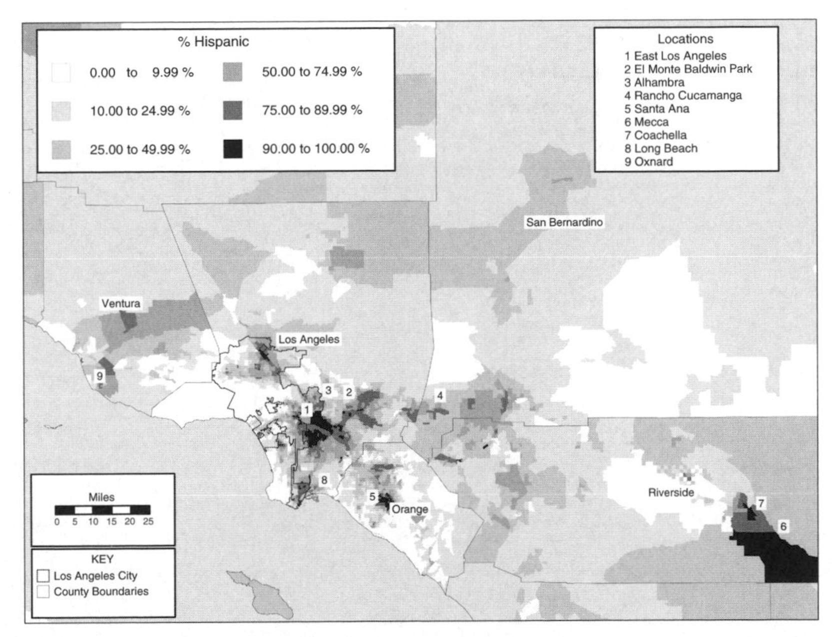

Figure 1.14. Los Angeles Metro Area: Percentage Hispanic, 2000, by Census Tract

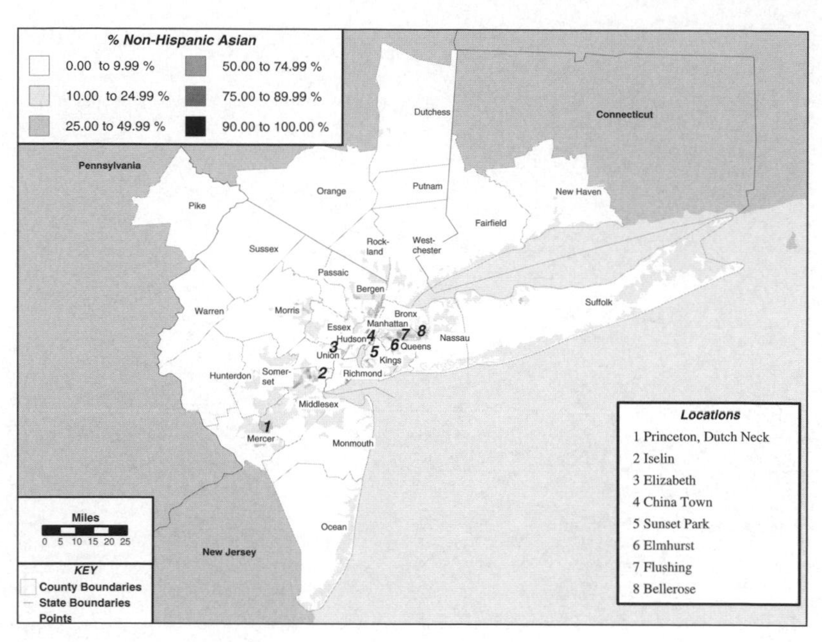

Figure 1.15. New York Metro Area: Percentage Non-Hispanic Asian, 2000, by Census Tract

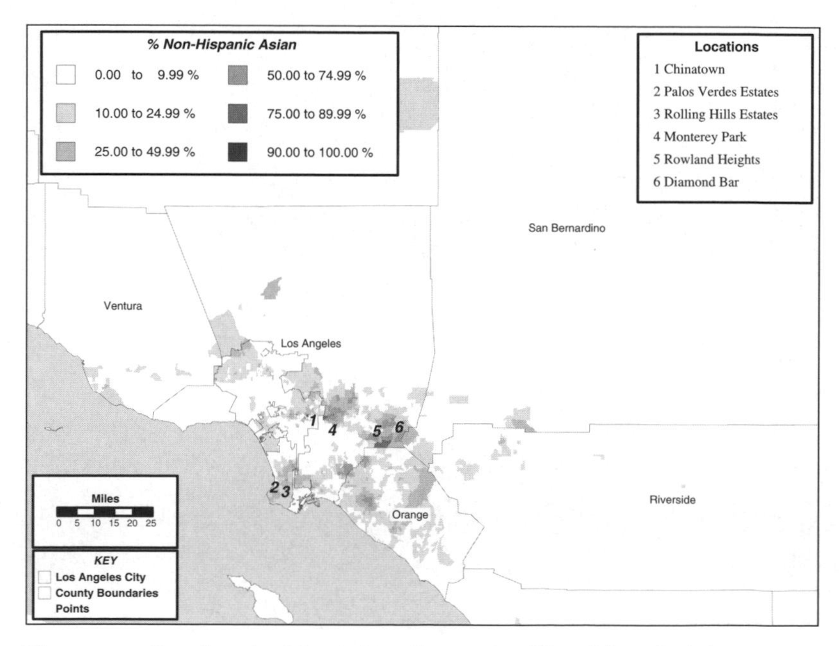

Figure 1.16. Los Angeles Metro Area: Percentage Non-Hispanic Asian, 2000, by Census Tract

some are close to concentrations of African-Americans, many are not. Further, very few parts of Los Angeles do not have at least a small percentage (10 percent) of Hispanics. Though Hispanics have grown rapidly in the New York area, they are nowhere near as pervasive.

The distribution of the Asian population in the New York CMSA, as presented in figure 1.15, reveals only a few places with notable concentrations. In New York City these include, of course, Chinatown in Manhattan, Flushing in Queens, and Sunset Park in Brooklyn. They also include areas in Middlesex and Bergen Counties in New Jersey. These Asian settlements are not usually close to those of African-Americans and Hispanics. In Los Angeles, too, as figure 1.16 shows, most of the areas of significant Asian concentration are distant from the black concentrations, in places like Monterey Park outside the city of Los Angeles, but not necessarily distant from the concentrations of Hispanics. Further, some areas of Asian settlement are located way beyond the city of Los Angeles, in very high-income neighborhoods. Examples are Walnut and Diamond Bar to the east. In the New York region, only a few areas, those already mentioned in New Jersey, seem to be following a similar pattern. These issues are discussed further in chapter 4.

WORKING IN THE METROPOLIS: A WALL AROUND THE CITY?

One reason for the persistent view that New York is different from Los Angeles may be that native New Yorkers, those living in the five boroughs, do not have much interaction with the suburbanites and vice versa, while in Los Angeles the city limits are more permeable and harder to define. Such a possibility, however, undercuts another stereotype that posits a constant to and fro of commuters from the suburbs to the city, one that has been given great literary life by Sloan Wilson's *The Man in the Grey Flannel Suit,* and numerous stories by Updike and Cheever. Indeed, in the midst of the yearly squabble over tax revenue for New York City, several years ago Mayor Giuliani opined that New York City probably had a higher proportion of workers coming into New York and earning more income than any other city.[6]

The stereotype of New York City's labor force being dominated by commuters from the suburbs is simply not true. In fact, as figure 1.17 shows, 78.6 percent of the workers in the city also live there. When the ten largest metropolitan areas are considered, New York City has the highest proportion of labor force living in the city, 12 percent higher than the next highest, Philadelphia, and 18 percent higher than Los Angeles, at about 61 percent. (What is true is that New York City has sev-

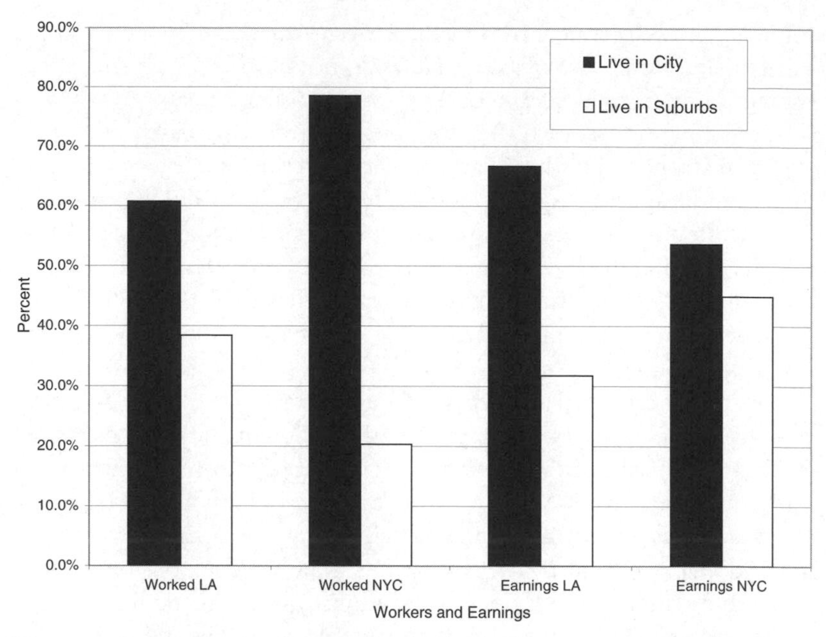

Figure 1.17. Residence and Earnings of City Workers, Los Angeles and New York City, 1990. (Source: table 1.A7.)

eral of the few counties in the United States where most people do not drive to work but, rather, take public transportation. This is true for all the boroughs but Staten Island. In Los Angeles, as in the New York suburbs, the usual mode of commuting is driving.)

However, it is also the case that the roughly 21 percent of the labor force that commutes into New York from outside earn more, are more highly educated, and are much less likely to be members of minority groups. So in a way, the stereotype about who commutes is correct, but the scale of the commuting is much less than the stereotype suggests. The same pattern holds true for Los Angeles.[7]

THE NEW YORK AND LOS ANGELES METROPOLISES INTO AN AGE OF EXTREMES

The patterns and trends discerned for the New York and Los Angeles metropolises do not bode well for the long-term viability of these cities. Until the economic recession in early 2001, which was exacerbated by the attack on the World Trade Center, the New York area was enjoying a relative boom fueled in large part by Wall Street. Los Angeles was also enjoying relative prosperity after undergoing a serious dislocation earlier in the decade.

Still, for eight straight years, the only county in the New York metropolitan area that had net migration from other parts of the United States was Putnam County. All of the others experienced substantial population outflow to other parts of the United States. These shifts have affected Queens, Brooklyn, and the other boroughs in major ways. Since 1990, New York City had a net loss, excluding immigration from abroad, of more than 1 million people to the rest of the United States. This has been made up by increases in migration from overseas and in births, which has lead to recent very modest overall gains in total population. At the same time, the composition of the population continues to change, as in Los Angeles. William Frey (1994, 1996) once dubbed this trend the "new white flight" but now prefers to call it "Balkanization." In short, it is the pattern of long-standing residents leaving areas of high immigration to go elsewhere in the United States.

Recent policy conflicts in New York point up some of the implications of these developments. The repeal of the commuter tax for New York State residents who commute to New York City largely benefits highly paid, well-educated suburbanites at the expense of New York City residents. Other sources must be found for the several hundred million dollars in lost revenue. Proposed tax cuts for those living in New York City may be scrapped. In this way, those who are most well off benefit. The massive changes in the New York metropolis have affected politics. George Pataki was the first New York governor who does not have a strong connection to the city. A lifelong Westchester resident, he served as mayor of Peekskill and as a state assemblyman. With the votes and power now outside of the city, things like the repeal of the commuter tax happen with ease. Funds to pay for improvements in New York City's school buildings, many of which are decrepit and in disrepair, are hard to come by. Resources to fund the City University, or to pay for other services, are similarly affected. Suburbanites and upstate residents must approve them. The most telling example may have been the governor's $54 billion proposed package to deal with the World Trade Center attack. Incredibly, it included much economic and transportation aid for upstate New York. All these developments reinforce the trend of long-standing residents leaving New York City. The World Trade Center attack will only exacerbate the exodus. Some estimate that as many as 15,000 of the lost jobs have moved to the suburbs. In Los Angeles the cap on property tax funding enacted by Proposition 13 began a long period of fiscal difficulty. Like New York City, Los Angeles City and County have difficulty paying for public services, and the state is often reluctant to redistribute resources to make it easier. These trends and the policies shaping and exacerbating them do not bode well for the overall health of the cores of the New York and Los Angeles metropolises.

Unlike a hundred years ago when Jacob Rijs wrote *How the Other Half Lives,* the other half on the whole no longer lives near the better half. Rather, the affluent now build suburban bedroom communities and edge cities' societies away from the urban core or retreat to urban enclaves, such as Beverly Hills and West Hollywood, or, in Manhattan, to doorman-guarded apartment buildings (co-ops) in select areas where potential residents are carefully prescreened by interview, a process that makes them far more exclusive than Los Angeles's famous gated communities. These enclaves aside, the urban core is "where the other half lives," at a safe distance from the "better half" who have no legal or other requirement to provide assistance. Instead, as Doug Massey pointed out in his essay "Into an Age of Extremes: Concentrated Affluence and Poverty in the Twenty-first Century" (Massey 1996), this is now a world trend, which the New York and Los Angeles metropolises are following, each in their own way.

APPENDIX

Table 1.A1. Growth of New York City and Los Angeles Areas, 1940–2000

	LOS ANGELES AREA				NEW YORK CITY AREA			
YEAR	Core	Near	Periphery	Total	Core	Near	Periphery	Total
1940	1,504,277 (46.22)	1,281,366 (39.37)	467,077 (14.35)	3,252,720	8,769,934 (65.64)	2,202,090 (16.48)	2,389,218 (17.88)	13,361,242
1950	1,970,358 (39.93)	2,181,329 (44.21)	782,559 (15.86)	4,934,246	9,253,788 (62.01)	2,764,506 (18.52)	2,904,857 (19.47)	14,923,151
1960	2,586,958 (33.37)	3,451,813 (44.53)	1,712,845 (22.10)	7,751,616	9,094,272 (52.42)	4,022,181 (23.18)	4,233,118 (24.40)	17,349,571
1970	2,944,878 (29.53)	4,087,197 (40.99)	2,939,962 (29.48)	9,972,037	9,138,671 (47.05)	4,519,537 (23.27)	5,763,662 (29.68)	19,421,870
1980	3,122,213 (27.16)	4,355,290 (37.88)	4,020,065 (34.96)	11,497,568	8,127,606 (43.17)	4,337,366 (23.04)	6,363,998 (33.80)	18,828,970
1990	3,647,301 (25.10)	5,215,863 (35.89)	5,668,365 (39.01)	14,531,529	8,274,892 (42.52)	4,313,450 (22.16)	6,874,108 (35.32)	19,462,450
2000	3,858,218 (23.56)	5,661,120 (34.57)	6,854,307 (41.86)	16,373,645	8,967,158 (42.49)	4,597,439 (21.78)	7,539,695 (35.73)	21,104,292

Source. Decennial Census Data. For New York metropolitan area, county-level data were used, and counties were arranged into the core, near, and periphery areas. For the Los Angeles metropolitan area, Los Angeles Minor Civil Division (MCD) was used as core, the balance of Los Angeles County as near, and the other four counties as periphery. For 1940 and 1950, the Bureau of the Census tabulated some "enclosed municipalities," those completely surrounded by Los Angeles City (e.g., Beverly Hills and West Hollywood), along with the city of Los Angeles. In 1960 and 1970, the enclosed municipalities were tabulated, and the MCD information did not contain the requisite detail. So for 1960 and 1970, the Los Angeles MCD tabulation was created using the city of Los Angeles and the enclosed municipalities. An insubstantial part of Los Angeles MCD was not incorporated in 1960 and 1970 (and still remains unincorporated). This area has negligible population. From 1980 on, the census tabulations were complete. These data were drawn from census publications or census machine-readable tabulations.

Note. For Los Angeles "core" is defined as the minor civil division of Los Angeles that includes the embedded municipalities of Beverly Hills, West Hollywood, Culver City, Ladera Heights, Marina Del Ray, and View-Park Windsor Hills, along with some unincorporated territory. This ensured that the same territory was considered over time. "Near" consists of the rest of Los Angeles County. "Periphery" is the other four counties of the CMSA, namely Ventura, Orange, San Bernardino, and Riverside. For New York "core" is defined as New York City minus Staten Island, plus Hudson and Essex Counties in New Jersey (which contain the cities of Jersey City, Hoboken, Bayonne, and Newark). "Near" includes Staten Island, Nassau, and Westchester Counties in New York and Bergen, Passaic, and Union Counties in New Jersey. "Periphery" includes the other seventeen counties of the CMSA. Numbers in parentheses are percentages. Percentages for a given year and for a given city may not total to 100, due to rounding.

Table 1.A2. White and Nonwhite, New York and Los Angeles Areas, 1940–2000

	LOS ANGELES AREA				NEW YORK CITY AREA			
YEAR	Core	Near	Periphery	Total	Core	Near	Periphery	Total
1940								
Nonwhite	97,847	27,754	11,560	137,161	559,799	85,676	83,890	729,365
	(6.5)	(2.2)	(2.5)	(4.2)	(6.4)	(3.9)	(3.5)	(5.5)
Total	1,504,277	1,281,366	467,077	3,252,720	8,769,934	2,202,090	2,389,218	13,361,242
1950								
Nonwhite	211,585	62,158	22,161	295,904	899,438	111,129	124,509	1,135,076
	(10.7)	(2.8)	(2.8)	(6.0)	(9.7)	(4.0)	(4.3)	(7.6)
Total	1,970,358	2,181,329	782,559	4,934,246	9,253,788	2,764,506	2,904,857	14,923,151
1960								
Nonwhite	310,741	274,164	54,360	639,265	1,356,304	198,234	231,564	1,786,102
	(12.5)	(7.7)	(3.2)	(8.2)	(14.9)	(4.9)	(5.5)	(10.3)
Total	2,479,015	3,559,756	1,712,845	7,751,616	9,094,272	4,022,181	4,233,118	17,349,571
1970								
Nonwhite	525,404	500,172	127,853	1,153,429	2,184,669	328,514	375,568	2,888,751
	(18.7)	(11.9)	(4.3)	(11.6)	(23.9)	(7.3)	(6.5)	(14.9)
Total	2,816,061	4,216,014	2,939,962	9,972,037	9,138,671	4,519,537	5,763,662	19,421,870
1980								
Nonwhite	1,003,651	1,338,312	604,130	2,946,093	3,172,107	530,934	572,503	4,275,544
	(33.8)	(29.7)	(15.0)	(25.6)	(39.0)	(12.2)	(9.0)	(22.7)
Total	2,966,850	4,510,653	4,020,065	11,497,568	8,127,606	4,337,366	6,363,998	18,828,970
1990								
Nonwhite	1,527,997	2,300,064	1,314,511	5,142,572	3,991,211	771,127	851,713	5,614,051
	(43.8)	(42.8)	(23.2)	(35.4)	(48.2)	(17.9)	(12.4)	(28.8)
Total	3,485,398	5,377,766	5,668,365	14,531,529	8,274,892	4,313,450	6,874,108	19,462,450
2000								
Nonwhite	2,018,936	2,863,340	2,462,496	7,344,772	5,043,776	1,195,653	1,367,411	7,606,840
	(52.3)	(50.6)	(35.9)	(44.9)	(56.2)	(26.0)	(18.1)	(36.0)
Total	3,858,218	5,661,120	6,854,307	16,373,645	8,967,158	4,597,439	7,539,695	21,104,292

Source. See table 1.A1.

Note. Core, near, and periphery are defined in table 1.A1. Numbers in parentheses are percentages.

Table 1.A3. Median Family Income in the New York and Los Angeles Areas, 1950–2000 (in 2000 Dollars)

	LOS ANGELES AREA			NEW YORK CITY AREA		
YEAR	Core	Near	Periphery	Core	Near	Periphery
1950	25,623	26,898	22,627	25,443	30,500	25,222
1960	41,190	41,939	38,389	36,189	46,713	40,306
1970	50,604	52,600	51,635	45,522	63,447	56,447
1980	47,918	53,520	55,922	41,018	64,398	59,273
1990	50,420	59,431	63,615	49,026	78,237	73,786
2000	40,709	54,207	56,402	42,900	74,374	71,887

Source. See table 1.A1.

Note. "Core," "near," and "periphery" defined as in table 1.A1.

Table 1.A4. Foreign and Native Born, New York and Los Angeles Areas, 1940–2000

	LOS ANGELES AREA				NEW YORK CITY AREA			
YEAR	Core	Near	Periphery	Total	Core	Near	Periphery	Total
1940								
Foreign born	215,248	124,468	46,377	386,093	2,333,097	407,653	399,857	3,140,607
Native born	1,191,182	1,129,144	412,215	2,732,541	5,877,038	1,708,761	1,782,661	9,368,460
% Foreign born	15.3	9.9	10.1	12.4	28.4	19.3	18.3	25.1
1950								
Foreign born	247,054	168,574	57,736	473,364	1,990,277	402,500	385,669	2,778,446
Native born	1,511,719	1,950,597	702,662	4,164,978	6,364,073	2,103,977	2,394,679	10,862,729
% Foreign born	14.0	8.0	7.6	10.2	23.8	16.1	13.9	20.4
1960								
Foreign born	329,555	246,825	109,301	685,681	1,631,178	447,832	396,512	2,475,522
Native born	2,257,403	3,204,988	1,603,544	7,065,935	6,106,790	3,376,115	3,605,042	13,087,947
% Foreign born	12.7	7.2	6.4	8.8	21.1	11.7	9.9	15.9
1970								
Foreign born	434,659	358,550	180,175	973,384	1,610,594	465,240	375,369	2,451,203
Native born	2,510,219	3,728,647	2,759,787	8,998,653	7,528,077	4,054,297	5,388,293	16,970,667
% Foreign born	14.8	8.8	6.1	9.8	17.6	10.3	6.5	12.6
1980								
Foreign born	843,013	821,780	459,234	2,124,027	1,875,835	549,281	510,326	2,935,442
Native born	2,279,200	3,533,510	3,560,831	9,373,541	6,251,771	3,788,085	5,853,672	15,893,528
% Foreign born	27.0	18.9	11.4	18.5	23.1	12.7	8.0	15.6
1990								
Foreign born	1,382,561	1,512,505	1,049,762	3,944,828	2,329,151	700,131	623,162	3,652,444
Native born	2,264,740	3,703,358	4,618,603	10,586,701	5,945,741	3,613,319	6,250,946	15,810,006
% Foreign born	37.9	29.0	18.5	27.1	28.1	16.2	9.1	18.8
2000								
Foreign born	1,562,875	1,886,569	1,618,171	5,067,615	3,201,137	1,000,008	994,656	5,195,801
Native born	2,295,325	3,774,569	5,236,136	11,306,030	5,766,021	3,597,431	6,882,303	16,245,755
% Foreign born	40.5	33.3	23.6	30.9	35.7	21.8	12.6	24.2

Source. See table 1.A1.

Note. Core, near, and periphery are defined in table 1.A1.

Table 1.A5. Hispanic Population in the New York and Los Angeles Areas, 1980–2000

	LOS ANGELES AREA				NEW YORK CITY AREA			
	Core	Near	Periphery	Total	Core	Near	Periphery	Total
Total Hispanics, 1980	815,305	1,250,198	688,709	2,754,212	1,609,549	240,331	247,595	2,097,475
Percent of population	27.5	27.7	17.1	24.0	19.8	5.5	3.9	11.1
Total Hispanics, 1990	1,370,476	1,935,640	1,408,289	4,714,405	1,982,926	398,468	399,288	2,780,682
Percent of population	39.3	36.0	24.8	32.4	24.0	9.2	5.8	14.3
Change 1980 to 1990 (%)	68.1	54.8	104.5	71.2	23.2	65.8	61.3	32.6
Total Hispanics, 2000	1,756,251	2,485,962	2,356,275	6,598,488	2,471,474	671,836	706,680	3,849,990
Percent of population	45.5	43.9	34.4	40.3	27.6	14.6	9.4	18.2
Change 1990 to 2000 (%)	28.1	28.4	67.3	40.0	24.6	68.6	77.0	38.5

Source. See table 1.A1.

Note. “Core,” “near,” and “periphery” are defined in table 1.A1.

Table 1.A6. Distribution of Hispanic Population in the New York and Los Angeles Areas, 1990–2000

	LOS ANGELES AREA			NEW YORK CITY AREA		
CLASS	1990	2000	% Growth	1990	2000	% Growth
Hispanic or Latino	4,714,405	6,598,488	40.0	2,780,682	3,849,990	38.5
Mexican	3,736,443 (79.3)	5,377,468 (81.5)	43.9	102,623 (3.7)	359,755 (9.3)	250.6
Puerto Rican	65,048 (1.4)	71,968 (1.1)	10.6	1,288,108 (46.3)	1,392,653 (36.2)	8.1
Cuban	60,302 (1.3)	58,231 (.9)	−3.4	161,529 (5.8)	141,549 (3.7)	−12.4
Dominican	3,356 (.1)	5,053 (.1)	50.6	407,349 (14.6)	782,361 (20.3)	92.1
Central American	503,400 (10.7)	792,495 (12.0)	57.4	184,316 (6.6)	383,745 (10.0)	108.2
Costa Rican	N.A.	16,694 (.3)	. . .	N.A.	28,903 (.8)	. . .
Guatamalan	139,650 (3.0)	213,472 (3.2)	52.9	29,852 (1.1)	71,322 (1.9)	138.9
Honduran	25,422 (.5)	43,224 (.7)	70.0	33,975 (1.2)	73,299 (1.9)	115.7
Nicaraguan	39,974 (.8)	48,033 (.7)	20.2	14,254 (.5)	16,776 (.4)	17.7
Panamanian	7,582 (.2)	10,094 (.2)	33.1	27,518 (1.0)	32,353 (.8)	17.6
Salvadoran	274,788 (5.8)	386,343 (5.9)	40.6	63,859 (2.3)	140,447 (3.6)	119.9
Other Central American	15,984 (.3)	74,635 (1.1)	. . .	14,858 (.5)	20,644 (.5)	. . .
South American	129,446 (2.7)	194,833 (3.0)	50.5	407,323 (14.6)	727,416 (18.9)	78.6
Argentinian	N.A.	31,181 (.5)	. . .	N.A.	33,015 (.9)	. . .
Bolivian	N.A.	7,337 (.1)	. . .	N.A.	8,662 (.2)	. . .
Chilean	N.A.	13,753 (.2)	. . .	N.A.	22,220 (.6)	. . .
Colombian	30,397 (.6)	41,370 (.6)	36.1	160,269 (5.8)	247,330 (6.4)	54.3
Ecuadorian	23,146 (.5)	27,181 (.4)	17.4	118,744 (4.3)	247,508 (6.4)	108.4
Paraguyan	N.A.	549 (.0)	. . .	N.A.	5,166 (.1)	. . .
Peruvian	29,298 (.6)	48,287 (.7)	64.8	56,946 (2.0)	110,662 (2.9)	94.3
Uruguayan	N.A.	1,976 (.0)	. . .	N.A.	11,249 (.3)	. . .
Veneuzulan	N.A.	5,117 (.1)	. . .	N.A.	18,708 (.5)	. . .
Other South American	46,605 (1.0)	18,082 (.3)	. . .	71,364 (2.6)	22,897 (.6)	. . .
Other Latino/ Hispanic	216,410 (4.6)	98,439 (1.5)	. . .	229,434 (8.3)	62,512 (1.6)	. . .

Source. 1990 and 2000 Decennial census tabulations. Hispanic group estimations based upon Current Population Survey Adjustments to 2000 tabulations.

Note. N.A. = not available. Numbers in parentheses are percentages. Due to classification changes within "Other Central American," "Other South American," and "Other Latino/Hispanic," these categories are not comparable for 1990 and 2000; therefore, % growth is not given.

Table 1.A7. Workers, Earnings, and Residential Location in the 10 Largest U.S. Cities, 1990

	HOUSTON		LOS ANGELES		NEW YORK		PHILADELPHIA		SAN FRANCISCO	
	Worked	Earned($)	Worked	Earned($)	Worked	Earned($)	Worked	Earned($)	Worked	Earned($)
Workers in city	1,121,091	29.2	1,818,009	50.3	3,682,214	117.0	740,733	19.5	552,969	17.5
Live in city	648,117	14.7	1,104,286	27.0	2,892,736	78.0	495,827	10.3	299,185	7.9
%	57.8	50.3	60.7	53.7	78.6	66.7	66.9	52.8	54.1	45.1
Live in suburbs	421,190	12.8	698,475	22.6	749,973	37.2	233,077	8.8	203,263	7.3
%	37.6	43.8	38.4	44.9	20.4	31.8	31.5	45.1	36.8	41.7
Live in other	51,784	1.7	15,248	.7	39,505	1.8	11,829	.4	50,521	2.3
%	4.6	5.8	.8	1.4	1.1	1.5	1.6	2.1	9.1	13.1
Residence in city	752,340	17.2	1,604,691	40.1	3,143,039	85.3	625,107	13.1	370,501	10.0
Work in city	648,117	14.7	1,104,286	27.0	2,892,736	78.0	495,827	10.3	299,185	7.9
%	86.1	85.5	68.8	67.3	92.0	91.4	79.3	78.6	80.8	79.0
Work in suburbs	94,306	2.1	489,337	12.7	229,686	6.6	120,875	2.6	68,381	2.0
%	12.5	12.2	30.5	31.7	7.3	7.7	19.3	19.8	18.5	20.0
Work in other	9,917	.4	11,068	.4	206,117	.7	8,405	.2	2,935	.1
%	1.3	2.3	.7	1.0	6.6	.8	1.3	1.5	.8	1.0

Table 1.A7. (*continued*)

	BOSTON		CHICAGO		DALLAS		WASHINGTON D.C.		DETROIT	
	Worked	Earned($)	Worked	Earned($)	Worked	Earned($)	Worked	Earned($)	Worked	Earned($)
Workers in city	477,939	15.0	1,459,693	40.4	715,116	19.3	707,142	24.3	363,476	9.9
Live in city	186,630	4.4	918,741	20.5	348,683	8.2	223,785	6.3	181,205	3.6
%	39.0	29.3	62.9	50.7	48.8	42.5	31.6	25.9	49.9	36.4
Live in suburbs	272,370	10.0	521,615	19.2	346,809	10.4	440,860	16.3	193,900	5.9
%	57.0	66.7	35.7	47.5	48.5	53.9	62.3	67.1	53.3	59.6
Live in other	18,939	.6	19,337	.7	16,624	.7	42,497	1.7	8,371	.4
%	4.0	4.0	1.3	1.7	2.3	3.6	6.0	7.0	2.3	4.0
Residence in city	270,371	6.5	1,167,900	26.0	469,958	11.2	290,787	8.1	322,368	6.6
Work in city	186,630	4.4	918,741	20.5	348,683	8.2	223,785	6.3	181,205	3.6
%	69.0	67.7	78.7	78.8	74.2	73.2	77.0	77.8	56.2	54.5
Work in suburbs	80,624	2.0	243,528	5.3	116,100	2.7	61,921	1.6	139,151	2.9
%	29.8	30.8	20.9	20.4	24.7	24.1	21.3	19.8	43.2	43.9
Work in other	3,117	.1	5,631	.2	5,175	.3	5,081	.2	2,012	.1
%	1.2	1.5	0.5	.8	1.1	2.7	1.7	2.5	.6	1.5

Source. Computed from 1990 Census Public Use Microdata samples.
Note. Dollar figures are billions.

CHAPTER TWO

The New York and Los Angeles Economies

David L. Gladstone and Susan S. Fainstein

New York and Los Angeles are the two American cities with the strongest claims to global city status. Their position in the world rests on the structure and size of their economies, of which substantial proportions involve activities with global reach. These include the provision of financial and other services to businesses around the world, the production of cultural transmissions with worldwide audiences, and the entertainment of visitors from other countries. Their global influence expresses itself in terms of their disproportionately large shares of certain industries relative to other American cities and, especially, in the sheer magnitude of employment in these sectors. The large number of employees and amount of value added within financial and producer services and hospitality industries, as well as motion pictures and other entertainment media, gives New York and Los Angeles their special character as global centers.

Despite their similarities, New York and Los Angeles do not occupy identical places in the world system of cities nor do they possess the same economic geographies. Their birth at different stages in American economic development led to different industrial structures (Abu-Lughod 1999). Even though both grew up around major ports, the effect of involvement in international trade differed. In New York it gave rise to dense development around the docks and an enormous financial industry supporting shipping activities, soon extending into a whole range of industries nationwide. By the time Los Angeles's port began to challenge New York's in size, Eastern banking institutions had acquired a dominant position that limited serious competition and, to the extent a West Coast financial rival developed to New York, it was San

Francisco not Los Angeles. In the meanwhile, Los Angeles benefited from a mild climate, nonexistent topographical boundaries to expansion, and, eventually, federal spending during World War II. These factors stimulated the growth of its vast aerospace industry and the development and wide dispersal of both commercial and manufacturing sites. Jewish moguls seeking a more open society than existed in the east moved to the west coast; their decision to locate the motion picture studios in Hollywood also contributed to differences between the two cities (Gabler 1988). In the postwar years, as will be discussed below, the critical path set in the earlier period led to the emergence of further dissimilarities.

If the two cities thus do differ in terms of industrial composition and spatial arrangements, they strongly resemble each other in labor force characteristics. Both display highly skewed income distributions, in part because both are hosts to huge numbers of low-skilled immigrants willing to accept work at very low levels of wages and benefits. At the same time, each offers extraordinarily high earnings possibilities due to the disproportionate presence of industries (investment banking, corporate law, broadcasting, and motion pictures) that pay their top executives and performers exceptionally well. In fact, inequality has increased substantially in global cities during the past three decades, not so much because the poor have become poorer and more numerous—although this has occurred—as because the rich have become so much richer (Fainstein 2001).

This chapter explores the components of and recent changes in the economic bases of New York and Los Angeles, the growth of high-tech and "new economy" industries, and the impact of immigration on the workforce. It looks also at the ways in which the economies of the two cities are becoming both more and less alike and the extent to which the prosperity displayed at the end of the millennium is likely to be stable. The assault on the World Trade Center and subsequent anthrax attacks seemingly directed at media headquarters make prediction of the economic future of these two global centers particularly perilous as of this writing (in October 2001).

Although we look briefly at the characteristics of the metropolitan economies to which these two cities belong, we mainly restrict our discussion to the five boroughs of New York City and Los Angeles County, which are roughly comparable in population and labor force. The city of Los Angeles occupies just 11.5 percent of the land area of Los Angeles County and, with a population of 3.7 million people, accounts for just 38.8 percent of the county's population.

GLOBAL CITIES

Global-city theorists generally point to three sets of characteristics that distinguish truly global cities from national or subglobal urban centers (Friedmann 1986; Castells 1989; Sassen 2000). The first is the global city's role as a command and control center in the international political economy. Global cities are places where key decisions get made; as such, they are home to large numbers of corporate headquarters, banks, and financial markets, as well as national and international economic and political institutions. Second, global cities are centers of global culture (Sassen and Roost 1999), accounting for a disproportionate share of the world's motion picture, music, news, entertainment, and artistic production. Third, global cities possess a distinctive industrial base: a decline in "traditional" manufacturing employment has been offset by rapid growth in the producer services, telematics, media, tourism, retail, and other service industries.

GLOBAL CITY FUNCTIONS IN THE TWO ECONOMIES

The three major characteristics of a global city—command and control functions, cultural production, and a distinctive industrial base—are present in varying degrees in the two metropolises. New York clearly exceeds Los Angeles in the first category. Few Fortune 500 firms are headquartered in Los Angeles—in fact, the New York metropolitan area is home to twice as many Fortune 500 headquarters as all of southern California. There are virtually no large banks or investment houses headquartered in Los Angeles, and although neither city is a state or national capital, New York possesses the United Nations and a large complex of nongovernmental organizations relating to it.

Los Angeles is highly specialized in global cultural production and, in terms of employment, much more so than New York. Its motion picture industry accounts for more than 5 percent of total employment and 13 percent of all services employment. Nevertheless, New York houses the headquarters of the major television networks. Both cities have very large tourism industries with a strong global component (Gladstone and Fainstein 2001). New York and Los Angeles are the leading destinations for foreign visitors to the United States (International Trade Administration 2001). Of the 18.4 million overnight tourists who visited New York in 2000, an estimated 6.8 million (37 percent) were international travelers. Los Angeles trailed only slightly, with 5.5 million inter-

Table 2.1. Overnight Visitors to New York and Los Angeles, 2000

	VISITORS	DOMESTIC VISITORS	INTER-NATIONAL VISITORS	INTER-NATIONAL VISITORS (%)
New York	18,400,000	11,600,000	6,800,000	37
Los Angeles	24,660,000	19,114,000	5,542,000	22

Sources. Los Angeles Convention and Visitors Bureau 2002; NYC and Company 2002.
Note. Figures shown are for New York City and Los Angeles County.

national arrivals constituting almost a quarter of its total 24.6 million overnight visitors (table 2.1).

Global-city theorists point to a particular type of service industry, producer services, as a key characteristic of global cities. Sassen ([1994] 2000) defines producer services as depository institutions (banks), non-depository institutions (credit), security and commodity brokers, insurance carriers, insurance agents, real estate, holding and other investment offices, business services, legal services, membership organizations, and miscellaneous business services. According to Sassen, global cities are production sites for highly specialized business, financial, and legal services. Consequently, global cities such as London, Tokyo, and New York (fig. 2.1) will have much higher concentrations of businesses and employment in these sectors than will nonglobal cities such as Manchester, Osaka, and Chicago.

An analysis of New York's producer-services industries underscores Sassen's contention that, by her definition, New York is a truly global city. It has a disproportionately large share of employment, as measured by location quotients (defined in the note to table 2.2), in nearly every producer-services industry: depository institutions (2.03), security and commodity brokers (8.25), real estate (2.47), holding and other investment offices (2.37), legal services (2.48), and miscellaneous business services (2.41 [table 2.2]). Moreover, New York's producer services are highly concentrated in space: location quotients for each producer service are higher in Manhattan than they are in the city as a whole. In some categories, such as security and commodity brokers, they are much higher. This centrality implies that these firms are primarily serving other businesses rather than retail customers.[1]

If we restrict our definition of a global city to one with a very high concentration of producer services, financial establishments, and law firms, then New York is much more "global" than Los Angeles is. Los Angeles has more than twice the national share of employment in only one producer-services category: unclassified business services (table 2.2).

Figure 2.1. Lower Manhattan Skyline (*on right*), without the World Trade Center, and the Emerging Jersey City Skyline (*on left*), January 2002. How far businesses will migrate from Manhattan to competing areas such as Jersey City has long been a central question.

Table 2.2. Los Angeles and New York, Location Quotients for Motion Pictures and Producer Services, 1997

	LOS ANGELES	NEW YORK
Depository institutions	.96	2.03
Nondepository institutions	.94	.70
Security and commodity brokers	.80	8.25
Insurance carriers	.83	1.43
Insurance agents and brokers	.90	1.05
Real estate	1.12	2.47
Holding and investment offices	1.18	2.37
Business services	1.22	1.13
Motion pictures	9.92	1.77
Legal services	1.34	2.48
Membership organizations	.75	.92
Unclassified business services	2.57	2.41

Source. U.S. Bureau of the Census 1977–97.

Note. A location quotient with a value greater than one indicates a higher than average representation of the particular industry in the local economy. A location quotient is a ratio of ratios. In our analysis, the numerator is the ratio of employment in a specific industry divided by total county or city employment and the denominator is the ratio of nationwide employment in the industry divided by total national employment.

In all others it conforms to national patterns much more than does New York. In fact, in all but two categories, miscellaneous business services and legal services, the location quotients for Los Angeles's producer-services industries have actually declined since the late 1970s. In other words, Los Angeles is becoming less specialized in the industries that Sassen defines as "global."

Not only is New York's relative share of producer-services employment much greater than Los Angeles's, but New York's largest producer-services firms are much larger than those of Los Angeles, regardless of how they are measured. For instance, New York's top ten accounting firms employ nearly five times as many accountants as do Los Angeles's (21,222 vs. 4,849), and New York's largest law firms employ more than 2.5 times as many attorneys (4,650 vs. 1,879). New York's top ten banks have assets in excess of $1.2 trillion; Los Angeles's top ten banking institutions have assets of $51.9 billion, or only 4.3 percent of the value of the assets commanded by New York's largest banks. Similarly, New York's largest commercial property management firms oversee more than twice the square footage of Los Angeles's largest property management firms (209.2 million square feet vs. 87.4 million square feet). Among the major producer-services industries, only Los Angeles's venture capital firms exceed New York's by any measure of magnitude, accounting for nearly twice the total investment ($4.7 billion vs. $2.3 billion [*Los Angeles Business Journal* 1999, 2000; *Crain's New York Business* 2000]).

The picture changes, however, when we consider absolute levels of employment in producer-services industries and when we compare the growth rates of various global city industries in Los Angeles and New York. During the 1977–97 period, Los Angeles's producer-services industries grew by 64 percent, adding more than 265,000 producer-services jobs to the economy. The corresponding figure for New York is 18 percent, with a net increase of 136,900 jobs. Not only did Los Angeles's producer-services industries add more jobs overall but also, during the recession of the late 1980s, Los Angeles's economy shed far fewer producer-services jobs than did New York's. For instance, between 1987 and 1992, New York lost more than 165,000 producer-services jobs, while Los Angeles gained more than 4,000 producer-services jobs during the same period.[2] Again, Los Angeles falls much closer to the national pattern with respect to growth in producer-services industries than does New York (the national increase in producer-services employment during the 1977–97 period was 108 percent [U.S. Bureau of the Census 1977–97]).

Markusen and Gwiasda, who have a less restrictive view of global-city functions than does Sassen, regard Los Angeles as unquestionably a global city. They define a world city as "one which successfully competes for major city status in at least one of the several important functions of integrating the transnational capitalist economy in a neo-mercantilist world" (Markusen and Gwiasda 1994, 168–69).[3] Those functions include trade, finance, business services, manufacturing, government, education, culture, health and social welfare, and immigration. For Markusen and Gwiasda, Los Angeles would clearly rank as a "world city" since it is a worldwide center of trade, business services, manufacturing, education, culture, health services, and immigration. In fact, in their view, Los Angeles may very well be more of a global city than New York, since it surpasses New York in more world-city categories.[4]

SERVICE AND MANUFACTURING SECTORS

In both New York and Los Angeles, as in the United States as a whole, the service sector, including consumer, producer, and public services, has been the driving force of employment growth. During the 1977–97 period, service-sector employment increased by 125 percent in Los Angeles, 75 percent in New York, and 165 percent nationally (table 2.3). But aggregating all service-oriented employment obscures important differences between the two cities. In Los Angeles, six service-sector industries more than doubled in employment terms between 1977 and 1997: two producer-services sectors (business services and legal services), two consumer-services sectors (motion pictures and museums), and two public services (educational services and social services). In New York, four service-sector industries grew by more than 100 percent during the 1977–97 period: amusement and recreation services, health services, social services, and museums.

In addition to growing faster than New York's, Los Angeles's service-sector industries have a larger number of people working within them: 1.44 million versus 1.35 million in New York (table 2.3). Significantly, Los Angeles leads New York in all categories of service-sector employment with the exception of five: health services, legal services, educational services, social services, and museums. Los Angeles's hotel, personal services, business services, auto repair services, motion picture, and amusement and recreation services industries are all substantially larger than New York's. Location quotient analysis reveals the particular service industries in which each city has a disproportionately large share of employment. New York's service-sector industries with a location quotient greater than two are legal services (2.48) and museums (3.52).

A major difference between New York and Los Angeles is the relative size of each city's manufacturing sector. In 1997, Los Angeles's manu-

Table 2.3. Los Angeles and New York, Employment in Selected Industries, 1977–97

	YEAR			GROWTH %
	1977	1987	1997	(1977–97)
Los Angeles:				
Total employment	2,647,263	3,546,393	3,588,831	35.57
Construction	110,550	136,818	115,339	4.33
Manufacturing	838,808	891,374	668,505	−20.30
Transportation, communications and utilities	153,084	222,244	210,691	37.63
Wholesale trade	207,136	278,263	291,436	40.70
Retail trade	474,034	617,794	592,001	24.89
Finance, insurance and real estate	200,051	291,228	240,603	20.27
Services	642,913	1,078,212	1,447,365	125.13
New York:				
Total employment	2,714,385	3,122,583	3,038,719	11.95
Construction	65,556	110,649	89,829	37.03
Manufacturing	594,539	422,888	254,590	−57.18
Transportation, communications and utilities	249,025	228,926	231,725	−6.95
Wholesale trade	230,306	231,459	200,691	−12.86
Retail trade	363,751	397,723	394,659	8.50
Finance, insurance and real estate	432,841	585,312	510,457	17.93
Services	769,588	1,129,957	1,351,112	75.56

Source. U.S. Bureau of the Census 1977–97.
Note. Los Angeles = Los Angeles County; New York = Bronx, Kings, New York, Queens, and Richmond Counties.

facturing industries employed nearly one in six workers. In New York, however, manufacturing firms employed only one in twelve workers or just over 8 percent of the city's total workforce. Los Angeles is now the largest manufacturing center in the United States in terms of employment, surpassing both Chicago and Detroit (Swertlow 1999). It differs, however, from the country's other major manufacturing centers in terms of its output: whereas Chicago and Detroit are specialized in heavy machinery, farm equipment, and automobiles, Los Angeles produces a wide range of products, "from ball bearings and flywheels, to medical devices and silicon chips, to elegant glassware and apparel" (Swertlow 1999).

New York / New Jersey and Los Angeles are home to two of the country's, and the world's, largest ports. The Port of Los Angeles, however, is significantly larger than the Port of New York and New Jersey, particularly with respect to containerized cargo. Goods exported through the Port of Los Angeles considerably exceed in value those passing through

New York's, although the value of air cargo exports from New York surpasses that from Los Angeles (Port Authority of New York and New Jersey 2000). Los Angeles's manufacturing industries benefit from their strategic position along the Pacific Rim, with large shipments of manufactured goods heading to both Latin America and East Asia.

The continuing importance of manufacturing in the Los Angeles economy, and its relative lack of significance in New York, is underscored by a comparison of the largest private-sector employers (table 2.4). Whereas the ten largest in New York include no manufacturing firms, Los Angeles's ten largest include three manufacturing companies: Boeing, Northrop-Grumman, and ABM Industries. That two of the county's top ten employers are military contractors is no accident. Throughout the postwar period, and particularly during the 1960–90 period, Los Angeles has received above-average levels of Pentagon dollars, a factor that has contributed to growth in the city's producer-services industries (Markusen et al. 1991; Markusen and Gwiasda 1994).[5]

Although Los Angeles continues to be a much more important manufacturing center than New York, like New York it is seeing the decline of manufacturing and the growth of services. Both trends mirror developments at the national level, but the degree of change in the two cities differs from national growth rates: whereas manufacturing employment declined by 5 percent nationally from 1977 to 1997, it declined by more than 20 percent in Los Angeles and by 57 percent in New York City.

Table 2.4. Largest Private Employers in New York City and Los Angeles County, 2001–2

LOS ANGELES		NEW YORK	
Employer	No. of Employees	Employer	No. of Employees
Kaiser Permanente	27,635	New York–Presbyterian Healthcare	30,020
Boeing	23,468	J. P. Morgan Chase	24,560
Ralphs Grocery	17,211	Citigroup	23,596
Bank of America	11,943	Verizon Communications	19,767
Target	10,993	Continuum Health Partners	16,807
SBC Pacific Bell	10,670	Federated Department Stores	13,220
CPE	10,245	New York University	12,960
Northrop Grumman	10,000	North Shore–Long Island Jewish Health System	12,792
University of Southern California	9,297	AOL Time Warner	12,500
ABM Industries	9,250	Saint Vincent Catholic Medical Centers	12,283

Source. *Crain's New York Business*, March 6, 2003; *Los Angeles Business Journal*, July 15, 2002.
Note. Figures for Los Angeles are based on 2001 data; for New York, on 2002 data.

Table 2.5. Employment Share in Select Industries, 1977–97

	LOS ANGELES COUNTY		NEW YORK CITY		UNITED STATES	
	1977	1997	1977	1997	1977	1997
Construction	4.2	3.2	2.4	3.0	5.5	5.3
Manufacturing	31.7	18.6	21.9	8.4	30.2	17.7
Transportation, communications, and utilities	5.8	5.9	9.2	7.6	6.2	5.9
Wholesale trade	7.8	8.1	8.5	6.6	7.0	6.5
Retail trade	17.9	16.5	13.4	13.0	20.6	21.0
Finance, insurance, and real estate	7.6	6.7	15.9	16.8	7.0	7.0
Services	24.3	40.3	28.4	44.5	21.6	35.6

Source. U.S. Bureau of the Census 1977–97.

Similarly, there was significant service-sector employment growth in Los Angeles and New York, 125 percent and 75 percent, respectively, although the service sector did not grow as quickly as it did in the country as a whole (165 percent [table 2.3]).

More revealing are the relative shares of manufacturing and service-sector employment in the two metropolitan economies, with Los Angeles mirroring national developments and New York sharply diverging from the national pattern. In Los Angeles, the share of manufacturing employment declined from just over 31 percent of all employment in 1977 to under 18 percent in 1997. In New York, the plunge in manufacturing employment has been precipitous; its share of total employment fell from 22 percent to less than 9 percent during the same period. New York's divergence from the national pattern has only emerged during the past thirty years; well into the past century, New York had the largest number of manufacturing jobs of any city in the nation.[6]

For both cities the decline in share of manufacturing jobs meant, of course, an increase in the proportion of service-sector jobs. The share of service-sector employment in New York grew by a larger percentage than in Los Angeles: from the late 1970s to the late 1990s service-sector employment increased its share in Los Angeles from 25 to 40 percent of all employment, while New York's share increased from 28 percent to nearly 45 percent of total employment (table 2.5). Nationally, service-sector employment increased from 21 to 35 percent; thus, it is less important on the national level than it is in either New York or Los Angeles.

TRENDS

A broad characterization of industrial organization reveals only a partial picture of economic change in New York and Los Angeles. A more finely detailed analysis of specific industries is necessary to capture the dynamics of growth and decline in the two cities. Whereas manufacturing employment has fallen in both New York and Los Angeles, not all manufacturing industries have shrunk at the same rate—or at all.[7] In Los Angeles, for example, the apparel and textile industries, archetypal "sweated industries," have grown by 50 percent over the 1977–97 period and now comprise nearly one in six manufacturing jobs in Los Angeles County. In New York, even though the apparel industry has steadily lost jobs, it still employs the most manufacturing workers, accounting for more than 25 percent of total manufacturing employment (U.S. Bureau of the Census 1977–97). (The other large New York manufacturing industry is printing and publishing, which accounts for nearly 25 percent of the city's manufacturing workforce.)

Overall employment increased in both New York and Los Angeles during the 1980s and the 1990s. From 1977 to 1997, employment growth registered 11.9 percent in New York and 35.5 percent in Los Angeles County. But even though the number of jobs increased in both cities, the rate of job growth in the balance of each metropolitan area was much higher. In Orange, Riverside, San Bernardino, and Ventura Counties, job growth exceeded 120 percent over the 1977–97 period. While not as dramatic as in the greater Los Angeles region, job growth in the New York metropolitan area (minus New York City) was nearly four times that of the central city, increasing by 43.8 percent from 1977 to 1997 (table 2.6).

Table 2.6. Los Angeles and New York, Total Employment in Central City and Metropolitan Areas, 1977–97

	LOS ANGELES		NEW YORK		
YEAR	County	Metropolitan Area	City	Metropolitan Area	UNITED STATES
1977	2,647,263	960,615	2,714,385	3,073,411	64,975,580
1982	3,130,772	1,296,713	2,896,979	3,528,370	74,297,252
1987	3,546,393	1,765,018	3,122,583	4,238,509	85,483,378
1992	3,536,964	1,959,323	2,903,470	4,156,300	92,800,870
1997	3,588,831	2,151,043	3,038,719	4,421,073	105,299,123
Growth %, 1977–97	35.6	123.9	11.9	43.8	62.1

Source. U.S. Bureau of the Census 1977–97.
Note. Los Angeles metropolitan area includes Orange, Riverside, San Bernardino, and Ventura Counties. New York City includes Bronx, Kings, New York, Queens, and Richmond Counties. New York metropolitan area includes Bergen, Essex, Hudson, Middlesex, Monmouth, Morris, Ocean, Passaic, Somerset, Union, Nassau, Orange, Putnam, Rockland, Sussex, Westchester, and Fairfield Counties.

DISTRIBUTIONAL EFFECTS

Economic change in the two cities has resulted in the growth of a top, extremely high-income sector, a shrinking middle, a vast, impoverished working class, and a smaller, very poor lower class (see Mollenkopf and Castells 1991; Fainstein et al. 1992). Expansion in both numbers of people and income at the top stems from the types of industries present in the two cities; likewise, the low-wage working class is a product of the new occupational structure, characterized by the decline of unionized jobs and the broadening of the poorly paid service sector. Service-sector jobs, including many in the advanced producer-services industries, pay lower-than-average wages, and in some service industries, such as tourism, they pay less than one-third the average wage. In both New York and Los Angeles (fig. 2.2), tourism industry jobs have grown faster than jobs in other industries, and tourism employment has increased its relative share in both cities, to about 12 percent of total employment. At the same time, average wage and salary increases in tourism-related industries have lagged behind wage increases in other industries, and in New York they have lagged very far behind other industries (Gladstone and Fainstein 2001).[8] And what is true of tourism jobs is also true of jobs in the retail-services industry and, in the case of Los Angeles, the growth sectors in manufacturing, apparel, and textile mill products.

Although poverty rates for the country as a whole remained fairly steady throughout the 1980s and 1990s, they increased sharply in Los Angeles and New York. In Los Angeles County, the percentage of the population living in poverty rose from 13.4 percent in 1979 to more than 20 percent in 1999. In New York, poverty rates varied by borough: Manhattan's poverty rate declined from 21.8 percent in 1979 to 20.7 percent in 1999, but rates rose in each of the other boroughs. Queens County experienced the sharpest increase, rising from 11.4 percent in 1979 to 17 percent in 1999 (U.S. Bureau of the Census 1980b, 1990b, 2000a). The slight decline in Manhattan's rate probably results from the increase in well-paid professionals who have moved into its new luxury housing complexes and gentrifying spaces, from Trump Tower to the Upper West Side to the East Village. Conversely, poverty rates may have increased much more rapidly in Queens, Brooklyn, and the Bronx because the outer boroughs account for most of the city's immigrant arrivals. The size of recent immigration to the two cities is one reason for the rise in number of the very needy. While not all immigrants are poor, many are, as indicated by the fact that the single largest occupational category of immigrants is "unskilled" (U.S. Immigration and Naturalization Service 2000b). Federal legislation makes even legal immigrants ineligible

Figure 2.2. Universal City Walk, Los Angeles. Owned by MGM Universal Studios and opened in 1993, City Walk is a "safety bubble," a secure environment where children and adults can stroll and enjoy themselves. It is typical of "walking city" Disney environments—for many visitors "a virtual urban scene preferable to the real thing just outside" (Pecora 2002).

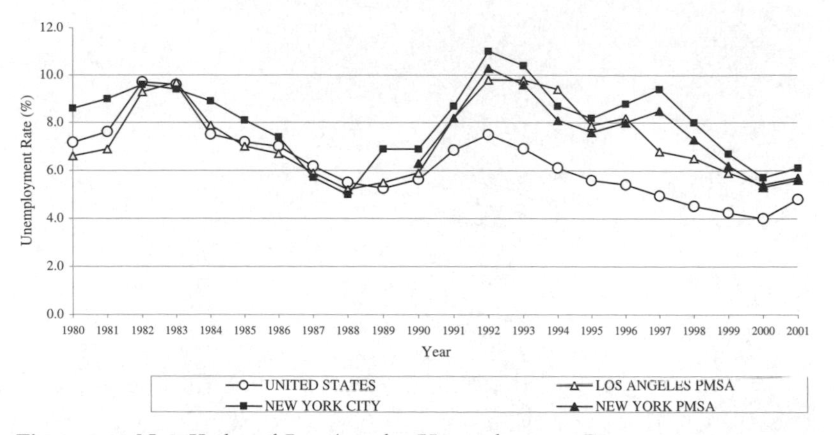

Figure 2.3. New York and Los Angeles Unemployment Rates, 1980–2001. Note that the Los Angeles PMSA is Los Angeles County and that the New York PMSA is New York City plus Putnam, Rockland, and Westchester Counties. Source: U.S. Department of Labor (http://data.bls.gov/cgi-bin/surveymost?la).

for much social assistance; illegal immigrants may find themselves in total destitution.

While the situation of the upper 80 percent of the income distribution curve can be explained in terms of labor market characteristics, the very poor owe their plight primarily to the failure of welfare measures. Their status is a consequence of processes of social exclusion—they are unemployed or detached from the labor force and suffer from serious deficiencies of language, education, and access to social networks. Although during the 1980s official unemployment rates in the New York and Los Angeles metropolitan areas were close to the national average, during the next decade they were well above it (fig. 2.3). Even in the 1980s, since labor force participation rates in the two cities were below the national level, the percentage of people lacking work exceeded the national proportion.[9] With nonexistent or declining support from the state sector, the poorest groups have seen their resources diminish over the past two decades.

In New York, the richest and poorest groups have gained in number at the expense of the middle. Whereas 43.6 percent of all New York City households were middle class in 1977, by 1997 they numbered less than 40 percent of the city's population (McMahon et al. 1998).[10] During the 1980s, the city's upper income groups grew rapidly, from 8 percent to nearly 16 percent of all families, declining slightly to 14.3 percent in

1997. The number of low-income households declined in the same period but increased throughout most of the 1990s. These facts led McMahon et al. (1998, 16) to conclude: "After seven years of a national economic expansion New York City's middle class is still waiting for the economic recovery to begin." New York City, in the last three years of the century, did see an acceleration of its growth rate, adding more than 80,000 jobs each year (Fredrickson 2000). The data on whether this prolonged economic robustness trickled down to lower-income groups are not yet available. The decline in employment that began in August 2001 and accelerated dramatically after the World Trade Center disaster, however, makes recent gains problematic, especially since service workers were the hardest hit in the aftermath of the attack (*Crain's New York Business* 2001).

In Los Angeles, the middle class also lost ground, both relatively and absolutely. From 1989 to 1996, income inequality increased 28 percent. Median household income in the city declined, from $50,336 in 1989 to $47,254 in 1996, a 6 percent drop.[11] Los Angeles's poorest households —those in the bottom twentieth income percentile—saw their income decline even more, by 15 percent (Assembly Select Committee on the California Middle Class 1998). Between 1994 and 1996, the fastest growing groups of households in Los Angeles were those with income below $40,000 and those with income exceeding $100,000 annually.[12] The number of households with income between $40,000 and $100,000 dollars per year declined in absolute terms. The greatest expansion (120 percent) occurred among households earning in excess of $25 million per year. As the Assembly Select Committee on the California Middle Class (1998, 5) bluntly reports, "Whether the measure is relative inequality or actual income, the seven years from 1989 to 1996—from recovery to recession to recovery again—saw the decline of the middle and working classes."

Three factors explain the contraction of the middle class: some middle-class families leave the city as household costs increase, some fall into lower-income categories, and some see their incomes increase. Income polarization in New York and Los Angeles is also fueled, at least in part, by the arrival of large numbers of immigrants from poor countries, who accept work in low-wage jobs and who replace the departing middle classes. In 1996, New York City led the nation with 133,168 legal immigrants, more than any other metropolitan area in the United States. Los Angeles was second, with 64,285 immigrant arrivals (U.S. Immigration and Naturalization Service 2000a). Of course, the number of illegal immigrants in New York and Los Angeles adds to these numbers.

STABILITY AND INSTABILITY

New York and Los Angeles both suffered sharp recessions at the beginning of the 1990s, doing worse than the nation. Then, once recovery began, they shared in the country's growing prosperity, albeit with the rewards distributed extremely unequally. At the time of this writing, in the immediate aftermath of the World Trade Center disaster, the future of the two economies, and particularly of New York's, cannot be predicted. Even without the events of September 11, 2001, the extent to which they could hold onto the gains of the 1990s was an open question.[13] The broader base of the Los Angeles economy makes its prospects appear stronger. Still, the rather surprising efflorescence of the "new economy" in New York during the 1990s could repeat itself in the future. One of the qualities of a global city not captured by quantitative measures is its attractiveness to creative people—it is this strength that perennially seems to make New York rebound from sharp economic downturns.[14]

New York is extremely dependent on its financial sector, particularly its securities industry. During the 1990–97 period, for instance, earnings in the city's finance, insurance, and real estate (FIRE) industries accounted for 57 percent of all earnings growth in Manhattan and nearly half of the city's total increase in earnings. Moreover, the city has become more dependent on Wall Street firms over time: between 1983 and 1987 earnings growth of Wall Street firms accounted for only 23 percent of the city's total earnings growth (Office of the State Comptroller 1998). In the 1990–97 period, earnings growth in the securities and commodities industry alone accounted for 44 percent of Manhattan's and 37 percent of New York City's earnings growth (U.S. Bureau of the Census 1990–97). During the latter part of the 1990s, the proliferation of Internet-content firms in New York's "Silicon Alley" (fig. 2.4) gave hope that the city's economic base was expanding once again. But a lot of these companies have proved highly fragile; as of this writing, many have gone out of business entirely (fig. 2.5), and others have laid off large proportions of their workforces. Whether consolidation within the industry will put it on a firmer footing remains to be seen.

In contrast to New York, the fortunes of Los Angeles are not as dependent on a single industry. Between 1990 and 1997, Los Angeles's FIRE industries accounted for 13.2 percent of the county's total earnings growth. The city is most dependent on business services, which accounted for just under a quarter of Los Angeles County's total earnings growth and which in Los Angeles are a more diverse sector than in New York. In comparison, Los Angeles's motion picture industry, despite its

Figure 2.4. "Silicon Alley," Sign on Twenty-third Street and Broadway/Fifth Avenue, with the Flatiron Building on the Extreme Right (January 2000). This area was packaged as the center of New York City's "dotcom" movement, with the term "Silicon Alley" explicitly invented to challenge Northern California's "Silicon Valley."

Figure 2.5. Same Scene as Figure 2.4, but with the "Silicon Alley" Sign Now Replaced (March 2002). This replacement, in early 2002, underscored the uncertainty of the dotcom movement's future in New York City.

high location quotient, accounted for just over 18 percent of total earnings growth.

CONCLUSION

Cities throughout the world have been promoting themselves as global cities. The implication is that strong linkages to the world economy will increase a city's well-being. The cases of New York and Los Angeles, however, make this faith questionable. They are enormous powerhouses of wealth, attributable to their dominance in certain industries. But it is precisely their "global" characteristics that make them particularly vulnerable to economic downturns and, evidently, especially important symbolic targets for terrorist wrath. New York, with its extreme specialization in finance and associated producer-services industries like corporate law, management consulting, and accounting, is highly sensitive to each economic downturn. The dependence of both cities on tourism makes every decline in discretionary spending a threat. Their large, poor populations constitute a continual strain on the public fisc, while their function as a haven for immigrants is double-edged in its contribution to economic strength.

The sheer size of the populations and economies of the two cities, the glamour associated with their leading industries, and their history of generativity probably mean that they will retain their places within the American system of cities. At the same time, if the past is any guide, they are likely to suffer high levels of volatility. They will continue to be destinations for international travelers and aspiring migrants from the heartland. But they will also continue to be the locations of the country's largest aggregations of impoverished people and to display extreme differences of wealth. The diversity of occupations and groups in New York and Los Angeles and the extent of both geographic and social mobility make the commonly used imagery of a dual city inappropriate. Other tropes that have been applied include fragmentation, quartering, division, and layering (Marcuse 1989, Marcuse and van Kempen 2000). We see in these two cities an ongoing dynamism, causing these more active descriptors to fit better the relationship between economy and society within their boundaries. In conclusion, then, our analysis points to certain commonalties of the two cities that distinguish them from other American metropolises: the absolute size of their leading industries, their sensitivity to perturbations in the world economy, and the extraordinary diversity of their populations. Despite the expansion of their suburban hinterlands and the flight of firms to other, less expensive locations around the world, they continue to be magnets for certain industries key to the global economy. The future of their economies depends on the continuing need of these industries for proximity to each other. Sassen (2000) contends that this cohesiveness has increased in the past decade and predicts that it will continue to do so. It is our view that firms involved in servicing the international economy do not necessarily require close contact with each other, and the faster growth rates outside these two central cities, even in producer services, undermines her argument. We do not, however, see the outcome as predetermined by either technology or cost structures.

CHAPTER THREE

From "Give Me Your Poor" to "Save Our State"

New York and Los Angeles as Immigrant Cities and Regions

Georges Sabagh and Mehdi Bozorgmehr

IMMIGRANT CITIES AND METROPOLITAN REGION

The number of foreign born in the United States reached 28.4 million in 2000, triple the number in 1970. But immigration is highly concentrated by states and by metro regions. Six states accounted for about 69 percent of all the immigrants residing in the United States in 2000. These included California (30.9 percent of the total), New York (12.8 percent), Florida (9.8 percent), Texas (8.6 percent), and New Jersey and Illinois (4.3 percent and 4.1 percent, respectively; table 3.1). Nine of the largest metropolitan regions in the United States accounted for 55 percent of all immigrants in 2000 (table 3.2).

New York and Los Angeles are the premier cities/metropolitan areas for immigration in America, in a close race with each other to rank first in terms of their numbers of immigrants (Bozorgmehr et al. 1996b). In 2000, the New York and Los Angeles consolidated metropolitan statistical areas (CMSAs) each contained about 4.7 million foreign-born persons, or about 23 percent and 30 percent, respectively, of each CMSA's total population (fig. 3.1).

In this chapter, we will compare immigration in the New York and Los Angeles metropolitan regions along several dimensions, including the composition, degree of diversity, and levels of socioeconomic achievement of their main immigrant groups, as well as their immigration histories. We will also discuss the contrasting attitudes of Angelenos and New Yorkers to the post-1965 immigrants, with the latter having been far more accepting and welcoming than the former. For example, the passage in November 1994 of the statewide anti-immigrant Proposition

Table 3.1. Foreign-Born Population by Selected States, 2000

SELECTED STATES	NUMBER	PERCENT OF TOTAL U.S. FOREIGN BORN	PERCENT OF THE STATE WHO ARE FOREIGN-BORN
California	8,781,000	30.9	25.9
New York	3,634,000	12.8	19.9
Florida	2,768,000	9.8	18.4
Texas	2,443,000	8.6	12.2
New Jersey	1,208,000	4.3	14.5
Illinois	1,155,000	4.1	9.5
Massachusetts	755,000	2.8	12.4
Virginia	526,000	1.9	10.8
Maryland	457,000	1.6	9.0
Washington, D.C.	55,000	.2	10.6
U.S. Total	28,379,000	75.8	10.4[a]

Source. Schmidley 2001.
[a]Percent of U.S. total population.

Table 3.2. Foreign-Born Population in Metropolitan Regions (CMSAs) with Populations of 5 Million or More in 2000

	NUMBER	PERCENT OF CMSA WHO ARE FOREIGN BORN
Los Angeles	4,706,000	29.6
New York	4,690,000	22.8
San Francisco	2,007,000	28.3
Chicago	1,070,000	12.3
Washington, D.C.	862,000	11.9
Boston	720,000	12.5
Dallas	673,000	12.8
Detroit	429,000	7.4
Philadelphia	310,000	5.1

Source. Schmidley 2001, tables 5.1 and 5.2A.

187 (Save Our State), which was initiated in the Orange County section of the Los Angeles region, was widely derided in New York (Kadetsky 1994). Indeed, immigrants in New York City, irrespective of their legal status, have since 1989 been officially protected by the mayor's Executive Order No. 124, proclaimed by Mayor Koch and later reaffirmed by Mayors Dinkins and Giuliani (Rathod et al., in press). We will account for these divergent attitudes in terms of differences in the pace, origins, and characteristics of immigrants to New York and Los Angeles, as well as in the political culture of these metropolitan areas. We will conclude

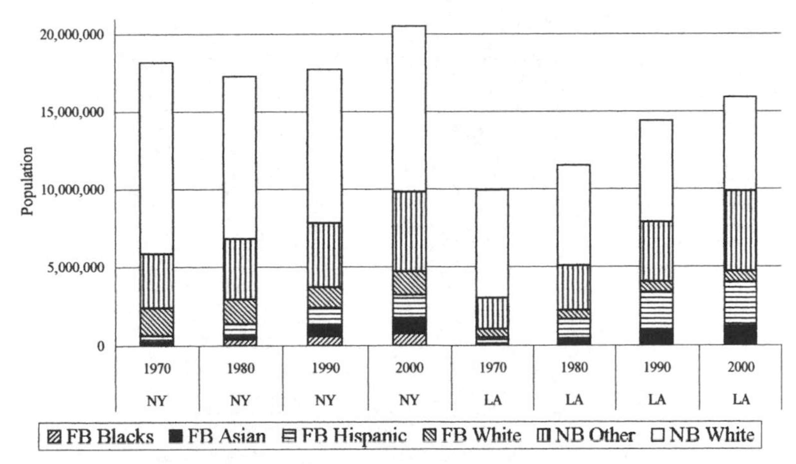

Figure 3.1. Foreign-Born Population by Major Ethnic Groups, Native-Born White Population, and Native-Born Other Population (Hispanics, Non-whites), Los Angeles and New York Metropolitan Regions, 1970–2000. Source: Data for 1970–90 are from the U.S. Bureau of the Census, full count. Data for 2000 are from the U.S. Bureau of the Census, Current Population Surveys, March Supplement and are the average for 1999, 2000, and 2001 in order to achieve greater accuracy since the CPS is a sample (U.S. Bureau of the Census 2001b).

by pointing out that the climate of opinion regarding immigrants has in recent years been growing more favorable in the Los Angeles metropolitan region as, for example, Latinos exercise increased political clout.

HISTORY

New York City has long been North America's premier immigrant city. It was "settled as an Anglo-Dutch colony, transformed by millions of Irish, Germans, Italians, Jews and others in the nineteenth century and early twentieth" (Groneman and Reimers 1995, 181) and then transformed again in the 1970s and beyond by immigrants from the Caribbean, Latin America, and Asia. At the height of twentieth-century immigration to the United States in 1910, 40 percent of the nearly 5 million people in New York City were foreign born. This percentage declined steadily until its nadir in 1970, when it was just 18 percent (table 3.3). The 1965 Hart-Celler Immigration Act rejuvenated immigration to New York. It resulted in a rise in the foreign born to about 36 percent of the population of New York City in 2000, just 4 percent below the city's twentieth-century peak in 1910.

Table 3.3. Population of New York City by Percent and Number of Foreign Born, 1860–2000

	%	NUMBER
1860	42.0	545,908
1880	35.0	723,660
1900	37.0	1,270,080
1910	40.0	1,927,703
1920	35.0	1,991,547
1940	28.0	2,080,020
1960	20.0	1,558,690
1970	18.0	1,437,058
1980	24.0	1,670,199
1990	28.0	2,082,931
2000	36.0	2,871,032

Sources. Data from 1860–1980 are reported in and calculated from Groneman and Reimers (1995, 582). Data from 1990–2000 are in New York City Department of City Planning (2002).
Note. Figures for 1860–1890 include the population within the present boundaries of New York City.

The Hart-Celler Act abolished the old country-of-origin quotas, which had allowed only small numbers of people from southern and eastern Europe and even smaller numbers of Asians to enter the country. These quotas were replaced by two main criteria for admission to the United States: first, possession of scarce and needed skills by people, such as engineers, doctors, nurses, and pharmacists, and, second, family ties to existing citizens or permanent residents. These criteria acted in tandem as those admitted with scarce skills later brought over their not necessarily skilled family members (Waldinger and Bozorgmehr 1996b, 9–10).

Before 1970, Los Angeles was a magnet for massive waves of migrants from other states but not from abroad. In 1970, 43 percent of the residents of Los Angeles County had been born in states other than California, and only 11 percent had been born abroad (table 3.4). For Los Angeles, the 1965 Immigration Act ushered in a new era of immigration. The proportion of foreign born in Los Angeles County tripled between 1970 and 1990 to 33 percent of the total population. In the Los Angeles CMSA, the number of immigrants doubled in a decade to more than 2 million in 1980 and then doubled in the next decade, so that by 1990 the numbers of foreign born in the Los Angeles CMSA (about 4 million) slightly exceeded those in the New York CMSA (about 3.7 million). This was the most dramatic increase in the foreign-born population for any large metropolitan area in the United States, and indeed for

Table 3.4. Population of Los Angeles County by Place of Birth (%), 1960–2000

PLACE OF BIRTH	1960	1970	1980	1990	2000
Born in California	34.5	39.5	40.7	40.8	45.3
Born in other states	51.8	43.3	37.1	27	17.7
Foreign born	9.5	11.3	22.3	33.3	35.8
State of birth not given	4.2	5.9	. . .	. . .	1
Total	100.0	100.0	100.1	101.1	99.8
Total population (millions)	6.0	7.0	7.5	8.9	9.5

Source. Data for 1960–90 are from the U.S. Bureau of the Census, full count. Data for 2000 are from the U.S. Bureau of the Census, Current Population Surveys (U.S. Bureau of the Census, 2001a).
Note. Percentages may not total to exactly 100 due to rounding.

the world, and led some observers to proclaim, prematurely as it turned out, that Los Angeles had replaced New York as America's premier immigrant city and region. By 2000 the New York CMSA's total foreign-born population had caught up with that of Los Angeles at about 4.7 million (fig. 3.1). The proportion of foreign born in New York City, at 36 percent, equaled the proportion of foreign born in Los Angeles County.

There is no major American city or county in which the majority population is foreign born, but several have a majority of foreign born if the second generation (i.e., children of immigrants) is also included (Rumbaut 1998). Such cities are called "immigrant cities." In 1997 foreign born and children of the foreign born made up 54 percent of the population of New York City and 62 percent of the population of the Los Angeles County (Rumbaut 1998, table 1a). A few other cities in the United States would also qualify as immigrant cities, for example, San Francisco, Miami, and Chicago (Schmidley 2001).

The presence of so many foreign born in the two metropolitan regions is further reflected in the language other than English spoken at home. According to the 1990 census, almost 40 percent of Los Angeles's population spoke a foreign language at home, compared to 30 percent of the population in New York. But the percentage of the population speaking Spanish in Los Angeles is twice the percentage of New York.

Since 1960, the Los Angeles region has ranked as the second largest metropolitan area after New York, but the gap in their population sizes has narrowed considerably. From 1970 to 2000 the total population of the New York CMSA rose only slightly, from 18.2 to 20.5 million, but the population of the Los Angeles CMSA surged from about 10 million

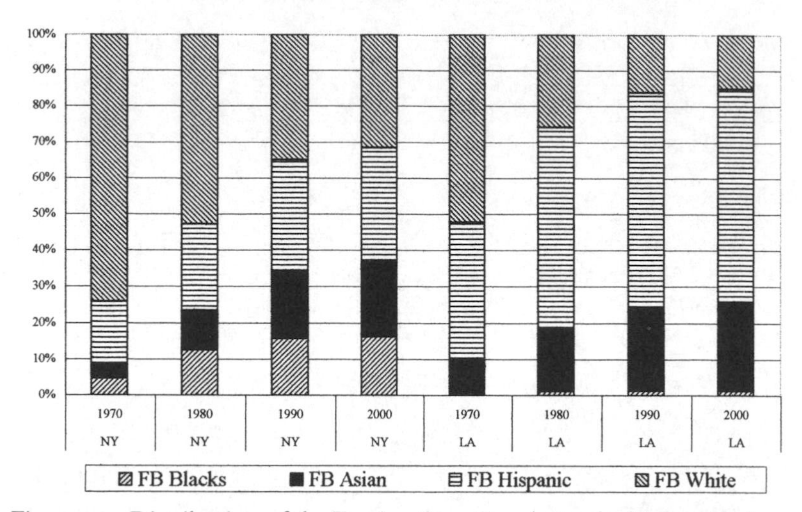

Figure 3.2. Distribution of the Foreign-Born Population by Major Ethnic Groups, Los Angeles and New York Metropolitan Regions (CMSAs), 1970–2000. Source: See figure 3.1.

to about 15.9 million (fig. 3.1). In each CMSA population, growth was due mostly to immigration.

IMMIGRATION TRENDS FOR MAJOR ETHNIC GROUPS

The national and ethnic origins of the immigrants groups in the New York CMSA are quite diverse, in general more so than in Los Angeles. By 2000 in New York, Hispanics constituted 32 percent of the total, as did non-Hispanic whites. Asians and blacks ranked third and fourth, constituting 21 percent and 16 percent of all immigrants, respectively (fig. 3.2). None of these four groups dominated, but none was especially small either. This mix was less diverse in Los Angeles. In 2000, Hispanics in the Los Angeles CMSA made up 60 percent of immigrants. Asian immigrants (24 percent of all immigrants) were also important. But blacks were a tiny 1.2 percent of all immigrants.

Hispanic Immigrants

New York's Hispanic immigrant population quadrupled, from about 410,000 in 1970 to about 1.5 million in 2000 (see fig. 3.3). The most significant trend in the composition of this population is the explosion of the number of Dominican immigrants in the CMSA, from about 53,000 in 1970 to about 479,000 in 2000. They accounted for 12 percent of the new arrivals in 1985–90. The number of Hispanic immigrants from all South American countries also increased dramatically, from about 114,000 in 1970 to about 733,000 in 2000. The three largest of these groups were from Colombia (about 202,000), Ecuador (about 180,000), and Peru (about 100,000). New York has recently become a magnet for Mexican immigrants. In 1970, the New York CMSA had only about 7,000 (by contrast the Los Angeles CMSA had about 268,000), but by 1990 Mexican immigrants had jumped to about 56,000 and in the next decade more than tripled, to about 196,000. This has caught the attention of many New Yorkers (Smith 2001) but still pales in comparison to the roughly 2.1 million Mexican immigrants in the Los Angeles CMSA in 2000.

Adding to the diversity of New York's Hispanic population is the special case of Puerto Ricans, who, as U.S citizens, are usually omitted from discussions of immigration. (Interestingly, they often fare worse economically than do blacks in New York City, as in, e.g., "Spanish Harlem.") As late as 1970, they encompassed two-thirds of New York's Hispanic population, but the heavy Hispanic immigration of the 1980s and 1990s has reduced their proportion to less than half (fig. 1.10).

Los Angeles, between 1970 and 2000, witnessed an explosion of Hispanic immigrants, from about 400,000 to about 2.8 million, with those born in Mexico accounting for about three-quarters of this total (fig. 3.3). The proximity of Los Angeles to the Mexican border has greatly facilitated moves back and forth across the frontier. But the facilitating factors amount to more than simply geographic closeness. The presence of a large native-born Mexican population in Los Angeles prior to 1970 has encouraged chain migration. Also, since California was part of Mexico until 1848, many Mexicans perceive immigration as a "return to Aztlan," hence the title of a book about Mexican migration by Massey et al. (1987). Los Angeles has certainly become "the capital of Mexican America" (Ortiz 1996, 247). In 1990, of the 13.4 million Americans who classified themselves as of Mexican origin, 4.7 million lived in the Los Angeles region.

Central American immigrants, mainly Salvadorans and Guatemalans, are the next most important Hispanic immigrant group in the Los Angeles CMSA, increasing dramatically from 23,000 in 1970 to 517,000 in 2000 (fig. 3.3). By 1990 Los Angeles contained more than half of the Salvadorans and Guatemalans in the United States (Lopez et al. 1996, table 10.1). In 1970, there were about as few Central Americans in Los Angeles as there were in New York. Although both populations have grown rapidly, by 2000 the total number of Central Americans in the

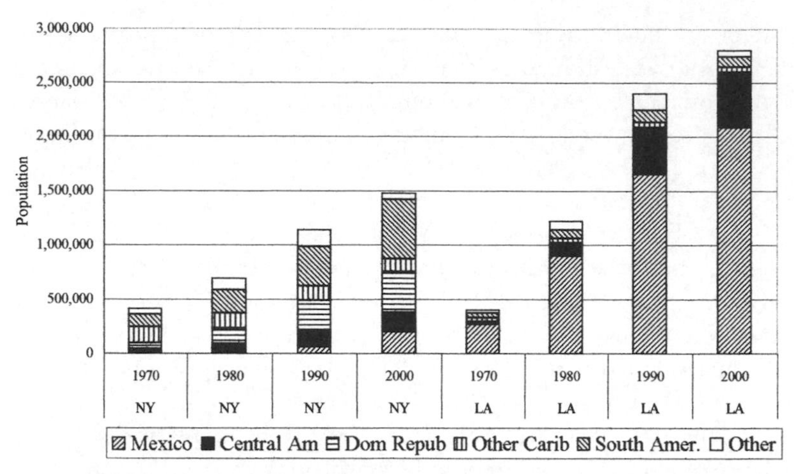

Figure 3.3. Foreign-Born Hispanic Population by Nativity, Los Angeles and New York Metropolitan Regions (CMSAs), 1970–2000. Source: See figure 3.1.

Los Angeles CMSA was more than twice that in the New York CMSA. Los Angeles's South American population, however, is still small, at about 94,000, only about 17 percent the size of New York's.

In sum, well over half of the immigrants to Los Angeles between 1960 and 2000 came from only three countries (Mexico, El Salvador, and Guatemala). This concentration would be much higher were we to take into account the census undercount of undocumented immigrants, most of whom are from these three countries as well. The problem with the undocumented is reflected in what some demographers have aptly called "counting the uncountables." The data for the United States as a whole and for specific cities are inadequate. Still, according to the best estimates of the Immigration and Naturalization Service (INS), there were an estimated 5 million undocumented immigrants in the United States in 1996, 40 percent of whom were from Mexico and another 10 percent from El Salvador and Guatemala (U.S. Immigration and Naturalization Service 1997, 198). Since these populations are heavily concentrated in California, this state received almost four times as many illegal aliens as New York State did. The total number of illegal aliens in Los Angeles County in 1992 was estimated at 1.5 million persons, composed of those who either had just received amnesty (under the 1986 Immigration Reform and Control Act) or were still unauthorized residents (Sabagh and Bozorgmehr 1996, 86). Based on INS data, the New York City Department of City Planning estimates that there were at least 400,000 undocumented immigrants in New York City in 1996 (Salvo and Lobo 1997). Whatever estimates are used, there is no doubt that the number of illegal immigrants is substantially higher in Los Angeles than in New York. Furthermore, illegal immigrants in New York are mainly visa overstayers and highly diverse, while those in Los Angeles are mainly undocumented Mexicans and Central Americans who entered the United States without any INS inspection (Tang and Tress 1999).

Asian Immigrants

In both New York and Los Angeles, there were hardly any Asian immigrants in 1970, just around 75,000 in each region. Their growth between 1970 and 2000 was phenomenal, particularly in the Los Angeles region. By 2000, there were just fewer than 1.1 million in the Los Angeles CMSA and about 907,000 in the New York CMSA (fig. 3.4).

In 1970 in New York, two-thirds of immigrant Asians were born in China, whereas in Los Angeles the Asian distribution was much more balanced and diversified, with Japanese (35 percent of the total), Chinese (29 percent), and Filipinos (28 percent) all well represented and a smaller group of Koreans (8 percent). But by 2000, the Asian distribution in the New York CMSA had also become much more diversified. Chinese were still the most important group (24 percent of the total), but Asian Indians were very close (23 percent of the total), followed by Filipinos (12 percent), Koreans (12 percent), and Japanese (6 percent). In the Los Angeles CMSA, the Asian population remained diversified, with Filipi-

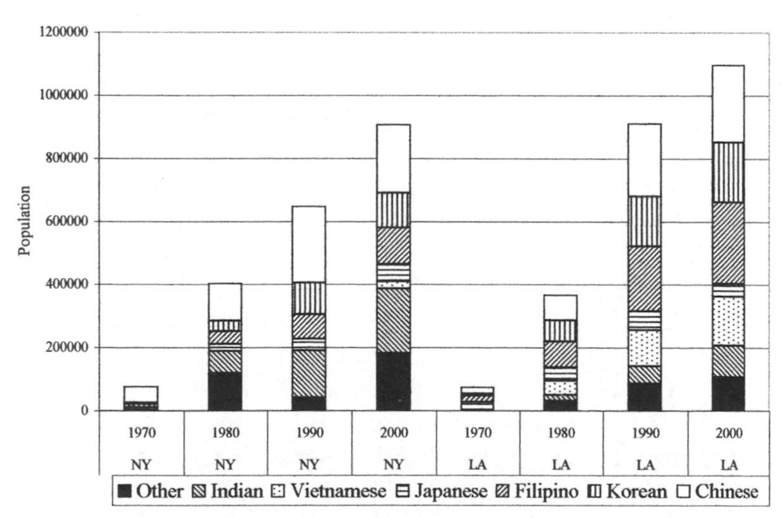

Figure 3.4. Foreign-Born Asians and Pacific Islanders by Nativity, Los Angeles and New York Metropolitan Regions (CMSAs), 1970–2000. Chinese includes those from mainland China, Taiwan, and Hong Kong. Source: See figure 3.1.

nos (23 percent), Chinese (22 percent), Koreans (17 percent) Vietnamese (14 percent), and Asian Indians (9 percent) as the five largest groups.

Black Immigrants

African-Americans have always been a much more important component of the population of New York than of Los Angeles. Unlike the Los Angeles CMSA, only 8 percent of whose population in 2000 was black, 17 percent of the New York CMSA's population was black. The recent heavy influx into the New York CMSA of Caribbean immigrants, most of whom are black, has greatly modified the internal composition of the black population. By 2000, immigrants from the Caribbean in the New York CMSA totaled about 1.1 million and made up 25 percent of all immigrants there. About 42 percent were Dominicans, who are mostly racially black but also Hispanic, followed by Jamaicans (19 percent), Haitians (13 percent), and Cubans (9 percent). Recently, New York has also received new immigrants from Sub-Saharan Africa, mainly from West Africa (Tang and Tress 1999). African immigrants in the CMSA now total about 128,000. As a result of these changes, fully one-quarter of the black population of the New York CMSA is now foreign born, with the Caribbean acting as the most important source area for New York City immigration.

In the Los Angeles region there are far fewer black immigrants. In 2000, there were about 80,000 immigrants from the Caribbean, only about 7 percent of the number in the New York CMSA. There were also about 37,000 immigrants from Africa, less than a third as many as in New York.

Moreover, there are two black Los Angeleses. The better-educated blacks, often found in the public sector, bypass competition with immigrants. The other black Los Angeles, that is, the less educated, which make up about one-quarter of all blacks, are more likely to face job competition from low-skilled immigrants. Waldinger's research shows that small firms in the private sector hire immigrants more frequently through informal channels, often through referrals by coethnic employees, while large firms hire blacks more through formal search and application processes comparable to those in the public sector (Waldinger and Lichter 2003). The formal dimension is undoubtedly connected to the fear of discriminatory lawsuits by black employees, a fear that is lessened when dealing with immigrants. An issue that deserves further research is whether immigrant blacks are a more serious competition to African-Americans than are immigrants of other racial backgrounds. This question is important for New York, with its significant populations of

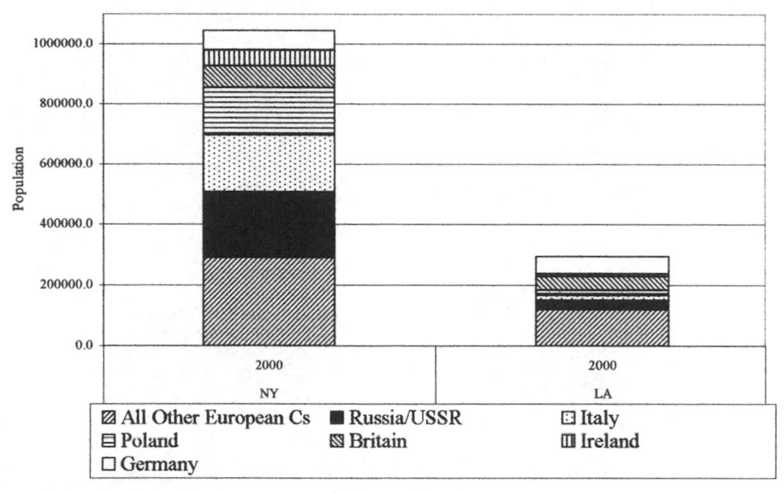

Figure 3.5. Foreign-Born Europeans by Nativity, Los Angeles and New York Metropolitan Regions (CMSAs), 2000. Source: See figure 3.1.

native- and foreign-born blacks. We do know that immigrant blacks (e.g., Jamaicans) frequently distance themselves from African-Americans to avert negative stereotypes and, in so doing, increase their appeal to prospective employers (Waters 1999).

Europe and the Middle East

In 2000 there were just over 1 million European-born persons in the New York CMSA, compared with about 290,000 in the Los Angeles CMSA (fig. 3.5). The largest and newest group was from the former Soviet Union (about 216,000), followed closely by people from Italy (about 190,000), and then from Poland (about 158,000). In view of the historical importance of European immigration, particularly in Manhattan, it is of interest to consider the areas of settlement of the new Europeans. Most of them have opted for the adjoining boroughs of Brooklyn and Queens, where housing is cheaper than in Manhattan. The two major areas of new European immigrant settlements in New York are Brighton Beach for Russian Jews (fig. 5.12) and Greenpoint for Poles. Greenpoint is unusual—one of the few old European ethnic neighborhoods that is still being sustained by an influx of coethnic newcomers.

In the Los Angeles CMSA, the largest group of European immigrants was from Germany (about 57,000) followed by England (about 46,000). Underlining how much less numerous are Europeans immigrants in Los Angeles than in New York, although the number of Ger-

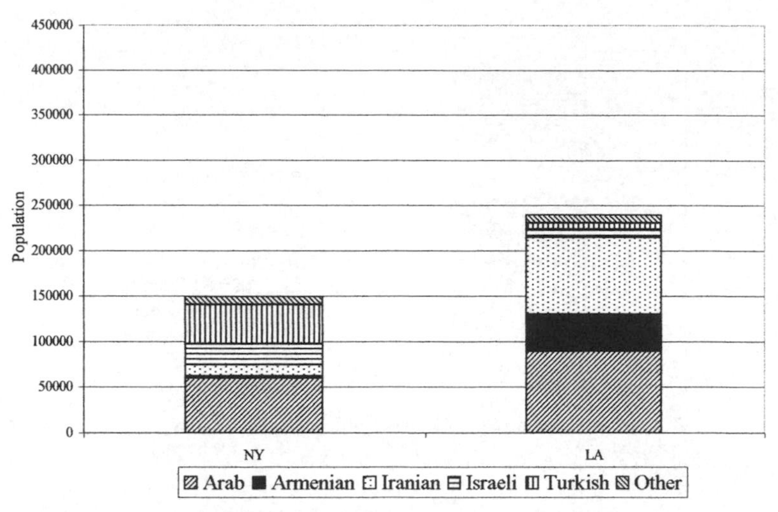

Figure 3.6. Foreign-Born Middle-Eastern Population by Nativity, New York and Los Angeles CMSAs, 2000. Source: See figure 3.1.

man immigrants in New York, at about 68,000, exceeds the number in Los Angeles, Germans in the New York CMSA are only the sixth largest European immigrant group.

The Los Angeles CMSA has about 240,000 persons who were born in the Middle East, substantially more than the roughly 150,000 Middle Easterners in the New York CMSA (fig. 3.6). Arabs, especially Egyptians and Lebanese, are the most important group in the New York CMSA's Middle Eastern population, 40 percent of the total. Turks, Israelis, and Iranians, in that order, are also important there. Arabs, mostly Lebanese and Egyptians, are also the largest Middle Eastern group in the Los Angeles CMSA, followed closely by Iranians, and then Armenians. Not surprisingly, these populations have received considerable media attention in the aftermath of September 11, 2001.

Diversity of Immigrant Population

We have argued that, despite the image Angelenos have of Los Angeles as the nation's most diverse city and region, New York is in many ways more diverse and closer to the U.S. immigrant profile as a whole. Indeed, many of New York's major immigrant groups are scarcely found in Los Angeles (e.g. Dominicans, Jamaicans, Haitians, and Guyanese). Furthermore, no group is dominant in New York among immigrants the way Mexicans are in Los Angeles.

Table 3.5. Immigrant (Foreign-Born) Population of the New York CMSA by Top 15 Countries of Origin, 2000

	NUMBER	% OF TOTAL
Dominican Republic	479,137	10.2
China	217,387	4.6
Russia	215,593	4.6
Jamaica	211,816	4.5
India	204,867	4.3
Colombia	202,317	4.3
Mexico	196,352	4.2
Italy	189,934	4.0
Ecuador	179,682	3.8
Poland	157,777	3.3
Guyana	150,445	3.2
Haiti	146,005	3.1
Philippines	112,822	2.4
South Korea	111,660	2.4
Peru	100,061	2.1

Source. U.S. Bureau of the Census, Current Population Surveys (U.S. Bureau of the Census, 2001a). The figures are the average for 1999, 2000, and 2001 in order to achieve greater accuracy since the CPS is a sample.
Note. Figure for China includes those immigrants from mailand China, Taiwan, and Hong Kong.

In the New York CMSA, Dominicans were the largest group at roughly 10 percent of the total, followed by Chinese from China, Taiwan, and Hong Kong (4.6 percent) and Russians (4.6 percent), and then Jamaicans (4.5 percent), Asians from India (4.3 percent), and Colombians (4.3 percent). (See table 3.5; for earlier data, see Lobo et al. 1996.) Because of its location on the Pacific Rim and its history of immigration from China, Japan, and Korea, the Los Angeles region used to have a much more diverse Asian population than that of New York, but, as we have seen, that has now changed.

Mexicans in the Los Angeles CMSA in 2000 constituted a colossal 46 percent of all immigrants, dwarfing the next four most common groups: people from El Salvador (6.2 percent), the Philippines (5.6 percent), China, Taiwan, and Hong Kong (5.3 percent), and South Korea (4.2 percent; table 3.6).

SOCIOECONOMIC ACHIEVEMENT

Compared to Hispanics, Asian immigrants in Los Angeles and New York, especially Chinese and Indians, are much more educated and include many professionals and entrepreneurs. This is the most salient as-

Table 3.6. Immigrant (Foreign-Born) Population of the Los Angeles CMSA by Top 15 Countries of Origin, 2000

	NUMBER	% OF TOTAL
Mexico	2,105,861	45.6
El Salvador	287,795	6.2
Philippines	257,234	5.6
China	243,406	5.3
South Korea	191,861	4.2
Ecuador	179,682	3.9
Guatemala	173,148	3.7
Vietnam	155,931	3.4
India	99,504	2.2
Iran	85,178	1.8
Canada	66,786	1.4
Germany	56,720	1.2
Honduras	51,559	1.1
England	45,566	1.0
Ghana	43,476	0.9

Source. US Bureau of the Census Current Population Surveys (U.S. Bureau of the Census, 2001a). The figures are the average for 1999, 2000, and 2001 in order to achieve greater accuracy since the CPS is a sample.
Note. Figure for China includes those immigrants from mailand China, Taiwan, and Hong Kong.

pect of Asian economic adaptation in the United States in general and in New York and Los Angeles in particular. Many quickly move into the middle class, and some even into the upper class. In 2000, nearly half of Asian immigrants aged twenty-five to sixty-four in the New York and Los Angeles CMSAs had at least a bachelor's degree, compared to less than 13 percent for Hispanic immigrants in New York and less than 6 percent in Los Angeles. Zhou and Kim, in chapter 4, show that a substantial number of new Chinese arrivals directly settle in affluent suburbs, thus bypassing stepwise mobility from urban immigrant ghettos to higher-status suburbs. Still, this pattern of settlement does not necessarily result in rapid acculturation, for we have seen the emergence of suburban enclaves of Chinese such as Monterey Park, Los Angeles.

While the educational levels of Asians somewhat exceeded those of non-Hispanic white immigrants (about 37 percent of non-Hispanic white immigrants in the New York and Los Angeles CMSAs had at least a bachelor's degree), their socioeconomic achievements were more or less comparable (see figs. 3.7 and 3.8). Thus the percentage of Asians and non-Hispanic white immigrants in both CMSAs in executive and professional jobs was high, ranging from about 34 to 48 percent. Unexpectedly, non-Hispanic white immigrants have a higher occupational

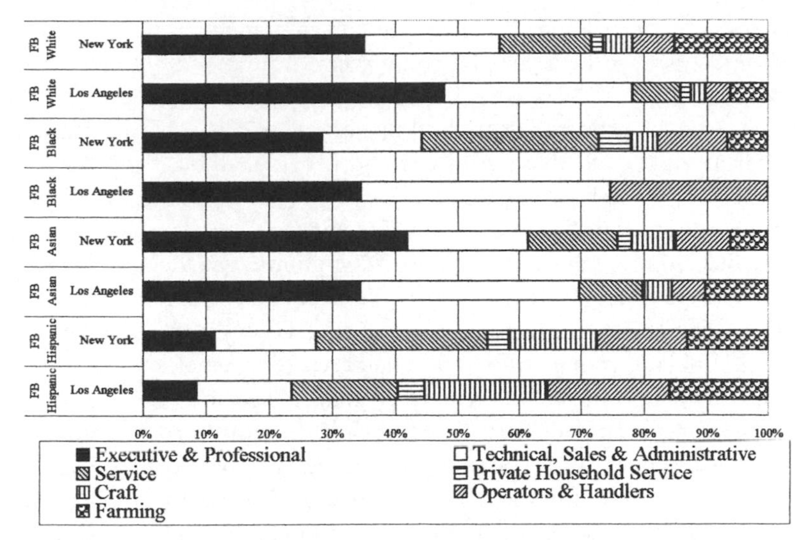

Figure 3.7. Occupational Distribution of Those Employed among Major Foreign-Born Groups, Ages 25–64, New York and Los Angeles (CMSAs), 2000. Source: See figure 3.1.

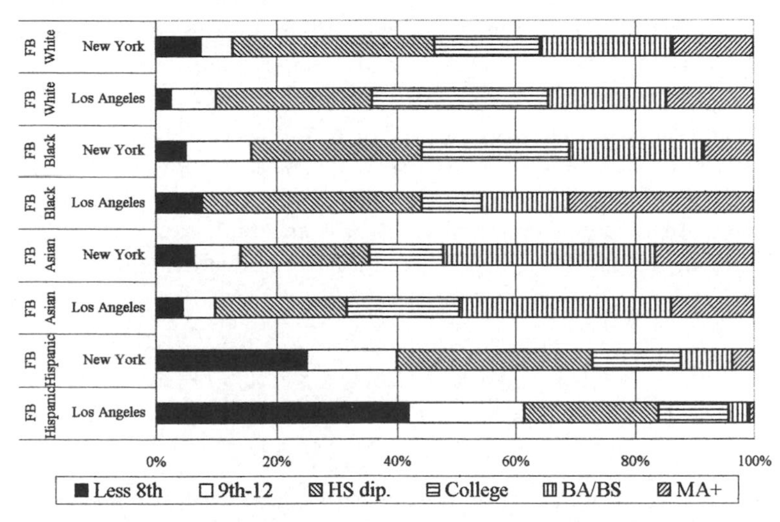

Figure 3.8. Educational Achievement of Major Foreign-Born Groups, Ages 25–64, New York and Los Angeles (CMSAs), 2000. Source: See figure 3.1.

status in Los Angeles than in New York. In Los Angeles, about 48 percent were in the two top occupations, compared with 35 percent in New York. One possible explanation for this difference is the greater relative importance of Middle Easterners among white immigrants in Los Angeles than in New York. Elsewhere, we have shown that, in the Los Angeles region, Middle Eastern immigrants have achieved a higher educational status than have non-Hispanic white immigrants (Bozorgmehr et al. 1996a, 354).

Los Angeles attracts a very small but highly selective black immigration from Africa, which constitutes roughly half of all black immigrants. About half of black immigrants have a bachelor's degree in Los Angeles and about 34 percent have executive and professional jobs. In New York, black immigrants have lower socioeconomic achievement because most are labor migrants from the Caribbean, but this is substantially higher than that of Hispanics in New York. Thus about 30 percent of New York black immigrants in 2000 had at least a bachelor's degree and about 28 percent had executive and professional jobs.

Mirroring their low levels of education, foreign-born Hispanics in each CMSA have the lowest socioeconomic achievement of all, with only about 9 percent of those in Los Angeles in professional and managerial jobs and only about 11 percent of those in New York. Foreign-born Hispanics are doing distinctly worse in Los Angeles than in New York in terms of both educational levels and occupational achievement, as we have seen. Mexicans and Central Americans, who predominate among Los Angeles Hispanics and have very low levels of education on the average (e.g., primary school for Mexicans), mainly account for the lower socioeconomic achievement of Hispanics in Los Angeles. Thus, Los Angeles attracts largely low-skilled working-class immigrants from these countries who find themselves at the bottom of the ladder, with little opportunity for upward mobility (Waldinger and Bozorgmehr 1996b). Since these immigrants also have the highest share of illegal aliens they are easily exploited economically and unwittingly provide ammunition for nativist reactions.

GEOGRAPHIC SEPARATION BY SOCIAL CLASS AND IMMIGRANT GROUPS

In Los Angeles, higher-status individuals reside in wealthy communities that are usually some distance from the segregated barrios and ghettos of poorer minorities and immigrants. The main contact that the wealthier populations have with poorer minorities and immigrants is sometimes only with the maids and gardeners they employ. During the 1992 riots, many of these higher-status Angelenos found themselves sheltered from all the violence, as if these riots happened in a faraway city.

Even in downtown Los Angeles, where there is more mixing, the new high-rise professional and financial area of the west side is worlds apart from an older and deteriorated shopping area in east downtown, where pedestrians are mostly poor minorities and immigrants. By skipping ethnic neighborhoods, Los Angeles's wide system of freeways discourages contact between various social groups.

This is far less true for New York City, particularly Manhattan, which, with its high pedestrian traffic, brings together the poor and the rich, the immigrant, the native, and the tourists. Furthermore, New York's heavily used public transportation system (bus and subway) encourages frequent exposure across class and ethnic and racial groups. This is vividly illustrated by a priest's personal observations (Principe 1997, 31):

> Any rider who cares to look around gets a chance to observe a daily sampling of the city's racial, religious, and ethnic groups: You see, for example, the entrepreneurial spirit of some of the newly arrived immigrants who go from car to car, offering discount prices on newspapers, gum, candy, incense sticks, flashing yo-yos, dolls, toys, even cellular phones. . . . Even more interesting, for me, are the outward signs of inward religious faith one sees on display in the subways—not the kind of thing non–New Yorkers would expect. An elderly couple speaking Yiddish, a young man topped by a yarmulke, a Hasidic couple wearing their distinctive garb: All testify to the still-strong Jewish presence in the city. An increasing Islamic element is reflected in the habit-like dress of some Muslim women and the neat dark conservative suits of men reading the Koran and wearing their skull caps. Here is a Sikh with his beard and turban; there a Hindu woman in a colorful sari; the Indian subcontinent and Eastern religions are well represented.

Thus, New Yorkers are often highly concentrated in a limited space as they commute or go about their daily business and are much more likely to be conscious of each other, in spite of the substantial residential segregation discussed in chapter 5. By contrast, the social and cultural separation between Angelenos accentuates the effects of residential segregation. This has important implications for the differences between the attitudes of New Yorkers and Angelenos toward immigrants.

PUBLIC SENTIMENT TOWARD IMMIGRANTS AND NATIVIST REACTION

Glazer and Moynihan ([1963] 1970) stressed the relative ease with which New York City had absorbed its newcomers compared to the cities in the West and Southwest, and they also stressed the sheer size of New York City and its immigrant populations. This is still true. For example, in 1990, the 585,000 Cubans in Miami made up 18 percent of its total population, but the 406,000 Dominicans in the New York region accounted for only 2.2 percent of its total population. Even though San Francisco is known as the center of Asian immigrants in the United States, it had the same number of Asians as the New York region in 1990. But, in relation to the total population, Asians were three times more numerous in San Francisco than in New York (15 percent as compared to 4.8 percent).

The economist Thomas Muller (1993) argues that the key difference between New York and other immigrant cities is not the numbers or even the characteristics of the immigrants but the attitudes of the receiving cities. New York's history of continuous immigration has created a political culture that is used to accommodating newcomers. This is a very important point, the implications of which we will shortly see for Los Angeles.

Anti-immigrant sentiments have become more widespread in the mid-1990s in the United States than when new immigration resumed after the passage of the 1965 Immigration Act. Whereas one-third of Americans wanted fewer immigrants in 1965, this percentage increased to more than half in the 1990s (Jaret 1999). But there are variations among immigrant cities. Southern California's nativist Anglos provided the needed funds and support to have the anti-immigrant Proposition 187 (Save Our State) included in the November 1994 state ballot. Proposition 187 made illegal immigrants ineligible for government-funded social and health services and attendance at public schools and required that illegal aliens be reported to the federal government. The authors of this proposition resided in Orange County, and its top contributors included a state senator from Orange County and a state assemblyman from Los Angeles (Kadetsky 1994). It passed "by a vote of 59 percent 'for' to 31 percent 'against'" (Clark 1998, 174). Seven counties in and around the San Francisco region voted against this proposition. But even though only 31 percent of Hispanics voted for this proposition, the Los Angeles region provided the needed votes to pass it (Clark 1998, 174).

In stark contrast, New York Mayor Ed Koch issued the pro-immigration Executive Order No. 124 in 1989. It stated that "the City shall provide services to all eligible persons without regard to their immigration status, and shall protect persons from the fear that they might be reported to the INS if they seek services such as emergency health care, police protection, or education for their children" (New York City 1999). Himself the son of an immigrant, Mayor Koch proclaimed, "Immigrant New Yorkers, it's your city too!" (quoted in Rathod et. al, in press). New Yorkers' favorable view of immigrants is mirrored by the fact that their mayors are very pro-immigration and have repeatedly and publicly argued that immigrants benefit New York City. No mayor of New York City can afford to be anti-immigrant. The grandson of Italian immigrants himself, Mayor Giuliani often broke ranks with Republicans on immigration policy. Giuliani challenged the provisions of the 1996 Personal Responsibility and Welfare Reform Act that deny supplemental security income (SSI) and food stamps to legal immigrant residents of New York City. He also launched "Citizenship NYC," an initiative to help elderly and disabled legal immigrants—at risk of losing SSI and food stamp benefits—to become naturalized citizens. Giuliani proclaimed that "as mayor of the largest city in America, which benefits more from the contributions of immigrants than any other place in the country, I see immigrants as assets. Immigrants are vital to our workforce, and add to the common prosperity. They do not detract from it. In our nations' urban centers, which provide a disproportionate amount of America's wealth, immigration constantly renews and rejuvenates the workforce. Our cities are the engines of the American economy and immigration is the fuel that powers those engines" (New York City 1999). Cynics may argue that this is a case of political opportunism since immigrants are increasingly entering the political process, but that case can also be made for Los Angeles.

True, the state of California is the land of propositions. Indeed, many have a hard time keeping track of anti-immigrant/minority propositions passed in California by number. However, lack of such initiatives in New York does not necessarily mean there is less anti-immigrant sentiment. To correct for these problems, we turn to other indicators of public sentiment toward immigrants, such as opinion polls, when available.

The *Los Angeles Times* has carried out a number of polls that include many questions about immigrants. That we could find only one comparable "official" poll by the *New York Times* for New York is itself indicative of New Yorkers' favorable view of immigrants, and that poll was not recent, despite the fact that the *New York Times* regularly polls New York City. For example, a 1999 poll on the Diallo police shooting case had questions about race relations, the treatment of minorities, and attitudes about the tragedy, but nothing on attitudes toward immigrants. The fact that Diallo is black is obviously considered more important than his being an immigrant, one more indicator of the racialization of ethnicity.

According to a survey carried out by the *Los Angeles Times* (1993a), 63 percent of the adults polled in the city of Los Angeles agreed with the statement that there are "too many immigrants in Los Angeles." Surprisingly, whites, blacks, and Latinos had the same negative view of immigrants. But when more specific questions were asked about the effects of high immigration, a substantial difference appears in the opinions of these three ethnic groups. Blacks were the most likely to agree that immigrants "take jobs away from Americans" and Latinos the least likely, with whites in-between.

According to a 1992 New York City survey, conducted about the same time as the above in Los Angeles, about 67 percent of those who expressed their opinions thought that "immigrants add to" rather than "detract from the quality of life in New York City" (Setlow and Cohen 1993, 16). This favorable opinion of immigrants was even higher among Jews and the Irish, who have a long history of immigration. Another survey of New York City obtained similar results in 1996. The question posed—that is, "Does immigration enrich New York City?"—was, however, biased in favor of immigrants. As many as 72 percent of New Yorkers agreed that "immigration enriches New York City." One respondent said "I not only think that NYC is enriched by immigrants but that this aspect of the City's population has made NYC what it is and will continue to be. It is the 'City of the World.'" Another New Yorker stated that "immigrants are the backbone of this City and keep the flavor of New York alive."

We could only find one other survey about the attitudes of New Yorkers toward immigrants, but its timing in 1993, shortly after the World Trade Center bombing, puts immigrants in a bad light. For instance, more than half of the respondents agreed that "illegal immigration" poses a serious "terrorist threat" to the United States (Behn and Muzzio 1993). In our opinion, the 1992 and 1996 surveys are much more representative of New Yorkers' favorable attitudes toward immigrants.

While there has been anti-Asian backlash, particularly among blacks, in New York (e.g., five long-term boycotts against Korean businesses), and some recent well-publicized disputes between Korean businesses and their Mexican employees, who claim they are not paid minimum wages, these pale in comparison to the burning and looting of Korean businesses that took place during the Los Angeles riots of 1992 (Min 1996). New Yorkers, in fact, often express appreciation for Korean grocery stores, nail salons, and, increasingly, ethnic restaurants for their around-the-clock service at rock-bottom prices. Although there have been complaints about signs in Hangul (the Korean alphabet) in Flushing, Queens, as well as in the Palisades and Fort Lee areas in New Jersey, such complaints have not reached the level of the English-only language initiative in Monterey Park, a suburban Chinatown (Horton 1995). When a longtime Flushing councilwoman made a remark that Asian immigrants have invaded Flushing, an Asian coalition of mostly

Korean and Chinese picketed against her. She retracted her words by stating that she was misquoted. Ironically, the mayor and governor of New York, both Republicans, attacked the councilwoman, a Democrat, in a press conference (see chap. 4). When southern Californians were asked about a proposal that "all foreign immigration to the United States be stopped for a period of three years," almost half of the white and black respondents, and nearly one-quarter of Asians, favored it strongly.

Several reasons account for the unwelcome extended to newcomers in Los Angeles, as opposed to a more receptive attitude in New York. First, New York has always been an immigrant Mecca, whereas the large influx of newcomers occurred in a very short time (thirty years) in Los Angeles. Simon and Lynch (1999) show that the American public has a tendency to express approval of immigrants who came earlier, but disapproval of the newcomers, in public opinion polls. Curiously enough, Angelenos' reactions to the new immigrants appear to be much more typical of the United States as a whole than are the views of New Yorkers. This is documented by several nationwide polls in the 1980s and the 1990s, which reveal that two-thirds of respondents expressed a preference for a decrease in the number of immigrants (Espenshade and Hempsted 1996, 538; Lapinski et al. 1997, 361). It is clear that nativist sentiments are strongest in the regions that have only recently received "floods of immigrants."

Second, as argued earlier, Mexicans and Central American labor migrants constitute the bulk of immigrants to Los Angeles, whereas no group dominates immigrant composition in New York nearly to the same extent. Perhaps the most significant implication of this immigrant composition is that a much larger number of these Los Angeles immigrants are undocumented, and they are perceived to put extra pressure on social services, especially in the economic recessionary times of the early 1990s. Opposition to high levels of immigration is generally greater when newcomers are seen as being largely undocumented, which is a distinctive feature of the new immigration to the United States compared to the old. According to a *Los Angeles Times* (1993d) survey carried out in a Los Angeles suburb (Orange County), two-thirds of white respondents considered illegal immigration a serious problem but only one-third had the same opinion about legal immigration. This pattern held for Latino and Asian respondents, except that fewer of them considered illegal immigration to be a serious problem. These results suggest that when a question is asked about immigration in general, many respondents are likely to think about the undocumented, particularly in Los Angeles. Another implication is that, compared to New York, immigrants to Los Angeles, particularly Mexicans and Central Americans, have lower education and skills than other immigrants as we stressed earlier. Consequently, we would expect a stronger nativist reaction in Los Angeles. Analysis of a 1983 survey in Southern California shows that "respondents who cast immigrants as poor and welfare dependents or as making little effort to learn English have some of the most unfavorable ranking of undocumented immigration and its impact" (Espenshade and Calhoun 1993, 210).

Third, New York and Los Angeles differ markedly in the origin of the dominant non-Hispanic white population and its impact on their attitudes toward immigrants. First- and second-generation immigrants account for more than half of New York's non-Hispanic white population but less than one-quarter of Los Angeles's non-Hispanic whites (Mollenkopf 1999, 419). Unlike Angelenos, many New Yorkers are the descendants of Jewish, Italian, Irish, and Greek immigrants. They are much less likely than the predominantly WASP Angelenos to be hostile to foreign newcomers. Historically, as argued by Laslett (1996), the WASP Angelenos were often intolerant to immigrants. Furthermore, many of Los Angeles's whites have been transplanted internal migrants, mostly from rural areas and small towns in the Midwest. Many of these migrants have the nativists' fear of all that is foreign and are quick to blame immigrants, particularly the undocumented, for the problems of living in large cities. For instance, in 1993, six out of ten whites residing in Orange County blamed illegal immigrants for "crime and street violence." It is significant that almost all of these whites had either moved from the city of Los Angeles or came from other parts of California. Middle-class whites are particularly sensitive to the deterioration of public schools and have responded either by a massive flight to the suburbs or by sending their children to private schools. This constituency ensured the passage of Proposition 187. In an analysis of the vote for Proposition 187 by communities in Los Angeles County, Clark (1998, 175) has shown that the strongest support for this proposition was in the predominantly white middle-class suburban areas of West Valley, Burbank, Glendale, Whittier, and West Covina.

Fourth, New York has historically had nongovernmental institutions (e.g., settlement houses, Jewish and Catholic hospitals) that helped immigrants. During the nineteenth and early twentieth centuries, lack of governmental involvement elicited a private response. Some of these duties are now carried out by the Mayor's Office of Immigrant Affairs and Language Services (MOIALS). New York is the only immigrant city that has an office devoted to immigrants; the only counterpart in Los Angeles is the Office of Human Relations, the main concern of which is to improve ethnic relations. The Office of Immigrant Affairs, started in the

Department of City Planning during the Koch administration (1985), became a mayor's office during the Dinkins administration (1989). In 1993, during the Giuliani administration, it became a cabinet-level office (MOIALS). "The Mayor's Office of Immigrant Affairs and Language Services promotes the interests and needs of immigrants and provides language-services to immigrants. . . . The Office works with community based organizations to improve city services to immigrants and encourage their participation in New York's political, economic, social, and cultural life" (New York City 1998).

FUTURE TRENDS

While in 1993 Los Angeles city residents were opposed to massive immigration, this opposition had markedly declined by 1999. In 1993, nearly two-thirds (63 percent) had agreed that there are "too many foreign immigrants in Los Angeles," but by 1999, less than half (45 percent) agreed with the statement, 7 percent stated they did not know, and as many as 18 percent said they "have not heard enough about that" to express an opinion (this last category was added in 1999). According to a *Los Angeles Times* poll conducted in March 2001, only 39 percent of Angelenos thought that "the growing immigrant population in Los Angeles is a bad thing for the city" (2001b). This further documents the decline in hostility to immigrants from its peak in 1993 in Los Angeles. In 1999 there were also marked differences between the attitudes of African-Americans and Latinos toward immigration, with 54 percent of African-Americans answering that the growing immigrant population was "a bad thing for the city," but only 34 percent of Latinos. A statewide 1999 survey shows that slightly more than three-quarters of Angelenos and San Franciscans disagreed with the statement that "children of illegal immigrants should be prevented from attending school" (Baldassare 1999, 24). Nevertheless, 45 percent of respondents in the Los Angeles region and 39 percent in the San Francisco Bay area still considered "illegal immigration from Mexico [a] big problem." On the whole, however, it is clear that Angelenos are now much less hostile to immigrants than they were in the early 1990s. The shift from a depressed economy to an economy that boomed is the most likely explanation of this change in public opinion. This is confirmed by an analysis of the November 1994 exit polls. Voters who were conscious of the economic crisis and felt threatened economically by illegal immigrants were more likely to support Proposition 187 (Alvarez and Butterfield 2000).

Ironically, anti-immigrant measures and sentiments have produced the opposite results from those intended by their advocates—they have led to a surge in naturalization that not only empowers immigrants to fight against such measures but also facilitates further immigrant influx through family reunification. The passage of Proposition 187 galvanized Latino community leaders to push for naturalization of immigrants and for voter registration among Latinos to increase their political power and to defend their rights in a hostile climate. For a variety of reasons, including the number of illegal immigrants and the low rate of naturalization, Latinos in California and Los Angeles have had a low rate of political participation. Thus, in 1990 only about 14 percent of the Hispanic population of voting age in Los Angeles County were registered to vote (Clark 1998, 179). But in California, between 1994, when Proposition 187 was approved, and 1996, the percentage of Hispanics registered to vote increased from about 25 to 29 percent of the voting age population. During the same period, the percentage actually voting increased from about 21 to 23 percent, to reach 1.3 million (U.S. Bureau of the Census 1996, 1998). The number of Latino voters increased even more by 1998 when "Latinos and Asians accounted for 1.7 million votes and gave Democrats a 900,000-vote margin" (*Los Angeles Times* 1999a). Furthermore, those who benefited from the 1986 amnesty were now eligible to become citizens. California Republicans, who championed Proposition 187 under the leadership of Governor Pete Wilson, subsequently paid a high political price for so doing. Since the passage of Proposition 187 in 1994, 1 million Mexican-Americans have become citizens, and 600,000 have registered to vote in California (*Los Angeles Times* 1999c). Nevertheless, on November 2, 1999, the chair of Save Our State, which launched Proposition 187, filed with the state attorney general a similar initiative for the November 2000 ballot to deny illegal immigrants most public services (*Los Angeles Times* 1999b). This time, however, the Republican Party and conservative organizations refused to support the new initiative, and it failed to get sufficient signatures to qualify for inclusion in the November 2000 ballot (*Los Angeles Times* 2000). But even if it had qualified, the substantial increase in the number of Latino and Asian voters was likely to have ensured its defeat.

The events of September 11, 2001, when nineteen hijackers sacrificed the hapless passengers of two planes to destroy the World Trade Center in New York and, with a third plane, damaged the Pentagon in Washington D.C., killing about 3,000 people, stunned the United States because it was the first attack on national territory since the War of 1812 (the Pearl Harbor attacks, in 1941, targeted military bases in two colonies). The aftermath testifies to the tolerance of New Yorkers. Since all the 9/11 terrorists were of Arab origin, the attack was a double shock to Middle Eastern–Americans, a fairly small minority group that, until then, had attracted little attention. Suddenly, however, they were at the center of national attention and, unfortunately, the subject of hostility, discrimination, and even violence in the United States. In the week after September 11, newspapers reported 645 bias incidents against Middle Easterners and South Asians in medium to large cities, including three shooting deaths (South Asian American Leaders of Tomorrow 2001). Yet in spite of the great loss of lives and destruction in New York, not to mention the negative economic reverberations, only isolated acts of hate crimes and bias incidents were perpetrated against Middle Eastern and South Asian immigrants. Of the above 645 hate crimes/bias incidents during the first week after the attacks, only thirty-eight occurred in the New York metropolitan area. New Yorkers may very well have been preoccupied with the losses they experienced right after the attacks. The consistent calls of Mayor Giuliani and Governor Pataki for tolerance and restraint in hatred toward members of specific ethnic and religious groups shortly after the attacks were effective. But the general tolerance of New Yorkers toward members of different racial and ethnic groups undoubtedly mitigated against extreme forms of backlash. Fifty-three hate crimes against Middle Easterners and South Asians were reported in the Los Angeles metropolitan area, including one shooting death, a somewhat higher number than in New York. So judging from this crisis, the population of the Los Angeles region is still not as tolerant of immigrants as is the population of the New York region.

CHAPTER FOUR

A Tale of Two Metropolises

New Immigrant Chinese Communities in New York and Los Angeles

Min Zhou and Rebecca Kim

Research on immigrant settlements has long stressed the transitory nature of inner-city ethnic enclaves as springboards for integration into mainstream host societies. Chicago's Stanislowowo, New York's Little Italy, and Los Angeles's Little Tokyo are living models, whereby immigrants toiled to allow their children or grandchildren to "melt" into suburbia as "indistinguishable" Americans. In the past three decades, however, this classic enclave-to-suburbia mobility model has been challenged. While many newcomers continue to converge in the central city as a first stop in the journey to attain the American dream, a visible number has bypassed the traditional staging place, moving directly into affluent urban neighborhoods or middle-class suburbs and situating themselves at the middle or upper-middle rungs of the mobility ladder. This seems to distort the correlation between levels of acculturation and residential mobility predicted by conventional assimilation theories; it opens up a possibility that the initial place of residence on arrival may be an end in itself.

As a result, many city neighborhoods that, though within the city boundaries, are beyond the inner urban core and that non-Hispanic whites once dominated have evolved into either resegregated enclaves, in which a single racial/ethnic minority group dominates, or "global" neighborhoods, in which diverse native-born minority groups live side by side with new immigrants of different national origins. Some of the resegregated neighborhoods experience decline, a phenomenon that has been studied in great detail. Others, however, are thriving and growing, with immigrants possessing higher than average education and incomes and capable of creating their own ethnic economies.

In this chapter, we focus on two emerging middle-class immigrant communities: Flushing in New York City, which, though an urban neighborhood, is located well beyond the inner-city core, and Monterey Park, the suburban municipality in Los Angeles County just beyond the boundaries of the city of Los Angeles.

Recent studies of immigration and new immigrant communities have shed fresh light on neighborhood transition in a number of important ways. (In addition to Sabagh and Bozorgmehr in chap. 3 of this volume, these studies include Winnick [1990], Fong [1994], Tseng [1994], Horton [1995], Y. Zhou [1996], Li [1997], and Saito [1998].) First, new immigrants are socioeconomically diverse. Second, tangible class resources that immigrants brought with them—money, skills, and other assets—are often linked to intangible ethnic resources, such as easy access to established ethnic and global networks and to foreign capital. This linkage enhances the value of individual holdings to create a new mode of immigrant incorporation: transnational entrepreneurship and overseas investment in local economic development. This mode of incorporation alters the way ethnic economies operate and facilitates their integration into the larger economy that is also increasingly globalized. Third, the large numbers and the economic power of newcomers heighten ethnic visibility. The influx of affluent Asian immigrants can be perceived as a threat to the established non-Hispanic white middle-class communities in which new immigrants have settled without going through the time-honored process of acculturation. Resistance from established residents, in turn, reinforces immigrant ethnicity, giving rise to a politics of diversity.

Our study examines the following questions with a focus on neighborhood transition: What are the new immigrant enclaves beyond the urban core like? How do different groups of immigrants negotiate their way into American metropolises? How may community development differ from place to place? What are the consequences and prospects of this new type of community development? Overall, we seek to understand the ways in which global neighborhoods challenge the notion of assimilation and speculate about how these new forms of immigrant enclaves contribute to our understanding of end-of-millennium urban and suburban dynamics.

GLOBALIZATION, IMMIGRATION, AND CHANGING PATTERNS OF SETTLEMENT

Globalization and Urban Transformation

Since the 1960s, two major trends have occurred simultaneously: globalization and immigration. Globalization leads to sweeping changes in the urban economy, dividing urban labor markets into a dominant core sector characterized by knowledge-intensive or capital-intensive jobs that offer high wages, good working conditions, career stability and promotion opportunities, and a marginal but sizable sector characterized by low-skill, labor-intensive work that offers minimum wages, poor working conditions, and little upward mobility (chap. 2; see also Edwards 1979; Tolbert et al. 1980). Of the low-wage manufacturing jobs that do exist, many have become highly concentrated in the central city, and access to these jobs depends largely on ethnic networks, making it harder for less skilled central-city residents to take advantage of economic growth and to move up socioeconomically (Waldinger 1996a). Accompanying globalization is speedy suburbanization of the non-Hispanic white population, a trend in New York, Los Angeles, and many other large metropolises across America (table 1.A2).

Such changing contexts of reception pose a daunting challenge for immigrants if they are to follow the conventional route of social mobility. On the one hand, the neighborhoods in which they first settle may be composed mostly of American-born minorities or other immigrants. New immigrants may have less contact with the native-born, middle-class, non-Hispanic whites with whom they are expected to assimilate. Further, many of the jobs available in the local labor markets either require advanced education and skills or do not pay decent wages, leading to possibilities of segmented assimilation outcomes. However, new patterns of assimilation have also become visible in light of these changing receiving contexts.

Post–World War II Chinese Immigration

Chinese immigration to the United States occurred several decades before the mass migration from southern and eastern Europe. Chinatowns in San Francisco, New York City, and the city of Los Angeles were typical of the nation's oldest immigrant enclaves. But unlike early immigrants from southern and eastern Europe, who were expected to assimilate into the mainstream society as quickly as possible, early Chinese immigrants were legally barred from naturalization and assimilation. They were forced to take refuge in a predominantly Chinese bachelors' society, creating jobs for themselves to avoid direct competition with native workers while enabling themselves to fulfill a sojourner's dream of returning to their homeland with gold and glory (M. Zhou 1992). The lifting of Chinese exclusion acts in the Second World War opened up other occupational channels for the Chinese. Many of them entered the military, the shipyards, and the civil service; and some were engaged in wholesale trade and operated grocery stores and other small businesses that were left vacant by the forced removal of the Japanese to internment camps (Waldinger and Tseng 1992).

Between 1960 and 2000, the number of Chinese-Americans grew dramatically from 237,292 to 2.8 million, with much of this growth attributed to immigration: more than 1.3 million Chinese from China, Taiwan, and Hong Kong were admitted to the United States as legal permanent residents between 1961 and 2000 (U.S. Immigration and Naturalization Service 2001). As of 1990, foreign-born Chinese accounted for about two-thirds of the Chinese-ancestry population nationwide and close to three-quarters in the New York and Los Angeles metropolitan areas.[1]

Unlike the "old-timers" who were uniformly unskilled laborers from the southern region of Guangdong Province, new Chinese immigrants come from more diverse origins and socioeconomic backgrounds. The three main sources of Chinese immigration are mainland China, Hong Kong, and Taiwan. In recent years, Chinese immigrants from Southeast Asia and the Americas have also been in evidence. Immigrant Chinese from different origins or different regions of the same origin do not necessarily share the same culture. Language is perhaps the most significant cultural barrier separating Cantonese-speaking coethnics from the Mandarin-speaking coethnics from Taiwan and from the mainland.

The new Chinese immigrants have been disproportionately drawn from highly educated and professional segments of the sending societies. The 1990 census showed that foreign-born Chinese (aged 25–64) with four or more years of college education were almost twice as common as U.S.-born non-Hispanic whites (42 percent vs. 21 percent). Foreign-born Chinese were also more likely to hold professional occupations than U.S.-born non-Hispanic whites (35 percent vs. 27 percent).

The New York and Los Angeles regions have continued to serve as the largest urban centers of Chinese settlement, with each accounting for more than 15 percent of the Chinese-ancestry population in the United States. The proportion of immigrant Chinese among all immigrants (Asians and non-Asians) in New York and Los Angeles is now about similar (4.2 percent and 5.7 percent of their respective regions in 2000).

In 1970, the Asian population of the New York region was predominantly (66 percent) Chinese, in contrast with Los Angeles where Filipinos and Japanese were about as numerous as Chinese. But by 2000 New York's Asian population was as diverse as Los Angeles's, and Chinese were now even slightly outnumbered by Asian Indians (fig. 3.4).

However, at least in 1990, the composition of the Chinese immigrant

Table 4.1. Selected Characteristics of the Chinese-American Population: New York and Los Angeles Metropolitan Areas (PMSAs)

	NEW YORK	LOS ANGELES
Total Chinese American population in 1990	246,817	245,033
Total Chinese American population in 2000	372,091	329,352
Place of birth (%):		
United States	21.9	23.1
Mainland China	47.5	27.0
Taiwan	7.9	19.9
Hong Kong	11.4	8.0
Other	11.3	22.0
Socioeconomic status (among the foreign born only):		
Average years of schooling	13.5	15.3
Managerial and professional occupations (%)	20.6	31.0
Median household income ($)	29,667	36,224
Residence (%):		
Chinatown, 1990	19.8	4.4
Chinatown, 2000	14.4	2.4
Flushing, N.Y., 1990	3.1	. . .
Flushing, N.Y., 2000	4.0	. . .
Monterey Park, Calif., 1990	. . .	8.9
Monterey Park, Calif., 2000	. . .	7.5

Sources. U.S. Bureau of the Census (1993, 2000c), full count 1990 and 2000, 1990 5% public use micro samples of the census and 2000 current population survey.
Note. The New York PMSA consists of New York City plus Rockland, Westchester, and Putnam Counties. The Los Angeles PMSA consists of Los Angeles County. The birth and socioeconomic status data are from the 1990 census, adapted from Y. Zhou (1998), tables 1, 3, 4, and 5. In 1990 and 2000, New York's Chinatown included fourteen census tracts (6, 8, 16, 18, 27, 29, 41, 2.01, 2.02, 14.02, 22.01, 43, 15.01, and 25), Los Angeles's Chinatown included six census tracts (2071, 1971.10, 1972, 1975, 1976, and 1977), and Flushing, N.Y., included eleven census tracts (797, 845, 851, 853, 855, 857, 859, 865, 867, 871, and 875). In 1990, Monterey Park, Calif., included thirteen census tracts (4817.02, 4817.11, 4817.12, 4820.01, 4820.02, 4821.01, 4821.02, 4822.01, 4822.02, 4826, 4827, 4828, and 5304) and in 2000 included fifteen (4817.11, 4817.12, 4817.13, 4817.14, 4820.01, 4820.02, 4821.01, 4821.02, 4822.01, 4822.02, 4826, 4827.01, 4827.02, 4828, and 5304).

populations of Los Angeles remained more diverse than New York's did. The Chinese population in the Los Angeles PMSA contained a much larger proportion from Taiwan than did the New York PMSA (19.9 percent compared to 7.9 percent) and a larger proportion from elsewhere (22 percent compared to 11 percent), as table 4.1 shows. New York's Chinese immigrant population was more heavily weighted to immigrants from the mainland than was that of Los Angeles (47.5 percent compared to 27.0 percent). Probably reflecting the greater diversity of their origins, Los Angeles's immigrant Chinese tended to show higher socioeconomic status than New York's did, measured by education, occupation, and income.

Neighborhood Transition

The suburbanization of the Chinese population, whether by direct immigration to the suburbs or by movement there from the inner city, has proceeded faster and is more dispersed in Los Angeles than in New York. Figures 4.1 and 4.2 show the residential concentrations of Chinese-Americans at the census tract level for the New York and Los Angeles regions, respectively. In New York, new Chinese neighborhoods are visible in Queens and Brooklyn (fig. 4.3), geographically distant from Manhattan's old Chinatown but within the municipal boundaries of the central city. There are new Chinese communities much farther out, many of which consist of middle-class Chinese immigrants associated with universities or high-technology corporations. Examples include Stony Brook on Long Island, the site of a campus of the State University of New York; Princeton Junction, Dutch Neck, and Plainsboro, associated with Princeton University and the Route 1 high-tech corridor; and Southeast Piscataway, associated with Rutgers University.

In the Los Angeles region, patterns of Chinese immigrant settlement have, as in New York, moved away from the inner-city old Chinatown, but they have grown way beyond the boundaries of the central city and become increasingly concentrated eastward into substantial suburban municipalities and areas—as close as Monterey Park (41 percent Chinese), San Marino (41 percent), Rosemead (29 percent), Alhambra (33 percent), San Gabriel (34 percent), Temple City (28 percent), and Arcadia (34 percent) and as far east as Hacienda Heights (22 percent), Rowland Heights (29 percent), Walnut (29 percent), and Diamond Bar (18 percent). (See table 4.2 and fig. 4.4.) Whereas in 1990 Monterey Park was the only city in the United States with an Asian majority, by 2000 there were five such cities in California, with three of these in the Los Angeles region—Cerritos, Monterey Park, and Walnut. By contrast, not a single city in the New York region came close to having an Asian majority, and none had even a high concentration of Chinese-American population ("high concentration" is defined as twice the group's proportional share in the total population of the region).[2]

Despite now being quite spread out compared with the past few decades, close to 15 percent of the New York metropolitan area's Chinese lived in old Chinatown in 2000, down from 20 percent in 1990. Old Chinatown is still highly concentrated by ethnicity—seven out of fourteen tracts contain a Chinese majority and another three contain 25 percent or more Chinese, and overall, about 56 percent of the residents are Chinese. But Los Angeles's Chinatown has witnessed a more

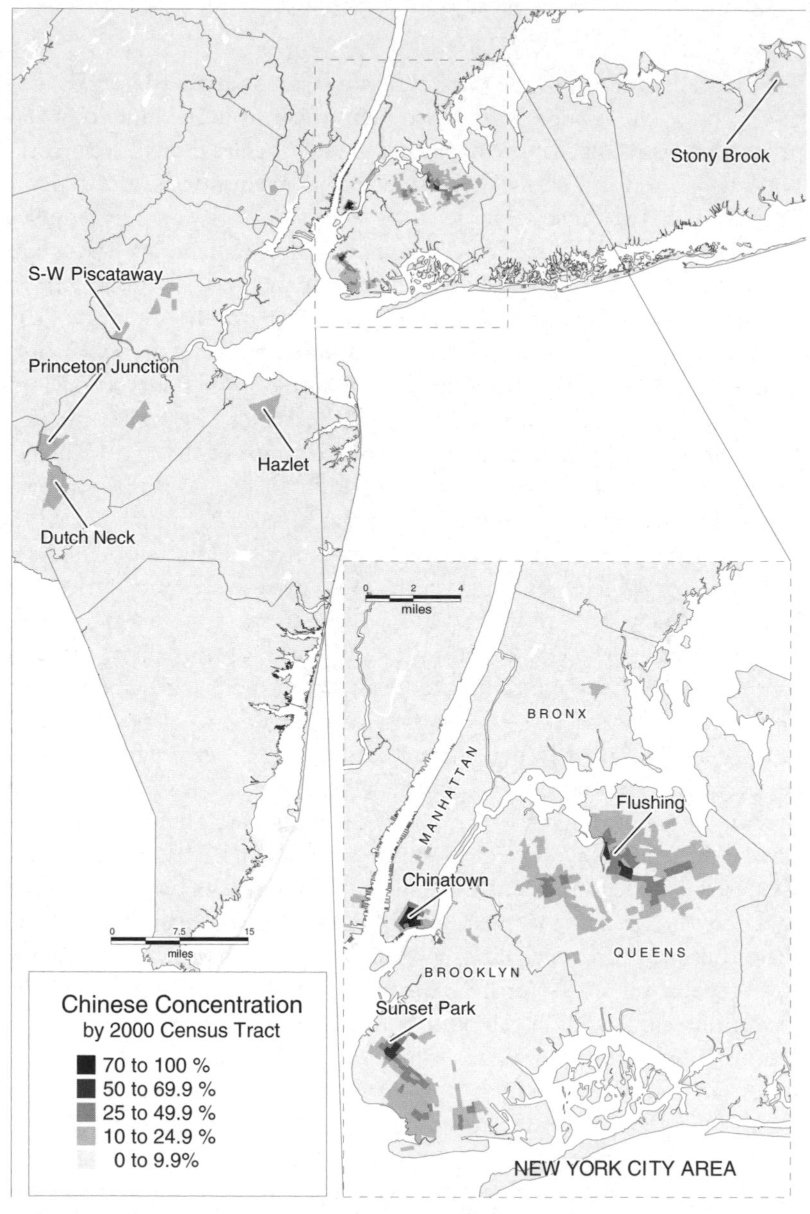

Figure 4.1. Residential Concentrations of Chinese: New York Region

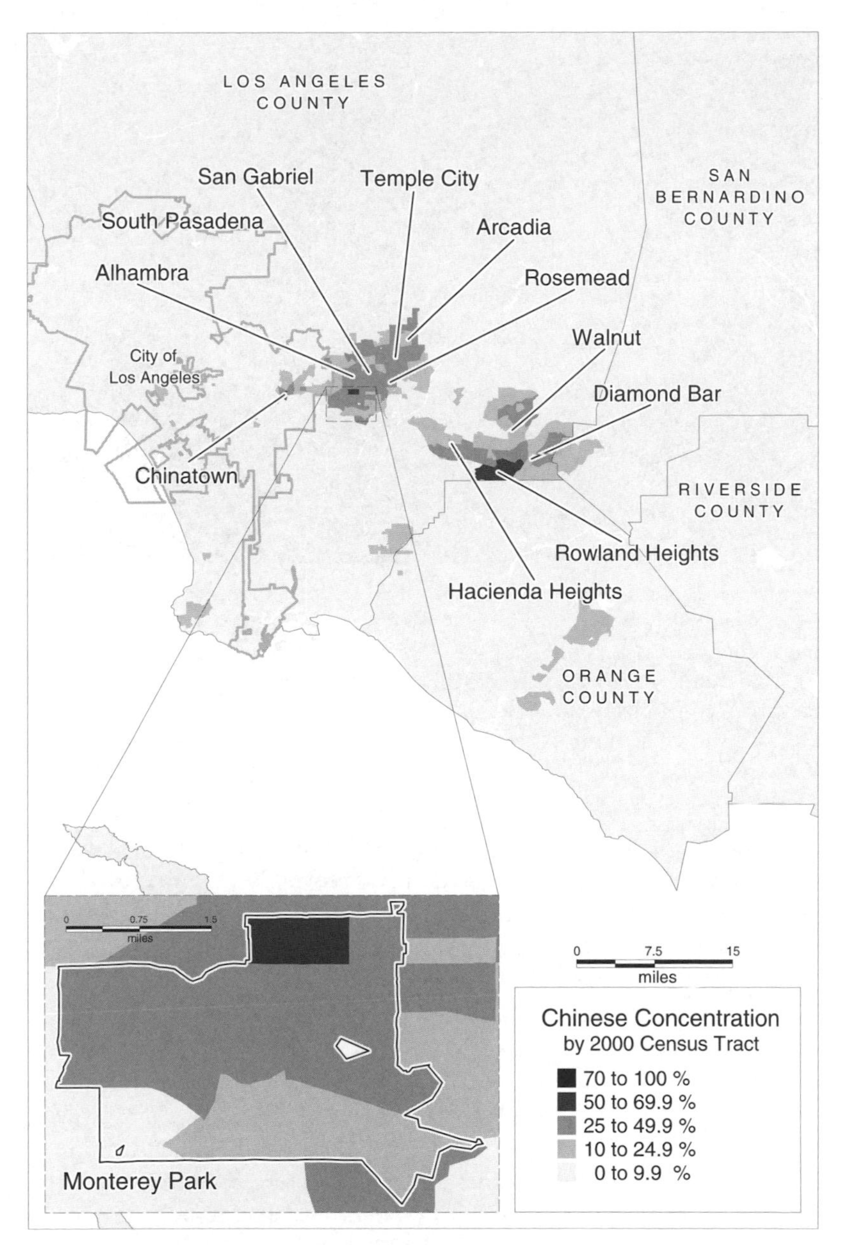

Figure 4.2. Residential Concentrations of Chinese: Los Angeles Region

Figure 4.3. Eighth Avenue (at Fifty-ninth Street) in Sunset Park, New York City, Now Called "Chinatown" by Many Residents of the Surrounding Areas. In the 1960s it was an undesirable no-man's-land that separated Borough Park, a Hassidic and orthodox Jewish neighborhood to the southeast, from Sunset Park, then a mainly Puerto Rican, Dominican, and Mexican neighborhood to the northwest. The no-man's status of Eighth Avenue gave the Chinese the chance to move in.

rapid decline of ethnic concentration. Less than a third of the residents are Chinese, only one of six tracts maintains a Chinese majority, and only 2 percent of the Chinese in the Los Angeles metropolitan area lived in old Chinatown in 2000 down from 4 percent in 1990.[3]

In sum, the recent surge of Chinese immigration has been accompanied by residential dispersion. The change is not necessarily associated with the disappearance of old Chinatowns—New York's, for example, has actually grown and expanded in new directions, taking over decaying adjacent neighborhoods (see fig. 4.5 and M. Zhou 1992). However, differences in place of origin, language/dialect, and class status, intertwined with ethnic networks and global market forces, contribute to the rise of new "satellite" Chinatowns or middle-class Chinese communities in areas away from the central city. Next, we describe two such communities and examine how immigration and new urban processes affect community development and immigrant adaptation.

Table 4.2. Cities in California for Which the Population Is More Than 40% Asian in 2000

CITY	% ASIAN	% CHINESE	TOTAL POPULATION
Alhambra (LACMSA)	47	33	85,804
Arcadia (LACMSA)	45	34	53,054
Cerritos (LACMSA)	58	15	51,488
Cupertino (SFCMSA)	44	24	50,546
Daly City (SFCMSA)	51	14	103,621
Diamond Bar (LACMSA)	43	18	56,287
Hercules (SFCMSA)	43	9	19,488
La Palma (LACMSA)	45	8	15,408
Milpitas (SFCMSA)	52	13	62,698
Monterey Park (LACMSA)	62	41	60,051
Rosemead (LACMSA)	49	29	53,505
San Gabriel (LACMSA)	49	34	39,804
Temple City (LACMSA)	39	28	33,377
San Marino (LACMSA)	49	41	12,945
Union City (SCMSA)	43	9	66,869
Walnut (LACMSA)	56	29	30,004

Source. U.S. Bureau of the Census 2000c.

Note. Rowland Heights, featured in figures 4.1 and 4.3, is a CDP (census designated place)—namely, an identifiable place that is not, however, a city. In 2000, Rowland Heights was 29% Chinese, 8% Korean and 13% other Asian. LACMSA = Los Angeles consolidated metropolitan statistical area; SFCMSA = San Francisco consolidated metropolitan statistical area.

FLUSHING: AN URBAN NEIGHBORHOOD IN TRANSITION

A Neighborhood within a Large City

Flushing is located in North-Central Queens, New York (see fig. 4.1). Although it is quite far from Manhattan's Chinatown, convenient access to the subway makes the commute relatively easy. Before the surge of contemporary immigration, Flushing resembled the main features of a suburban bedroom community—tranquil, cozy, and relatively low density. It shared the postwar suburban development that affected all of Queens, resulting in a mixture of housing types, including block after block of development-style single-family units, as well as numerous mid- and high-rise apartment buildings and projects. As is the case in all parts of New York City, there are pockets of considerable affluence and old stately homes in Flushing. Since the 1960s, the total number of year-round housing units in Flushing has doubled, or tripled in the surrounding area, and the housing stock has been dominated by multi-family dwellings and apartment units. Overall, the owner occupancy rate of Flushing's housing stock is much lower than that of Queens (38 per-

Figure 4.4. Korean-Dominated Shopping Center, "Super Market Mall," Rowland Heights, on Fullerton Street near Highway 60 (the Pomona Freeway). One block away is a much larger Chinese-dominated shopping center. Rowland Heights is 50 percent Asian (29 percent Chinese, 8 percent Korean). Suburban concentrations of middle-class and wealthy Asians continue to grow eastward beyond such concentrations as Monterey Park and San Gabriel (see fig. 4.2). The location in this photo is twenty-five miles east of downtown Los Angeles.

cent) and the city (23 percent) as a whole as of 1990, and the immigrant population is more likely than natives to be living in small rented apartments. As in any typical urban neighborhood, there are also low-income housing projects in Flushing within walking distance of bus stops, the subway, and the Long Island Railroad station.

The Newcomers

In demographic terms, Flushing is clearly a neighborhood that has experienced rapid transition and is in this sense similar to many other neighborhoods in New York. However, at least in relative terms, Flushing is booming with the arrival of new immigrants. Between 1980 and 1990, Flushing's population increased by 14 percent, four times higher than the rate of growth for metropolitan New York as a whole. The population growth has continued into the 1990s.

Before the surge in contemporary immigration, Flushing was a neighborhood of mostly non-Hispanic white, moderate-income, working-class residents. In the early days, Chinese and other minorities were not welcome in the neighborhood. A long-time Chinese resident who was married to a white American recalled that, when she and her husband decided to move to Flushing, she did not go with her husband to look for housing. She explained, "Because they [whites] didn't want to see Chinese here. At that time, there were few Chinese around in the community. I was not the only one, but there weren't many." According to this resident, there was only one Chinese restaurant and one Chinese laundry in Flushing in the early 1960s.[4]

Since the mid-1970s, Flushing has rapidly emerged as a multiethnic neighborhood. Two demographic trends—non-Hispanic white flight and Asian influx—contributed to the transformation. Between 1970 and 1980, the non-Hispanic white population of Flushing fell by 55 percent and declined further by another 42 percent between 1980 and 1990, far exceeding the rate of decline in Queens and New York City as a whole. By 2000, non-Hispanic whites were a small minority (from 2 to 20 percent) in every census tract in Flushing, while the proportions of Asians had risen to a majority in all but two tracts. Non-Hispanic whites in Flushing as of 2000 made up only 13 percent of the neighborhood's population (down from 24 percent in 1990), compared with 33 percent in New York City as a whole. Flushing' s black population

Figure 4.5 Expanding Chinese Neighborhood, at the Foot of the Manhattan Bridge, Division and Forsyth Streets. New York City's Chinese-dominated area around traditional Chinatown has been growing north for twenty years to accommodate new Chinese immigration and has now reached the Manhattan Bridge (see fig. 4.1).

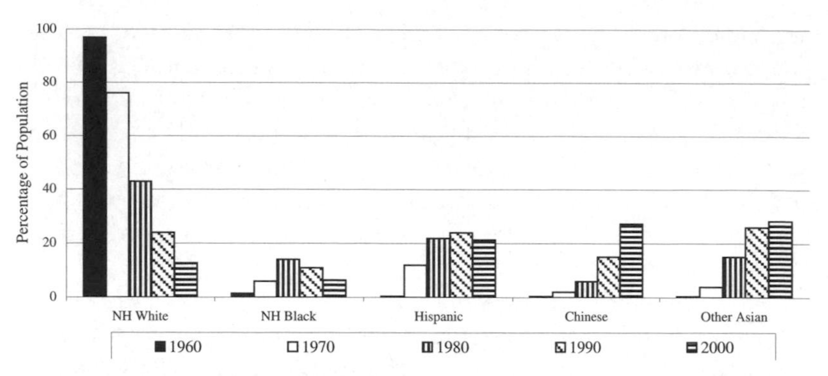

Figure 4.6. Changes in Racial and Ethnic Composition by Decade, Flushing, N.Y. Source: U.S. Bureau of the Census 1960, 1970, 1980a, 1990a, 2000b.

has also declined, making up about 6 percent of the total in 2000 (down from 11 percent in 1990). As of 2000, Chinese and other Asians made up 56 percent of the neighborhood's population (up from 41 percent in 1990), and Latinos comprised 21 percent. Figure 4.6 represents these changes.

Superimposed onto the base of the remaining residents, most of whom are of European ancestries, are three large groups of Asian immigrants: Chinese (27 percent of Flushing's population), Korean (13 percent), and Indian (10 percent). There are also many new immigrants from virtually all parts of the world. Representatives of the three largest Asian groups are all clearly visible in the central business district of Flushing, although the concentrations rarely extend more than a few blocks. Flushing is often referred to as the "satellite" Chinatown or Little Taipei, though there is nothing in Flushing that matches the ethnic concentration of old Chinatowns in Manhattan.

Flushing is clearly a new immigrant neighborhood. The most significant characteristic is the high proportion of the foreign born. As of 1990, 43 percent of the residents were born aboard, which was distinctively higher than the corresponding figure for the whole of Queens Borough (29 percent), and the rest of the New York metropolitan area (27 percent). Fifty-seven percent of residents moved into Flushing since 1975; 46 percent of the residents spoke a language other than English at home, and 11 percent reported that they speak English poorly. Flushing had a lower unemployment rate, a lower poverty rate, a higher median household income, and lower proportion of single-parent households than the borough of Queens and metropolitan New York as a whole. One plausible explanation is that Flushing's Asian immigrants are considerably better educated than either the average immigrant or the average U.S. resident. In Flushing, college graduates were almost two times as common among immigrants from mainland China, and nearly four times as common among immigrants from Taiwan, as compared with other residents.

The Chinese immigrant community in Flushing was initially built by foreign capital from Taiwan and Taiwanese immigrants. Many Taiwanese came to Flushing because they had few ties to Manhattan's old Chinatown and did not identify with the old-timers and their family-sponsored immigrants who are predominantly Cantonese. Their superior educational backgrounds and abundant economic resources enabled them to build their own enclave away from the existing center of Chinese settlement (Zhou and Logan 1991). It appears that once the movement to Flushing began, other Chinese followed suit; some moved in from Chinatown as a step up the socioeconomic ladder, while others moved in directly from abroad. Thus, Chinese immigrants in Flushing are more diverse in their places of origin and class backgrounds than those in Manhattan's Chinatown.

Ethnic Economies and Neighborhood Revitalization

Before the urban transformation, the retail scene in Flushing was dominated by an amalgam of small specialty shops and services. There was a mix of furniture and appliance stores, restaurants, and discount establishments, most of which were operated as typical mom-and-pop stores; there were also a small number of large department stores. New York's overall economic recession in the early 1970s hit the Flushing business community heavily, causing many small shops and commercial enterprises to close down, commercial vacancy rates to increase, and property values to drop. The same structural disadvantages that plagued the New York metropolitan area—a significant net loss of manufacturing jobs—was also encountered in Flushing.

This trend, however, was dramatically reversed with the arrival of immigrants from different parts of Asia since the 1970s. With the injection of massive amounts of immigrant capital and entrepreneurship from Taiwan, and to a lesser extent from Korea and India, Flushing is well positioned to come to the forefront of an urban economy dominated by the service, commercial, and consumption sectors. Since 1975, new retail and office development has sprung up regularly in Flushing's downtown area. Property values in Flushing increased from 50 to 100 percent during the 1980s, and commercial vacancy rates have plummeted from 7 percent in the late 1970s to less than 1 percent in the early 1990s (Parvin 1991, 22).

Today, commercial development is extraordinarily active with new businesses ever enlarging the commercial core. In the very heart of the downtown commercial and transportation hub, the multilingual signs of several mainstream bank branches and Asian-owned banks stand at the busiest intersection. Just a few blocks from the subway station, in what was until recently an aging neighborhood rapidly falling into decay, stands a fourteen-story, pink granite and limestone tower—the Sheraton La Guardia East Hotel—which is Taiwanese owned. Such a sight in downtown Flushing would have been unimaginable in the early 1970s. In the immediate vicinity of the subway station, upscale Chinese restaurants and full-service supermarkets, interspersed with small cafés, green grocers, drugstores, and fast-food restaurants, give the area an unmistakable look and feel of Chinatown. But it is not quite a new Chinatown. There are modern office complexes that house banks and service-oriented firms owned by Taiwanese immigrants and transnational Taiwanese, as well as subsidiary firms from the Asian Pacific. The commercial core is also filled with Korean, Indian, Pakistani, and Bangladeshi restaurants and stores, packed into the shop fronts along the main streets. The expanded downtown is now a bustling, vibrant commercial area.

Suburban Chinese come to the neighborhood for multiple purposes. For example, many Chinese families come from the outer suburbs to bring their children to the Chinese language schools and other tutoring and recreational facilities for Saturday afternoon language classes and recreation. While children engage in these activities, their parents usually shop at the local grocery and specialty shops. Others come to Flushing to study or browse at the crowded public library that possesses books, magazines, and newspapers in different Asian languages, staying afterward to do some shopping and, perhaps, to eat at one of the many ethnic restaurants. The development of Flushing as a comprehensive ethnic business center means that suburban Chinese residents no longer have to go into the Manhattan Chinatown to visit a restaurant, do their shopping, or satisfy their need for Chinese cultural activities.

Some of our respondents describe what has happened as the "Flushing miracle," in which a once struggling neighborhood has been revived economically with capital imported from Asia and with the entrepreneurial spirit and hard work of Asian immigrants. Ethnic entrepreneurs, however, tend to attribute the boom in ethnic enterprises to persistent attempts to achieve the American dream and the cultural fear of losing face. Aside from cultural norms, investment in Flushing is continually being stimulated by the prospect of a growing Asian community, which in turn perpetuates confidence in the neighborhood and ensures further population growth.

Political Participation

Historically, Chinese immigrants were denied the right to become naturalized citizens and were thus indifferent to politics. Much of the political activity in Chinatowns across the nation was oriented either toward the homeland or toward the defense of ethnically defined interests within the immigrant community. New York City had a segmented political system that was organized along ethnic lines and was used as a vehicle for the expression of ethnic interests (Waldinger and Tseng 1992). Because of their small numbers, early immigrant Chinese were not only economically marginalized and socially isolated, they were hardly visible in local politics.

In recent years, more and more immigrant Chinese have become naturalized citizens and have become more active in local politics than ever before. In Flushing, immigrant Chinese have formed various civic organizations serving multiethnic interests in the local community rather than narrowly defined ethnic interests. These new ethnic organizations work with other civic organizations in the neighborhood to mediate intergroup misunderstandings and conflicts. They also routinely mobilize local business owners and residents to participate in civic activities, such as street-cleaning campaigns, voter registration drives, and lobbying the Community Board and city hall on urgent neighborhood issues. However, the scale and the effectiveness of Chinese immigrants' participation in local politics have remained limited. For example, the electoral numbers in the Twentieth Council District are far from favoring Asian challengers. In 1990, Asians made up almost a third of Flushing's population but only 7 percent of registered voters. Councilwoman Julia Harrison was twice challenged by Asian-American candidates. But she won both elections in the 1990s, even though she was depicted as an "anti-Asian bigot," publicly referring to the influx of Asian immigrants and Asian-owned businesses as an "invasion" and making a calculated effort to gather white voter support by attacking the Asian immigrant community (Dugger 1996; Lii, 1996). Now that Asians make up the majority in Flushing, their increasing political participation and power will be predictably stronger in the years to come.

MONTEREY PARK: A GLOBAL CITY IN AN AMERICAN SUBURB

A Suburb by a Large City

Unlike Flushing, which is an urban neighborhood toward the outskirts of a large city, Monterey Park is an incorporated suburban municipality with its own elected city council. From the beginning of World War II until 1960, Monterey Park prospered as the wartime economy brought new people from across the country to southern California (Fong 1994). In the early days, Monterey Park was one of the most affordable suburban bedroom communities—a cozy town with various single-family homes, tree-lined streets, and spacious green lawns. In the 1960s, about 85 percent of housing consisted of detached single-family homes, and 4 percent consisted of ten or more units. About two-thirds of the housing was owner-occupied, and the vacancy rate was about 5 percent.

Beginning in the early 1970s, newcomers and foreign capital from Taiwan brought drastic changes to Monterey Park. In contrast to the tradition of immigrants starting out from the bottom of the socioeconomic ladder, many wealthy Taiwanese investors poured money into the suburb's real estate development and lured wealthy immigrants from Taiwan and potential emigrants in Taiwan to buy into the best neighborhoods immediately on arrival or even prior to their arrival (Tseng 1994). As more Taiwanese immigrants arrived in the 1980s, housing prices increased with a clear surge in both residential and commercial construction. Huge luxurious homes were built on joint lots alongside multiple-family apartments and condominiums. The total number of housing units in the city jumped from 12,833 in 1960 to 19,331 in 1980. Median housing value in 1990 was $238,800. The proportion of multiunit apartments (ten units or more) also jumped from 5 percent in 1960 to 14 percent in 1990; and the proportion of owner-occupied housing decreased from 65 percent in 1960 to 55 percent in 1990.

Commercial development in Monterey Park also experienced drastic changes beginning in the early 1980s, with the arrival of many Taiwanese realtors, developers, investors, entrepreneurs, and, later, the mainland Chinese nouveau riche. These wealthy immigrants and transnationals played a crucial role in reinvigorating a formerly inactive economy and boosting real estate values. In many cases, profits were not the focus. Many investors and entrepreneurs were willing to take losses to secure a place in the United States. Opening businesses and establishing settlement enabled Chinese newcomers to obtain immigrant visas or certain types of nonimmigrant visas that could later be adjusted to permanent residency. The heavy infusion of foreign capital investment, rapid economic growth, and sudden influx of affluent immigrants from Taiwan and mainland China stirred up the once tranquil bedroom community, transforming it into a cosmopolitan hub of the Asian Pacific where property prices skyrocketed and various Chinese-owned businesses sprang up along main streets with discernible Chinese-language signs, replacing old and familiar diners and specialty shops.

Demographic Transformation

Like Flushing, postwar Monterey Park was predominantly non-Hispanic white. But due to its cozy middle-class suburban atmosphere and proximity to downtown Los Angeles, Monterey Park, in the 1950s, began to draw upwardly mobile Mexican-Americans from neighboring East Los Angeles, Japanese-Americans from the Westside, and Chinese-Americans from Chinatown (Fong 1994; Horton 1995). By 1960, Monterey Park's ethnic makeup was 85 percent non-Hispanic white (down from 99.9 percent in 1950), 12 percent Latino, 2.9 percent Asian, and .1 percent black. Many of the Latinos and Asian-Americans arriving in Monterey Park during the 1950s and 1960s were educated, acculturated, and middle-class second- or third-generation immigrants who were driven by the American dream of upward mobility and suburban life. By 1970, Latinos and Asian-Americans were well represented in the community (34 percent and 15 percent, respectively), yet Anglos were still a majority (50.5 percent). The process of ethnic integration was fairly smooth, since the new residents were mostly acculturated second- or third-generation members of ethnic minorities and were not perceived as a threat to existing Anglo political and institutional dominance (Horton 1995).

Drastic demographic change, however, was set off by the arrival of immigrants and investors from Taiwan and the Pacific Rim and an influx of foreign capital. By the mid-1980s, the city had been transformed from an Anglo bedroom town into a cosmopolitan city with an Asian majority, a visible presence of immigrant Chinese, and a vibrant ethnic economy. As shown in figure 4.7, non-Hispanic white residents declined rapidly from 51 percent in 1970 to 26 percent in 1980 and to just 7 percent in 2000. In contrast, the proportion of Asian residents increased from less than 15 percent in 1970 to 34 percent in 1980 and 62 percent in 2000. By 2000, Monterey Park was one of five California cities with an Asian majority (see table 4.2). Two of the others, Cerritos and Walnut, were also east of the city of Los Angeles. Rowland Heights, which is near Walnut and is a "census designated place" rather than city, is 50 percent Asian (fig. 4.2).

The majority of Monterey Park's Asian-Americans are of Chinese ancestry (67 percent), and the rest include U.S.-born Japanese-Americans (12 percent) and other immigrants from Southeast Asia, such as Vietnamese (8 percent). In 1980, 31 percent of the Monterey Park population was foreign born, in 1990 increasing to 51 percent. Not surprisingly, 73 percent of those in Monterey Park spoke a language other than English at home as of 1990.

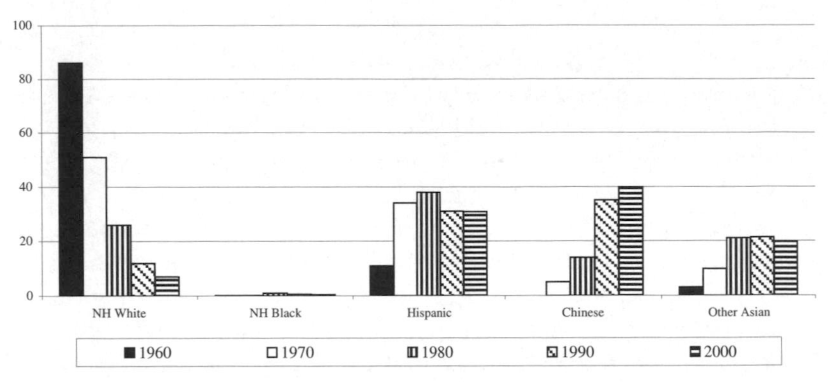

Figure 4.7. Changes in Racial and Ethnic Composition by Decade, Monterey Park, Calif. Source: U.S. Bureau of the Census 1960, 1970, 1980a, 1990a, 2000b.

Unlike earlier Chinese immigrants who were mainly from rural regions in South China, Monterey Park's newcomers were initially from Taiwan, either as investors or professionals at the outset. Once the Chinese community took shape, family migration and migration from mainland China, Hong Kong, and Southeast Asia followed. By the mid-1980s, the number of mainland Chinese immigrants surpassed that of the Taiwanese. According to the Immigration and Naturalization Service, among Chinese immigrants who selected Monterey Park as their preferred destination between 1983 and 1990, 44 percent were from the mainland and 42 percent from Taiwan. Yet, the visibility of Taiwan money, Taiwanese-owned businesses, and Taiwanese involvement in local politics earned Monterey Park the nickname Little Taipei, with which both Taiwanese and mainlanders are identified. What makes Taiwanese immigrants in Monterey Park distinct is that they are disproportionately highly skilled and capital-rich and that many of them obtained immigration visas through direct investment in or employment by either Chinese-owned businesses or mainstream American businesses. Overall, the Chinese immigrants are more highly skilled than Los Angeles County's population: as of 1990, about a quarter of the adult Chinese population had completed four years of college and another 17 percent had postcollege education, compared to 14 percent and 8 percent, respectively, county-wide; close to 40 percent held professional occupations, compared to 27 percent county-wide; and 16 percent of the work force were self-employed, compared to 10 percent county-wide (Tseng 1994, 54).

Another distinct characteristic of Monterey Park's new Chinese immigrants is the visibility of transnational migrants. In contrast to the traditional male sojourner who left his family behind to find riches in America, a new group of Chinese transnationals—"spacemen" as the media calls them—have settled their wives and children in Monterey Park while shuttling back and forth between both sides of the Pacific Ocean (Fong 1994). And in other cases, the children—known as "parachute kids"—are left in the United States alone to obtain an education, while both parents remain in Asia (M. Zhou 1998). Transnational household arrangements have become an alternative model of immigrant settlement. Indeed, Monterey Park's newcomers represented a brand new stream of immigrants and a new mode of incorporation. Instead of moving from immigrant enclaves like other native-born Latinos or Asian-Americans, the new Chinese immigrants inserted themselves directly into the middle-class suburb without much acculturation.

Development of Ethnic and Transnational Economies

In the 1960s, a few small specialty shops, supermarkets, and restaurants dominated commercial activities in Monterey Park. At night, streets were quiet as residents retired to their comfortable homes. A former police chief recalled, "You could shoot a cannon off at Atlantic and Garvey, and it could fly through the air and roll to a stop without hitting a soul" (quoted in Arax 1987, 1). Today, Chinese-owned supermarkets and mini-malls have replaced this small-town commercial core with various stores and restaurants that have become part of a greater commercial hub for ethnic and transnational businesses. The vibrant commercial center expands block after block and is active from early in the morning till late at night, seven days a week. As a resident recalled, "At 3:30 in the morning . . . I counted 34 cars stopped at a red light at Atlantic and Garvey [one of the main intersections]. It looked like rush hour" (quoted in Arax 1987, 1).

The Chinese ethnic economy in Monterey Park cannot be measured in traditional terms. While many Chinese-owned businesses still resemble those in Chinatowns—such as mom-and-pop or husband-wife restaurants, gift shops, food stores, and other small-scale services, newly created business establishments are bigger and more Westernized. Many of them are upgraded and improved through combinations of ethnic and Western skills to sell Asian products and services. The pace of these capital flows accelerated in the following decade as Hong Kong, China, and Southeast Asia started to transfer capital to the United States. Another important source of economic development has been the family assets and savings that immigrants brought to their new country.

Real estate development is perhaps Monterey Park's most notable economic activity. Foreign capital has been channeled into the community by Chinese-owned banks and financial institutions, as well as by individual family savings. In the 1980s, rampant and speculative land development all over southern California turned many small bedroom towns into cities with high-density commercial and residential overdevelopment. Monterey Park was simply part of the trend. What made it unique, however, was that the development had an Asian face, and the economic boom responded mainly to the demands of coethnic immigrants (Horton 1995). Investors from Taiwan targeted the place because of its growth potential and its convenient location—accessible to Chinatown and to the Pacific Rim. With sufficient capital, these investors bought up properties and converted or developed them into a wide array of housing: residential housing ranged from luxury homes and condominiums to high-density apartment complexes and commercial developments focused on mini-malls. By the late 1980s, few vacant lots were available, and the price of land skyrocketed. Many lots for commercial development sold at $40–$50 per square foot, much higher than the price of $8–$10 per square foot that supermarkets or department stores could afford to pay. With these inflated prices, developers had to recoup their costs through intensive development—building smaller and denser mini-malls and office buildings. As a result, Monterey Park has also become a commercial and banking hub for an even bigger Chinese community that resides in San Marino, Arcadia, and throughout the San Gabriel Valley.

The proliferation of commercial development in Monterey Park, however, has gone far beyond the city's geographic boundaries, mirroring a new trend of Chinese immigrant settlement in Los Angeles. Unlike New York's Chinese-owned businesses, which are concentrated in Chinatown, Flushing, and Sunset Park, Los Angeles's Chinese-owned businesses are as spread out as the ethnic population. As of 1992, there were about 11,000 Chinese-owned firms in Los Angeles. About 12 percent were located in Monterey Park and another third in neighboring cities in the San Gabriel Valley. Nonetheless, the ethnic economy in Los Angeles's eastern suburb plays a pivotal role in the local economy as well as in the economic adaptation of Chinese immigrants. According to Yenfeng Tseng (1994), the new ethnic economy was highly diversified and transnational, with operations ranging from franchised American-style supermarkets to banks and accounting firms.

Monterey Park and its neighboring cities have become producer service centers for Chinese businesses and a hub for cross-cultural and transnational business services (Tseng 1994; Li 1997; Y. Zhou 1998).

Much of the economic growth is linked to economic development in the Pacific Rim.

Political Participation

From the 1940s to the mid-1970s, politics in Monterey Park was dominated by an "old-boy network"—a local power structure consisting of predominantly non-Hispanic white Republican professionals and businessmen (Horton 1995). This power structure was challenged by the arrival of Japanese-Americans and Mexican-Americans in the 1950s and 1960s and the unprecedented arrival of Asian immigrants, mainly Chinese, during the mid-1970s and 1980s. The addition of Chinese immigrants tipped the power balance and transformed local politics into the politics of diversity (Horton 1995).

In the 1980s, some Democrats showed varied levels of willingness to adapt the city's institutions to suit new immigrants and minorities, while others sided with conservatives against the Chinese newcomers. However, when immigrants with strong economic resources form a numerical majority, city politicians cannot possibly ignore them. The shrinking non-Hispanic white population along with the decreasing influence of the old white conservative elite have created an opportunity for young multiethnic businessmen, minorities, immigrants, women, and multiculturalists, as well as nativists, to engage in politics, opening up a new political order in Monterey Park (Horton 1995).

In 1983 when Lily Lee Chen, a Chinese-American, was inaugurated as mayor, Monterey Park's five-member city council was truly multiethnic with one non-Hispanic white, two Mexican-American, one Filipino-American, and one Chinese-American.[5] *Time* magazine featured this "majority minority" city council as representative of multiculturalism and as a "successful suburban melting pot." Growing resentment against demographic, cultural, and economic changes relating to the Chinese newcomers, however, soon swept the minority incumbents out of office. In 1986, three of the city council members were replaced by long established non-Hispanic white residents, returning the city council to white control in pursuit of anti-immigrant campaigns under the name of the defender of Americanism: "English, the family, God, the nation, and the neighborhood" (Horton 1995, 95). Backlash against ethnic politics in the mid-1980s was short-lived, however, as more and more immigrant Chinese became naturalized citizens and were mobilized into participation in local politics. In 1988, Judy Chu, a Chinese-American was elected to the city council, was reelected to serve on the city council until 2001, and was elected mayor of Monterey Park three times. In 1990, Samuel Kiang, a China-born naturalized citizen, was elected to the city council. As of 2001, two of the city's elected officials were Chinese-American (a council member and the city treasurer), but only one of the ten appointed officials was Chinese-American.

Most recently, however, there was another severe setback for Chinese-American political participation. In 1999, all four Chinese-American candidates out of eleven candidates on the ballot lost their bids for the three city council seats for which they were vying. Again in 2001, all five Chinese-American candidates (one withdrew before Election Day) out of seven candidates on the ballot lost their bids for the one city council seat that was open. Even though none of the Chinese-American candidates won city council seats in the 1999 and 2001 elections in Monterey Park, the latest electoral politics indicated the greater political maturity of Monterey Park's Chinese-American community. Despite the current losses, Chinese-Americans in Monterey Park are using their increasing demographic presence and electoral and economic power to challenge traditional Anglo domination in the city council. Today, the Asian constituency extends beyond Monterey Park to other Chinese communities in the San Gabriel Valley and recognizes the election of a Chinese or Asian candidate as supporting the overall "development of Chinese- and Asian-American power in Los Angeles, California and the United States" (Horton 1995, 108). The formation of the West San Gabriel Valley Asian Pacific Democratic Club and the burgeoning of immigrant political organizations in the 1980s has further strengthened Chinese-Americans' political power base. Judy Chu's successful bid for the Forty-ninth District seat of the California State Assembly in 2001 signifies growing Asian-American political clout.[6]

CONCLUSION AND THE IMPLICATIONS FOR THE FUTURE

Monterey Park may be an outlier since there are so few cities in the United States where Asian-Americans constitute a majority and where Chinese immigrants make up such a significant part of that majority. However, middle-class immigrant Chinese communities are growing rapidly and visibly not only in New York and Los Angeles but also in San Francisco, San Jose, Boston, Houston, and other major immigrant-receiving metropolitan areas. Similar developments are also evident in Toronto and Vancouver in Canada.

Broadly speaking, the two modern enclaves studied here, Flushing and Monterey Park, share certain common characteristics with older Chinatowns but are distinct from Chinatowns in many other ways; and they also differ from each other. Like Chinatowns, new middle-class immigrant communities serve those needs of new arrivals that are unmet in the mainstream society, and they provide opportunities for self-employment and employment.

But in both Flushing and Monterey Park, the pattern of ethnic succession is distinct from that of the past. Rather than an ethnic minority that arrives to bring down the average economic level of the populace, the incoming ethnic minority arrives with higher than average education and economic resources and with the capability of creating its own ethnic economy. These communities are better connected to the outside world on economic, social, and political terms. Moreover, they can no longer be narrowly defined as the "ethnic enclave" or "staging places" just for the poor and the unacculturated.

Yet the social class composition of both Flushing and Monterey Park is fluid and dynamic. These communities were started by affluent immigrants, investors, and professionals; but as time goes by, the pioneers have began to send for their relatives, who may not be as resourceful. Many family-sponsored immigrants, especially those from mainland China, are of urban working-class backgrounds, and most lack English language proficiency and transferable job skills. They have come to Monterey Park to join their families. Also, many low-skilled immigrant workers are drawn to Monterey Park because the expanding ethnic economy needs their labor and they can easily find housing through relatives and friends. As a result of intertwined ethnic ties, the Chinese populations in Flushing and Monterey Park are becoming more socioeconomically diverse. Such class diversity has implications for both immigrants and the native-born. For Chinese immigrants, class segmentation would mean greater social service burdens and a high risk of bearing a dual stigma—both foreigner and poor. As a way to avoid association with working-class coethnics, the more affluent Chinese immigrants are under pressure to migrate out further. Several immigrant Chinese business owners in Monterey Park that we interviewed told us that they had recently moved to avoid "overcrowdedness" and "gangs in schools." Some newcomers even express a reluctance to settle in Monterey Park. A Chinese home buyer from New York told us, "I wouldn't want to buy into Monterey Park . . . because it's so congested, crowded, and so many [poor] Chinese."[7] Interestingly, these feelings mirror those of established residents. For middle-class non-Hispanic whites, Latinos, and Asian-Americans alike, the influx of working-class immigrants may now mean a disruption of middle-class lifestyles and the threat of importing inner-city or Third World social problems.

Flushing and Monterey Park both have a strong ethnic economy that goes beyond the traditional model of small business and, instead, follows a mixed model of "East meets West" development driven by the market and economic globalization. Rapid economic growth propelled by the influx of foreign capital and immigration creates opportunities but causes pains associated with soaring real estate prices, overcrowding, noise, traffic congestion, and crime. Some long-time residents in Flushing lamented that the new Flushing "looks like hell. . . . It's really a disaster. There is too much traffic, filth and chaos."[8] Monterey Park residents would echo these feelings. A Japanese-American on his return to Monterey Park complained, "Damn it, Dad, where the hell did all these Chinese come from? Shit, this isn't our town any more" (cited in Horton 1995, 10). Among established residents in Monterey Park, there is a deep-seated fear that their neighborhoods are turning into Chinatowns or microcosms of Taipei, Shanghai, or Hong Kong, which as they imagine are among the most crowded, congested, and polluted cities in the world. While established residents voice their concerns with a sense of nostalgia for small-town life and resentment of the "Asian invasion," more established Chinese immigrants also cite these problems as their primary reasons for leaving Monterey Park.

Also, Flushing and Monterey Park have become increasingly multiethnic, unlikely to be dominated by a single national-origin group. Diversity at the local level has made intraethnic and interethnic relations key community issues. The mixing of coethnics from different class backgrounds gives the community the power and vitality to combat the trends of ghettoization and social isolation encountered in the inner city but, simultaneously, turns the place into another type of "staging place" for the more affluent immigrants. Living side by side with members of different ethnic group members provides opportunity for intimate social contact but also garners potential tension. Flushing has not witnessed any explosive ethnic tensions. But when conflicts do surface, Flushing's multiethnic immigrant groups may have relatively little solidarity to mobilize politically because the power of ethnic immigrants is fragmented in New York City's huge political maelstrom. In contrast, conflicts are much more overt in Monterey Park, often focusing on growth control movements and English-only resolutions, but ethnic mobilization seems more effective because native-born Latinos and Asian-Americans tend to align with immigrant Chinese to act on racial issues in a city where minority groups form the numerical majority and political power is concentrated locally.

Tracing the development of Chinese immigrant settlement, we have seen that long-standing immigrant enclaves in the inner city seem to have absorbed the sheer numbers and the successive waves of immigrants fairly smoothly, and with largely salutary results, and that there are few substantive regional variations. In suburbia (or the outer boroughs in the case of New York), however, complacent "bedroom" communities have experienced widespread in-migration of middle-class immigrants and rapid economic growth, and the results have been confrontational. Recent suburban immigrant concentrations have tipped the suburban balance of power, raising nativist anxiety. In Flushing and Monterey Park, immigrants from Asia, no less than blacks and Latinos, can be perceived as a threat to non-Hispanic white middle-class communities when they achieve a substantial presence. Their high socioeconomic standing, contribution to the local economy, and adaptive attitude do not make them immune to criticism. Rather, they can pose a different kind of threat, one that undermines longtime residents' sense of place and identity (Horton 1995) and their notion of "Americanness." As immigration continues into the twenty-first century with its long-lasting impacts on American cities, a reconceptualization of neighborhood change and residential mobility is much needed.

CHAPTER FIVE

Residential Separation and Segregation, Racial and Latino Identity, and the Racial Composition of Each City

David Halle, Robert Gedeon,
and Andrew A. Beveridge

As large numbers of southern and eastern European immigrants—Italians, Russians, Austrians, Romanian Jews—came to New York City and other industrial cities in the late nineteenth and early twentieth centuries, they mostly settled in areas that were heavily populated by others from the same national origin. Typically living in tenements, the new immigrants were definitely separated and, one could say, segregated from the wider population. At the same time, those of English, Irish, and German origin, who had arrived earlier, were mostly spread throughout New York City (Beveridge 2001). Initially, the newer immigrants were often thought to be, and were treated as, different from the longer-standing residents. For example, while the Census Bureau classified both the newer and older immigrants as "white" (i.e., basically the same) a Congressional commission implicitly disagreed, publishing a report that defined more than 170 races (Dillingham Commission 1911).[1] By mid-twentieth century, such groups as Italians, Greeks, Jews, and Russians were all considered completely "white" together with Germans, English, and Irish, and little residential segregation remained between them.

The black community of New York City had been traumatized by the draft riots of July 13–16, 1863, when mostly working-class Irish rampaged though the small black neighborhoods of Manhattan, seeking vengeance on the community that they blamed for the war they were being drafted to fight. With a verified body count of 119, this was the single largest incident of civil disorder in the history of the United States (Burrows and Wallace 1999, 895). More than three times as many people were killed in the draft riots as in the 1965 Watts riots and over twice as

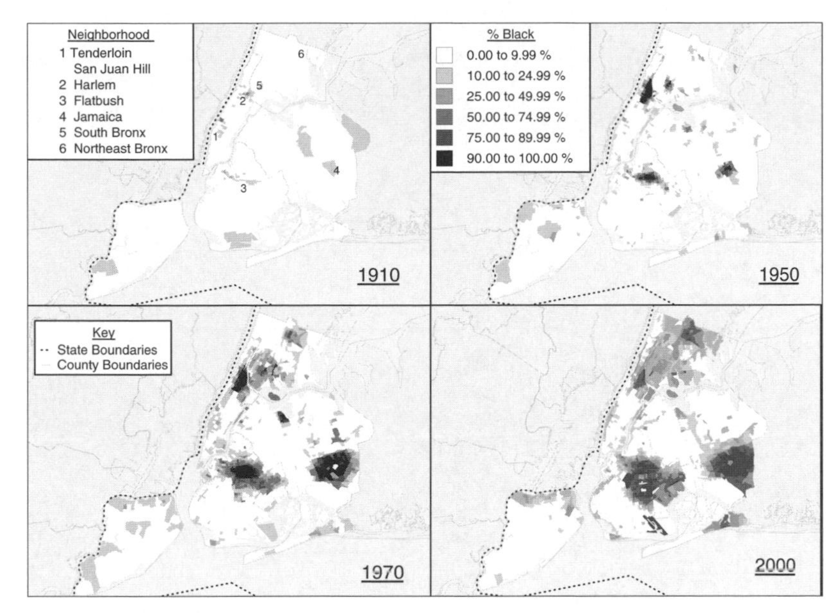

Figure 5.1. Growth of Black Neighborhoods, New York City, 1910–2000

many as in the 1992 Rodney King riots in Los Angeles (table 12.3). Many blacks fled to the city of Brooklyn, establishing neighborhoods in places such as Fort Greene Park and Atlantic Avenue west of Bedford, and New York City's black population shrunk to 14,804, 5,000 fewer than in 1840 and just 1.4 percent of the population. From 1865, a small but steady influx of blacks from the south began to replenish the black population of New York City and Brooklyn, but by 1900 the two cities still had just 66,666 black residents, less than 2 percent of the population. This included 3,552 foreign-born blacks, most of them recently arrived from the West Indies, the largest such settlement in the United States. The main black communities in Manhattan were in the Tenderloin and San Juan Hill areas from about Twenty-fourth to Forty-second Streets and between Fifth and Seventh Avenues, the "Hell's Kitchen" area from Thirty-seventh to Fiftieth Streets and from Eighth to Tenth Avenue, smallish sections of Greenwich Village, and sections of Harlem (see fig. 5.1 and Burrows and Wallace 1999, 895, 993, 1112). There were also black communities in well-defined sections of Queens, Brooklyn, and Staten Island.

When African-Americans began arriving in large numbers in the 1910s in New York City and other northern cities, they were also segregated into "black quarters." The "color line" was well defined through-

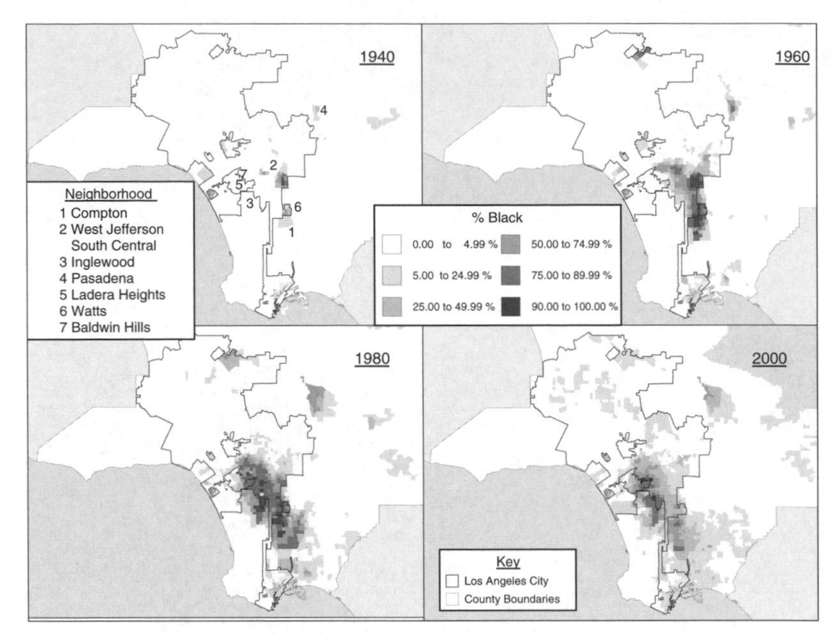

Figure 5.2. Growth of Black Neighborhoods, City of Los Angeles, 1940–2000

out the industrial northern cities. Harlem became the center of black New York (fig. 5.1).

In contrast, when the pueblo of Los Angeles was first established in 1781, persons of part-African ancestry made up roughly half of the population, and until 1915 blacks were not rigidly segregated by residence. The numbers involved, however, were small. For example, according to the 1850 census, there were only twelve blacks. But from about 1915 until various legally imposed mechanisms for maintaining segregation were weakened by U.S. and California Supreme Court decisions made between 1948 and 1967, Los Angeles had one main black ghetto. This extended from downtown southward on either side of Central Avenue and came to be known as South Central Los Angeles. There were also two smaller concentrations of blacks—in the West Jefferson area and in Watts (fig. 5.2; Allen and Turner 1997, 79).

Since World War II, African-Americans have made major economic gains, and a sizable proportion in both New York City and the city of Los Angeles have moved out to the suburbs; but unlike the European immigrants and their children, a sizable proportion of African-Americans still live in highly segregated, inner-city ghettos, while those who moved to the suburbs may still live in African-American concentrated residential settings. The 1968 Fair Housing Act, the main legislation passed to outlaw discrimination in the residential market, was weak. Unlike civil rights legislation in employment and education, the Fair Housing Act did not provide for a government agency with responsibility for investigating and prosecuting violations of the law. Individuals who believed they were the victims of discrimination in the housing market had the burden of bringing their own private suits (Massey and Denton 1993). Overall, the Fair Housing Act has probably had more effect in somewhat deterring discrimination in the sale of new homes than in reversing patterns of discrimination in older, already highly segregated neighborhoods.

The city of Los Angeles developed much later than New York City did, has a far lower proportion of African-American residents, and largely depends on the automobile for transportation. But the bulk of suburban development outside New York City occurred after World War II, and much of it resembled that of the Los Angeles consolidated metropolitan statistical area (CMSA). In both metropolitan areas, developers built tract housing, corporate parks, and edge cities, though in a more complex pattern than concentric rings around an urban core. Finally, the 1965 changes in the immigration law ensured continued increases in the large numbers of Latinos and Asians in addition to African-Americans. Figures 5.3 and 5.4 show the growth of Latino concentrations. How these groups would be incorporated into these two major metropolises was an important question. Would they face segregated living conditions to the same degree as blacks? What sort of housing choices would they make? Census data allow us to answer some of these questions by assessing the levels of residential separation and integration in the Los Angeles and New York regions for 1970–2000 for blacks, Latinos, and Asians.

Using census data we argue that, in these complex settings, four main patterns of minority group settlement are apparent (summarized in table 5.1). First, there is the classic, highly segregated urban ghetto and barrio, which is a plausible account of the situation for most blacks and many Hispanics in much of New York City and the city of Los Angeles.

A second pattern consists of usually suburban areas of heavily concentrated middle-class African-Americans, Hispanics, or Asians (figs. 1.11–1.16 show the location of most of those mentioned here below). African-American examples in the New York CMSA are Baldwin and Freeport in Long Island, Runyon Heights in Yonkers, and the Walworth area in White Plains/Scarsdale. Some such areas are within the city, as in the case of Laurelton, Saint Albans, and Cambria Heights in southeast Queens located toward the outskirts of the city and geographically separated

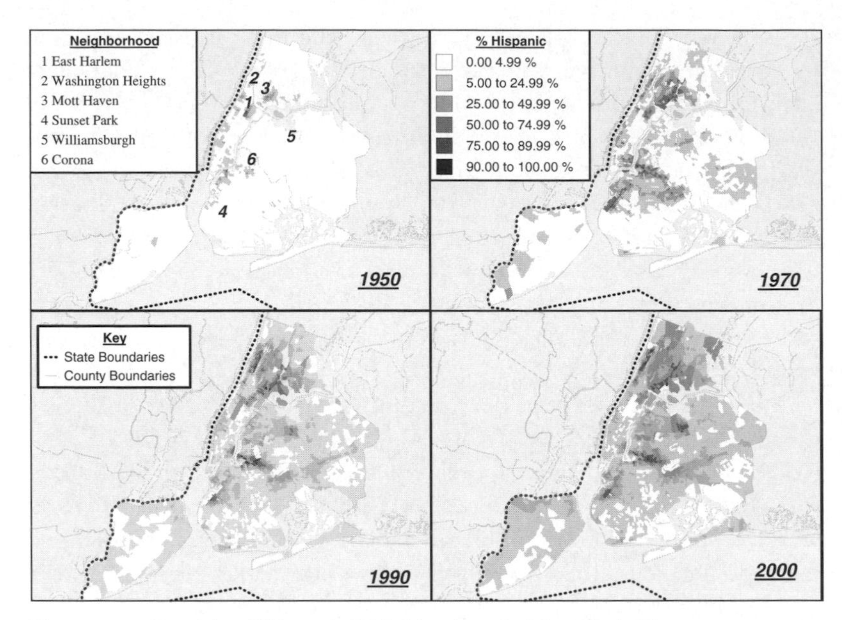

Figure 5.3. Growth of Hispanic Neighborhoods, New York City, 1950–2000

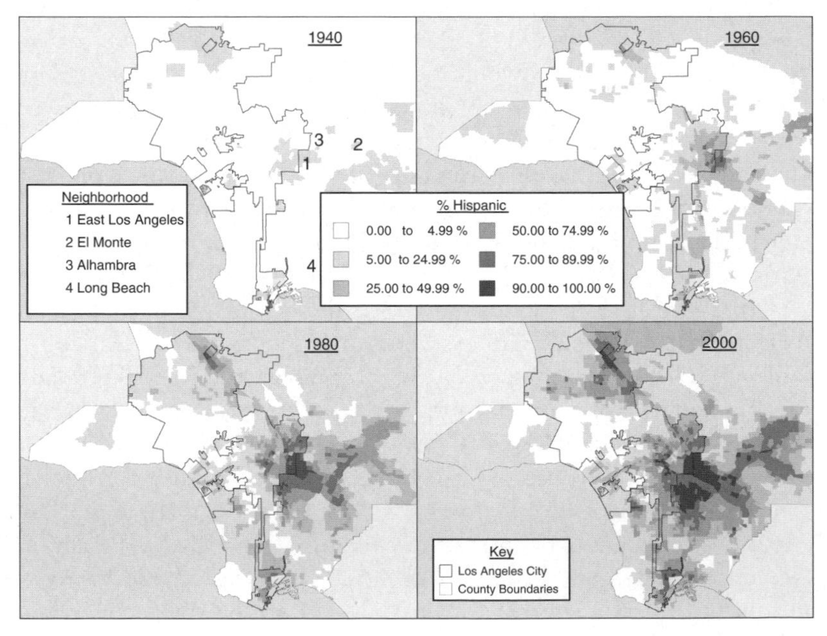

Figure 5.4. Growth of Hispanic Neighborhoods, City of Los Angeles, 1940–2000

Table 5.1. Patterns of Black, Latino, and Asian Settlement, Los Angeles and New York

PATTERN/TYPE	LOS ANGELES EXAMPLES	NEW YORK EXAMPLES
1. Classic, highly segregated urban ghetto/barrio composed of blacks or Latinos	South Central, Compton, East Los Angeles	Harlem, Bedford-Stuyvesant, East Harlem
2. Middle-class areas with large concentrations of middle-class minorities—African Americans, Hispanics, or Asians—surrounded by areas that are predominantly nonminority; usually, but not always, located beyond the urban core	Monterey Park, Alhambra, Diamond Park, Rowland Heights	Baldwin, Runyon Heights, Walworth, Laurelton, Saint Albans, Cambria Heights, Flushing, Sunset Park
3. Areas where blacks, Latinos, or Asians reside but represent a very small proportion (under 5%) of the total	Several areas located throughout the CMSA though more frequently well beyond the boundaries of the city and often closer to the periphery of the CMSA; also, some condo complexes in the city	Several areas located throughout the CMSA though more frequently well beyond the boundaries of the city and often closer to the periphery of the CMSA; also, some cooperative and condo complexes in the city
4. Suburban areas where a minority group resides in large proportions (over 30%) and that are geographically so extensive that it cannot be said that these areas are enclaves surrounded by areas where nonminorities predominate (as in type 3)	Much of San Bernardino and Riverside Counties	. . .

Note. The classic, integrated community, where blacks and non-Hispanic whites reside together over a long period (30 years or more) is a fifth type. It is not common so far. In the New York CMSA, parts of Freeport may qualify. Just beyond the southern part of the CMSA, Levittown, N.J., is an example. In the Los Angeles CMSA, several of the newly developed areas to the east, in San Bernardino County (e.g., Moreno Valley) or San Bernardino (e.g., Highlands) look as though they may qualify but have not yet passed the test of time.

from inner-city black neighborhoods. Asian examples, analyzed in the previous chapter, include Monterey Park, Alhambra, Diamond Bar, and Walnut in the Los Angeles CMSA and Flushing and Sunset Park, which, though in New York City, are not in the center. These are all middle-class areas, in terms of income levels and housing stock, dominated by a particular minority group and surrounded by residential areas that are dominated by nonminorities.[2] The traditional language of segregation cannot adequately define the situation here since we are mostly discussing voluntary separation—the rapid growth of predominantly minority suburban or suburban-like developments, composed of minorities who have chosen to live with members of their own group. Albeit this is in some cases because they wish to avoid the problems of trying to live in areas dominated by possibly hostile nonminorities and albeit that blacks are likely to face more serious hostility than Latinos or Asians. (Note that we use the term "segregation" in this chapter to refer to a situation in which, on the whole, one group resides in an area because it has been excluded from other areas by noneconomic constraints. We use "separation" for when the situation on the whole results from a group preferring to live apart.)

A third type of minority residential setting is far less segregated or separated but also has less of a concentration of African-Americans, Latinos, or Asians. Examples exist throughout both CMSAs, though the pattern is especially represented by several areas located well beyond the boundaries of both New York and Los Angeles and often closer to the periphery of their CMSAs as well as in some cooperative and condo complexes in the cities themselves. Here, small numbers or proportions of minority groups live by choice in areas or buildings that are predominantly nonminority.

The fourth pattern is represented by Latinos in areas in the two eastern counties of the Los Angeles region, San Bernardino and Riverside (known as the "Inland Empire"). Latinos have moved into new suburban housing there in numbers and proportions that have already made them a third or more of the population of these areas and will surely lead them to become a majority (fig. 1.13). The geographic spread of Latinos is so extensive there that there are no identifiable boundaries that clearly separate them from nonminority-dominated areas, which is what distinguishes this from the third pattern. Here, too, the traditional language of segregation seems hard to apply since the "minority" group is also the largest group over an enormous geographic area. Hence these areas of the Inland Empire are a unique laboratory for studying the evolving dramas over racial and ethnic identities in the United States.

A final pattern, which can be called "classic integration," consists of areas in which blacks and non-Hispanic whites reside together in stable, not transitional, communities, with both groups making up sizable proportions of the total, around 30 percent or higher. These areas are not common. Possible examples include parts of Freeport, Long Island and several areas in Riverside and San Bernardino Counties, such as Moreno Valley and Highland. But these are all too recent to have met the test of being stably integrated for about thirty years.

BLACKS, LATINOS, AND ASIANS IN THE CITIES OF NEW YORK AND LOS ANGELES

Before presenting this analysis in detail, we need to discuss the black, Latino and Asian composition of the two cities and CMSAs since the overall proportions of these groups affects the question of how they are distributed residentially and why. We also need to understand how the census defined and redefined the various categories used to characterize minorities and to measure segregation. As in the earlier era of large-scale migration, the definitions of "race" and of "minority" are contentious terrain, both politically and scientifically. How data are collected and tabulated here strongly influences the conclusions drawn. For example, our data discussion will challenge a major assumption that has dominated the understanding of the racial composition of many large U.S. cities at least since 1980, namely, that the proportion of whites is dwindling. We argue that, for the cities of New York and Los Angeles, this is true only if whites are defined in a restrictive manner that is hard to justify.

In New York City from 1990 to 2000 the proportion of Hispanics/Latinos rose from 24.2 to 27.0 percent and the proportion of Asians (and Pacific Islanders) rose from 7.6 to 10.2 percent.[3] The proportion of blacks fell from 29.4 to 26.9 percent, despite the large increase in black immigrants from the Caribbean (see table 5.2). The largest proportion of Hispanics/Latinos in New York City in 2000 was in the Bronx with 48 percent, followed by Manhattan with 27 percent, Queens with 25 percent, Brooklyn with 20 percent, and Staten Island with 12 percent. The largest concentration of Asians, by far, is in Queens, 18 percent of the borough's population, followed by Manhattan with 9 percent, Brooklyn with 7.5 percent, Staten Island with 6 percent, and the Bronx with 3 percent. The largest proportion of blacks is in the Bronx and Brooklyn, with 36 percent of the population for each of these counties, followed by Queens with 20 percent, Manhattan with 17 percent, and Staten Island with 10 percent.

Table 5.2. Black, Latino, Asian, and White, New York and Los Angeles, 1990–2000

	1990	2000
New York City:		
% Hispanic/Latino	24	27
% Black	29	27
% Asian	7	10
% White	52	45
% White (using CPS)	64	60
% Non-Hispanic white	43	35
New York CMSA (including New York City):		
% Hispanic/Latino	16	21
% Black	20	20
% Asian	5	8
% White	68	58
% White (using CPS)	77	74
% Non-Hispanic white	61	50
City of Los Angeles:		
% Hispanic/Latino	39	47
% Black	14	11
% Asian	10	10
% White	53	47
% White (using CPS)	74	81
% Non-Hispanic white	38	30
Los Angeles County:		
% Hispanic/Latino	37	45
% Black	11	10
% Asian	11	12
% White	57	49
% White (using CPS)	N/A	80
% Non-Hispanic white	41	31
Los Angeles CMSA (including Los Angeles County):		
% Hispanic/Latino	35	40
% Black	9	8
% Asian	9	11
% White	61	55
% White (using CPS)	82	81
% Non-Hispanic white	46	39

Note. All data are from the decennial census except the data identified as from the Current Population Survey (CPS). Data are rounded to the nearest percentage point. The 2000 decennial census data are for those choosing one race on the census's race question (see n. 4 in this chapter). In New York City and the New York CMSA, 4.9 percent and 3.4 percent, respectively, of respondents chose more than one race. For the city, county and CMSA of Los Angeles, 5.2, 4.9, and 4.7 percent, respectively, of respondents chose more than one race. Asian in this table includes Pacific Islanders and Native Hawaiians, a numerically tiny group. The CPS does not offer the category "other race" on the race question, leading a higher proportion of Latinos to select "white" than on the decennial census where they can select "other race." N.A. = not available — the CPS has no Los Angeles County code for 1990.

The direction of change was similar in the city of Los Angeles. The proportion of Hispanics increased from 39 to 47 percent, though Asians (and Pacific Islanders) stayed constant at 10 percent. The proportion of blacks, which for decades has not been large—around 14 percent—fell by about 3 percent from 14.2 to 11.5 percent. Thus in both New York City and the city of Los Angeles the proportion of blacks is declining.

Looking at the entire New York CMSA, the proportion of African-Americans has remained constant at around 20 percent between 1990 and 2000. Hispanics have increased from 16 percent to 21 percent, while the Asian population went from 5 percent to 8 percent. The growth of the Asian and Latino population is especially marked in some areas of New Jersey, in addition to Queens as noted. Figures 1.11–16 show the current distribution of this population in the New York region.

Looking at the entire Los Angeles CMSA, the percentage Hispanic/Latino rose from 35 to 40.3 percent from 1990 to 2000. The largest percentage of Hispanic/Latinos was in Los Angeles County (45 percent, up from 37 percent in 1990). The Hispanic/Latino profiles of San Bernardino (39 percent, up from 26 percent), Riverside (36 percent, up from 26 percent), Ventura (33 percent, up from 26 percent), and Orange County (31 percent, up from 24 percent) resemble each other. In all these counties, Latinos are set to be the majority or close to it by the end of this decade. The percentage of Asians (and Pacific Islanders) in the five-county region overall went from 9.1 to 11.3 percent. It rose from 11 to 12 percent in Los Angeles County, from 10 to 14 percent in Orange County, from 5 to 6 percent in Ventura County, from 4 to 5 percent in San Bernardino County, and remained unchanged at 4 percent in Riverside County.

The overall percentage of blacks throughout the five-county region declined slightly, from 9 to 8 percent. During that time, it declined from 11 to 10 percent in Los Angeles County, rose from 8 to 9 percent in San Bernardino County and from 5 to 6 percent in Riverside County, and remained constant at 2 percent in Ventura and Orange Counties. That the percentage of blacks has remained almost constant in the overall Los Angeles region, while declining by 3 percent in the city of Los Angeles, supports the view of a black shift from the city to the suburbs in the Los Angeles CMSA.

COUNTING WHITES

How about the proportion of "whites"? Measured in the manner mandated by the government for the 2000 census tabulations, the proportion of "whites" (without regard to their Hispanic/Latino status) is not dropping sharply in the two cities, contrary to a common view. This is mainly because a significant proportion of Latinos classify themselves as white when asked by the census, and is also, secondarily, because the proportion of residents who classify themselves as black is declining as already described. (Further complicating the issue for the 2000 census was the ability of respondents to choose "multiple races." On this important topic, see the accompanying note.)[4]

In order to grasp the problems with the conventional view that the proportion of whites is dropping sharply, it is important to understand how one obtains and reports statistics on who is white, black, Hispanic, and so on in the United States. It is the Office of Management and Budget that has jurisdiction over how race and Hispanic/Latino status are defined. The standard practice has been that everyone is classified as either Hispanic/Latino or non-Hispanic/Latino. Then the category race, and its subcategories, is also used to classify everyone again but without offering a subcategory for Hispanics/Latinos.[5] As a result the 2000 census uses two separate questions, one to investigate race and the other to investigate Hispanic/Latino origin.

On the 2000 census, the "Hispanic origin" question asked, "Is Person x Spanish/Hispanic/Latino?" Respondents were given the choices of "No, not Spanish/Hispanic/Latino," "Yes, Puerto Rican," "Yes, Mexican, Mexican Am., Chicano," "Yes, Cuban," and "Yes, other Spanish/Hispanic/Latino." This was followed by what is called the "race question," which is our source of data on whites, blacks, and Asians but not Hispanics. This question asked respondents if they were "white," "black, African Am., or Negro," "American Indian or Alaska Native," various categories of Asian such as "Chinese," "Japanese," "Indian," or "Korean," or "some other race." Figure 5.5 reproduces these two questions from the census form.

By looking at how people who said they were Hispanic/Latino on the "Hispanic origin question" classified themselves on the race question, we determine the proportion of Hispanics/Latinos who classify themselves as white. Fully 36 percent of Hispanics/Latinos in New York City and 37 percent in the city of Los Angeles classified themselves as (only) white. Another 51 percent in New York and 59 percent in Los Angeles classified themselves as "some other race," with only 8 and 1 percent, respectively, choosing "black."

That more than a third of Hispanic/Latino residents of the cities of New York and Los Angeles classified themselves as white on the 2000 decennial census explains why, though the proportion of all whites (as opposed to non-Hispanic whites) has declined somewhat in the two cities, from 52 to 45 percent in New York City and from 53 to 47 percent

United States
Census
2000

→ NOTE: Please answer BOTH Questions 7 and 8.

7. **Is Person 1 Spanish/Hispanic/Latino?** *Mark* ☒ *the* ***"No"*** *box if **not** Spanish/Hispanic/Latino.*

- ☐ **No**, not Spanish/Hispanic/Latino
- ☐ Yes, Puerto Rican
- ☐ Yes, Mexican, Mexican Am., Chicano
- ☐ Yes, Cuban
- ☐ Yes, other Spanish/Hispanic/Latino -- *Print group.*

8. **What is Person 1's race? *Mark* ☒ *one or more races to*** *indicate what this person considers himself/herself to be.*

- ☐ White
- ☐ Black, African Am., or Negro
- ☐ American Indian or Alaska Native -- Print name of enrolled or principal tribe.
- ☐ Asian Indian
- ☐ Japanese
- ☐ Native Hawaiian
- ☐ Chinese
- ☐ Korean
- ☐ Guamanian or Chamorro
- ☐ Filipino
- ☐ Vietnamese
- ☐ Samoan
- ☐ Other Asian -- *Print race.*
- ☐ Other Pacific Islander -- *Print race.*
- ☐ Some other race -- *Print race.*

→ **If more people live here, continue to Person 2.**

Figure 5.5. 2000 Census Questions on Race and on Hispanic/Latino Origin

in the city of Los Angeles from 1990 to 2000, it has not collapsed and indeed is still just under half of the total population of each city.[6]

This estimate of the proportion of Latinos/Hispanics who classify themselves as white, based as it is on the 2000 decennial census tabulations, is conservative. In fact, the figures are highly dependent on the precise wording of the census's race question, most especially whether the option "some other race" is offered. The Census Bureau conducts an annual "Demographic Survey," which is a supplement to its monthly Current Population Surveys (CPSs). This annual CPS supplement—the data for which are based on a sample of respondents rather than on the full population of the decennial census—is the main way we know how the racial composition of America is changing between decades. The race question on this CPS omits "some other race" from the options offered to respondents.[7]

When asked the race question without the "some other race" option, a much higher proportion of Latinos/Hispanics classify themselves as white than on the 2000 decennial census. Thus in the 2000 CPS, 83 percent of those residents of New York City and an enormous 98.7 percent of those residents of the city of Los Angeles who classified themselves as Hispanic/Latino on the "Hispanic or Latino Origin" question also classified themselves as white on the race question.[8] Clearly most Latinos who would choose "some other race" opt to choose white if "some other race" is not a possible selection. Using this CPS data gives a picture that flatly contradicts the stereotype of a collapsing population of whites. In the city of Los Angeles, the proportion of whites in 2000 was 81 percent of the total population, and in New York City it was 60 percent. All five New York City counties remain majority white.

The merits of these two ways of wording the census race question—that is, with the "some other race" option (2000 decennial census) or without (CPS)—can be debated, along with the two different pictures they produce of the direction of the "white" population of the two cities in the past decade (i.e., declining moderately by 6–7 percent or in Los Angeles rising moderately by 7–8 percent). Neither position can be said to be the obviously correct one. Those who favor using data that excludes the "some other race" option can say that it is meaningful to know how Latinos classify themselves when asked to choose solely between "black," "white," and various categories of Asian. They can also point to the fact that, after reporting the results of this category just for census tabulation purposes, the Census Bureau for all other official reporting purposes uses a statistical procedure to reallocate all respondents who answered "some other race" to one of the "official race" categories—white, black, Native American, Asian or Pacific Islander. This is because the Office of Management and Budget does not consider "some other race" a viable category that can stand alone and indeed the Census Bureau needed a special dispensation from the Office of Management and Budget to collect and tally "some other race" on the decennial census.[9]

In contrast, people who favor using the data that includes the "some other race" option can reasonably argue that although a large proportion of Hispanics classify themselves as "white," a slightly larger proportion see themselves as somehow other than white or black, perhaps "between" these categories or simply on a different dimension (Rodríguez 1992; Rodríguez and Cordero-Guzmán 1992).[10]

The only approach to the topic that seems hard to justify is the one that produces the results that suggest that the white population of these cities has collapsed. This common approach simply excludes all Hispanics/Latinos from the white category and, thus, brackets all these issues and debates. This approach decides that the white category will not include the substantial proportion of Hispanics/Latinos who classify themselves as white on either the decennial census or the CPS and, then, "discovers" that the proportion of whites in the cities of Los Angeles and New York and other comparable cities is in steep decline.[11] For example, in New York City, non-Hispanic whites dropped from 43 to 35 percent of the total population from 1990 to 2000, while in Los Angeles non-Hispanic whites dropped from 38 to 30 percent (see table 5.2).

Thus, it may be time to abandon the view that the cities of New York and Los Angeles contain a rapidly dwindling minority of whites in favor of the view that the composition of whites in the two cities is changing, as it always has done. Nowadays the white component of each city is more Latino, just as in the past, for example, New York City's white component became more Irish and, then later, more Italian and Jewish and so on. Many of these older groups of whites have been leaving the cities for some time now, but groups such as Latinos are replacing them; and the fact that a large proportion of Latinos classify themselves as whites when given the opportunity to do so by the census has as much right to be noted as does that of the Irish or Italians or Jews to so self-classify.[12]

RESIDENTIAL INTEGRATION AND SEGREGATION

We now turn to measuring residential segregation/separation in the two regions, a topic that could not be adequately addressed without an understanding of the interrelated demographic and definitional issues just discussed. Some think that residential Los Angeles is more highly segregated than is residential New York City. This image is based on several factors, each of which is open to challenge or modification. For example, it is true that in sections of New York City, especially in Manhattan, racial and ethnic groups are mixed on the streets, in stores, and on public transport. Still, there are neighborhoods in New York City where a black man simply walking down the street is known to risk attack by teenagers and young adults (e.g., Bensonhurst, in Brooklyn—see below). It is true that in the 1980s and early 1990s, the city of Los Angeles had one geographically enormous black ghetto—the South Central/Watts/Compton area—while New York City had several, smaller in geographic extent—Harlem, Bedford-Stuyvesant, southeast Queens, Brownsville. This might suggest that the black population of New York City is more dispersed. But from 1980 to 2000 the black population in South Central/Watts/Compton became considerably less concentrated and is now, on the whole, far less dense than the black neighborhoods of New York City just mentioned, as figure 5.2 shows, and is arguably therefore less ghettoized. Finally, the fact that large sections of South Central Los Angeles were, in the 1980s and 1990s, rapidly changing from predominantly black to predominantly Latino, especially Mexican, might imply that ghettoization, involving one minority group or another, is a more permanent feature of the city of Los Angeles than of New York City. At the same time, in New York City, too, Latinos have long moved into areas that were predominantly black, as in the recent move of Dominicans south toward Harlem from Washington Heights or the steady Latino movement west into Harlem from "Spanish Harlem" (figs. 5.6, 5.7).

Indeed, scholarly studies of segregation/separation undertaken on 1990 census data and earlier imply that Los Angeles should be less segregated than New York. These studies find that, in general, newer housing tends to be less segregated than older housing, in part because it was built after the weak but not totally ineffective Fair Housing Act (Lee and Wood 1991; Massey and Gross 1991). Housing in Los Angeles, often built in the past thirty years, should be less segregated than in New York, where much housing, especially that in the urban core, was built years ago. Scholarly studies have also found that unique racial segregation dynamics are emerging in multiethnic areas, particularly in the West, and that high levels of Latino and Asian immigration provide the basis for greater mixed-race neighborhood living (Frey 1991; Farley and Frey 1994; Clark 1996, 113).[13] The following analysis will address these issues.

The most commonly used, and in many ways the best, single measure of racial separation is the "index of dissimilarity" or "*D*." (For a review of segregation measures, see Massey and Denton [1988].)[14] The *D* index measures the degree of difference between the ways that two groups are distributed among the smaller geographic units that compose a larger geographic unit. For example, it would tell us whether blacks and whites in a county are distributed in a similar way among the

Figure 5.6. Storefront Black Church alongside Latino Beauty Salon, 4056 South Central Avenue (November 2001). Such juxtapositions are common in South Central Los Angeles, where the Latino presence is growing alongside a diminishing African-American presence.

Figure 5.7 Dominicans in Washington Heights with George Washington Bridge in Background

census tracts that compose that county. These *D* scores can also be interpreted in such a way as to indicate the percentage of one group that would have to move in order for the distribution of that group over the larger geographic area to be identical to the distribution of the comparison group over the same area. The range for *D* scores is from 0 to 1. The higher the *D* score, the higher is the level of separation between two groups. For example, when comparing whites and blacks, if all the blacks in a county lived in census tracts that were 100 percent black, then the *D* score would be 1—perfectly segregated. In contemporary America, *D* scores of 0.7 or above are usually taken to indicate major levels of segregation/separation, though scores in the 0.6 region are also high and scores in the 0.5 region indicate moderate levels of separation (Ethington 2001).

The *D* score is dyadic in that it compares just two groups at a time. In the following analysis the county is usually the larger geographic unit (though data for New York City and the city of Los Angeles are also presented), the many census tracts into which the county is divided are the smaller geographic units, and the focus is on two comparisons, first between non-Hispanic whites and blacks; second between non-Hispanic whites and Hispanics. Although the comparison group in each case is non-Hispanic whites, the intention is not, of course, to imply that Hispanics are not white. It is simply to compare the residential patterns of blacks and Hispanics—the two largest minority groups—with those of the rest of population who classify themselves as "white."

Non-Hispanic White–Black Segregation

Figure 5.8 compares non-Hispanic whites and blacks using 2000 census data. The complete data are laid out in the appendix (tables 5.A1 and 5.A2). Both cities display a high level of separation between blacks and non-Hispanic whites. All five counties that constitute New York City have levels of segregation that are well above 0.7, and two (Brooklyn and Queens) are above 0.8, indicating enormous separation/segregation. Manhattan, the core county in the New York City area, has the next highest score (0.77). The city of Los Angeles (0.73) has a score that is high, though markedly lower than that of Brooklyn and Queens. Los Angeles County, with a score of 0.68, is less segregated than the city of Los Angeles or the New York City counties.

The image of an "integrated" Manhattan, based on the truth that in many parts of Manhattan there is much mixture on the streets and on public transportation especially the subway and also at work, is clearly not accurate when it comes to where people live. Indeed, there are some obvious mechanisms that support Manhattan's residential segregation.

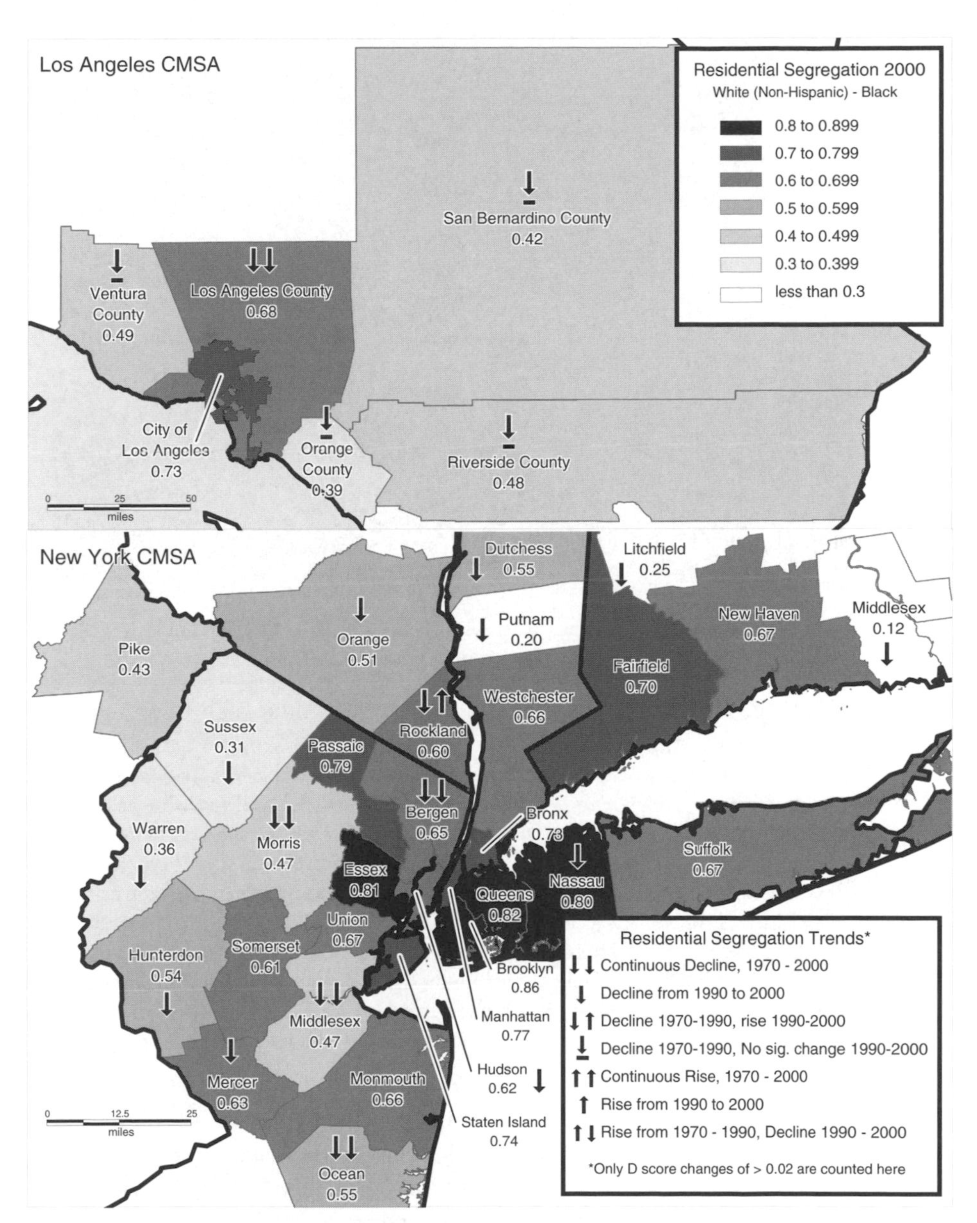

Figure 5.8. Residential Segregation between Whites (Non-Hispanic) and Blacks, 2000

Figure 5.9. 1230 Park Avenue (Intersection of Ninety-sixth Street) Co-Operative Building, Designed by Rosario Candela in the 1920s (*inset*), Looking North toward Harlem. This wealthy section of Park Avenue is just three blocks south of one of the densest concentrations of public housing in New York City. Although several sections of Harlem have expensive and desirable brownstones mostly inhabited by well-to-do blacks, the latter have been unable to move south along Fifth Avenue and Park Avenue into fashionable apartment buildings, in part because of the exclusive co-op system, which combines a private housing association, the residents of which are screened by admissions committees, and a gated (doorman) community. By contrast, blacks in Los Angeles have been able to move into very desirable areas on the fringe of the ghetto, such as Ladera Heights. Residential segregation between non-Latino whites and blacks is extremely high in Manhattan, and residential segregation between non-Latino whites and Latinos is higher in Manhattan than in any other county in the New York or Los Angeles regions.

For example, about 80 percent of the apartment market in Manhattan consists of cooperative buildings, which are both "gated communities" (with doormen or secured entry systems) and private housing associations with the right to interview and screen potential new purchasers (fig. 5.9). The courts have ruled that the boards of these residential cooperatives are free to turn down anyone they wish provided the grounds are not race, national origin, gender, sexual orientation, familial status, or disability. Since the boards were not required to give, and rarely in fact gave, the reason for turning someone down, there has been plenty of room for informal discrimination based on, for example, race or Latino origin. In September 2002 the New York State Assembly passed a bill (pending before the State Senate as of November 2002) that would require co-op boards to provide written reasons for rejecting an applicant but with no penalty for failing to do so (Romano 2002).

The stereotype of Queens County as one of the most ethnically and racially diverse places in the country needs modification, too, given its *D* score of 0.82. While Queens County as a whole does contain a very diverse racial and ethnic population, its large black population is highly separated from its non-Hispanic white population, with much of it concentrated in the large area of southeast Queens, as figure 5.1 shows. At the same time, the next section will show that the Hispanic population of Queens is much less separate from its non-Hispanic white population than is the black population.

Brooklyn's score of 0.86 is higher than any county in either CMSA examined here. The Brooklyn neighborhood of Bensonhurst is worth studying in detail (fig. 5.10). It is a "traditional ethnic" neighborhood that has long contained a large proportion of Italians and Jews. The area has a reputation as hostile to blacks. In a notorious 1989 incident, a young black man, Yusef Hawkins, who had come to Bensonhurst with three black friends to view a used Pontiac they had seen advertised in the newspaper, was killed by young white residents of Bensonhurst who

Figure 5.10. Bensonhurst, Brooklyn, Avenue Cristoforo Columbo. Inhabited mainly by Italians and Jews, with a small proportion of Latinos and Asians, Bensonhurst is notoriously hostile to blacks.

did not believe blacks should be there. In the community, few spoke out against the killers and several agreed that blacks should not have been there in the first place (*Newsweek* 1989). The black Reverend Sharpton was stabbed while leading a march to protest Hawkins's murder. In both CMSAs, census tracts that do not contain a single black even though the total population of the tract is more than 200 (i.e., the population is not trivial in size) are rare. For the 2000 census, there are only eighteen instances of such tracts in the New York CMSA out of a total of 5,202 tracts. There are only three instances in the Los Angeles CMSA out of a total of 3, 338 tracts.[15] Ethnographic research indicates that, at least in the New York–New Jersey region, these kind of tracts may indicate the kind of neighborhood where blacks are not only unwelcome but may even be in physical danger should they stray into them (Halle 1984).

Bensonhurst contains nine of the eighteen tracts in the New York CMSA that do not have a single black, and a tenth such tract is about a half mile north of Bensonhurst in the heavily Hassidic section of Gravesend.[16] Of these nine Bensonhurst tracts, eight are contiguous and are inhabited by 12,280 people, an astonishingly large number given that they contain not a single black. The population of these tracts is by no means uniform in other respects—in addition to the large proportions of Italians and Jews already mentioned, it includes small proportions of Asians (from 1 to 20 percent, depending on the tract) and Hispanics (from 2 to 8 percent, depending on the tract). Bensonhurst retains its segregated character in regard to blacks despite not being a gated community and having no physical barriers, such as highways, railroad tracks, or disused land, that wall off its population. Indeed, nearby is a largely African-American housing project, Marlboro Houses, which contains a concentration of low-income, mostly welfare dependent, female headed families, of whose existence most Bensonhurst residents are well aware.

Bensonhurst is known as hostile territory for blacks. The terms "segregation" and "separation" are equally applicable here. Some, perhaps many, residents of Bensonhurst do not wish blacks to live there, and, given the physical danger that they might face if they tried, it is likely that most blacks have no desire to live there anyway. Bensonhurst is an extreme case, but there are some smaller, less extreme versions (fig. 5.11). In Queens, for example, parts of the neighborhood of Middle Village contain two noncontiguous tracts with a total of 2,278 people and not a single black. Blacks know Middle Village as inhospitable.[17] It is no accident that neighborhoods like Bensonhurst and Middle Village exist in Brooklyn and Queens—the two counties where segregation/separation between blacks and non-Hispanic whites is higher than any county in either the New York or the Los Angeles CMSA.

Figure 5.11. Brighton Beach, Boardwalk (March 2002), a Shore Neighborhood Just South of Bensonhurst. During the summer, its beach is informally segregated, with blacks and many Latinos preferring to occupy the neighboring Coney Island Beach. A large immigrant Russian community (discussed in chap. 3) lives in Brighton Beach.

The Los Angeles CMSA has only three tracts that contain more than 200 people with not a single black, and all three are in Los Angeles County. Two are Hispanic enclaves, one in East Los Angeles with 97 percent Hispanic (the tract contains 2,187 people), the other in El Monte with 91 percent Hispanic (the tract contains 2,174 people). The third tract without a single black is very different in character from these two and resembles, though in a more moderate version, Bensonhurst or Middle Village. It is in the city of La Cañada Flintridge, a neighborhood located in the hills just west of Pasadena, with spectacular views of the cities of Los Angeles and Pasadena below. La Cañada Flintridge has a variety of sizes of houses, from small townhouses to mini-mansions. The tract without a single black contains huge and expensive houses; its population of 4,430 classify themselves on the race question as 73 percent white and 23 percent Asian, and on the Hispanic origin question as only 4 percent Hispanic. The tract is just a quarter of a mile from the northwest section of Pasadena, whose population is more than 50 percent black. This black section of Pasadena is separated from La Cañada by a reservoir and a gully, and there are no residences for a strip of about a quarter of a mile between the two towns, although a road crossing the gully joins them easily by automobile. La Cañada Flintridge was rumored to have once had an active Klu Klux Klan, and only in the past decade have there been any Jewish residents. It is, therefore, reasonable to suspect that blacks are, or feel, unwelcome there.

Looking beyond the counties that constitute the urban core of New York City and the city of Los Angeles, the four counties surrounding Los Angeles County were markedly less segregated by race than Los Angeles County—all scored below 0.5, with the lowest scores in Orange county (0.39) and the highest scores in Ventura (0.49) and Riverside (0.48).[18] Thus, in all four of these counties levels of separation between blacks and non-Hispanic whites are below levels considered serious. This may be, in part, because the proportion of the black population in these counties is not high, in all cases below 10 percent and in Ventura and Orange Counties as low as 2 percent.

The picture for the counties surrounding New York City is more mixed than for those surrounding Los Angeles County. Nassau County on Long Island, with a score of 0.8, has a segregation level that approaches the highest levels in the city. Indeed, in terms of black and non-Hispanic white residential patterns, parts of Nassau County resemble, and are in some ways an extension of, adjoining Queens. In the middle of Nassau County, a small group of townships that contain significant proportions (20–90 percent) of blacks and include the towns of Baldwin and Freeport are surrounded by townships and villages with very low proportions of blacks (e.g., to the west, Floral Park, New Hyde Park, Mineola, and Old Westbury), as figure 1.11 shows. Much of the housing in Nassau County was built immediately after World War II and excluded blacks, with Levittown on Long Island, developed beginning in 1947, a famous example. Even now, only a handful of blacks (fewer than 200) live in this community of more than 50,000 (Lambert 1997).

Still, residential race relations in these areas of Nassau County do not just replicate those in the inner-city ghetto. These areas constitute a second type of minority residential setting, in which the group (here blacks) enjoy middle-class life styles and housing and often income levels. Indeed, a developing pattern of black suburbanization on the periphery of New York City is that of large black sections—black suburbs—surrounded by larger residential sections, the population of which contains very small proportions of blacks. Though highly segregated with respect to the *D* index, such a pattern does allow some housing choice for African-Americans, offering many more amenities than the inner-city ghetto and far more housing choice. It allows minority group members who have the financial resources to live in attractive neighborhoods with decent schools. Other examples are the area of southeast Queens, including Laurelton (fig. 5.12), Saint Albans, and Cambria

Figure 5.12. Laurelton, Southeast Queens, 228th Street and 141st Avenue. Located toward the outskirts of the city, predominantly black areas of southeast Queens such as Saint Albans, Cambria Heights and Laurelton are geographically separated from inner-city black neighborhoods. Residents are mostly a mixture of American blacks and immigrants from the Caribbean The residences tend to be medium- or modest-sized detached houses or largish row houses, but there are also some very large houses, especially in Laurelton south of Merrick Boulevard. Twenty-thirty years ago these areas were mostly inhabited by Italians and Jews.

Heights; Runyon Heights in Yonkers; and the Walworth area in White Plains/Scarsdale. All these areas are predominantly black, middle-class areas that allow for continuing upward movement economically.[19] They have some affinities with a certain older type of black suburb in the region, which consists of a smallish black enclave, tucked in or near a predominantly nonblack area. Spinney Hill in Great Neck is an example (Halle 1993, 12). However these newer black suburbs tend to be much larger than the latter and are growing in size, with newer housing and more affluent residents.

These large, black middle-class suburbs, separated from the inner-city ghettos, have not really developed in the Los Angeles region, perhaps partly because the black population's smaller size, only about one-sixth that of New York City's in 2000, makes it less able to sustain them. The closest equivalent is a neighborhood like Ladera Heights (fig. 5.13), known locally as the "black Beverly Hills," which is just south of Century City on the westernmost edge of the black ghetto that extends

Figure 5.13. Ladera Heights, City of Los Angeles. Known locally as the "Black Beverly Hills," this affluent neighborhood, about two-thirds black, is just south of Culver City on the western edge of the black ghetto that extends from South Central Los Angeles. Like neighboring Baldwin Hills, Ladera Heights is raised above the black ghetto of which both are otherwise a contiguous part. Los Angeles does not, at this point, have the kind of separate black suburbs that have developed in New York, partly because the black population of the city of Los Angeles is only about one-sixth as large as that of New York City.

from South Central. Raised above the ghetto, Ladera Heights consists of very large homes, about two-thirds of which are occupied by an affluent black population that first moved in when whites abandoned the area after the 1965 Watts riots. Still Ladera Heights is a contiguous extension of the large central black ghetto, albeit on the fringe.

Parts (though only parts) of Freeport in Nassau County have the reputation of being residentially racially integrated, with significant proportions of blacks and non-Hispanic whites (at least 30 percent of each group) residing together in the same blocks in stable communities, at the time of writing. Here, further out from New York City, some blacks and non-Hispanic whites coexist in neighborhoods where the commonalities of a "middle-class" lifestyle and home allow people to transcend differences of race within the same community. Still, such classically integrated areas are unusual in the New York CMSA, and skeptics will predict that over time they, too, will become either predominantly non-

Hispanic white or predominantly black. (See the note to table 5.1 for the few other examples.)[20]

Other counties surrounding New York City that have segregation scores approaching the highest in New York City are Essex County (0.81) in New Jersey, which contains the old, racially troubled city of Newark; Passaic County in New Jersey (0.79), which contains the likewise troubled city of Paterson; and Fairfield County, Conn. (0.70), which contains the old city of Hartford. Several other counties surrounding New York City and Newark have segregation levels in the 0.6–0.7 range. These include, in New Jersey, Bergen, Hudson, Monmouth, Somerset, Union, and Mercer; in New York, Rockland, Suffolk, and Westchester; and in Connecticut, New Haven.[21]

In contrast, some counties in the New York CMSA, especially those near the periphery, have segregation levels as low as those of the four peripheral counties of the Los Angeles CMSA. These include Middlesex, N.J. (0.47), Morris, N.J. (0.47), and Pike, Pa. (0.43). (Scores of below 0.5 are compatible with the existence of high concentrations of blacks, as in the smallish and old black suburbs that are found in the region including the counties just mentioned. The scores in such cases show that elsewhere in the county blacks are more evenly distributed.) A few counties, again all located near the periphery of the CMSA, have segregation levels that are 0.36 or lower, which is below the lowest scores of any county in the Los Angeles CMSA. These counties include Litchfield, Conn. (0.25), Middlesex, Conn. (0.12), Putnam, N.Y. (0.20), Sussex, N.J. (0.31), and Warren, N.J. (0.36). These very low segregation levels are likely related to the small percentage of blacks in these counties, in none of which was the percentage of black residents in 2000 above 2 percent while in two (Litchfield and Middlesex) it was below 1 percent.[22] Other studies have suggested that, in the United States, when the percentage of minorities, especially blacks and Hispanics, is well below 10 percent, segregation levels are often low, too, though if later the proportion of minorities approaches 8–10 percent, then a tendency toward segregation or resegregation often also appears (Massey and Gross 1991; Mumford Center 2001).[23] In similar fashion, a survey of residents of Los Angeles County found that most non-Latino whites (81 percent) said they would be comfortable if up to 20 percent of their neighbors were blacks, but the percentage expressing comfort fell as the hypothesized percentage of blacks rose beyond 20 percent. Expressed comfort with Latinos as neighbors was somewhat greater and with Asian neighbors greater still (Charles 2000, 182–88). Thus these areas with low proportions of minorities and low levels of segregation constitute a third model of residential relations that differs clearly from the urban core/ghetto model exemplified by blacks in South Central, Harlem, Bedford-Stuyvesant, and so on or from the model of minorities living in large concentrations in the suburbs (see table 5.1).

Black–Non-Hispanic White Segregation/Separation over Time

The data discussed so far are for 2000. How about the trend in separation between blacks and non-Hispanic whites? Dissimilarity indices by decade from 1970 to 2000, for each county of the two regions, can assess this. The arrows in figure 5.8 summarize some major separation/segregation trends for those counties. (The absence of arrows indicates that the data for the county in question do not fall into any of the patterns foregrounded here.) Only *D* score changes from one decade to another that exceed 0.02 are noted; smaller changes are too minor to consider significant.

Separation/segregation patterns are stable, at their very high levels, in New York City. None of the five counties/boroughs that compose New York City displayed any significant change during the entire period 1970–2000. Indeed, in New York City, as in many comparable urban areas of the United States, a significant level of segregation was already set in the early twentieth century when the black population was small and increased as that population grew. The *D* score for New York City in 1910 was already 0.64, even though the black population (about 92,000) was only 1.9 percent of the total population. By 1930 blacks constituted 4.7 percent of the population, and the *D* score had risen to 0.79. In 2000 it was 0.82, while the black population was about 27.0 percent of the population.

Of the New York counties that are contiguous with New York City, separation/segregation levels declined very slightly in Nassau, though are still very high (0.8), and remained stable at fairly high levels in Suffolk and Westchester. Levels of black and non-Hispanic white separation/segregation are more fluid in some of the New Jersey counties on the periphery of the major urban area of Newark. Thus from 1970 to 2000 there were continuous declines in the levels of such separation in Middlesex, Ocean, Bergen, and Morris counties. In other counties (Mercer, Hunterdon, Sussex, and Warren) there were declines between 1990 and 2000. But in Essex County, where the city of Newark is located, and in Passaic County, where Paterson is, levels of separation between blacks and non-Hispanic whites have stayed pretty constantly high from 1970 to 2000, as they have in Fairfield County, Conn., where Bridgeport is located. Thus in the older major cities in the New York

CMSA, not just in New York City, there has, in general, been no decline in levels of segregation/separation.

Separation between whites and blacks declined continuously from 1970 to 1990 in all five counties that compose the Los Angeles region (see also Clark 1996). However from 1990 to 2000, this decline ceased in each of the four counties surrounding Los Angels County and indeed began to reverse itself, though the rise is small—less than 0.02 in each county—which is why it is not noted as a rise in figure 5.8. This leaves Los Angeles County as the only county in the CMSA in which the level of black-white separation declined continuously from 1970 to 2000. The ongoing decline in Los Angeles County is striking, especially in view of the fact that in the major older cities of the New York region (New York City, Newark, Paterson, Hartford) such separation is frozen at very high levels. It is probably related to the fact that sections of the black population are moving farther out and, in many ways, being replaced with Latinos more rapidly than in New York City and that the black population of the city and county of Los Angeles has now declined to around 10 percent. (The percentage of blacks in New York City has declined, too, from 1990 to 2000 without a corresponding fall in levels of segregation but remains high, at 27 percent.) In contrast, it will be noted in the next section that levels of separation between Hispanics and non-Hispanic whites in Los Angeles County have risen continually from 1970 to 2000, as the Hispanic immigrant population has grown.

The fact that, in the four counties surrounding Los Angeles County, the decline in levels of separation between blacks and non-Hispanic whites from 1970 to 1990 has now ceased would support the view of those who have argued that over time patterns of black-white segregation would reappear somewhat in these more recently developed areas (Clark 1996).[24] The reasons suggested for this are that, as the proportions and numbers of minorities increase, pressure to resegregate/reseparate rises both from the other residents, who feel more threatened and uncomfortable, and perhaps also from blacks, who prefer to live together. But it is too soon to be sure about what is, and will be, going on in these four peripheral counties, especially since the data show only a modest tendency toward black-white resegregation over just one decade, 1990 to 2000, and in none of these counties has separation moved to a level that is usually considered to indicate major segregation. Also, the proportion of blacks in the four counties surrounding Los Angeles County has grown only slightly in San Bernardino (from 8 to 9 percent) and in Riverside (from 5 to 6 percent), while remaining constant at 2 percent in Ventura and Orange. Given the always modest proportion of blacks in the city of Los Angeles, whose correlate is that the size of the black population seeking to suburbanize is not large, it is possible that the counties surrounding Los Angeles County will not develop the sizable black suburbs that have developed in New York.

Separation between Hispanics and Non-Hispanic Whites

Figure 5.14 summarizes the separation/segregation picture for the comparison between Hispanics and non-Hispanic whites. The highest levels of such separation in the New York region exceed those in the Los Angeles CMSA. (This parallels the case for levels of separation between blacks and non-Hispanic whites.) Thus two counties in the New York region have *D* scores for segregation between Hispanics and non-Hispanic whites that exceed the score in the city of Los Angeles (0.66) and in Los Angeles County (0.63), which is the most segregated county in the Los Angeles region. In the New York region, the highest *D* scores for separation between Hispanics and non-Hispanic whites were in Manhattan (0.72) and Passaic County, N.J. (0.69). Manhattan is no more a residential melting pot between Hispanics and non-Hispanic whites than it is for blacks and non-Hispanic whites. Passaic contains the old town of Paterson, which has a large Hispanic population. The Bronx (0.67), Brooklyn (0.67), and Essex County (0.64) have scores that compare with the city and county of Los Angeles.

At the same time, some counties of New York City display levels of separation between Hispanics and non-Hispanic whites that are not especially high, as do some counties that adjoin New York City. These include Queens (0.52) and Staten Island (0.42) in New York City and, bordering New York City, Nassau (0.47), Suffolk (0.46), and Westchester (0.54) Counties. In Queens County, as was mentioned, the levels of separation between non-Hispanic whites and Hispanics are moderate, although they are enormous between non-Hispanic whites and blacks. Evidently in New York City there is a diversity of Latino settlement just as the composition of the Latino population is diverse, as noted in chapters 1 and 3. Many Puerto Ricans, the original highly concentrated Latino group, have moved out of New York City. Dominicans now reside heavily in East Harlem, as well as in Washington Heights and the South Bronx where levels of separation are high.[25] But other Latino groups, including Mexicans and other Central and South Americans, have settled, among other places, in Queens, where levels of separation with non-Hispanic whites are low. The northwest portion of Queens, where the Number 7 train travels, is a polyglot immigrant area, including also sizable groups from East and South Asian and European origins (fig. 5.15).

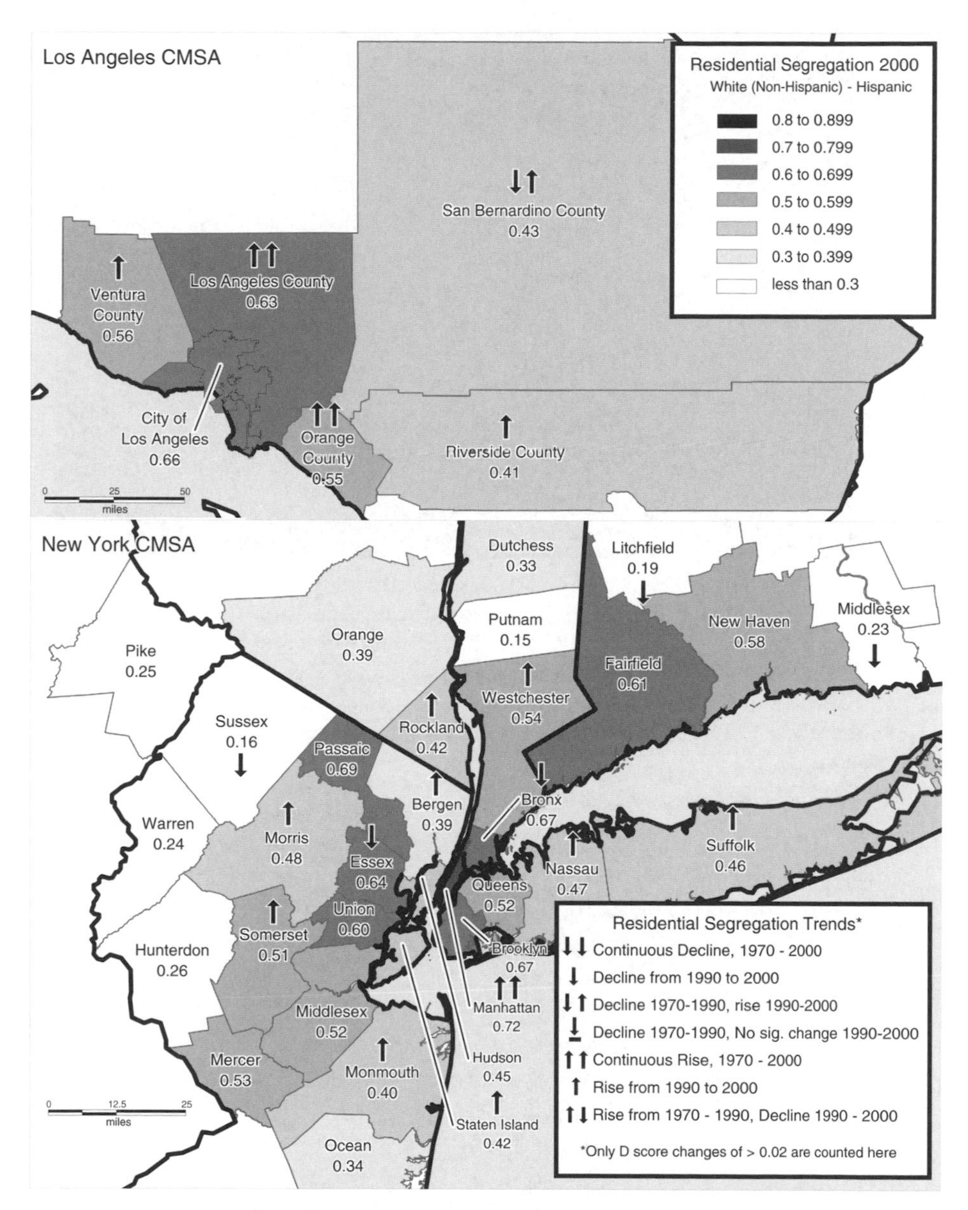

Figure 5.14. Residential Segregation between Whites (Non-Hispanic) and Hispanics, 2000

Figure 5.15. Roosevelt Avenue (and Seventy-third Street), the Commercial Center of Jackson Heights, Queens. Roosevelt Avenue runs under the number 7 subway, making it easily accessible. This section of northwest Queens is ethnically highly diverse, with many Mexicans and other Central and South Americans and many Asians, including Chinese and Indians (see chap. 3). But northwest Queens has very few blacks, who instead tend to reside in southeast Queens.

In the Los Angeles CMSA, the four counties that border Los Angeles County have separation levels that are comparable to these moderate to low levels of separation in counties such as Queens. They range from Ventura (0.56) and Orange (0.55) Counties to Riverside (0.41) and San Bernardino (0.43) Counties.

Latino and Non-Hispanic White Separation Compared with Black and Non-Hispanic White Separation

A striking characteristic of the Los Angeles region is that levels of separation between Hispanics and non-Hispanic whites in 2000 are about comparable to levels of separation between blacks and non-Hispanic whites in the region. Indeed in two counties, Orange and Ventura, the levels of separation between Hispanics and non-Hispanic whites were higher in 2000 than the levels of separation between blacks and non-Hispanic whites in those counties, with the difference being quite marked for Orange County, where the *D* score for the black with non-Hispanic white comparison is 0.39, compared to 0.55 for the Hispanic with non-Hispanic white comparison. In the three other counties in the Los Angeles region the levels of separation between Hispanics and non-Hispanic whites were only a little lower than those between blacks and non-Hispanic whites.

In the New York region, by contrast, when comparing counties with each other, the highest levels of separation between Hispanics and non-Hispanic whites are lower than the highest levels of separation between blacks and non-Hispanic whites. Thus the highest *D* scores for separation between Hispanics and non-Hispanic whites (Manhattan, 0.72; the Bronx, 0.67; and Passaic, 0.69), although high, do not approach the levels of separation between blacks and non-Hispanic whites found in Brooklyn, Queens, and Nassau, all of which were 8.0 or above. Further, within the same county in the New York CMSA, the level of separation between blacks and non-Hispanic whites usually substantially exceeds the level of separation between Hispanics and non-Hispanic whites.

Latinos in the Inland Empire

An area with low levels of separation between Hispanics and non-Hispanic whites that is especially interesting is the eastern part of the Los Angeles CMSA—eastern Los Angeles County, San Bernardino County, and Riverside County. The large and rising proportions of Hispanics here contradict the dictum that low levels of separation are often confined to areas where the proportion of the minority group is small, less than 10 percent of the total population. This makes these areas a unique case study of evolving residential patterns, rich in possibilities for analysis over the next decades (fig. 5.16).

Known jointly as the Inland Empire, San Bernardino and Riverside Counties are one of the most economically vibrant areas of the United States. They are, for example, the primary distribution center for goods in southern California and the western United States. A large proportion of the new homes in the Los Angeles region are built here and are attractively priced, with a median price in 1999 of $205,000, less than half that of comparable new units in Orange County and older urban areas of Los Angeles County. For such reasons, the Urban Land Institute in 2000 pronounced Riverside and San Bernardino to be the "consummate suburban location" (Urban Land Institute 2000, 283–84).

Much of the Latino suburbanization in the Los Angeles CMSA is located here, in areas where the overall proportion of the population that is Latino already ranges from at least 60 percent (eastern Los Angeles County) to 39 percent (San Bernardino County) and 36 percent (Riverside County) and is growing at the rate of about 10–20 percent a de-

Figure 5.16. Mexican-Owned House in LaPuente, in Southeast Los Angeles County, Corner of Alterio and Deepmead Avenue. Swathes of often contiguous new suburbs, whose Latino populations are already 35 percent or more and are increasing at about 10 percent a decade, stretch through eastern Los Angeles County and much of San Bernardino and Riverside Counties.

cade. In the entire history of American suburbanization, dating from 1814, there is no comparable instance of an ethnic or linguistic group moving to the suburbs in such overwhelming numbers and density.

The demographics of the Inland Empire suggest a new suburban phenomenon, which the traditional language of residential segregation/separation may not capture. The proportions of one key minority group, blacks, may be too small for sizable black sections to develop, either voluntarily or by the actions of a threatened, nonblack population. By contrast, the proportions of a second key minority group, Latinos, may be so large as to dominate the region. Still, as figures 5.8 and 5.14 show, the level of separation between non-Hispanic whites and both blacks and Latinos in these two counties does not exceed 0.48. Further, the fact that half or more of Latinos classify themselves as white lends additional support to the view that the traditional language of residential segregation is probably inadequate to capture the phenomenon of Latinos in the vast suburbs of the Inland Empire.

Adding to the interest of this area are the small residential enclaves of middle-class or wealthy Asians, discussed in chapter 4, such as Walnut, Rowland Heights, and Diamond Bar. In Walnut, a wealthy Asian section, new homes in 2001 sell at prices from $800,000 upward.

As regards trends over time, in the Los Angeles region from 1990 to 2000 the separation/segregation trend has been uniformly toward greater separation between Hispanics and non-Hispanic whites in all five counties (though the 1990–2000 rise in Los Angeles County was slight, just below 0.02). This was not the case for the period 1970–1990, where the picture was mixed.[26] Still, levels of separation between Hispanics and non-Hispanic whites in San Bernardino and Riverside Counties remain below those usually considered even moderately segregated. Hence, as the proportion of Latinos rises to a majority and beyond to saturate these new suburban areas, it is not clear whether any of the traditional models of separation/segregation might come into play.

In the New York region, the 1990–2000 trends in levels of segregation between Hispanics and non-Hispanic whites are mixed. Some counties that compose New York City or are close to it show significant increases in the level of separation from 1990 to 2000. These include Staten Island, Westchester, Nassau, and Suffolk. In Manhattan, levels of separation between Hispanics and non-Hispanic whites rose continually from 1970 to 2000, though for some decades, for example, 1990–2000, the rise did not quite exceed 0.02. In Queens, there was a very small rise too but just below 0.02. In contrast, levels of separation in the Bronx declined slightly. For the New Jersey counties in the New York CMSA, the picture is also mixed over the period 1990–2000, with seven of the fourteen New Jersey counties in the CMSA displaying no significant change during that time. Of the rest, four saw increased levels of separation between Hispanics and non-Hispanic whites, and three saw decreased levels.

CONCLUSION

The residential composition of each city and region cannot be summarized in a single headline (e.g., "segregation is rising" or "segregation is falling"). Above all, several models are needed to capture the diversity of the two regions. And it is important to make basic distinctions, such as between the urban core (and within the urban core between, e.g., the various counties that compose New York City) and the outer and the peripheral areas.

Thus New York City and, though to a somewhat lesser degree, the city of Los Angeles provide one clear model for residential patterns between blacks and non-Hispanic whites, which can be called the traditional ghetto/barrio model. This consists of urban areas of high concentrations of blacks surrounded by areas with low concentrations of blacks. Levels of residential separation between blacks and non-Hispanic whites are high in the urban cores of both CMSAs—in New York City and in the city of Los Angeles and in Los Angeles County—though the highest levels of such separation are found in parts of New York City, especially Brooklyn, Queens, and Manhattan. Also, while in Los Angeles County the level of separation between blacks and non-Hispanic whites has declined continually from 1970 to 2000, in New York City these segregation patterns are stable at extremely high levels, as they are in the other older cities in the New York CMSA and, in many ways, as they have been throughout the twentieth century. There is nowadays almost no political constituency in New York City that is trying to reduce these segregation/separation levels, since black and Latino politicians clearly benefit from the existence of black and Latino voting constituencies. A corollary of the model, not inevitable but not unexpected either, is a shameful neighborhood like Bensonhurst, without a single black resident and known as place where blacks who try to move in may be in physical danger. This "traditional" model is also a reasonable approximation of the situation of Latinos in the inner cities of the two regions—for example, East Harlem and Washington Heights in New York and sections of South Central Los Angeles.

A second model consists of African-Americans, Latinos, or Asians who have achieved middle-class status and move to areas, beyond the urban core, with high concentrations of their group. There are several areas in the New York region that fit this profile for African-Americans, and a few for Latinos and Asians. There are, overall, many more in the Los Angeles area, though for Latinos and Asians rather than for blacks.[27]

A third model for residential patterns between blacks and non-Hispanic whites can be found everywhere in the CMSA but is especially represented by some of the New Jersey, New York, and Connecticut counties toward the periphery of the CMSA as well as by some areas in the counties surrounding Los Angeles County. Here levels of segregation are fairly low, as however, are the percentage of minorities who reside there (but not Latinos in Los Angeles). The future direction of separation levels in such areas is unclear. There are those who argue that over time patterns of segregation will start to reappear in these more recently developed areas, as the proportions of minorities there increase (Clark 1996). But the proportions of minorities may remain low in many of these areas. This is especially true for blacks in the Los Angeles region since the proportions of blacks in the central city, the main source of black migration to these peripheral areas, is not large to start with. It is also the case that many of the African-Americans in such areas will be middle class and therefore less threatening to non-Hispanic whites (Farley and Frey 1994).

A fourth model, in some ways the obverse of the previous model, is represented by relations between Hispanics and non-Hispanic whites in eastern Los Angeles County and the adjoining Inland Empire—San Bernardino and Riverside Counties. In these newly developed suburbs the overall proportion of the population that is Hispanic now ranges from 36 to 60 percent and is growing. Levels of separation between Hispanics and non-Hispanic whites are low, perhaps because the blanketing of the area by Latinos is proceeding so rapidly that there is little opportunity for traditional patterns of segregation to emerge. These low levels of separation are also likely related to the fact that, as we have seen, at least around half of the Latinos classify themselves as "white" when asked by the census. Thus if the low levels of separation in the third model derive partly from the fact that the minority group at issue—blacks—is a small proportion of the total population, the low levels of separation in the fourth model derive from the fact that the "minority" group at issue—Latinos—is an enormous proportion of the total population. These two counties of the Inland Empire constitute a fascinating experiment in suburbanization and will provide material for study for several decades.

Finally, it is arguable that the categories around which this entire discussion has revolved—categories such as black, white, and even Latino and Asian—lend legitimacy to racial and quasi-racial categories that decades ago progressives insisted were unscientific. Scholars such as the members of the American Anthropological Association have long recoiled from race, viewing it as an antiquated concept (Beveridge 2001). Even when the use of these terms is justified, as it usually is these days, not in biological but in sociopolitical terms, for example, in order to target less privileged groups for help, it can reasonably be said that such quasi-racial categories should be avoided. The French practice, where since 1848 the government has been forbidden from collecting data about the racial composition of the population, is exemplary here (Lamont 2000). In the United States, by contrast, the government requires the Census Bureau to collect such data. It might also be objected that nowadays progressive analysts stress the diversity of each of these broad categories, referring, for example, to Jamaicans and Nigerians and Somalians and American blacks rather than to blacks and referring to the many subcategories of Spanish origin peoples rather than to Latinos.

These are all valid points and should be born in mind. The census specifically notes that the classifications found on the "race" and "Hispanic origin" question are "not intended to be scientific in nature."[28] Still, the overall categories of black, Latino, Asian, and white are, for better or for worse, in constant scholarly and public use and so the next best strategy to avoiding them is to ensure they are used with care and a critical awareness of their origins and limitations.

Following this line, it has been argued here that we should retire a stereotype that has dominated our understanding of the residential composition of cities like New York and Los Angeles for much of the post–World War II period, namely, the view that as the proportions of minorities—blacks, Hispanics, and Asians—rise the proportion of "whites" is rapidly declining. The main problem with the stereotype is that a significant number of the Hispanics/Latinos in Los Angeles and New York classify themselves as white when asked by the census. A second problem is that the proportion of blacks has fallen between 1990 and 2000 in both cities. The stereotype of a dwindling band of whites in these cities can only be maintained by excluding Hispanics/Latinos from the white category, a practice that is part of a long history of opinion leaders acting as though a newly arrived group does not really belong in the white club. In their early histories in New York City the Irish, the Italians, and the Jews were each initially viewed by existing groups as nonwhite and attempts were made to suggest that groups from southern and eastern Europe, such as Italians and Jews, or Catholics, such as the Irish, were of a different race than the English or Germans. This practice has been carefully documented and is now seen as quaint and bizarre—another chapter in the history of racial and ethnic prejudice (Williams 1990; Brodkin 1998). This simultaneous movement—a strong numerical and proportional increase in two of the three main minority groups, Latinos and Asians, together with a change in the composition of the population of those classifying themselves as white to include more Latinos—is one of the most interesting facets of contemporary race and ethnicity in the cities and metro regions of New York and Los Angeles.

APPENDIX

Table 5.A1. Dissimilarity Indexes by Time: Los Angeles CMSA

	NON-HISPANIC WHITE/ BLACK	NON-HISPANIC WHITE/ ASIAN	NON-HISPANIC WHITE/ HISPANIC	BLACK/ ASIAN	BLACK/ HISPANIC	ASIAN/ HISPANIC
Los Angeles Co.:						
2000	.683	.500	.631	.679	.541	.555
1990	.730	.462	.611	.693	.593	.511
1980	.809	.470	.572	.761	.724	.496
1970	.901	. . .	.458	. . .	.841	. . .
Orange Co.:						
2000	.391	.418	.551	.373	.345	.497
1990	.375	.332	.499	.356	.395	.460
1980	.447	.305	.424	.473	.473	.404
1970	.853	. . .	.322	. . .	.748	. . .
Riverside Co.:						
2000	.483	.386	.414	.366	.397	.440
1990	.467	.332	.348	.336	.424	.460
1980	.541	.415	.396	.518	.548	.453
1970	.642	. . .	.389	. . .	.608	. . .
San Bernardino Co.:						
2000	.420	.407	.428	.420	.298	.429
1990	.402	.316	.364	.363	.356	.357
1980	.525	.311	.371	.497	.452	.434
1970	.734	. . .	.388	. . .	.592	. . .
Ventura Co.:						
2000	.493	.308	.561	.330	.328	.471
1990	.478	.300	.523	.329	.336	.450
1980	.554	.403	.527	.409	.423	.488
1970	.741	. . .	.443	. . .	.533	. . .

Note. Ellipses dots indicate years for which data were not available for that variable.

Table 5A.2. Dissimilarity Indexes by Time: New York CMSA

	NON-HISPANIC WHITE/ BLACK	NON-HISPANIC WHITE/ ASIAN	NON-HISPANIC WHITE/ HISPANIC	BLACK/ ASIAN	BLACK/ HISPANIC	ASIAN/ HISPANIC
Connecticut:						
Fairfield:						
2000	.696	.322	.615	.550	.228	.446
1990	.692	.341	.603	.591	.317	.505
1980	. . .	. . .	. . .	. . .	. . .	. . .
1970	. . .	. . .	. . .	. . .	. . .	. . .
Litchfield:						
2000	.252	.176	.191	.200	.173	.185
1990	.386	.276	.313	.232	.299	.313
1980	. . .	. . .	. . .	. . .	. . .	. . .
1970	. . .	. . .	. . .	. . .	. . .	. . .

Table 5A.2. *(continued)*

	NON-HISPANIC WHITE/ BLACK	NON-HISPANIC WHITE/ ASIAN	NON-HISPANIC WHITE/ HISPANIC	BLACK/ ASIAN	BLACK/ HISPANIC	ASIAN/ HISPANIC
Middlesex:						
2000	.125	.121	.227	.076	.192	.197
1990	.286	.308	.366	.390	.442	.652
1980	...	...	...	...	...	...
1970	...	...	...	...	...	...
New Haven:						
2000	.667	.337	.578	.579	.379	.554
1990	.686	.455	.575	.607	.464	.643
1980	...	...	...	...	...	...
1970	...	...	...	...	...	...
New Jersey:						
Bergen:						
2000	.648	.349	.393	.644	.487	.400
1990	.688	.307	.329	.705	.543	.393
1980	.743	.316	.298	.705	.598	.375
1970	.801	...	.657	...	.820	...
Essex:						
2000	.808	.302	.644	.765	.641	.643
1990	.822	.270	.680	.777	.651	.705
1980	.805	.347	.670	.761	.655	.720
1970	.790	...	.814	...	.632	...
Hudson:						
2000	.624	.451	.448	.541	.628	.507
1990	.661	.434	.430	.605	.650	.519
1980	.739	.468	.488	.706	.765	.542
1970	.745	...	.604	...	.756	...
Hunterdon:						
2000	.542	.257	.256	.537	.400	.293
1990	.619	.256	.293	.669	.411	.346
1980	...	...	...	...	...	...
1970	...	...	...	...	...	...
Mercer:						
2000	.634	.395	.530	.743	.455	.628
1990	.686	.404	.548	.735	.465	.627
1980	.712	.414	.564	.752	.489	.651
1970	.674	...	.798	...	.559	...
Middlesex:						
2000	.465	.408	.521	.433	.400	.610
1990	.525	.349	.523	.508	.446	.590
1980	.573	.401	.562	.584	.524	.636
1970	.642	...	.708	...	.699	...
Monmouth:						
2000	.659	.379	.397	.646	.430	.499
1990	.666	.360	.354	.681	.484	.475
1980	.672	.421	.397	.721	.540	.542
1970	.668	...	.585	...	.612	...

Table 5A.2. *(continued)*

	NON-HISPANIC WHITE/ BLACK	NON-HISPANIC WHITE/ ASIAN	NON-HISPANIC WHITE/ HISPANIC	BLACK/ ASIAN	BLACK/ HISPANIC	ASIAN/ HISPANIC
Morris:						
2000	.466	.350	.476	.466	.305	.505
1990	.508	.312	.451	.506	.420	.501
1980	.594	.339	.437	.642	.593	.524
1970	.707	. . .	.797	. . .	.777	. . .
Ocean:						
2000	.545	.325	.341	.464	.294	.304
1990	.600	.463	.336	.544	.358	.391
1980	.696	.441	.427	.719	.404	.520
1970	. . .	. . .	. . .	. . .	. . .	. . .
Passaic:						
2000	.790	.355	.693	.712	.391	.551
1990	.812	.433	.719	.735	.386	.593
1980	.815	.431	.722	.789	.433	.667
1970	.765	. . .	.735	. . .	.500	. . .
Somerset:						
2000	.606	.266	.511	.480	.461	.562
1990	.594	.261	.408	.545	.468	.477
1980	.708	.386	.384	.662	.609	.482
1970	.755	. . .	.855	. . .	.594	. . .
Sussex:						
2000	.314	.236	.161	.253	.248	.195
1990	.478	.365	.255	.507	.444	.395
1980	. . .	. . .	. . .	. . .	. . .	. . .
1970	. . .	. . .	. . .	. . .	. . .	. . .
Union:						
2000	.670	.265	.603	.633	.477	.570
1990	.710	.275	.620	.696	.523	.535
1980	.716	.350	.597	.685	.575	.535
1970	.700	. . .	.705	. . .	.581	. . .
Warren:						
2000	.356	.265	.241	.344	.245	.185
1990	.435	.270	.238	.485	.351	.307
1980	. . .	. . .	. . .	. . .	. . .	. . .
1970	. . .	. . .	. . .	. . .	. . .	. . .
New York:						
Bronx:						
2000	.729	.502	.673	.586	.317	.465
1990	.733	.537	.694	.610	.316	.504
1980	.712	.461	.664	.646	.356	.556
1970	.687	. . .	.698	. . .	.287	. . .
Dutchess:						
2000	.547	.297	.332	.556	.294	.390
1990	.586	.356	. . .	.664	. . .	. . .
1980	. . .	. . .	. . .	. . .	. . .	. . .
1970	. . .	. . .	. . .	. . .	. . .	. . .

Table 5A.2. *(continued)*

	NON-HISPANIC WHITE/BLACK	NON-HISPANIC WHITE/ASIAN	NON-HISPANIC WHITE/HISPANIC	BLACK/ASIAN	BLACK/HISPANIC	ASIAN/HISPANIC
Kings (Brooklyn):						
2000	.856	.456	.668	.822	.601	.585
1990	.862	.445	.679	.784	.589	.559
1980	.869	.484	.672	.751	.611	.582
1970	.818	. . .	.726	. . .	.545	. . .
Nassau:						
2000	.804	.354	.473	.731	.470	.467
1990	.828	.321	.430	.771	.536	.449
1980	.831	.378	.353	.779	.613	.440
1970	.783	. . .	.645	. . .	.697	. . .
New York (Manhattan Co.):						
2000	.765	.460	.718	.732	.441	.670
1990	.765	.519	.694	.744	.424	.652
1980	.760	.549	.652	.755	.509	.631
1970	.756	. . .	.634	. . .	.567	. . .
Orange:						
2000	.506	.282	.389	.430	.201	.350
1990	.543	.366	.396	.546	.239	.454
1980	.560	.558	.418	.749	.373	.695
1970	. . .	. . .	. . .	. . .	. . .	. . .
Putnam:						
2000	.199	.133	.148	.219	.172	.188
1990	.410	.261	.175	.446	.470	.261
1980	.515	.415	.290	.636	.531	.459
1970	. . .	. . .	. . .	. . .	. . .	. . .
Queens:						
2000	.816	.442	.515	.780	.693	.413
1990	.817	.450	.494	.782	.661	.356
1980	.831	.468	.498	.825	.704	.394
1970	.840	. . .	.548	. . .	.665	. . .
Richmond:						
2000	.742	.332	.424	.649	.371	.345
1990	.746	.353	.373	.702	.447	.423
1980	.729	.295	.366	.700	.413	.389
1970	.661	. . .	.612	. . .	.353	. . .
Rockland:						
2000	.604	.316	.430	.468	.469	.422
1990	.573	.318	.404	.482	.501	.473
1980	.587	.284	.382	.604	.544	.495
1970	.660	. . .	.587	. . .	.650	. . .
Suffolk:						
2000	.670	.329	.465	.620	.407	.472
1990	.692	.349	.429	.680	.517	.488
1980	.711	.422	.382	.724	.580	.531
1970	.685	. . .	.554	. . .	.727	. . .

Table 5A.2. *(continued)*

	NON-HISPANIC WHITE/BLACK	NON-HISPANIC WHITE/ASIAN	NON-HISPANIC WHITE/HISPANIC	BLACK/ASIAN	BLACK/HISPANIC	ASIAN/HISPANIC
Westchester:						
2000	.663	.285	.545	.585	.419	.480
1990	.673	.310	.515	.654	.456	.509
1980	.672	.390	.476	.648	.473	.527
1970	.668	...	.776	...	.716	...
Pennsylvania:						
Pike:						
2000	.434	.197	.246	.300	.223	.150
1990	.440	.304	.242	.629	.246	.438
1980	...	...	...	...	...	...
1970	...	...	...	...	...	...

PART II

SOCIAL AND URBAN PROBLEMS

CRIME, EDUCATION, AND POVERTY

CHAPTER SIX

Metropolitan Crime Myths

Jack Katz

INTRODUCTION

Over the past twenty years, two very different stories have dominated the popular understandings of crime in New York and Los Angeles. To judge from the major metropolitan newspapers and the stated views of political and community leaders, Los Angeles has been plagued by gangs, and when law enforcement has tried to respond to the problem, the results have been worse than simply ineffective (Christopher and Independent Commission on LAPD 1991). In 1992, the release of the verdict acquitting Los Angeles policemen on charges of beating Rodney King set off an episode of urban anarchy; in retrospect, earlier antigang law enforcement crackdowns in the late 1980s and early 1990s were seen as contributing substantially to its causes. A series of subsequent scandals and reports of disorganization in law enforcement led to the replacement of two chiefs of police and the loss of elected office of two successive heads of the Los Angeles County district attorney's office. As of this writing, in spring 2001, the Los Angeles Police Department (LAPD) and the Los Angeles County district attorney's office remain mired in revelations that antigang officers in the Rampart and other divisions of the LAPD regularly stole and sold drugs, and on occasion even shot and framed alleged gang members (Chemerinsky 2000; Parks 2000). While crime declined in Los Angeles in the 1990s, virtually no one has seriously suggested that local law enforcement deserves the credit.

In New York in recent years, the media and political leaders have not attributed crime to youth gangs but to a diffuse culture of chaos, and the police department, closely controlled by the mayor, has been seen as extraordinarily successful in reducing crime through tight professional management of police personnel. Notorious instances of police abuse have occurred, but in contrast to the experience in Los Angeles, they have been resolved relatively quickly through locally organized prosecutions. And, while suspicions of racism and brutality haunt the New York Police Department (NYPD), New York's mayor, police chiefs, and local prosecutors have enjoyed widespread support and enviable professional reputations. New York's police leadership has been disseminating its management philosophy throughout the country and, indeed, the world (Bratton and Knobler 1998). New York's Mayor Giuliani, credited by the usually reserved *New York Times* for having produced a "marvel" of law enforcement (Silverman 1999, 3), was easily reelected in 1997 and was set to run for the U.S. Senate when health problems intervened.

In short, it would seem that the fundamentals of crime and law enforcement in the two largest metropolitan areas in the United States must be strikingly different. But if we look at crime rates and the routine realities of law enforcement over the past fifteen years, the differences evaporate. The overall picture is one of basic similarity colored by differences that do not consistently support either the understanding of the particulars of crime and law enforcement in New York or the perspectives held on them in Los Angeles that are conveyed by media, popular culture, and law enforcement leaders.

The contrast between the divergent portraits represented in popular cultures and the similar histories of criminal violence and police activity in the two cities are so extreme as to warrant an inquiry into metropolitan crime myths. By characterizing the views of crime and law enforcement in the two coastal cities as myths, I do not mean only that they are fundamentally wrong. Myth, a concept familiar in anthropology and historical theology but unfortunately usually heard only as a summary criticism when voiced in application to contemporary Western societies, is a useful technical term in the analysis of culture.

Three features are salient in assessing whether a belief is a myth. First, myths are not necessarily false; they are ideas about matters that, under current states of evidence and by the use of the logic of empirical research, cannot be established as true or false. Second, myths are not just guesses about the unknown; they are beliefs that resonate deeply because they address immediate existential concerns that they would resolve with presumptions. Third, myths are not simply emotionally evocative fantasies about central matters; they are profoundly consequential for the distribution of power in society.[1]

The sharp differences between Los Angeles and New York in their stories about crime and law enforcement call for at least three inquiries.[2]

First we need to document and reveal the systematic patterns in how crime and law enforcement are differentially interpreted in the two cities. Second, we should look at the actual evidence of crime and law enforcement activity in order to analyze the patterns of difference and similarity in the two cities. When we find that the myths are powerfully contradicted by the two metropolitan histories of crime and law enforcement, we are led to a third question. If patterns of crime and law enforcement cannot explain differences in the popular cultures that have emerged to interpret crime in Los Angeles and New York, what does? The evidence bearing on this question is neither as neatly organized as are statistics on crime and police activity nor as ready-at-the-fingertips as are the publications of major metropolitan newspapers. But three critical causes can be suggested: different immigration experiences, the structure of the two criminal justice systems, and the parochial concerns of metropolitan crime news.

Overall, we find that to explain differences in the stories told about crime and law enforcement in Los Angeles and New York, we must look at institutional and contextual factors that shape the generation of popular culture in the two regions. There are vast institutional stakes involved in sustaining a presumption that something as telling about collective life as crime must tell a fundamentally unique story in each city. In the end, we are left intrigued about a larger question, whether the more basic myth that is shaping metropolitan crime myths is that New York and Los Angeles are fundamentally different metropolitan areas.[3]

CRIME NEWS IN NEW YORK AND LOS ANGELES

Newspapers in New York and Los Angeles have promulgated many similar themes about crime and law enforcement in recent years: a terrifying rise of criminal violence in the late 1980s, amazing declines in the 1990s, a concentration of violence among youth and minorities, and stunning instances of police brutality. But closer inspection reveals patterned differences.

In each city's news, crime has been portrayed with an organizational character that is juxtaposed against the character of the organization of law enforcement; but the relationship between crime and official control in each city has been the obverse of the other. In New York, crime has been depicted as produced chaotically, with law enforcement agencies portrayed as professionally managed. In Los Angeles, crime has been attributed significantly to organized street gangs, with law enforcement described as chaotic, professionally compromised, and struggling un-

Table 6.1. Stories on Gangs in Metropolitan Newspapers

	1990 AND 1991	1997 AND 1998	SUM OF THE 4 YEARS
Los Angeles Times	1,393	775	2,168
New York Times	136	176	312

Source. Based on a search in Lexus/Nexus for the word "gang" in the headline and lead paragraph of all articles in the 1990, 1991, 1997, and 1998 *New York Times* and *Los Angeles Times,* Home Edition.

successfully with its own organizational disorder. If we take the coverage by the major city newspapers as an indication of popular culture, the general, everyday, presumptive understandings in the two urban areas appear to form a dialectic of dialectics.

Organization and Chaos in Images of Street Violence

In Los Angeles, gangs have long been the leitmotif for understanding crime.[4] In the early 1990s, the *Los Angeles Times* used "gang" in its headline or first paragraph to refer to local street youth groups at about ten times the rate as did the *New York Times* (table 6.1).[5] The relationship diminished somewhat through the decade, but a recent check shows that the comparison remains extreme.

At first glance, "gang" suggests that some form of organization is at least partially governing crime. When we look beyond the raw counts and examine how the two newspapers use the word "gang," subthemes emerge to enrich the contrast. In New York, "gang" more often takes on the nature of a verb, while in Los Angeles's constructions "gang" functions more like a noun. New York stories may be of offenders who "gang up" on someone, or who, in an adverbial phrase, attack "in a gang." Note that when used as a verb or adverb, "gang" describes a kind of attack but does not conjure up explanatory ideas or suggest why the attack occurred. Even when "gang" is used grammatically as the subject, as in "A gang of youths attacked," the reference to gangs often functions as a description of the kind of action rather than as a cause.

In Los Angeles's crime stories, gangs are postured as entities that preexist criminal victimizations, providing the motivation that explains them. There are many Los Angeles crime stories of the following sort (all taken from the *Los Angeles Times Index* of its 1991 editions). "Martha Naverette . . . became the 100th victim of street-gang violence in greater Los Angeles during 1991." Here the victim was not necessarily "ganged up" on but the message is that street gangs caused her death.

"Gang" in Los Angeles's crime culture is used as an adjective in ways that indicate not how violence was done but why: crimes are characterized as "gang confrontations," described as part of "gang warfare," labeled "gang-related" or as "drive-by" shootings, even when the only direct evidence reported is that of an assailant acting alone or of a victim's injuries. "Retaliation" is another common way that the gang idea implies an explanation. As situationally specific behaviors, retaliatory shootings may look no different than other shootings; the message is that they have presituationally formed motives.

Sometimes particular gangs (Bloods, Crips, White Fence, 18th Street, Trucha Salvadoreña) are named as the symbols that violence honors, but even when they are not, classic formulas such as "gang-infested area of Los Angeles" implies that gangs exist as live creatures, here as vermin, with ongoing destructive appetites. Just mentioning that a victim was in or associated with a gang or that attackers were gang members brings an explanatory thrust: "One youth was shot to death and two were wounded by gang members." "Gang," here, is a powerfully resonant part of a noun phrase; reading such descriptions, we already have images of why the event occurred: because revenge or territory claiming or even senseless attacks are the sorts of things gangs do.

When there is no description of ganging up or some other distinctive way that violence was situationally enacted, the assertion that, in any case, the crime was gang violence suggests that there was organization independent of the moment of victimization. Note how this formulation can ironically work a lack of evidence so that it satisfies the classic form of causal explanation. In order to avoid tautology, explanatory variables should be "independent," that is, they should vary or be shown to exist independent of the dependent variables that they would explain. "Ganging up" doesn't explain crime because it does not imply organization independent of the situation of victimization. It tells how the crime was done but not why. But an article asserting that situationally undistinguished violence was by a gang can suggest why, because it implies the existence of an entity that transcends moments of violence. Such a report can lend a hard sense of causality to an account of crime just because it does not describe how the crime was done. In Los Angeles, the very fact that there is no situational evidence of distinctive gang activity supports rather than undermines the gang myth.

Gang news organizes the reader's otherwise chaotic perception of crime. What is available for reporting on violence is usually mute result and brute fact, most commonly, that someone was shot. By suggesting gang involvement, what otherwise might be nothing more than a naked, unnerving description of victimization is immediately encased in explanatory imagery. If it does not put readers at ease, the gang connection at least suggests that order and discipline is available for their understanding. Often no offender is identified, either in the Los Angeles or New York stories on crime. But as the news in Los Angeles uses "gang" in crime stories, even if readers do not know who to target, they learn what to aim at: those gangs!

If New York does not use the street youth gang as a central trope for conceptualizing its problems of urban criminal violence, what does it use? Significantly, youths and street violence also loom large in New York's crime news coverage. But if the hermeneutic lenses for perceiving youth crime in Los Angeles come in a variety of gang colors, in New York the prevailing interpretive posture has been a caricature of existential philosophy. News coverage in New York stresses the randomness, wildness, and senselessness of crime. Images of chaos prevail.

One of the most famous street crimes in the nation in the early 1990s was the rape and near-fatal violent assault of a young female Wall Street professional who was jogging in Central Park. This attack was characterized as a "wilding," a term introduced into popular culture by this application. In early 1990 (January 19), the *New York Times* found it advisable to provide a definition of "wilding" as a phenomenon in which brazen urban youths rampage through streets. In this case, the attack had been a group effort, the attackers had been youths, many of the assailants had prior involvements with criminal law enforcement, and the attackers had associated with each other in their neighborhood before the event. Yet no effort was made to characterize the offenders as members of a gang. Recent revelations have underscored the wisdom of resisting the urge to impute gang causality to the event. (See the comments by David Halle at p. 41 of this volume.)

In another story from 1990, the *New York Times* reported that "loosely organized groups of young people who rob, rape or kill for money or fun are on the rise in New York City" (Lee 1990, B3). Just when the facts would seem to invite a gang label, the interpretation turns sharply away, leaving an overall impression not of social organization but of youth running in, around, and over superficial symbols of order. In other stories, the New York public learns that stabbings in Central Park are the work of a random, deranged killer (June 23, I1), that there is a wave of brutal, random crime in New York City (August 9, B1), that the increase in the murder rate in 1990 was caused by drug-related random violence (April 23, A1 and September 6, B1), and, to quote newspaper pidgin English, "New York City like Wild West" (August 6, B1). For their crime mythology, Manhattan writers here favor the symbolic world of the frontier, of humanity forced by the accumulated, incomprehensible forces of history to live on a territory that, while old, has evolved beyond the reaches of civilization.

The suggestion of chaos is heightened in stories about "drug gangs," which, despite the intersection of youth, collective associations, and illegal drug markets everywhere, are rare in Los Angeles's crime news. Gangs in Los Angeles are youth "street" gangs, associations that form around collective symbolic identities, which are understood to be compelling for adolescents and young adult men independent of specific acquaintance fights, assaults on strangers, or drug sales. But in New York, the imagery is of drug markets giving rise to vicious collaborations to exploit illegal opportunities. Thus even where there are gangs in New York's crime news, they tend to be indicators of the inherently chaotic realities of contraband markets.

One can already see how the style of reporting criminal violence in New York leads the public to look in wild desperation to criminal justice officials, not only for practical action but also for cognitive direction. This inclination is promoted more directly when gang news is about the mafia or organized crime gang, for example: "Law enforcement officials said yesterday that Vincent Gigante's racketeering conviction was unlikely to immediately weaken the Genovese crime family's powerful. . . ." (Raab 1997). Note the reliance on law enforcement expertise. We learn about crime families with the assistance of law enforcement expertise. When New York crime is not described as chaotic but as organizationally produced, as in news on organized crime, professional criminal justice officials are already at least partially in cognitive control, even if the "family's" power remains unchecked.

In Los Angeles, the contrast of organized street gangs and the disorganized law enforcement system opens a distinctive cognitive space for intermediary actors. One genre of crime stories reports the efforts of neighborhood organizations and community groups to mobilize resistance to gang violence. Representative stories include topics such as the head of the "Community Youth Gang Services Project" denying that they are operating as informants for police and United Neighborhoods Organization mobilizing against gang violence.

Another intermediating organization often mentioned in Los Angeles gang stories is the school: a "31-year-old 'gang counselor' suffers anxiety attacks from stressful occupation but refuses to give up." Vandalism does $27,000 damage to an elementary school, and gang graffiti is found in the bathrooms. A "fight erupted between rival gangs and escalated into a brawl between black and Latino students" at Inglewood High School.

In contrast, along with the small number and special category of organized crime stories, the drug gang story in New York stresses barbarism, a set of people beyond the reach of sympathetic efforts at social control:

> They called themselves the Cut Throat Crew, and the authorities say that in one horrific incident, the drug gang more than lived up its name—by beating, trying to rape and then throwing a customer off an apartment roof to her death.
>
> When the gang was not demanding payment from its customers, investigators said, it was solidifying control of a $150,000-a-week heroin empire on the Lower East Side, squelching competition through violence and using children as young as 14 to ferry drugs to customers. (Roane 1998)

One would not expect to find counselors employed to work with New York's drug gangs or mafia families. The New York conception of local gang problems does not set the stage for innovative programs of intervention through schools, neighborhood associations, and city-funded alternative activity programs such as night basketball and summer camps; it cries out to law enforcement agencies as a desperate community's last chance.

Organization and Chaos in Images of Law Enforcement

Los Angeles's gangs shade into youth culture and, thus, into the social worlds of schooling. Los Angeles's crime news thus carves out a large role for amateur intermediaries, such as community groups, and non–law enforcement professionals, for example, school counselors. The trope of the non–law enforcement intermediary amplifies the dialectic between gang-organized youth and the police. The work of the intermediaries implicitly casts the police as, at best, irrelevant and, at worst, through alienating at-risk youth, routinely counterproductive, even when they are not racist and corrupt.

The cognitive space that is filled in Los Angeles with neighborhood groups, charitable and publicly funded antigang programs, school counselors, and school-sponsored conflict resolution sessions is filled in New York by references to the multiple law enforcement offices that are constantly supervising disorder, each poised within its particular jurisdictional boundaries to sweep down and pick up some of the bad guys. Robert Morgenthau, who long ago became a venerable institution as Manhattan's district attorney, is credited with descending on the "Cut-Throat" gang of drug dealers. Strike Force agents, from the Federal Bureau of Investigation and prosecution offices of the Justice Department, track the destinies of mob families. A police expert on Chinatown gangs, commenting on the background to acts of violence by young men in the Flying Dragons, explains the gang's links with economic power groups in Chinatown, immigrant labor management, and home country tongs.

The contrasting images of the etiology of criminal violence in New York and Los Angeles have been complemented by opposite images given to law enforcement over the past decade. In Los Angeles in the 1990s, the image of organized street gangs was first used to create an inverse portrait of a disorganized police force in the context of the spring 1992 rebellion/riot following the verdict in the prosecution of LAPD officers for beating Rodney King. Early news reports attributed the outbreak of the anarchy to marauding bands of gang youth. Indeed, the LAPD set up this interpretation by its dramatic "gang sweeps" in the late 1980s and early 1990s. Drawing personnel from distant bureaus, the LAPD assembled large forces that on given nights entered South Central, low-income African-American neighborhoods in a kind of blitzing action, arresting scores of young men based on perceptions of their gang affiliation. For lack of evidence of criminal behavior other than curfew violations, the vast majority were released after a night or two in jail. When the verdict acquitting LAPD officers of beating King was announced in far off Simi Valley, it instantly reverberated through South Central, and young men were soon seen on TV, vandalizing stores, setting buildings on fire, moving in carloads through the center of the city, and beating non-African-Americans whom they had dragged out of cars. The most famous videotaped street assault was carried out by a set of young men including "Football Williams," who was identified as a gang member and was later arrested in a publicity event personally led by LAPD chief Daryl Gates.

In a report scheduled to be released on May 1, 1992, but which was delayed several weeks since May 1 turned out unexpectedly to be the third day of the King riots, Ira Reiner (1992, 1), then district attorney of Los Angeles, opened with the declaration: "As the 20th century draws to a close, Los Angeles is generally acknowledged to have the worst street gang problem in the United States, if not the world." According to this report, every other black adolescent in Los Angeles was a member of a street gang.

The King riots added to the disgrace that the much-aired videotape of the police beating of Rodney King had already brought the LAPD. Gates was removed as chief (although his removal had to await his decision to retire), a new chief was brought in from Philadelphia and, after his penchant for accepting free hotel accommodations in Las Vegas was publicized, his contract was not renewed. For years, the department was depicted in Los Angeles politics and news as in chaos. Later in the 1990s, when a veteran LAPD African-American police officer took over as chief, it appeared for a brief period that the LAPD was on its way toward tight internal discipline and a recovery of professional respectability. Then, as the ironic result of an internal investigation launched by the new chief, Bernard Parks, the Rampart scandal broke, in which it was revealed that LAPD officers had extorted money from drug dealers, had themselves dealt drugs, and, apparently in connection with these crimes, had shot citizens and covered up the shootings by framing the victims. The events initially reported occurred in the Rampart division, although similar allegations later appeared in other areas of the city. Notably, the officers involved had been acting in antigang units. As the scandal grew more intense, reports began to appear of widespread abuse of youths' rights by antigang officers.

Thus the dialectical relationship in Los Angeles in the 1990s between images of gang-organized criminality and organizationally undisciplined police officers was not a matter of coincidence. The former image was the solid foundation on which the latter image was rapidly constructed. An obverse dialectic emerged at more or less the same time in New York. Just as the perception in Los Angeles about the nature of crime as organized by gangs led to the disorganization of law enforcement, in New York the perception of a baffling chaos as the breeding ground of crime shaped the organization of law enforcement.

Under Mayor Rudolph Giuliani, the NYPD became famous for a zero-tolerance policy, which in police rhetoric and popular understanding meant two things. One was that, if the law did not mandate less punishment for first offenses, neither would the police. The second was that minor infractions would be treated as seriously as major crimes. New Yorkers were treated to a series of stories describing the NYPD not only punishing homeless men for urinating in public but also arresting well-dressed Wall Street workers for smoking marijuana in public. Property was seized from unlicensed street vendors; trespassers and "squeegee men" were arrested; parking law scofflaws had their cars impounded and sold. Earlier, the transit police had mounted a campaign against graffiti, and for the first time in years, subway trains began to appear free of graffiti. William Bratton, the chief of the transit police, rode on his subterranean success to become the first of Mayor Giuliani's appointees to the head of the NYPD.

Chaos, not just crime, was being attacked. Citing the "broken windows" theory promoted by university academics James Q. Wilson and George Kelling (Wilson and Kelling 1982), Giuliani and his police chiefs argued that signs of disorder regularly escalated through a series of steps into serious criminal violence. Broken windows, graffiti, and abandoned cars left for weeks on the streets were interpreted by street criminals as signs that an area was not being supervised and, thus, as a license to use areas criminally, for example, to hold drug markets openly. Contraband drug markets in turn bred chaotic struggles over distribution rights that led to violence.

But the broken windows theory was only the street side of the alleged transformation of law enforcement. Within the NYPD, the leadership proclaimed a revolution in management style, and it was this new internal policy, particularly a tightening of discipline within the supervisory ranks, that was said to have given effect to zero-tolerance policies (Bratton and Knobler 1998). Within police administration, the antidisorder effort was thought to decrease crime not by garnering a newfound respect for order in the hearts of the masses but through more practical means. When the police stopped young men on minor infractions, such as jumping subway turnstiles, they would check them for outstanding warrants and unpaid fines, and they would frisk them for concealed weapons. It became riskier to carry guns, and the suppression of spontaneous gun violence, it was reasonably thought, would significantly reduce homicide.

The mayor and the police leadership took great pride in claiming that they had reduced crime not simply by being tough with all miscreants but by exercising sophisticated discipline within police ranks as well. Computer tracking of crime trends began in this period, and the top echelon of NYPD leaders began holding review meetings with subordinates in which they would be held accountable for knowing what the data showed about their areas of responsibility and for allocating their personnel in response. On one side, the audience for police leaders was the bad guys on the street, on the other, perhaps more personally important side, it was elite business school–trained CEOs on whom they modeled their administration (Bratton and Knobler 1998; Silverman 1999, 89).

If we compare the experiences of the two cities in terms of police brutality cases in the 1990s, we get a sobering reminder that we are dealing with mythology. One might think that the greater public respect, apparent managerial discipline, and organizational unity of the NYPD made a difference in lowering the level of police brutality, but there is no clear evidence to that effect. As the LAPD was rocked in the 1990s by publicity over the brutalization of Rodney King and of Latino gang members by Rampart Division officers, NYPD officers were revealed to have engaged in mind-boggling brutality against Abner Louima and Amadou Diallo. Louima, a black Haitian immigrant, had been arrested for a brawl outside a nightclub. In a Brooklyn precinct station, a white officer "shoved a broken-off broom handle up his rectum, then waved the feces-covered stick under his nose and threatened to kill him" (Morgenthau 1999, 42). Amadou Diallo was killed in a gratuitous, tidal wave assault by four white members of "the city's élite Street Crime Unit" (Chua-Eoan 2000, 26). Diallo, a West African immigrant, was at the time isolated, unarmed, and innocently engaged. The police fired forty-one bullets at him in a matter of seconds on the apparent perception that he was acting evasively and pulling out a gun (it was a wallet). Addressing more routine practices of the NYPD, the New York State attorney general issued a probing critique suggesting racism in stop-and-frisk practices (Spitzer 1999).

But there are notable differences in the social meanings and organizational implications of police scandals in the two cities. In New York, even when extreme police brutality has surfaced, there has been no parallel in recent years to the Los Angeles riots following the verdict in the prosecution of officers in the Rodney King case. The Mollen Commission investigated a scandal about NYPD drug dealing that broke in 1992, eventually implicating six precincts in widespread drug trafficking, massive perjury, and brutality related to corruption. Mayor Giuliani responded by abolishing a city council–created police oversight committee in favor of a new commission of his creation; his police chief, Bratton, developed a plan to train police to testify truthfully. Both Giuliani and Bratton continued to enjoy widespread public support. The ink on the Mollen report was barely dry when the *New York Times* was celebrating the achievements of the NYPD. Even in reporting the police killings, local and national news media treat the NYPD with respect. *Time* magazine, for example, wrote of the elite Street Crime Unit that "it had been tremendously successful. Though making up less than 2 percent of the police force, the SCU [Street Crime Unit] accounted for more than 20 percent of the city's gun arrests. . . . The murder rate plummeted" (Chua-Eoan 2000, 26).

In New York, scandals lead to commissions that recruit locally prominent lawyers, who use their experience as a stepping-stone to prosecutorial and judicial office. (See the review in Chin 1997, 1:xii–xvi.) The same process through which the city officially damns the police department functions as a moral certification for new legal leaders. This pattern, which is barely known in Los Angeles, is so well established in New York that, when police scandals break, New York's would-be elite appreciate the opportunities for professional elevation through public service that will ensue.[6]

In the two famous New York police brutality cases of the late 1990s, prosecutions were handled by African-American-led district attorneys. While Robert Johnson, the black Bronx district attorney, lost in the Diallo case, the racial composition of the legal drama was evident to the public. The Louima cases were successfully handled by Zachary Carter, the African-American head of the U.S. attorney's office for Brooklyn. If the public could not take assurance that police brutality would be less likely in New York in the future, there were grounds to believe that, in some fundamentally important respects, the law enforcement system in the area works admirably.[7]

Meanwhile in Los Angeles, not only was the LAPD in crisis during virtually the entire decade of the 1990s, the Los Angeles district attorney's office has suffered continuous public attacks. Two successive heads of the prosecution office, Ira Reiner early in the decade and Gil Garcetti at the end, lost reelection bids. And the Los Angeles police commission and mayor have failed to regain apparent control of the LAPD, with the mayor firing the head of the police commission and the U.S. Justice Department threatening to take over control of the LAPD because of a lack of responsiveness to the civil rights violations revealed by police scandals. Three years after a beating of a suspect, eighteen months after the revelation of the beating in an internal LAPD investigation, there is no end in sight to the probe of the Rampart Division antigang officers for brutalizing suspects, stealing drugs from them and from the police evidence lockup, and in one instance, for planting a gun and framing a defenseless suspect who became paralyzed from a police shooting.

CRIME AND POLICING PATTERNS

The New York and Los Angeles myths about crime and law enforcement imply several patterns in the histories of the two cities. In Los Angeles, where youth gangs were portrayed as responsible for crime, one might reasonably expect to find that youth violence rose relatively more rapidly when overall crime rates in both cities soared. Given the claims made in New York that policing policies uniquely brought about a turnaround in crime, one might think that there was a dramatic decline in New York's crime unmatched in Los Angeles's experience. With respect to measures of law enforcement activity, the two metropolitan crime cultures lead us to expect an unusual concentration of police activity against adolescents in Los Angeles, at least in the period before the LAPD scandals of the 1990s; and in New York, an intensification of law enforcement activity that could have brought about the decline of crime in the 1990s.

What data may we consult to assess these implications? Apart from public medical examiners' offices, the police generate virtually the only readily available, regularly produced data about crime and police activities, but we must be especially wary of police statistics here. After all, the police in Los Angeles and New York have been strong advocates of their respective city's myths. Although we have no satisfactory alternative to the data generated by law enforcement activity, some police data are generally accepted as being "harder" than others. For measuring crime, these are data describing the annual number and some demographic characteristics of victims of homicide, while for measuring police activity, they are statistics describing the annual number and some demographic features of people arrested for homicide.[8] In the following discussion, I cite only population data, homicide counts by year and age, and arrest counts by year and age. With these limited resources we can still generate telling analyses.

We are especially interested in gang crime and police action against gang crimes, but the police never have reliably produced gang statistics over a period of several years, much less by using the same coding procedures in different cities.[9] Still, to measure events relevant to gang-aged youth, we can carve out a reasonable age category for organizing the standard victimization and arrest data. Homicides generally drop significantly after early childhood and rise sharply in late adolescence, thus adolescent homicide is defined here as crime by or to sixteen- to nineteen-year-olds.

We note first that overall homicide rates over time do not sustain the claim that the police in New York did something distinctive to lower the crime rate.[10] If we look at the changes between 1990 and 1998, the perception in New York of a greater decline is modestly consistent with the New York myth. The drop in Los Angeles is 57 percent compared to a drop in New York of 73 percent. Something miraculous arguably happened, but the difference in the decline in the two cities does not make an overwhelming case for attributing saintly powers to the police in New York, and if we look within a longer time frame, the city differences diminish further. Thus, contrasting the rates in 1984 and 1998, the rate of homicide dropped 60 percent in New York and 50 percent in Los Angeles (table 6.2). At the least, there would seem to be reason for substantial celebration in Los Angeles as well as in New York. It is not the historical experience with crime victimization but the lack of morally eligible candidates that explains why no one has been raised to hero status on Los Angeles's collective shoulders.[11]

Table 6.2. Homicides: Number and Rate per 10,000 Population

					RATE CHANGE (%)			
	1984	1990	1994	1998	1984–98	1984–90	1990–94	1994–98
Los Angeles	2.39 (758)	2.81 (983)	2.37 (845)	1.20 (426)	−50	18	−16	−49
New York	2.00 (1,450)	3.00 (2,262)	2.02 (1,566)	0.81 (638)	−60	50	−33	−60

Sources. Population data: U.S. Bureau of the Census 1982, pts. 6 and 34; 1992, pts. 6 and 34; 2000a. All intercensus years estimated from differences between prior and postdeccenial year figures. Homicide data from California Department of Justice, Criminal Justice Statistics Center; Special Request Section; State of New York, Division of Criminal Justice Services, Office of Justice System Analysis, Bureau of Statistical Services.
Note. Unless otherwise noted, in all tables and figures in this chapter, Los Angeles refers to the city of Los Angeles, not the county. Figures in parentheses are numbers of homicides.

It is especially revealing to observe that New York started this period, in 1984, with a substantially lower homicide rate than Los Angeles did. Homicides in New York jumped up much more in the late 1980s than they did in Los Angeles, rising fully 50 percent from 1984 to 1990, as compared to only 18 percent in Los Angeles. Much of the perception of an incredible decline in New York in the 1990s can be explained by the city's exceptionally accelerated increase in crime in the late 1980s. As a mayoral candidate in 1993, Rudolph Giuliani was eager to blame the incumbent administration for New York's crime crisis, but a rapid rise in criminal violence was a national phenomenon in the late 1980s (the national homicide rate of fourteen- to seventeen-year-olds tripled from 1984 to 1998, rising from 4.2 to 12.1 per 100,000; from 1984 to 1991, the homicide victimization rate of black males aged fourteen to seventeen went from about eighteen to about seventy-two per 100,000 [Fox 2000, 295, 300]), and there has been no serious argument that a breakdown in police activities was the cause. New York and Los Angeles were part of this national rise, and if there was any miracle in the New York story it was that the rising wave moved through the two cities with a slightly different historical timing that was blessedly fortuitous for Rudolph Giuliani's career.

Note that, looking only at the drop in New York, the details do not fit the story that credits the toughness of the new mayor or the new management policies that his police chiefs brought in. Giuliani and his new police chief, William Bratton, only came into office in January 1994. Their new policies started at the earliest in 1994. But in the period 1990–94, the homicide rate in New York had already dropped 33 percent. It appears that whatever was happening to reduce crime in New York started before Giuliani's administration took office, and then essentially continued, picking up a slightly greater pace in the overall period 1990–98. Had there been no acceleration in the rate of decline, and had the pre-Giuliani trend simply continued, the 1998 rate still would have been less than half the 1990 rate. Note, also, that the drop in New York during the period 1994–98, when the NYPD/Giuliani regime was touted as having achieved miracles, was only slightly faster than the drop in Los Angeles. In the period 1990–94, however—before Giuliani and Bratton came into power—homicide in New York was dropping twice as fast as it was dropping Los Angeles. If mayoral policies and police management are to be credited with lowering crime rates, these comparative data suggest that it was the regime of Mayor David Dinkins that should be credited.

The image of New York's exceptional drop, and the exuberant crediting of its police for it, was not created out of whole cloth. The New York crime myth was a product of three powerful and common biases in the popular reading of crime data. The first is a practice of not looking comparatively at the experience in other cities, especially the experience in Los Angeles. As the country's second largest city and because of police debacles of the 1990s, Los Angeles was strategically positioned for any serious examination of the effects of police management on crime rates.

The second bias in the New York view was due to the habit of looking at raw homicide numbers, not rates. New York newspapers and politicians could correctly and with great emotional impact point to a much larger number of lives saved by the crime decline. The decline in New York is given powerful additional human weight when it is observed, as it frequently was, that a specific large number of people, 1,624, were alive at the end of 1998 but would have been dead had rates remained what they were in 1990. In Los Angeles, the comparable figure would be 557, and even if the difference is significantly due to the much larger size of the New York city population as compared to the city of Los Angeles (8 million vs. 3.7 million), politicians in New York were eager to brush aside statistical niceties about "rates" versus raw numbers by invoking images of the very numerous bodies they could claim their policies had kept warm and mobile.

Finally, the time spans guiding the New York perceptions were misleading. The decline in the 1990s in New York seemed to be especially dramatic in part because the decline started from a significantly higher peak relative to rates in the prior decade. And more generally there seems to be a lag in media and popular cultural recognition of changes in crime rates. Rates began falling significantly during the mayoral administration of David Dinkins, but the search for someone to credit only began after Rudolph Giuliani was in office.

Table 6.3. Male Homicide Victims 16–19 Years Old per 10,000 Males 16–19, Rates and Numbers

	1984	1990	1994	1998
Los Angeles	6	12	12	5
	(63)	(125)	(135)	(60)
New York	5	12	9	3
	(110)	(232)	(164)	(57)

Sources. On victimization: for New York—1984, New York Police Department, Office of Management and Planning, Crime Analysis and Program Planning Section; 1990, 1994, 1998, State of New York, Department of Criminal Justice Services, Office of Justice System Analysis, Bureau of Statistical Services; and for Los Angeles, all years— California Department of Justice, Criminal Justice Statistics Center, Special Request Section. On population: for New York—1984 figure estimated from 1980 and 1990 census figures; 1990, 1994, 1998, figures from U.S. Census Bureau, Population Division, Administrative Records and Methodology Research; and for Los Angeles—1984 figure estimated from 1980 and 1990 figures faxed from census; 1998 figure from Current Population Survey (CPS); 1994, estimated from 1990 census and 1998 CPS figures.
Note. Figures in parentheses are the number of victims.

If a comparative view of the historical record of homicide victimization substantially undermines the celebration of law enforcement policies in New York, what light is shed on the myth of gang violence in Los Angeles by a similar inquiry? Here we can usefully focus on data describing adolescent homicides and arrests of adolescents for homicide.[12] Table 6.3 shows that the adolescent homicide victimization rates in Los Angeles and New York are strikingly similar, especially for the period from the mid-1980s to 1990. As we have seen, these were the years in which the news media, law enforcement, politicians, and community groups were intensely alarmed about youth street gangs, attributing to them major responsibility for the increase in the city's crime rate. Again, as we saw in detail above, no similar attribution was made in New York.

Now, these data can be still reconciled with a view that youth street gangs are much more prevalent in Los Angeles. It is not inevitable that a city with a distinctive problem of violent youth gangs would have a higher youth homicide rate. But if youth gangs are not raising the homicide rate beyond what it otherwise would be, it is not immediately clear why political, police, and communal demands for punitive attentions should focus on them. Note, moreover, that to the extent that there is a difference between the increase in youth violence in the two cities during the 1984–90 period, it was New York that had the greater increase not just in overall homicide but specifically in adolescent homicide. These data make one doubly curious—in terms of not only why in Los Angeles in this period there were community-supported, mayoral-encouraged, district attorney– and police-organized "sweeps" of black poverty areas to arrest gang members but also why a distinctive story about subcultures of youth deviance did not arise in New York.

Table 6.4. Percent of All Homicide Victims Who Were 16–19

	1984	1990	1994	1998
Los Angeles	9	14	17	15
New York	9	11	11	10

Sources. See table 6.3.
Note. Percentages include both males and females.

Consider now the comparative change in the two cities over the entire fifteen-year period. In both cities there was a startlingly rapid rise in the victimization of adolescent males in the late 1980s, the homicide rate doubling on both coasts. And there was a startling drop in victimization of adolescent males in both cities in the late 1990s. As with the total homicide rates reviewed earlier, New York shows slightly more dramatic changes, rising more up to 1990, but only because it started at a slightly lower base rate, and then dropping further in the 1990s.

The doubling of youth homicide in the late 1980s was, of course, phenomenal; it would provoke a search for understanding among the most somnambulant organs of popular culture. In table 6.4, we begin to see why popular culture in Los Angeles might especially focus its imagination on youth gangs. Even if adolescents were not becoming more violent in Los Angeles more rapidly than in New York, it is true that in the late 1980s, and ever since, they have been a bigger part of the Los Angeles crime story than they were earlier and than they are in New York. Note (from table 6.3) that between 1990 and 1998, adolescent homicide rates dropped enormously in Los Angeles, by 58 percent. But (see table 6.4) the 1998 percentage of all Los Angeles homicide victims who were adolescents was still 67 percent higher than it had been in 1984, while in New York, adolescents contributed a relatively steady percentage to the overall city homicide victim statistics.

It was easy to look too quickly at elements in this historical picture and believe that youth gangs were becoming more violent in Los Angeles or at least a bigger problem in the city, even when youth homicide victimization plummeted. Youth violence was becoming worse in Los Angeles over this fifteen-year period but only as compared to other forms of violence. Youth violence did shoot up in the 1980s, and when it declined significantly in the 1990s, other forms of violence declined even more rapidly, leaving youth violence as a larger part of the overall violence problem in Los Angeles.

Some of the biases that we previously found to be sustaining the myth of a police-engineered turnaround in New York have supported the gang myth in Los Angeles. In particular, news reports and official commentary on crime in Los Angeles almost never make a comparative reference to trends in New York or any other city. But something else has been distorting the understanding in Los Angeles: the changing absolute size of the foreign-born youth population. From 1970 to 1990, the number of foreign born in the population aged fifteen to nineteen years old rose from 50,000 to 246,000 in Los Angeles County and from 92,000 to 126,000 in New York City. This rapid increase in the presence of foreign-born adolescents in the Los Angeles area in the 1980s may have enhanced sensitivities that were profoundly irritated by concurrent crime rate increases.

In the 1980s, the gang myth was literally institutionalized in Los Angeles's culture. The California attorney general's office pressed police departments across the state to label more and more events as gang crimes. Los Angeles's police chief and district attorney in the late 1980s and early 1990s invented catchy labels, such as "Operation Hammer," for mass arrests of alleged gang members. Community groups, including many that had been severely critical of Los Angeles's police chief Daryl Gates, thanked him for organizing the sweeps and remained supportive up to the release of the videotape of the Rodney King beating.

> Reactions of South Los Angeles residents to the police incursions into gang-infested neighborhoods over the past two nights were nearly unanimous: Get the gang-bangers off the streets—fast and for good.
>
> And while some argued that innocent people often get caught up in the sweeps, most of the residents agreed that the Police Department must increase its raids to eradicate gang violence. (Dawsey 1989, 26)[13]

The *Los Angeles Times* published stories on gang crimes at a frenetic pace up through the early 1990s, as we have seen. Once set so powerfully in motion, the fact that youth violence in the 1990s declined to a fraction of its earlier rate was not sufficient to kill the gang myth.

The histrionic mobilizations of Los Angeles law enforcement against gangs in the first half of the fifteen-year period obscured the double structure of the gang myth. The gang myth is not only a superficial popular cultural lens for interpreting Los Angeles's crime, it is also superficial in terms of understanding what has been happening with the area's law enforcement.

Arrests are key tools for investigation. If homicides are thought to occur because of the activities of gang youths, then arrests of youths thought to be gang associates would be a logical investigative strategy. When a set of criminals is suspected of involvement, it makes sense to arrest members and try to develop evidence by turning each against the others. One might reasonably expect an aggressive police department to be making a lot of homicide arrests, especially where it is thought that

Table 6.5. Homicide Arrests of Males Aged 16–19: Number and Percent of All Homicide Arrests

	1984	1990	1994	1998	% CHANGE IN HOMICIDE ARRESTS 1984–90	1990–98
Los Angeles	243	343	179	98		
	(19)	(33)	(32)	(27)	41	−71
New York	198	413	339	168		
	(18)	(29)	(27)	(21)	108	−50

Sources. California Department of Justice, Criminal Justice Statistics Center, Special Request Section; New York Police Department, Office of Management and Planning, Crime Analysis and Program Planning Section.
Note. Numbers in parentheses are percentages.

there are communication networks, like gangs, among those who are likely to know about homicides.

If youth gangs are thought to contribute significantly to criminal violence in Los Angeles, we might expect the police in Los Angeles to intensify arrests of adolescents when crime rates soar more than the police do in cities that also have soaring crime rates but where there is no prevailing belief that youth gangs distinctively contribute to crime. Table 6.5 shows that from 1984 to 1990, when crime rates soared in Los Angeles, adolescent arrests did rise by 41 percent, and when crime rates fell in the period 1990–98, adolescent arrests dropped by 71 percent. But the swings in New York do not indicate that the gang myth actually guided police arrest practices in Los Angeles. As we saw earlier, homicide jumped even more in the 1980s in New York, where, from 1984 to 1990, arrests of adolescents for homicide rose much more than they did in Los Angeles, by 108 percent, and then dropped by 50 percent in the 1990s.

A comparison of police practices in arresting adolescents in New York and Los Angeles continues the portrait of substantial similarity that we saw in homicide rates in general, a portrait that reveals somewhat more extreme shifts in New York. Read as reflections on the myth of a distinctive police policy in New York, these data are also disconfirming. Before the Giuliani administration took office, when crime soared in New York in the 1980s, the police were hardly passive in their response, nor did they respond more vigorously in the 1990s, at least as regards arrests of adolescents for homicide.

But these data do not allow us directly to compare crime rates with police practices. Perhaps myth-consistent differences between the two cities would appear if we examine how many adolescents the police ar-

Table 6.6. Adolescent Homicide Arrests per Adolescent Homicide Victim

	1984	1990	1994	1998
Los Angeles	3.5	2.5	1.2	1.5
New York	1.6	1.6	1.9	2.7

Sources. For Los Angeles and for New York victims, as in table 6.3; for New York arrests: New York Police Department, Office of Management and Planning, Crime Analysis and Program Planning Section; "adolescent" is defined as persons aged 16–19, combined male and female.

rest in each city for each adolescent homicide, during each of these four years. Perhaps the police in Los Angeles are consistently arresting more adolescents for each adolescent homicide than are the police in New York, and perhaps the New York police under Mayor Giuliani brought about their city's crime decline in part through an unusual commitment to arrest a great excess of adolescents per youth homicide.

Table 6.6 indicates a difference between the two cities over this fifteen-year period but again, not one that sustains the myths about crime and law enforcement in either city. In Los Angeles, arrests of youths for homicide, per homicide victim, drop in the 1980s, when youth homicides soar, as well as in the 1990s, when youth homicides dramatically decline. It is notable that the decline in police activity in Los Angeles was substantial in the late 1980s, even as crime rates were soaring, the gang myth was raging, and the police had broad community support to act aggressively against young suspects. The decline of police activity in rounding up adolescents on murder charges to get evidence on adolescent homicide, and to intimidate or otherwise deter would-be youth killers, did not wait for the early 1990s, when the Los Angeles police were supposedly "demoralized" by the publicity about police racism that was stimulated by the O. J. Simpson trial and by the historical staining of the reputation of the LAPD when the videotape of the beating of Rodney King was played and replayed around the world. The per-homicide arrests of adolescents dropped by half in the late 1980s and again by half from 1990 to 1994.

The sweeps against gang members staged by the LAPD in the late 1980s and early 1990s, and the damning of gang criminals by Los Angeles's police chief and district attorney in appearances on national TV news shows as well as in the local news media, were essentially publicity stunts. Other than the capture of a handful of youths on outstanding arrest warrants, it appears that these mass arrests made no significant contribution to law enforcement. The gang myth in Los Angeles is thus revealed to be a double myth, one that not only misleads with regard to the causes of crime but that has also masked what the police fundamentally do to enforce laws against major crimes.

Note also that in both cities, throughout this fifteen-year period, the direction of change in police practices runs either independently of or opposite to the direction of change in crime. At the end of the period, in 1998, the number of adolescent homicides in Los Angeles is about equal to the number in 1984 (sixty-five and sixty-nine, respectively), but the average number of adolescents arrested per adolescent homicide is less than half what it was in 1994. In New York, as murders of adolescents more than doubled in the late 1980s, the number of adolescents arrested per adolescent homicide remained constant. There was little change in this measure of police activity up to 1994. It was only at the end of this fifteen-year period, when adolescent homicide rates were at a celebrated low point, that youth arrests per homicide reached their height. To put it conservatively, it is far from clear that the intensification of law enforcement in New York preceded and caused rather than followed the decline in violent crime, at least for adolescent homicides. One might reasonably suggest that in the 1990s, the NYPD become more active only after crime began to drop dramatically.

It is arguable that rises and declines in criminal activity control the confidence and vigor of police activities more directly and obviously than that police action controls criminal activity. For the police to deter crime, they must reach an audience that is diffuse, indefinite, and at best only partially and loosely organized. With regard to the police, there are much more easily identifiable hearts and minds to control. The police continuously engage in a closely inspected discourse with the local media and politicians about official versions of crime realities. And a declining crime rate makes it easier for police to arrest more suspects per offense. Instead of imagining that what the police do affects the level of criminal activity, we should investigate how the historic reputations of law enforcement leaders are indirectly shaped by criminals as they cumulatively produce what becomes an official image of the ebb and flow of the sources of disorder.

HOW METROPOLITAN CONTEXTS SHAPE CRIME MYTHS

If a comparative examination of the histories of crime and policing in Los Angeles and New York does not justify the distinctive stories developed in the two metropolitan cultures, why have they taken such divergent forms? That the answer is far from simple is indicated by the impermanence of the dominant themes. The image of gang organized crime and chaotic law enforcement is no more rooted in the southern California landscape than is the obverse image of chaotic street violence and professionally organized law enforcement in New York. Indeed, today's myths reverse earlier images.

In the 1950s and 1960s, New York, not Los Angeles, was the ethnic city where gangs flourished. Organized crime covered not just the current entertaining interest in marginal remnants of mob families but labor racketeering, as in *On the Waterfront,* a successful movie in which Marlon Brando played a longshoreman caught between loyalties to a neighborhood-based gang, a girlfriend, and the welfare of his coworkers. *West Side Story,* first a Broadway musical and then a successful movie, depicted interrelations of school, urban youth, and immigrant cultures shaping street gang violence. Social research followed suit (Bloch and Niederhoffer 1958). Writing in the mid 1970s about *New York Times*'s gang stories, Walter Miller noted that "media coverage in New York . . . has been characterized by a period of considerable attention to certain types of gangs, a period of virtually no attention, and a period of renewed attention" (Miller 1976, 98).[14] Los Angeles was still a predominately non-"ethnic," white, native-born American city well into the 1960s. Carefree blond surfers, not black and Latino street gangs, dominated the image of Los Angeles youth. This image changed abruptly during the Watts riots of August 1965, but even as late as 1970, the county population was still 80 percent white (Sabagh and Bozorgmehr 1996, 87).

On the law enforcement side, for decades after the Second World War, the LAPD enjoyed a reputation for professionalism, lack of corruption, and disciplined internal management. Indeed, popular culture in Los Angeles often contrasted the LAPD with the corruption and slovenly appearance of the NYPD. In New York, there were six major scandals about bribery, contraband sales, and brutality by policemen and, at times, about prosecutors and judges as well, over the period 1894–1994, known under labels that described the heads of investigating commissions: Lexow, 1895; Curran, 1913; Seabury, 1932; Hefland, 1954; Knapp, 1972; and Mollen, 1994. Mollen Commissioner Harold Baer noted that, over "the past hundred years, New York City has experienced a twenty-year cycle of corruption, scandal, reform, backslide and fresh scandal in the New York City Police Department" (Chin 1997, 1:xvii–xviii).

The LAPD, in contrast, enjoyed a relatively pristine image for over half a century, stretching from a corruption scandal in the 1930s to the Rodney King beating in the early 1990s, much of it under the leadership of a police chief revered for imposing militaristic discipline within the department, William H. Parker. The image of the LAPD was established nationally by the TV show *Dragnet,* whose star, Jack Webb, wrote scripts in close association with the LAPD.[15] As the neatly attired detective Joe Friday, Webb each week would confront the disorganized lives of Los Angeles residents. Often still dressed in house robes at midday, the witnesses that Webb/Friday confronted were routinely messy in reporting the relevant evidentiary details, and the policeman as routinely had to exercise patient indulgence as he pressed witnesses for "the facts, Ma'am, just the facts." The chaos was out there in the socially unorganized sprawl of Los Angeles, not in the police department. Arrests, controlled by careful preparation, were relatively inconsequential parts of the show.

It is, however, not simply a matter of chance that the urban cultures of crime have developed in a contrasting fashion in the two cities. In the late 1980s, criminal violence shot up across the nation, and all organs of popular culture were exercised to make sense of the very real heightened level of terror on many city streets. The materials available for weaving narratives were distributed differently on the two coasts.

In southern California, the extraordinary demographic transformation documented elsewhere in this volume was well in progress. As noted above (see fig. 6.1), from 1980 to 1990, in Los Angeles but not in New York, there was a dramatic change in the percentage of the adolescent population that was born outside of the United States. In Los Angeles County, the figure changed from 14 to 39 percent in only ten years; in New York City, there was a modest rise, from 23 to 27 percent.

It has long been a pattern in U.S. cities that rapid increases in migrant youth population (which after the First and Second World Wars significantly included blacks coming to northern cities from the rural south) lead to gang formation (Thrasher 1963). Even though the evidence here indicates that gangs may not raise the level of violence beyond what it otherwise would be, gangs are, if nothing else, flashy symbolic vehicles that dramatically change the urban cultural landscape (Katz 1988, chap. 4).

Gangs should be understood as one crystallization of a much broader phenomenon. Immigrant youth are brought beyond neighborhood boundaries and into contact with each other, and with adolescents from older resident populations, by the urban school system. Home styles reflecting adult sensibilities, both immigrant and "country" identities, are massively replaced after primary school. Middle schools or junior high schools become steaming grounds of cultural creativity, where adolescents energetically devise new cultural clothes, seeking to mediate their interactions with masses of peer strangers through daily efforts

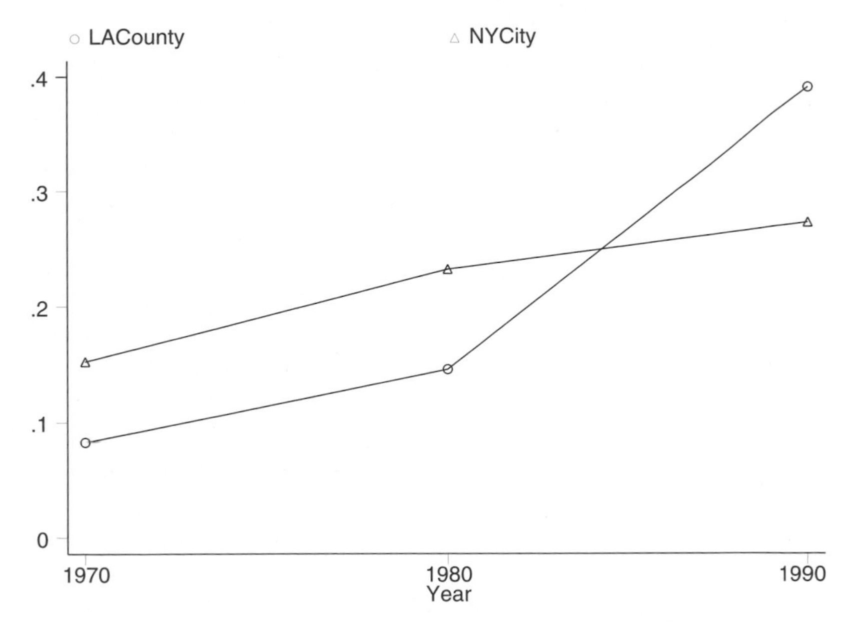

Figure 6.1. Proportion of 15–19-Year-Olds in Los Angeles County and New York City Who Were Born Outside the United States, 1970–90. "Born outside the United States" means that the person was not born in the fifty states or in Washington, D.C. It should be noted that this is slightly different from the commonly used variable "foreign born." Individuals who were born in U.S. territories (including Puerto Rico, Guam, American Samoa, etc.) are not foreign born but they are born outside the United States. Based on one-in-100 samples extracted from Ruggles et al. (1997).

to block, provoke, and dominate emotionally powerful attentions. The collective activity of fashioning new styles for wearing clothing, encoding hand gestures and novel body postures, writing graffiti, and designing bizarre hairstyles offers compelling audiovisual materials for popular culture, whether in the form of music videos, Hollywood movies, or city news coverage. Even while adolescent violence in Los Angeles jumped in parallel with adolescent violence in New York, it was the Los Angeles area that was featured in entertainment culture, such as Compton (MTV music videos on "gangsta rap" and hip hop music), East Los Angeles (the movie *Colors*), and South Central (the movie *Boyz 'n the Hood*).[16] Gangs are a small part of this feverish cultural creativity, but a part disproportionately represented by all popular culture institutions.

As put by Sabagh and Bozorgmehr in this volume, Los Angeles has experienced, over the past thirty years "the most dramatic increase in the foreign-born population for any large metropolitan area in the

United States, and indeed for the world" (102–3). Moreover, a great segment of the area's population remains in shadows because of illegal residential status. By 1992, "The total number of illegals in Los Angeles County in 1992 was estimated at 1.5 million persons" (106).

The institutions of popular culture in Los Angeles have been heavily pressed to provide some summary understanding of this sea change in the region's collective life. The very swiftness of the increase in population size and in the immigrant population has created a vast gap between social reality and the official representation of Los Angeles, for example, in political office. Further, if the immigrant population was not being officially counted or represented in the area's public life, still in everyday life Los Angeles residents, or anyone who moved around the city outside of the most affluent, most western neighborhoods, were confronted on all sides with blaring evidence of these changes. In New York, by contrast, much of the new Spanish-speaking residential population was never hidden in the shadows in a similar manner because, as Puerto Ricans, they entered as citizens. The extraordinarily seductive appeal of the gang trope in Los Angeles must be understood against a background of a huge demographic "dark figure." In lieu of alternative representations of the area's new realities, the colorful visibility of youth gangs struck an especially high profile.

The social worlds of immigrant and minority youth produce more than just an entertaining culture, of course. They also regularly produce a range of what are defined as problems, not only by the police but by school and other social welfare authorities as well. Even neglecting the stories on given acts of interpersonal violence, gang news would be a major phenomenon in Los Angeles because, in what has become a recurrent American pattern, the funding and mission of numerous urban social intervention programs are tied to the gang metaphor. The city council often supports, as "gang-intervention programs," a variety of social welfare services (job training, personal counseling, recreation facilities) that in other Western societies would not need the guise of crime prevention to get governmental support.

Gang news in Los Angeles is thus elaborately fabricated but not out of whole cloth. It is, in fact, supported by a distinctive if ironic pattern in Los Angeles's crime. As we have seen, although youth homicide rose and fell in Los Angeles as in New York, in Los Angeles the remarkable decrease in adolescent homicide was exceeded by an even more remarkable decrease in homicide in other age groups in the population. In the 1990s, youth crime ironically became an increasing problem in Los Angeles even as it fell dramatically. In these circumstances, the visibility of gangs as ubiquitous social phenomena in Los Angeles has become an irresistible explanatory resource.

What, then, of the contrasting images of law enforcement professionalism? In Los Angeles, the disgrace of law enforcement in the 1990s has been closely related to the gang myth. As noted, the county district attorney, which is the office with the immediate responsibility for supervising and enforcing legal constraints on the police department, was deeply complicit in the civil liberties abuses of the LAPD's antigang campaigns. Local district attorneys are always somewhat implicated in police abuses, since they depend on police-generated evidence in their routine criminal prosecutions and since the police apparently routinely fabricate or misrepresent evidence (e.g., by using anonymous "informant" evidence to ground requests for search warrants) throughout the nation. But in Los Angeles, when the county district attorney is compromised, there is no realistic alternative office to supervise the police department.

Consider the comparative structures of the criminal justice systems in New York and Los Angeles, particularly the relationship of police to prosecution offices (fig. 6.2). The LAPD is only one of forty-nine police departments overseen by the Los Angeles County district attorney, and the federal prosecutor, the central California U.S. attorney's office, has an even larger jurisdiction. In contrast, the NYPD is within the jurisdiction of seven prosecution offices, one for each borough (or county) that makes up New York City, plus two federal-level U.S. attorney offices. Just across the Hudson River, the U.S. attorney's office in New Jersey has occasionally come across evidence of official corruption crossing state lines and worked with New York prosecutors. The attorney general in New York State has occasionally played an important role in supervising the NYPD, for example, in a recent investigation on racial profiling (Spitzer 1999). And special prosecution offices are established from time to time to focus on official corruption.

One might think that the monopoly status and larger size of the county prosecutor in Los Angeles would make it more powerful with regard to the city police department, as compared to the smaller offices whose jurisdiction covers only parts of the NYPD's operations. But the social interaction within law enforcement offices in the two cities works in a manner opposite to this commonsense view. It is revealing that, within recent years, the Los Angeles law enforcement officials who have made political careers have come from the police department (Tom Bradley, Ed Davis), not the prosecution offices. In New York, the opposite has been the case, with Rudolph Giuliani first coming into the

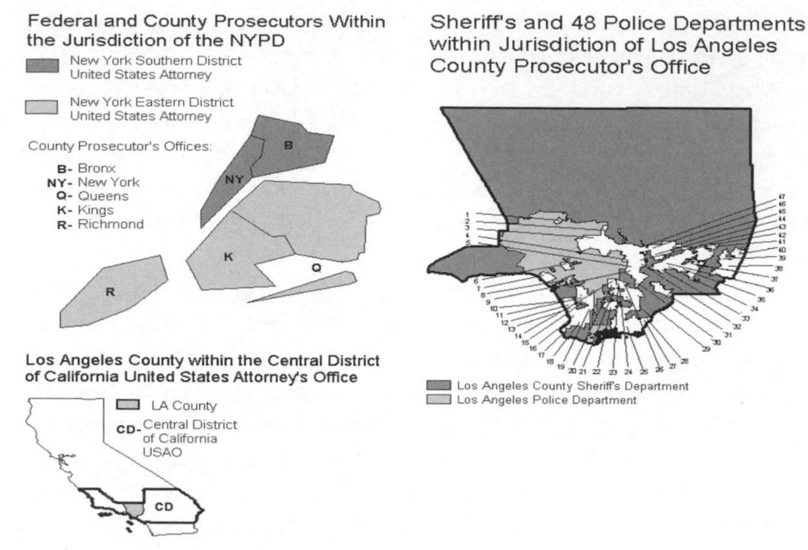

Figure 6.2. Prosecutorial and Police Jurisdictions, New York and Los Angeles. The jurisdiction of the Los Angeles County Prosecutor's Office includes the areas covered by the Los Angeles Police Department, the County Sheriff's Department, and areas policed by 47 smaller city departments, identified as follows: *1*, San Fernando; *2*, Glendale; *3*, Burbank; *4*, South Pasadena; *5*, Alhambra; *6*, Beverly Hills; *7*, Santa Monica; *8*, Culver City; *9*, Monterey Park; *10*, El Segundo; *11*, Inglewood; *12*, Manhattan Beach; *13*, Hermosa Beach; *14*, Vernon; *15*, Redondo Beach; *16*, Hawthorne; *17*, Palos Verdes Estates; *18*, Torrance; *19*, Gardena; *20*, Huntington Park; *21*, South Gate; *22*, Compton; *23*, Maywood; *24*, Bell; *25*, Signal Hill; *26*, Bell Gardens; *27*, Hawaiian Gardens; *28*, Long Beach; *29*, Downey; *30*, Montebello; *31*, Whittier; *32*, San Gabriel; *33*, El Monte; *34*, Baldwin Park; *35*, West Covina; *36*, Irwindale; *37*, Covina; *38*, Pomona; *39*, La Verne; *40*, Claremont; *41*, Glendora; *42*, Azusa; *43*, San Marino; *44*, Arcadia; *45*, Sierra Madre; *46*, South Pasadena; *47*, Pasadena.

public eye through anticorruption prosecutions he conducted as an assistant U.S. attorney in Manhattan.

In both metropolitan areas, the district attorney's office is an attractive stepping stone in a political career. But in Los Angeles, there is essentially only one stone available. For the chief district attorney, there is no need to take the risk of bringing innovative or controversial cases. One can rely on sensational murder cases or, if they are not conveniently available, antigang actions, to launch name recognition. If the Los Angeles County district attorney can survive his tenure without scandal, he is virtually guaranteed a clear shot at statewide office. The inability of Los Angeles district attorneys to avoid implication in LAPD scandals unexpectedly undermined their political prospects in the 1990s.[17]

In New York, the situation is more complex. Seven prosecution offices, each with its own public relations or press officers, each with its own social network in legal, business, and political communities, continuously jockeys for professional, sometimes public, esteem. As in Los Angeles, New York prosecutors are compromised by the routine necessity to rely on police evidence that they cannot independently test. But there is a tradition in some of the New York prosecution offices of taking risks in bringing cases against other law enforcement agencies.[18]

The revelation of police misconduct generates a distinctive ambivalence in the image of law enforcement in New York. On the one hand, there is no good evidence that police corruption or brutality is better controlled in New York than in Los Angeles. On the other hand, whenever the NYPD is officially condemned, some other part of the area's law enforcement community emerges with more prestige, and the image of law enforcement often takes on new appealing elements. As pointed out, the Diallo and Louima cases, in which blacks were brutalized or killed by white policeman, were handled by African-American-led prosecution offices, at the county level in the Bronx and at the federal level in Brooklyn. The Thomas Dewey model of advancing a political career through targeting official misconduct is deeply embedded in New York culture but virtually unknown in Los Angeles.

CONCLUSION

A dialectical relationship between the themes of chaos and organization, as applied to crime and law enforcement, has emerged within each metropolitan area through systematic if not inevitable processes. Los Angeles's immigration history has generated a youth culture represented vividly by street gangs, whose visibility provided the basis for a thoroughgoing, open conspiracy in local law enforcement to violate the civil rights of minority youth. When the law enforcement conspiracy unexpectedly backfired, the gang myth became the basis of law enforcement's disgrace.

In New York, the rapidly rising wave of criminal violence demanded some metaphoric effort at comprehension, and the slower growth in the immigrant youth population during the 1980s and the early years of the 1990s, plus the fact that the city's long history of absorbing immigration made it less plausible to finger immigrants as the new phenomenon to be blamed for the new crime wave, led to "chaos" as an interpretive solution.[19] The zero-tolerance law enforcement policy of the Giuliani administration made compelling local sense against this popular cultural background. And even when extraordinary evidence of extreme police brutality indicated a lack of management control and professionalism in the NYPD, some arms of the unusually differentiated local law enforcement system have emerged out of the ensuing climate of outrage with even brighter images of professional respectability.

That there is a dialectic of dialectics in the myths generated by the two cities is also not accidental because the image of each city has not developed independently of the image of the other. Many of the gang stories in the *New York Times* have actually been about Los Angeles gangs, especially in the early 1990s. New Yorkers understood the chaos of their youth violence against the background of Los Angeles's gang-organized violence. And in Los Angeles, New York's strange wilding assaults highlighted the long-familiar outlines of comprehensibly motivated drive-bys. Meanwhile, as Los Angeles has emerged as the nation's second largest city, popular culture in Los Angeles has quietly switched alter ego from San Francisco to New York. (Would the current volume be as obviously compelling a project were it a comparison of Los Angeles and San Francisco?) Looking at the two cities, it becomes clear that the relative lack of management leadership in Los Angeles is not simply myth. Apart from agencies representing artists, Los Angeles is now the central home office of virtually no major institutions. The leadership gap in prosecutorial law enforcement in Los Angeles receives little comment because it fits smoothly into the invisibility of political power, which resides not in the city's recent affable mayors but in distant and low profile county supervisors and with the invisibility of economic power that is exercised in distant institutional headquarters.

That the crime stories in New York and Los Angeles have been myths is not, however, due to any difference in the residents' gullibility. Crime news everywhere is never essentially about crime (Katz 1987). Like crime in the movies, crime in the news is about portraying existentially ambiguous features of personal identity and of the social landscape, for example, the nature of urban collective identity. It is not surprising that the popular cultures in Los Angeles and New York generate distorted views of the area's criminal realities. When looking at sensational cases of deviance, people are not so much curious to see what is most typical but what is most hidden in the backgrounds of their lives. In both cities, the institutions of popular culture offer people a series of broken mirrors to catch a reflection of faces they cannot otherwise see. What may be a bit surprising in all of this is that New York and Los Angeles seem to be working out a dialectical culture of fantasies in which they will increasingly find each other as their distorted reflections.[20]

CHAPTER SEVEN

Centralization versus Fragmentation

The Public School Systems of New York and Los Angeles

Julia Wrigley

At first sight, the similarities between the New York and Los Angeles school systems are striking. The largest and second-largest school districts in the country, they face severe problems with overcrowding, low student achievement, and crumbling buildings. Each has experienced the mass departure of middle-class students to suburbs and private schools. The two school systems absorb waves of immigrant students, who often live in poverty and speak limited English. Neither district has stable leadership, with superintendents routinely coming and going, who are hailed as saviors on first arrival only to be booted out unceremoniously a few years later. In both cities, the districts can barely muster the funds or the managerial will to build new schools. Construction projects frequently involve years of delays, confusion, and cost overruns. The loss of middle-class students has meant the loss of political clout. The Los Angeles and New York school boards have served as targets for the mayors of those cities, who assail them for ineptitude and protection of hidebound bureaucracies. Critics differ on proposed solutions to the problems of the public schools of New York and Los Angeles but not on the need for radical change. At the turn of the century, frustrated boards of education in both cities hired noneducators as superintendents, hoping for renewal from outsiders.

Despite these similarities, the Los Angeles and New York school districts also differ in ways that reflect the distinctive histories and political cultures of the two cities. Educational history is often written as if politics did not matter (Henig et al. 1999). This slights the unique social forces that have created institutions with distinct educational practices and modes of organization. Education is local in the United States, and every city has a school system marked by its own history and the residue of battles between contending political and social groups (Wrigley 1982). Even the huge social changes that have led to impoverished, segregated large cities have not diminished the impact of the local political context.

In Los Angeles, the school district faces problems of fragmentation. The district covers 707 square miles and is far bigger even than the 498 square miles of the city of Los Angeles. The school district includes other cities (Bell, Carson, Cudahy, Gardena, Huntington Park, Lomita, Maywood, San Fernando, South Gate, Vernon, and West Hollywood), as well as parts of eighteen other cities and of unincorporated areas of Los Angeles County. District leaders and school advocates fear this unwieldy conglomeration will be broken up into smaller units. The district has also faced problems of political fragmentation, as it has contended for decades with incoherent policy making at the state level. In New York the school district has had a very different political evolution and context, with a history of educational centralization at both the local and state levels. The New York City school bureaucracy is famous for its size, rigidity, and inertia. It operates on principles of hierarchy that have penetrated the school system down even to the classroom level. At the state level, the board of regents has maintained an unusual degree of curricular control, a control it intensified at the turn of the twenty-first century as it put into place a demanding set of high school exit exams.

In this chapter, I will assess the differences between the Los Angeles and New York school systems in relation to their political histories and cultures. At one level of abstraction, New York and Los Angeles are very similar, but at another level, they differ in the composition of their immigrant populations, in their political structures, in their relationships to their surrounding political environments, and in their cultural traditions (Siegel 1997; Abu-Lughod 1999). All of these bear on the ways their school systems have taken shape and on people's efforts to reform those systems.

NEW YORK: THE FACTORY MODEL WRIT LARGE

The New York City school district stands out as a model of one type of school district, a highly bureaucratized, rule-bound, centralized system, where schools were known by numbers, indicative of their status as standardized, interchangeable units. As the exemplar of modern, standardized schooling, the district absorbed wave after wave of immigrants into a vast system, almost deliberately impersonal. In New York early in the century, reformers struggled to create a professionally driven school bureaucracy, one that would operate on the basis of merit and principle rather than patronage and corruption (Tyack 1990). In truth, the schools never lived up to this ideal. Ethnic politics operated beneath the surface and teachers struggled with overcrowded classrooms and lack of supplies (Rousmaniere 1997). Reformers never created the smooth, scientifically based machine they hoped for, but they did create a vast system with an overlay of bureaucratic control. The bureaucracy they helped create became ever more byzantine, ever more elaborate and entrenched (Rogers 1968; Tyack and Hansot 1990; Ravitch and Viteritti 1997). In part, this arises from the sheer size of the New York school district. With 1 million pupils and 65,000 teachers, it dwarfs even the Los Angeles district, with its 705,000 students and 35,000 teachers (Young 2002). The New York City school system is the largest public agency outside of Washington, D.C. (Ravitch and Viteritti 1997, 19). It enrolls an astonishing 38 percent of the students in the state, with the next-biggest district, Buffalo, lagging far behind at only 47,000 students (New York State Education Department 2001).

In a system so vast, administrators put a premium on control by standardization. With unionization, teachers won some autonomy, but traditionally the New York City schools were highly regulated. This extended to the classroom, with every room containing a portrait of George Washington, a flag, and an approved arrangement of student desks (Markowitz 1993). Teachers had to punch time clocks, and if they failed to arrive twenty minutes before classes started a notation was made in their permanent record. Principals, too, were hemmed in by rules, spending much of the day "filling out forms in triplicate and weighing every educational decision against a vast compendium of rules and regulations imposed from above" (Fliegel 1993, 25). Procuring supplies required extensive paperwork and local schools had minimal budgetary control.

As in any bureaucratic enterprise, the selection and sorting of personnel (both students and teachers) loomed large. In New York at both local and state levels, a culture of testing operated strongly, with educational authorities producing their own tests, rather than buying commercial products. Every year students were tested in writing, spelling, arithmetic, silent reading, and vocabulary; they also took IQ tests (Rousmaniere 1997, 64). The city's large high schools were extensively tracked and, even more important, admission to the city's elite science schools (Bronx Science, Stuyvesant [fig. 7.1], and Brooklyn Tech) was gained through exams. Nothing else counted, not attendance, grades, or parents' connections, just performance on written tests of math and English skills, devised by New York City teachers. Even as exam schools be-

Figure 7.1. Stuyvesant High School, Lower Manhattan. Places in New York City's handful of elite public high schools, which are allocated solely on test scores, are highly prized, with only about one in ten student applicants admitted.

came rare in other cities, New York's retained their place, with roughly 21,000 students a year competing for 2,500 spots (MacDonald 1999). Selection by exam benefited generations of striving immigrants, with Asian-Americans occupying many of those coveted science school spots at the turn of the twenty-first century. In 2000, they were 48 percent of the student population at Stuyvesant, 46 percent at Bronx Science, and 39 percent at Brooklyn Tech.

In New York, teachers, too, were selected by written exams that were unique to the city. Until 1970, a board of examiners was charged with evaluating teacher candidates. A candidate "had to take a highly competitive and difficult written examination to demonstrate general intelligence and correct use of language skills. If she was applying for a license to teach in the high schools or to teach special subjects, the exam would also test her knowledge of her subject matter or technical skills" (Markowitz 1993, 76). The much-feared board of examiners also evaluated candidates on their demeanor and speaking skills.

With its centralized control and elaborate systems of evaluation, the New York City school system commanded considerable prestige until well into the 1960s. Intensely hierarchical, the New York City schools served their most academically talented students well, but despite the emphasis on standardization, schools in the city's impoverished neighborhoods were more crowded and in worse repair than those in affluent areas (Markowitz 1993). They also had less experienced teachers. Bureaucratic operation did not translate into genuine equity; instead, the schools reinforced the residential segregation of the city. Racial issues became explosive in the 1960s. The New York City school bureaucracy was so large that it weathered many storms by simple inaction; in the late 1960s, however, the district faced a crisis it could not finesse.

In frustration over the failure of desegregation efforts, civil rights groups turned to community control of schools in the late 1960s, a goal also fostered by the Ford Foundation. In 1968, black and Puerto Rican activists engaged in an explosive battle with the teachers union over control of an intermediate school in Ocean Hill–Brownsville (Gittell 1973; Jacoby 1998). The conflict precipitated a bitter teachers strike, with the original issues soon overlaid by ethnic strife, as ugly charges of racism and anti-Semitism flew between a heavily Jewish teaching force and black protesters (Abu-Lughod 1999, 352). What had begun as a local struggle brought the city's ethnic politics to a boil and created lasting divisions between former allies in the civil rights movement. In response to the pressure for community control, the state legislature responded in 1969 by creating thirty-two decentralized districts. Teachers union lobbying helped limit the power of the local bodies. They were given control only over elementary and intermediate schools, while the high schools and special education remained under the control of the central administration.

The Ocean Hill–Brownsville conflict exposed racial fault lines deep within the city and the school system. While the school bureaucracy had been able to absorb and deflect many other conflicts, racial politics cut too deep. Critics blasted the school bureaucracy as out of touch and pathological, addicted to "compulsive rule following" (Rogers 1968, 297), and suffering from inbreeding and insulation. The address of school district headquarters, 110 Livingston Street, became shorthand for a bureaucratic sinkhole.

Although the demand for community control was specific to the era, the political eruption reflected a broad set of changes as non-Hispanic whites lost their numerical predominance. By 1999, the New York City school district was 84.6 percent minority (35.2 percent non-Hispanic black, 37.7 percent Hispanic, 15.4 percent non-Hispanic white, .4 percent American Indian, and 11.3 percent Asian-American). Segregation was pronounced, with 832 of the city's schools having a more than 80 percent minority population (with "minority" defined as any student other than those who were non-Hispanic white). More than three-fifths of the students in New York were eligible for the free lunch program, and 62 percent lived in areas of concentrated poverty. In 1998, almost 142,000 New York City students had individualized educational programs; these students alone equaled the enrollment of the twelfth largest school district in the United States (Young 1999).

New York's schools had once exemplified the achievements of a modern, standardized system, but as the district's bureaucracy met the problems of urban America, the school system became a target of both left and right, denounced for incompetence and waste. Academic achievement faltered, with deficiencies becoming painfully apparent as more high-stakes tests were imposed. In 1999, 77 percent of the city's eighth-graders failed a statewide math test and 65 percent failed in English (compared to statewide failure rates of 54 percent and 46 percent, respectively). Figure i.14 shows the dismal disparity between the reading skills of many of the city's sixth-graders and those of the rest of the state. Large city high schools tried to combat violence by installing metal detectors, substituting technology for the control exerted by a more intimate community (Devine 1996).

The best of the thirty-two local school districts allowed some innovation to flourish (Fliegel 1993), but for the most part they became vehicles for intensely local politics. Tiny bands of politicians on the make rounded up votes to install themselves in power; with turnouts in the range of 5 percent, it was not hard to gain control of a local district and then direct patronage and supply money as desired. The school district was battered by charges of corruption issued by a full-time investigator, who documented fraud at both piddling and grand levels, ranging from theft of supplies to one local district's diversion of $6 million to private schools (Goodnough 1999; Hatocollis 1999, B8). After numerous scandals, the state legislature stripped the boards of some of their powers in 1996, and in 2002 it put them on a fast track toward abolition as part of a shift toward direct control of the schools by the mayor. Once seen as an expression of direct democracy, ultimately they were decried as exemplifying "amateur hour" (Mitchell Moss, quoted in Berger 2002, 25).

The school district's decline was reflected in its inability to deal with its physical plant. New York's schools were once grand edifices, dominating their local communities, but by the end of the twentieth century teachers and students labored in dirty, noisy buildings in bad repair (fig. 7.2). Not until 2001 did the district replace the last of the manually stoked coal furnaces in the city's schools. To remove the influence of organized crime from school construction projects, in 1988, the state legislature took building power away from the board and gave it to a new

Figure 7.2. John F. Kennedy High School, Maple Hill, the Bronx. The New York City school system has fallen far short in building sufficient new schools or adequately staffing and maintaining existing schools. The address 110 Livingston Street, school district headquarters, was long synonymous with the worst features of bureaucracy, leading Mayor Michael Bloomberg to move the district brass to a building near city hall soon after his election as a sign of change. Schools in the Bronx are especially deficient. Many qualified observers believe that, apart from Bronx Science, which is an elite testing school, almost none of the other twenty-one high schools in the Bronx are even adequate.

agency, the School Construction Authority (SCA). This was a radical step, as almost every other school district in the country oversees its own building program (Steinberg 1999, B6).

The School Construction Authority suffered from the same problems that the district as a whole did. A critic charged that "the SCA builds too few schools for too much money, wastes tax dollars wantonly, and treats its customers, from principals to the public, with disdainful arrogance" (Kontorovich 1998). Graft has declined, but that decline has come at a price: the creation of a rigid organization that is unresponsive to public pressure. Ironically, the state legislature had opted for the same fix as the city's progressive reformers early in the century—the creation of a rule-driven organization—but with much the same outcome: replacing "malfeasance and responsiveness" with "honest mediocrity"

(Rothstein 1999, B9). In 2002, the mayor acquired the power to appoint the members of the SCA's board, bringing it under his control.

Lack of Civic Capacity

By the end of the twentieth century, New York public schools no longer appeared able to function well academically or operationally. In 2002, a Quinnipiac Poll of New York City voters found that 78 percent said they were dissatisfied with the city's public schools (Quinnipiac University Polling Institute 2002). Exit polls from the 2001 mayoral election showed that education had become the second most important issue for voters; only the economy worried them more (table i.2).

With the city's schools widely perceived to be in crisis, longstanding opposition to mayoral control over the schools diminished. Commentators had hailed the improvement of Chicago's schools under mayoral control, and nationally, this appeared to be the wave of the future for failing urban school systems. Rudolph Giuliani had fought for mayoral control during his eight years in office but had to settle for using his aggressive style and vengeful public persona to get the school board to do his bidding. Giuliani was able to drive two superintendents from office when they lost his favor, but he could not directly run the schools. In his farewell speech on leaving office, he cited this as his major regret. The lack of mayoral control was a striking anomaly in a city charter that gave the mayor of New York vast powers, far greater than those of the mayor of the city of Los Angeles, as Sonenshein shows in chapter 10.

Rudolph Giuliani's successor, Michael Bloomberg, made it clear when running for office that he would aim for control of the schools. He declared that "change has to happen now, and I want to be in the position to make it happen as the next mayor of the city of New York. If I fail, the voters can—and should—throw me out" (Tomasky 2002). In June 2002, only six months after Bloomberg took office, the state legislature granted his wish, less afraid of what he would do with his new power than they had been of Giuliani. Under the new law, the board of education was expanded to thirteen members (including the chancellor), but the mayor appointed eight of those members and had sole authority to select the chancellor. The law also gave the mayor direct control of the School Construction Authority. The community school boards were effectively disbanded, although actual abolition had to await review by the U.S. Department of Justice, which had to insure that minority voting rights had not been violated (Berger 2002).

Black and Hispanic legislators did not rally for the community boards. Ironically, as the boards faced extinction, it was Republican legislators who favored them, perhaps because they had operated more effectively in middle-class areas than poor ones. Polls showed, however, that black and white voters differed on whether they thought mayoral control would improve the schools; 51 percent of white voters thought it would, compared to only 30 percent of black voters (Quinnipiac University Polling Institute 2002).

In New York, power shifted to the mayor in the absence of other strong players. In the suburbs, mobilized parents and other citizens can bring about school change if they set themselves to it. In New York City, however, the sheer complexity of school politics deters all but the most sophisticated and determined parents from activism. Not many parents imagine that they can influence an $11 billion a year organization. Most are active only at the local level, engaging in what could be called a politics of maneuvering as they try to raise money for their own school or seek advantage for their own children. Even New York's decentralized districts are far larger than the average suburban school system. The voting system is so convoluted, the candidates are so unknown, and the issues are so obscure, that few go to the polls. Those running the New York schools have little to fear from a mobilized parent force, although symbolic issues occasionally erupt, as in the early 1990s when Queens parents denounced a "Rainbow Curriculum" that encouraged tolerance for gays and lesbians. Their protests helped drive Chancellor Jose Fernandez from office.

Minority leaders in New York City, like parents, have also not succeeded in playing a major role on school matters. This contrasts with the situation in a number of American cities, including Baltimore, Detroit, Washington, D.C., Newark, and Atlanta, where white elites have effectively ceded public school systems to African-American political leaders (Henig et al. 1999). In these cities, white corporate figures have retained power over economic decision making but have seen the schools as an arena for black control, one with little personal relevance to them but with high salience to newly emergent politicians. In New York, this transition did not take place, or only very partially. Except for the brief mayoralty of David Dinkins, political leadership has remained largely in non-Hispanic white hands, partly due to the city's highly diverse immigrant stream, which gives no single group numerical dominance, while continuing to include a minority of non-Hispanic white immigrants (among whom people from the former Soviet Union are the largest contingent) that builds on an earlier base of massive immigration from Europe, as Sabagh and Bozorgmehr discuss in chapter 3.

Reformers often look to the business community for leverage over the schools, hoping their labor force concerns will lead them to act. New York City employers are not happy with the schools. A survey showed that fewer than 5 percent considered city graduates to have "good" writing, spelling, or math skills (Johnson et al. 1998). Only 2 percent said they thought the city's public schools were doing well, while 95 percent said they needed either "fundamental change" or "complete rebuilding." Eighty-six percent said that high school diplomas offered no guarantees that students had mastered basic skills.

Despite this displeasure, New York's business leaders have paid little attention to the schools, focusing more on crime and economic matters and drawing skilled workers from the suburbs when necessary (Johnson et al.1998). This contrasts with the situation in Chicago, where business leaders, stung by the city's schools being labeled the worst in the nation, joined civic groups and the mayor to bring about far-reaching changes in the school system. Chicago's business leadership, however, has a long history of cohesion and civic action (Wrigley 1982; Shipps 1997). In New York, business leaders have had more of a national or international than a local focus (Gittell 1994). As in many other cities (Henig et al. 1999), they see the public schools as unproductive arenas for intervention, with problems too deep, costly, and racially charged to be easily addressed. In New York, "large numbers of employers believe getting deeply involved in schools or school issues is likely to be a frustrating, time-consuming, and ultimately unrewarding exercise" (Johnson et al. 1998, 18).

Middle-class reformers in New York, the heirs to the progressive reformers early in the century, have shown little stomach for futile jabs at the bureaucratic leadership of the city's public school system. Instead of challenging the school system, they have tried to go around it (Fliegel 1993; Meier 1996). They used school decentralization, partial as it was, as an opening wedge for their innovations, under the initial leadership of Deborah Meier, who created the innovative high school Central Park East, which has drawn thousands of visitors from around the world. With Central Park East as a model, private civic groups, in cooperation with district authorities and the teachers union, have set up a network of more than a hundred alternative public schools in New York that are designed to be the opposite of the ordinary city public schools (McDonald 1999).

Where the standard New York public school has been large, the creators of alternative schools argue that small is better. Where New York's public schools have been based on a deeply engrained culture of testing, the alternative schools rely on portfolios and student projects. Where the New York schools are impersonal, the alternative schools aim to be nurturing. While it can be very difficult for parents to talk with teachers in regular schools, the alternative schools demand some level of parent involvement as a condition for their children's admission. They ask for teacher commitment as opposed to union rules, asking teachers to give extra time to help create a "learning community."

Some of the alternative schools in New York City have won extensive publicity and millions of dollars in foundation support. They enroll, though, only 5 percent of the district's students and have mainly been given freedom to recruit the poor, often serving as "last resort" schools for students who would otherwise drop out (Ancess and Ort 1999). They face unremitting bureaucratic impediments and the envy of colleagues in regular schools who begrudge them their freedom.

The city's homegrown reformers have tried to change one school at a time; to some extent they have succeeded, but due to their small numbers and focus on individual schools, they cannot be a powerful force for district-wide change. Their educational agenda has been shaped in reaction to the district, but they want only to be free to pursue their own goals. Already they have, as one observer notes, "operated with a degree of autonomy and creativity unusual in big-city school systems" (McDonald 1999). Some hope to leave the school district entirely, re-creating themselves as charter schools.

State Inequalities

Within New York City, no coalition has emerged to improve the city's schools, with mayoral control a response to the failure of other alternatives. In the state political arena, the city has also been disadvantaged. Upstate and suburban politicians in Albany have manipulated the state's complex school aid formulas to provide New York City with 34 percent of state aid, while it has 38 percent of the state's students (Anderson 1999; McCall 2000). New York City is unique among major U.S. cities in spending less than the statewide per-student average on schools (Campaign for Fiscal Equity 2000). *Education Week* gives New York state a D− on funding equity. In January 2001, Judge Leland DeGrasse declared New York state's school funding system unconstitutional, ruling that resource shortfalls had deprived New York City students of their right to a sound basic education. Republican Governor George Pataki promptly announced that the state would appeal the decision, and in June 2002, the Appellate Division of New York State's Supreme Court overturned it. The court ruled that the state did not have to provide students with a decent education, just a "minimally adequate" one that enabled students to perform at about an eighth-grade level in such jobs as messenger and flipping hamburgers. The Court declared magisterially, "Society needs workers in all levels of jobs, the majority of which may very well be low level."

Funding inequities take a direct toll on New York City's schools. When suburbs want to improve school quality, they hire better teachers and reduce class size. New York City has serious problems doing either. While the district does better than average at putting its money into instruction, it still maintains much bigger classes than those found in the suburbs. New York City's elementary school classes average twenty-eight students, while those in the rest of the state average only 22.4 students (*EPP Monitor* 1998, 3). The city has distinct problems recruiting and keeping well-prepared teachers. Outside the city teachers can easily earn $20,000 more and they can work in a more pleasant environment (Campaign for Fiscal Equity 2001). Principals in New York City find their jobs so demanding and so low paid compared to the suburbs that in the late 1990s as many as 300 principals' jobs and 1,200 assistant principals' jobs were unfilled (Johnston 2000). Few candidates apply for open positions (New Visions for Public Schools 1999).

Given the low wages and harsh working conditions of teachers in New York City, it is not surprising that on average they are less skilled than elsewhere in the state. Ninety percent of the state's uncertified teachers work in New York City, with many concentrated in poor neighborhoods. A report by Hamilton Lankford, an economics professor at the State University of New York, Albany, "found that 42 percent of city elementary school teachers who have failed the Liberal Arts and Sciences Test work in schools with the highest need index, based on the proportion of students having limited English proficiency and receiving free lunch" (Campaign for Fiscal Equity 1999). Those teachers who are certified have often passed the teachers' exam only marginally. Almost a third of the city's teachers with the basic liberal arts and sciences certification have failed that test at least once, while in the rest of the state only 4.7 percent had ever failed the test (Campaign for Fiscal Equity 2001). Those who fail are often later hired as uncertified teachers. The city has particular problems recruiting qualified math and science teachers. In New York City, 47 percent of teachers who took the math test failed, compared with 17 percent elsewhere in the state. In the city, 48 percent of those attempting the physics test failed and 37 percent failed the biology test (Campaign for Fiscal Equity 2001; Lankford, Loeb, and Wyckoff 2002).

Problems of teacher quality can severely affect students' chances to learn. A national study found that that "measures of teacher preparation and certification are by far the strongest correlates of student achievement in reading and mathematics, both before and after controlling for student poverty and language status" (Darling-Hammond 2000). Small classes and high-quality teachers are particularly important for students from low-income families (Jencks and Phillips 1998). When poor students have several bad teachers in a row, many never regain the ground they lose. Students from middle-class homes can more easily recover from academic setbacks. With more than half of New York City's students coming from areas of concentrated poverty, large classes and underprepared teachers can be educationally devastating.

Across the country, state education departments are increasingly becoming active players in educational policy making (Lee 1997). In New York, this is not a new role for the state's education commissioner, where traditions of centralization have operated. State education officials have responded to New York City's educational problems by drawing on the same culture of exams long found in the city. State Education Commissioner Richard Mills championed a different educational agenda when he was the top education officer in Vermont, pioneering in the use of portfolios for student assessment. When he took the New York post, though, he persuaded the state board of regents to intensify its written exam requirements for graduating from high school. He explained this switch by saying that standards built on exams made sense for New York, given its educational practices and history.

New York traditionally offered two forms of diplomas. Regents' diplomas required passing academically challenging exams; students could also receive a less prestigious form of diploma if they passed the Regents Competency Test, which required an eighth-grade reading level and a sixth-grade math level. As only about one-fifth of New York City high school students have received regents' diplomas in the past, educational observers anticipate that many New York City students will not be able to graduate from high school once the more stringent requirements are fully implemented in 2003.

While critics of every political persuasion have railed at what they have seen as an ineffective school system, no coalition has arisen with the ability to create a new model of schooling. New York lacks the civic capacity to change schools its ordinary citizens, business leaders, and politicians define as inadequate. In New York, the schools reflect the problems of the city; the wealthy do business in New York but do not depend on its public services. With some exceptions (including, most notably, the city's exam high schools), the schools have the low quality of services reserved for the poor. The city's most active school reformers are dedicated to avoiding the bureaucracy as much as possible, simply going about the business of creating their own schools, perhaps leading by example but not attempting anything as ambitious as the systemwide school reform that occurred in Chicago. New York's early twentieth century reformers had a grand vision: they wanted to build a school system and insulate it from political control. They succeeded, in part, but their successors have found what they built an obstacle rather than an aid.

It remains to be seen whether the shift to mayoral control will bring school improvement. Once district control was in his grasp, Mayor Michael Bloomberg began sounding more cautious about what he could accomplish than he had been as a candidate, saying, "Keep in mind, if you change governance so the mayor has the tools, it doesn't mean the schools are going to get better" (Tomasky 2002).

FRAGMENTATION IN LOS ANGELES

The problems of the Los Angeles schools are similar in broad outline to those of New York. It, too, is a large district serving a poor population, including many immigrants, and it faces problems of low achievement and a crumbling infrastructure. It differs, though, in that fragmentation, or the risk of it, has loomed larger than problems of centralization. For the Los Angeles school district, the risk of fragmentation has been both physical—that the district would be dismembered—and political, in that it has operated in a chaotic political environment. The sheer multiplicity of government bodies creates confusion. Analysts note that "local government in Los Angeles County includes the county government (84,000 employees in 37 departments), 88 cities, and over 200 special districts. The result is a multilevel bureaucracy that is difficult for the public to understand and access" (Baldassare et al. 2000, 1). Above all, the Los Angeles school district has operated in a political situation where those it primarily serves—the children of immigrants—have their futures controlled by non-Hispanic white voters at the state and city levels.

California's history once appeared to contrast sharply with that of New York. Reformers never had to battle corrupt machines (Sonenshein, chap. 10), and they never had to create powerful bureaucracies to keep the schools out of politics (Abu-Lughod 1999). The schools were out of politics, just as other public agencies were removed from the political arena. Elections were nonpartisan for all offices, not just for schools. Politicians such as Governor Pat Brown were able to build a massive state infrastructure, including a highly regarded public school system capped by a three-tiered university system. State institutions had prestige, and the schools, in particular, appeared to have avoided the problems of decay and overcentralized control found in New York. In truth, California's schools were highly segregated, and the 1965 Watts riot made it clear that hidden in Los Angeles's sprawl were festering problems of racial inequality. The latent problems in California's development emerged still more powerfully in the last quarter of the twentieth century, when the state's political structure proved unable to deal with deep economic and ethnic cleavages within the population. In Los Angeles, the schools suffered from political instability and limited resources as the district struggled to cope with an enormous change in its clientele.

In New York, a strongly multiracial immigrant stream entered channels already carved out by immigrant predecessors, allowing the city to absorb huge numbers of immigrants without much sense that its overall ethnic structure had been decisively changed or would be likely to change in the near future. In Los Angeles, the city has changed very rapidly from being predominantly non-Hispanic white, with newcomers who were mainly native-born Midwesterners, to becoming a port of entry for the vast wave of Hispanic immigrants, as documented in chapter 3. In a remarkably short period of time, Los Angeles's cultural ambience and its political economy have been radically altered (Waldinger and Bozorgmehr 1996b). The city's restaurants, sweatshops, and small manufacturing plans depend on the new labor force; Hispanic immigrants also provide a vast service class that has enabled even non-Hispanic whites with modest incomes to hire gardeners, nannies, and housecleaners.

The city's population changes have been felt even more in the schools than in other areas of the city's life, due to the age distribution of the immigrants. In 1970, non-Hispanic whites made up half the district (Colvin 1999, A1), but by 1999, they had fallen to 10 percent. Neighborhood segregation once maintained ethnic lines within schools, but by the turn of the century non-Hispanic whites were too few to dominate in more than a few pockets of the school district. Only three of the Los Angeles district's 645 schools are more than 80 percent non-Hispanic white. Overall, Hispanic students make up nearly 70 percent of enrollment, with African-Americans at 13 percent and Asian-Americans at 6.5 percent.

Political Incoherence at the State Level

California's public schools have been buffeted by political and economic turmoil arising from use of the initiative process. In 1978, the state's voters passed Proposition 13, which sharply cut property taxes and restricted school districts' ability to raise funds (see Sears's discussion in chap. 13). Proposition 13 became "the third rail" of California politics, untouchable by politicians who wanted to maintain their careers, with huge (and partially unanticipated) consequences for many areas of California's public life. With its radical cut in property taxes, the historic source of funding for schools, Proposition 13 left the state's school districts reeling. The state moved to fill the gap, an effort that helped equalize funding disparities but also reduced local loyalty to schools (Schrag 1999). With the state controlling 90 percent of district revenues, districts no longer mobilized local supporters to help raise funds. Business leaders, in particular, lost interest in schools when the link to property taxes was severed (Sonstelie, Brunner, and Ardon 2000). Formal authority over schools remained lodged with school boards, but the state, without any long-term educational strategy, controlled resources, leading a school superintendent to comment that "California has an education system with no conceptual framework" (Legislative Analyst's Office 1999, 5).

Fragmentation and turf wars at the state level have hampered strategic planning. Policy making is divided between the governor, the legislature, the state superintendent of public instruction, and the eleven members of the state board of education (Mendel 1999, A3). The state superintendent is elected independently, while the governor appoints the state board of education. Conflicts have been most intense when the governor and state superintendent have been from different parties, as occurred during the 1980s when state superintendent Bill Honig, identified with Democrats, battled Republican Governor George Deukmejian. Conflicts between the two helped create an educational impasse; for ten years, the state was unable to decide on what statewide tests to use, which meant the extent of the state's educational slide was unknown in a critical period (Mendel 1999). Even when the state superintendent and the governor are from the same party, they can engage in political rivalry (Skelton 1999, A3), with the diffusion of power leading to "conflict and confusion about state policy" (Legislative Analyst's Office 1999, 14).

Authority is so diffuse, and political ambitions can be so distorting, that during a critical period in its history, when the state's schools were adjusting to the enormous change in their circumstances produced by massive immigration and Proposition 13, California was unable to formulate coherent educational strategies. The state became known for educational fads. In one year, 1983, the state legislature passed more than forty separate school reforms. In the 1990s, the pace intensified, with an array of new plans, including new state testing systems, the abolition of bilingual education (unless local parents fought to keep it), class-size reduction, a mandated end to children's social promotion, and the introduction of school choice plans featuring charter schools (Ruenzel 2000). Policy analysts begged the state to pause and allow time for reforms to be digested before plunging into new arenas.

Uncertainties have been exacerbated by the initiative process, which has allowed voter intervention into basic aspects of educational functioning in California. Initiatives have become increasingly common; while between 1956 and 1976, voters faced only twenty-nine initiatives, they voted on 106 in the next twenty years (Gerber 1998). Voters have struck out against affirmative action and bilingual education, while defeating measures to create school vouchers. Each initiative has created confusion over implementation and intense political controversy. The initiative process adds a dramatic level of uncertainty to the normal functioning of public institutions in California. It has also allowed for white voters to retain a higher level of control over the political process than might otherwise have been the case. They moved to the arena where they held the greatest power: statewide campaigns outside the regular political process. Berkeley political scientist Susan Rasky has commented, "Of course racism is a part of it. Initiatives are a game where only white people play. It's a parallel universe, having no resemblance to the real population of the state" (Ivins 1998, F3). Sears refers to the semihidden racial agendas underlying many of these initiatives as "symbolic racism" (chap. 12).

The shift to state funding also created severe economic problems for the schools. California's spending per pupil fell more than 15 percent relative to spending in other states between 1970 and 1997 (Sonstelie et al. 2000). In 1975, California ranked eighteenth in school funding among the states, while in 1995 it ranked forty-first (Kiewiet 1999). *Education Week* gave California a grade of F in resource adequacy (*Education Week on the Web* 2002). The schools drastically cut back on extracurricular activities, maintenance, textbooks, and school supplies. Classrooms became overcrowded. Cutbacks in school funding coincided with massive changes in the school population in Los Angeles and many other cities in California. It was hard to escape the conclusion that non-Hispanic white voters, older than average and most without children in the public schools, had little interest in paying the freight for the children of immigrants (Schrag 1999). In 1998, only 21 percent of the state's electorate was made up of parents with children in the public schools, while twenty years earlier the figure had been 42 percent (Miller 1998).

The Los Angeles area, in particular, was riven by an enormous cleavage between those who held the financial levers and those who used public services, whether those services were public transportation, county hospitals, or schools. Immigrants in Los Angeles were less likely to have become citizens than those in New York and were less likely to have been incorporated in the city's political bargaining process (Mollenkopf, Olson, and Ross 2001). New York had established mechanisms for incorporating immigrants, while in Los Angeles, native residents, predominantly non-Hispanic white, made few moves to share power with the city's burgeoning, and generally very poor, immigrant population (despite Mayor Bradley's multiethnic electoral coalition). In the city, the disparity between residents and voters was stark, with non-Hispanic whites making up less than a third of the population but more than half the voters (Gold 2001).

Political analysts have pointed to other reasons for California's school cutbacks, including the long-term effects of the shift to state funding. About half of property tax revenues had come from taxes levied on commercial, industrial, and agricultural property, revenues that were lost when taxation was shifted to the state level (Sonstelie et al. 2000). This led the state to cut per-pupil spending relative to elsewhere in the country. The power of the state's teachers unions precluded cuts in teachers' salaries, so the impact of the cuts was felt mainly in the teacher/pupil ratio. By 1997, the ratio was 38 percent higher than the average for other states.

California faced an extraordinary concentration of educational problems in the last decades of the twentieth century, including a severed connection between the governing authority and the taxing power for the schools; an unpredictable and incoherent political environment; a major demographic challenge, with a massive influx of non-English-speaking immigrants; and a large decline in per-pupil spending relative to other states. The extent of California's educational problems became fully evident only in the 1990s, when the state's residents woke up to the fact that not only were the schools shabby and overcrowded but they were functioning very poorly as well. In 1994, the state's fourth-graders tied for last with Louisiana's in the National Assessment of Educational Progress (NAEP) reading test. California, once filled with promise and seemingly able to avoid the traps of the rundown cities of the northeast and Midwest, had slid to the bottom of the educational heap. In 1998, California's students continued to score poorly on reading, doing better only than those in Hawaii. In 2000, nearly half (48 percent) of California's fourth-graders scored below basic on the NAEP math test.

Class-Size Reduction and Unexpected Results

California's economy improved in the 1990s, which helped the state's political leaders focus on the schools. Spurred by the disastrous educational performance revealed by the 1994 NAEP test results, Governor Pete Wilson and the legislature responded in 1996 by adopting a plan to reduce class size in the early elementary grades. They did this in a distinctively Californian style. Almost overnight, they created financial incentives for school districts to reduce class sizes from more than thirty to a maximum of twenty, and most districts responded. "With virtually no planning time, school districts managed to put hundreds of thousands of students in small classes by the time school started, just six weeks after the legislation passed" (Carlos and Howell 1999, 1). Critics charged that the real purpose of the plan was to keep a budget surplus from falling into the hands of the teachers' union. Whatever its origin, the plan was typical of educational policy making in the state in that there was little thought given to how thousands of extra teachers and classrooms would be found.

The problems hit hardest in the poorest and most overcrowded districts. In schools already overflowing with students, there were no extra classrooms available for new, smaller classes to be formed. With demand for teachers at high levels throughout the state, teachers flowed to the districts that offered the most attractive teaching environment (Carlos and Howell 1999, 1). Before the class-size reduction initiative, schools serving low-income students had teachers with roughly the same credentials and levels of experience as those serving middle-class students. By 1999, however, three years after the initiative began, wide differences had emerged. Schools serving poor and minority students were far less likely to have experienced, credentialed teachers than were their more affluent counterparts. In schools enrolling mainly black students, with three-quarters of the students needy enough to be on the school lunch program, 30 percent of the students had uncredentialed teachers. Only 5 percent of white students attending schools with fewer than a quarter of the students enrolled in the school lunch program had teachers without full credentials (Jepsen and Rivkin 2002). Researchers warned that inexperienced teachers might have a negative impact on the quality of education provided to Hispanic students, in particular (Ogawa et al. 1999), obviously a special concern for the Los Angeles district.

The hasty implementation of California's class-size reduction plan solved the problem of large classes, but it intensified inequalities in the state's schools (Ogawa et al. 1999). The hurried development of California's plan contrasted with the careful and systematic approach that Tennessee took in reducing class size; in a highly unusual step, Tennessee carried out a well-designed experimental study to assess its class-size reduction program before carrying it out statewide. Texas school reform has also been notable for its systematic development.

In California in the 1990s, political leaders—including, particularly, Governor Gray Davis, elected in 1998—strove to reverse the decline of the state's schools. They created statewide educational standards and a high school exit exam that would be required for graduation by 2004 and implemented a system of statewide testing and of ranking of schools. The state was rebuilding an educational infrastructure that had been largely destroyed in the preceding two decades. The sheer onslaught of reform initiatives threatened to create confusion, though, and continued California's fragmented approach to educational change (Ruenzel 2002). It was not clear that the state's change of direction could help its largest district, which continued to suffer from an erratic political course and which had suffered educational damage, as well as educational gain, from the class-size reduction initiative.

Los Angeles: Schools without Direction

The Los Angeles school district was buffeted by many forces beyond its control in the last quarter of the previous century, including a chaotic state political environment and rapid growth and demographic change within it. It would have been hard for any district to contend with the economic, political, and demographic forces that affected southern California. Seventy-five percent of Los Angeles students are from families below the poverty line and half speak only limited English (White 1998). The district faces severe problems recruiting qualified teachers; teachers in Los Angeles County earn less than 40 percent above the average real earnings per job in the county, while in other districts they can earn 75 percent above the real earnings per job in their counties (Pogodzinski 2000). The Los Angeles school district, though, has faced managerial and political problems that have led it to lurch from crisis to crisis rather than engaging in any long-range planning. The New York district is rigid in its bureaucratic intensity, but it has a kind of institutional stability that is hard to find in Los Angeles. The Los Angeles district's dysfunctionality reached a peak in the fall of 1999, when efforts by new school board members to depose a superintendent led to a tragicomedy in which even district officials did not know who was in charge (Sahagun 1999, A1).

This instability has been heightened by simmering secession efforts. A 1978 school desegregation plan, although soon overturned, fomented opposition to the district in the San Fernando Valley, organized around the antibusing organization Bustop (described in chap. 13). Los Angeles is the only school district in the country where there is "a powerful move to create smaller, fully autonomous districts within the current systems' borders" (Hendrie 1998). The threat of secession has been contained by a state law that puts obstacles in the way of would-be defectors, but it looms large in the political consciousness of those running the schools and the city of Los Angeles (Schmidt 1995). Powerful politicians advocate breaking the district into smaller units, and a state watchdog group, the Little Hoover Commission, has recommended breakup, arguing that the district as it stands is "disturbingly dysfunctional"

Figure 7.3. Hooper Avenue School, South Central, Fifty-first to Fifty-second. These prefabricated classrooms were intended to be temporary but have often been in use for decades due to lack of funds (above all caused by Proposition 13) for new construction. The classroom shown above is laid on a foundation. Sometimes the structure's construction is even more temporary, merely resting on concrete blocks. The Los Angeles Unified School District is widely known for its permanent use of temporary structures, though the practice is widespread in Chicago, too.

(Little Hoover Commission 1999, 1). When district officials strike reformers as being recalcitrant in supporting change, those demanding change threaten that the alternative could be breakup (Hendrie 1997).

The threat of future breakup looms over the district, but on a less dramatic level, district leaders also have failed to deal with basic operational issues, including building new schools. It takes strategic planning to create new schools as needed, and by any standard, the Los Angeles district has failed spectacularly in this endeavor. Since 1978, it has built only eight new schools, despite great overcrowding in immigrant areas. More than 160,000 students attend school in 4,400 portable classroom buildings (Willman 1999; Sauerwein 2000), and in excess of 15,000 are bused to less-crowded schools outside their neighborhoods (see fig. 7.3). Over one-third of the district's schools operate on year-round schedules to maximize building use (Friedman 2000).

The Los Angeles district's problems with building schools have been so severe that they have plunged the district into political crisis. These problems have surpassed even those of New York. In New York, most problems have centered on construction issues, while in Los Angeles, these have been overshadowed by the even greater problem of finding sites for schools. Until 2000, the board refrained from taking residential property for school purposes. This meant that the district sometimes had to assume the risk of building schools on contaminated industrial land. The district poured $200 million into the Belmont Learning Center, making it the most expensive school in American history, only to face years of turmoil after the site turned out to contain explosive toxic gases. Bitter conflict over whether to proceed with the project or to abandon it helped lead the school board to replace Superintendent Ruben Zacarias and other top officials. The district has built other schools on toxic sites as well. It also could not complete projects. The Los Angeles Unified School District (LAUSD) spent $36 million on a new elementary school and high school in South Gate but after twelve years had not begun construction (see fig. 7.4).

Ironically, the Little Hoover Commission recommended that the Los Angeles district shift responsibility for building schools to an independent agency like New York's School Construction Authority (1999). New York officials, invited to a hearing in Los Angeles to discuss their system, in all candor advised them not to follow the New York model.

The Los Angeles district's problems with long-range planning stemmed in part from a governance system that led board members to focus on narrow interests. Conflict over the 1978 school desegregation plan had led to a shift in the method of electing school board members, with the district broken into seven electoral zones, instead of board members being elected citywide (Schmidt 1995). Increasingly, school board members were elected as representatives of the ethnic groups that predominated in their electoral districts. Favor trading and identity issues loomed large at board meetings, which one former board member described as being about "pork, pork, pork." The Belmont Learning Center debacle occurred in part because the district proved unable to pull the plug even when it became apparent that the site was contaminated; board members who represented Hispanic districts had incentives to continue supporting a school that would have reduced overcrowding in their districts.

As in New York, in Los Angeles there are few powerful civic forces able to restore strategic direction to the schools. Problems with the schools have been highly visible and Mayor Richard Riordan first rose to public prominence from within the business community with promises to revolutionize the public school system. Actual programs, however, have

Figure 7.4. Hacienda Village, Head Start Preschool, Watts. This school, surrounded by barbed wire, is run by the Urban League. Beset by fragmented political authority, the Los Angeles Unified School District has been unable to do effective strategic planning. For example, it failed to adequately expand school capacity to meet burgeoning enrollment in immigrant areas, building only eight new schools from 1978 to 2001. The most notorious example of poor planning was the Belmont Learning Center, abandoned because it was built on a toxic waste site after absorbing $200 million of funds, making it the costliest school in American history.

been limited. Along with Helen Bernstein, the president of United Teachers Los Angeles, Riordan spearheaded a group of civic leaders in the creation of a school reform plan called LEARN (Los Angeles Educational Alliance for Restructuring Now), which the district adopted in 1993. Individual schools were to devise their own reform strategies with participation by all local stakeholders. The district aimed to have all schools "go LEARN" in five years, but the program was voluntary and many schools chose not to participate (Hendrie 1997). This laissez-faire approach differed both from Chicago's energetic systemwide school reform effort and from reformers' highly purposeful, focused efforts to create alternative schools in New York City. The New York reformers had a specific educational vision, while in Los Angeles the LEARN plan was as diffuse as other initiatives in the district. By 1997, LEARN was widely conceded to have been a disappointment.

Overall, Los Angeles does not have powerful constituencies pressing for school reform. Its business community has displayed only intermittent interest. Its middle-class reform community is weaker than in New York; the lack of elite schools has meant that the most upwardly mobile immigrants have removed themselves from the district when possible. Private school enrollment has not grown in California, despite the problems of the public schools, but evidence on housing prices suggests that parents move to find good schools. Economists analyzing housing prices in the Los Angeles metropolitan area have noted that the large premiums they found suggested that homebuyers perceived substantial quality differences between school districts (Sonstelie et al. 2000). Residential relocation is relatively easy for those with resources because, as of 1999, there were ninety-nine school districts in Los Angeles and Orange Counties.

In Los Angeles, Mayor Richard Riordan was far more identified with school issues than his counterpart in New York City. Los Angeles mayors are similar to those in New York until 2002, though, in not being able to take direct command of the schools. The problem is even more complex in Los Angeles because the school district includes other cities (White 1998). Frustrated by his lack of influence, in 1998 and again in 2000, Mayor Richard Riordan funded a slate of candidates for the school board. In 1998 his slate won and the newly constituted board replaced the superintendent, an operation that caused considerable confusion and ethnic antagonism. In 2000 his candidates were less successful, despite growing public attention to the schools. *Los Angeles Times* exit polls found that education was the most important issue to those who voted for either of the top mayoral candidates in 2001.

CONCLUSIONS

The problems of urban school districts are familiar ones: low levels of student achievement, a shortage of well-prepared teachers, difficulty repairing and building schools, and continuing patterns of racial segregation (Orfield and Eaton 1996). In each district, problems compound each other, with those schools that serve the poorest students having the least-qualified teachers, including, disproportionately, those who are uncertified (Betts et al. 2000; Fruchter 2000). It is not surprising that these problems are found in the nation's two largest districts, New York and Los Angeles. It is also not surprising that these districts exhibit what has been called "policy churn": the constant search for quick fixes for deep-lying educational problems (Hess 1999). The two districts have basic political problems in addressing educational issues. The New York state legislature has favored upstate and suburban interests over those of New York City. Los Angeles operates in a state that for several decades was unable to devise or carry out long-range educational programs. And in both cities, local constituencies have proven unable to coalesce around public school issues.

The most deeply rooted problem arises from the lack of political and economic power of those served by the public schools of New York and Los Angeles. The middle class has found other educational options in both cities, leaving the public schools for the children of the poor. This has occurred simultaneously with deepening economic inequality in the two states. New York State has the greatest gap in income between its top and bottom fifths of any state in the country and California ranks fifth (Economic Policy Institute 2000). The public school parents of New York and Los Angeles lack clout in proportion to their numbers, and the growing gap between rich and poor in California and New York presages further loss of political power for those using public services.

Despite the structural similarities between the situations of the New York and Los Angeles schools, it is also evident in reviewing the histories and circumstances of the two districts that there is substantial variation in how educational politics play themselves out in different cities. The schools of Los Angeles and New York are not identical, and the political coalitions that have intermittently formed around them are also not cut from one cloth. The differences between the two districts suggest that educational policy does matter, even if profound economic inequalities are hard to overcome.

While the two districts are shaped by their histories, increasingly their futures are likely to be shaped by state-level action. At one time, states took fairly passive roles in educational politics, but they are now major players. The state context has enormous influence on the functioning of big-city schools. In California this has been strikingly evident as initiatives have reworked the political landscape and as the state has increasingly come to control the educational purse strings. Less dramatically, in New York the board of regents has shaped the high school curriculum and the state legislature has created funding formulas that disadvantage the New York City schools.

The problems of the New York and Los Angeles school districts stem in part from their relative disadvantage compared to their suburbs. Each has trouble recruiting qualified teachers, who can easily get less stressful jobs at higher pay in surrounding communities. These problems of relative disadvantage cannot be addressed without educational planning that transcends the district itself. New York City and Los Angeles schools are unlikely to be healthy institutions without committed, long-term, planful, and effective support from their state governments, which control curricular standards, the licensing of teachers, and the distribution of resources. Media attention focuses on the drama of superintendents coming and going from office, first triumphant and then defeated, and on the promise of eagerly awaited reform plans. Superintendents, however, have little power to alter unwieldy institutions and their deeply entrenched practices without stable political environments that allow long-term change to take root. While New York and Los Angeles differ in the specifics of their problems, both cities have been short on the effective provision of educational resources. Only changes in the political culture of New York and California are likely to address successfully the educational problems of their largest cities.

CHAPTER EIGHT

It Did Happen Here

The Rise in Working Poverty in New York City

Mark Levitan

The recent debate over welfare reform centered on two issues neatly captured by the title of the 1996 federal legislation, the Personal Responsibility and Work Opportunity Reconciliation Act. Advocates for reform argued that the welfare system's open-ended entitlement to cash assistance sapped recipients' sense of personal responsibility (see, most famously, Murray [1984]). Reform's critics focused on the impact of a five-year lifetime limit to cash assistance and expressed skepticism about whether the nation should be embarking on an employment based antipoverty strategy after a two-decade-long decline in job opportunities and real wages for workers with less than a college degree. Some worried that the jobs would just not be there (Carlson and Theodore 1995; Frendt and Levine 1996; Kleppner and Theodore 1997). Others thought that the market could absorb an influx of less-educated workers but only at the cost of still lower real wage rates (Mishel and Schmitt 1995; Bernstein 1997; Burtless 2000).

By 2001 the welfare rolls had been more than halved and "dependency" had lost its force as a hot-button issue. Concerns about the low-wage labor market also receded as the economic recovery that began in 1991 "found another gear" middecade. In the booming economy of the second half of the 1990s, unemployment rates dropped to thirty-year lows and real wages for workers at the bottom of the wage ladder climbed dramatically (Mishel et al. 2001). Most impressively, poverty rates for many demographic groups fell to levels equal to or less than their prior all-time lows (Dalaker 2001). The coincident plunge in the public assistance rolls, decline in poverty, and rise in wages and labor market participation made for a prima facie case that welfare reform had worked (see, e.g., Council of Economic Advisors 2000, 187–204). The fear that the effort to move people off the welfare rolls and into the labor market would swell the ranks of the working poor abated.

This chapter questions the degree to which this collective sigh of relief is justified. It reexamines the connections between welfare reform, the labor market, and poverty by presenting New York City as a counterfactual to many of the national trends just noted. New York's "outlier" status is an opportunity to revisit some of the concerns voiced during the national welfare debate. In a less than ideal economic context, the chapter finds that poverty rates for working families rose and that working families became a larger proportion of the city's poor families.

The chapter begins with an overview of some of the relevant disparities between New York and the rest of the nation. It then considers the ways in which welfare reform may have affected the city labor market. A third section profiles the New York City low-wage labor market in the 1990s. It explores a skewed pattern of job growth, an unprecedented influx of less-skilled jobseekers, and the effect of these supply-and-demand side forces on real wage rates. The subsequent section traces the shifting demographic profile of poor families with children in New York City from the late 1980s to the late 1990s. The final section draws some conclusions for policy making.

This chapter takes its story through 2000, the last year of a record long economic expansion. The nation entered a recession in March of 2001 and the city economy began to falter soon after. Hope that New York would be able to sidestep the worst of the contraction was dashed by the terrorist attack of September 11. The city lost some hundred thousand jobs in the following months, and the local unemployment rate, which had begun to creep upward in the summer, reached 7.3 percent in December. And, for the first time in more than six years, the welfare rolls expanded. It is much too early to know the degree to which the various trends examined here will be reversed or accelerated by these events. But the short-run prognosis for New York's poor is painfully obvious: greater hardship.

NEW YORK CITY AND THE UNITED STATES

Mirroring the national experience, New York's welfare rolls plummeted in the second half of the 1990s. And along with that of the nation, the city's economy boomed. From 1996 to 2000 the city added 354,000 jobs to its payrolls. By the end of the decade, a higher proportion of New York City's population was participating in the labor force than at the

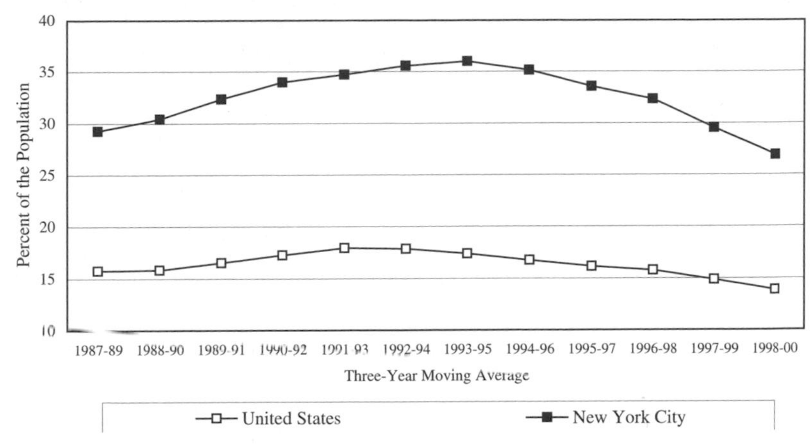

Figure 8.1. Poverty Rates for Families with Children, United States and New York City. Source: tabulated from the *Current Population Survey, Annual Demographic File* (U.S. Bureau of the Census, various years b).

last business cycle peak (the late 1980s). But that is where the similarities end. Despite the four years of record-setting job growth, the citywide unemployment rate in 2000 (5.7 percent) was both well above the national rate (4.0 percent) and the 5.0 percent rate New York achieved in 1988 (see fig. 2.3). In another contrast to national trends, real wages of New York City residents at the end of the nineties remained below prerecession levels throughout most of the wage distribution. Median weekly earnings for New York City residents who were full-time workers in 1999–2000, for example, were 1.5 percent below their 1988–89 level, after adjusting for inflation, while for the nation weekly earnings had exceeded their prerecession high by 3.3 percent.

Did these comparative weaknesses in New York's labor market result in a growing disparity between the city and national poverty trends? Figure 8.1 plots three-year moving averages in the poverty rate for families with children in New York City and across the United States.[1] It indicates that for city residents this poverty rate rose from 29.3 percent in the late 1980s to 36.0 percent for 1993–95 and subsequently declined to 26.9 percent in the late 1990s. The cyclical pattern evident in the city poverty rate is paralleled by the national trend, albeit at a rate that is consistently close to half that of New York's.[2] The poverty rate for all U.S. families with children rose from 15.8 in the late 1980s to an 18.0 percent average for 1991–93 and then dropped to 13.9 percent at the end of the 1990s.

While figure 8.1 suggests a stable, albeit large, disparity, another per-

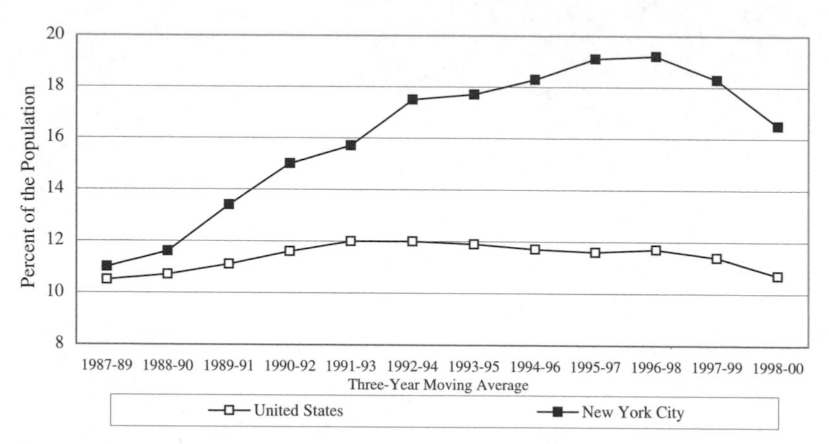

Figure 8.2. Poverty Rates for Families with Children That Include a Worker, United States and New York City. Source: tabulated from the *Current Population Survey, Annual Demographic File* (U.S. Bureau of the Census, various years b).

spective reveals a striking divergence between New York City and the nation. Figure 8.2 plots the poverty rate for U.S. and New York City families with children that include at least one worker. The U.S. working family poverty rate follows the familiar countercyclical pattern: it rose from 10.5 percent in the late 1980s to 12.0 percent in the early and mid-1990s and then declined later in the decade, to 10.7 percent, as economic growth first faltered, then recovered, and later accelerated. The New York City poverty rate for this group of families, by contrast, rose dramatically (from 11.0 percent in the late 1980s to 19.2 percent in 1996–98), only edging down (to 16.5 percent) in the final years of the decade.[3]

The two figures make several points that inform subsequent analysis. Figure 8.1, illustrates the typically cyclical character of poverty rate trends; year-to-year changes usually reflect the ebb and flow of economic conditions. The end points of figures 8.1 and 8.2—the late 1980s (the average of 1987, 1988, and 1989) and the late 1990s (the average of 1998, 1999, and 2000)—are both periods when the economy was at or approaching cyclical peaks. Because they are comparable phases in the business cycle, these two time periods provide a vantage point for looking at longer-term trends rather than shorter-term changes in poverty.

Figures 8.1 and 8.2 also suggest that there could have been changes in the composition of the kind of New York City families that are poor. Because the city poverty rate was rising rapidly for a specific segment of families (those that include a worker) while it edged down for all families, the composition of the city's poor from the late 1980s to the late

1990s may well (barring a compensating shift in the make up of the city population) have changed. The peak-to-peak analysis that follows indicates that this is just what happened. In this chapter, I show that poverty rates rose not only for families with workers but also in families where household heads had more than a high school degree, and even in families that included fathers as well as mothers. These poverty rate increases along with shifts in the composition of the population produced a dramatic transformation in the composition of the city's poor families. In addition to an "old" poor—made up of families who are outside the economic and social mainstream—there emerged "new" poor—made up of families who are impoverished despite their participation in the mainstream. Most notable of all these changes is the striking rise in the proportion of poor families that include at least one worker.

In sum, the New York experience looks much like the pessimistic scenario predicted by some critics of welfare reform. The public assistance rolls fell, more of the city's population found work, and the poverty rate for New York City's working families climbed. I contend here that what separated the city from the nation was that while labor—even less-skilled labor—was scarce across the country as reform was being implemented, welfare leavers in New York faced stiffer competition for jobs. The rise in working poverty in the city suggests that if the U.S. economy cannot sustain its recent vigor, working poverty may increase nationally as it has in New York. Today's optimism about welfare reform may prove premature.

WELFARE REFORM

For more than a decade, the dominant theme of welfare policy has been the need to transform public assistance from an open-ended entitlement to a program that promotes work. To some degree, attempts to foster work have been a consistent element in federal welfare policy since the 1960s. But the 1996 reform was unprecedented. First, it established a five-year lifetime limit on federal cash assistance. Second, it set out a new principle for effectuating the transition from welfare to work. Reform rejected the long-held concern that recipients did not have sufficient skills to make it in the labor market. It adopted a "work first" approach, insisting that properly motivated recipients could find work without training and education programs and that any job they might be able to obtain was preferable to welfare. Federal law required that an increasing share of the adult caseload be engaged in a prescribed set of work activities. And it was up to the states to devise ways to meet these participation rates by establishing a system of sanctions—the partial or complete loss of benefits—for welfare recipients who failed to comply with the demands of the new system.

A sharp shove into the labor market has not been the only theme of recent antipoverty policies. Welfare reform occurred along with greater funding of federal child care, transportation, and welfare-to-work block grants, an expansion of the Earned Income Tax Credit, and an increase in the minimum wage. While the goals of and performance measures contained in the Personal Responsibility and Work Opportunity Reconciliation Act clearly reflect the post-1994 Congress's priority with ending dependency, these other federal, along with state-level initiatives also reflect an (only partially fulfilled) commitment to the notion that government should assure that people who work can live at some minimum level of dignity.

There is conflicting evidence at the national level as to the success or failure of these programs that are intended to support workers' efforts to make it in the low-wage labor market. The most overarching indicators suggest that in the context of a red-hot economy, they have been effective enough to prevent a measurable erosion of living standards for workers at the bottom of the job ladder as a significant number of welfare recipients have moved into the labor market. But a number of studies that specifically focus on recent welfare leavers and their families find a pattern of erratic work, low wages, and significant hardship even in a period of low unemployment (Cancian et al. 1998; Braunder and Loprest 1999; Loprest 1999).

Across the United States, welfare reform was a sea change in public policy that affected the lives of millions of welfare recipients, welfare leavers, and low-income people who have sought welfare but have been diverted from the public assistance rolls by efforts to "convince" them that they were better off without it. New York City's implementation of welfare reform generated more local controversy than elsewhere in the nation. But, with the exception of the heated battles brought on by the city's nearly singular reliance on workfare—work in exchange for welfare benefits—as its "one size fits all" work activity, many of the local controversies focused on issues that are not unique to New York, such as the widespread use of sanctions, curtailed access to food stamps and Medicaid for qualified families, and diversion of eligible people at the point of application for welfare (fig. 8.3).

Perhaps welfare reform in New York affected labor market outcomes for public assistance leavers (and other participants in the low-wage labor market) in ways that are unique to the city. The data needed to make such a judgment are simply unavailable.[4] What can be stated with

Figure 8.3. Union Square Being Cleaned by Three Groups of Workers (January 2002). These included Work Experience Program or WEP workers, who wear orange vests with a parks department logo; Community Service Workers, who wear green shirts and green hats with parks department logos and who are atoning for infractions of the law; and employees of the Union Square Business Improvement District (BID), who wear blue vests with the BID logo.

confidence is that the city is exceptional in the very high proportion of its population that was receiving welfare in 1995, 16.5 percent (the year local reform efforts began), and the size of the decline in the adult caseload (50,000–60,000 per year) relative to the post-1995 expansion of the city's labor force (about 75,000 on average each year). The relative magnitude of the caseload decline makes it hard to imagine that it did not have a significant impact on the city labor market.

NEW YORK CITY'S LOW-WAGE LABOR MARKET IN THE 1990S

The national recession at the beginning of the 1990s hit New York hard.[5] Payroll employment declined by more than 327,000 (an average of 3.1 percent annually) from 1989 to 1992. By the latter year, the unemployment rate for city residents reached 11.0 percent. The local economy, moreover, was slow to recover. But in the second half of the 1990s, employment in the city grew impressively. Payroll growth has averaged a record-setting 2.5 percent per year from 1996 through 2000, and the unemployment rate fell to an annual average 5.7 percent in 2000.[6]

These aggregate figures set a context for what happened at the bottom end of the labor market. In brief, there was a sharp increase in employment in New York's low-wage service sector. At the same time a massive influx of less-skilled jobseekers kept unemployment rates among those demographic groups most dependent on the low-wage labor market high and their wages low. As a result, there was a dramatic expansion in the fraction of the city's workforce that was earning low wages.

The Demand Side

Recent job growth in New York City was not only robust in aggregate, it also generated employment opportunities for less-skilled workers. Throughout the expansion, employment growth has been disproportionately located in low-wage retail and service industries. As illustrated in figure 8.4, employment in the "low-wage service sector" (defined as retail and service-sector industries paying an average annual wage of less than $30,000 in 2000) rose by 19.1 percent (112,073) from 1989 to 2000, while employment in all other industries was essentially unchanged (up 2,948).[7] The lack of growth in the latter group is largely attributable to declines in goods-producing industries.[8]

Despite the strength of employment growth in the low-wage service sector, inflation-adjusted wages in this group of industries rose by a mere 1.4 percent from 1989 to 2000 (fig. 8.5). By contrast, real wages in the all-other-industries group increased by 41.2 percent over the eleven-year period. The lack of real wage growth in the low-wage service sector, despite its robust expansion, suggests that employers had an ample supply of workers willing to take low-wage jobs.

The Supply Side

The number of workers readily available to employers is typically measured by the size of the labor force. That group is composed of persons who are either employed or are "making specific efforts" to find employment (i.e., those defined as "unemployed" by the U.S. Bureau of Labor Statistics). Labor force participation rises and falls with the business cycle. When economic activity contracts, the labor force shrinks, as fewer people are working and more of the unemployed become discouraged and give up the hunt for a job. In recoveries, more people are working and more people are inclined to actively look for work when they think there is a strong possibility of finding a job. New York City's labor force declined by 179,000 during 1989–95. But then, from 1995 to

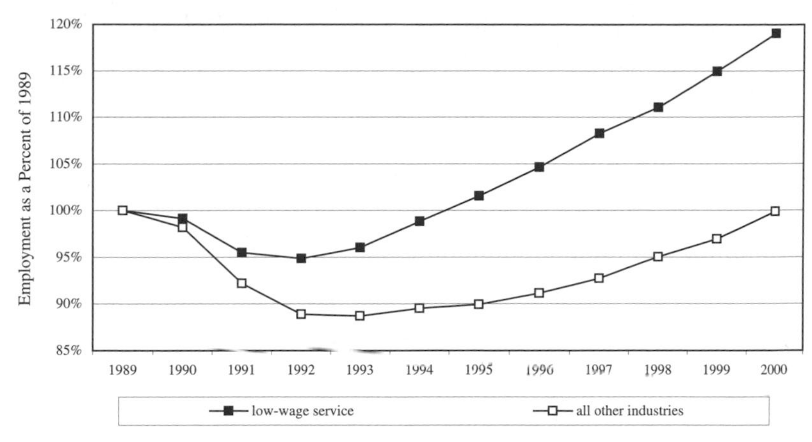

Figure 8.4. Employment Growth in Low-Wage Service and All Other New York City Industries. Source: tabulated from *Covered Employment and Wages* data provided by the New York State Department of Labor (2001).

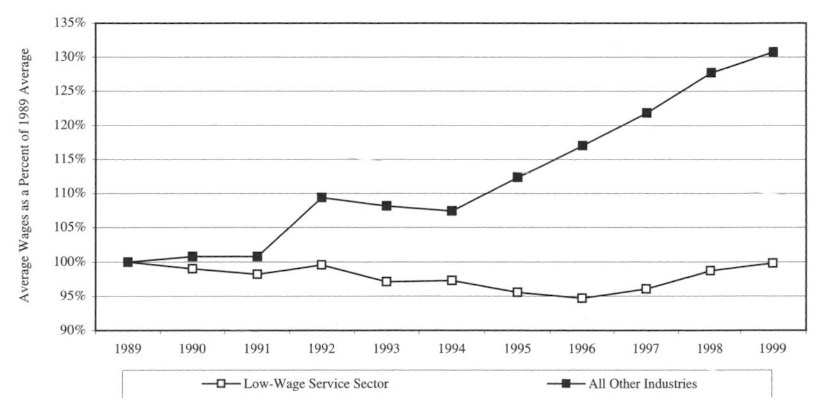

Figure 8.5. Real Wage Growth in Low-Wage Service and All Other New York City Industries. Source: tabulated from *Covered Employment and Wages* data provided by the New York State Department of Labor (2001).

2000, the city labor force expanded by 376,000. The growth in participation has been particularly striking among those most likely to be working or looking for work in the low-wage sector of the economy: women, minorities, the less educated, and younger workers.

Table 8.1 details the rise in the labor force participation rate (the proportion of the working age population that is in the labor force) between 1994 and 2000 for a variety of demographic groups. New York City's labor force participation rate has grown rapidly since 1994, the

Table 8.1. Labor Force Participation Rates for Working-Age New York City Residents, 1994 and 2000 (as Percent of the Population)

	1994	2000	DIFFERENCE
Total	64.8	69.2	4.4
Female	56.5	62.2	5.7
Male	74.4	77.0	2.6
Females by race/ethnicity:			
Blacks	58.2	63.1	4.9
Hispanics	43.1	57.8	14.7
Whites	63.6	66.7	3.1
Males by race/ethnicity:			
Blacks	68.3	70.4	2.1
Hispanics	70.6	77.1	6.5
Whites	79.9	80.7	.8
Females (25–64) by education:			
Less than high school	34.8	45.0	10.2
High school degree	58.2	61.9	3.7
Some college	69.7	72.3	2.6
Bachelor's or more	81.6	79.5	−2.1
Males (25–64) by education:			
Less than high school	66.3	74.1	7.8
High school degree	80.5	81.1	.6
Some college	83.8	83.2	−.6
Bachelor's or more	90.6	91.4	.8
Both sexes, by age:			
16–19	25.1	29.3	4.2
20–34	68.4	74.3	5.9
35–54	73.7	77.3	3.6
55–64	52.0	54.0	2.0

Source. Data are annual averages tabulated from the U.S. Bureau of the Census, Current Population Survey.
Note. Working age refers to residents 16–64 years of age. Difference is the percentage point change from 1994 to 2000.

year before resident employment began to recover from the recession and the city administration made cutting the welfare rolls a top priority. The growth in participation has been particularly rapid among those most likely to be working or looking for work in the low-wage sector of the economy.

1. Labor force participation grew more rapidly for females than males (5.7 percentage points as compared to 2.6 percentage points).
2. Among both females and males, participation rates rose most dramatically for Hispanics: 14.7 percentage points for Hispanic females and 6.5 percentage points for Hispanic males.
3. The rise in labor force participation was also most conspicuous among women and men with less than a high school education (10.2 and 7.8 percentage points, respectively).

4. Younger adults (persons age twenty through thirty-four) had the sharpest rise in participation among the age groups: 5.9 percentage points.

The flow of people into the low end of the labor market is not only suggested by which groups have experienced the largest increases in participation, it is also suggested by estimates of inflows of jobseekers from specific sources. Perhaps most salient in this regard is the striking coincidence between the decline in the number of adults on the city's welfare caseload and the growth of the labor force. Since 1995, when the city's welfare rolls began their dramatic decline, an estimated 50,000–60,000 adults have been leaving public assistance each year. Also contributing to the influx are the 40,000–50,000 working-age immigrants and 30,000–40,000 young people exiting the city's high schools.[9] It is unlikely that any other city in the nation (with the possible exception of Los Angeles, which also has both a large proportion of its population on public assistance and a large influx of immigrants) has experienced anything like this surge in job seekers.[10]

The number of job openings that were available to absorb this inflow is difficult to estimate directly. It includes the increase in the number of jobs in low-wage industries and occupations as well as the vacancies created by people moving either up the wage ladder or out of the local labor force. The available data, however, do allow us to see, on an aggregate level, how successful job seekers were in finding employment.

New York City's unemployment rate averaged 5.7 percent in 2000, compared with the national average of 4.0 percent. The citywide unemployment rate was not only high relative to that of the nation; it was also an average that masks wide disparities among New Yorkers. Table 8.2 provides unemployment rates for 2000 by a variety of demographic characteristics. Unemployment rates were highest for those demographic groups that are overrepresented in the low-wage labor market.

1. The unemployment rates were particularly high for black men (8.7 percent) and Hispanic women (10.4 percent).
2. Women with less than a high school degree faced an 11.9 percent unemployment rate.
3. Nearly a fifth of the labor force's teen and 6.5 percent of its twenty-through-thirty-four age groups were unemployed.

In sum, despite record-breaking rates of employment growth, joblessness remained a problem for those seeking work in the low-wage sector of the labor market. This undoubtedly contributed to the lack of real wage growth for workers in the bottom half of the city's wage distribution.

Table 8.2. Unemployment Rates for Working-Age New Yorkers, 2000 (as percent of the labor force)

	FEMALE	MALE	BOTH SEXES
Total unemployment rate	6.1	5.4	...
By race/ethnicity:			
Blacks	6.7	8.7	...
Hispanics	10.4	6.0	...
Whites	3.7	3.6	...
By education (age 25–64)			
Less than high school	11.9	5.8	...
High school degree	5.4	5.0	...
Some college	4.2	4.5	...
Bachelor's or more	2.6	2.3	...
By age (both sexes):			
16–19	...	...	19.3
20–34	...	...	6.5
35–54	...	...	4.7
55–64	...	...	2.9

Source. Data are annual averages tabulated from the U.S. Bureau of the Census, Current Population Survey.
Note. Working age refers to residents 16–64 years of age.

Real Wages of New York City Residents

By the end of the 1990s, real wages for workers on the lowest rungs of the national wage ladder had surpassed their prerecession peaks. Yet, inflation-adjusted earnings throughout much of the New York City wage distribution failed to climb above their 1988–89 level.[11] Figure 8.6 depicts real wages at five percentile cut-offs relative to their value in 1988–89. It indicates that weekly earnings for full-time workers declined sharply throughout the New York City wage distribution during the last recession and well into the subsequent recovery. Only workers near the top of the wage distribution (those at the ninetieth percentile) have seen their wages rise above their prerecession levels. Workers at the bottom of the wage scale suffered both the steepest declines and weakest recoveries in their wage rates. Real wages at the tenth and thirtieth percentiles declined by 5.0 percent and 6.6 percent, respectively.

The increasing numbers of city workers who are employed in low-wage industries and the sharp and widespread declines in real wages throughout the wage distribution have eroded the ability of a significant fraction of New York's workers to earn a family-supporting wage. For example, the proportion of the full-time resident workforce earning a weekly wage that could not lift a family of three above 150 percent of the poverty line rose from 23.9 percent to 29.5 percent from 1988–89 to 1999–2000.

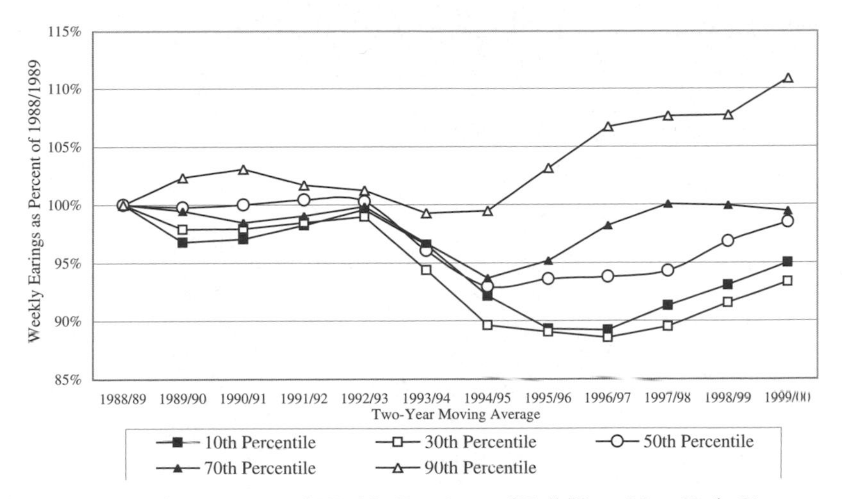

Figure 8.6. Changes in Real Weekly Earnings of Full-Time New York City Wage Earners by Selected Percentile. Source: tabulated from the *Current Population Survey* (U.S. Bureau of the Census, various years a).

A TRANSFORMED POOR

While the citywide poverty rate was little changed from the business cycle peak of the late 1980s to the business cycle peak of the late 1990s, the composition of the city's poor underwent dramatic transformations.[12] In this section, I explore these changes in three stages, beginning with a look at shifts in the kinds of families that live in the city. I then detail changes in poverty rates for these different kinds of families. Finally, I examine the changing demographic makeup of families who live below the poverty line. The focus in each step is on the three characteristics of families that have been targets of antipoverty policy: education, marriage, and work.

Poverty rates are relatively high in New York and other cities, it is often argued, because of the kind of people who live in them. Indeed most explanations of "urban decay" focus on the exodus of higher-income groups to suburbia and the growing concentration within central city areas of groups who are at greatest risk of being poor. Between the late 1980s and the late 1990s, New York's families with children were changing in ways that should have reduced the city poverty rate. First, educational levels rose. As table 8.3 indicates, people with more than a high school degree headed a growing share of the city's families. The proportion of families headed by a person with "some college" (those who attended college but have not earned a bachelor's degree) increased by

Table 8.3. Who Lives Here? Percentage Distribution of All New York City Families with Children, Late 1990s versus Late 1980s

	1990S	1980S	DIFFERENCE
By educational attainment of household head:			
Less than high school	26.2	32.7	−6.5
High school degree	27.9	34.0	−6.1
Some college	22.5	16.4	6.1
Bachelor's or more	23.3	16.8	6.5
By presence of a worker:			
No worker	17.4	23.0	−5.6
At least one worker	82.6	77.0	5.6
By family type:			
Husband-wife	54.7	56.8	−2.1
Female headed	40.0	40.2	−.2*
Male headed	5.2	3.0	2.2

Source. Tabulated from the U.S. Bureau of the Census, Current Population Survey, Annual Demographic File, various years.
Note. Column totals may not sum to 100% due to rounding. 1990s = average of 1998, 1999, and 2000; 1980s = average of 1987, 1988, and 1989. Difference is measured as the percentage point change.
*Not statistically significant.

6.1 percentage points, and the share of families headed by someone with a bachelor's degree or more climbed by 6.5 percentage points. Conversely, families headed by someone with less than a high school degree fell by 6.5 percentage points and those headed by someone with no more than a high school degree declined by 6.1 percentage points. Over the same period of time, the proportion of New York City families with children that included at least one worker increased to 82.6 percent, a 5.6 percentage point rise from the late 1980s.

In contrast to these positive developments, the proportion of families with both a husband and wife (families that tend to have a relatively low poverty rate) fell by 2.1 percentage points, due primarily to a 2.2 percentage point rise in male-headed families. (The 0.2 percentage point drop in female-headed families was not statistically significant.) This last trend did not fully offset the first two changes. Indeed the poverty rate for families with children edged down by 2.4 percentage points from late 1980s to late 1990s.

Rising Poverty Rates for Families with Higher Education, Workers, and Fathers

The impact of the poverty-reducing demographic changes on the citywide poverty rate was muted by changes in poverty rates for subgroups of New York City families with children. Indeed, in each of the three population breakouts described in table 8.4, poverty rates rose for the

Table 8.4. Who Is Getting Poorer? Poverty Rates for New York City Families with Children, Late 1990s versus Late 1980s

	1990S	1980S	DIFFERENCE
By educational attainment of household head:			
Less than high school	47.7	53.8	−6.1
High school degree	28.5	24.7	3.8
Some college	23.6	13.5	10.1
Bachelor's or more	5.0	6.1	−1.1
By presence of a worker:			
No worker	76.5	90.2	−13.7
At least one worker	16.5	11.0	5.5
By family type:			
Husband-wife	12.0	9.5	2.5
Female headed	48.2	58.3	−10.1
Male headed	20.6	15.4	5.2

Source. Tabulated from the U.S. Bureau of the Census, Current Population Survey, Annual Demographic File, various years.
Note. Column totals may not sum to 100% due to rounding. 1990s = average of 1998, 1999, and 2000; 1980s = average of 1987, 1988, and 1989. Difference is measured as the percentage point change.

kinds of families that have historically been the least likely to be poor (and fell for those most likely to be poor). As the table indicates:

1. Poverty rates rose by 3.8 percentage points for families headed by persons with a high school degree. The poverty rate for those with some college jumped by 10.1 percentage points. At the same time, the poverty rate for families headed by a person who did not complete high school declined by 6.1 percentage points.
2. Poverty rates climbed dramatically for families that included at least one worker, from 11.0 to 16.5 percent. Surprisingly the poverty rate fell, by 13.7 percentage points, for families with no worker present.
3. The changes in poverty rates by family type also narrowed the difference between families at greater and families at less risk of being poor. The poverty rate for husband-wife families rose by 2.5 percentage points. Male-headed families (a very small share of the city's families) also suffered a 5.2 percentage point rise in their poverty rate. By contrast, poverty rates declined (by 10.1 percentage points) for female-headed families.

The Changing Face of Family Poverty

The combined impact of these population shifts and poverty rate changes has dramatically altered the composition of the city's poor. A decade ago, New York City's poor neatly fit the stereotype of urban

Table 8.5. Who Are New York City's Poor? Percentage Distribution of Poor New York City Families with Children, Late 1990s versus Late 1980s

	1990S	1980S	DIFFERENCE
By educational attainment of household head:			
Less than high school	46.4	60.2	−13.8
High school degree	29.5	28.7	.8*
Some college	19.7	7.6	12.1
Bachelor's or more	4.4	3.5	.9
By presence of a worker:			
No worker	49.5	71.1	−21.6
At least one worker	50.5	28.9	21.6
By family type:			
Husband-wife	24.4	18.4	6.0
Female-Headed	71.6	80.0	−8.4
Male-Headed	4.0	1.6	2.4

Source. Tabulated from the U.S. Bureau of the Census, Current Population Survey, Annual Demographic File, various years.
Note. Row totals may not sum to 100% due to rounding. 1990s = average of 1998, 1999, and 2000; 1980s = 1987, 1988, and 1989. Difference is measured as the percentage point change.
*Not statistically significant.

poor families; they were overwhelmingly headed by jobless, poorly educated, single mothers. By the end of the 1990s, each of these groups represented a declining share of New York City's poor families with children. Conversely, poverty moved upscale. As detailed in table 8.5, the proportion of families headed by someone with a high school degree or more education constituted one-half of the city's poor. The proportion of poor families with both a husband and wife climbed by 6.0 percentage points and made up nearly one-quarter of poor families. Most dramatically, the share of poor families that include at least one worker leaped by 21.6 percentage points. These families now make up one-half of all New York's poor families with children. Evidently, more poor families were doing the things policymakers have insisted would lift them out of poverty. But, because the rewards for "good behavior" weakened over the decade, the proportion of New York City families with children who live below the poverty line was little changed.

CONCLUSION

Has welfare reform created a new working poor in New York City? I noted, in this chapter, the magnitude of the decline in the adult caseloads relative to the size and timing of the sharp increase in the size of the city labor force. I also focused on how changes in the labor market (most notably the surge in job seeking by less-skilled workers and employment in low-wage industries) were generating a growing segment of the New York City workforce that is earning low wages. In a subsequent section, I documented a reflection of those changes in a dramatic increase in the fraction of poor families that included a worker. The picture drawn of the city's labor market is certainly consistent with the scenario predicted by some critics of welfare reform—a rise in job seeking by less-skilled workers, high levels of unemployment (despite strong employment growth), and a decline in real wages relative to the prior business cycle peak. The increase in the poverty rate for working families and the rising share of poor families that include a worker rounds out that picture.

The data marshaled in this chapter, however, do not support an argument that welfare reform belongs at the top of some chain of causality. Welfare leavers were not the only source of the impressive influx of people looking for work in the low-wage labor market. As noted above, immigration from abroad has also been a major source of less-skilled labor. In fact, it has been argued that many of the labor market and poverty trends noted here are mostly the result of immigration (New York Observer 1999; Hymowitz 2000). Moreover, as the rise in working poverty depicted in figure 8.2 makes clear, welfare reform postdates the onset of some of the labor market changes and poverty shifts described in this chapter. The argument in this chapter is not that reform was the only cause of the city's relatively high unemployment rates and declining real wages. The point, rather, is that a welfare policy that aggressively promotes caseload reduction through "work first" may indeed contribute to a rise in working poverty in a labor market in which welfare leavers face stiff competition for jobs.

It is beyond the scope of this chapter to sort out the relative contribution of the shifts in policy, demographics, or labor markets that have been driving the growth of New York City's working poor throughout the 1990s. From a policy perspective, that task may be less important than an understanding of the magnitude of the problem and an identification of the factors that are at work creating it. Without fully acknowledging all its implications, the 1996 watershed in social policy marked the adoption of a new antipoverty strategy: work in the low-wage service sector. Whether a job as a cashier, janitor, security guard, home health care aid, or day-care worker is indeed a "path out of poverty" is still an unsettled question. The answer to it will depend on the future performance of the labor market. It will also depend on the evolution of social policy—the extent to which the nation makes further progress in developing a comprehensive system of benefits that support all low-wage workers regardless of where they are coming from. An adequate system of supports for low-wage earners and their families would go well beyond the modest measures taken to date. It would raise incomes directly by expanding the Earned Income Tax Credit and raising the minimum wage; it would foster upward mobility by establishing lifetime access to job training and education; and it would support families by providing health insurance, child care, and housing assistance.

In the meantime the case of New York City stands as a warning. The work-based antipoverty strategy that emerged from welfare reform has been declared a success in the context of a half decade of vigorous economic growth. Across the country, the strong economy of the second half of the 1990s reversed a nearly thirty year–long decline in the labor market position of less-skilled workers. Yet the factors that have driven the longer-term trend—technological change, global competition, and eroding union power—have not waned. Unless the economic performance of the late 1990s is soon restored, the warnings that reform would result in too many workers chasing too few jobs may ultimately prove prophetic.

CHAPTER NINE

The Local Welfare State in Transition

Welfare Reform in Los Angeles County

Geoffrey DeVerteuil, Heidi Sommer,
Jennifer Wolch, and Lois Takahashi

INTRODUCTION

The American welfare state was fundamentally altered in 1996. In August of that year, President Clinton signed the Personal Responsibility and Work Opportunity Reconciliation Act (PRWORA), essentially devolving responsibility for welfare provision and administration to the states and their constituent localities. Moreover, the focus of the welfare state shifted from entitlements and income maintenance to personal self-sufficiency through employment.

Devolution of responsibility and welfare-to-work provisions implies a greater role for the local welfare state, the welfare apparatus rooted in a particular locality, generally a city or county. In effect, welfare reform puts into sharper focus the capacity of the local welfare state, its autonomy and constraints. The purpose of this chapter is to illustrate the concept of the semiautonomous local welfare state, by examining the transitions in local welfare state policies and programs brought on by welfare reform in Los Angeles County. In the second section, we trace the evolution of the American welfare state, paying particular attention to its downsizing over the past twenty years. Conceptually, we position the local welfare state within these larger trends as constrained by economic and political frameworks yet able to exercise some measure of autonomy. This idea is then translated into a policy continuum between autonomy and constraint.

In the third section, the concept of the semiautonomous local welfare state is applied to Los Angeles County. We focus on the policy changes and caseload impacts of welfare reform on three distinct programs/populations: indigent adults receiving General Relief (GR); legal immigrants receiving federal programs, particularly food stamps; and families receiving Temporary Aid to Needy Families (TANF). The experience of each program in the postreform era illustrates different facets of the semiautonomous local welfare state. In turn, we position each program along the continuum between autonomy and constraint.

THEORETICAL AND HISTORICAL PERSPECTIVES ON LOCAL WELFARE STATE FORMATION

Local welfare state formation can be understood as the interaction of global, national, and local processes (Laws 1989). Accordingly, local welfare state formation is necessarily complex and defies any single theoretical approach. We begin with a broad historical review of the changing American welfare state and then propose a theory of the semiautonomous local welfare state that recognizes the role of larger economic and political forces while also appreciating the semiautonomous process of local welfare state formation and action.

The Federal Welfare State in Transition

Most social policy scholars do not recognize an American welfare state until the New Deal of the 1930s, although Skocpol (1992) does point to the existence of a "precocious" welfare state in the late-nineteenth and early-twentieth centuries on the basis of pensions for Civil War veterans and widowed mothers. Nonetheless, most welfare functions were locally funded and controlled until the Great Depression. At that time, with the nation threatened by social instability, Roosevelt instituted the New Deal. This legislation initiated the basis for the federal welfare state, encouraging the active intervention of government in the national economy to minimize its extremes. The national welfare state emerged as a "system of supports for those who for one reason or another were not expected, or were unable, to meet the demands of labor in an industrial economy" (Cope 1997, 182). Its political and financial bases secure, the federal welfare state would grow substantially, reaching its apogee with the War on Poverty programs in the mid-1960s.

Over the past twenty years, the national welfare state has been increasingly devolved, privatized, and dismantled (Wolch 1990; Kodras 1997, 80–82). Devolution has resulted from internal transformations that shift responsibility for public assistance programs to lower levels of government. Privatization has seen the transfer of traditional government functions to external commercial or nonprofit entities. And finally, the dismantling of the national welfare state has involved reduction in

Table 9.1. Federal Welfare Reform, 1996

	KEY ELEMENTS
Title I: Block Grants for Temporary Assistance for Needy Families (TANF)	Removes the entitlement of individuals to government assistance Gives federal money to states in the form of block grants, instead of need, based on 1994 levels Devolves responsibility for TANF to the states Requires a percentage of families to engage in work activities, increasing incrementally with time Imposes a five-year (over a lifetime) limit on family use of block grant funds Requires recipients to engage in approved work activities within two years of application
Title II: supplemental security income (SSI)	Restricts access for less severely disable children Substance abusers lose their benefits
Title IV: restricting welfare and public benefits for aliens	Makes all legal noncitizens in the United States before the act ineligible for SSI and food stamps Restricts legal noncitizens arriving after the act from access to all means-tested benefits for five years Renders illegal immigrants generally ineligible for all federal benefits Provides additional state options to deny legal noncitizens access to other federal/state programs such as TANF and Medi-Cal (Medicaid)
Title VII: food stamps and commodity distribution	Requires that able-bodied recipients ages 18–50 (without dependents) receive benefits for a maximum of three months out of any three-year period, unless working a minimum of 20 hours per week Reduces the maximum food stamp benefit by 3 percent

Source. Adapted from Legislative Analyst Office (1996).

or withdrawal of federal funding or alteration of program guidelines, significantly transforming existing government programs at all levels.

These trends culminated in the 1996 Personal Responsibility and Work Opportunity Reconciliation Act. This legislation was the product of several forces: dramatic caseload increases in the early 1990s (an astounding 27 percent between 1990 and 1994), as well as a consensus around the need for federal welfare state change (U.S. House of Representatives 1996, 386; Lake 1997). This act fundamentally altered the federal welfare state, dismissing any entitlement to government assistance and shifting the focus from income maintenance to job training and employment. The act consisted of nine separate sections (titles), each focusing on separate policy themes. In table 9.1, we outline those provisions most likely to have significant impacts upon the local welfare state, particularly in localities with large service-dependent and immigrant populations.

While some of these key provisions have subsequently been revised, the 1996 act set into motion three fundamental shifts to the federal welfare system: (1) the increased localization of welfare provision and administration to state and local levels through block grants and devolution of welfare provision responsibilities; (2) emphasis on individual rather than collective responsibility for poverty in the form of lifetime limits on benefit; and (3) the preference of self-sufficiency over basic entitlements, embodied in the welfare-to-work provisions.

Understanding the Transition at the Local Level

What is the local welfare state's position within this increasingly devolved, privatized, and dismantled federal welfare state? Does the local welfare state merely follow these larger trends, or can it actually exercise some measure of local autonomy? One way to approach this question is to incorporate both "top-down" and "bottom-up" theories of local welfare state formation. As a result, the local welfare state emerges as constrained by economic and political frameworks yet able to exercise some measure of autonomy.

From a top-down perspective, the local welfare state is severely constrained by a number of larger political and economic forces. According to the regulationist perspective, the local (welfare) state simply mimics larger political shifts, namely, the drive to streamline the federal welfare state in the increasingly post-Fordist and globalized system (Kirby 1990; Goodwin et al. 1993). In this respect, Lauria (1997) argues that regulation theory obscures and underestimates "the causal efficacy of local agents and institutions" (viii). Moreover, regulation theory is ineffective at conceptualizing the spatial unevenness among localities, preferring instead to advance assumptions of internal homogeneity and unproblematic translations of regulations from the national to the local level (Goodwin et al. 1993).

Similarly, theories of the capitalist state relegate the local (welfare) state to a subordinate position, its constrained existence "predicated upon the need for directed long-term crisis avoidance at the local level" (Clark and Dear 1984, 133). From such a perspective, the local welfare state emerges as a "purposively constituted apparatus of higher tiers of the state [functioning] . . . largely to facilitate state actions of crisis management and control" (Clark and Dear 1984, 138). Accordingly, this encourages a necessarily constrained view of the local state (e.g., Peterson 1981), limited in its ability to raise and attract capital, and therefore avoiding redistributive practices, including welfare provision, in favor of (developmental) policies that expand local fiscal capacity.

Top-down theories, however, provide only partial understandings of local welfare state formation. The larger economic and political context cannot wholly determine (or constrain) local policy decisions. Thus, we need to incorporate more bottom-up insights that recognize the local state as both "passive medium and an active expression" of larger forces (Kirby 1990, 741). This more nuanced, less structuralist account focuses on local state semiautonomy, where autonomy refers to the ability to enact local policies without undue constraint.

As a semiautonomous democratic institution, the local state and its welfare apparatus emerge as both an agent of and obstacle to larger changes, including efforts at federal welfare reform (Pinch 1992; Lee 1994). It is agent in the sense that it must implement federal guidelines and initiatives, and an obstacle in the sense that the local welfare local state may prove a reluctant, if not rebellious, participant in the larger effort (e.g., Mayor Sam Yorty's reluctance to conform to federal guidelines during the 1960s). Moreover, the local state has its own agenda that may confound federal directives. For instance, after welfare reform was enacted, mayors of cities with large immigrant populations subsequently mobilized in opposition to the federal restrictions (Rohrlich 1997a). Local officials were able to keep the issue of benefit cuts to immigrants in the public eye, fostering subsequent revisions.

As the arena of local common sense, the nature of the local welfare state is also subject to pressure from local groups. For instance, in New York City, many church groups have refused to participate in Mayor Giuliani's workfare program (Sexton 1997). In this case, local groups were able to resist, if not shape, the form and function of the local welfare state. The bottom-up perspective also recognizes the unevenness of local welfare states. Each local welfare state is a unique repository of larger processes and local histories and geographies. For instance, a city with a relatively long history of generous welfare benefits, such as New York City, would differ greatly from a city where welfare was always viewed with suspicion. Moreover, given the devolution of responsibility for welfare provision and administration to the local level, welfare reform has the potential to exacerbate interlocality differences.

By combining the top-down and bottom-up perspectives, we are able to recognize local welfare state formation as a geographically uneven process, marked by both larger constraints and localized autonomy. However, the combination of both perspectives necessarily engenders a somewhat contradictory picture of the local welfare state: at once constrained by longstanding economic and political frameworks, yet able to exercise some measure of local autonomy. One approach to understanding this apparent contradiction is to imagine a continuum for local welfare state programs, ranging from complete autonomy to complete constraint. Most programs would fall somewhere in the middle, the outcomes of both local autonomy and broader constraints. We propose several key internal and external factors that influence the degree of autonomy/constraint of local welfare state programs, including those following.

- *Larger economic context:* This broader factor can help determine the degree of policy options at the local level.
- *Legal/administrative framework:* This broader factor embodies the range of legal and administrative rules and procedures that constrain or enable local action, including recent federal and state guidelines for welfare reform.
- *Local characteristics:* These local factors include local labor market conditions, local demographics (e.g., immigration, language, poverty), and the ability of local groups to access the policy-making process.
- *Local state capacity to act:* This political/institutional factor incorporates the internal constraints on local state actions, such as the inertia associated with large local bureaucracies, lack of information systems, and political rivalries or stalemates.

In what follows, we apply this semiautonomous perspective when considering the local welfare state in post–welfare reform Los Angeles County.

LOS ANGELES COUNTY AND WELFARE REFORM

Los Angeles County is an important case study for several reasons. As the most populous county in the nation, Los Angeles is characterized by significant welfare dependency, as well as extreme economic and demographic variability. In 1995, when most U.S. residents were rejoicing over a rebounding economy, Los Angeles County still suffered a higher poverty rate among residents of all ages (22.7 percent) than the state (16.5 percent) and national average (13.8 percent [Dalaker and Naifeh 1998]). With such exposure to poverty, it is not surprising that so many Los Angelenos and Los Angelenas require some form of public assistance. In June 1999, nearly 1.7 million individuals, or 15 percent of county residents, received aid from at least one public assistance program (Department of Public and Social Services [DPSS] 1999a). Furthermore, one in five of the individuals aided in Los Angeles County were noncitizens and nearly one in two spoke a primary language other than English (DPSS

1998b). Few local welfare states must contend with implementing welfare reform among a service-reliant population of equal size and diversity.

We begin with a brief overview of historical trends that have shaped the current local welfare landscape. From there, the bulk of our analysis consists of critically examining three distinct welfare populations: single adults without dependents receiving General Relief (GR); legal immigrants receiving all types of federal assistance, with a focus on food stamps; and families with dependent children receiving TANF. By examining each population/program, we are able to position each program along the continuum between local autonomy and local constraint, thereby illustrating the broader theory of semiautonomy of the local welfare state.

Historical Trends

In the late 1970s and early 1980s, a confluence of events engendered a crisis of the local welfare state in Los Angeles County. The first of these events was the passage of Proposition 13 in 1978, which drastically limited the revenue-raising capabilities of local governments in California. Subsequently, "under the guise of the 'New Federalism' and the promise of greater flexibility at the state level, the federal government began a series of retrenchments and cutbacks" (Wolch and Sommer 1997, 8), beginning with the 1981 Omnibus Budgetary Reconciliation Act. The legislation effectively restricted eligibility for federal programs as well as cut federal funding for state and local health and social welfare programs. Third, a deep national recession dramatically increased rates of unemployment, fostering a greater need for public assistance. Despite increasing need, Los Angeles County responded to the larger cuts and exploding demand by retrenching its own welfare systems, especially the health and mental health sectors, as well as imposing stricter rules on access to local welfare benefits (Lee 1994).

Although Los Angeles County experienced a dramatic economic boom in the mid- and late-1980s, demand for local public assistance continued to increase. Caseloads surged dramatically again in the early 1990s, when Los Angeles County experienced its most severe recession since the 1930s. In 1992, the county aided 1.6 million people, up from fewer than 1 million in 1989 (Wolch and Dear 1993; Wolch and Sommer 1997). Once again, the State of California further cut benefit levels for families in need and enabled counties to reduce steadily General Assistance payments to individuals. Nonetheless, the recession deepened, and by 1995 close to 2.1 million needed some sort of assistance from the local welfare state (Wolch and Dear 1993; Wolch and Sommer 1997). The county flirted with outright bankruptcy, with major local public hospitals slated for closure until the federal government provided financial relief.

By the time the local economy began to show signs of recovery, a new wave of federal welfare reform was on the political agenda, leaving not a single safety-net program untouched. For the local welfare state, still operating under a fiscal deficit in 1996, this new agenda generated uncertainty with regard to federal and state funding and program guidelines. In light of such uncertainty, maintaining a fairly restrictive local welfare state seemed the safest policy. Local and state legislatures aimed to mitigate some of the potential negative impacts of reform and help prevent counties from being financially overburdened by individuals falling through a greatly reduced federal safety net. However, these political responses would have an uneven impact on different welfare programs.

Able-Bodied, Employable Individuals: General Relief and the Semiautonomous Local Welfare State

Single, able-bodied individuals represent an important, if traditionally neglected, segment of the service-dependent population. In California, single, able-bodied individuals have historically been eligible for government aid through the locally funded and operated General Assistance programs. In 1931, Los Angeles County created its version of this program, called General Relief (GR), as aid of last resort for single, able-bodied individuals (Lee 1994).

Even before 1996 welfare reform, the local welfare state was under pressure to streamline the GR program. Between 1976 and 1993, the number of persons on GR grew by more than 400 percent (17,569 to 88,925 [Wolch and Sommer 1997, 14]). Since GR is locally funded, Los Angeles County was able to respond to this exploding demand by repeatedly curtailing GR benefits and restricting program eligibility. The most drastic cuts came in 1993, when the Los Angeles Board of Supervisors decreased GR benefits 25 percent, from $285 to $221 a month, in order to cut local expenditures. While subsequent lawsuits would render this decrease illegal, the county's strategy demonstrated its considerable ability to shape the local welfare landscape. Indeed, while the initial cuts in 1993 were only temporary because of lawsuits, the county was subsequently successful in reducing its expenditures on local welfare state benefits using other strategies, so that current benefits are now set at $221. Able-bodied recipients (approximately 60 percent of the total GR population) not already employed at least forty hours per month were required to participate in community service, with the end result that recipients effectively worked off the cost of their assistance (Freese 1997).

The capacity of the local welfare state to fund public assistance programs is an important constraint influencing a county's ability to adapt in times of transition. As Proposition 13 and the past recession made clear, Los Angeles County's position is severely limited. It cannot raise necessary revenues to increase public assistance in times of increased need without also decreasing expenditures in other categories of public goods and services. Unlike federal programs, including Aids to Families with Dependent Children (AFDC), food stamps and Supplemental Security Income (SSI), locally funded assistance programs are subject to fiscal constraints at the local level.

Within this constrained context, the passage of PRWORA stimulated further calls for more stringent restrictions on GR benefits. Some counties, fearing that former welfare recipients would turn to local General Assistance, began to pressure the State of California to change the laws regarding locally funded aid. In January 1997, Senate Bill 681 allowed counties to decrease benefit levels and impose time limits on able-bodied GR recipients ("employables") to three months. The legislation also allowed options to further reduce benefit levels; provide $40 of the grant as in-kind medical benefits; and make ineligible recipients suspected of having substance abuse problems. The latter was one way to preclude substance abusers who had lost their federal SSI benefits from turning to GR.

As an indication of the county's reluctance to deal with increased local need, the board of supervisors opted to restrict GR eligibility to five months a year for employable recipients and to deny benefits to individuals identified as having substance abuse problems unless enrolled in treatment programs. The five-month rule began February 1998 for most recipients, and the first recipients lost their benefits in July 1998. In the month of December 1998, of the 7,046 cases dropped from the rolls, 20 percent were due to time limits, a proportion that is sure to grow over time (DPSS 1998c).

Local advocacy groups were, however, once again successful in pressuring the County Board of Supervisors to reconsider this time limit and opened up the potential for a more comprehensive local safety net. In December 1998, the board of supervisors approved a plan to extend welfare benefits for GR recipients participating in a job-training program (*Los Angeles Times* 1998). Effective February 1, 1999, the new program, titled General Relief Opportunities for Work (GROW), allows all employables who comply with program guidelines to qualify for six months of aid a year. An additional three months of benefits will be available for those who continue job training and job-search activities through GROW.

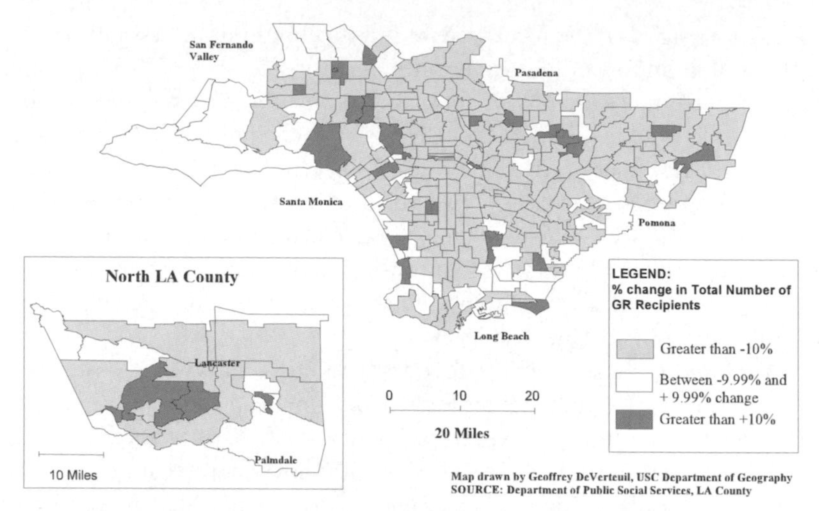

Figure 9.1. Percentage Change in General Relief Recipients by Zip Code in Los Angeles County, May 1997–April 1999

These post-PRWORA measures have had an important impact on caseloads. In the period just preceding welfare reform (August 1994–August 1996), GR caseloads were stable at a monthly average of 90,000 persons. However, in the period just after welfare reform (August 1996–August 1999), GR caseloads declined 32 percent to a monthly average of 62,000 persons (DPSS 1999a). Between August 1999 and April 2002, GR caseloads have stabilized at around 64,000 persons per month (DPSS 2002). Of course, given the improving local economy, not all of this decline can be attributed to stricter GR policies. Nonetheless, benefit cutbacks and restrictions have radically "hardened" the GR landscape.

Figure 9.1 shows the changing geographic distribution of GR recipients between May 1997 and April 1999. This map shows the widespread, though not complete (especially in peripheral areas), pattern of decline within zip codes.

Currently, the GR landscape primarily reflects the confluence of three factors: the fiscal constraint on the local welfare state; its ability to shape policy in a semiautonomous fashion; and the effectiveness of local advocacy groups (DeVerteuil, Lee, and Wolch 2002). In effect, GR is a case of the weak link in the larger welfare system, beyond the legal bounds of recent federal welfare reform but an important barometer of the local welfare state's capacity and willingness to provide for its indigent. In terms of the larger continuum between local autonomy and local constraint, the GR system reflects relatively strong local autonomy, with the local welfare state able to play an important role in fashioning its own welfare landscape.

Legal Immigrants and Federal Programs: The Autonomous and Constrained Local Welfare State

In August 1997, almost a quarter of all TANF, GR, Medi-Cal, and food stamps–only recipients were noncitizens, mostly legal immigrants. In particular, legal immigrants were concentrated within the food stamps–only and SSI programs. In August 1997, a full 21 percent of food stamp–only recipients were legal immigrants. Food stamps are a federal means-tested program that helps low-income households (individuals and families) obtain a more nutritious diet by supplementing their income with food stamp benefits. Supplemental security income refers to federal cash benefits that guarantee a minimum level of income for needy aged, blind, or disabled individuals; SSI recipients also receive Medi-Cal (but not food stamps).

Until the advent of PRWORA, legal immigrants were eligible for food stamps and SSI benefits. Afterward, however, new immigrants were barred from any federal means-tested programs for five years. More specifically, initial federal law stipulated the following for legal immigrants who arrived prior to August 22 1996: (1) those not yet receiving SSI are only eligible in the future if they become disabled and not for simply reaching the age of sixty-five, and (2) no eligibility for federal food stamps unless they are under eighteen or over sixty-five years of age. In each of these cases, benefits can be restored only when the legal immigrant becomes a citizen or reaches forty work quarters (i.e., forty three-month periods) in the United States. States were given the option to continue to provide or deny eligibility for additional programs.

Faced with important cuts to a large and vulnerable population, the State of California did not exercise these options and even created a state-funded food stamp program for legal immigrants under eighteen and over sixty-five. Since that time, federally funded benefits for many legal immigrants who arrived prior to August 22 1996, have been reinstated, but many of these immigrants no longer know their eligibility status or are simply afraid to apply. Moreover, some legal immigrants who lost their SSI benefits were covered by a new state program. This state program, known as Cash Assistance Program for Immigrants (CAPI), provided SSI-level benefits as of December 1, 1997, to those legal immigrants who arrived prior to August 22, 1996, but who have reached the age of sixty-five since that date. The program has already attracted significant demand: in November 1998 alone, more than 1,800 elderly immigrants applied in Los Angeles County, and by August 1999, 4,319 people were being supported (Ellis 1998; DPSS 1999a).

Despite these countermeasures, impacts were initially negative. Even though California did not adopt all of the available restrictions open to states, more than 150,000 children, adults, and elderly in the state lost their federally funded food stamps in August 1997, although 56,000 of these regained their food stamp benefits the following month (Government Accounting Office [GAO] 1998). In Los Angeles County, 91,000 legal immigrants lost food stamp benefits, with 29,000 later having benefits restored through the state-funded program. The impact of these cuts on the county's overall food stamps–only caseload has been substantial. Even with restoration, total persons aided decreased 29 percent from August 1997 to August 1999, while the proportion of food stamp–only recipients who were legal immigrants fell by a third, and their total number plummeted from 30,000 to 18,000 (DPSS 1999a). By April 2002, total persons aided had dropped another 7 percent (DPSS 2002).

This type of decline was not evident for other assistance programs for which similar information was available, including TANF or GR. The proportion of GR recipients who were legal immigrants (19 percent) fell slightly between August 1997 and August 1999, while the proportion of legal immigrants among TANF recipients dropped from 9 to 7.1 percent for one-parent families and from 32 to 26 percent for two-parent families (DPSS 1997a, 1998a, 1999a).

Although comparable data on SSI caseload change were not available, it seems unlikely that significant change has occurred. This is not only because SSI benefits were reinstated for most legal immigrants who arrived prior to August 22, 1996, but also because those not reinstated could be covered by CAPI.

Welfare reform has also slowed rates of public assistance caseload addition among legal immigrants in Los Angeles County. Despite the fact that a majority of legal immigrants are eligible for most welfare programs, the percentage of immigrant families applying for aid among all applicants dropped from 23 percent in January 1996 to only 8 percent in August 1998 (DPSS 1997a, 1998a, 1999a). An Urban Institute report (Gallagher et al. 1998) indicated that legal immigrants were facing a greater degree of fear and confusion with regard to receipt of public assistance, translating into greater hesitancy to apply for programs for which they are in fact eligible. Not only have the recent changes made seeking assistance more invasive than ever before, but now there is also the added fear of being considered a "public charge," undermining immigrants' naturalization efforts and denying them the possibility to travel abroad. Legal and undocumented immigrants also fear that the

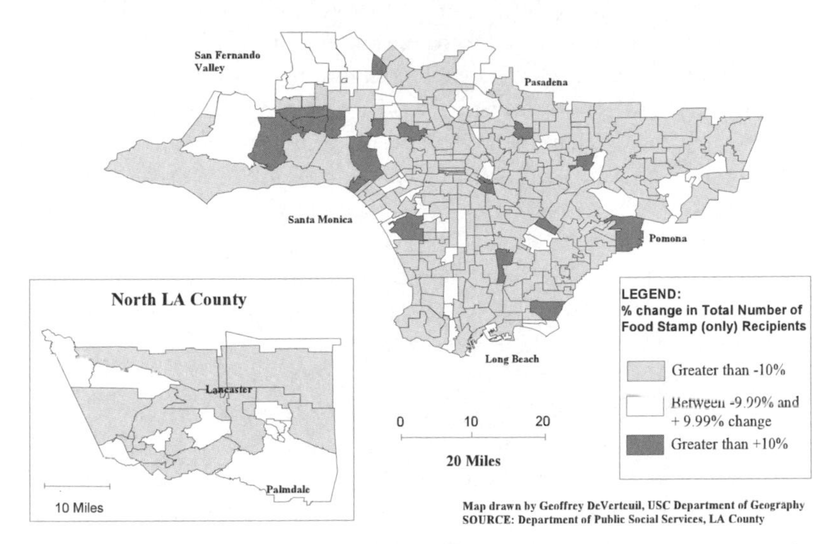

Figure 9.2. Percentage Change in Food Stamp–Only Recipients by Zip Code in Los Angeles County, May 1997–April 1999

receipt of public assistance on behalf of their citizen children will raise public ire. The language barriers that exist for many immigrants can only compound the issue, as those who did apply had to deal with the lengthy and byzantine program application. For example, the publicly funded health program for children, the newly created Healthy Families, initially required a twenty-seven-page application. Figure 9.2 shows a pattern of marked decline, with the few increases generally located in peripheral zip codes.

In Los Angeles County, such changes in the welfare application process for legal immigrants necessarily imply a much greater state role in the regulation and surveillance of immigrants. The devolution of these programs also means that the responsibility for such functions fell to lower levels of government. For example, welfare administrators now have the additional burden of checking citizenship status and the date on which an immigrant arrived in the United States, as well as seeking affidavits of support and attempting to enforce these when necessary. In terms of regulation, welfare reform has created additional pressure among legal immigrants to naturalize so as not to lose desperately needed benefits, present or future. Pressure to naturalize led to a massive backlog of 400,000 applicants in the Los Angeles District (a seven-county region) who await their fate for two years or more (Ellis 1999).

In sum, the expanded mandate for surveillance of legal immigrants granted to the local welfare state would imply greater autonomy. However, devolution has meant the development of an expanded bureaucratic apparatus, at times replacing programmatic functions of the local welfare state and forcing the dedication of more staff time to matters once largely the domain of the federal government. Moreover, the initial federal restrictions and the crucial role of the State of California in filling the funding gaps for immigrant welfare programs underline the relative weakness of the local welfare state in dealing with larger shifts. Therefore, when placed along our continuum, the food stamp–only and SSI benefits among legal immigrants occupy a middle position between local autonomy and local constraint.

Families and Children: TANF and Constrained Local Welfare State

Federal welfare reform initiated a complete overhaul of the largest public assistance program, Aid to Families with Dependent Children (AFDC), replacing it with Temporary Aid to Needy Families (TANF). Simply put, the goal was to reduce welfare dependence among families by requiring able-bodied adults to make the transition into the workforce and ensuring that individuals turn to TANF only as a temporary solution to financial hardship. Families receiving TANF, including those that are highly dependent (i.e., who receive at least 50 percent of their income over a two-year span from welfare, including at least 25 percent through TANF), constitute another group that is extremely vulnerable to welfare reform (MaCurdy and O'Brien-Strain 1997, xii–xiii).

Although the impacts will not be as immediate as for legal immigrants dependent on federal programs, the shift from AFDC to TANF and the accompanying welfare-to-work provisions fundamentally alter the way the local welfare state interacts with welfare families and children. In 1996, the federal government insisted that states formulate their own welfare-to-work plans. In California, this plan is known as the California Work Opportunity and Responsibility to Kids (CalWORKs). As part of the state plan, each of the state's fifty-eight counties had to formulate its own local plan, ensuring an increasingly uneven welfare landscape.

In Los Angeles County, most new applicants for public assistance now have to enroll in the primary welfare-to-work program, Greater Avenues for Independence (GAIN). This application process involves screening for domestic violence, substance abuse, and mental health problems, orientation, job search, vocational assessment, a welfare-to-work contract, and employment/community service. Once the application process is completed, applicants begin a "job-first" program, for which services include job-finding workshops and supervised job searches. Failure to find a job invokes vocational assessment, remedial education, and vocational-skills training. Postemployment services are also available to help employed participants retain their jobs, work toward a better one, and ultimately move to financial independence. Moreover, GAIN offers help with transportation, child care, and special job-related expenses, such as uniforms and tools. Child care is provided for all children aged ten and under and, when funding allows, for those twelve and under. Conversely, individuals can be sanctioned prior to the initial cut-off date for failing to comply with GAIN program requirements. Sanctions involve a reduction in assistance equal to the parent's share of monthly benefits.

The most immediate impact of such welfare reforms has been a decline in caseloads. On the eve of welfare reform, the number of persons on AFDC had stabilized at about 875,000 persons. However, between August 1996 and August 1999, the number of persons on TANF dipped by 30 percent to 613,000 (DPSS 1999a). Between August 1999 and April 2002, persons aided dropped another 19 percent. Of course, this decline masks many trends, not all of which are tied to successful welfare-to-work strategies or increased self-sufficiency among dependent families with children. Certainly, some former recipients have secured employment in the buoyant economy and are either no longer eligible for assistance or are choosing not to access it, reserving benefits for more desperate circumstances. Penalties (reduction in benefits) and sanctions (loss of adult's share of benefits) are a further source of caseload decline and can occur within the framework of both CalWORKs and GAIN. Within CalWORKs, families can receive penalties for not declaring their child's paternity, failing to provide their child's immunization records, and not verifying school attendance. In December 1998, penalties were in effect for 807 parents, 62 percent of these for failing to meet child-support requirements (DPSS 1998d). Parents can also be sanctioned for committing criminal violations as well as failing to meet the work requirements linked to GAIN. As of December 1998, more than 11,000 sanctions were in effect, nearly all of them for parents failing to meet work-participation requirements (DPSS 1998e). Between April and December of 1998, a total of more than 19,000 such sanctions were recorded (DPSS 1999b). Figure 9.3 shows the pervasive geographic pattern of declining percentages of those receiving TANF between May 1997 and April 1999, by zip code.

Beyond the matter of caseloads is the onerous challenge presented by welfare to work, a challenge that amply illustrates the considerable constraints facing the local welfare state. In effect, the county is primarily responsible for getting TANF recipients to make the transition into the

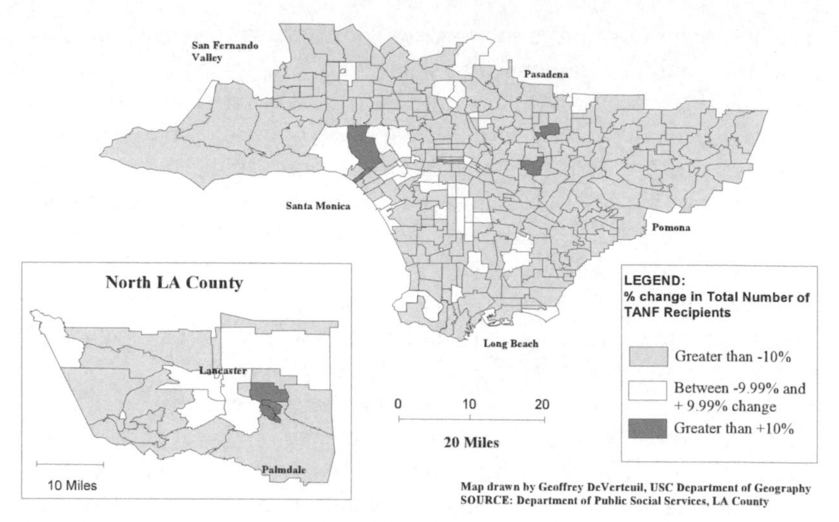

Figure 9.3. Percentage Change in TANF Recipients by Zip Code in Los Angeles County, May 1997–April 1999

workplace, with some 193,000 adult TANF recipients (80 percent of total) in Los Angeles County facing a five-year cap (Sommer 1998). However, the county was behind its goal of enrolling 150,000 recipients in the GAIN program by the beginning of 1999 and moving 60,000 of those into employment by June 1999. As of November 1998, there were just over 75,000 GAIN participants enrolled. One response has been to further devolve responsibilities, by subcontracting GAIN service provision in major county subregions to private for-profit firms (in this case, Maximus and Lockheed Martin). These trends reflect the troubling drift toward a local workfare state (Jessop 1994; Peck 2001), premised on the need to find jobs, any kind of jobs, for former welfare recipients.

Consequently, the local labor market will play a significant role in the county's ability to help recipients from GAIN and TANF make a successful transition into the workforce. Although the labor market has improved in the postrecession period, the modest gains in new jobs created and rates of employment should be viewed against the larger context, as of 1997, that follows.

- Though Los Angeles County lost 436,700, or 10 percent, of its jobs between 1990 and 1994, it had regained only 168,800 of them by 1997 (Force et al. 1998, 72).
- The true unemployment could be closer to 10.5 percent if discouraged workers are taken into consideration (72).

- Among occupations in which welfare recipients have experience, there was a decline of 315,700 jobs in the county between 1990 and 1994. Between 1994 and 1996, a gain of only 61,000 jobs (or 2.2 percent) was recorded (107).
- In occupations appropriate for most welfare adults, in three-fourths of the projected annual job openings, the median wage offered for new job applicants was $6.99 per hour or less (108).

Indeed, most welfare workers have been unable to move beyond jobs that are either part time or short term, or both. Less than one-fifth of these workers are able to gain entry into industries paying sustaining wages and work for at least three-quarters of the year over a multiyear period, which are the prerequisites for rising above the poverty threshold (Drayse et al. 2000). Therefore, even if the stagnant economy is able to provide employment opportunities to the expanding number of former TANF recipients, there seems to be little likelihood that these jobs offer long-term permanent exits from poverty. Recent reports indicate that nearly three-quarters of long-term GAIN workers and their families were still below the poverty threshold by the late 1990s (Drayse et al. 2000).

In one particular segment of the welfare-to-work population, the two-parent family, California (and by extension Los Angeles County) lags far behind other states. Ellis (1999) reports that the state failed to get 75 percent of its two-parent cases into the workforce for 1997 and is also likely to fail such requirements for 1998. The heavy proportion of legal immigrants among this population is a likely explanation for the minimal progress. Seventy-three percent of two-parent families in Los Angeles County reported a primary language other than English. Such a challenge illustrates the constrained ability of the local welfare state to secure promising work for its dependent citizens and legal residents.

In summary, the inability of the local welfare state to get the bulk of TANF recipients to make the transition into sustainable jobs reflects constraints on its autonomy. The local welfare state is unable to create jobs on its own effectively, relying instead on the vagaries of the private job market and attempting to increase the competitiveness of its recipients through new funding from the federal and state levels for job training and education. It becomes clear that welfare to work is another crisis for the local welfare state, but not a crisis of its own making. Rather, it is a federal crisis, devolved to localities. The consequences are apt to affect seriously those inner-city communities least able to weather the shifts and to become overwhelming if or when the economy slows down significantly. As such, along the continuum between local autonomy and local constraint, the county's limited ability to move recipients from welfare to work clearly demonstrates the limits of its local autonomy.

With welfare reform, the State of California and the county of Los Angeles have responded in varying and at times contradictory ways, depending in large degree on current political conflicts and changing economic and fiscal trends. Although it may appear that localities merely reflect the larger trends expressed by international and national political economic shifts, localities also enjoy political, regulatory, and bureaucratic spaces that allow them flexibility in responding to welfare reform.

CONCLUSIONS: A NEW MODEL OF LOCAL POVERTY MANAGEMENT?

Welfare reform has sharpened our understanding of the limits and abilities of the local welfare state. The cases of GR and unattached individuals, food stamps and legal immigrants, and AFDC/TANF and families with children illustrate different facets of the semiautonomous local welfare state. In our analysis, GR emerged as the most autonomous program at the county level, while AFDC/TANF better reflects the more constrained options of the local welfare state.

By closely analyzing these programs in the postreform era, we are able to reveal the complexities of the semiautonomous local welfare state. Beyond this consideration, however, our study contains larger implications about the way in which poverty is managed at the local level. As local programs shift in favor of job training and workfare over income maintenance and welfare, certain segments of the service-dependent population, particularly those deemed "nonemployable," will be negatively affected. At this point, we speculate that the local welfare state is increasingly implicated in the management of these economically marginal people. Driven by federal devolution, a lack of resources, and bureaucratic expediency, the local welfare state must rely on increasingly privatized modes of service administration and delivery, including private shelters, public and for-profit jails, and private sober-living homes. Paralleling this strategy of privatization is the demise of a locally provided continuum of care for service-dependent populations. In its place, evidence is pointing toward an increasingly circulatory approach to poverty management, whereby certain people are cycled across an array of unrelated (and uncoordinated) institutional settings (Wolch and DeVerteuil 2001). As a consequence, the everyday paths of the service-dependent and other vulnerable populations are now increasingly subject to circulation across jails, prisons, hospitals, rehabilitation centers, single-room occupancy (SRO) hotels, voluntary and public shelters,

Figure 9.4. Homeless Encampment, Downtown, Los Angeles, San Julian near Sixth Street (February 2002). The U.S. Department of Housing and Urban Development dubbed the city of Los Angeles as the "homelessness capital" of the United States in 1984.

public and for-profit jails, for-profit out-of-home placement facilities (e.g., a sober-living home for someone leaving detox), and the street (fig. 9.4). These expedient tendencies may be amplified by the existing recession, as well as a post–September 11 climate in which localities must dedicate resources to new issues such as homeland defense.

The concept of a "new poverty management" raises many implications for future research. For instance, poverty management strategies (localization, privatization, cycling) address different marginalized populations and, most critically, promote different institutional settings. For instance, different marginalized groups are institutionalized according to different rhetorics: emergency aid for shelters, social order for jails, and family values for out-of-home placement facilities. While offering apparently distinct settings, recent poverty management strategies essentially compartmentalize poverty-related problems, camouflaging their structural origins and confusing policy goals. The study of these new institutional settings, of how they reflect changing bureaucratic priorities, and of their locations across the metropolis all constitute important concerns for future research.

Further research should also explore the experiences of service-dependent populations as they cycle through settings such as jails, shelters, hospitals, and out-of-home placements. Such research would require tracking individuals across time and space to better understand their cycles across settings, the frequency and mix of institutional settings used, and the circumstances under which different settings are employed. Ultimately, the new poverty management approach reflects the growing crisis of the local welfare state and its drift toward the local workfare state, implying a deepening marginalization of service-dependent populations now defined primarily by their ability to compete successfully in the formal labor market.

PART III

POLITICS, POWER, AND CONFLICT

CHAPTER TEN

Gotham on Our Minds

New York City in the Los Angeles Charter Reform of 1996–1999

Raphael J. Sonenshein

"People here have not the faintest interest in taking anything but maybe pizza and bagels from New York," said Los Angeles city employee labor leader Julie Butcher. . . . Laura Lake, a Westside activist who was a leader of the 1980's slow growth movement, which she called Not Yet New York, said she still has leftover buttons, if anyone needs some. . . . Lake observed: "The way I view New York is as the Old Country. It's as if someone were coming from Europe to tell us how to run a democracy."
Rohrlich (1998)

The belief in the structural reform of government has been most widely held in American local government. The strength of this belief in structure reflects the remarkable impact of reformers on urban government. These efforts provide an opportunity to evaluate and improve urban democracy, which consists of the institutions, structures, and processes that connect people in cities to those who govern them. The movement to build new structures of citizen participation has encouraged some hope for a "rebirth of urban democracy." (Berry et al. 1993).

Increased attention to urban reform and urban democracy reverses a tendency in recent decades to treat cities as dependent entities whose residents cannot enjoy the benefits of democratic control. For an extended period, we risked losing the value of the vast database of local government as laboratories of democracy. According to Gittell (1994, 136), failing to come to terms with the reform of urban democracy has consequences for how we view cities and "has provided reinforcement for labeling cities as dependent and further discouraged active concern with the formulation of political solutions to city problems. There has been a visible lack of interest in structural and process reform of cities. The vitality of the grassroots reform efforts of the 1970's, which looked to expansion of citizen participation and the role of neighborhood and community organizations, was depreciated by the pessimism of growth politics. This change in the emphasis of urban scholarship took its toll on the political and intellectual status of the city in American political life."

The study of American urban reform inevitably pulls us westward. The reformers' strength has been far greater in the West and Southwest than in the East and Midwest (Shefter 1983). Although reform has always been important in the East and Midwest (with a long heritage in such big cities as New York and Philadelphia), it has been overshadowed by the great party machines. The history of the traditional big cities is the history of party organizations and their opponents. Reform in those regions has often been the province of "silk stocking," upper status constituencies.

In her book *Morning Glories,* Amy Bridges (1997) recast the history of urban reform by placing her focus not on the part of the country where reform is weak but in the Southwest and West, where reform has been central to urban government. To study government west of the Mississippi River is not to study the fine points of the party machine; it is to explore the nature of reform: "Although the municipal reform movement eventually had profound effects on city politics everywhere, in the large cities of the Northeast and Midwest, municipal reformers celebrated few victories at the polls, and when they did win, their time in office was most fleeting. . . . In the Southwest municipal reformers enjoyed a different history. . . . Just as the big cities of the Northeast and Midwest were commonly governed by political machines, and the cities of the South by Bourbon coalitions, so the cities of the Southwest have in the twentieth century been governed by municipal reformers" (1997, 3).

The politics and government of reform cities are there to be studied, and unusual innovations develop. Urban reformers of the Progressive era have the reputation—not without justification—for being conservative and for intending to exclude minorities (Welch and Bledsoe 1988). But Finegold (1995a, 1995b) has shown that in a number of cities, Progressive reformers worked closely with working-class constituencies to develop liberal governing coalitions.

GOVERNMENT IN THE CITIES OF NEW YORK AND LOS ANGELES: HISTORY AND CULTURE

The broadest and strongest biracial coalition at the big-city level developed not in the partisan cauldrons of New York City or Chicago but in the presumably "apolitical" and conservative metropolis of nonpartisan Los Angeles (Sonenshein 1993). The Tom Bradley coalition of blacks and liberal Jews, all active in the reformers' wing of the Democratic Party, applied the time-honored principles of municipal reform to the call for inclusion of the city's diverse population into its government. In New York City, Bradley and his reform allies might have seemed like "morning glories." But in reform Los Angeles, they were especially well suited to win power and to govern.

These differences in emphasis between reform and "regular" politics suggest a broader comparison between America's two largest cities, New York City and Los Angeles. In her study of New York City, Los Angeles, and Chicago as global cities, Abu-Lughod (1999) has shown that while these great metropolises are affected by similar global forces, they respond in ways that are shaped by local political culture and structure. Barbara Ferman's (1996) comparative study of neighborhood empowerment in Chicago and Pittsburgh also highlighted the impact of differing political structures in different cities. In that light, the experiences of such vastly different cities as New York City and Los Angeles should lead us to speak not of urban democracy but of urban democracies.

Advocates of a "Los Angeles School" have presented Los Angeles as a fundamentally different sort of metropolis from New York City and Chicago. In this view, Los Angeles is polycentered and highly dispersed, in contrast to the more center-based, traditional model usually associated with the so-called Chicago School and now with the New York School (Halle, in the introduction to this volume). The Los Angeles School theorists also make political comparisons. They tend to see Los Angeles as politically fragmented, with political authority highly dispersed, in comparison to more centralized political forms in more traditional cities. The literature has long characterized Los Angeles as a fragmented, dispersed entity (Fogelson 1967; Fulton 1997).

There is much to recommend this notion of a Los Angeles School. If Los Angeles is developing in a manner different from the more traditional metropolis, then we need to do further exploration of its urban democracy. Perhaps the entire framework of urban democracy and reform in Los Angeles will differ from that in New York City.

Los Angeles and New York City can be compared on the basis of political culture and political structure. The most striking aspect of this comparison is the extent to which the political culture and structure of Los Angeles were influenced by the desire not to be like New York City, or at least as people thought New York City to be. Images of New York City influenced the design of early Los Angeles government at the beginning of the twentieth century and even played a role in the debate over a new city charter at the end of the century. At the same time, the differences in the actual structure of the two cities' governments are in some ways not as great as might be imagined.

Los Angeles was constructed in its modern form to avoid all the presumed pitfalls of big-city machine politics. The largest influx of migrants to Los Angeles came from Midwestern cities at the turn of the twentieth century. They sought to have the virtues of the small Midwestern town in the clothes of a great metropolis: "The people of Los Angeles desired the size but not the character of the modern metropolis . . . to combine the spirit of the good community with the substance of the great metropolis" (Fogelson 1967, 191). These founders carried with them a vision of a homogeneous community, free of corruption but uninviting to immigrants and other groups who had to struggle mightily to gain acceptance in the growing metropolis (Singleton 1979; Sonenshein 1993). In the desire to build such a city, many residents were politically excluded who might otherwise have thrived in the politics of New York City: African-Americans, Jews, Latinos, Asian-Americans, and others.

Los Angeles government was intentionally established not to be New York City or any other traditional big city with party organizations and machines. That difference bespeaks a relationship between the governments of the two cities, at least from the standpoint of Los Angeles.

The 1925 City Charter that placed its stamp on Los Angeles government incorporated the reform philosophy that would mark Los Angeles as "a different kind of city." The mayor would have considerable authority but would face a strong city council. Citizen commissions whose members would be appointed by the mayor would direct the day-to-day operations of highly autonomous city departments (Abrahams 1967; Schockman 1996). Utilities would be publicly owned through proprietary departments of harbor and of water and power. Because of the power of citizen commissions and city bureaucrats, elected officials would be limited in their ability to "interfere" with efficient operation of government.

In this area, Los Angeles government is different from that of New York City. The Rodney King case (1991–92) made this difference abundantly clear. It was truly baffling to outsiders that Mayor Tom Bradley could not fire Police Chief Daryl Gates because the chief had civil service protection. The autonomous political power of the Los Angeles Police Department stands as one of the most remarkable and at times disastrous features of Los Angeles government. In the search to avoid corruption, the city instead created an unaccountable, unresponsive (if efficient) police department. Ironically, the search for efficiency created devastating inefficiencies, the most damaging of which has been the costly police scandals and the huge bills the city has had to pay for them.

The most important reform aspect of Los Angeles democracy was its thoroughgoing nonpartisanship, lasting to this day. Elections are held among candidates with no party designations listed on the ballot. Party organizations are nonexistent in city politics. In his study of nonpartisan elections, Charles Adrian (1959) found that some cities have the form but not the reality of nonpartisan elections. He listed Los Angeles as a city that really meant nonpartisan, a characterization that could hold today as well.

By comparison, New York City government developed around a very strong mayoralty and powerful party organizations. For most of the twentieth century, New York mayors were far more powerful than Los Angeles mayors. Partisan elections created and sustained strong party organizations. The five boroughs that comprise New York City generated their own party organizations, creating almost a federal system of power. A citywide Board of Estimate made critical budget and land-use decisions, with appointments to the board made by the mayor and the borough presidents. A large but weak city council could not compete with either the mayor or the Board of Estimate. The city council was a cipher, about which it was said that it was worse than a rubber stamp, because at least a rubber stamp leaves an impression (Schwartz and Lane 1998).

At the same time, there are areas in which the two cities have had similarities of political structure. While many Western and Southwestern cities adopted the most popular form of reform government—the council manager system in which an elected council selects a professional city manager—Los Angeles retained the mayor-council structure typical of Eastern and Midwestern cities (McCarthy et al. 1998). While other reform cities adopted at-large elections for city council, Los Angeles utilized elections by individual districts (Dykstra 1925). Although the Los Angeles mayor does not have the level of authority of a New York City mayor, the office is not nearly as powerless as some have said (Dykstra 1925; Greene 1998a).

Regardless of the structural comparison, the political cultures of the two cities are considerably different. New York City is a highly politicized community, best described by Sayre and Kaufman in 1960: "Nearly everyone in the city takes part in the city's political and governmental system. Taking part in 'politics'—that is, engaging in deliberative efforts to determine who gets public office (whether elective or appointed) and to influence what public officials and employees do—is an almost universal avocation among New Yorkers" (39).

By contrast, Los Angeles has a low-key political system, described well by Carney in 1964:

> Los Angeles has a low quotient of civic feeling. As a political community, it is highly attenuated. As a body politic, it is gangling and loose, and the nervous system which co-ordinates that sprawling body is haphazard and

> feeble. . . . One feels that the Angelenos are drawn together more on one of those sorrowing nights when the Giants bomb Koufax early in the game than they are on a day of municipal election. . . . It is not that politics seems futile or ugly or threatening to the Angelenos. To most of them, politics seems unnecessary. (Carney 1964, 116)

It is a mistake, however, to underestimate the coherence of Los Angeles politics. Los Angeles is capable of great achievements, such as the 1984 Olympics or the incorporation of minority groups through an astoundingly successful and durable interracial coalition behind five-term Mayor Tom Bradley (Sonenshein 1993). In the first half of the century, when Los Angeles completed vast public works, its leaders were able to accumulate political power and the local state developed considerable autonomy (Erie 1992). Balanced against its successes are its stunning failures, such as the 1965 and 1992 civil disorders and the possibility that twenty-first-century secession movements would tear it apart.

As a result of both structure and culture, Los Angeles is a city in which the spirit of reform (if not always reform structures) is central to the city's government. New York City has had a long and varied history of municipal reform, placed alongside its colorful saga of party organization (Viteritti 1989, 19). Reformers are contenders in New York City and can put a real scare into the regular party forces; but they are certainly not dominant.

In Los Angeles, the battle for power is fought not between parties and reformers but over the control of reform itself. As Bridges (1997) has shown, reform is so powerful an ideal in such communities that those who are in power and those who are out seek to compete to be the best reformers.

Thus, a battle over charter reform in Los Angeles should not be confined to high-status "do-gooders," and the League of Women Voters but should draw into its vortex top city officials, business, labor, and many others. The battle will not be only for the material spoils of government (jobs, patronage, etc.) but for leadership itself. To the victor go not thousands of patronage jobs but the credibility to exert leadership in a city built around the doctrines of reform.

The debate will be dominated by a search for the high ground of reform. Charter reform in Los Angeles will not be a struggle between elite reformers and party regulars running the system; it will be a battle in which all can portray themselves as reformers. In other words, both the advocates of change and its opponents will describe themselves as crusaders against corruption and avatars of greater efficiency.

Los Angeles residents, particularly those in government, often make reference to the most corrupt regime in local political history, the mayoralty of Frank Shaw (1933–38). The Shaw regime stands as the great moral lesson of Los Angeles reform. Shaw operated under the 1925 Charter, but before it had been amended to provide civil service protection to all general managers of departments.

Before his unprecedented recall by the voters in 1938, Shaw built a powerful political machine through widespread abuse of his mayoral powers. The depth of the local fear of corruption is reflected in the frequent references to the Shaw regime in charter reform discussions.

In addition to exploring the role that images of New York City played in the Los Angeles charter debate, this chapter ventures some comparisons between charter reforms in the two cities. Despite differences in structure and culture, pressure to reform the city charters in both cities led to changes that made the governmental systems of the two cities more alike than before.

Charter reform in New York City brought a degree of convergence with Los Angeles, just as Los Angeles charter reform brought elements of New York City government to Los Angeles. At the end of the two cities' charter reforms, however, the fundamental nature of the political structures of each city remained significantly different.

In 1986, a federal court declared the New York City Board of Estimate to be an unconstitutional violation of the one-person, one-vote doctrine, leading to a successful comprehensive revision of the New York City Charter. The court ruled that boroughs of unequal population could not have equal representation on a citywide decision-making body. While New York City has had several major charter revisions, there was no mistaking the importance of the 1989 revision (Mauro and Benjamin 1989; Schwartz and Lane 1998).

A guiding assumption of the New York City charter reform was that the Board of Estimate should be eliminated and the council should obtain new powers but that the system should continue to be marked by a strong mayoralty (Schwartz and Lane 1998). Even with the continuance of the strong mayor system, the charter reform in New York City made the system more "normal," more like the average American big city than it had been before and even a little bit more like Los Angeles, with its dominant city council. The Los Angeles charter reform increased the authority of the mayor and scaled back some of the council's administrative authority. But just as the New York City reform did not fundamentally alter the strong mayoralty, the Los Angeles reform did not adopt a strong-mayor form of government.

THE LOS ANGELES CHARTER REFORM OF 1999

In the mid-1990s, Los Angeles moved to revise its charter comprehensively in the face of well-organized efforts by some in the San Fernando Valley to secede from the city. In a sense, Los Angeles had to decide whether in its desire to avoid being like New York City, it had lost some of the assets of a strong, visible political system. If Los Angeles government was perceived to be in need of improvement, how far in the direction of New York City's model would the city's residents be willing to go?

Born out of a desire to reduce the appeal of those in the San Fernando Valley who called for secession from the city of Los Angeles, Los Angeles charter reform developed into a complicated political struggle between the mayor and the city council, with important involvement by other elected officials, business, labor, civic groups, and minority organizations.[1] In addition to changes in the authority of the mayor and city council, the new charter included a major change in participation by establishing a citywide system of neighborhood councils and by creating area planning commissions.

The context for charter reform in Los Angeles was the conjunction of the election of a Republican businessman, Richard Riordan, as mayor in 1993, and the rise of a credible movement for secession in the San Fernando Valley in 1995. Riordan, who was strongly critical of the city bureaucracy and of the city council, sought in charter reform to upgrade the mayor's authority. He was the political actor most motivated to implement charter reform.

Riordan was part of a wave of white moderate-to-conservative centrist mayors, some Democrats, some Republicans, who succeeded African-Americans in the four largest American cities (Sonenshein et al. 1995). National attention to these new mayors, with their promises of new models of service delivery and urban governance, raised the possibility that Los Angeles would become somewhat more like the other two major cities, New York City and Chicago.

But the real wind in the sails of charter reform came from the movement for Valley secession. The San Fernando Valley contains roughly one-third of the city's population, and as many as 45 percent of its registered voters. Separated from the rest of Los Angeles by the Santa Monica Mountains (fig. i.5), the San Fernando Valley had long entertained notions of independence. Dominated by single-family homes, this bastion of the white middle class became the center of opposition to school busing in the 1970s and provided massive support for tax-cutting Prop-

Table 10.1. Population of the San Fernando Valley, 1990 and 2000

	1990		2000	
	Number	Percent	Number	Percent
Non-Hispanic whites	697,389	57.5	561,301	41.8
Blacks	45,304	3.7	59,838	4.5
Asian	91,489	7.5	119,889	8.9
Hispanic	373,110	30.7	566,470	42.1
Other	6,544	0.5	36,357	2.7
Total	1,213,836	99.9	1,343,855	100.0

Source. 1990 data derived from the Economic Alliance of the San Fernando Valley (2000, 62). 2000 data derived from Census 2000 by the San Fernando Valley Economic Research Center at California State University, Northridge.
Note. Asian includes Pacific Islanders. Percentages may not total to 100 because of rounding.

osition 13 in 1978. By the time secession made it onto the city's central agenda in 1995, the Valley had become much more diverse as Latinos moved there in large numbers. The 2000 census revealed that non-Hispanic whites comprised a minority (41.8 percent) of the Valley's population, while Latinos now comprised 42.1 percent (see table 10.1).

Backed by new state legislation that eased the path to secession, Valley insurgents had by 1996 gotten the full attention of city leaders. A Valley businessman and political ally of Riordan, David Fleming, proposed that if the city reformed its charter, it could blunt the impetus for secession by making government more efficient and responsive. Riordan was naturally in agreement, since such an approach might help him reach his goal of greater mayoral authority.

The biggest obstacle to the implementation of Fleming's plan was the vitriolic dislike between Riordan and the council. After an early honeymoon, Riordan's abortive plans to privatize or contract out some city services led to severe conflict with city employees and with the council. It was downhill from there, as Riordan vowed to find new ways to work his will over the council, and the council adopted various resistance strategies. It was hard to imagine the two sides joining together to create a consensus charter revision. But an effort was made anyway.

The charter reform process began in earnest in 1996, when City Councilman Michael Feuer, whose Fifth Council District was half in the Valley, proposed with David Fleming that the city create an appointed charter reform commission. Under the Feuer-Fleming plan, the appointed commission, whose members would be selected by the three citywide elected officials (the mayor, the city attorney, and the controller) and the city council, would send its recommendations directly to the ballot without council review. Feuer entered into negotiations with Mayor Riordan and Council President John Ferraro to bring his motion to fruition. However, the council defeated the measure, on the grounds that the normal procedure of council review of ballot measures should be maintained.

The city council then dusted off a motion originally made by Councilwoman Ruth Galanter in 1991 for the appointment of a charter reform commission that would make recommendations to the city council for placement on the ballot. With the failure of the Feuer-Fleming plan to win council approval, an angry Fleming proposed the creation of an elected commission, the recommendations of which could go straight to the ballot.

Unbelievably, both alternatives were implemented. The council created an advisory commission in the fall of 1996, with members to be appointed by the council members (the council president acting as mayor when Riordan chose not to make his appointments), the city controller, and the city attorney. Backed by funds raised by Riordan, a ballot measure to create an elected commission was passed by the voters in April 1997, and members were elected in the April primary and June runoff elections.

Thus, by July 1, 1997, the city had the altogether remarkable situation of two legal and legitimate charter reform commissions, pursuing different visions of comprehensive charter reform. In a further oddity, most of the mayor's candidates for the elected charter reform commission were defeated by candidates supported by his opponents in organized labor. It took Riordan some months of patient effort, as well as divisions within organized labor, to regain control of the body Riordan had created.

The crucial dividing issue for the city's powerbrokers became the power of the mayor. And here the perception (not always the reality) of New York City government emerged strongly as a factor in the debate. On this issue, Los Angeles charter reform had "Gotham on its mind."

It was perhaps inevitable that Riordan, a businessman with little patience for legislative politics, would find the mayor-centered governments of New York City and Chicago appealing. He saw Richard M. Daley and Giuliani appear to shuffle and reshuffle their governments with barely an effective squeal from other powerbrokers in the system. Riordan was deeply concerned about the governance of the Los Angeles Unified School District. He could see that Daley had won authority from the Illinois legislature to appoint the school superintendent and to control the schools directly. Giuliani had less authority, since the schools were run by an appointed school board. But he could appoint two of the seven members of the school board, and through influence with borough presidents who appointed other members, he could exercise considerable control. And of course power perceptions are relative. Giuliani, possessor of a vast mayoral authority, was constantly trying to expand it, calling for the abolition of the board of education and even establishing his own charter reform commission, the recommendations of which were rejected by the voters.

By contrast, Riordan not only felt hamstrung by the city council but also felt blocked from influencing a school district operated by a separately elected school board. On the education front, Riordan finally decided midway through his mayoralty to go outside the structural reform approach and raised money for reform candidates who were successful in winning a majority of school board seats.

Riordan frequently referred to the mayor's office as weak and powerless. His argument resonated among business leaders and to some degree in the San Fernando Valley, where his many political supporters regarded him as a friendly force in an unfriendly government. Others argued that the mayor's office in Los Angeles, while not nearly as strong as the mayor in New York City and Chicago, was much stronger than believed (Greene 1998a; McCarthy et al. 1998).

In any case, a guiding assumption of the Los Angeles charter reform was that there would be some enhancement of mayoral authority and some diminution of council authority. By contrast, a guiding assumption of the 1989 New York City charter reform was that the mayor's vast authority needed to be circumscribed and held accountable by a strengthened city council (Schwartz and Lane 1998). One of the additional outcomes of charter reform in New York City was the creation of the office of public advocate, elected citywide to replace the previous office of the citywide elected council president and to further help hold the mayor accountable.

For the purposes of this chapter, the Los Angeles City Charter will be discussed as the old charter (1925–2000) and the new charter (ratified by the voters in 1999 and implemented on July 1, 2000). The old charter had little detail about the role of the mayor and, by contrast, granted considerable explicit authority to the council. The council was defined as the "governing body" of the city.

The New York City Charter, even as amended in 1989, is far more mayor-centered. (Table 10.2 summarizes the comparisons between the two city charters.) The New York City Charter contains extensive detail on the authority of the mayor. According to the appointed commission's research (Appointed Los Angeles Charter Reform Commission 1998b), New York is the only city that grants to the mayor all residual powers of

Table 10.2. New York City and Los Angeles: Old and New Charter Comparisons

	NEW YORK CITY		LOS ANGELES	
	Old Charter	New Charter (1989–)	Old Charter (1925–2000)	New Charter (2000–)
Council size	35	51	15	15
Council election	District	District	District	District
Partisanship	Partisan	Partisan	Nonpartisan	Nonpartisan
Governing body	Mayor	Mayor	Council	No governing body
Budget	Mayor and council	Mayor and council	CAO advises mayor and council	CAO advises mayor and council
Neighborhood government	Boroughs/community boards	Boroughs/community boards	None	Neighborhood councils/area planning commissions
School board	Appointed, with mayor making two appointments and each borough president making one	No change[a]	Elected by district	Elected by district
Department heads	Called "commissioners"; serve at pleasure of mayor; no civil service protection	No change	Called "general managers"; mayor appoints and removes with council majority; no civil service protection for department heads[b]	Mayor appoints with council majority; mayor removes with right to appeal to council and two-thirds council may over-ride, no civil service protection for department heads
Council authority	Extremely weak due to role of Board of Estimate	Council legislative and oversight roles strengthened	Great administrative authority	Reduced administrative authority; greater focus on oversight and legislative roles
Board of Estimate	Immense power	Abolished	None	None

Note. New York City's community boards are basically advisory only, although their views are often taken quite seriously. By contrast, the new area planning commissions in Los Angeles will make decisions on land use. New York's board of estimate had to approve every contract signed with the city, which gave it enormous power and also facilitated corruption. It was composed of the five borough presidents, plus the mayor (who had two votes), the city comptroller, and the city council president.

[a] As of 2002, the mayor appoints the school chancellor directly as well as eight members of the thirteen-member board.

[b] In 1995, a charter amendment took department heads out of civil service.

the city (in other words, those powers not explicitly given to other bodies). In most cities, such powers rest with the city council, and a few cities (such as Philadelphia) are silent on the issue.

Before the New York City charter reform of 1989, the mayor was even more powerful through his or her role in appointing key members of the powerful Board of Estimate. Even after the 1989 charter reform eliminated the Board of Estimate, the mayor remained a huge force in New York City. When Mayor Giuliani became irked that his police commissioner had his picture on the cover of a national magazine, he sacked him. When he tired of his schools chief, he worked with his appointees and allies on the school board to force him out. When he became disenchanted with the new superintendent, he showed him the door, too. The mayor is expected to be in charge, and when he or she is not, the penalty is severe, as David Dinkins discovered after the rioting in Crown Heights. Some have described the New York City mayoralty as the closest equivalent to the presidency, and mayors are often featured as potential candidates for higher office although they are very unlikely to succeed in that upward step.

The mayor of Los Angeles is a very important politician in city, state, and nation but is not the focus of saturation news coverage. The mayor operates in an atmosphere that is less political and less public, in a city where politics have much lower visibility than in New York City.

The Los Angeles mayor had considerable influence and power under the old charter, but that power was hemmed in by the council. For example, the mayor appointed and removed general managers of city departments but in each case required a majority vote of the fifteen-member council. Until a 1995 charter amendment, mayors had even less scope to direct general managers. Department heads had civil service protection and were hired and fired by city commissions appointed by the mayor. The 1995 measure ended the civil service status of general managers and placed the hiring and firing authority for most general managers in the hands of the mayor with the consent of the council. In New York City, by contrast, top officials of city departments serve "at the pleasure of the mayor," a phrase that was very popular with Mayor Riordan's staff.

The City Administrative Officer (CAO) in Los Angeles, a position established in 1951, served both the mayor and the council and provided a single set of budget numbers for deliberations by elected officials. The office was originally established as a mayoral tool to design a coherent budget in the face of the tradition of semiautonomous departments. Riordan's hostility to the shared authority of the CAO drove the CAO into the arms of the city council. There is no equivalent office in New York City.

The remarkable system of citizen commissions also distinguishes Los Angeles government from New York City. Most Los Angeles city departments have citizen commissions, the members of which are mayoral appointees, that provide either policy direction or in some cases direct management of the department. Over the years, the commission system has eroded, and few still manage departments. Mayors have become adept at using commission positions as rewards to allies, and the commission system has become an adjunct to mayoral authority. While a "commissioner" in New York City is normally the equivalent of a Los Angeles "general manager," there is no real parallel in New York City for a Los Angeles city commissioner.

Even under the old charter, the Los Angeles mayor had great authority in the development of the city budget. It was difficult for the council to interfere with the mayor's budget because there were strict time limits to council action. If the council did not act by a set date, the mayor's budget would take effect. Even the governor of California has no such power. (The new charter largely retained the mayor's budget authority.)

A consensus had emerged from a series of charter reform commissions as far back as 1934 that the mayor of Los Angeles should have enhanced authority, but there was disagreement among the various commissions about the nature and extent of such changes. Thus the two commissions in 1997 were left with a general view that the mayor needed more authority but with often bitter disagreements about the nature of that change. And the mutual dislike between Riordan and the council made it difficult to find a common ground on how much would be enough.

The question of mayoral authority emerged as a crucial stumbling block to building consensus on a range of issues. After his initial defeat in the campaign for the elected commission, Mayor Riordan recouped by building a close relationship with the elected group. Organized labor found it increasingly difficult to compete with the mayor for influence over the elected commission.

With the vehicle of the elected commission, Riordan placed all his energy into the drive for mayoral authority. He set out three main goals for charter reform: (1) to have the mayor appoint the city attorney, instead of being elected as under the old charter, (2) to reduce or eliminate the role of the city administrative officer, which reported both to the mayor and council under the old charter, and (3) to give the mayor the authority to unilaterally fire general managers of city departments. In all three areas, Riordan's proposals would have aligned Los Angeles practice with that of New York City. There were a host of less important Riordan priorities, all aimed at reducing the council's influence and increasing that of the mayor (Rohrlich 1997b). While the final charter proposal made significant changes to increase mayoral authority, and was attacked by opponents of the charter for that reason, Riordan gained none of the three core goals he originally set forth.

The mayor's arguments not surprisingly found greater support in the elected commission than in the appointed commission. But even in the elected commission, Riordan faced defeat on his proposed changes to the office of the city attorney. Both commissions decided to keep the city attorney largely as it was.

On the removal of general managers, and on the role of the CAO, a vast and bitter debate developed, which took months to resolve. Early in the deliberation process, both commissions tentatively voted to grant to the mayor unilateral authority to fire general managers. The appointed commission voted to give the mayor this power on March 25, 1998, matching a similar action by the elected commission in the same week. A half-year later, after public meetings disclosed widespread public opposition to this proposed charter change, the appointed commission reversed itself and voted to maintain the existing procedure requiring a majority vote of the council to remove general managers.

On the role of the City Administrative Officer, the elected commission largely sided with the mayor against the position of the appointed commission. On August 24, 1998, the elected commission voted to transfer many of the CAO's functions to the mayor. Keith Comrie, the CAO since his appointment to the post by Mayor Tom Bradley in 1978, entered the debate with a dramatic flourish. He issued public denunciations of the mayor's position, bringing into the open a battle that had been developing between himself and Riordan since 1993.

The image of New York City government became a key part of the local debate. Comrie cited New York City government as the model that Los Angeles had consciously rejected and argued that the mayor's proposals, if enacted, would bring east coast corruption to Los Angeles and bring Los Angeles back to the days of the Shaw regime (Greene 1998b). While Comrie was not well known outside city hall, his attacks on the elected commission were warmly received in city hall, where he became something of a hero (Merl 1998). (In actuality, the image of New York City government as corrupt in the traditional sense was more appropriate to the old days when the Board of Estimate had to approve every city contract, providing huge opportunities for graft. Exposed under this system, one borough president, Donald Manes of Queens, committed suicide while another, Stanley Simon of the Bronx, went to jail.)

Comrie was joined in his assault on the elected commission by unions representing city employees, which blasted increases in mayoral power and called for retaining the CAO. Comrie maintained the New York City theme: "Progressive governments don't look to New York for good government and leadership. . . . Does it make good common sense to look to New York, the only large city that went bankrupt, as a model that we want to follow?" (McGreevy 1998; Newton 1998a).

On September 10, 1998, Comrie issued a scathing attack on the proposals of the elected commission regarding mayoral authority and the CAO's office. He announced that he would delay his January retirement because, he said, "I consider this such a threat to honest and good government that I'm going to stay on." An aide in Riordan's office blasted back, "Keith is just proving that he's denying a village somewhere in the world its idiot" (Newton 1998b).

The New York image became more entrenched as Comrie spoke about the staff of the elected commission. The staff director and legal drafting specialist on the elected commission were both from New York City. They were open, avowed fans of the New York City government system. Comrie blasted them as New York City hacks and blamed them for the drift of the elected commission toward the mayor's position, relying on what Comrie called "the New York model."

On September 17, 1998, Comrie's office released a study contending that consolidating power in the mayor's office would severely damage good government. His report was titled, "Prescription for Incompetence and Corruption." For key political actors, the firing of general managers and the CAO emerged as do-or-die issues. Council members were adamant about retaining a majority vote for the firing of general managers and, in addition, were fearful of losing access to the research role of the CAO. Organized labor was vehement in its opposition to changing the rules on firing general managers as well as in its support of the CAO. The appointed commission, sympathetic to Comrie's arguments and to intense resistance by the council and organized labor, largely endorsed retaining the CAO in its existing form.

The appointed commission released its preliminary recommendations to the public in early August 1998. The commission then conducted a series of eight interactive open houses, where the measure to authorize the mayor to fire general managers unilaterally drew a very negative reaction from the public in all quarters of the city. The appointed commission's survey found that 61 percent of all respondents opposed unilateral firing authority, with 34 percent in favor. Fully a third of all participants expressed strong disapproval of the proposed change to the charter on firing of general managers (Appointed Los Angeles Charter Reform Commission 1998a).

On October 6, 1998, the appointed commission reversed its earlier decision and recommended maintaining the current council role in the removal of general managers. George Kieffer (1998), chair of the appointed commission, set out in an op-ed article the view that "the mayor's office is not as weak as it has been portrayed. . . . The authority of the mayor of Los Angeles should be increased. But the sole and unfettered authority to remove general managers is not so necessary to effective leadership as to outweigh the risks of mischief, incompetence and political abuse."

The general manager issue represented a fundamental area of disagreement between the two commissions, which had been seeking to agree on a single charter for months through a joint conference committee. On November 16, 1998, Mayor Riordan transmitted a letter to the elected commission making his case for unilateral removal authority. Council President John Ferraro followed with a letter on December 4 (Ferraro 1998) stating: "*I am absolutely and unequivocally opposed to giving any mayor of the City the unilateral authority to remove its general managers*. . . . The Mayor feels that the involvement of the Council will have a corrupting influence on the process, but allowing the Mayor to act alone will not. I don't find that to be a valid argument. It seems that it would be easier to corrupt one person than 15."

The issue of mayoral authority tapped into elements of the local political culture. Both sides were claiming the mantle of reform. In a city where politics have low visibility, the granting of great power to one politician raised suspicions.

A compromise on general managers soon began to circulate around city hall. The proposal would change the existing system in which a majority of the council had to approve a removal of a general manager. Under the compromise proposal, a fired general manager could appeal removal to the council, which could, with a two-thirds majority, reinstate the official. The compromise proposal quickly gathered substantial support on both charter reform commissions and among council members, other elected officials, business, and labor.

By that time, the compromise process was largely in the hands of the two chairs, George Kieffer (appointed) and Erwin Chemerinsky (elected). In constant contact with each other, they forged a wide range of agreements, which they then presented as joint recommendations to a conference committee made up of members of both commissions.

They also spearheaded the search for community support of the emerging Unified Charter. In the absence of coalition behavior among elected officials, the two chairs built mutual trust (Hinckley 1981) and created their own coalition.

Riordan remained outside the evolving consensus. On November 2, 1998, the mayor announced his full support for the elected commission's proposed new charter and his disappointment with the appointed commission's approach. He then actively lobbied the elected commission to go it alone without the appointed commission. Riordan's involvement brought the joint conference committee process between the two commissions to the verge of breakdown. When the chair of the elected commission, Chemerinsky, resisted Riordan's pressure to go it alone without the appointed commission, the mayor's chief aide pointedly suggested that Chemerinsky step aside as chair. Chemerinsky refused. Yet with pressure growing from all sides for a compromise, and with editorials in the *Los Angeles Times* accusing Riordan of "lobbing grenades," the two commissions inched toward a compromise charter and toward the two-thirds solution.

In early January 1999, the Service Employees International Union (SEIU) Local 347 released a poll of registered voters on the removal of general managers that supplemented the less systematic data gathered by the appointed commission in its open houses (Service Employees International Union 1998). The results indicated that it was not just politicians who opposed the mayor's position; the public was vehemently opposed to taking the city council out of the process.

Only 15 percent of registered voters favored granting the mayor the power to fire general managers unilaterally. The old charter provisions were supported by 39 percent, and the two-thirds compromise by 33 percent. Even in the San Fernando Valley, there was as little support for unrestricted mayoral firing authority as there was in South Central Los Angeles. In the Valley, only 14 percent favored the mayor's position compared to 12 percent in Central/South Los Angeles.

The most dramatic week in charter reform came after New Year's Day 1999. In a heavily attended meeting on January 5, 1999, the elected commission considered the Unified Charter. Chemerinsky made an impassioned plea for passage. Many community activists spoke in favor of the package. Mayor Riordan spoke against it. Rumors of political threats against commissioners swirled around. Finally, "in a stunning moment of political drama" (Newton 1999a), the elected commission voted down the Unified Charter, and all seemed lost.

The next day, the appointed commission met to consider the Unified Charter in the wake of the elected commission's rejection. Kieffer made an eloquent plea that despite the other commission's actions the appointed commission should adopt the Unified Charter anyway. The commissioners unanimously voted to adopt the Unified Charter. The large audience, demoralized by the apparent breakdown of consensus the night before, stood and cheered the appointed commission's rescue of the imperiled Unified Charter. Charter reform was back in business.

Blistering editorial criticism of the mayor and the elected commission soon led to a turnaround. A week after rejecting the compromise, the elected panel approved the package with some relatively minor modifications. After weeks of further negotiation, a single charter emerged and was placed on the ballot with the two-thirds compromise in place. The Unified Charter also left the CAO's office largely unchanged.

Lack of compromise on one key issue may have saved the charter. Both commissions had voted to increase the council's size but could not agree on the exact number. Informal discussions with public opinion experts later made it clear how lucky the charter commissions had been in not agreeing. An increase in the size of the council would have been hugely unpopular, and the failure to agree on the number removed a key stumbling block to passage.

The different fate of council size in the two cities exemplifies another difference in their political cultures. The New York City charter reform had incorporated an increase in the size of the city council from thirty-five to fifty-one, which became a popular part of the measure. Voters in Los Angeles are far more reluctant to increase the number of elected officials than are voters in New York City. The commission kept the size of the council unchanged in the main charter proposal and attached additional ballot measures for twenty-one and twenty-five seats, respectively. Both council increases were crushed at the polls.

Although the final agreement lacked the three main elements that Riordan had wanted, he did gain significant authority for the mayor in the charter. The mayor received authority to grant pay raises to general managers within guidelines set by the council; to direct the city's intergovernmental relations; to structure the mayor's office within budget guidelines; to remove the designation of the city council as the city's governing body; to authorize the mayor to remove appointed city commissioners without council veto; to remove general managers more easily through the two-thirds compromise; to prevent the council from modifying decisions by city commissions; and a number of other provisions.

The mayor also gained an earlier implementation date for the new charter than either commission had contemplated. Both commission chairs had recommended that the new charter take effect on July 1,

2001, when there would be a new mayor in office. One unnamed source quipped, "Giving this mayor this charter is like giving a teenager a Testerosa" (Newton 1999b). With the support of City Attorney James Hahn and Council President John Ferraro, Riordan won a change in these recommendations to July 1, 2000.

Much of the bitterness in the charter debate concerned issues of "the center," namely, power at city hall and who would exercise it. The other dimension of charter reform concerned the "periphery," in this case, the structures for neighborhood empowerment. As a consequence of a reform process that was meant to discourage secession, the new charter included a major pair of Los Angeles innovations: a system of advisory neighborhood councils and decision-making area planning commissions.

In fact, the final proposal on neighborhood councils—advisory bodies, rather than elected, decision-making councils—was supported by the New York City experience of community boards. In that area, at least, the New York City analogy was not particularly damaging. The appointed commission relied heavily on the New York City case because it represented the only city of Los Angeles's size to have a system comparable to what was being proposed.

Although the New York City experience bolstered the argument that citizen advisory bodies could play a valuable role in a big city, the meaning of neighborhood councils was quite different in Los Angeles than in Gotham. Community boards, as they are called in New York City, were implemented by the State of New York as part of a revision of the State Constitution in 1974. In an era of citizen participation, and in the wake of the disastrous battle over community school boards in the late 1960s, the state created the institution of advisory citizen boards. These boards received further definition in the New York City Charter Reform of 1989, when they were given a role in the new land use review process involving the borough presidents. In a city with a diverse array of local party organizations and other well-organized bodies, community boards would be unlikely to become the central symbol of citizen participation.

In Los Angeles, by contrast, neighborhood councils became the spirit of charter reform and the main vehicle for enhanced citizen participation. For a city without party organizations, with few bodies other than labor unions, chambers of commerce, and homeowner associations able to influence city policy, neighborhood councils were a dramatic departure that seemed to promise a new connection to city hall.

Even further, the area planning commissions were genuine innovations in urban governance. By contrast to the advisory role of neighborhood councils, area planning commissions would make decisions on local land use matters and thereby decentralize elements of the complicated land use approval process in the city. Some of these powers might be seen as precursors of a borough system, much discussed among secession advocates as an alternative to breaking away. Ironically, New York City's charter reform was moving away from the major powers held by boroughs and was transforming them into semiadvisory bodies in the land use process.

The increases to mayoral authority in the proposed charter brought opposition from six members of the city council, including the council president. Three members of the council, Mike Feuer, Cindy Miscikowski and Joel Wachs, backed the new charter, while three others remained neutral. The opposing side recruited major labor organizations to its camp and raised money principally from city lobbyists and from council members' political war chests.

The pro-charter coalition included the mayor, Riordan's enemies Comrie and City Attorney James Hahn, City Controller Rick Tuttle, Chief of Police Bernard C. Parks, the three council members, numerous business and civic organizations, and even leaders of the secession movement. Riordan took the lead in raising money for the pro-charter campaign and was able to generate a war chest substantially larger than that of the opponents.

The ballot arguments presented by the pro and con sides clearly indicated that the language of reform permeated both sides of the debate. The pro side argued that the new charter would increase efficiency and responsiveness while preserving checks and balances against corruption. The con argument charged that the new charter would be costly and inefficient and would set the city back to a period of mayoral corruption. It would be up to the voters—the ultimate reformers—to decide. And on election day, a strong majority of 60 percent of the voters cast their ballots for the new charter.

The new charter passed in all areas of the city except the African-American community, where opposition to Riordan ran high and where public employees were well represented. The core base of support for the charter was on the Jewish west side, with secondary support from the San Fernando Valley and from the Latino east side. In that sense, the winning coalition was the mirror image of the New York City charter vote. The heaviest support in New York City was in minority neighborhoods that would gain representation; the strongest opposition was in Staten Island, which had disproportionate power under the Board of Estimate in the old charter (Schwartz and Lane 1998).

The differing coalitions for charter reform in New York City and Los Angeles are largely explained by the differing impacts of the new provisions on various communities. Those communities that might lose influence under the new charters (African-Americans in Los Angeles; Staten Island in New York City) stood out in opposition.

Despite all the battles over mayoral authority, the greatest appeal of the new Los Angeles charter to the voters was the system of neighborhood councils. The real driving force of the charter from the public's standpoint was not the new arrangement at the center of government but the dispersal of authority to the periphery. The participatory elements of the new charter bolstered the argument of city leaders that the city government was reforming and that secession was therefore not necessary.

The reform of the Los Angeles City Charter was an example of how leaders and activists can surmount the structural difficulties in the way of collective action. The threat of secession might suggest political fragmentation but the ability to use the charter to help fend off that threat demonstrated a coherent political and governmental response to a crisis of legitimacy.

The battle over secession continued after the passage of the new charter, influencing the election of a new mayor in 2001, James Hahn, who had the support of secession advocates and Valley voters. After becoming mayor, Hahn campaigned vigorously against secession arguing that the participatory mechanisms in the new charter now made secession unnecessary. In a November 2002 vote on the secession of the San Fernando Valley, secession lost by a roughly two-to-one majority citywide but passed narrowly (51 percent to 49 percent) in the San Fernando Valley. The success or failure of the new charter in making city government more efficient and responsive will likely play a major role in future battles over whether to stay together or break up. As the city continues to refine its new charter, there has already been discussion of additional participatory mechanisms, one in particular that is characteristic of New York City: the system of boroughs.

CONCLUSION

In Los Angeles, where there are multiple and divided authorities, charter reform seemed doomed to collapse when two competing charter reform commissions were established. But in a pattern that has appeared before in Los Angeles, the hole created by the lack of enduring political institutions was temporarily filled by individuals outside government who forged the agreements necessary to bridge the differences over the authority of the mayor. As a consequence, the new charter offered the chance to create new mediating institutions: neighborhood councils and area planning commissions.

On the issue of mayoral authority, the battle over charter reform in Los Angeles revealed long-standing beliefs prevalent in the local political culture about executive power. While the new Los Angeles Charter enhances the mayor's management authority in significant ways, the main changes sought by the mayor were derailed by reference to the contrast between local tradition and images of New York City government.

Despite the animus held toward New York City government in Los Angeles, the new charter made Los Angeles's government a little bit more like that of New York City. Los Angeles strengthened its mayoral office and built a system of neighborhood councils. As New York City eliminated its Board of Estimate and greatly strengthened its city council, it became a little bit more like Los Angeles. But in the realm of politics and government, no one could mistake one city for the other. Their differences continue to be profound and reinforce the notion that, in America, rather than a single urban democracy, we have urban democracies.

Los Angeles charter reform was consistent with the historical quest of Los Angeles to be a great city but to be a community unlike the older metropolises of New York City and Chicago, to build a political system without political parties. As its population continues to grow, and as it is increasingly seen as a city of world importance, Los Angeles residents will likely keep trying to improve on the reform model, to overcome the fragmentation that threatens effective collective action, in order to have the virtues of the great metropolis and the small town.

CHAPTER ELEVEN

The Mayoral Politics of New York and Los Angeles

Karen M. Kaufmann

There is perhaps no more potent symbol of political inclusion than the ascension of a group member to the mayoralty of ones' city. While all mayors are not equally powerful, the presence of a minority mayor in a large city nonetheless provides important material and psychological benefits to minorities who reside there. For much of the 1970s and 1980s, Los Angeles represented a model of minority incorporation, while New York City, arguably the more liberal city of the two, was run by a conservative coalition that debatably offered few symbolic or material rewards to its large minority community. Then in the 1990s, both cities were run by conservative regimes, causing speculation that liberalism, as illustrated by the "new" politics of the nation's two largest cities, had been banished from the urban landscape. The new millennium, however, witnessed a rebirth of urban liberalism with Los Angeles electing a liberal Democrat, James Hahn, to succeed Richard Riordan. Early polling in the New York mayoral contest also pointed to a Democratic victory, with the liberal Mark Green running strongly against his Republican opponent Michael Bloomberg. In the post–September 11 environment, and after an acrimonious Democratic primary, however, New Yorkers opted for the billionaire businessman, Bloomberg. This chapter explores the similarities and differences in the mayoral politics of Los Angeles and New York.

From 1977 to 1989, New York City politics were dominated by the outspoken and sporadically conservative, Ed Koch, during which time Los Angeles was led by a black liberal Democrat, Tom Bradley. Los Angeles was in fact the first large city with a small black population to elect a black mayor. And as noteworthy as Bradley's election in 1973 was, his ability to sustain his biracial electoral coalition for five consecutive terms was equally exceptional. During the 1980s, racial polarization in the vote was increasingly observed in New York City mayoral elections, yet was much less characteristic of Los Angeles politics. From this narrow perspective then, it appeared that Los Angeles voters were simply more receptive to liberal candidates than were voters in New York. At minimum, it appeared that these two electorates engaged in largely different types of voting considerations. In 1993, however, both Los Angeles and New York elected moderate Republican mayors. Extreme racial polarization in the vote, once notably absent in Los Angeles, was now characteristic of both cities. For the first time in several decades, political behavior in Los Angeles and New York appeared strikingly similar. Thus one focus of this chapter is to explore how such dramatic changes in voting behavior can occur.

The following analyses pay particular attention to the mayoral politics of New York City and Los Angeles over the past ten years. Relying on the insights of group interest theory, these cases illustrate the importance of electoral context with regard to voting behavior. The central theoretical argument is that the political context in local elections determines the extent to which race and racial attitudes become salient voting considerations. In particular, heightened perceptions of intergroup competition and conflict are argued to create a conflictual decision context that makes racial and ethnic concerns salient to voting behavior. In the absence of such conflict, the group interest perspective anticipates that traditional political cues, such as party identification, will be more important than alternate group attachments, such as race or ethnicity. Thus from a group interest point of view, the apparent differences between New York and Los Angeles during the 1970s and 1980s can be explained by intercity differences in the level of interracial conflict. The 1992 Los Angeles riots, however, are credited for a change in the political context of Los Angeles. In this more conflictual environment, racial issues became salient voting considerations to white Angelenos, much as they had been in New York for several decades. Furthermore, the continuing salience of interracial competition in New York and Los Angeles, coupled with booming local economies in both cities, enabled rather easy reelections for both Rudolph Giuliani and Richard Riordan in 1997. By 2001, however, the tenor of racial conflict in these two cities had shifted. Notable police scandals in both cities put conservatives on the defensive and portrayed racial minorities in a victimized light. The reframing of racial discord in New York and Los Angeles, coupled with low crime rates, low unemployment, and fiscal solvency for their municipal governments, constituted an important shift in the political context of these cities. The ability of liberal mayoral candidates to appeal to white voters in the 2001 elections is then largely explained by this change.

The political environment in New York, unlike Los Angeles, has a long history of salient racial and ethnic cleavages. The relative strength of ethnically based regular party organizations, the persistent racial and ethnic residential segregation, the acrimonious political competition among blacks, Latinos, and white ethnics, large amounts of public sector employment, the rapid transformation of the city's demography due to large influxes of foreign immigrants, and the enormous power located in the mayor's office all contribute to heightened and quite tenacious intergroup competition in New York City (Glazer and Moynihan [1963] 1970; Arian et.al. 1991; Mollenkopf 1992). David Dinkins's narrow victory in 1989 was achieved in spite of this acrimonious backdrop.

By contrast and in an absolute sense, Los Angeles represents a vastly different trajectory of racial and ethnic conflict. New York City's long history of racial and ethnic diversity can easily be contrasted with the historical homogeneity of Los Angeles. While Los Angeles today may be, like New York, a consummate multicultural city of the twenty-first century, it is within the past forty years that this dramatic demographic transformation has taken place, as Sabagh and Bozorgmehr showed in chapter 3. And while the Los Angeles political landscape has certainly been punctuated with dire outbreaks of racial unrest over the past thirty-five years, the majority of the "Bradley years" represented a tacit racial accord in this rapidly transforming city (Siegel 1997). Buffered by a robust economic expansion, profound demographic changes in Los Angeles were reasonably well tolerated throughout the 1980s. The 1992 civil unrest in Los Angeles coupled with the dire economic circumstances during this period, however, effected a notable shift in the social and political climate. The atmosphere of interracial accommodation so prevalent in the 1980s had been replaced by considerable fear and distrust. And in this context of heightened intergroup competition, white Democrats supported a white Republican mayoral candidate in large numbers.

THE GROUP INTEREST THEORY OF LOCAL VOTING BEHAVIOR

The central claim of group interest theory is that perceived competition among subgroups within the larger community makes group identities and perceived group interests salient to voter choice. In the absence of perceived competition, group interests are considerably less salient. In their stead, this theory maintains that traditional political cues such as partisan affiliations are likely be more influential to the vote than are alternate group identities.

Most traditional theories of voting typically point to political identities such as party identification as central to voter choice (Campbell et al. 1960; Fiorina 1981.) While social identities such as race, religion, and ethnicity indirectly influence political choices, party identification is argued to be more influential to political behavior as it is more proximate and salient to electoral choices. The group interest perspective, however, proposes that in the case of local politics, partisan identities are not always the most proximate and salient group identities and that other group memberships may supplant partisan leanings as salient voting cues. Unlike national-level politics, the issue debates that characterize local politics do not necessarily lend themselves to traditional partisan cleavages. The essential questions that dominate many, if not most, local elections focus on the priorities and allocation of local government services—that is, who will receive how much and at the expense of whom. The who and whom within the realm of local politics do not, of course, refer to individuals but, rather, to subgroups within the larger municipality that at times represent opposing priorities and interests. Thus, the inherent focus of local government on the distribution of resources and the competitive nature of the allocation process tends to reinforce the importance of secondary group memberships in relation to the political world. Furthermore, and insofar as many of the issues in local campaigns invoke competing group interests within the electorate, these interests become salient political cues that motivate political behavior.[1]

Group interest theory also maintains that group interested voting behavior is contingent on the degree of individual identification with the group and with the cohesiveness of the group. Thus, depending on the baseline strength of in-group identification and group cohesiveness, different types of groups will generally exhibit different levels of group voting. The mere presence of a group member on the ballot will likely draw support from those most highly identified within the group, even if there are no compelling group interests that accompany this candidacy. When group-member candidates are coupled with group-specific agendas, however, there is a much greater likelihood of a substantial group vote as well as countermobilization from groups that perceive their interests to be at risk. The promotion of a group interest agenda thus acts to enhance the cohesiveness of in-group members as well as the cohesiveness of opposing groups. For this reason we should expect to see evidence of group voting when racial or ethnic group members are on the ballot and, even more so, when group interest agendas are pursued within a campaign.

Finally, political ideology and partisan identification have potential direct effects on the individual voting decision. This theory presumes that as intergroup rivalries escalate, the importance of group identity as a political cue will increase relative to the independent effects of partisanship and ideology. Conversely, when intergroup competition is low, partisan beliefs should be more strongly related to voting behavior than are other group identities. The relative strength of partisan and ideological commitment also influences the extent to which interest motivations become politically manifest at the individual level. The theory suggests that strong partisans are less susceptible to interest-driven motivations than are their weaker partisan counterparts. Strong partisanship acts to constrain individuals from shifting to interest-driven voting cues (Tedin 1994). Thus the group interest approach maintains that intergroup rivalry will have the greatest impact on weak partisans and on moderate ideologues.

NEW YORK CITY: 1989 AND 1993

The 1993 mayoral election in New York City was a rematch of the 1989 election between David Dinkins and Rudolph Giuliani. Dinkins had won the 1989 election by a slim margin, and while Dinkins was able to craft a winning coalition comprising blacks, Latinos, and non-Latino white liberals, only 26 percent of non-Latino white voters supported the black Democrat. To a degree, Dinkins's candidacy in 1989 had been aided by a white liberal backlash against Ed Koch and a relatively strong local economy. By 1993, however, the local economy in New York City was plagued with enormous job losses. The entire nation was mired in recession in the early 1990s, and New York City's unemployment rate hit a ten-year high in 1993. Accompanying the economic downturn was increased concern over crime and interracial violence. Survey results from 1989 indicated that many voters believed a black mayor would mitigate interracial tensions in the city. Dinkins apparent difficulty in coping with the Korean grocery boycott and the Crown Heights riots (see chap. 12) dampened much of this hope.

As much as the political context did not favor Dinkins's reelection, the surprising fact is that the swing vote from Dinkins to Giuliani constituted fewer than a 100,000 out of 1.8 million total votes. These results certainly suggest that these two election outcomes were largely based on a set of stable attitudes that were central to voter choice in both elections. Racial attitudes were enormously salient in the 1989 contest, and the changes in political environment between 1989 and 1993 only enhanced this salience. Table 11.1 compares the 1989 mayoral vote with 1993, and its findings do suggest that racial considerations were somewhat more salient in 1993.[2] Whereas 71 percent of non-Latino white voters supported Giuliani in 1989, this percentage increased to 77 percent in 1993. Latino voters were slightly more supportive of Giuliani in the latter contest, with the percentage of their support increasing from 35 to 37 percent. Conversely, black support for Dinkins increased from 91 percent in 1989 to 95 percent in 1993.

Also, these data suggest that small movements within a variety of subgroups were responsible for Giuliani's victory—that no single group defection can be held solely responsible for the change in outcome. Among non-Latino white liberals, Dinkins's support remained a stable 51 percent. Among white ideological moderates and conservatives, however, he lost approximately 7 percentage points within each group. There was great concern in the Dinkins camp that the death of a rabbinical student at the hands of black youths in Crown Heights, and the political fallout from this incident, would substantially damage his support among Jewish voters. Support for Dinkins among Jews did fall but only three percentage points, from 35 percent in 1989 to 32 percent in 1993. More detrimental to Dinkins than the decline in the Jewish vote, however, was the increased turnout and increased loyalty to Giuliani among white Catholics. White Catholics represented 24 percent of the electorate in 1989 and 30 percent in 1993. Much of this increase in white Catholic turnout is credited to a Staten Island secession measure that was also on the general election ballot. While the total number of votes cast in the other four boroughs remained constant or declined in 1993, total votes cast in Staten Island increased by more than 25,000. Over half of Guiuliani's margin of victory can be attributed to the increase in white Catholic turnout in Staten Island and to their expanded support for Giuliani —82 percent in 1989 versus 88 percent in 1993 (Mollenkopf 1995).

In spite of the different election outcomes in 1989 and 1993, these two elections were indeed quite similar. The racial polarization so evident in 1989 was even more so in 1993. The group interest hypothesis proposes that, similar to 1989, racial attitudes will be a strong determinant of the vote in this election as well. Table 11.2 presents a series of logistic regression analyses that explore this claim.[3] The dependent variable in the 1993 analyses is vote choice, coded 0 for Dinkins and 1 for Giuliani. The independent variables represent a range of competing explanations for the vote, including partisan identification, political ideology,

Table 11.1. Comparison of Four New York City Mayoral Votes

	% of total voters				% who voted for:							
					1989		1993		1997		2001	
	1989	1993	1997	2001	*Giuliani*	*Dinkins*	*Giuliani*	*Dinkins*	*Giuliani*	*Messinger*	*Bloomberg*	*Green*
Total					48	50	51	49	57	41	50	47
By race/ethnicity:												
Non-Latino White	56	56	53	52	71	26	77	21	76	21	60	38
Black	28	29	21	23	7	91	5	95	20	79	25	75
Latino	13	12	20	18	35	64	37	60	43	57	47	49
Asian/other	2	3	4	...	...	...	...	...	...	...	...	...
By ideology:												
Liberal	29	30	33	37	30	69	34	65	43	55	36	60
Moderate	39	43	43	45	48	51	56	43	61	38	53	44
Conservative	23	27	23	17	65	32	67	33	72	25	64	32
Non-Latino whites:												
Liberal	14	17	17	...	47	51	48	51	54	43	...	...
Moderate	23	25	23	...	78	22	85	15	82	16	...	...
Conservative	15	12	14	...	86	10	97	3	92	3	...	...
By party:												
Democrat	57	61	61	65	30	70	33	67	45	54	34	64
Independent	18	22	20	16	62	38	69	31	65	32	60	33
Republican	21	17	19	19	81	17	93	7	92	6	88	9
By religion:												
Protestant	27	24	24	24	27	73	26	74	40	58	40	58
Roman Catholic	39	45	41	37	62	38	69	31	66	32	60	37
Jewish	16	17	23	19	65	35	68	32	72	27	52	46
Non-Latino whites:												
Protestant	8	6	7	...	70	30	82	18	78	18	...	...
Catholic	24	30	21	...	82	18	88	12	85	12	...	...

Source. CBS News/New York Times 1991; Voter Research Exit Poll 1993; Voter News Service Exit Poll 1997; Edison Media Research Exit Poll 2001.

Table 11.2. Logistic Regression Results for New York City Mayoral Voting, 1993

	ALL NON-LATINO WHITES	NON-LATINO WHITE DEMOCRATS	NON-LATINO WHITE MODERATES
Party identification	1.04*	. . .	.28
	(.52)		(.87)
Ideology	1.40*	1.18	. . .
	(.55)	(.63)	
Attitudes regarding race relations	3.87**	3.78**	7.43**
	(.76)	(.82)	(1.96)
Crime/safety attitudes	2.05**	2.57**	2.59**
	(.58)	(.68)	(1.28)
Attitudes regarding local government and immigrants	1.13*	1.05*	2.28*
	(.49)	(.53)	(1.03)
Attitudes regarding Dinkins and the local economy	4.04**	3.70**	5.36**
	(1.03)	(1.07)	(1.95)
Constant	−5.90**	−5.97**	−8.33**
Number of cases	281	191	117
Percent cases correctly predicted	87	84	91

Source. WCBSTV/New York Times, New York City preelection survey (May 1993).
Note. Dependent variable is vote choice (Dinkins = 0, Giuliani = 1). Entries represent unstandardized logistic regression coefficients. Standard errors are in parentheses. All independent variables are scaled from 0 to 1. Attitudes regarding race relations and immigrants are scaled from liberal to conservative. Party identification is scaled Democrat = 0, Republican = 1. Crime/safety attitudes and attitudes regarding Dinkins and the local economy are scaled from good to bad.
*Significant at the .05 level.
**Significant at the .001 level.

attitudes regarding Dinkins and race relations, attitudes regarding crime and safety, attitudes regarding local immigrants, and attitudes regarding Dinkins and the local economy.

Clearly in both of these elections racial concerns were enormously salient, and as such, racial attitudes should constitute a significant factor with regard to electoral choice. The "attitudes regarding race relations" measure comprises three questions and is scaled from 0 to 1, approve to disapprove (Cronbach's $\alpha = .72$). The questions ask respondents if they approve of Dinkins's handling of race relations, if they feel that he has helped or damaged race relations, and if he has shown favoritism to blacks over Jews. Thus a positive and significant coefficient suggests that increasing dissatisfaction with Dinkins's management of race relations corresponds with higher probabilities of a Giuliani vote.

The crime/safety measure consists of one question assessing the relative safety of the city compared to four years ago. Similarly, the local economy question asks respondents to judge whether Dinkins has helped or hurt the local economy over the past four years. Both of these retrospective evaluations are scaled from 0 to 1, safer/helped to less safe/hurt. The final attitudinal measure relates to the degree of attention paid by city government to recent immigrants. The rapid escalation of foreign immigration over the past ten years has contributed to the increasingly multicultural make-up of the city and has also contributed to increased tensions among racial and ethnic groups. This measure represents another potential dimension of group conflict that may fall outside of the domain of more traditional racial themes. The survey question used for this measure asks whether local government pays too much attention, the right amount of attention, or too little attention to immigrants. The measure is scaled from liberal to conservative, with the expectation that people who feel that local government pays too much attention to immigrants will be more likely to support Giuliani than will those who offer more liberal responses.

The results of three logistic regression analyses are presented in table 11.2.[4] The findings from this analysis provide strong support for the group interest hypothesis. With regard to the total white electorate, retrospective evaluations of Dinkins's management of race relations and the local economy are the two most significant factors with respect to the vote. Crime/safety attitudes, immigrant attitudes, partisan identification, and political ideology also attract significant, albeit smaller, coefficients. These findings provide strong evidence that racial attitudes were extraordinarily salient in the context of electoral choice, even when controlling for a variety of other important political factors.

White Democrats and white moderates were important swing constituencies in this election. The regression results in table 11.2 demonstrate that, for both groups, racial attitudes were more significant than were economic concerns, crime/safety attitudes, and attitudes toward recent immigrants. The relative strength of racial attitudes was especially profound for white moderates. In this case, the racial attitude coefficient was more than twice the size of the coefficient for crime/safety attitudes and was almost one and a half times the size of the local economy coefficient. The relative strength of this factor, controlling for other traditionally important political concerns, strongly bolsters the claim that racial considerations were influential to this electoral outcome.

While the findings from the New York election analyses strongly implicate racial attitudes in the electoral preferences of white voters, the fact that David Dinkins was a black candidate, surely enhanced the extraordinary salience of race in these two elections. In the case of Los Angeles, however, neither of the 1993 mayoral candidates were black. The following section turns to an analysis of the 1993 Los Angeles mayoral election. The main hypothesis is that racial attitudes were also deeply implicated in the voting behavior of Los Angeles whites and that even in the absence of a black candidate, race and racial attitudes were salient and influential to mayoral voting.

LOS ANGELES: 1993

The 1993 mayoral election in Los Angeles represented the end of an era in Los Angeles politics. Mayor Tom Bradley had decided not to run for his sixth term, and this would be the first time in twenty-four years that Bradley was not on the ballot. Furthermore, the 1993 political climate in Los Angeles was uncharacteristically turbulent. In April 1992 there had been widespread rioting by blacks and Latinos in response to the initial Rodney King verdict. Although the civil unrest lasted less than a week, there nonetheless remained a sense among many Los Angeles residents that peace within the city was fragile and that the police force was too small or otherwise unprepared for future outbreaks of urban violence. To compound this situation, the city was deep in an economic recession.

The unique circumstances surrounding this election—Bradley's intention to retire, the recent violence, and the serious economic recession facing the city—brought forth large numbers of primary contenders.[5] The two runoff candidates that emerged from this primary were Michael Woo and Richard Riordan. Mike Woo was, from the beginning, the perceived frontrunner. A Chinese-American, he had represented Hollywood's thirteenth council district since 1985. Woo was a liberal with strong financial backing who had cultivated political ties within the black, Latino, and Asian communities. He announced his candidacy early and was considered by most political insiders to be Bradley's probable successor.

The wildcard in the primary race was millionaire attorney and businessman Richard Riordan. Whereas Riordan was well known in and around city hall, he was a virtual stranger to the Los Angeles electorate. A venture capitalist, Richard Riordan had made millions in partnership with junk bond king Michael Milken and had been a frequent campaign contributor in the city. Riordan had enormous personal wealth and financed his own campaign. And although it was true that he could afford to buy the name recognition that he initially lacked, a white Republican millionaire who had amassed his fortune through junk bond deals with Michael Milken just seemed an unlikely successor to the black Democratic mayor of Los Angeles.

In Los Angeles's postriot environment, Woo promoted himself as the "multicultural" candidate who would bring groups together and mend the city's interethnic fissures. A liberal Chinese-American with ties to the black and Latino communities, he argued that he was uniquely positioned to secure future peace in Los Angeles. Riordan, by contrast, did not embody the racial healer but rather argued that he was "tough enough to turn L.A. around." He portrayed himself as a pragmatic manager concerned with the physical safety and economic future of the city. He ran a decidedly nonideological campaign and focused much of his campaign resources on the conservative San Fernando Valley, which at that time was 57 percent non-Latino white (table 10.1), and on the generally more liberal, predominantly non-Latino white west side. The Woo campaign painted Riordan as a ruthless, corporate-raiding Republican. The Riordan campaign painted Woo as an ineffectual bureaucrat and pointed to his spotty record within the thirteenth district. Registered Democrats outnumber Republicans in Los Angeles by a margin of 2 to 1. Had partisanship mattered much to this election, Woo would have been the mayor. In the end, however, Riordan prevailed by a margin of 54 to 46 percent.

A demographic description of the 1993 mayoral vote is found in table 11.3. Several important conclusions may be drawn from these data. First, substantial racial polarization in the Los Angeles vote is evident. Sixty-seven percent of non-Latino white voters supported Riordan compared to only 14 percent of Los Angeles's black electorate. Among Latino voters, Woo was more successful, capturing 57 percent of the vote. Second, Woo was only moderately successful at securing his natural white constituency—Democrats and liberals. Thirty-nine percent of white Democrats and 31 percent of white liberals defected to the Republican Riordan, and among white moderates and independents, Woo lost 75 percent and 70 percent of the vote, respectively. Even among Jewish voters, Woo was only able to attract a slight majority—51 percent of the vote.

Woo did not ignore the white vote, but it appears that he miscalculated their interests in this election. Woo, like Riordan, recognized the need for a larger police force and publicly committed to this. His desire to build multicultural harmony in the city, however, was in contrast to Riordan's "get tough" approach. That Riordan was so successful among the non-Latino white electorate implies a disinclination among many white voters toward further accommodation of minority interests.

Table 11.4 displays three logistic regression analyses that explore the group interest hypothesis. As in the New York City analysis, the samples are restricted to non-Latino white voters, the dependent variable is vote choice (Woo = 0, Riordan = 1), and all of the independent variables are scaled from 0 to 1.[6] The independent variables in this analysis include partisanship, political ideology, retrospective evaluations of Bradley, attitudes regarding racial and ethnic minorities, attitudes regarding illegal immigrants, and income.[7] The retrospective Bradley evaluation was included to assess the extent to which Riordan voters were simply looking for a change in the nature of local leadership. Although Mike Woo was not endorsed by Bradley, he nonetheless was a Democrat and represented many of the same constituencies that were associated with the Bradley coalition. Thus the inclusion of this measure tests the possibility that voting for Riordan was connected to dissatisfaction with the Bradley regime.

The "attitudes regarding minorities" measure is a scale comprising two survey questions. The first asks respondents to assess whether city government is paying too much attention to racial and ethnic minority groups. The second question asks respondents to assess responsibility for problems facing minority groups in the inner city. These questions are combined and scaled from 0 to 1, liberal to conservative (Cronbach's $\alpha = .68$). This measure is particularly well suited for this analysis as it links individual attitudes toward minority groups with government responsibility for and accommodation of these groups. A positive and significant coefficient thus suggests that higher levels of resistance to minority accommodation is associated with higher probabilities of a Riordan vote.

In addition, I include a measure referred to as "attitudes regarding illegal immigrants," which probes individual respondents on the degree to which they believe that city agencies, such as the police, should aid the Immigration and Naturalization Service in their efforts to identify and deport illegal immigrants. City policy at the time opposed using local police in this capacity. Given that the issue of illegal immigration and its purported drain on city resources was prominent at the time of this election, this question appeared to be an appropriate and timely measure of perceived intergroup conflict. Thus a positive and significant regression coefficient implies that increasing concern over illegal immigration is positively associated with voting for Riordan.

Table 11.4 displays logistic regression results from three independent analyses. The first analysis includes the entire non-Latino white sample, and there are several interesting findings. Although racial attitudes significantly correspond with the vote, the single most important factor in this election appears to be ideology. The coefficient in this case is almost three times as large as any other coefficient and suggests that among

Table 11.3. Description of Three Los Angeles Mayoral Votes

	% OF TOTAL VOTERS			% WHO VOTED FOR:					
				1993		1997		2001	
	1993	1997	2001	*Riordan*	*Woo*	*Riordan*	*Hayden*	*Hahn*	*Villaraigosa*
Total				54	46	61	35	54	46
By race/ethnicity:									
Non-Latino white	72	65	52	67	33	71	26	59	41
Black	12	13	17	14	86	19	75	80	20
Latino	10	15	22	43	57	60	33	18	82
Asian/other	4	4	6	31	69	62	35	65	35
By ideology:									
Liberal	30	27	49	27	73	33	62	41	59
Moderate	43	47	29	63	37	66	30	62	38
Conservative	27	26	22	79	21	81	16	73	27
Non-Latino whites:									
Liberal	22	...	26	31	69	...	...	38	62
Moderate	31	...	15	75	25	...	...	71	29
Conservative	20	...	12	92	8	...	...	88	12

By party:									
Democrat	63	60	70	39	61	47	49	48	52
Independent	6	7	8	70	30	58	34	48	52
Republican	30	31	20	91	9	91	7	79	21
By income:									
Under 20,000	14	16	11	42	58	53	42	47	53
20,000–39,999	25	24	19	52	48	54	41	54	46
40,000–59,999	22	23	18	60	40	62	34	52	48
60,000 and up	39	37	52	62	38	67	30	57	43
By religion:									
Protestant	39	37	32	63	37	64	32	69	31
Roman Catholic	24	28	28	63	37	65	31	40	60
Jewish	19	15	18	49	51	71	26	54	46
By region:									
Westside	18	18	18	55	45	64	33	48	52
San Fernando Valley	44	42	42	71	29	74	22	55	45
Central Los Angeles	21	22	21	40	60	55	41	42	58
South Los Angeles	17	18	19	27	73	35	61	67	33

Source. Los Angeles Times Exit Poll, June 1993, June 1997, and June 2001.

Table 11.4. Logistic Regression Results for Los Angeles Mayoral Voting, 1993

	ALL NON-LATINO WHITES	WHITE DEMOCRATS	WHITE MODERATES
Party identification	.86*	. . .	.43
	(.38)		(.58)
Ideology	5.74**	8.45**	. . .
	(.91)	(1.44)	
Attitudes regarding minorities	1.44**	1.18**	3.06**
	(.46)	(.60)	(.73)
Attitudes regarding illegal immigrants	.27	.14	1.11
	(.44)	(.62)	(.81)
Bradley approval	.26	.16	.36
	(.53)	(.73)	(.86)
Income	1.81**	2.83**	1.03
	(.57)	(.84)	(.93)
Constant	−4.65**	−6.02**	−.27
	(.74)	(1.08)	(1.15)
Number of cases	307	141	114
Percent cases correctly predicted	86	85	81

Source. Los Angeles Times, Los Angeles preelection survey (May 1993).
Note. Dependent variable is vote choice (Woo = 0, Riordan = 1). Entries represent unstandardized logistic regression coefficients. Standard errors are in parentheses. All independent variables are scaled from 0 to 1. Attitudes regarding minorities and immigrants are scaled from liberal to conservative. Party identification is scaled Democrat = 0, Republican = 1. Bradley approval and income are from low to high.
* Significant at the .05 level.
** Significant at the .001 level.

non-Latino whites, increasing conservatism corresponds with an increased probability of a Riordan vote. Similarly, among white Democrats, the effect of ideology is substantially larger than that of racial attitudes. These initial analyses suggest that the results of this election were driven, to a great degree, by ideological divisions in the electorate.

As indicated in table 11.3, Riordan performed extremely well among ideological conservatives and almost as well among ideological moderates. The strength of Riordan's showing among these groups is obviously reflected in this analysis and, at first glance, might suggest that Mike Woo was simply too liberal for the largely moderate and conservative white constituency. Woo's showing among moderates was unusually low in this election, however, suggesting that the response from the ideological middle in this election may have been driven by factors specific to this electoral context. The following, therefore, focuses particularly on the voting behavior of white ideological moderates.

The regression analysis conducted for non-Latino white moderates provides strong evidence of racially motivated voting. The only factor that significantly predicts the moderate vote in this analysis is racial attitudes. Income differences, retrospective evaluations of Bradley, party identification, and attitudes regarding immigrants did not produce any significant prediction of the mayoral vote. As moderate voters generally represent an important swing constituency in any election (and represent more than 30 percent of voters in this election), their overwhelming support of Riordan and the racially motivated nature of this support strongly implicate racial attitudes in the outcome of this contest. This finding provides support for the group interest hypothesis and suggests that white resentment toward minority groups and their respective demands on city resources was crucial to Woo's losing this pivotal constituency.

During the four elections preceding 1993, white voters overwhelmingly supported Los Angeles's black mayor, Tom Bradley. The lack of racial animosity among white voters in Los Angeles was so politically pronounced during this period that not only did Bradley win each of the last four elections in the at-large primary, but there were also no significant challenges made to his mayoralty. In the context of economic distress and in the wake of the Los Angeles riots, the city elected its first Republican mayor in more than thirty years. The findings from the 1993 analysis provide evidence that the election of Richard Riordan was, in large part, tied to the conflictual political context and to the salience of racial attitudes in this election.

NEW YORK 1997: STABILITY IN MAYORAL POLITICS

For both Richard Riordan and Rudolph Giuliani, reelection was a relatively easy task. Local economies in New York and Los Angeles had improved substantially over the prior four years and crime rates had dropped significantly. Public approval rates of both mayors were, in the aggregate, very high, yet approval rates showed substantial racial variation. Given the continuing racial conflict evident in both cities, however, it is not surprising that racial identities continued to retain their political significance.

Table 11.5 displays job approval rating for incumbent mayors in New York and Los Angeles during the 1980s and 1990s, and there are several interesting patterns in these data. In New York, from 1985 to 1997 there were persistent racial differences in the approval ratings of mayors Koch, Dinkins, and Giuliani. While Koch's initial support from black voters had been quite high, increasing racial acrimony in the city coupled with Koch's racially insensitive remarks as mayor led to growing polarization between blacks and whites. By 1989, Koch was largely unpopular among

Table 11.5. Incumbent Mayor Approval Ratings by Race, New York and Los Angeles, 1979–2001

	PERCENT WHO APPROVE OF INCUMBENT MAYOR'S JOB PERFORMANCE		
	Non-Latino Whites	Blacks	Latinos
New York:			
1985 — Koch	75	39	56
1989 — Koch	43	28	41
1993 — Dinkins	33	83	50
1997 — Giuliani	82	34	62
2001 — Giuliani (pre-9/11)	63	25	43
2001 — Giuliani (post-9/11)	87	58	81
Los Angeles:			
1979 — Bradley	72	81	74
1981 — Bradley	71	89	82
1985 — Bradley	73	84	79
1989 — Bradley	70	77	78
1993 — Bradley	29	58	44
1997 — Riordan	66	24	65
2001 — Riordan	66	59	73

Source. New York Times, Quinnipiac University Poll, and Los Angeles Times Polls from selected years.

all groups; however his job performance was least appreciated within the black community. David Dinkins's election in 1989 evoked similar levels of racial disagreement. This time, however, blacks were the most supportive of Dinkins while white voters were the least approving and Latinos fell squarely in between. The Giuliani mayoralty also evoked racial disparities in job approval, with whites and Latinos overwhelmingly supporting the mayor while blacks largely disapproved.

The shifting patterns of support seen in table 11.5 highlight the disparate interests of blacks and whites in New York City politics. In each of the past four mayoral administrations, black and non-Latino white voters appear to be on largely opposite sides of the political divide. Latino voters represent less political homogeneity than blacks and whites, however, and illustrate a greater degree of fluidity in mayoral support. While 50 percent of Latinos approved of Dinkins in 1993, over 60 percent supported Giuliani in 1997. Furthermore, and to a large degree, Giuliani's support from the Latino community resulted from his explicit efforts at courting them.

The group interests of the black and Latino communities in New York and elsewhere are rather distinctive. Latinos, like blacks, are typically poorer than whites, yet the demands from poor Latinos are often more particular and less institutional than are the desires of urban blacks. Similar to the white ethnic immigrants that preceded them, the political agenda of urban Latinos focuses on greater economic and educational opportunities. Unlike blacks, however, there is less demand for the redress of social injustice or for systemic overhaul. The greater ethnic and cultural diversity within the Latino community further implies less political homogeneity. For a "law-and-order" mayor like Giuliani, then, the Latino community represented greater coalition-building opportunities than did the black community. The mayor built working relationships with Latino leaders such as Herman Badillo. And Giuliani's public opposition to state policy proposals to deny legal immigrants social services during their first year of residence (chap. 3, 116–17) was most certainly a nod to Latino interests.

The central point of contention between blacks and the Giuliani administration was over the issue of the police. Giuliani promoted a larger and more vigilant police force. His crackdown on quality-of-life offenses such as graffiti, vandalism, and the ubiquitous "squeegee men" was praised by many New Yorkers. His new and more aggressive street crimes unit was also credited for declining crime rates; however many black political leaders argued that reductions in crime were being achieved at the expense of the civil liberties of poor minorities, blacks in particular. The brutal beating of Haitian immigrant Abner Louima during Giuliani's first term and the police shooting of African immigrant Amadou Diallo are particularly high-profile examples of the types of incidents that constantly fueled the political battle between the black community and Giuliani's police force. From the time of his election in 1993, the mayor, a former federal prosecutor, gave broad support to the police and consistently opposed proposals for their independent oversight. His continued support of the police force created an impenetrable breach between his administration and leadership in the black community. In this context, the racial polarization in his support is quite understandable. Non-Latino white voters and Latinos, to a lesser degree, were willing to accept incidents of police brutality in exchange for a 40 percent decline in the city's crime rate. Black voters apparently were not.

NEW YORK CITY VOTING—1997

While Giuliani beat his Democratic opponent, Ruth Messinger, by a large 57 to 41 percent margin, his electoral coalition was largely the same as it had been for years prior. Giuliani received 76 percent of the non-Latino white vote, 20 percent of the black vote (compared to only 5 percent when Dinkins was running against him), and 43 percent of the Latino vote, a six-point increase over 1993 (see table 11.1). While the voting behavior of the New York City electorate was largely stable, more significant changes could be seen in the 1997 turnout. The overall turnout rate in 1997 was a low 38 percent. The reduced turnout in 1997, however, was not randomly distributed throughout the city. Turnout in black neighborhoods declined the most precipitously, averaging 23 percent. Notable levels of decline in predominantly non-Latino white neighborhoods were also evident, an average of 21 percent. The vote in Latino neighborhoods was the most resistant to decline and on average only decreased by 16 percent.[8] For the first time in the history of the city, the Latino vote nearly equaled the black vote. Whereas blacks represented almost 30 percent of mayoral voters in 1993, they were only 21 percent of the total electorate in 1997. And equally telling, Latino voters, who were only 12 percent of the electorate in 1993, now equaled 20 percent. While it is difficult to know the impetus for this sustained Latino mobilization (in light of the many factors that discouraged turnout among blacks and non-Latino whites), their enhanced status in the governing coalition (relative to the position of blacks) may have been an important reason.

LOS ANGELES IN 1997—EVIDENCE OF A BROADENING COALITION

The circumstances surrounding Richard Riordan's election in 1997 were in many ways very similar to those in New York. Much like Giuliani, Riordan had taken over the helm of city government during a period of economic retrenchment. By 1997, the city economy was on the mend, jobs were coming back to the city and the crime rate had declined. In spite of the improving local economy, racial tensions still ran high in the city of Los Angeles. The O. J. Simpson criminal and civil trials continued to fan the flames of racial discord for most of Riordan's first term, and Riordan's lack of support for the black chief of police, Willie Williams, was another source of conflict.

Comparing the approval ratings during the Bradley and Riordan administrations provides further insight into the effect that the change in political context had on the city of Los Angeles and its politics. During the Bradley years—from 1979 to 1989—approval rates of the mayor by all groups did not dip below 70 percent. While approval was notably higher among blacks, the relatively high and consistent rates of support among non-Latino whites and Latinos strongly suggests a lack of racially motivated politics. In the wake of the riots, Bradley's approval ratings plummeted among non-Latino white voters to 29 percent and his support within the Latino community also dropped, to 44 percent. Blacks continued to support Bradley—albeit at a lower level, 58 percent. Nonetheless, the salience of racial sentiments became pronounced in mayoral politics for the first time in many years. Riordan's approval ratings in 1997 reflect the continuing polarization between black and white interests in city politics. While 66 percent of non-Latino white voters approve of Riordan in 1997, only 24 percent of black voters do. The opinions of Latino citizens appear to mirror those of non-Latino whites in Los Angeles, with 65 percent approving of the mayor's job performance.

The pattern of support for Riordan in Los Angeles is strikingly similar to Giuliani's in New York. Only in this case, Riordan was more successful in attracting Latino support than Giuliani was. Certainly part of Riordan's success among Latinos could be attributed to his conscious inclusion of Latinos in his administration and his personal generosity to many schools and community groups in Latino neighborhoods. As important as these factors may have been, Riordan's personal commitment to children and to education was also appealing to Latinos. Educational reforms were a centerpiece of Riordan's mayoral agenda. While having no statutory control over the massive Los Angeles Unified School District (LAUSD), Riordan nonetheless focused much of his personal political energies on resuscitating the languishing Los Angeles schools. The Los Angeles Educational Alliance for Restructuring Now (LEARN) program and the push for more charter schools in Los Angeles were both largely attributed to Riordan's efforts. Latinos comprise approximately 70 percent of the LAUSD, and education is typically a top priority among Latino voters, mirroring the increased importance of this issue to the general electorate as well (see table i.1). Thus Riordan's success in attracting Latino support can be credited to both personal and political choices that he made while mayor. Furthermore, Riordan was able to build political alliances with many prominent Latino leaders, and the 1997 endorsements of council members Richard Alatorre and Richard Alarcon most certainly gave Riordan additional credibility in Latino neighborhoods.

Riordan was much less successful in building support in the black community. His lack of support for then Police Chief Willie Williams was particularly alienating to black voters. Williams had been hired in the wake of the riots and after former Police Chief Daryl Gates resigned. Riordan and Williams had strained relations throughout Williams's tenure and his firing was perceived by many blacks as a power grab to replace Williams with a more accommodating chief. Support for Williams was so high in the black community that his reappointment was listed among the top three most important issues facing the city in 1997—behind crime and education but ahead of jobs (*Los Angeles Times* 1997). In spite of this vocal opposition from the black community, Williams was fired and Riordan was held accountable.

MAYORAL VOTING IN LOS ANGELES IN 1997

Riordan's opponent in 1997 was Democratic State Senator Tom Hayden. Hayden's record was a laundry list of liberal causes and his political objective was to revitalize the Bradley coalition of non-Latino white liberals, blacks, and Latinos. While Hayden was successful in appealing to black voters, he was not able to attract meaningful numbers of non-Latino white or Latino voters and was beaten by a margin of 61 to 35 percent in the low-turnout at-large primary.

A comparison of the 1993 and 1997 mayoral votes can be found in table 11.3. The findings from this analysis suggest that Riordan's electoral coalition had expanded considerably since his first term. Riordan's electoral support in 1993 came predominantly from non-Latino white voters, while his opponent, Michael Woo, received majorities of the black, Latino, and Asian vote. In 1997, Riordan captured large majorities among non-Latino whites, Latinos, and Asians, and his only electoral weakness was among black voters. Given the heightened racial tensions in the city and the declining relative importance of the black vote, Riordan did not risk alienating the numerically important non-Latino white vote by accommodating the political demands of blacks. Furthermore, as he was able to bolster his support within the increasingly mobilized Latino community, black votes were not necessary to sustain his electoral viability.

Like the mayoral contest in New York, the 1997 mayoral election in Los Angeles drew an extremely low citywide turnout, and declining turnout was especially prevalent among non-Latino white and black voters. Latino participation, as a percentage of the total electorate, was a record 15 percent and, for the first time, Latinos outnumbered black voters at the polls. The increasing importance of Latino voters in Los Angeles and New York reflect both demographic and political trends. In New York, even by 1990 the Latino community, with 24 percent of the population, was already close in size to the black community, which was 29 percent of the total population, and by 2000 Latinos and blacks each constituted 27 percent of the population. But the Latino community has been typically accorded less political clout due to the relatively low voter participation rates of Latinos compared to blacks. In Los Angeles, Latinos were 39 percent of the city population in 1990 and 47 percent in 2000, yet have also, as in New York, traditionally participated in low numbers. Blacks—while only 14 percent of the population in the city of Los Angeles in 1990 (and only 11 percent in 2000)—amassed disproportionately high levels of political incorporation because of the high rates of mobilization within the black community during much of the 1970s and 1980s. To a great degree then, turnout differences between blacks and Latinos in both cities traditionally rendered blacks a more desirable coalition partner. The confluence of increasing Latino mobilization and a decline in black turnout, however, may have dire consequences for future black incorporation in these two cities.

The conservative shift in the politics of both cities also closed off many political opportunities for black/white coalitions. On both the national and local levels, blacks constitute large proportions of the Democratic Party, and Democratic leaders cannot politically afford to alienate black voters. Republicans, like Giuliani and Riordan, have no similar impetus to include blacks in their governing coalitions and, in fact, may risk their white voter base if perceived as too accommodating. The increasing political participation of Latino voters, coupled with their greater receptivity to conservative politics, has created new opportunities for the political incorporation of Latinos. These new opportunities, however, appear to have come largely at the expense of previously empowered black voters.

LIBERALISM REBORN: THE 2001 ELECTION IN LOS ANGELES

While a number of pundits and academics saw the respective electoral successes of Giuliani and Riordan as a death knell of urban liberalism in these two cities, group interest theory sees them in a much different light. The political context that had made these Republican candidates and their respective messages so viable in the early 1990s had changed substantially by 2001. Economic vitality in both cities translated into low unemployment, declining crime rates, and relatively plentiful municipal coffers. Racial conflict, while present in both cities, had taken a somewhat different public form, with white police officers, scandal, and abuses at the center of many controversies and with racial minorities perceived more as victims than aggressors. In this new political and economic context, the racial interests of non-Latino white voters became somewhat subsumed by nonracial policy concerns, and Democrats behaved more like traditional Democrats, supporting liberal policies and liberal candidates. In particular, the 2001 mayoral election in Los Angeles provides an apt illustration of how changes in political context effect changes in the political behavior of urban voters.

In 2001, Mayor Riordan was term limited from running again, and the nonpartisan primary, much as in 1993, offered Los Angeles voters a wide array of political choices, from Riordan's handpicked Republican successor, Steven Soboroff, to a liberal Latino, Antonio Villaraigosa. Unlike Los Angeles's electoral choices in the early 1990s, however, almost 70 percent of the primary electorate supported Democrats of one stripe or another, including 53 percent of white primary voters who cast ballots for the Democrats. In the end, two liberal Democrats—City Attorney James Hahn and former speaker of the California State Assembly, Antonio Villaraigosa—met in the June runoff. While the hopes of many Latinos were pinned on Villaraigosa's becoming the first Latino mayor in more than a hundred years, Hahn nonetheless defeated Villaraigosa in the runoff by a comfortable 54 to 46 percent margin. But in spite of Villlaraigosa's loss, liberal dominance in the nonpartisan primary certainly signaled a Democratic reascendancy in the mayoral politics of Los Angeles.

The basis for the Democrats' electoral success in 2001 is much the same as that of Riordan's success eight years earlier—just in reverse. The vibrant Los Angeles economy, with its attendant low unemployment, low crime rates, and fiscal abundance, constituted a promising backdrop for liberal politicians. The riots and the O. J. era that had so transfixed the non-Latino white electorate during the first half of the decade were fading memories. Instead, the racial incidents of the late 1990s were exemplified by rampant police misconduct, putting the conservative white establishment in a defensive posture while strengthening the political fortunes of more moderate and liberal voices. Steven Soboroff, the lone Republican in the primary field, was strongly endorsed by the popular Riordan, and he tried to invoke, in his campaign, the tough love and law-and-order themes that had been so successful for his benefactor. The intense conflict and interracial angst that had made Riordan's 1993 campaign appeals so successful were not, however, present in 2001. The relative calm and fiscal health of the city had deemphasized racial interests in favor of the more typical political fare: jobs, education, and police reform. And in this context, the largely Democratic Los Angeles electorate behaved in kind and elected a liberal Democratic mayor.

MAYORAL POLITICS IN NEW YORK 2001

For most of the campaign season it looked as though New Yorkers would also replace their incumbent Republican mayor with a Democrat. Low crime rates and impressive economic growth had diffused much of the overt racial conflict that often typifies New York City politics. Furthermore, a growing concern over police brutality, so prevalent during the Giuliani administration, seemed to be drawing non-Latino white liberals back to the Democrats. A *New York Times*/CBS survey conducted in August 2001 showed Mark Green, one of the two front-running Democrats, leading the Republican Bloomberg by a twenty-five-point margin (*New York Times* 2001). Yet in the end, Michael Bloomberg would indeed win this contest by a 50 to 47 percent margin.

On September 11, the day of the Republican and Democratic primaries, two hijacked commercial airliners crashed into the World Trade Center in Downtown Manhattan—changing the political focus of New York City politics dramatically. Almost overnight, economic issues became of paramount concern (table i.2). Giuliani, whose popularity had waned considerably over the course of his two terms, was politically reborn with soaring approval ratings (table 11.5), and the issue of leadership came to dominate the political concerns of voters. This new political context greatly enhanced Michael Bloomberg's electoral viability.

The September 11 primaries were postponed until September 25, and Bloomberg, a billionaire businessman and recent convert to the Republican Party, who spent $20 million in the primary season alone, easily beat his opponent Herman Badillo by a 66 to 25 percent margin. The Democratic primary was considerably more competitive, and the top two vote getters—Public Advocate Mark Green and Bronx Borough President Fernando (Freddie) Ferrer—headed into a runoff to be held on October 11. Ferrer's campaign aggressively foregrounded his "two cities" argument, according to which New York City was now divided between the rich or well-to-do and the poor and disadvantaged, with the latter group composed disproportionately of minorities, especially blacks and Latinos. Ferrer also castigated Green for planning to rehire Bill Bratton as police commissioner, complaining that Bratton, in his first term as commissioner, from 1993 to 1996, had disregarded the rights of minorities in his eagerness to lower the crime rate. In the first round of primary balloting, Ferrer had received 72 percent of the Latino vote and 52 percent of the black vote but only 7 percent of the non-Latino white vote. By contrast, Green had run well among non-Latino whites (40 percent) and relatively well among blacks (34 percent) and had received a small but significant proportion of the Latino vote (12 percent). In order for Ferrer to survive the runoff, it was apparent that he would need a much higher number of non-Latino white voters. For Green, the calculus was much the same. The Green campaign decided to go negative against Ferrer in a television ad that described Ferrer's philosophy regarding the rebuilding of the financial district as "borderline irresponsible" and that ran the tagline, "Can we afford to take a chance?" In addition, leaflets began to show up in predominantly Jewish neighborhoods with a grotesque cartoon of Ferrer kissing the behind of the Reverend Al Sharpton. Green disavowed responsibility for the leaflets; nonetheless, a higher level of racial consideration had clearly been injected into this campaign. Mark Green won the Democratic primary by slightly fewer than 45,000 votes. However, his racially divisive campaign choices would haunt him in the general election as unprecedented numbers of Latinos and black voters would defect from the Democratic Party and vote for Bloomberg.

Leaders of the African-American and Latino communities were outraged over the "Can we take a chance?" ad, and demanded an apology from Green. Reverend Al Sharpton threatened Green with a call for a black boycott of the polls on election day. The nasty Democratic primary campaign had created an enormous rift within the Democratic coalition—a rift that most certainly contributed to Bloomberg's general election victory. Mark Green received 38 percent of the non-Latino white vote in the general election—considerably more than the 21 percent garnered by Dinkins and Messinger in the two previous races. With 75 percent of the black vote and only 49 percent of the Latino vote, however, Green lost to Bloomberg by slightly more than 35,000 votes. Clearly Bloomberg's extravagant campaign spending ($74 million, according to the *Washington Post* [2002]) and his last minute endorsement by Giuliani were important to this election. Nonetheless, had Green been able achieve the same levels of minority support accorded Ruth Messinger four years earlier, he would have won this race. In this case, it was not the non-Latino white defections from the Democrats but, rather, black and Latino defections that gave Bloomberg his victory. Interracial conflict still played an enormously important role in the choices of New York City voters, only this time it was a new variation on an age-old theme.

CONCLUSION

While it has been argued that the political differences between New York and Los Angeles reflect a distinction between the old machine politics of the East and the reform tradition of the West, such arguments seem less weighty today. The 1990s witnessed many more similarities than differences in the politics of the nation's two largest cities. Group interest theory maintains that political contexts matter and that heightened group conflict elicits group interested voting behavior and often undercuts the importance of traditional political cues. Thus the relative stability of New York City politics, the conservative retrenchment in Los Angeles during the past decade, and the "rebirth" of urban liberalism in both cities in 2001 can be explained from this contextual perspective.

Several interesting conclusions are drawn from these cases. First, it is important to point out that, in the context of the persistent racial tensions that characterize much of New York City politics, a confluence of circumstances in 1989 brought about a unique opportunity for the election of a black mayor. The relative strength of the local economy, coupled with a liberal backlash against Koch's inflammatory racial rhetoric, opened the door, ever so slightly, for Dinkins. In 1993, however, he was unable to hold on to his narrow electoral margin as the political environment shifted to a worsening local economy, rising crime rates, and public accusations of racial favoritism. In other words, the Giuliani coalition, his Republican roots notwithstanding, was not much of a departure from the Koch coalition in 1985.

A second important observation is that, under conditions of heightened intergroup conflict, electoral behavior in Los Angeles was strikingly similar to that in New York. The multiracial coalition that had supported Bradley for so many years was effectively undone by the infusion of racial interests. There are an enormous number of factors that distinguish the structure and character of New York City politics from those in Los Angeles. Nonetheless, mired in a poor economy and beset with interracial unrest, white Los Angeles voters opted for a conservative Republican attorney in much the same way that white New Yorkers did. On its face, the Los Angeles electorate appeared to be more ideological than racial in its electoral motivations. On further study, however, there is evidence of racially motivated voting behavior, especially among the critical swing constituency of ideological moderates. These results are especially profound given that neither of the candidates in 1993 was black.

The reelection campaigns in 1997 offered voters in Los Angeles and New York little racial variation in their candidates. All four major candidates in the 1997 elections were non-Latino whites, and yet the white liberals were as unsuccessful in appealing to non-Latino white voters in 1997 as had been their liberal minority predecessors in 1993. The persistence of interracial competition in both cities gave white voters little impetus to revert to their Democratic roots and gave black voters little hope at enhanced political incorporation. Furthermore, the more conservative leanings of Latino voters coupled with their increasing mobilization made them attractive coalition partners in these Republican-led administrations, especially in relation to the black community. And given the persistent outsider status accorded to Latinos in both cities, it is not surprising that many jumped at the chance to take a more prominent role in these conservative administrations.

The shifting support of Latino voters, especially in Los Angeles, highlights the importance of group interests in relation to local politics and further underscores the inherent instability of "rainbow coalitions." In Democratic-led urban administrations, black voters are typically essential to electoral success. In Republican administrations, however, black voters can be virtually shut out with little electoral repercussion. Latino voters have often been accorded a secondary status in Democratic administrations given their history of poor electoral participation. Increasing levels of political activity within the Latino community coupled with a more moderate political agenda, however, created new opportunities for political incorporation in New York and Los Angeles. The lesson from Los Angeles in 2001, however, suggests that the Latino/Republican alliance during the Riordan years may have been little more than an instrumental short-term relationship. The Villaraigosa candidacy garnered more than 80 percent of the Latino vote, but only 21 percent of the Republicans in the general election. Rather, moderate and conservative white voters banded together with more than 80 percent of black voters to elect James Hahn. The schism between black and Latino voters in this most recent election may merely reflect the effect of Hahn's somewhat unique pedigree. His father was a much beloved county supervisor, who had represented the black community for many years. Nonetheless, these results also likely point to increasing competition between blacks and Latinos in Los Angeles. To no small degree, the candidates, the issues, and the political context will undoubtedly shape the future of these new urban regimes, as will perceived levels of interethnic and interracial conflict between increasingly powerful Latinos electorates and their white and black counterparts.

The most recent New York City election also points to the increasing independence of Latinos from their traditional Democratic coalitions. Over the course of the past ten years, Latinos in Los Angeles and New York have periodically supported Republican candidates in rather large numbers. And in the short term, acrimonious campaigns waged against Latino candidates have resulted in hard feelings and electoral retribution. Only time will tell how the intensifying competition between African-American, Latino, and non-Latino white voters will play out, but it is almost certain that perceived conflict and salient group interests will continue to play a primary role in the mayoral politics of these two cities.

CHAPTER TWELVE

Riots in New York and Los Angeles

1935–2002

David Halle and Kevin Rafter

The precariousness of public order is perhaps a lesson
that needs to be relearned by every generation.
David Sears (1994, 252)

The only mega riot of the 1990s that was comparable in scale to some of the biggest urban riots of the 1960s occurred in Los Angeles after four white policemen were acquitted in the beating of African-American Rodney King, despite the fact that the beating had been videotaped. The 1992 Rodney King verdict upheavals, together with the enormous Watts riots of 1965, gave the city of Los Angeles the reputation of being as prone to riots as any other American city.[1] The main perceived rival here is Miami, which during the 1980s was the only American city to experience three major riots including the massive 1980 Liberty City uprising (Portes and Stepick 1993, 179).[2]

One sign of this view that Los Angeles suffers more serious and more frequent riots than New York is the difference in the number of academic studies of riots in the two cities/regions. Scholars have analyzed the Watts and Rodney King riots but have written far less about post–World War II riots in or around New York City.[3] There is, for example, no study by an academic of the 1967 Newark riots, although these were among the worst riots of the 1960s and Newark is just a mile from New York City's Staten Island border. (There are two accounts by community activists, including one by the young Tom Hayden [1967] who had been working in Newark as a community organizer for four years before the riots occurred and who, much later, became a major political figure in Los Angeles.)[4] Nor is there an academic study of the 1977 blackout-related riots in New York City, even though the number of stores and businesses damaged then was more than 50 percent higher than in either of the two mega riots in Los Angeles (see tables 12.1 and 12.2).[5]

Yet in the 1990s New York City has hardly been riot free. It had two

Table 12.1. Mega Riots and Major Riots, Los Angeles Region, 1933–2002

		RIOT INTENSITY CRITERIA					
NAME/LOCATION	START DATE	Duration in Days	Arrests	Injuries	Deaths	Business/Property Damage	Geographic Spread
Zoot suit riot	June 3, 1943	5*	ca. 606	N.A.	0	Very little	Mexican neighborhoods of Los Angeles*
WATTS RIOT	August 11, 1965	6*	3,952*	1,032*	34*	ca. 1,000 buildings*	Large area in and around Watts*
RODNEY KING RIOT	April 29, 1992	5*	9,500*	2,383*	45*	700 businesses*	Central city and numerous inner-city suburban areas*

Sources. The sources for the data in tables 12.1 and 12.2 are contemporary newspapers, especially the *Los Angeles Times* and the *New York Times,* as well as the following studies: Governor's Commission on the Los Angeles Riots [McCone Commission] (1965), Hayden (1967), National Advisory Commission on Civil Disorders [Kerner Commission] (1968), Wright (1968), Mayor LaGuardia's Commission (1969), Sears and McConohay (1973), Capeci (1977), Stein (1978), Curvin (1979), Curvin and Porter (1979), Romo (1983), Mazon (1984), Nash (1985), Newton (1991), Report to the Governor on the Disturbances in Crown Heights [Girgenti Report] (1993), Verge (1993), and Baldassare (1994). Numbers of arrests, injuries, and amount of property damage sometimes vary from source to source for the same riot. The numbers cited above are those that seemed most reliably based. None of the variation in numbers is large enough to change whether a particular riot is classified as major or mega.

Note. A "mega riot" (shown in all capitals here) is a riot in which at least three of the measures or components of a riot's intensity reached very intense levels, as specified in the text. A "major riot" is a riot in which one or two, but not more, of these measures or components reached very intense levels.

* Qualifies as "very intense," as defined in the chapter.

Table 12.2. Mega Riots and Major Riots, New York Region, 1933–2002

NAME/ LOCATION	START DATE	RIOT INTENSITY CRITERIA: Duration in Days	Arrests	Injuries	Deaths	Businesses Looted/ Damaged	Geographic Spread
Harlem, N.Y.	March 19, 1935	2	50	100	1	200 or 1,000 stores/ businesses[a]	Inner city*
Harlem, N.Y.	August 1, 1943	1	c.550	c.500	6	About 1,450 stores/ businesses*	Inner city (110–145th streets, 8th–Lenox Aves.)
Harlem–Bedford-Stuyvesant	July 19, 1964	6*	219 Harlem, 316, B-S	124 Harlem, 19 B-S	1 Harlem	122 stores Harlem, 415 stores B-S	Two large inner city areas*
NEWARK, N.J.	July 13, 1967	5*	1,600*	1,500*	26*	1,029 stores/ businesses*	. . .
Plainfield, N.J.	July 14, 1967	5*	. . .	. . .	1	. . .	. . .
Jersey City, N.J.	July 16, 1967	3*	50	. . .	1	. . .	. . .
Englewood, N.J.	July 16, 1967	3*	8	. . .	. . .	. . .	. . .
Jersey City, N.J.	June 10, 1970	4*	. . .	. . .	. . .	. . .	. . .
NEW YORK CITY blackout riots	July 13, 1977	2	3,076*	622	2	1,616 stores/ businesses*	Total of 31 neighborhoods (mostly poor) in all five boroughs of the city; also sections of Westchester County*
Crown Heights	August 19, 1991	4*	110	38–43	2	6	Two city neighborhoods (30 blocks)*
Washington Heights	July 3, 1992	6*	139	90	2	3–5	Several adjoining city neighborhoods from 183st to 135st*

Sources. See sources for table 12.1.

Note. Mega riots are shown in all capitals here. The Harlem, Harlem–Bedford-Stuyvesant, New York City blackout, Crown Heights, and Washington Heights riots occurred in New York City. B-S = Bedford-Stuyvesant. Ellipses dots indicate no data available.

[a] The *New York Times* (March 20, 1935) said 200 store windows were broken. In a telegram to Governor Lehman, quoted in the *New York Times* (March 21, 1935), the Harlem Merchants Association said more than 1,000 stores had been damaged.

* Qualifies as "very intense" as defined in the text.

major riots, one just before and one just after the Rodney King verdict. The August 1991 riot between blacks and orthodox Jews in Crown Heights, Brooklyn, lasted four days and was probably the most important reason why New York's incumbent mayor David Dinkins lost the 1993 mayoral election to Rudolph Giuliani, as Kaufmann stresses in chapter 11. An investigative report commissioned by the governor of New York characterized the Crown Heights riot as "the most widespread racial unrest to occur in New York City in more than a twenty-year period" (Report to the Governor 1993, 133). A July 1992 riot in Washington Heights (northwest Manhattan), triggered by a police officer's fatal shooting of a Dominican resident whom observers said was unarmed, lasted six days, as long as the Rodney King riot. Los Angeles (the city and region), in contrast, had no major riot in the 1990s other than in 1992.

There are, as well, some striking similarities between riots in the two cities. Latino participation in the Rodney King riots has been widely noted. For example, Latinos constituted 51 percent of those arrested (Morrison and Lowry 1994, 34). Latino participation in the Washington Heights riots in some ways went beyond that, since almost all the rioters were Dominicans. A second feature of the Rodney King riots was that looters often targeted Korean stores, especially liquor stores. Korean stores were also targeted in the Washington Heights riots. Further, in New York City there were, during this period, major tensions between Koreans and blacks, with five well-publicized black boycotts of Korean stores.

This chapter systematically compares and contrasts riots in the two cities/regions since 1930. One aim is to see whether, in fact, either city/region is markedly more riot prone than the other. Since it is not practical to consider every riot since 1930, the discussion will focus on the two most serious kinds of riots, called here, in ascending order of gravity, "major" riots and "mega" riots. An important prelude to this discussion will be to define what is meant by a riot, something that a surprising number of discussions do not do, and to do so in such a way that riots can be classified by their level of seriousness.[6] Although the city of Los Angeles appears to have had two mega riots in the past thirty-six years, and the 1967 Newark riot, close to New York City, was also an apparent mega riot, a formal definition is needed to confirm these perceptions. We will argue that, once such a formal definition is made, it is apparent that New York City's 1977 power blackout was a mega riot, too. Overall, this chapter will raise doubts about the impression that the city of Los Angeles is markedly more riot prone than New York City. Further, looking beyond the two city boundaries, the region around

New York City actually looks more riot prone than the region around the city of Los Angeles.

A second result of this chapter will be to underline the fact that socio-political stability cannot be taken for granted in either city/region. Mega riots have occurred in each city even though neither the national nor the local context was more inflamed and volatile than usual. For example, the Rodney King verdict riots in Los Angeles in 1992 and the New York 1977 power blackout riots show that if a major cause presents itself, such as a manifestly unjust trial verdict or the temporary removal of the security provided by night lighting, then the most serious of riots can take place in either city.

A further aim of this chapter is to consider these riots in the context of the history of social order and disorder in American cities. The major and mega riots in New York and Los Angeles over the past seventy years have been, loosely, a product of their times, though some clearly came toward the tail end of a riot era while others pointed forward to new riot eras. For example, the 1943 "zoot suit" riots in Los Angeles, in which Anglo servicemen turned on young Mexican-Americans, came toward the end of an era of rioting that spanned the nineteenth and first half of the twentieth century. This era involved ethnic or racial groups attacking one another, often with deadly consequences, and especially whites attacking ethnic or racial minorities.[7] A prime example is the New York City draft riots of July 13–17, 1863, probably the most serious civil insurrection in American history, resulting in about 119 deaths (see table 12.3). In the worst phase of these riots, mostly Irish laborers turned on and lynched local blacks whom they blamed for the draft on the grounds that the civil war was being fought on behalf of blacks (Cook 1974; Bernstein 1990).[8] As immigration was restricted from the 1920s on, this form of rioting, which social historians have called "interethnic/racial" or "communal" riots, became less frequent and, in the 1960s, was largely replaced by a new era of rioting, involving above all blacks destroying property amid symbolic protests about perceived inequalities, a form of rioting that social historians have called "property-oriented" or "commodity riots" (Gilje 1996, 9–11; Sears 1973, 24–54; Janowitz 1969, 317–39).

This chapter will suggest that the 1990s riots in Los Angeles and New York imply a partial return to that earlier, pre-1960s, era of interethnic rioting. Certain features of 1992 in Los Angeles—when Koreans were victimized by blacks and Latinos—and Crown Heights in 1992—where blacks, including a large proportion of immigrants from the Caribbean, and Jews fought each other—suggest this may be happening. Nor would

Table 12.3. Other Selected Mega Riots in U.S. History

		RIOT INTENSITY CRITERIA					
NAME/LOCATION	START DATE	Duration in Days	Arrests	Injuries	Deaths	Business/Property Damage	Geographic Spread
New York City draft riots	July 13, 1863	5*	. . .	Several hundred	119*	. . .	Many neighborhoods*
Chicago	1919	5*	. . .	Just over 500*	38*	. . .	Several neighborhoods*
Detroit	June 20, 1943	2	700	600*	34*	. . .	Several neighborhoods*
Detroit	July 23, 1967	8*	7,200*	2,000*	43*	477 (including homes)	Several neighborhoods*
Miami (Liberty City)	May 17, 1980	5*	1,100*	. . .	18*	150 buildings	Several neighborhoods*

Sources. See sources for table 12.1.

Note. Ellipses dots indicate no data available.

*Qualifies as "very intense" as defined in the text.

a partial return to interethnic rioting be improbable given the massive increase of immigration into the United States since 1965 and especially into Los Angeles and New York. Indeed, it looks as if Los Angeles, New York, and Miami, too, the three cities most affected by immigration in recent decades, are now the most riot prone.[9]

RIOT DEFINED

A "riot," as defined here, involves at least one group publicly, and with little or no attempt at concealment, illegally assaulting at least one other group or illegally attacking or invading property. Property may be either real estate or areas of public or civil space that rioters use in ways that suggest that the authorities have lost control. In order to constitute a riot, rather than a serious disturbance or melee, the attacks on another group or on property need to reach a certain threshold of intensity (see below). Once they have reached that threshold, riots can be further classified by their level of gravity, with a mega riot as the most serious.[10]

Notice three features of this definition of a riot. First, the actions of a riot are mostly done publicly and without any attempt to hide them, although individual rioters may try to hide their own identities while they are performing the actions. This is one important distinction between riots and other types of illegal behavior, which are usually done with care to conceal. (For example, from 1978 to 1982 landlords in the South Bronx who saw that they could recover far more in fire insurance than their buildings were worth intact burned about 10,000 buildings—residential or commercial—a year.[11] This far exceeds the 700–1,000 buildings damaged during either the Watts or the Rodney King riots. Such arsonist activities were not riots both because they were concealed and because they were done individually, not in groups.) Second, riots do involve behavior that is clearly illegal. This distinguishes them from, for example, major demonstrations or state-sponsored lynching. Third, any group can, in principle, riot, including the police and the armed forces. The zoot suit riots were an armed forces riot. An infamous police riot occurred in New York City in September 1992 when a crowd of 10,000 officers and their supporters massed outside city hall to protest Mayor Dinkins's proposal to replace the existing police civilian complaint review board, an agency of the New York City Police Department, with an independent panel.[12] The police blocked traffic on the Brooklyn Bridge and surged through the doors of city hall, and some punched reporters and jumped on cars, all of which led the media plausibly to label this a police riot (McKinley 1992).

A riot's level of intensity is best captured by considering several factors: how long the riot lasts, how many people are killed or injured, the number of arrests, the amount of property damage, and the riot's geographic spread. These criteria are the basis for classifying riots by their level of seriousness.[13]

The most serious riots of all—mega riots—are marked by the fact that several of the factors that constitute a riot's level of intensity are very high. To determine exactly what counts as very high requires some benchmarks. The following will be used here to ensure that the same criteria are applied to riots in each region.

For length of time, a riot that lasts longer than two days will count as very high. For number of people killed, more than ten will count as very high. For number of arrests, more than a thousand will count as very high. For number of injuries, more than 500 will count as very high. For amount of property damage, more than 500 stores or other buildings suffering damage will count as very high.[14] For geographic spread, rioting that spreads beyond two adjoining neighborhoods will count as very high unless the neighborhood is very large (e.g., Watts), in which case a riot that covers much of the neighborhood will count as very high.

A "mega riot" can now be defined as a riot in which at least three of the measures or components of a riot's intensity reached very high levels, as specified above. The next level of seriousness, a "major riot," can be defined as a riot in which one or two, but not more, of these components reached very high levels.

Tables 12.1 and 12.2 present all the major and mega riots in the two regions since 1933.[15] Figures 12.1 and 12.2 illustrate their locations. For comparison, table 12.3 outlines some of the other worst riots in U.S. history.

MEGA RIOTS IN NEW YORK AND LOS ANGELES

In the city of Los Angeles, the 1965 Watts riot and the 1992 Rodney King verdict riot were mega riots. There were no other mega riots in the region. In the New York region, the 1967 Newark riot was a mega riot. Though mostly forgotten by social analysts, the blackout-related looting that occurred through much of New York City in 1977 was also a mega riot. The following are sketches of these mega riots.

Watts, August 11, 1965

On a hot summer evening on August 11, 1965, Marquette Frye, a black man who was speeding and driving erratically on the freeway, was pulled

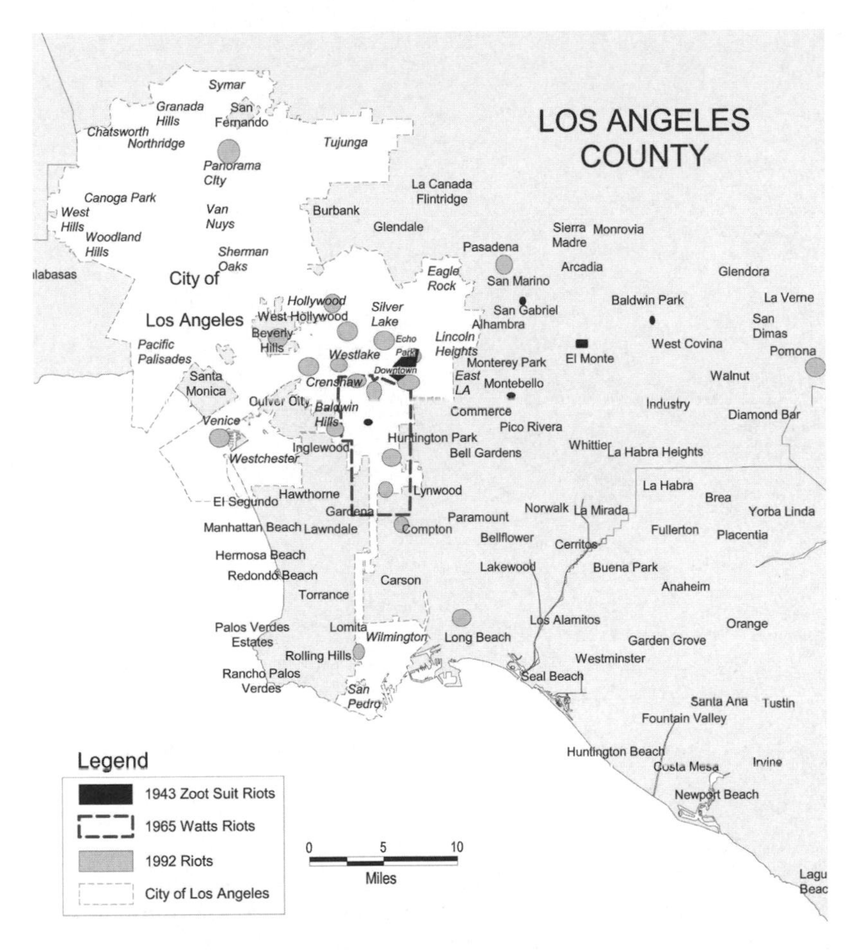

Figure 12.1. Major and Mega Los Angeles Riots: 1943, 1965, and 1992

over in the heart of Watts by a motorcycle officer of the California Highway Patrol. Frye's brother was in the car, and the two had drunk several screwdrivers to celebrate the return of Frye's brother from the service. After answering a number of questions in a cooperative way, Frye became angry as he was being arrested. He had been joined, at this point, by a crowd of bystanders who also became angry. Frye's mother arrived and argued on his behalf. Other officers were called to the scene, who beat Frye with batons and took him, his mother, and his brother into custody. The crowd threw bottles, rocks, and bricks at the departing police. This was the start of the Watts riots.

For the first two days, the police department, following its usual pro-

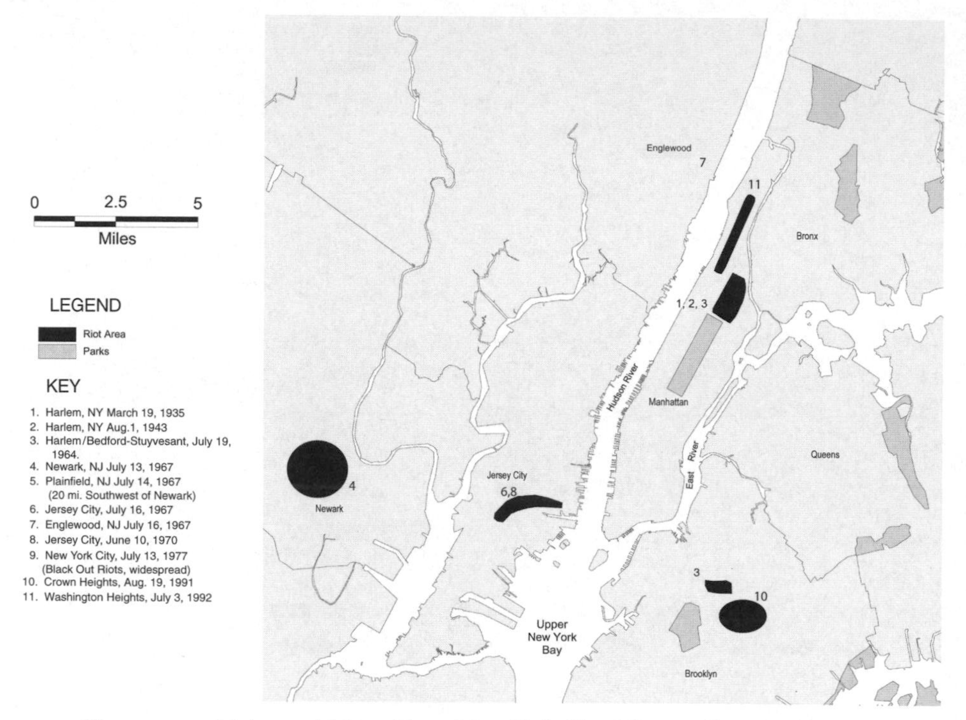

Figure 12.2. Major and Mega Riots, New York City Metropolitan Region, 1935–2002

cedures for riot activity, withdrew from the riot area so as not to create further provocations. Although there was much rock and bottle throwing, there was no looting, burning, or shooting during this period. But the rioting had not ceased by the afternoon of August 12, at which point Police Chief William Parker declared himself "perplexed." The deputy police chief then ordered his officers to return in force. Massive looting and burning quickly occurred, followed the next day by major shootings. By the afternoon of August 14, sixteen people were already dead.

The riots lasted six days, with thirty-four people dead and almost 4,000 arrested. During the riots, the National Guard and police cordoned off an area of 46.5 square miles, an area one and one-half times as large as Manhattan and larger than the city of San Francisco (Sears 1994, 238). The Kerner Commission characterized Watts as "the worst [riot] in the United States since the Detroit riot of 1943. [It] shocked all who had been confident that race relations were improving in the North, and evoked a new mood in the Negro ghettos around the country" (National Advisory Commission on Civil Disorders 1968, 38).

Rodney King Riots, April 29, 1992

Four police officers, on trial in Ventura County's predominantly white Simi Valley for the widely televised beating of black motorist Rodney King, were acquitted by an all-white jury. King had refused to stop his car when approached by police, who then caught up with him after a long chase and gave him a beating that, unknown to them at the time, was videotaped by a local resident. The jury acquittal triggered rioting in South Central Los Angeles. Although police had been assembled outside the Simi Valley courtroom to anticipate trouble, the Los Angeles Police Department was woefully unprepared for disturbances in the inner city thirty miles away. At first the rioters were mainly blacks, but then Latinos in South Central joined in.

The first recorded disturbance took place in the predominantly black, South Central Los Angeles neighborhood of Hyde Park and involved brick throwing and the beating of a white pedestrian. The most infamous incident of the riots occurred about two hours later at Normandie and Florence Avenues when a white truck driver, Reginald Denny, was pulled from his cab and beaten almost to death, while TV cameras recorded the scene. He was finally rescued by several black men and women who drove him to a hospital. The rioting spread during the evening and next day to numerous parts of the city and continued for several days (fig. 12.3). By Friday, the third day of the riot, the National Guard was

Figure 12.3. Corner of Normandie and Manchester, South Central Los Angeles, 1992 after the Riots

in place. Overall, there were forty-five deaths, 2,383 injuries, and 9,500 arrests.

A feature of the rioting and arson was the targeting of Korean stores. Relations between blacks and Korean merchants had been troubled for some time, culminating in two 1991 incidents in which Korean merchants shot blacks whom they suspected of stealing from their stores. One such incident, captured on the store's security system and later publicly televised, showed the execution of the teenager Latasha Harlins, deliberately shot in the head at point blank range by the merchant. In neither case did those doing the shooting receive jail terms.

Newark, July 12, 1967

Although by 1967 the city was 52 percent black and 10 percent Puerto Rican and Cuban, the non-Hispanic white population retained firm control of the mayoralty, city council, and board of education. In the months before the riot, a number of incidents angered several black residents of the city. The city's planning board had announced its intention to turn over 150 acres in the heart of the city to build the state's new medical and dental college. Many blacks saw this as an attempt to reduce the size of the black residential presence, involving, as it would, the displacement of some 22,000 people from the predominantly black Central Ward. Repeated allegations of police brutality against blacks constituted an additional grievance. The black community wanted, and the police adamantly opposed, an independent police review board to investigate charges of police brutality. Blacks were also angered by the mayor's intention to appoint a white, not a black, as head of the board of education (Wright 1968).

Then on July 12 a black cab driver, John Smith, was arrested in Newark on a traffic violation. He was an "unlikely candidate to set a riot in motion" (National Advisory Commission on Civil Disorders 1968, 60). Honorably discharged from the army as a corporal, he played chess and the trumpet and had worked as a musician and in a factory before turning to cab driving, which was not his strength. Within a few years, he had eight or nine accidents and his license had been revoked. On July 12, he was stopped by the police for tailgaiting a police car. Residents of a high-rise housing project overlooking the police precinct saw the police dragging Smith into the precinct house. He either could not or would not walk. Residents called civil rights leaders in Newark and word spread among other taxi drivers that the police were beating one of them. Crowds gathered and violence erupted. The next day, the mayor said it was an isolated incident. Inflammatory rumors spread, including one that Smith had died. In his bail hearing, Smith said that he had been held with his head over a toilet bowl in the police station and beaten (Hayden 1967, 10). Rioting broke out when a group of protestors at the police station dismissed as inadequate a mayoral announcement that a citizen commission would be formed to look into the incident. During the next five days, major riots took place all over the city, accompanied by much shooting on the part of police and some sniper fire. On July 15, the National Guard and State Troopers were called in. Overall, there were twenty-six deaths, about 1,500 injuries, and about 1,600 arrests.

This was one of the most widely publicized and consequential riots of the 1960s (Smith's picture appeared on the cover of *Time* magazine.) A statistical analysis of all racial disturbances in American cities during the 1960s that involved more than thirty people concluded that 168 out of 341 of them were associated with one of two "extraordinary events," either the July 1967 Newark riots or the April 1968 assassination of Martin Luther King (Spilerman 1976, 773). The Newark riot, for example, was followed within days by several riots in northern New Jersey—notably Englewood, Jersey City, Plainfield, and New Brunswick (see fig. 12.2). Of these, the riots in Plainfield, which lasted five days, and in Englewood and Jersey City, which each lasted three days, were major riots as defined here. A mega riot in Detroit on July 23 closely followed Newark in time (National Advisory Commission on Civil Disorders 1968, 69–108; see table 12.3).

The Newark riot also symbolized the not-always-consistent way some New Yorkers viewed their city's propensity to riot during this period. New York City, it was noted, had no major or mega riot in 1967, unlike so many other cities. Some people implied this was because New York City just did not have mega riots. At the same time, New York City's liberal Republican mayor John Lindsay, who went to Harlem to calm the crowds after Martin Luther King's assassination, was given much of the credit for the city not having riots in 1967, which is not especially consistent with the idea that New York City cannot have mega riots.[16]

In each of the mega riots just discussed, a very high level was reached on every measure of a riot's intensity, not just the minimum number of three required for a mega riot as we have defined it. The riots all lasted from five to six days and they involved from twenty-six to forty-five deaths, just over 1,000 to more than 2,000 injuries, major property damage, and a very large number of arrests—the lowest number of arrests was Newark, with about 1,600, and the highest was Los Angeles in 1992, with about 9,500. Further, these riots all went beyond a local neighborhood of a few blocks. The Watts and Newark upheavals spread to a large section of the central city, while the Rodney King riots spread much further, beyond the core central city to the inner suburbs.

Figure 12.4. Spanish Harlem, Day after the 1977 "Blackout Riots" in New York

Power Blackout, New York City, July 13, 1977

Though featured in the 1999 Spike Lee movie *Summer of Sam,* the 1977 blackout is often ignored in discussions of civil disorder.[17] Yet this event contradicts the stereotype that New York City does not have mega riots. An evening power outage in northern Westchester County triggered a general power failure in New York City, which lasted about twenty-five hours for most residents. During this time, there was widespread looting—just over 1,600 stores were affected—in every city borough, a total of thirty-one mostly poor neighborhoods (fig. 12.4). Economics seemed an important motivator for many of the rioters, about 70 percent of whom were unemployed. Clothing and food stores were especially targeted. There were also about 1,040 fires, many of them arson (Curvin and Porter 1979).

Never before or since have all of New York City's five boroughs been simultaneously involved in a civil disorder. There was no police plan for such a contingency, and it is unclear how there could have been one. As a captain in the Bedford-Stuyvesant section of Brooklyn said: "The whole strategy during disorders is to move men from where you don't need them to areas where you do need them. We can get anywhere from 100 to 1,000 men to a trouble spot in pretty quick time. But there's nothing you can do if it goes up everywhere at once" (Curvin and Porter 1979, 69). Despite the enormous amount of looting, the number of deaths was small: two killed by storeowners and none by police. But almost all the experts agreed that the outcome would likely have been far more violent had the police not kept to an unusually strict no-shooting policy, laid down by the former police commissioner, which stressed that an officer firing without full justification would face disciplinary action (Stein 1978, 81). One officer who had been in the middle of one of the most extensive looting areas, Broadway in Brooklyn, commented: "If we'd have shot just one person that night we'd have had a war on our hands" (Curvin and Porter 1979, 58–59).

Most of the rioters were black and Hispanic. Thus in New York City, Hispanics were involved in major riots long before the much-noted Latino involvement in the 1992 Los Angeles riots. Hardest hit in the blackout riots were the black and Hispanic neighborhoods of Harlem, East Harlem, the South Bronx, the High Bridge and Grand Concourse sections of the Bronx, Jamaica in Queens, and the Bedford-Stuyvesant, Bushwick, Williamsburg, and Crown Heights sections of Brooklyn. In Brooklyn, almost every business in the neighborhoods that ran from Saint John's place through Crown Heights had been looted by the morning of July 17, and along Broadway from Myrtle Avenue to Flushing Avenue in Bedford-Stuyvesant, untouched stores were the exception. The looting pushed many of these neighborhoods, whose commercial life was already fragile, into much more serious decline. There was also some looting in Westchester County, in the cities of Mount Vernon, Yonkers, and New Rochelle.

These blackout-related disorders arguably constitute a mega riot because of their geographic spread, amount of property damage, and number of arrests. The number of looted or damaged stores—assessed to be 1,616 (Curvin and Porter 1979) in all five boroughs of the city, with damage least intense in Staten Island—was far higher than the other mega riots discussed here. (But the 1,450 damaged stores in the major 1943 Harlem riot, discussed later, are comparable to the blackout damage). The number of arrests in the blackout (3,076, the vast majority for looting) exceeded those in Newark though not those in 1992 in Los Angeles.

The main reason why the significance of these blackout-related disorders is often overlooked is that ideological themes—for example, protests against government or against police misbehavior or against social and racial inequities—did not appear as prominent motives of the rioters. This contrasts with the other mega riots discussed already and with the major riots to be discussed later. Yet the 1977 disorders are, arguably, a bona fide kind of riot, the kind Gary Marx (1972) has labeled "issueless riots." Issueless riots occur when external controls are absent or severely weakened, as when the police go on strike.[18] The 1977 power blackout provided just such a weakening of external controls.

To call these riots "issueless" is, of course, to exaggerate. Many of the rioters in these situations surely have in mind a variety of issues and grievances. For example, targeting of clothing and food stores by the 1977 blackout rioters suggests economic factors as a major issue.[19] Still, the term "issueless" is designed to stress the opportunistic quality of these riots—the major precipitating cause is the removal of police controls, not an economic or political or social grievance, though the latter are doubtless often also present in major ways.

To discuss riots in the two regions without taking these blackout-related events seriously would be misleading. For one thing, it would overlook the fact that a set of future circumstances that similarly weakened or temporarily removed the sources of social control might have a similar outcome. Also, the adverse economic consequences of the blackout riots were real enough for the neighborhoods where they were concentrated.

MAJOR RIOTS IN NEW YORK AND LOS ANGELES

Major riots are those in which one or two, but not more, of the components of a riot's intensity reach very high levels. From 1933 to 2002, Los Angeles has had, besides its two mega riots, just one major riot—the 1943 zoot suit riots. This counts as a major riot because of the time it lasted, at least five days, and its geographic spread to many of the neighborhoods with concentrations of Mexicans. A historian of riots in America characterized it as "the most notable example of ethnic conflict of the mid century" (Gilje 1996, 150). The following is a sketch.

Zoot Suit Riots, June 3, 1943

In the early 1940s, the ethnic populations of California as a whole, and of Los Angeles in particular, were under siege. In March and April of 1942 the entire Japanese and Japanese-American populations on the West Coast were placed in "relocation centers." Racial ire then turned on Mexicans. Local newspapers announced a "Mexican crime wave," which the city of Los Angeles appointed a special grand jury to investigate. The chief expert witness for the Los Angeles County Sheriff's Department testified that "Mexican Americans had inherited their 'naturally violent' tendencies from the 'bloodthirsty Aztecs' of Mexico who were said to have practiced human sacrifice centuries ago." The central event here was the "Sleepy Lagoon" trial in which, amid enormous national publicity, seventeen Mexican-American youths were convicted in

January 1943 of the murder of another Mexican-American. The noted author and attorney Carey McWilliams, who attended the trial, wrote that "from the beginning the proceedings savored more of a ceremonial lynching than a trial in a court of justice" (McWilliams 1949, 230–31). The Second District Court of Appeals agreed with Williams when in October 1944 it dismissed the charges (Mazón 1984, 21).

The "zoot suit" or "sailor" riots occurred in this context of hatred and paranoia. On the evening of June 3, 1943, eleven sailors on shore leave said that they had been attacked by a group of young Mexicans wearing zoot suits. "Zoot suits" were the distinctive clothes—a long coat, tight-bottomed pants, a pancake hat, pointed shoes—worn at that time by rebellious teenagers, especially in major American cities (New York, Detroit, Chicago) as well as abroad. In Los Angeles, they had been adopted by a minority of Mexican-American youths known as *pachucos* (and the Sleepy Lagoon defendants had been portrayed by the prosecution as "zoot-suiters"). Many Angelenos resented this clothing, which they saw as a wartime extravagance worn by people identified as "foreigners" (Romo 1983, 166; Nash 1985, 110–11; Mazón 1984). Los Angeles, meanwhile, had one of the largest concentrations of military personnel in the United States, with as many as 50,000 servicemen from all branches of the armed forces in the city on any given weekend. The evening of June 3, on hearing that a group of sailors claimed they had been attacked by young Mexicans, more than 200 uniformed sailors went to the Mexican-American community in East Los Angeles, looking for zoot-suiters whom they beat. Over the next three nights, sailors, joined by uniformed soldiers, rampaged through East Los Angeles as well as other communities in Los Angeles where Mexicans lived, such as Watts, Boyle Heights, El Monte, and San Gabriel, beating the many Mexican youths they found in bars, movie theaters, or just on the sidewalks. The Los Angeles police accompanied the crowds of soldiers and sailors in police cars, watched the beatings, and then jailed the victims. The local press—which had helped whip up the crowds with unattributed quotes from zoot-suiters along the lines of, "We're meeting 500 strong tonight and we're going to kill every cop we see"—proclaimed the soldiers and sailors as heroes.

On June 8, the military authorities concluded that they had lost control of their personnel. A military commander reported: "Hundreds of servicemen prowling downtown Los Angles mostly on foot, disorderly, apparently on the prowl for Mexicans. Groups vary in size from 10 to 150 men, and scatter immediately when shore patrol approach. Men found carrying hammock clews, belts, knives, and tire irons when searched by patrol after arrest." Realizing that they now had a mutiny on their hands, the military placed Los Angeles off limits for military personnel. But rioting continued for several more days in Southern California including San Diego (Mazón 1984, 73). No soldier or sailor was ever charged with any crime, although seven were arrested for disorderly conduct.

The zoot suit riots were among the last of a genre of riot that had been happening in America for a hundred and thirty years. Such riots often involved bloody attacks on persons, especially entailing strife between ethnic groups, white lynching of blacks, and violent labor confrontations. Perhaps because these kinds of attacks were now becoming less acceptable, no one was killed or very seriously injured in the zoot suit riots (Mazón 1984, 1).

By contrast with this single major riot in Los Angeles, New York City has had five major riots from 1933 to 2002, two of them in the past decade. These include the Harlem riots of 1935 and 1943, the Harlem–Bedford-Stuyvesant riots of 1964, the Crown Heights riots of 1991, and the Washington Heights riots of 1992. In the New York region in the 1960s, there were, in addition, the three major riots already mentioned that followed the Newark mega riot in 1967 and that involved mostly blacks. There was also a major Jersey City riot in 1970 in which Puerto Ricans protested police brutality (see fig. 12.2). Narrative accounts of these major New York City riots follow.

Harlem, 1935

A sixteen-year-old black youth was caught stealing a penknife in a large, crowded department store. Employees took the boy into a back office and called the police. Word spread among the customers that the boy was being beaten. A riot began in the store and spread to the streets as protesters claimed yet another instance of store and police brutality against blacks. A hearse that by chance was parked across the street, and a summoned ambulance that left empty, led to false rumors that the boy had been beaten to death. About 3,000 blacks roamed the streets of Harlem in protest until 6 A.M. the next day, with widespread smashing of store and business windows and looting. Estimates ranged from between 200 and a 1,000 stores or businesses having been damaged. There were fifty arrests, about a hundred injuries, and one death. Mayor La Guardia appointed a commission to investigate. Local leaders argued that the root causes were racial segregation and high unemployment—50–55 percent of the people of Harlem were unemployed—and the commission agreed (Mayor LaGuardia's Commission 1969).

Harlem, August 1, 1943

By the summer of 1943 racial tensions were high in several American cities. One of the major issues was the understanding by blacks that while they were being asked to risk dying for their country in World War II, they were doing so in armed forces that were segregated. In June a mega riot broke out in Detroit, a major war production site that had attracted many black workers. In New York City, blacks had been especially angered by Mayor LaGuardia's decision to contract the Metropolitan Life Insurance Company to construct a large, quasi-public housing project in lower east Manhattan at Stuyvesant Town. Metropolitan Life's history of discrimination led many to conclude that blacks would not be permitted to live there (Capeci 1977, 12–13, 68–70).

Then on August 1 in Harlem a white policeman shot in the shoulder a black soldier who was trying to prevent the arrest of a black woman accused of disorderly conduct. False rumors circulated that the soldier had been killed while protecting his mother. Groups of rioters, many in their teens or early twenties and some wearing zoot suits, roamed the streets for two days throwing stones and bottles and looting on a widespread scale. The looting centered on 125th Street but extended north to 145th Street and south to 100th Street and involved 1,450 stores throughout the main commercial areas (Capeci, 1977).

Although neither of the Harlem riots lasted longer than two days, each spread to a substantial area of the inner city, which qualify them as major riots, and the 1943 Harlem riots left more stores damaged than either the Watts or the Rodney King verdict riots. The two Harlem riots also pointed forward to a new era in riots, an era that culminated in the 1960s and involved black attacks on property (often white owned) in ghetto neighborhoods but far fewer of the interethnic attacks on people that had characterized riots of the earlier period. As Gilje has pointed out in his history of riots in America, in the Harlem riots of 1935 and 1943, "Angered and frustrated by racial oppression, and eager to seek advantage in the moment of disorder, blacks destroyed and confiscated white property in black neighborhoods. . . . The parallels between the two Harlem riots, the urban rioting of the 1960s, and many ghetto disturbances since then is striking" (Gilje 1996, 157; see also Capeci 1977, 170–71).

Harlem and Bedford-Stuyvesant, 1964

The riots in Harlem and Bedford-Stuyvesant were some of the earliest of the 1960s. On July 16, responding to a dispute between a group of young blacks and a white building superintendent, an off-duty police lieutenant shot and killed a fifteen-year-old black youth who had attacked him with a knife. Trouble started in Harlem, where teenagers smashed store windows, then spread to Bedford-Stuyvesant in Brooklyn. The troubles were partly also precipitated by anger at the lynch murders of three civil rights workers in Mississippi in June. The Harlem and Bedford-Stuyvesant disturbances lasted six days and included throwing of bottles and Molotov cocktails, looting, and fighting with the police.

Crown Heights, August 1991

In 1991 the section of Brooklyn known as Crown Heights consisted of about 207,000 people, composed of three main groups. The smallest group, about 10 percent of the total, were Lubavitch Hasidim, Orthodox Jews who migrated from Eastern Europe in the 1940s and who chose to remain in Crown Heights while other whites moved out in the years after World War II. The second group was African-Americans who moved in after Word War II, often from the South. The third, and fastest-growing group, were immigrant blacks from the Caribbean, who had been coming to Crown Heights in especially large numbers since the mid-1960s. For example, more than 18,000 came between 1983 and 1989 (Report to the Governor 1993, 41–43).

On a hot summer evening, a car carrying four Hasidic Jews went through a stoplight, collided with a crossing car, and ricocheted into two black children riding their bikes. One, a seven-year-old, was killed. The Hasidic car was the last in a three-car motorcade. The first was a police car while the second was carrying the Hasidic Grand Rebbe. A Hasidic-run ambulance arrived and was told by police officers to take the Hasidic Jews, who were being beaten by individuals in the crowd, to safety. A New York City ambulance, which had arrived moments after the Hasidic-run ambulance, treated the black boys. The police just stood around. A rumor spread that the Hasidic ambulance had deliberately ignored the critically injured black children.

The black crowd became angry. The anger built on a general feeling that the Hasidim were given preferential treatment in the community. The issues included the perception that, in the 1970s, Community Board 9 (community boards in New York City allow citizens to influence local planning and resource decisions—see table 10.2) had been gerrymandered in favor of the Hasidim and that Hasidim had been paying high prices for the homes of black residents in order to drive them out. It was also charged that the police discriminated against blacks and favored the Hasidim, for example, by closing local streets to traffic on the Jewish Sabbath to the inconvenience of blacks. In 1978 a prominent black civic leader was strangled in a choke hold by police when he tried to prevent his brother from being arrested for a traffic violation (Report to the Governor 1993, 43–47).

The crowd grew larger and began yelling racial epithets such as "the Jews killed the kids." Later in the evening, Yankel Rosenbaum, a rabbinical student from Australia, was fatally stabbed by one of a crowd of black youths. Rioting continued for four days, fed by the view that the Hasidim were treated specially well (Report to the Governor 1993, 58). The Hasidim, in contrast, believed that Mayor Dinkins allowed the riot to get out of hand because, as an African-American, he was reluctant to use force against blacks. Certainly Police Commissioner Brown did too little for the first three days of the rioting. The official governor's report on the riot concluded that: "much of the criminal activity in Crown Heights was targeted against the Hasidic community in a way rarely witnessed in recent New York City history" (Report to the Governor 1993, 135). Crown Heights thus had some of the hallmarks of the interethnic/racial riots of a much earlier era.

Washington Heights, July 3, 1992

By 1992, immigrant Dominicans were just over half the population of Washington Heights, an upper Manhattan neighborhood to the northwest of Harlem. Considerable drug dealing by Dominicans contributed to the neighborhood's having the largest number of murders in the city (122 in 1991). At the same time, many hard-working Dominicans lived in cramped quarters and resented both the drug dealers and the police's tendency to assume that most Dominicans were in the drug trade.

On July 3, a police officer, whom some residents said had himself long been involved in stealing drugs from dealers, fatally shot a Dominican resident, whom observers said was unarmed and was not involved in the drug trade. (This picture was complicated ten days later when an autopsy revealed the victim had recently consumed cocaine.) Six days of violent protest followed, with large crowds of people surging though the streets protesting and attacking police. About 2,000 police in riot gear were, after a while, deployed throughout the area. Looting was not extensive, but targeted were several Korean stores, especially those selling sneakers. The senior police commanders responsible for dealing with events were absent during the first few days—the police commissioner himself was in Los Angeles for days one through three.

All five of these New York riots took place in an area that went way beyond just a few blocks, qualifying them as major riots. Also, the

Harlem–Bedford-Stuyvesant riots and the Washington Heights riots lasted six days, as long as any of the mega riots, while Crown Heights lasted four days.

CONCLUSION

We can first conclude that the attacks on Koreans in Los Angeles in 1992 and the black-Jewish hostilities that framed the 1991 Crown Heights riots (recall that the fastest growing group in Crown Heights were immigrant blacks from the Caribbean) suggest a return, in the context of rising immigration, to the interethnic and racial violence that characterized many riots in America in the nineteenth century and first four decades of the twentieth century. The governor's inquiry into Crown Heights specifically noted this return to an earlier era (Report to the Governor 1993, 133).[20]

The progression of Miami's three riots in the 1980s also support this analysis. The May 1980 Liberty City mega riot occurred after an all-white jury acquitted four white former Dade County police officers of charges in the fatal beating of African-American businessman Arthur McDuffie, despite the legal and medical evidence that showed he had been beaten to death.[21] Blacks, already angered by a series of recent perceived injustices by white police and others in authority toward blacks, directed their rage and violence against whites rather than property, in striking contrast with riots of the 1960s (Porter and Dunn 1984, xiii, 27–33). Perhaps one reason for this interethnic violence was rising anxiety in the black community about competition for resources created by the steady arrival to South Florida, from 1977 to 1981, of about 60,000 Haitian "boat people" desperate to leave their country, and the highly publicized arrival, starting in April and ending in September 1980, of about 125,000 Cubans from the port of Mariel, roughly 45 percent of whom had some kind of delinquent background (Portes and Stepick 1993, 18–60). By the time of the Miami riot of 1984, interethnic conflict, this time between blacks and Hispanics, had moved to the foreground. The rioters, almost all blacks in Liberty City, Overtown, and Coconut Grove, were angered by a jury's acquittal of a Hispanic police officer who shot in the head a black man who was being arrested in a video arcade. The Hispanic officer was staunchly defended by the Hispanic-American Confederation, an organization of Latino police officers that helped pay his legal fees. Five years later, black-Hispanic conflict was also in the foreground of Miami's 1989 riot, triggered when a Hispanic off-duty cop shot to death a black motorcyclist who was doing nothing worse than speeding. Black officials and residents were quoted as saying that underlying the violence of the riots was "a belief by blacks that Hispanic immigrants had taken over the city, prospering at the expense of poor blacks" (Schmalz 1989).

Thus riots in the 1980s and early 1990s in the three premier immigration cities, New York, Los Angeles, and Miami, seem to harbinger a return to interethnic conflicts. (However, Cincinnati's major riot of April 2001, triggered by black perceptions of police misbehavior toward blacks [Sack 2001], shows that 1960s- and 1970s-style riots involving urban blacks protesting socioeconomic injustices and destroying property have not disappeared.)

A complete analysis of why heightened immigration might bring some return of interethnic rioting is surely complex, but four major reasons seem clear: first, greater competition for scarce resources on the part of groups who may not have much to start with; second, the fairly sudden and, to those loosing out, disturbing shifts in interethnic power relations that can accompany the immigration of new groups;[22] third, as a city becomes less homogeneous its neighborhoods are more likely to consist of groups who do not understand and do not sympathize with each other;[23] and fourth, the increasing probability that the ethnic or racial composition of the city's leadership (mayor, police chief, etc.) will differ from that of subordinate groups, further increasing tension. That such interethnic or racial riots have not occurred in New York and Los Angeles in the middle and latter 1990s may be, in part, because the long economic expansion that ended in 2001 softened resentments between ethnic and racial groups. Time will show if this was the case.

A second conclusion is that the sociopolitical fabric of the city of Los Angeles does not seem markedly more fragile than New York City's, either in the past twenty years or going further back to the 1930s. In the 1930s and 1940s, Los Angeles had one major riot, the zoot suit riot; New York City had two major riots during this period, the Harlem riots of 1935 and 1943. In the 1960s, Los Angeles had the Watts mega riot. New York City had the major Harlem–Bedford-Stuyvesant riots in 1964 and, in 1977, what was arguably a mega riot, the blackout riots. In the 1990s Los Angeles had one mega riot, New York City had two major riots.

Further, when the comparison moves from the cities to the two regions, the New York region looks far more riot prone in the past forty years than does the region around the city of Los Angeles. In the 1960s and early 1970s, the New York region had the Newark mega riot, as well as several major riots in cities in New Jersey. The region beyond the city of Los Angeles has been free of major or mega riots during that time. This difference between the two regions mostly reflects the fact that the

New York black and Latino populations have for long been far more dispersed in a series of older urban ghettos both around New York City and around the New York region than is the case in the city of Los Angeles and the surrounding region (see the maps in chaps. 1 and 5). This greater dispersal in a series of older urban concentrations or ghettos of the black and Hispanic population of New York City and the surrounding region probably has much to do with the greater availability of public transport, for example, the New York City subway system and the Port Authority Trans-Hudson, or PATH, train that connects New York City with New Jersey. By contrast, the major urban or inner-city concentrations of the black and Latino populations in Los Angeles have for long been in far fewer areas, notably South Central Los Angeles, East Los Angeles, and Pasadena. Of course, beyond these older urban concentrations, a large proportion of the Latino population of the Los Angeles consolidated metropolitan statistical area (CMSA) is also very dispersed, but these concentrations are in suburban communities that lack the ghetto-like atmosphere of older urban concentrations, as chapter 5 shows.

A third conclusion is that, in either city, a major event or combination of events can present itself that can precipitate even a mega riot (Rodney King, the blackout riots), even if the general context of inequality and residential segregation is not already seriously inflamed. Indeed, the preceding review suggests an important distinction between two kinds of situations or causes that can lead to riots. In the first, typical of the context of American cities in the 1960s, the general context of inequality and residential segregation is already highly inflamed by several other factors (in the 1960s, the civil rights struggles and Vietnam War), so that a local event that is not especially different from many that commonly occur (e.g., the arrest of a motorist for speeding as in Watts in 1965; the shooting by an off-duty police officer of a black youth who had attacked him with a knife, as in Harlem in 1964) can trigger a riot (National Advisory Commission on Civil Disorders 1968, 116-118).[24] Here the concept of a triggering event is exactly appropriate, since the situation is already tense and volatile, and therefore an event that is not unusual may be sufficient to precipitate a major or even a mega riot. In other situations, the general context of inequality and residential segregation or separation is not highly inflamed. In these situations a major or mega riot can still occur if a major cause or set of causes presents themselves. This was the case both for New York City's blackout riots and Los Angeles's Rodney King riots.

Thus in 1992 in Los Angeles two events fused to create a major, but highly unusual, cause. The first event was the videotaping of the Rodney

King beating. For the first time in U.S. history, an incident of police brutality toward an African-American was fully taped so that it could be, and was, seen and seen again by the entire population of the region. The second event was the verdict and the circumstances associated with its delivery. Not only did the jury deliver a manifestly unjust vote to acquit, but the verdict—eagerly awaited by many of the city residents—was also publicly announced so that everyone got the news at the same time.[25] Further, the LAPD were poorly prepared to deal with civil disorder associated with the verdict. This analysis suggest that it might be a mistake to think that the Los Angeles riot of 1992 occurred because the city of Los Angeles has, in contrast with New York City, particular structural conditions such as particularly tense race relations or particularly tense police relations. For example, although Los Angeles clearly has poor police relations and considerable racial segregation, the analysis of census data in chapter 5 suggested that residential segregation in New York City was even more pronounced than in Los Angeles during the early 1990s.

In 1977 in New York City a general power blackout likewise acted as a major, unusual cause leading to a mega riot. Underlying the importance of contingency in 1977 is the comparison with 1965 when New York City also had a large-scale blackout but on that occasion little or no looting. An important reason for the different outcomes of the two blackouts had to do with several weather- or time-related factors, none of which concerned differences in the degree of inequality or injustice in the two periods. Thus the 1965 blackout occurred on a cool evening when people in poor neighborhoods were not on the streets in large numbers and during a full moon, which provided some light, and it began at 5:30 P.M., while owners were still in their stores—many owners, in fact, stayed the night to deter looting. By contrast, the 1977 riot occurred at 9:35 P.M. after many owners had gone home. Also, in 1977 people had experienced the blackout of 1965 and knew the power would probably be out for a long time (Curvin and Porter 1979, xiv–xv).

In New York City in the late 1990s a trilogy of widely publicized instances of police brutality had, together, the potential of producing a major riot. The first incident, in August 1997, was the torture by a white police officer of the Haitian immigrant Abner Louima. Incriminating evidence from other police officers induced the officer to plead guilty at his trial in May 1999 and especially angered and alarmed the black community. The second event occurred in the midst of the concern over the first when, on February 4, 1999, four undercover police officers gunned down Amadou Diallo, the twenty-two-year-old immigrant from West Africa, standing innocently outside his doorway in the Bronx. In the third incident, in March 2000, Patrick Dorismond a twenty-six-year-old security guard was shot by an undercover detective outside a Manhattan bar after Dorismond responded angrily when the detective tried to entrap him by asking to buy marijuana.

Of these three police incidents involving innocent blacks, the Diallo case came closest to triggering a major riot. For two months, there were almost daily protests involving major acts of civil disobedience by hundreds of ordinary and prominent citizens in front of city hall. At least 1,200 people were arrested, including several prominent politicians (Charles Rangle, Floyd Flake, Earl McCall, David Dinkins, Jesse Jackson, and even the daughter of Justice Stephen G. Breyer of the U.S. Supreme Court). Tension was diffused by a grand jury indicting the police officers involved. A second buildup of tension, after the officers were found not guilty, was limited because of factors such as that four of the jury members were black and, in sharp contrast with the Rodney King riots, that there was no videotape of exactly what happened. The officers claimed that Diallo resembled the profile of a wanted rapist and that they, albeit in error, believed that he had fired a gun at them.

While, fortunately, the Diallo events did not lead to a major riot, the preceding analysis suggests that they might have. There is little reason for complacency when considering the social fabric of either New York City or the city of Los Angeles.

CHAPTER THIRTEEN

Black-White Conflict

A Model for the Future of Ethnic Politics in Los Angeles?

David O. Sears

I begin this chapter by describing the racialized politics in Los Angeles, revolving around conflicts between blacks and whites, that has occurred since the passage of landmark civil rights legislation in the mid-1960s. The key events here, in Los Angeles and in California as a whole, include the rejection of fair-housing legislation through the passage of Proposition 14 in 1964; the Watts riot, the largest race riot in the postwar period up to that time; racially charged mayoralty campaigns; busing programs and antibusing protests; the California tax revolt; gubernatorial races that pitted black against white candidates; the beating of the black motorist Rodney King, eventuating in a massive ghetto riot in 1992; and the 1996 ballot measure that eliminated governmental affirmative action programs. These events produced both sharp racial polarization and, among whites, deep divisions between racial liberals and racial conservatives. I also make, in this chapter, some comparison with New York City.

However, not all the news on the racial front was bad. Despite these tensions and the relatively small black minority in Los Angeles, a liberal biracial coalition produced five victories for the black mayor Tom Bradley beginning in 1973, a near-victory in his 1982 gubernatorial campaign, and important black representation in several legislative bodies. Indeed, Los Angeles was the only major American city with a small black minority that had a black mayor in the 1970s and early 1980s; in other cities such as Chicago, Atlanta, and Detroit, black political success was primarily due to the mobilization of large black populations. Moreover, in Los Angeles, none of the electoral events that went against blacks triggered urban rioting.

I then question whether this history of racial conflict provides an appropriate model for understanding the urban politics of the future in which the new immigrant groups to Los Angeles, dominated numerically by those from Latin America and Asia, will play a key role. Is the conflict between whites and blacks likely just to expand to incorporate these groups into a new "racial order" with still broader ethnic balkanization? Some observers have suggested that the historic model of black-white conflict is indeed a good fit. In this view, a wide variety of such peoples of color, not just blacks, have been dominated and oppressed by white racism. For example, Sucheng Chan (1991, 42) argues that "racial discrimination is what separates the historical experience of Asian immigrants from that of Europeans, on the one hand, and makes it resemble that of enslaved Africans and dispossessed Native Americans and Mexican-Americans, on the other hand."

According to this general point of view, the 1992 rioting might well be a harbinger of an unhappy future. It seemed initially a "classic" race riot within the black ghetto, in the mode of the 1960s, expressing the anger of African-Americans at the police because of the acquittal of the police officers who had beaten Rodney King. But it ultimately incorporated heavy Latino participation and spread far out of the black ghetto. Soon thereafter came intense Latino protest against Proposition 187, which was intended to bar illegal immigrants from receiving many forms of government services. These events could be interpreted as reflecting the expansion of the racial order beyond black-white conflicts to incorporate conflicts between whites and all peoples of color, especially including Latinos as another subordinated racial group, in a larger "ethnic hierarchy" (Fredrickson 1999; Bobo and Massagli 2001).

I am skeptical about this simple view and will argue that many of the difficulties confronting these new immigrants may be transitional, as were the obstacles facing European immigrants nearly a century ago. The new immigrant groups may, indeed, be replicating that European experience rather than the black experience.

RACIALIZED POLITICS IN LOS ANGELES

An important starting point for any discussion of racialized politics is the relative size of the black and white populations. At the climactic moment that civil rights legislation was passed in 1965, tolling the death knell for the Jim Crow system in the South, Los Angeles was an overwhelmingly white city in an overwhelmingly white metropolitan area, with a relatively small black population. In the 1960 census, blacks constituted only 14 percent of the population of the city of Los Angeles, and only 8 percent of the population of Los Angeles County. By 1990, the black population of the city of Los Angeles was still only 14 percent, and only 9 percent of the Los Angeles metropolitan region (CMSA), far below almost any of the other ten largest metropolitan areas in the country (Russell 1996; Allen and Turner 1997).[1] Further, by 2000 the proportion of blacks in the city of Los Angeles had actually fallen to 11 percent (table 5.2). Politics in Los Angeles has nevertheless been quite racialized for almost four decades as I will show, despite this absence of either equivalent and highly competitive black and white populations or an outnumbered white minority trying to hang onto power. I will use two criteria of racialization: the polarization of the races in evaluating these political events and the role of racial prejudice in generating cleavages among whites about them.

An appropriate starting point for the discussion is 1964, the year when the Civil Rights Act was passed, finally declaring racial discrimination to be illegal throughout the nation. Though proposed by the Kennedy and Johnson administrations, it ultimately passed with strong Republican support and was opposed mainly by Southerners (90 percent of the Southern Democrats in the House opposed it [Carmines and Stimson 1989]). The 1964 presidential election seemingly provided a strong endorsement of such liberal civil rights policies in California. Despite the overwhelmingly white electorate, President Lyndon Johnson beat his Republican opponent, Senator Barry Goldwater of Arizona, who had opposed the Civil Rights Act, by nearly a 2-to-1 margin. But this overlaid a more complex, and racialized, story. On the same ballot, California voters passed Proposition 14, repealing the recently enacted Rumford Fair Housing Act by a 2-to-1 margin. Paradoxically, both Johnson and this repeal won big in Los Angeles County, receiving 58 percent and 67 percent of the vote, respectively (Sonenshein 1993, 70). The Proposition 14 vote was strongly polarized by race, supported by 70 percent of the whites and only 16 percent of the blacks in the final statewide preelection poll. Moreover, white support for Proposition 14 was strongly and positively correlated with the voters' levels of racial prejudice (Wolfinger and Greenstein 1968, 766).

Almost a year later, in August 1965, the arrest of a black motorist in the heart of the major black ghetto in Los Angeles evolved into the Watts riot, the most destructive race rioting that postwar America had seen up to that point. Extensive research on the rioting was conducted by a team of University of California, Los Angeles, social scientists (Cohen 1970; for the interpretation found here, see Sears and McConahay 1973). First of all, the response to the riot was highly polarized by race,

Table 13.1. Attitudes toward the Watts Riot (Los Angeles County, 1965–66)

	BLACKS (%)	WHITES (%)
What caused (the riot)?		
Specific grievances (discrimination, police mistreatment, etc.)	38	20
Pent-up hostility (revenge, etc.)	26	14
Total sympathetic	64	34
Triggering incident	11	18
Undesirable groups (communists, etc.)	9	29
Accident, weather	0	10
Total antagonistic	20	57
Did the authorities handle (the riot) well or badly?		
Authorities handled riot badly	65	32
Authorities handled riot well	28	66
Do you think (the riot) helped or hurt the Negro's cause?		
Helped their cause	38	19
No difference, don't know	30	5
Hurt their cause	24	75

Source. Sears and McConahay 1973, 160, 161, 164.
Note. The respondent was allowed to select his or her own term to refer to the rioting. "Other," "don't know," and "no answer" not shown for the causes of the riot question.

as shown in table 13.1. Most whites were critical of the rioters, were inclined to dismiss any broader political meaning of the rioting, supported the handling of the rioting by the authorities, and thought it would damage the civil rights cause. Most blacks, too, were critical of the lawlessness and violence displayed by the rioters but attributed the rioting to politically meaningful causes such as pent-up black hostility, racial discrimination, or police mistreatment of blacks. Most blacks were critical of the authorities and had more optimistic expectations about its effects. Second, whites' divisions of opinion about the rioting were significantly associated with conventional indicators of traditional racism. For example, 81 percent felt the riot would hurt the Negro's cause among those who would find it distasteful to have a Negro marry someone in their family, whereas only 59 percent felt it would be damaging among those not finding intermarriage distasteful (Morris and Jeffries 1970). Watts, too, hastened white flight from certain neighborhoods close to predominantly black sections of the city, including Ladera Heights, which then became an affluent black neighborhood (chap. 5).

In the mayoral contest four years later, the incumbent white mayor, Sam Yorty, was challenged by the first major black candidate in city history, Tom Bradley, a moderately liberal city councilman who had been a former police officer. The campaign became racialized even though Bradley himself did not emphasize his race. Yorty had been a vigorous critic of blacks during the 1965 rioting, dismissing charges of police brutality as mere propaganda by communists and demagogues. In 1969, the Yorty campaign stirred up whites' concerns about black crime and racial integration. Bradley ran well in the early going and held a healthy lead in the primary, 42 to 26 percent, despite the small black electorate. The polls continued to show him in the lead right up to election day. Nevertheless in the end, Yorty won handily, by 53 to 47 percent.

Voting choices in that election were strikingly polarized by race. For example, Sonenshein (1993) reports that Bradley received the vast majority of the votes in black council districts but ran about even in a white liberal district (51 percent), and lost badly in a white conservative district. However the "old-fashioned racism" common among Southern whites, reflecting stereotypes of blacks' biological inferiority and support for segregation and legalized discrimination, was almost completely absent in Los Angeles: in one suburban sample of whites, 96 percent felt that Negroes should be able to use the same public facilities as whites, and 99 percent that Negroes should have the same chance as whites to get any job (Sears and Kinder 1970). Nevertheless, white voters also were split as a result of racial prejudices. Much more common than old-fashioned racism was a new form of racial prejudice, "symbolic racism," defined as beliefs "that are almost wholly abstract, ideological, and symbolic in nature . . . [about matters that] have almost no conceivable personal relevance to the individual, but have to do with his moral code or his sense of how society should be organized" (Sears and Kinder 1971, 66). Its content reflects four basic beliefs: racial discrimination has nearly disappeared; blacks do not show sufficient work ethic; they are too demanding of special treatment; and they get too many special favors from government and other institutions (see Sears 1988; Kinder and Sanders 1996; Sears et al. 1997). Whites tended to be about evenly divided about each belief. And symbolic racism was closely associated with preferences for Yorty, as can be seen in table 13.2 (see also Kinder and Sears 1981). Moreover, symbolic racism contributed to Yorty support above and beyond the effects of general political conservatism: liberals and conservatives alike were strongly influenced by symbolic racism.[2]

A year later, a local judge, Alfred Gitelson, ruled that the Los Angeles Unified School District (LAUSD) was illegally segregated on the basis of race. His decision was strongly attacked, and he was defeated for reelection shortly thereafter. In 1976, the California Supreme Court affirmed the Gitelson decision but did not specify a remedy. The standard remedy for school segregation at the time was to bus children of both races to schools outside of their own largely segregated neighborhoods. So the LAUSD school board put a mandatory busing plan into

Table 13.2. Percentage Supporting Yorty as a Function of Symbolic Racism and Ideological Conservatism (San Fernando Valley, 1969)

	CONSERVATIVES	LIBERALS
Do LA city officials pay more, less, or the same attention to a request from a black person as from a white person? (more)		
High symbolic racism	80	67
Low symbolic racism	43	4
Effect of symbolic racism	+37	+63
Negroes shouldn't push themselves where they are not wanted. (agree)		
High symbolic racism	71	45
Low symbolic racism	50	15
Effect of symbolic racism	+21	+30
Could most Negroes get along without welfare if they tried? (yes)		
High symbolic racism	76	58
Low symbolic racism	42	17
Effect of symbolic racism	+34	+41

Source. Sears and Kinder 1971, 77.
Note. Each entry is the proportion preferring Yorty to Bradley among those with the specified combination of symbolic racism and political ideology. The high symbolic racism responses to the three items are "more attention," "agree," and "could get along without it," respectively. "Effect of symbolic racism" refers to the size of Yorty's greater advantage among those high, as opposed to low, in symbolic racism.

effect in 1978. Busing was the most emblematic of all racial issues in the 1970s because of the symbolic importance of *Brown v. Board of Education* to the civil rights movement, the painful ongoing integration of school districts in the South, and the occasionally violent white protest against busing even in non-Southern cities. An antibusing organization, Bustop, quickly formed in the San Fernando Valley, forced the recall of school board members who had supported the busing plan, including the board chairman, and took control of the board. In 1979, a constitutional amendment was passed in a special statewide election voiding the legal basis for the busing order.

Blacks and whites were strongly polarized on the issue of busing. Though we have no readily available Los Angeles data for that period, busing was supported by 17 percent of the whites and 53 percent of the blacks in a national survey in 1978 (Schuman et al. 1997, 123, 248). And racial prejudice was a far stronger predictor of whites' attitudes toward busing than any other variable measured, as shown in four surveys conducted in Los Angeles between 1976 and 1979 and nationally (Sears and Allen 1984).

Simultaneously, a strong tax revolt movement developed in California. It came to a head in 1978 with the passage statewide of Proposition 13, providing radical cuts in property taxes and capping them for the future. A year later its proponents followed with the successful Gann Amendment capping state spending, and then, in 1980, an unsuccessful effort to cut state income taxes. Our study of this tax revolt analyzed nine statewide surveys (Sears and Citrin 1985). It showed that the issues central to the tax revolt, concerning tax cuts and the preferred size of government, had themselves become strongly racialized even though they had little or no manifest racial content. First of all, every survey showed very large differences between blacks and whites; for example, a preelection poll showed that 66 percent of the whites supported Proposition 13, whereas only 18 percent of the blacks did (Sears and Citrin 1985, 98). Race remained one of the strongest predictors of attitudes toward the tax revolt even controlling on other relevant variables, including homeownership. Second, racial prejudice was one of the strongest predictors of support for the tax revolt even with controls on ideology, party identification, and cynicism about government. In an overall model containing twenty-one predictors, racial prejudice, along with general political ideology, had the largest total effect on support for the tax revolt and was also a strong predictor of preferences for smaller government. These findings might seem puzzling, since the debates about taxes and government spending generally did not make even indirect reference to race. It is noteworthy, though, that the preferred spending cuts best explained by racial attitudes had to do with welfare, public schools, and public health, areas of public expenditure that had already become implicated in racial disputes in California.[3]

Shortly thereafter, in 1982, Tom Bradley became the first major black candidate for governor in California history. This time both the late preelection polls and the early exit polls showed a Bradley lead, despite the fact that only 6 percent of the eligible voters were black (DiCamillo and Field 1996). Nevertheless, he was narrowly defeated. Racial polarization was extreme; the exit polls showed that 95 percent of the blacks, as against 42 percent of the whites, had voted for Bradley (Pettigrew and Alston 1988, 18). Symbolic racism was again a strong predictor of divisions among whites: for example, among whites who felt government was paying too little attention to blacks and other minorities, 79 percent voted for Bradley, while only 32 percent of those who felt government had given them too much attention voted for him. Indeed such racial attitudes proved to be nearly as strong a correlate of the white vote as party identification or ideology. And by this time, the racialization of California politics had gone beyond strictly racial issues, reaching into basic partisan divisions as well. Symbolic racism predicted the white vote against white Democratic candidates just as strongly as it did the vote against Bradley (Citrin et al. 1990).

In the 1990s, affirmative action became a powerfully racialized issue. In 1995, the University of California Board of Regents made a highly controversial decision to end affirmative action in admissions. Proposition 209 was then placed on the 1996 statewide ballot, seeking to eliminate all state and local affirmative action programs. Ward Connerly, a black member of the board of regents and cochair of the pro-209 campaign, further racialized this issue by relying heavily on quotes about a "colorblind" society from Martin Luther King, Jr. It passed with 54 percent of the vote. Again, the races were quite polarized, and our own research showed that racial prejudice had a significant effect on whites' attitudes (Sears and van Laar 1999).

THE BOUNDED SEVERITY OF RACIAL CONFLICT

Throughout the period from the mid-1960s to the present, then, race has repeatedly been a central focus of politics in California and in Los Angeles. It has arisen in all the usual contexts: race riots, elections pitting black against white candidates, policy issues directly relevant to race (such as fair housing, busing, and affirmative action), as well as in policy issues only indirectly relevant to racial equality or in standard partisan elections. In all these cases, black and white Californians have been sharply polarized, and racial prejudice has sharply divided whites.

During this period, race has not affected all of local politics, of course, and it has had its ups and downs. It seems clear that the two major riots produced a quite intense white racial backlash. That backlash may well have contributed in an important way to Sam Yorty's successful race-baiting mayoralty campaign in 1969, and Richard Riordan's successful law-and-order candidacy in 1993, as Karen Kaufmann argues in chapter 11. Whether that postriot backlash had a lasting and general effect on whites' political preferences or simply caused white racial conservatism to surface in some areas and not in others, as it has throughout this period, is less clear. For example, the discredited white conservative police chief, Daryl Gates, was replaced after the Rodney King rioting by first one black police chief and then another, rather than by another hard-line white conservative.

In any case, what seems clear is that racialized politics has been a recurrent, if episodic, theme in Los Angeles and statewide over the past three decades. Having said that, it is important to note that the severity of racialized politics has been bounded. To place it in perspective, compare it with the levels of ethnic polarization in Yugoslavia and other trouble spots around the globe. In Bosnia and Kosovo, Serb leaders and military and paramilitary units carried out extensive "ethnic cleansing," including displacement of whole populations from their homes, massive destruction of property owned by ethnic minorities, and mass murder. Leaders and ordinary citizens alike often express general denial of any wrongdoing. Some factions have often only accepted any election results or other agreements that would place their opponents in power at the point of a gun. Indeed after the Dayton Accord that divided Bosnia, the Serb minority in Sarajevo left en masse, burning down their own homes so that Muslims could not benefit from them. These events, though scarcely unique, provide a well-known benchmark against which to measure the much less severe racial polarization and intergroup animosity in Los Angeles.

Numbers and Coalitions

Despite their being a relatively small minority in Los Angeles and California, blacks have enjoyed considerable political success. In 1973, Tom Bradley faced Mayor Yorty again and won with 54 percent of the vote. In 1977, 1981, and 1985 he handily defeated conservative white opponents in the primary elections for mayor, with an average of 64 percent of the vote. In 1989 he won with 52 percent of the vote in the primary, a closer race, but his closest challenger was another black candidate, who himself took 28 percent of the vote. So after the narrow defeat in 1969, black candidates received healthy majorities in the next five mayoral elections—in a city whose black population never exceeded 18 percent (Sonenshein 1993).

In this respect Los Angeles has been somewhat unique. Of the largest twenty cities in the country, only one, Detroit, had a black mayor as early as did Los Angeles, and as of 1990 Detroit was 76 percent black (U.S. Bureau of the Census 1994). Of the other nineteen cities, almost all of those with black mayors who overlapped substantially with Bradley's tenure had far larger black populations.[4] New York City (29 percent black in 1990) did not have a black mayor until Bradley's last term in office. Of these twenty largest cities, only five cities have had a smaller proportion of blacks than Los Angeles, and only one of those has had a black mayor—Willie Brown in San Francisco, which is 11 percent black —and he was elected only recently, after Bradley completed his fifth full term.

Part of Bradley's success was surely due to his generally nonconfrontational stance on racial issues. But the best analysis of Bradley's electoral success focuses on the coalitions he was able to form with Jewish and other relatively liberal white voters in Los Angeles, even during the peaks of hostility over busing and other racial issues (Sonenshein 1993). The durable biracial coalition that supported Bradley also gave an important role to the business community and, later, included Latino and Asian-American leaders as well. Sonenshein's analysis highlights the strength of biracialism in Los Angeles in the midst of strongly racialized centrifugal forces. In his view, it contrasts with the "sad history of interracial conflict in New York City and Chicago" (1993, xvi–xvii).

Comparing Los Angeles and New York

It is impossible to make a rigorous comparison of Los Angeles with New York in terms of the racialization of politics during this period. No comparable race-related ballot measures provided a simple expression of racial sentiments at the ballot box. The first major black candidate for mayor of New York, David Dinkins, did not run until 1989, two decades after Bradley's first campaign in Los Angeles.

However, there were several celebrated racial incidents in New York that provided pollsters with occasions for gauging public opinion, such as racial violence in Crown Heights and Bensonhurst, Tawana Brawley's false accusations of being racially victimized, and police malfeasance resulting in the sodomizing of a Haitian refugee. And in fact we can compare public opinion in Los Angeles and New York about two quite analogous racial incidents: the videotaped beating of the unarmed black motorist Rodney King by several Los Angeles police officers in 1991 and the killing of the African immigrant Amadou Diallo by New York police officers in 1999. Both events received a great deal of publicity, and whites' and blacks' opinions were surveyed shortly after each incident by the *Los Angeles Times* and the *New York Times.* Table 13.3 presents some of the data from roughly parallel items used in the two cities.

Most obvious is the strong racial polarization in both cities about these events. For example, in both cases blacks tended to disapprove of the job the police were doing while whites were more favorable toward them. Blacks were much more likely than whites to believe that the police often commit acts of police brutality and use excessive force and were more likely to believe that the police are biased against blacks. And blacks were more likely to defend the black critics of police behavior (Los Angeles Mayor Tom Bradley and New York black activist Al Sharpton) while whites were more likely to defend the white supporters of the police (Los Angeles Police Chief Daryl Gates and New York Mayor Rudolph Guiliani).

But racial polarization seems to have been greater in New York City

Table 13.3. Whites' and Blacks' Attitudes about Police Incidents in Los Angeles (1991) and New York (1999)

	WHITES (%)	BLACKS (%)	DIFFERENCE (%)
Los Angeles — the beating of Rodney King:			
The way the LAPD is handling its job:[1]			
Approve	48	17	
Disapprove	44	79	35
Incidents of police brutality involving LAPD:[2]			
Uncommon	37	13	
Very/fairly common	58	87	29
LAPD tougher on:[3]			
Whites	0	0	
Same	21	11	
Blacks	66	84	18
Rodney King incident racially motivated?[3]			
Nonracial	29	10	
Racial	48	73	25
Job approval for Daryl Gates:[1]			
Approve	45	13	
Disapprove	46	82	36
Job approval for Tom Bradley:[1]			
Approve	41	64	23
Disapprove	48	31	
New York — the killing of Amadou Diallo:			
The job the New York City police are doing:[4]			
Favorable	65	24	
Unfavorable	31	74	43
In a dangerous situation, the New York City police use:[4]			
Necessary force	54	19	
Excessive force	33	72	39
New York City police treatment favors:[4]			
Blacks	1	0	
Treats both fairly	32	9	
Whites	45	81	36
Diallo shooting tragic thing:[4]			
But understandable	27	6	
And no excuse for it	61	89	28
Job approval for Rudolph Giuliani:[4]			
Approve	62	15	
Disapprove	32	74	42
Job approval for Al Sharpton:[4]			
Favorable	12	47	35
Unfavorable	56	18	

Sources. 1 = *Los Angeles Times* poll, April 4, 1991; 2 = *Los Angeles Times* poll, March 21, 1991; 3 = *Los Angeles Times* poll, March 8, 1991; 4 = *New York Times* poll, March 14, 1999.

Note. The beating of Rodney King was first televised on March 5, 1991. Amadou Diallo was killed on February 4, 1999. These surveys sampled the city of Los Angeles and New York City, respectively. The "difference" column refers to the greater antipolice attitudes among blacks than among whites.

than in Los Angeles. Most whites in Los Angeles thought police brutality was at least fairly common, whereas most in New York City believed that the police use only necessary force. In Los Angeles, almost as many whites disapproved of the police as approved of their performance, whereas in New York City, the police had the support of the overwhelming majority of whites. Such findings, placed alongside the contrast of the early and consistent victories of Tom Bradley in Los Angeles with the much later term of the black David Dinkins in New York City, defeated after a single term, suggest that Los Angeles politics may not be so severely racialized after all, at least not by a relative standard.

A broader point might be made about both cities. Despite considerable polarization of the races over the King and Diallo incidents, whites surveyed in both cities were quite prepared to criticize the behavior of the police. They were frank about their perceptions that their police forces are generally biased in favor of whites and against blacks and were highly critical of police behavior in both the King and Diallo cases. This seems to represent a substantial change from the 1960s. Whites then tended to defend harsh treatment of racial minorities by the police. For example, after the Watts riot, only 4 percent of the whites felt that the police engaged in too much force; they criticized the police only for letting the rioting get out of hand (Morris and Jeffries 1970, 493). This too stands in stark relief to the apparent widespread Serb defense of ethnic cleansing in Bosnia and Kosovo.

Dogs That Didn't Bark in the Night

Most observers would take for granted that the major civil disturbances in Los Angeles in 1965 and 1992 represented strong racial fractures in the community. Both the Los Angeles rioting and the broader ghetto rioting in the 1960s have been subjected to a great deal of empirical analysis (e.g., National Advisory Commission on Civil Disorders 1968; Cohen 1970; Baldassare 1994). There is no dearth of explanations for these events. Structural conditions such as poverty, racial discrimination, mistreatment of various kinds, family breakdown, and a climate of lawlessness, whether treated as objective conditions or as subjective grievances, are usually prominent (e.g., Sears and McConahay 1973). So are the dynamics of crowd behavior (e.g., McPhail 1971; Tierney 1994).

Much attention also is usually given to the triggering events. The event that triggered the Watts riot was the bungled arrest of a black driver suspected of driving under the influence in South Central Los Angeles. It was a hot summer night, and a crowd quickly assembled, largely through a word-of-mouth process, as the commotion grew. Such triggering events and this pattern of information diffusion about them were familiar elements in the ghetto violence in the 1960s. The event that triggered the 1992 rioting was the acquittal—in a courtroom in a predominantly white suburb more than fifty miles away from South Central Los Angeles—of the four police officers accused of misconduct in the beating of Rodney King in 1991. As the news spread through radio and television, and then word of mouth, African-Americans began to congregate in the streets, and the violence slowly grew. Even in the 1960s, the triggering event at times occurred far away. In 1968, news of the assassination of Martin Luther King, Jr., presumably spread through black communities mainly through the mass media (National Advisory Commission on Civil Disorders 1968).

Social scientists usually analyze civil disorders that did happen, not those that did not happen. But almost all of the structural conditions invoked to explain riots are and have been present throughout this era, rarely stimulating a disturbance. The conditions usually described for the assembling of a crowd also would seem to be quite common. Why have they not stimulated more disorders?

Quite a few events in Los Angeles in this era did not trigger any racial violence even though they seemingly had great potential for doing so. A number of events could plausibly have been portrayed as significant and direct expressions of whites' disrespect of blacks and repudiation of blacks' clearly expressed preferences. These are Sherlock Holmes's "dogs that did not bark in the night." Prominent among them are several of the election results chronicled above, including the rejection of fair housing in 1964, after its overwhelming passage by the legislature and support by the governor; Yorty's come-from-behind defeat of Tom Bradley in the 1969 mayoralty campaign with a race-baiting campaign; and Bradley's narrow last-minute defeat for governor in 1982. Blacks could easily have viewed other events as a collective statement by white voters that they did not want their children mixing with black children. Examples would be the recall of pro-busing members of the Los Angeles school board in 1978, the 1979 constitutional amendment eliminating busing in Los Angeles, and the elimination of official affirmative action programs in 1996. In all six cases, white voters either defeated favored black candidates or passed ballot propositions that eliminated programs expressly designed to reduce racial inequality. Each could easily have been read as a collective insult by whites to the black community. But none in fact led to civil disorders.

This suggests two things. First, it tells us something fundamental about the bounded severity of racial conflict in this era. Racial violence is not an inevitable consequence of political losses suffered by racial and ethnic minorities. Second, the two major ghetto riots that did occur involved the police and individual black motorists. Police mistreatment of individual blacks triggered civil disorder while a collective loss in an election did not. Why? One clue may come from social psychological research on perceptions of social justice. Its central conclusion, well summarized by Tyler and his colleagues (1997), is that individuals' satisfaction or dissatisfaction with their outcomes often are more closely linked to judgments about whether the norms of justice have been violated than to personal or group interests. Although blacks represent a particularly alienated minority group in America, they nonetheless overwhelmingly support the fundamental tenets of American democratic ideology (Gurin et al. 1989). Like other ethnic groups, they believe that valuing equality is the most central component of American identity (Citrin et al. 1990). And nothing expresses equality more clearly than the principle that each individual is equal at the ballot box. Perhaps the will of a popular majority has considerable legitimacy even in the eyes of a minority group that has been abused in the past by the majority, so a popular election may not be seen as an occasion for taking to the streets.[5] Brutal, violent police actions against individual members of a group long abused by the police would seem to strike a rawer nerve. Of course many black motorists have been arrested before and since, with no civil disorder occurring, but those arrests, too, may contribute to the strength of these occasional violent reactions.

THE NEW IMMIGRANTS: FOLLOWING THE BLACK TRAJECTORY?

I have argued that racial conflict, bounded but often intense, has been at the heart of much of Los Angeles's politics over the past three decades. This conflict has involved the efforts of blacks to achieve greater equality and the resistance of conservative whites to this. But while three decades ago Los Angeles could fairly be described as having an overwhelming white majority, by 2000 non-Hispanic whites were only 30 percent of the city and 39 percent of the Los Angeles CMSA. The "new immigrant" groups, Hispanic and Asian-Americans, have expanded rapidly, with Hispanics now 47 percent of the city of Los Angeles and 40 percent of the Los Angeles CMSA, and Asians 10 percent of the city and 11 percent of the CMSA. Indeed, Asians now constitute about the same proportion of the city as do blacks and constitute a substantially higher proportion of the Los Angeles CMSA (see table 5.1).

How will the growth of these two new immigrant groups—Hispanics and Asians—affect the pattern of racialized politics in Los Angeles?

Perhaps racial conflict will simply be broadened to include them, producing a four-way ethnic balkanization. A future of four warring tribes, each walled off in its own political enclave, pursuing its own group's interest, has sometimes been described as a Hobbesian war of all against all or, drawing on the local ubiquity of cinematic metaphor, as a "Blade-runner" scenario (e.g., Tierney 1994). A number of social-structural theories might lead us to expect just this. They posit a "racial order" or an "ethnic hierarchy" ranging from the dominant (or hegemonic) to the most subordinated racial and ethnic group. For example, the "sense of group position" theory suggests that the outlooks of dominant groups "exhibit a feeling of superiority . . . a belief that the subordinate group is intrinsically different and alien . . . a sense of proprietary claim over certain rights, statuses, and resources . . . [and] a perception of threat from members of a subordinate group who harbor a desire for a greater share" (Bobo 1999, 9). Social dominance theory also assumes a highly stable hierarchy of groups ranging from the dominant and hegemonic whites, followed in order by the minority groups comprising "people of color": Asians, Latinos, and African-Americans (Sidanius and Pratto 1999). Such theories predict "in-group favoritism" in which in-groups give preferential outcomes to their own, in terms of group evaluations, stereotypes, policy preferences, and so on (also see social identity theory [Tajfel and Turner 1986]).

An alternative theory emphasizes "black exceptionalism" (Sears et al. 1999). This suggests that American society may contain two rather different "racial orders," if that is the appropriate term, rather than one. It views black-white racial conflicts as deriving principally from the long-term consequences of subjecting Africans to an involuntary system of chattel slavery beginning in the seventeenth century and then maintaining them (and to a large degree, them only) in an explicitly and formalized lower caste status for nearly 350 years. In 1903, W. E. B. DuBois forecast that the defining problem of the twentieth century would be the "color line." The "one drop of blood" rule as applied to blacks has not been historically flexible or permeable, as reflected in such contemporary indicators as their severe residential segregation and low rate of intermarriage with other groups. Today the color line continues to be a key element in enforcing black exceptionalism.

To be sure, on occasion voluntary immigrant groups may also have been regarded as coming from a different "race" than that of Europeans, as Asians and Mexican Indians certainly were initially. But there is an important difference between the political history of the black population, on the one hand, and today's Latino and Asian populations in Los Angeles, on the other. Today's blacks are almost all descendants of those slaves brought to North America in the seventeenth and eighteenth centuries. They and their ancestors have been living in the United States as a stigmatized lower caste for centuries. In contrast, the Latinos and Asians in Los Angeles today are for the most part not descendants of hyphenated-Americans who had been confronting discrimination and mistreatment for generations. Rather, most are recent voluntary immigrants, with little experience with or even knowledge of the American past: in 1990, nearly three-fourths of the Asians and over half the Latinos in the Los Angeles region were foreign-born (Farley 2001, 39).

Because the experiences of blacks and other minority groups have been so different, one should be cautious about drawing parallels between them. Nathan Glazer has made this point well: "The separateness of blacks is real. . . . For this one group, assimilation, by some measures, has certainly failed. . . . For Hispanics and Asian Americans, marked in varying degree by race, it is in large measure a matter of choice, their choice, just how they will define their place in American society. . . . But the difference that separates blacks from whites, and even from other groups 'of color' that have undergone a history of discrimination and prejudice in this country, is not to be denied" (1997, 120–21). Indeed the frequent classification of Asians and Latinos with blacks as "people of color" or at least as "nonwhite," a practice criticized in chapter 5, may itself be temporary. With time, like earlier groups of voluntary immigrants, they may move toward assimilation into the broader society (Alba 1990). Chapter 5 pointed out how the Irish were often regarded as "black" in the early years of mass immigration to the United States but, with time, were increasingly regarded as "white" (also see Roediger 1999). The Chinese living in Mississippi were initially classified as black in that state's rigid Jim Crow system, but gradually they too were informally reclassified, and by the mid-twentieth century were generally treated as being on the white side of the color line (Loewen 1971).

Signs of a Broader Ethnic Balkanization

We nevertheless do have some evidence for the view that racialized politics is indeed giving way to an expanded ethnic balkanization. Each of these four contemporary ethnic groups prefers the policies that benefit its own members over policies that benefit other groups, much like the polarization of blacks and whites over racial issues seen earlier. Table 13.4 provides several typical examples from research on both national and Los Angeles samples (Sears et al. 1999). The heavily immigrant populations of Hispanics and Asians are considerably less favorably disposed than are the largely nonimmigrant whites and blacks toward reducing

Table 13.4. Support for Multicultural Policies in Los Angeles County by Respondent Ethnicity

	NON-HISPANIC WHITES (%)			BLACKS (%)			HISPANICS (%)			ASIANS (%)
	1994	1995	GSS	1994	1995	GSS	1994	1995	GSS	
Immigration policy:										
Change the level of legal immigration? (% increase minus % decrease)	−50	−50	−61	−55	−65	−55	−24	−29	−31	−13
Spend more to deport illegals (no)	24	33	. . .	30	36	. . .	60	64	. . .	49
Spend more for border security (no)	15	. . .	. . .	15	. . .	. . .	48	. . .	. . .	17
Affirmative action policy:										
Preferential hiring and promotion of blacks due to past discrimination (favor)	10	15	8	. . .	46	61	19	32	16	28
Preferential hiring and promotion of Hispanics due to past discrimination (favor)	12	12	. . .	36	45	. . .	. . .	53	. . .	24
Ethnically based descriptive representation:										
Should congressmen match constituent ethnicity? (yes)	8	. . .	6	18	. . .	27	23	. . .	15	9
Racial/ethnic experience should be taught by one's own. (agree)	33	. . .	22	46	. . .	46	47	. . .	26	38
Should teachers match student ethnicity? (yes)	6	. . .	6	13	. . .	18	10	. . .	18	11

Sources. 1994 and 1995 Los Angeles County Social Surveys, 1994 General Social Survey. Entries for Asians pool the first two surveys. See Sears et al. (1999).

Note. Entries are the percent taking a liberal, prominority group position. GSS = General Social Survey. Ellipses dots indicate that no data were available.

the level of legal immigration to the United States or toward increasing money spent to deport illegal immigrants and increase border security. The two "new immigrant" groups differ from each other in ways that make sense, as well: Hispanics, for instance, show much more opposition to increasing border security than do Asians, presumably because the vast majority of Hispanics come directly across the border from Mexico. Preferential treatment targeted for blacks tends to be favored by blacks, but it is met with massive opposition from all three other groups. Preferential treatment targeted for Hispanics receives majority support only among Hispanics. In each of these cases, then, each ethnic group seems to have adopted preferences for policies serving its own interest at the expense of policies serving the interests of other groups.

Similar evidence of apparently increasing ethnic balkanization comes from the 1992 civil disorder in Los Angeles. Initially, the events seemed quite similar to those of the Watts riots of 1965 in that the rioters were predominantly black and the targets predominantly white. As a result, the events were often interpreted in the familiar terms of 1960s-era ghetto rioting. Conservatives once again saw street hoodlums (this time local gang members, not "outside agitators") as using the pretext of political events to pillage, loot, and injure the innocent, and so it was a "riot." Their critics saw it as yet another in a long line of black protests against social injustice, and so it was a "rebellion" or an "insurrection" of an oppressed people (Sears 1994). But others maintained that it was "a new form" and "the first urban unrest of the 21st century" because it was "the first multiethnic riot," based on "territorially-based ethnic tensions" (Morrison and Lowry 1994; Tierney 1994). Was that, in fact, the case?

To some extent it clearly was new. The participants in the rioting in 1965 had almost all been black, but in 1992, 51 percent of those arrested were Latino and only 36 percent were black, paralleling the dramatic change in the ethnic composition of South Central Los Angeles over that time (Sears and McConahay 1973; Petersilia and Abrahamse 1994). The targets of looting and burning changed as well. In 1965 they had been primarily white police and merchants (Governor's Commission 1965; Cohen 1970). In 1992 the violence again targeted the predominantly white Los Angeles police force, but much of it also was aimed at Korean merchants: 54 percent of those businesses that were totally lost had been owned by Koreans (Tierney 1994).[6] This would be consistent with the notion that the 1960s racial-conflict model, of ghetto blacks rioting against whites, had simply expanded to incorporate the two new immigrant groups in a broader racial order, with the more disadvantaged blacks and Latinos rioting against the more privileged whites and Asians.

Departures from the Black-White Model

However, the preponderance of the evidence suggests a different pattern, that the new immigrant groups are not simply assuming predictable slots in an expanded racial order in Los Angeles. First of all, the great majority of Hispanics and Asians in Los Angeles, when asked directly, say they are more likely to think of themselves politically more as "just an American" than as "a member of some ethnic group." Given a third choice, of a hyphenated-American description as both an American and a member of an ethnic group, somewhat over half prefer "both" (Sears et al. 1999). Second, once immigration has been accomplished and people settle into life in America, they seem not to see themselves increasingly as a member of an American ethnic group in a rigid group hierarchy. In fact, with time, these new immigrant groups move away from strong identification with their own ethnic group as defined in the American political context. It is the foreign-born, not those most fully socialized into the American political and social system, who are most likely to think of themselves in ethnic terms. For example, in a 1994 survey in Los Angeles, only 27 percent of the foreign-born Latino adults thought of themselves as "just an American" always or most of the time when it came to political issues, but 65 percent of the U.S.-born thought of themselves that way (Cheleden et al. 1996). That is, longer experience with the American stratification system actually leads Latinos to see themselves less in terms of their own ethnic identity.

Moreover, the longer the new immigrants and their families live in the United States, and the more familiar they become with the realities of American politics, the less they support policies that distinctively favor their own groups' interests. Latinos born in the United States and/or who have spent the longest time in the United States had the most conservative attitudes about immigration and language policy (Sears et al. 1999). In other words, the new immigrants, not those most fully socialized into the American racial order, display the sharpest ethnic balkanization. With time, political assimilation becomes more common, and Latinos and Asians tend to behave politically less and less like balkanized ethnics.

Finally, when asked for their normative views, even the relatively disadvantaged minority groups that would benefit most from specific ethnic entitlements tend to reject them. Most Hispanics and Asians oppose an ethnically balkanized society in which each group is represented according to its numbers. Both Los Angeles County and national samples were asked for their views of such descriptive representation schemes as allocating congressional seats or teaching jobs to specific ethnic groups in proportion to their fractions of the population. Such schemes were rejected by the great majority within each ethnic group (Sears et al. 1999). As can be seen in table 13.4, this was true in the national General Social Survey data as well as in Los Angeles.

THE FUTURE ETHNIC ELITES

One noteworthy feature of black-white racial conflict is that the most privileged blacks have, in the past two decades, been the most vigorous proponents of their own race's political interests. Better-educated blacks tend to have a stronger sense of common fate with other blacks, supported Jesse Jackson's presidential bid more, and support black nationalism more than do less-educated blacks (Gurin et al. 1989; Bobo and Johnson 2001). Middle-class blacks tend to perceive greater racial discrimination and are more pessimistic about racial progress than are less-affluent blacks (Hochschild 1995).

The future leaders of the new immigrant groups, Asians and Latinos, are today being educated in America's colleges and universities. Is higher education providing them the same strong sense of group identity and common fate and perceptions of group discrimination as it does for better-educated blacks? A large panel survey of the University of California, Los Angeles (UCLA), freshman class entering in 1996 tested this.[7] First of all, the Asian and Latino students come primarily from recent immigrant families. Almost half of the Asian freshmen (49 percent) are first-generation Americans, and only 7 percent had even one grandparent born in this country. Only 2 percent of the freshman class were Japanese-American, the group exposed to internment during World War II, the harshest recent form of discrimination against Asian-Americans. Similarly, almost two-thirds of the Latino students are first- or second-generation Americans; only 36 percent had even one parent, and 33 percent, even one grandparent, born in this country. Most of their families' experiences are of having grown up far from the American-style ethnic discrimination that Mexican-Americans have historically experienced in California and the Southwest. In other words, these future Hispanic and Asian elites in Los Angeles are primarily the products of immigrant families, rather than of families with long experience as subordinate groups in an American racial and ethnic hierarchy. Unlike blacks, they and their families do not carry the scars of centuries of treatment in America as a lower caste group. In that sense they may be more like turn-of-the-century European immigrants than like the descendants of African slaves.

These students' own sense of ethnic identity also focuses more on their national origins, and therefore on recent immigrant experience, than on their place in an American racial order. When asked the open-ended question, "Which ethnic/racial group do you most closely identify with?" whites and blacks readily provided the politically constructed categories historically identified with America's racial hierarchy: 89 percent of the whites said "white" or "Caucasian," while 99 percent of the blacks said "black," "African American," or "Afro-American." However, few of the Asian-American students used the artificial ethnic identities politically constructed for them: only 11 percent described themselves as "Asian American" and only 1 percent as "Pacific Islander." Rather, the majority (63 percent) represented their identity in terms of their specific nations of origin, such as "Chinese," "Korean," "Filipino," or hyphenated nationality–American (e.g., "Chinese American"). Only about half of the Latino students (49 percent) used the standard American political labels, "Hispanic," "Latino," or "Chicano," with the other half describing themselves in terms of their national origins, even though the vast majority (83 percent) had been born in the United States (Sears et al. 2001). So unlike whites and blacks, most members of these new immigrant groups do not identify themselves as members of the large American ethnic categories depicted in discussions of the American racial order.

Finally, the longer the Asian and Latino students and their families had been in the United States, the weaker their ethnic identities became.[8] The UCLA freshmen with the strongest ethnic identity were from the most recent immigrant families: students who lived in a household in which some language other than English was spoken, had parents and grandparents who had been born in other countries, and had mainly same-ethnicity friends in high school. This is shown in table 13.5. Interestingly enough, greater parental education was associated with weaker, not stronger, ethnic identity among Latinos. Other analyses of later waves of this panel study show that Asian students' own ethnic identities tend to weaken as they progress through college, and Latinos' ethnic identities did not strengthen at all (Sears et al. 2001). This provides further evidence that parallels between blacks and these other peoples of color may be misleading. Longer and deeper exposure to American culture strengthens blacks' sense of racial distinctiveness but seems to weaken it for the new immigrant groups.

Table 13.5. Predictors of Strength of Ethnic Identity at Entry into College (UCLA, 1996)

	ASIANS		HISPANICS	
	r	b	*r*	b
Foreign language spoken at home	.23**	.29** (.08)	.33**	.23 (.15)
Born outside United States:				
Self	.10*	.00 (.11)	.08	.03 (.25)
Parents	.15**	.03 (.18)	.28**	.13 (.20)
Grandparents	.13**	.03 (.12)	.32**	.20 (.12)
Close friends in high school:				
Same ethnicity	.39**	.35** (.05)	.11*	.39** (.09)
Different ethnicity	−.09	−.17 (.10)	−.08*	.00 (.19)
Demographics:				
Mother's education	−.04	.05 (.03)	−.24**	.04 (.06)
Father's education	−.08*	−.04 (.03)	−.29**	−.06 (.05)
Religiosity	.15**	.04* (.01)	.09	.03 (.03)
Adjusted R^2 (%)		14.8		21.0

Source. UCLA Class of 2000 Study.

Note. Entries in columns 2 and 4 are unstandardized regression coefficients with standard errors in parentheses.

*$p < .05$.

**$p < .001$.

CONCLUSIONS

In a variety of ways, then, the model of racialized politics built up over the past several decades of conflict between blacks and whites in Los Angeles does not seem to transfer well to the new political situation generated by the recent heavy immigration from Asia and Latin America. Blacks are, of course, America's oldest racial minority group. Today's African-Americans are overwhelmingly the descendants of nineteenth-century slaves. They have been shown to have strong racial consciousness and great political solidarity. However, most of the Asians and Hispanics now living in the Los Angeles metropolitan area are first-generation immigrants and are rarely more than second generation. Few are the descendants of those victimized by such instances of blatant discrimination as the Chinese Exclusion Act, the internment of Japanese-Americans in World War II, or the shabby farm labor practices to which Mexican-American field workers have long been subjected. Their ethnic identities tend to focus on their national origins rather than their position in the American racial order. Moreover, the longer they and their families remain in the United States, the less they identify with their own ethnic group, the weaker their ethnic identity, and the less they prefer policies that serve the distinctive interests of their ethnic group. And they seem to show little normative appetite for ethnically balkanized representation schemes.

Even the 1992 rioting in Los Angeles may have a different interpretation than initially thought. It may, in fact, have been multiple riots at once, in which continuing high levels of black-white tensions undergirded a wholly different and complex set of dynamics involving the interethnic hostilities consequent to foreign immigration. As Tierney says (1994, 167), "The Los Angeles case involved multiple interracial and interethnic antagonisms that are not easily reducible to a single model." The city continues to struggle with its historic white-black conflicts and at the same time has to confront the realities of absorbing large numbers of new immigrants.

Even if one assumes that a hegemonic racial order exists in the United States that arrays ethnic and racial groups according to power, resources, and status, it is not evident that the new immigrant groups are falling into their assigned places in that hierarchy. The kind of racial isolation and polarization between blacks and whites that marked Los Angeles, New York City, and many other metropolitan areas in the years following the civil rights revolution may well be a misleading model for understanding the future trajectory of the new immigrant groups. Rather, they seem to be settling into a less permanently distinctive and ethnically conscious role in the American political system than blacks have.

In the short run, the political future of Los Angeles would seem more likely to involve the kind of ethnic coalition-building that marked New York City and other Eastern and Midwestern cities in the aftermath of heavy European immigration. This may not always take a predictable form: in the New York City mayoralty race of 2001, blacks and Latinos did form a reasonably tight, though in the end losing, coalition behind the Hispanic Fernando Ferrer, while in the Los Angeles mayoralty race earlier that year, most blacks supported the winning white candidate, James Hahn, and Latinos gave their strongest support to the Latino Antonio Villaraigosa. In the longer run, it would not be surprising if we saw, over the generations, a trajectory of gradual political assimilation in the United States, again with the European immigrants' overall experience of assimilation perhaps serving as a better model than the more separate black experience.

PART IV

CULTURE

CHAPTER FOURTEEN

Hot and Cool

Some Contrasts between the Visual Art Worlds of New York and Los Angeles

András Szántó

I see that I have made my first comparison of Los Angeles and New York, something I swore not to do. Comparisonitis, relentlessly malicious, is something every New Yorker comes down with here, like the flu. Recovery is possible. It comes from the realization of just how *peculiar* a place L.A. is and what a radical sense of the human it breeds.
Peter Schjeldahl (1981)

When New Yorkers tell me what's wrong with L.A., everything they say is wrong—no tradition, no history, no sense of a city, no system of support, no core, no sense of urgency—they're absolutely right, and that's why I like it.
Robert Irwin (quoted in Weschler 1982)

As joint custodians of virtually all art activity of consequence in America, New York and Los Angeles have costarred in a stunning success story. In a mere five decades these cities have leapt from cultural oblivion to global domination in the visual art field. Here the similarities end. All along, Los Angeles trailed New York in terms of size, wealth, and power. Their art scenes revolve around diverse people and places, and their moments of glory follow different timelines. New York has long had an edge with respect to some resources essential to a vibrant art scene—connections to Europe, an elite that's willing to spend lavishly on cultural pursuits, a certain sophistication of mind—and Manhattan has almost always led the way whenever art came into contact with money. But there were also eras in which California embodied the zeitgeist, enhancing the cogency of its art: during the antiauthoritarian late 1960s and early 1970s, in particular, and in the globalized, technology-and-media obsessed 1990s. In briefly surveying the art scenes of the two cities, it is important to realize that the art world that matters is tiny, even though the art world in sum is huge. There may be 700–800 art galleries and museums in New York today, and half as many in Los Angeles, but only a precious few of them play a lasting role in the shaping of art history. I will leave much of the larger art world out of the picture so that I can sketch the parameters of the geographical and institutional space that art has colonized on both coasts over the years.

GENESIS

The year is 1825, and church spires are still the tallest structures in Manhattan. With the opening of the Erie Canal, New York City begins to grow into the largest metropolis in the Western Hemisphere. Artists have already established the National Academy of Design, the center of art life in the city. In four years the *New York Mirror* will laud "the rapid progress of the arts in a city whose advancement in wealth, refinement, and useful knowledge has no precedent in the annals of any nation on the globe" (Voorsanger and Howat 2000). The Hudson School is growing into the first nationally recognized art movement linked to the city. By 1851 the *Republic* newspaper could boast that the "Empire City" is the undisputed "art centre of America" and is "destined to give tone and direction to American art effort." Art can be studied and bought in dozens of schools and galleries in this bustling place (the first art gallery, Knoedler, opens in 1848). By 1872 Manhattan has a magnificent Metropolitan Museum.

The stirrings of a modern art scene in New York date back to 1910, when Alfred Stieglitz exhibited impressionist and postimpressionist artists in his 291 Gallery on Fifth Avenue. The Armory Show of 1913, featuring 1,600 works, was a landmark event: a bridge to the avant-garde. In its wake emerged a handful of galleries and artists' associations and, in 1929, the Museum of Modern Art. But before World War II, "the sense of important movements being touted alike by the press and by the artists themselves was notably absent" (Davidson 1994, 294). Artists who made pilgrimages to Paris returned lamenting "the complete absence of an artistic milieu in the United States . . . a total lack of discourse" (Ashton 1979, 13).

The Depression, surprisingly enough, was the crucible for a more tangible art world. The federal government's Works Projects Administration (1935) paid artists to paint and sculpt, and in so doing, it fostered a sense of community.[1] Such new organizations as the Artist's Union and the Artist's Committee for Action (1934), the American Artist's Congress (1936), and the Organization of American Abstract Artists (1937) were soon helping to sustain the avant-garde. After 1936, the atelier of Hans Hoffman served as a gathering spot for avant-garde artists. The recently established Whitney Museum of American Art launched its biennial exhibitions in 1932. And in the most vivid testament to how the city and its elite had warmed up to modern art, in 1939 the Museum of

Modern Art moved into its permanent quarters, with funds from Abby Rockefeller, on the site of the former family mansion. This dynamic buildup occurred against a backdrop of decline in Europe. With the rise of Nazi rule, Jewish artists, critics, dealers, and collectors were forced to leave the continent. Profiting from the cataclysms, New York, hub of a flourishing war economy and first port of call for émigré artists (including Dali, Léger, Mondrian, Chagall, and others) was poised to "steal modern art from Paris" (Guilbaut 1983, 91).

If New York was waking up, Los Angeles art was still comatose. The oft-heard claim that "Los Angeles art has no history" (Colpitt 1983) is an exaggeration, but the city had a lot of catching up to do. Los Angeles was young: in 1885 its population numbered only 11,000. When the first artists set up studios downtown, "there was no support community of art organizations, no display space, and no patrons" (Moure 1993). An art club and an art association (the first art gallery) were formed in 1890, but what little support artists got was issued mainly by women's associations. Los Angeles had a distinctive painting style—impressionistic plein air landscapes—but unless an artist was lucky enough to have his own means, his outlooks were rather dim. During a slump in 1896–97, many dispirited painters packed up and left.

Things took a turn for the better as Los Angeles swelled in size and importance. In 1910, the city established an "exposition park" to showcase its new achievements, crowned by a $250,000 Museum of History, Science and Art. The art wing, which subsequently evolved into the Los Angeles County Museum of Art (LACMA), couldn't be opened until 1913, due to the scarcity of work by local artists (Higgins 1963, 7). But LACMA's "art annuals" began to attract more and more attention. Key institutions appeared: the Otis Art Institute (1918) and the Chouinard Art Institute (1921); the Pasadena Art Museum (1921); Art Center, a California version of Bauhaus (1930); and the Jepson Art School (1945), forerunner of the School of Fine Arts at the University of Southern California. The schools were of exceptional importance, and so they would remain for the duration of Los Angeles art's history, given the paucity of commercial support through private galleries and collectors.

A feeling of working in the shadow of New York—and even in the shadow of the wealthier and more refined San Francisco—was already in the air. Then as later, Los Angeles artists and critics gave vent to a defensive second-city mentality that at times manifested itself as a plea simply to be taken seriously. A good example is this 1981 rant by Peter Plagens: "Artists in Los Angeles are—minor preferences for surfing and Mexico and racquetball and Nantucket aside—quite like artists in New York. They are not examples of quaint forms of tribal life requiring explication by latter-day Margaret Meads; they are serious people deserving serious criticism" (1981, 26). New York artists would never need such a baseline defense of their raison d'être (and certainly not by the time Plagens penned those words). But before the war, the situation in Los Angeles was miserably bleak. The city didn't provide the bare essentials of an art world, and its best artists would frequently try their luck in Manhattan instead (Philip Guston and Jackson Pollock, e.g., moved out east in 1930). Interviews with Angeleno artists vividly recall their isolation in those early years: "[There] were a couple of artists, and if you wanted to visit them, you had to take two or three days"; "there were no galleries of the kind we understand"; "the interest in creativity, contemporary creativity, just didn't exist. Nobody would even think about this. It had no meaning" (Colpitt 1983, 19, 22).

GESTATION

The relentless expansion of the New York art world in the second half of the twentieth century can be told as a tale of three booms. Each one added scale and complexity to the art world, and each was linked to major creative breakthroughs, especially in painting (the most marketable art form): abstract expressionism in the 1950s, pop art in the 1960s, and neo-Expressionism in the 1980s. In between the booms, recessions cleared the way for younger artists and dealers, and they cleansed the art world, as it were, of boom-time excess. Such "creative destruction" of a thoroughly American kind locked in New York's supremacy in visual art.

The first-generation New York School scene revolved around only a few individuals and gathering places. By the early 1950s, Franz Kline, Robert Motherwell, Mark Rothko, Willem de Kooning, and especially Jackson Pollock became cultural heroes; still, their milieu consisted, at first, mainly of grubby downtown venues where habitués talked and drank. The Greenwich Village scene involved about a hundred artists, poets, writers, and hangers-on. The dozen or so painters at its core earned the support of a few enterprising, wealthy, committed dealers on Fifty-seventh Street and Madison Avenue. Betty Parsons, the best known among them, is credited with creating the idiom of the art gallery as studio—plain white walls declaring allegiance to artists, not patrons.

Between 1939 and 1946 the number of galleries in New York quadrupled, to 150 (and their sales tripled between 1944 and 1945). The media began its dalliance with the avant-garde when *Life* magazine on August 19, 1949, inquired: "Is Jackson Pollock the Greatest Living Artist in the United States?" By the late 1950s, second-generation New York

School artists could expect to exhibit at a young age with commercial dealers or in nonprofit galleries, like the Hansa and the Tanager. By 1961 there were 300 art galleries in the city, capable of presenting 4,000 exhibitions each year. A poignant symbol of the prestige of modern art was the unveiling of Frank Lloyd Wright's futuristic spire for Solomon R. Guggenheim's Museum of Non-Objective Art, in 1959.

But there were costs associated with this success. By 1952, what postwar American art chronicler Irving Sandler called the "loose fraternity of Abstract Expressionists" had more or less disintegrated, though the art market was "boiling with an activity never known before" (1978, 17). In 1960 "there was almost nothing left of the camaraderie that small numbers can sustain" (Ashton 1979, 229). Calvin Tomkins pinpointed 1958 as the demise of the abstract expressionists' "tribal solidarity" and the dawn of a "disunified art world" (1980, 149). As the halo of collectors and dealers surrounding the artists expanded, questions about merit would increasingly be settled in the marketplace. The bond between art and money had cemented.

New York's first bout of exuberance was already in remission when the foundations of the Los Angeles art world were still being laid down. Modernism's influence was felt on the West Coast only after World War II (the presence of Marcel Duchamp and Man Ray helped). In the midst of an improving postwar economy much of the early activity took place in genteel Pasadena. A 1951 bequest of 600 modern works to the Pasadena Art Museum (fig. 14.1) provided a source of inspiration for artists. "Los Angeles art" was assuming an identity. Peter Voulkos's ceramics workshop at Otis (1954) marked the beginnings of a California abstract expressionism. In the ensuing years, Edward Kienholz and Ed Ruscha, quintessential Los Angeles artists both, arrived in the city and started making a name for themselves. So did Walter Hopps, an influential art historian, curator, and art dealer whose activities lent a great deal of credibility to Los Angeles art. Circles formed around these men.

The signal event was the 1957 opening of Hopps's Ferus Gallery on La Cienega Boulevard. The legendary gallery, "which, almost single-handedly, spawned a contemporary art collecting scene in Los Angeles" (Weschler 1982, 51), exhibited many of the local artists who would go on to make national reputations, including Kienholz (Hopps's founding partner in Ferus), Ruscha, John Altoon, Billy Al Bengston, Robert Irwin, Ed Moses, and Larry Bell. The La Cienega gallery strip came alive around Ferus and art dealers Felix Landau, David Stuart, and Irving Blum (who became a partner and front man in Ferus after 1958). The dealers coordinated their openings for Monday night "art walks." Local collectors were warming up to the new art (Paul Kantor and Frank

Figure 14.1. Norton Simon Museum, Pasadena, View from Colorado Avenue (February 2002). One of the earliest influences of modernism on the West Coast was in Pasadena, thanks to a large gift of art works to the Pasadena Art Museum in 1951. The museum closed during the art market recession of the late 1960s and in 1974 reopened as the important Norton Simon Museum.

Perls in Beverly Hills were selling them works from Europe and New York). It was a self-contained bohemian society, not unlike Greenwich Village a decade before.

Out East, painters and sculptors were already saddled with a larger, denser, more commercial milieu and a formidable, dignified history. Not in Los Angeles. "The absence of a tradition gave Los Angeles art an open field, without the obstacles of history or heroes" (Plagens 1974, 29).[2] For the past fifty years, as long as such comparisons have been made at all, there has been a presumption about the integrity, innocence, and purity of Los Angeles art, which arose out of its distance from the tribal conflicts that ravaged the career-obsessed art life of New York. "You have a certain purity here," the sculptor Carl André once said. "You know people in New York think of you as something isolated and pure and you have a certain integrity that's not corrupted by being mixed up in this lowlife New York art world" (Newman 2000, 158).

The new energy fermented mainly in the schools. The progressive Chouinard was on its way to fusing (controversially) with the Conservatory of Music, to form the California Institute of the Arts (CalArts), with funding by Walt Disney. University art departments, notably UCLA, and galleries added another training ground and forum for artists. But while the advances of the 1950s kindled a sense of optimism, they must be put in perspective. As happened in New York a decade earlier, aesthetic effervescence wasn't matched by a similarly sturdy art infrastructure. There weren't enough dealers promoting contemporary art, and those who were could only sell local work with difficulty. Art remained a low priority in a city of 4 million that, as late as 1950, spent only $131,000 on arts facilities. The real action was still in New York.

GOLDEN AGE

In the 1960s New York got its first taste of a real art boom. Moving past abstract expressionism, artists were realizing aesthetic breakthroughs. The period's reigning style—pop—was eminently salable, and in the midst of unprecedented prosperity, artists of every segment of the art market thrived. The suddenness of the ascent in values was staggering. Jackson Pollock's *Blue Poles,* which sold for $6,000 in 1953 and $32,000 in 1956, aptly illustrates the trend: by 1972 its price topped $2 million. Complaints predictably followed: "If the artist was in hell in 1946," critic Allan Kaprow famously fumed in 1964, as the art market swelled to $2.5 billion, "now he is in business" (Kaprow 1964).[3]

The art world as we know it today was coming into view, and so were its iconic figures. The sixties gave us the quintessential art star, Andy Warhol (America's best-known contemporary artist), and the prototypical art dealer, the worldly and erudite Leo Castelli. This legendary supporter of Warhol, Jasper Johns, Robert Rauschenberg, Frank Stella, and Roy Lichtenstein had "a lingering European patrician distaste for the idea of being 'in trade'" (Tomkins 1988, 21), and as such was a model to his peers (among them, Sidney Janis, André Emmerich, and Richard Bellamy)—dealers who were in the game mainly for the art, not the money. But the dealers' good fortunes were improving along with those of their artists. American and European collectors were now flocking to New York, and the art boom that they fueled presaged some of the "excesses" of the 1980s: glitzy openings, links between fashion and art, speculation, instant careers, media hype. Dealers saw their power increase vis-à-vis museums; auction houses made headway against dealers; collectors asserted themselves as never before.

Yet, if the art world was now infused with money to a degree that many of its denizens found distasteful, it also retained a healthy spirit of progressivism and marginality. Artistic debates, unfazed as yet by postmodernism, were played out with an earnest commitment to working through a more or less shared avant-garde agenda. The art world remained modest in size, and its members were "conditioned by a common culture: they received a similar education, lived in Manhattan, saw the same shows in galleries and museums, read the same art books and magazines" (Sandler 1988, 108). Serious collectors and public collections were not yet priced out of the market. Critics, such as the all-powerful Clement Greenberg, earned unprecedented respect. The art world had become "a far larger and more visible, cohesive, dynamic and commanding force" (Mamiya 1992, 1), and yet, conditions for sustaining a discourse about art were close to ideal. It was a happy medium between the obscurity of the early years and the all-out commercialization that followed.

Vietnam and the oil crisis popped the bubble. Suddenly, buying art was no longer fashionable, and the money dried up in the recession. Wary of art's co-option into the market system, artists turned to creating unwieldy, unsalable objects and events: performance art, concept art, earthworks. Pluralism and theoretical argument thrived; dealers foundered. "Art didn't disappear during the years between 1968 and 1978, but it went into hiding" (Levin 1988, xiii.).

The art world, however, always finds rejuvenation in a crisis, and so it did in the 1970s. Nonprofit cooperative galleries and alternative art venues proliferated. There was refreshing openness to photography, film, video, graffiti art, junk, and natural materials, and the arts absorbed feminism, environmentalism, and politics. At last, there was more room for minorities: El Museum del Barrio in New York (founded in 1969) moved to upper Fifth Avenue in 1979, and the Studio Museum of Harlem (created in 1968) established its permanent collection in 1979. International ties were strengthened as "other nations' styles and approaches to art-making became an integral part of America's aesthetic Pluralism" (Robins 1984, 5). The edges of the art world were pushed outward even as the city and many of its galleries teetered on the edge of bankruptcy.

The real silver lining, however, was in a rat-infested grid of blocks below Houston Street that until 1962 didn't even have a name. Paula Cooper opened the first art gallery in one of Soho's majestic cast-iron buildings in 1968. Two years later, almost 2,000 artists were living and working in the area (Simpson 1981, 188). In 1973 Leo Castelli and other uptown dealers moved to 420 West Broadway, making it New York's most prestigious address for new art for the next quarter century. The giant loft galleries—there were eighty-four in Soho by 1975—shaped a new architectural idiom that expressed the heightened ambitions of New

York artists. These monumental spaces proclaimed that the artworks inside them were destined for museums, not simply private homes.

The quiescent seventies turned out to be a staging ground for the go-go eighties. The art market swelled steadily after 1975.[4] Christie's and Sotheby's were transformed into publicly traded companies, answering to more nakedly commercial ambitions. An army of young graduates headed toward art careers from the nation's mushrooming arts schools. New York had a reputation for crime and sleaze, but it was easy to start a life in art there. By the early 1980s, 10,000 artists could be considered for a museum show in America (Crane 1987, 2–5). Most of them dreamed of making it in Manhattan.

In Los Angeles, the art world was also hitting its stride. By the early sixties, complained art dealer Irving Blum, the "the earlier camaraderie and real affection that these people had for one another . . . began to shift with the spectre of money, the spectre of commerce, the spectre of greater interest, the spectre of greater collecting activity, the spectre of competition" (Colpitt 1983, 39). Yet, these pressures were not as pronounced as in New York, and nostalgia for the heroic days was a small price to pay for the first "golden era" of Los Angeles art.

There was new art: "hard edge" abstraction and other important styles were simultaneously emerging, earning new labels like "Cool School," "California Light and Space" and "Finish Fetish." There were new artists, including such soon-to-be-celebrated newcomers to the city as Sam Francis and Richard Diebenkorn. The schools went from strength to strength.[5] Influential New York painters began to show their work in Los Angeles, and the Gemini lithography workshop attracted more artists still. The Los Angeles County Museum of Art moved from its cramped wing at the Museum of History, Science and Arts to a new building in Hancock Park in 1965, devoting galleries to new art and local artists. In the years 1964–67 the city even had a strong art magazine: *Artforum,* which promoted the "L.A. look" and connected it to debates and events in the East. With Michael Fried, Lucy Lippard, Robert Pincus-Whitten, Max Kozloff, Rosalind Krauss, Peter Plagens, Annette Michelson, and Barbara Rose unleashing their intellectual firepower, *Artforum* got behind Los Angeles art, and especially behind Ferus (the magazine's offices were conveniently situated above the gallery), and this boost was exactly what Los Angeles art needed.

The La Cienega scene between Melrose and Santa Monica Boulevards exploded, with hangouts like Barney's Beanery (immortalized in Kienholz's 1965 sculptural installation) adding to the mix in what was soon to be called West Hollywood. The Monday night art walks would wind their way from Ferus to Esther Robles, to Felix Landau, to the Ankrum Gallery, to the Los Angeles Art Association galleries, and on. The West Coast began to attract collectors from New York (in a short-lived experiment, Ferus joined up with Manhattan's Pace Gallery to exploit this interest). Santa Monica Boulevard became a second stop on the gallery circuit; Nicholas Wilder and other dealers there were showcasing artists from Venice (Peter Alexander, Chuck Arnoldi, Laddie and Guy Dill, Jo Bear, and others).

It was the beginning of a decade-long shift to the West Side, the newly popular home of young professionals and artists. In Venice, the new artists' quarter, influential galleries like ACE (Sam Francis, Michael Heizer) and L.A. Louver (Jim Dine, David Hockney, Frank Stella) forged links to New York and to pop art. It was all part of a bigger story. By now the third-largest city in the country, Los Angeles was on a roll. "'Culture' meant 'art,' and 'art' implied 'new,' and 'new,' as everybody was informed, meant California—particularly Los Angeles" (Plagens 1974, 27).

For a while, anyway. The "Los Angeles aesthetic momentum" didn't last. Its commercial and institutional foundations proved too weak. By 1968 Ferus had closed, *Artforum* had moved to New York, and Walter Hopps had departed to the East. As in New York, many artists turned "from object to experience," eschewing art easily marketed to collectors. Local museums, especially LACMA, were derided for being undependable friends of local artists. The Pasadena Museum, where Hopps had once worked miracles, was forced to close owing to financial problems (it reopened later on as the Norton Simon Museum). La Cienega Boulevard went downhill, a victim of flagging interest and ebbing money supply from New York. Several artists left the city, and some notable collections dispersed. "Los Angeles art crept into [the 1970s] like a mugging victim: battered, impoverished, scared and disgusted"; then the oil crisis spiked, in 1973, "knocking the remaining wind out of the gallery commerce by doing in several regional industries" (Frank 1978, 42). Ed Ruscha's seminal painting *The County Museum on Fire* was a prescient message about the condition of the Los Angeles art world by the seventies—a symbol of sophistication but also vulnerability.

From the helter-skelter 1960s and 1970s emerged the outlines of a bicoastal art system that would seem familiar in our present day. And as the two art worlds matured on opposite ends of the country, their contrasts became more noticeable. The recession of the early seventies underscored Los Angeles's debt to its nonprofit institutions. More than ever, academic galleries and alternative spaces like the Los Angeles Institute of Contemporary Art (LAICA) and Los Angeles Contemporary

Art Exhibitions (LACE), as well as newly assertive feminist initiatives like the Woman's Building shouldered the burden of promoting new art.

To be sure, distance from the market had some salutary effects. It encouraged and tolerated experimentation. Then as now, Angeleno artists were at liberty to foray into "difficult" or unfashionable aesthetic ground. Their academic base offered consistent support, no matter where their pursuits led them. In New York, in contrast, "the juggernaut of commerce" created a "necessity to enter the marketplace in order to be an artist" (Hap Tivey, quoted in Wortz1983, 69–70).[6] Free of galleries' demands to be self-important, Los Angeles artists could explore the humorous and the decorative side and indulge in "visual hedonism" (Zelevansky 2000, 300). The school-heavy support structure gave rise to a specific kind of university-based artist in Los Angeles. Where New York had its Andy Warhol and its Jasper Johns, Los Angeles had John Baldessari and Chris Burden—men whose reputations were based in their student following, not so much their gallery conquests. Los Angeles has been called the research and development arm of the New York art world precisely because its all-important schools are able to function as a laboratory for pure, disinterested aesthetic exploration.

By the 1970s, it was also clear that Los Angeles would be perennially dogged by two problems. One of them was geography. The more the art world grew, the more it was absorbed into Los Angeles's isolating sprawl. As a result, "artists' out-of-studio debates, dealing, informal teaching, and clique-forming do not take place with the intensity of activity at the Cedar Bar, the Club, or Subjects of the Artists, in New York" (Plagens 1974, 28). This kind of observation is a recurring theme of comparisons between the two cities. "New York has a sheer energy that seems self-perpetuated," the Los Angeles painter Lari Pittman said more recently. "Los Angeles on the other hand is much more diffuse, so that it's up to you—both as an artist and as a citizen—to make things happen" (quoted in Cotter 1987, 169).

The other chronic problem was "regionalism": a disconnect with artistic debates taking place elsewhere. "One of the things that I think was most damaging and criminal about the provincialism here during the '50s, '60s, and early '70s," complained Los Angeles art historian Howard Singerman in the late 1980s, "was the assumption that our art was more real than New York art. New York was just all this theory stuff, and artists there weren't working from their 'real-from-birth' selves" (Singerman and Knight 1987, 56). Isolation had its advantages—it incubated a distinctive style and attitude—but once a professional art world formed, it turned into a liability. As Ferus dealer Irving Blum recalled: "Urgency was the thing that drove me out of California finally, the lack of urgency. . . . And that lack of urgency filters down to the art making as well. You can do it in two months from now just as easily as today, with the same result, and in the mean time, the beach is beckoning" (Weschler 1982, 51).

On a deeper level, regionalism exposed Los Angeles art to charges of anti-intellectualism. "The most depressing thing about the Los Angeles art scene," a critic wrote in 1977, "is that ideas are thought, or perhaps felt, to be subversive. . . . Los Angeles is seemingly cut off from the ideational framework that sustains the art of the rest of the world" (Brennan 1977, 23). This complaint, too, has echoed through the decades. A 1985 commentary bristled about "a clear lack of interchange of ideas that results in a highly inbred, and therefore somewhat retarded, approach toward creating and exhibiting art" (Kohn 1985, 37–39). A 1993 article summed up the trade-offs thus: "Young artists in Los Angeles aren't often terribly interested in what everyone else is doing. This is both an unfortunate offshoot of Los Angeles's aforementioned historical amnesia and a liberating facet of its unique intellectual landscape" (Greene 1996, 9).

BOOM AND BUST

In New York, where both art and theory were flourishing, it was time for the greatest art boom in history. It escalated through most of the 1980s and, after boiling to a frenzy around 1987, climaxed in 1990, when Van Gogh's portrait of Dr. Gachet was auctioned for $82.5 million at Christie's—a world record that still stands unbroken. In 1989 Sotheby's and Christie's sold 402 works for more than $1 million. In November 1989 (the single most profitable month in the history of the art market), 305 artworks were sold for more than $1 million apiece, and fifty-eight for more than $5 million.

The boom recast the landscape of contemporary art. In 1980 Jasper Johns's *Three Flags* became the first painting by a living artist to sell for $1 million. Nine years later, publisher S. I. Newhouse paid seventeen times that amount for another of Johns's works, *False Start.* Top emerging artists such as Ross Bleckner, Julian Schnabel, David Salle, and Eric Fischl, along with members of the European "Trans-Avantgarde," formed a generation without precedent. Never before had so many artists achieved such fame en masse, and so quickly.

The revival owed much to the return of painting and, especially, to neo-Expressionism, a macho, painterly style that was "not supposed to happen," in the words of one critic, but that proved irresistible to collectors. Schnabel, its main proponent, was the personification of the publicity-hungry art star. His success was engineered by Mary Boone, an ambitious young dealer, who was to the hard-nosed 1980s art world what the patrician Leo Castelli had been to the 1960s. A surprisingly diverse constellation of larger forces stoked the boom. Unprecedented wealth accumulation and concentration, coupled with a deeply consumerist culture, set the stage. Art prices were fueled by billions of dollars from Japan, rampant speculation, investment schemes, media hype, the energy of Soho and the East Village (Manhattan's new art neighborhood), scores of new dealers and consultants, entrepreneurial collectors, acquisitive corporations, and aggressive auction houses. The unlikely alliance of forces even included unprecedented government and nonprofit support of the arts and favorable tax laws. A different cast of characters appeared on the stage, from insurers and bankers to appraisers and lawyers specializing in art.

At the epicenter of the boom, the dimensions and mood of the art world were shifting—for good. Concerns were mounting that the art world was abandoning its cherished autonomy from the norms of mainstream society. In a faster, commercial art world dominated by newcomers and speculators, how could agreement be reached about aesthetic principles, and how could such agreements dominate over the irrepressible logic of prices? And if the art world became only a rarefied niche of the entertainment industry, as it seemed to many critics of the changes, why should it merit extra prestige and privileges, such as tax exemptions?

These anxieties had simmered, off and on, ever since the 1950s, when art emerged from its bohemian cocoon. Now they were far more urgent. But the skeptics didn't have to wait long until their predictions about the boom's self-defeating trajectory were confirmed. An economic slowdown, the onset of AIDS, and a military standoff in the Gulf brought on a full-scale market meltdown after 1990. As galleries folded and prices tumbled, there was little to cushion the blow. The art world's core validating system had been enfeebled by the boom-time euphoria, by vestigial suspicion over art quickly made and sold. The New York gallery world completely froze up in 1990–94, leaving Zurich, Cologne, London, and the reunified Berlin to grab the spotlight, temporarily reversing a half-century-long trend.

In Los Angeles, it was time for a day in the sun. In 1984 the city became the second largest in the United States. Its empowerment drew strength from the music industry and Hollywood's mounting significance, from vital connections to the Pacific Rim, and from an ongoing experiment in multiculturalism. Between the 1970s and the year 2000, Los Angeles profited twice from its second-city status. In the 1980s it

Figure 14.2. The Geffen Contemporary MOCA, First Street and North Central Avenue in Little Tokyo. Opened in 1983 as an interim space while MOCA was under construction, the so-called Temporary Contemporary, renovated by Frank Gehry, was quickly successful. The structure was originally built in the 1940s as a hardware store (notice the remnants of the original sign at the top of the building) and was then later used as a city warehouse and police car garage. Part of Gehry's idea was to show respect for the old structure by retaining its façade.

reaped the economic boom's benefits while avoiding the hype and overheating that marred the New York art world. In the nineties, after the bubble burst, Los Angeles artists stepped into the void. The past ten years have definitively put Los Angeles art on the national and international visual art stage. In this second "golden age," the city has finally backed up its exceptional talent with a solid institutional base.

It was clear by the early 1980s that Los Angeles desperately needed additional contemporary-art infrastructure (Wortz 1980). The answer was a temporary building for a new Museum of Contemporary Art (the Temporary Contemporary), which opened in a Little Tokyo warehouse in 1983 (fig. 14.2) and has stayed open and remarkably popular ever since. In 1986 MOCA opened a permanent museum on the edge of downtown in a postmodern edifice designed by Arata Isozaki (fig. 14.3). The museum's total exhibition space now rivaled that of MoMA in New York (Failing 1986). In 1986 LACMA inaugurated a four-level contemporary art wing. Three years later, the Santa Monica Museum of Art was installed in a former dairy redesigned by Frank O. Gehry. Nearby, Eli Broad opened a contemporary art education center and museum in an old phone-company building overlooking Venice beach. And the most impressive change was yet to come. The J. Paul Getty Trust was drawing up plans for a hilltop museum and research center near Bel Air. It would consume more than a billion dollars in the largest single-phase construction project ever undertaken. "The Los Angeles art scene was headed at long last for international cultural respectability" (Clothier 1989a). Even the city got into the act, upping its arts budget eightfold to $20 million.

Some of the earlier problems (apathy, collector disinterest, and a callous press) persisted, but there were new signs that Los Angeles was catching up. The catalyst, once again, was the school system, especially the University of California, Irvine, and CalArts. At CalArts, under the charismatic Baldessari, graduates were taught not only about art skills and history but also about art-world survival skills. With graduates such

Figure 14.3. Museum of Contemporary Art (MOCA), California Plaza and South Grand Avenue, on the Edge of Downtown Los Angeles. Designed by Arata Isozaki, MOCA opened in 1986. Its genesis was the realization by artists, curators, and politicians that Los Angeles was the only major American city without a significant museum devoted solely to contemporary art.

as Ross Bleckner, Eric Fischl, David Salle, Mike Kelley, and Barbara Bloom, CalArts became the preeminent feeder school of the art world on both coasts. "As early as 1980, there was talk in New York art circles of a 'CalArts mafia,' complaints of old school chums helping each other get a foot in gallery doors," wrote Los Angeles critic Ralph Rugoff in 1989 (331).

Still, by some counts Los Angeles had only thirty galleries of critical interest in 1985 (Kohn 1985, 123). But dealers were proliferating and showing a wider array of work. Santa Monica was the city's main art center now, with galleries relocating there in droves from the La Cienega area. A cluster of thirty galleries formed near the ocean—a "SoHo by the beach" (Clothier 1989b, 130). A boosterish article reported that "in L.A.'s increasingly image-conscious art world nothing but the best will do" and that the "crescendo of activity" extended to "commercial galleries, artist-run spaces plus a growing mass of millionaire private collectors" (Clare 1987, 40). By 1989 the *Artscene* guide listed some 300 galleries in the greater Los Angeles area; its editor boasted that he ran seven or eight new listings in every issue (Clothier 1989b, 128). "Certainly the consensus . . . seems to be that things in Los Angeles are better for art than they've been for a long time," wrote Holland Cotter in 1987. But, he added cautiously, "the unspoken context of this conviction is that things could not have gotten much worse than they were during the last decade or so" (163).

When the 1980s bubble burst, Los Angeles was far from immune to recession. The downturn decimated California's defense and aerospace industries, and it forced a predictable slowdown in art acquisitions. But, by hitting New York even harder, the bust also created "a level playing field" (Scarborough 1993, E11). Los Angeles could once again count on its noncommercial institutions; Hollywood patrons, meanwhile, having recently warmed up to collecting, could still afford to buy art.[7] By the mid-1990s there was more "cause for optimism" (Muchnic 1995). "What is most exciting about Los Angeles right now," wrote Terry Myers in 1995, "is that even in the midst of many probable and incessant disasters (whether economic or natural), the 'bottom' and the 'middle' of the art market seem to be thriving" (24).

THE LANDSCAPE: LOS ANGELES

In recent years—a period marked by historically unprecedented wealth creation on the West Coast and elsewhere, which has also been the most prosperous chapter in the brief history of Los Angeles art—galleries have further dispersed in Los Angeles and its environs. This drift has been a hallmark of the scene over the years, and it's accelerating. Los Angeles galleries constantly splinter into minidistricts, colonizing empty blocks and buildings and, often as not, vanishing as quickly as they appear. The gyrations of the art market routinely wipe out dealers. Some activity is squeezed out of galleries altogether into a patchwork of homes, garages, offices, and studios. There are deeper reasons for Los Angeles's diffuse art topography: "The very word 'center' is a solecism here. The downtown may sprout skyscrapers and institutions forever, as some anticipate, yet never feel like the center of anything" (Schjeldahl 1981, 25). Dealers take advantage of this open playing field by moving freely into areas with good auto access, architecture, or rents. The flux is destabilizing, but it's appropriate for today's multinodal art world. If New York had been a perfect staging ground for modernism's tightly focused narrative, Los Angeles seems naturally suited to the diffuse, pluralistic discourse of postmodernity.

A handful of Los Angeles dealers date back to the 1950s and 1960s, but most gallery districts are new. There are no less than ten in central Los Angeles alone; half of them are less than a decade old. Some of the five districts in the outlying areas are just as new. Each zone is a distinct microcosm, with its own key dealers, museums, and schools. Some emerge gradually and randomly; others result from planned development. Recently, the historic migration of galleries to the West Side has begun to reverse. Deterred by high rents, young dealers are moving east, leaving behind traces of the older and more established gallery scene near the ocean.

Moving eastbound from the coastline, one first encounters Santa Monica (figs. 14.4, 14.5).[8] There, out of the energy of the mid-1980s and spearheaded by art dealer Wayne Blank, grew Bergamot Station (fig. 14.6), a former trolley depot housing several dozen galleries and a museum (the site, still owned by the Transit Authority, may eventually be razed to make way for a subway station). This complex (with notable Los Angeles dealers such as Rosamund Felsen, Patricia Faure, Craig Krull, and Patrick Painter) is one of the most densely packed gallery concentrations in America. Bergamot is gradually turning into a haven for veteran artists, but it remains the anchor of the West Side art scene—the "closest you'll get to one-stop shopping" for art in Los Angeles (McKenna 1996, 56). The Getty Center in Brentwood (fig. 14.7), meanwhile, has cemented the West Side's overall dominance in the visual arts in the Los Angeles area. The sumptuous collections and epic scale of the 105-acre complex have confirmed prognoses that the Getty would "surpass every prestigious museum or exhibition centre" in the city (Zirkzee 1995, 62-65).

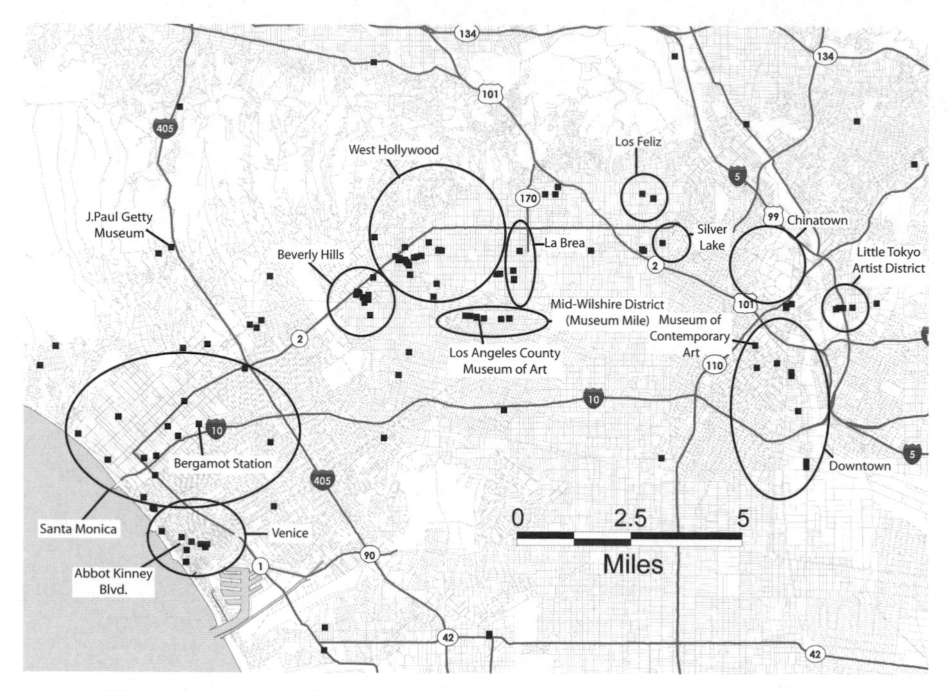

Figure 14.4. Art Galleries and Museums in Los Angeles

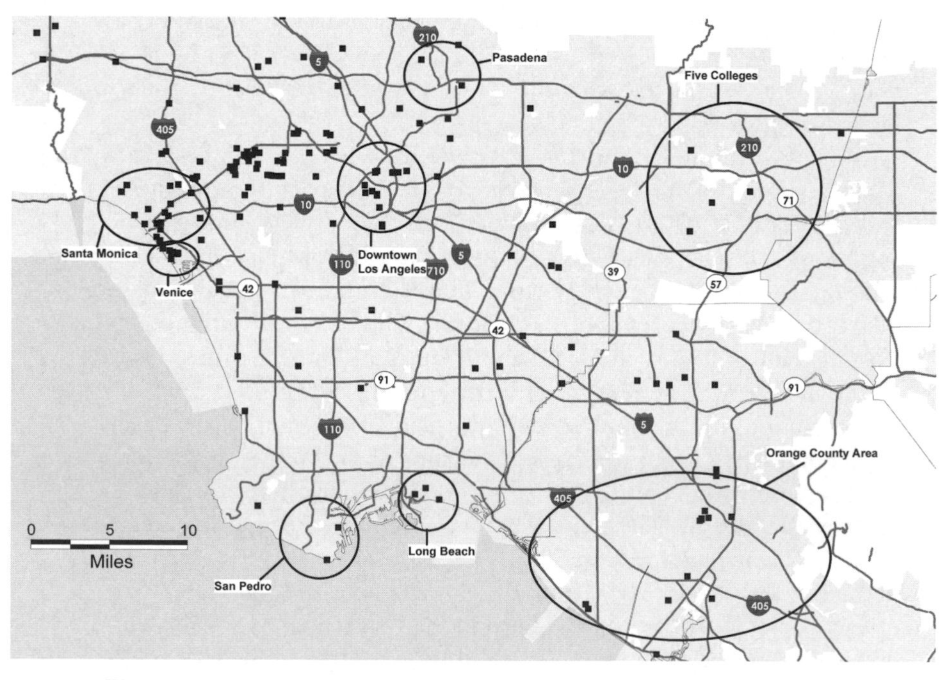

Figure 14.5. Greater Los Angeles

Figure 14.6. Bergamot Station Arts Center, with the Santa Monica Museum in the Background. The Bergamot Center is the largest fine art complex on the West Coast, with about forty galleries. Built originally in 1875 as the terminus for the Red Line Trolley from Los Angeles to the Santa Monica Pier, the arts center opened in 1994. The driving force behind its creation was the city of Santa Monica.

Venice, to the south, has been overshadowed by Santa Monica, but some dealerships established by the beach in the 1960s and 1970s (notably L.A. Louver) remain extremely influential. The past half decade has seen a robust commercial revival near the beach and around Abbot Kinney Boulevard, a new mecca for architects and artsy types. Fashionable new galleries like Sandroni Rey and a cluster of urbane design businesses and boutiques have colonized this area since 1998.

On a good day it is a twenty-five-minute drive from the coast to a group of interconnected districts that lie about halfway between the ocean and downtown. The wealthiest but smallest of these is in Beverly Hills. Despite the proximity of the University of California, Los Angeles, and the prosperity that is synonymous with the area—or because of it—Beverly Hills has never been a significant venue for contemporary art. Most of the galleries in the area trade in resale material or offer grist for interior decorators. But there are a few notable exceptions. In 1996 the Pace and Gagosian galleries of New York joined a handful of well-regarded dealers and opened satellites in Beverly Hills to attract movie industry clients. Unfortunately, their multimillion dollar investments

Figure 14.7. The Getty Center, New Campus, Opened 1997. The Getty Center's wide-ranging collection, modern architecture, and spectacular location have propelled it to the forefront of the Los Angeles cultural scene. Built high on an isolated hilltop, its inaccessibility has made it a target of social critics.

have failed to spark a major surge in collecting interest (Pace has already scaled back its presence). Another exception is the Timothy Yarger Fine Arts Gallery (fig. 14.8) on North Rodeo Drive, which handles blue-chip contemporary artists, including David Hockney, Pierre Brisson, and LeRoy Neiman, alongside works from the estates of Picasso, Chagall, and Miró.

There is more art in West Hollywood, a neighborhood of young creative people that is currently on the upswing for contemporary art. West Hollywood is a melting pot: internationally renowned dealers of the 1960s such as Margo Leavin (John Baldessari, Alexis Smith, Stephen Prina, etc.) work alongside galleries featuring artists who rose to prominence during the past two decades, such as Regen Projects.

The Mid-Wilshire district, two miles further east along "Museum Mile," is notable for its blend of public exhibition spaces and commercial galleries, all drawn here by interesting architecture and affordable rents. The Los Angeles County Museum of Art serves as a magnet for dealers, more than a dozen of whom have relocated from the West Side in the past decade (ACME and ACE are among the top names). To the north of Wilshire lies the last of the midcity zones, a pocket of reputable galleries along La Brea Boulevard. Several date back to the 1960s and 1970s, when this was the most lively spot on the art scene (Ferus was around here; the Apex and Jan Baum galleries are also links to that era). Like Fifty-seventh Street in New York, La Brea is mainly a haven for historically established, costly art.

Another important agglomeration of gallery districts lies in and around the downtown business district. Of these, Little Tokyo/Artist District looks back on the longest history: artists were turning industrial spaces into studios here some thirty years ago, and the stalwart Cirrus and Post galleries have maintained a sense of continuity through much of that history. Migration to the loft area accelerated after the 1978 opening of the LACE artists' cooperative. During the 1980s, plans were drawn up for a cohesive artist district. Artists moved in, and galleries (like the artist-run Deep River) soon followed. The developers have purposefully mixed together several kinds of creative activity. The Brewery complex, for example, includes galleries, studios, and lofts, and it regularly hosts live musical events.

Urban renewal has recently spread to downtown Los Angeles, which is undergoing the latest of several attempts to breathe life back into one of America's least hospitable urban centers. The grim business district has absorbed major investments into arts infrastructure from the city

Figure 14.8. Timothy Yarger Fine Arts Gallery, Rodeo Drive, Beverly Hills

and private institutions. The current effort began with MOCA's temporary and permanent buildings, now among Los Angeles's top public attractions featuring new art. The Japanese American National Museum opened a spectacular building nearby in 1999. Other high-profile cultural projects, such as Gehry's Disney Hall, are nearing completion. As life returns to downtown, its derelict buildings and empty lots hold great promise for art.

Silver Lake and Los Feliz are rapidly being settled by artists and young creative types who are fostering a do-it-yourself scene. Houses, parking lots, empty cinemas, and storefronts have become provisional art galleries; weekend-long interdisciplinary minifestivals are publicized mainly by word of mouth. The atmosphere recalls the old La Cienega days, but the gentrification of these formerly working-class neighborhoods is unrelenting. Commercial galleries and hip boutiques are already moving in.

The forward guard is therefore advancing into Chinatown, on the north end of downtown, as Chinese residents move to the suburbs (chap. 4). Chinatown is quickly emerging as a small art community unto itself. A cluster of galleries (including China Art Objects, Goldman Tevis, INMO Gallery, and others) have opened along a 500-foot alley named Chung King Road since 1998, lured by cheap rent, recent beautification, safety management coordinated by a business improvement district, and a Los Angeles oddity: foot traffic. The new dealers showcase mostly conceptual work and, like their La Brea forebears, coordinate openings on Saturday afternoons. This is the red-hot new frontier of the art scene—at least until new areas and dealers capture the art crowd's attention.

The review of the art map wouldn't be complete without a glance at some of the outlying areas. Los Angeles encompasses several sub–art worlds, which flourish at a considerable degree of independence from each other. Closest to the center is Pasadena, the oldest residential community in Los Angeles. Historic institutions such as the Huntington Library hark back to Pasadena's early, graceful affluence, while the Norton Simon Museum, housing one of California's top collections, boasts a popular new renovation by Gehry. The modernist campus of the Art Center College of Design up in the hills (which is also adding several new structures) and the presence of a few art dealers downtown makes Pasadena a more lively spot than its gentle suburban streetscapes suggest. Affluent families priced out of the West Side are infusing a new cultural energy, providing support for entities like Pasadena Art Space and the Armory Center for the Arts, which mount innovative programs to lure art enthusiasts.

The Claremont Colleges, about thirty miles east in Pomona (Harvey Mudd, Claremont McKenna, Scripps, Pomona, and Pitzer) are another archipelago of arts activity. Several of the colleges have strong art programs, each contributing to a milieu served by both academic galleries and independent dealers. To the south, Orange County has used its recent high-tech wealth to invest in arts-driven development projects, such as the one in Santa Ana. A dusting of galleries has cropped up over this expansive area. The same is true for San Pedro, with its cluster of studios and live-work spaces on a repurposed demilitarized naval base, and Long Beach, where planners are building an arts district for local residents.

Rare is the artist from Santa Monica, the Wilshire district, or Silver Lake who ventures into these distant corners of greater Los Angeles. But new and growing neighborhoods are precisely what give Los Angeles its artistic vitality: as soon as the status quo is established, upcoming areas ascend in popularity, prompting a healthy cultural osmosis.

NEW YORK CITY

The New York art world is more concentrated, but it, too, is rapidly dispersing in the wake of the spectacular economic boom of the 1990s (fig. 14.9). The early-1990s recession, it seemed, was a brief flashback to the 1970s. Only those seriously committed to art hung on as the "excesses" of the 1980s came to be deplored, and a slower, more political art took center stage. But it was only a fleeting interlude. With the return of prosperity, strictures against conspicuous consumption soon eased and a stealthy art boom gave way to an overt one. The peaks of 1989–90, however, were not revisited even in the heady years of 1999–2000 (when the London Art Sales Index of the U.S. auction market still hovered at one-half its level of a decade earlier). Nevertheless, by the onset of the millennium extraordinary art prices (such as the $55 million sale at Christie's of Picasso's *Woman with Crossed Arms* or the $1.8 million paid for Jeff Koons's *Pink Panther* sculpture) were again making headlines.

The art world has been steadily absorbing new artists, especially young, attractive, marketable ones. More than ever, it takes its cues from the art market, and, reminiscent of the late 1960s and late 1980s, it has once again rekindled its cozy relations with fashion and media. Photography is commanding prices once reserved for paintings and sculptures. Aided by boom-time hyperbole, online distributors have made inroads into the market for prints and multiples. Galleries, too, are thriving: in 1996 the *Art in America* guide listed 366 galleries in

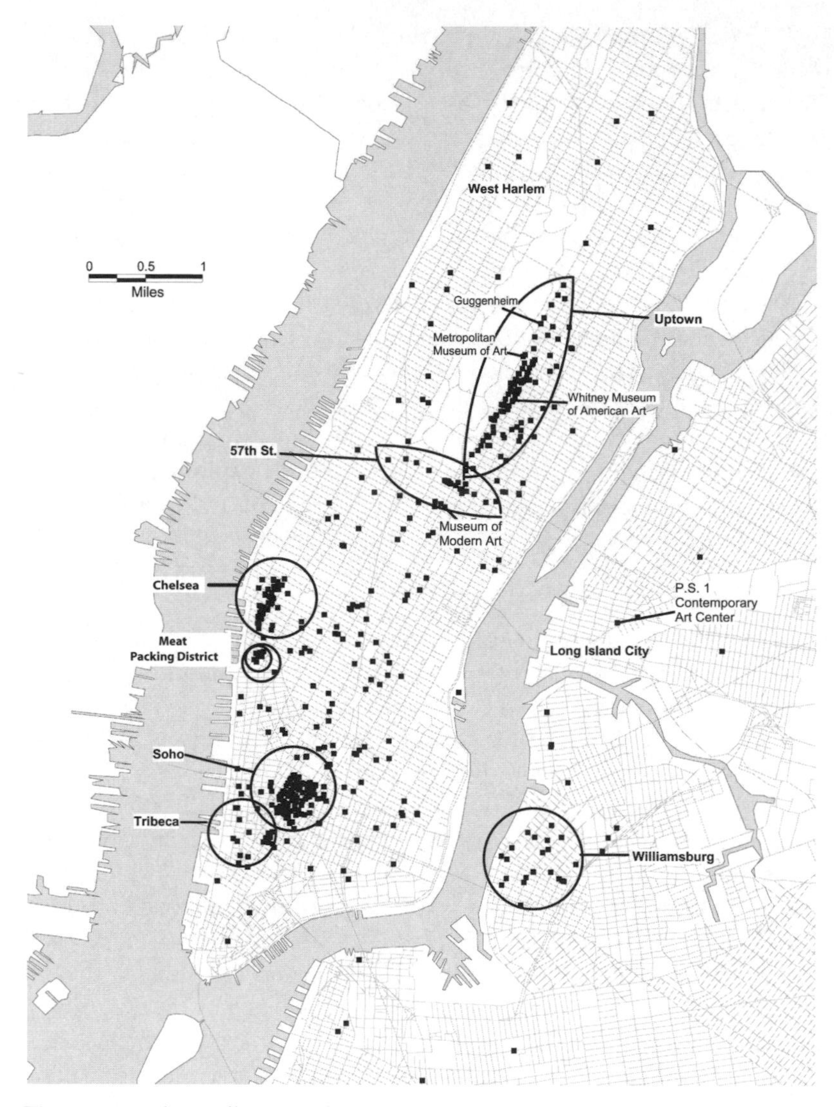

Figure 14.9. Art Galleries and Museums in New York City

New York, up 15 percent from 1990, and their numbers have significantly multiplied since then, especially in the outer boroughs. Last but not least, the city has significantly expanded its portfolio of art institutions: new facilities for the Whitney Museum and the International Center of Photography; a huge art center in Long Island City, P.S. 1 Contemporary Art Center (recently absorbed by MoMA, which is revamping its

Fifty-third Street headquarters); an enlarged New Museum in Soho and an expanding Studio Museum in Harlem; a relentlessly metastasizing Guggenheim and a sprawling miniempire in Chelsea—the Dia Foundation—which spearheaded the influx of galleries to the far West Side and is currently building a massive upstate museum.

Around 1999 Chelsea overtook Soho as New York's main contemporary art district. The origins of the shift date back to 1994, when the intrepid art dealers Paul Morris, Tom Healy, Pat Hearn, and Matthew Marks acquired spaces on far West Twenty-second Street, on a scrappy block formerly inhabited only by Dia's headquarters (fig. 14.10) and a few taxi garages. In 1996 a group of established Soho veterans (Paula Cooper, Barbara Gladstone, Anina Nosei, and the owners of Metro Pictures gallery) announced plans to move their operations to Chelsea, and the trickle swelled into a stampede. The pioneers bought their spaces cheap and broke an historical pattern: they achieved protection from escalating rents. The latecomers, however, were forced to saddle their businesses with hefty mortgages and operating costs. These days, Chelsea is turning into a neighborhood of haves and have-nots. The wealthy

Figure 14.10. The Dia Foundation on West Twenty-second Street, Manhattan. The foundation was a pioneer in the redevelopment of Chelsea into a contemporary-art center.

galleries are here to stay, but the smaller ones will likely be wiped out or forced to move when their leases come up for renewal or when future recessions take their toll.

Chelsea's main physical axis is now Twenty-fourth Street between Tenth and Eleventh Avenues. That thriving block has supplanted not only other Soho locations but also Fifty-seventh Street as Manhattan's top address for high-end contemporary art. It now houses the Gagosian, Luhring Augustine, Metro Pictures, Barbara Gladstone, and Andrea Rosen galleries, among others. The indefatigable Mary Boone opened a gallery space on the block on November 16, 2000. That event was a symbolic bridge to the glitzy 1980s: a series of dramatic Eric Fischl paintings were offered for $350,000 apiece, and just like in the old days, conspicuously placed red dots announced that the works were already sold. The largest Chelsea galleries—Sonnabend, John Miller, and the new PaceWildenstein satellite on Twenty-fifth Street are examples—are once again redefining the architectural norms of art promotion, sending a supremely confident message about the commercial art world's ever-growing aspirations. These galleries conclude the evolution that transformed the operating metaphor of gallery design from the salon to the art studio to the warehouse filled with museum-worthy goods. With their multiple viewing rooms and gargantuan floor plans, these Chelsea spaces seem to announce that they are no longer antecedent to museum display, as mere proving grounds for artists before their work is absorbed into the canon of art history. For all purposes, these mega-galleries *are* museums.

The more than 150 art galleries spread around Chelsea now form a seamless agglomeration with the Meat Market district to the south, a trendy zone around West Fourteenth Street that has, since the decline of the wholesale meat-packing business, steadily changed into a loft and gallery area.[9] Chelsea and the Meat Market now form the largest gallery district in the world: roughly a fifty-block concentration of exhibition spaces bounded by Twelfth Street to the south, Thirty-first Street to the north, Sixth Avenue to the east, and the Hudson River to the west. Galleries near Fourteenth Street (such as Gavin Brown's Enterprise, which operates Manhattan's last real artists' bar) tend to be a bit more edgy. But rents are of course rising, and the days of the upstart galleries are numbered.

Fifty-seventh Street between Sixth Avenue and Park Avenue has been a home to high-end contemporary art galleries for more than half a century. The midtown dealers represent internationally acclaimed living artists and major estates, often operating only on the secondary market. Some have been stalwarts of the gallery scene for decades (e.g., Goodman, Fischbach, Hammer, Marlborough, Miller, Zabriskie, etc.), while others (such as the Grant Selwin, Danese, and Greenberg van Doren galleries) have moved in more recently to be nearer to major patrons and museums. Pace, the world's largest art gallery (now operating as PaceWildenstein), is headquartered on Fifty-seventh Street, with satellite operations distributed on seven floors. Its museum-quality installations, glossy catalogs, six-figure artist stipends, and full-service collector support predated the Chelsea mega-galleries by twenty years.

The food chain continues up Madison Avenue to the art world's top tier. The "gilded ghetto" of the Upper East Side is populated mainly with old-master dealers (Wildenstein, Knoedler & Co., Hirschl & Adler, Acquavella, and others). They share the area with New York's top museums and auction houses. But with few exceptions (e.g., Gagosian, C&M Arts, Richard Gray), the uptown dealers have little or no connection with the current conversation about visual art. They trade in history.

That leaves Soho, Manhattan's final contemporary art hub. But not for long. The cast-iron district is being overrun by fashion boutiques and restaurants. Only a smattering of galleries carry on (among them Deitch Projects, Ronald Feldman Fine Arts, and Tony Shafrazi) along with several highly respected nonprofit spaces (Artists Space, Drawing Center). Although about a hundred galleries, exhibition spaces, and private dealers are still listed in Soho and adjacent Tribeca, this part of town is destined to become another phantom art neighborhood, much like Greenwich Village or the East Village, which contain traces of activity still but no longer count for much in the real art scene.

Soho's demise is the latest chapter in the unending revitalization of the New York art world. Other neighborhoods are now ascending the same ladder of gentrification that changed Soho from an industrial wasteland into a chic fashion mall in three decades. Williamsburg is New York's true center of artistic production nowadays (i.e., where artists actually live and work), and it already has dozens of galleries. Greenpoint, another Brooklyn neighborhood, trails not far behind. As soon as rents in Dumbo (the Brooklyn waterfront under the Manhattan Bridge) turn too expensive for artists, lofts will sprout in Red Hook. If P.S.1 (fig. 14.11) and subway access draw artists to Long Island City, lower taxes and reliable PATH trains make Jersey City and Hoboken attractive propositions. The next candidate for gentrification is Harlem. Studios and lofts are already mushrooming north of West 125th Street (the Project gallery on 126th Street is a lively outpost of downtown art life); Columbia University and several art institutions are eyeing the area for expansion. The real estate brokers trail not far behind.

Figure 14.11. P.S. 1 Contemporary Art Center, Long Island City, Queens

The fact that art has, as it were, escaped the ghettos of Soho and Chelsea and taken over the entire city is a striking sign of the New York art world's vitality and capacity for reinvention. The marginal pursuit of a handful of bohemians in Greenwich Village half a century ago has become a multibillion-dollar professional industry that reaches into almost every corner of New York City and well beyond.

WHAT NOW?

The dispersion of galleries and lofts has produced one surprising outcome: the New York art world's topography is beginning to resemble the sprawl of Los Angeles. And the cities are converging in other respects. New York is still the larger and more powerful art city, but Los Angeles is catching up. Critical debates emanate mainly from the East Coast, but theory is not as important as it once had been. Regionalism —the old curse of Los Angeles art—hardly poses a handicap in a postmodern art world that accepts, even demands, distinctly individuated expressions from artists. "The idea of a regional conflict between the art of the West and East coasts may have had some validity in the 1960s, but it has less meaning in the pluralistic art world we now inhabit," wrote Melinda Wortz as far back as 1983 (68).

The art produced on the two coasts is looking more and more alike.

Artists are similarly educated; they travel and communicate with each other constantly. Los Angeles artists follow the same trends; they make the rounds of the same museums and galleries; they see the same magazines, books, and Web sites. Many East Coast artists are recruited from Los Angeles schools, and successful Los Angeles artists have dealers in New York. The Los Angeles gallery system is less stable than the one in New York, but as the art world goes global and embraces new media, instability will mount on both coasts. The one lasting disparity is a difference in tone, in attitude, in outlook, and in demeanor that flows from the unique flavor of Los Angeles life—from just "how *peculiar* a place Los Angeles is," to repeat Peter Schjeldahl's poignant words, and "what a radical sense of the human it breeds" (1981, 25).

It should be noted that growth and convergence have not empowered commercial art galleries on either coast. On the contrary, the hegemony of the art gallery—art's lifeblood since the debut of modernism—is fading. Stable and exclusive relationships between artists and their representatives are morphing into all kinds of flexible arrangements. "Despite the renewed activity, what characterizes the present moment is a sense of frustration with the gallery itself" (Kino 1996). Traditional artist-gallery relationships are counterproductive in a global art world because complexity demands freedom. If the last century gave artists permission to "paint what they think best and then look around for a buyer" (Baxandall 1972, 3), usually with the help of a dealer, our own time is testing the parameters of the gallery system. Many successful painters and sculptors now work with multiple dealers or as free agents. In addition, the limited capital and time a dealer can devote to his artists sets a margin on how large any single gallery can grow; boosting the number of artists is not usually an option. The result has been an exponential increase in the number of galleries, a proliferation of sociological microorganisms inside an ever more crowded and ever less transparent art world. No one knows how long such a system can sustain a meaningful discourse about art.

The largest galleries are continuing to rationalize and globalize their operations. New York's giant galleries certainly have no precedent in art dealing. Larry Gagosian has built up an empire that allows him to tour artists around the world. In the fall of 2000 he was exhibiting Cy Twombly on Madison Avenue, Damien Hirst in his museum-size outpost in Chelsea, Philip Taaffe in Beverly Hills, and Dexter Dalwood in London. In the same year, the PaceWildenstein conglomerate had two galleries in New York and one in Los Angeles and was planning to add satellites in Europe and Asia. It is hard to miss the analogy between these galleries and the Guggenheim Museum's network of global affiliates. They follow a similar strategy of building international brands that maximize interest, exposure, and market demand for visual art.

Such powerhouses will dominate in the future. They will offer works from all across the art-historical spectrum and provide a gamut of services to artists and clients. Only such behemoths can manage the reputations of the major art stars, commission expensive works of public art, or deflect the hostile forays of the auction houses onto contemporary art turf. Midsize galleries will have to equip themselves to do business in an increasingly professional, globalized art marketplace, where artists and collectors will expect more and better services. At the bottom of the food chain, upstart galleries and nonprofit spaces will still be there to ferret out new talent. However, they will be destined to lose their best artists to the more prominent dealers, because artists' needs evolve and those of galleries usually don't. Artists who are upwardly mobile in their careers almost always part company with their early galleries. If the artist is up, his dealer is out—that's as close as the art world gets to a sociological law.

Much has been made of the Internet as a substitute venue for art discourse, but it will be a long time before it can truly rival the rich interactions of a dense urban center like Los Angeles or New York. Globalization, if anything, has enhanced the allure of big cities. Obituaries about New York's waning dominance have appeared in the media for twenty years. But New York's power has been reinforced precisely because the art world is becoming more international and, therefore, more reliant on hub cities where globetrotting artists, dealers, and collectors can intercept each other. The same trends are putting Los Angeles on the map of indispensable cities. We are witnessing today the emergence of a cosmopolitan network of artists and experts who properly belong neither here nor there. If they belong anywhere, it would be in New York, a place that transcends the limitations of all other cities, or in Los Angeles, a megalopolis that embodies the very idea of the "posturban," placeless future.

CHAPTER FIFTEEN

"Hollywood Is a State of Mind"

New York Film Culture and the Lure of Los Angeles from 1930 to the Present

Saverio Giovacchini

The progressive lawyer and activist Carey McWilliams famously termed California "an island on the land," separated from the rest of the continent by a set of geographical, historical, and cultural circumstances. Within California, Hollywood appeared to the Denver born McWilliams even more detached from the United States than the rest of the state. Because of its connection to the movies, McWilliams wrote, Hollywood "exists only as a state of mind, not as a geographical entity" (McWilliams [1946] 1983, 330). Indeed, our first encounter with Hollywood rarely occurs at the physical level. Rather, we become acquainted with Hollywood through the legends about Hollywood. Leo Rosten, the author of a famous 1930s portrait of the Hollywood community, noted that next to the real, physical Hollywood was the legendary Hollywood created by the fan magazines. This legendary Hollywood ignored the reality of studio politics, union strikes, and aging stars and depicted instead "a sort of Venice without canals, full of glittering conveyances, dazzling maidens, and men like gods" (Rosten 1941, 3).

This popular version of the Hollywood legend is complemented by another legendary discourse about the film community that relates Hollywood to the intellectual landscape of the nation and to its cultural hierarchies. This second Hollywood legend is different from the one created by the "fan-zines" and yet is just as fictive. While fan magazines rose-tinted Hollywood into a "Venice without canals," American literati have crafted a different image of Hollywood marked by desperation and loneliness. Often using or implying an invidious comparison between Los Angeles and New York, this discourse sees Hollywood as the land of what Dwight Macdonald defined as "mass-cult," the intellectual sell-out, and the "low culture" (Macdonald [1960] 1983; Gorman 1996, 137–85; Giovacchini 1998, 437–43). Within this legend, Hollywood and artistic endeavors are as antithetical as air-headed Los Angeles is to the intellectual capital of the nation, New York.

The starting point of this essay is that the bipolarism and the dichotomy between Hollywood cinema and intellectual endeavors and between Los Angeles and New York cultures do not speak to the reality of the Los Angeles film community nor do they define with any precision the relation between American mainstream cinema and avant-garde. This discourse about Hollywood is, in a sense, a "state of mind"—the mind of a largely New York–based American intelligentsia that manufactured this cultural image of the movie citadel as the anti-intellectual "sausage factory." Furthermore, it is important to note that this anti-Hollywood state of mind became dominant only after World War II when the New York intellectuals defined mass culture in general, and Los Angeles in specific, as the opposite of art, modernism, and New York City. In the 1930s the boundaries were not staked as clearly, and New York film culture was much more open to Hollywood and to the hybridization of mass culture and modernism (fig. 15.1). In turn, the generation of New York filmmakers that emerged from the "cineclubs" and the film schools at the end of the sixties also felt the lure of Hollywood. The Hollywood that attracted them, however, was again ageographical and immaterial. It was the "movie-made" Hollywood constituted by the classical cinema of the studio era and had nothing to do with Los Angeles or southern California that these filmmakers often continued to define using the same language and images of the anti-Hollywood consensus of the 1950s.

A HYBRIDIZED CINEMA: NEW YORK–HOLLYWOOD, 1930–45

In the New Deal era, the attitude of many New York modernist intellectuals toward Hollywood was certainly ambiguous and largely unscathed by what Andreas Huyssen has called the contemporary "anxiety of contamination" between "high and low," mass culture and modernism (1986). In the early thirties, New York avant-garde magazine *New Theater* articulated the rather porous relation between Hollywood and New York and avant-garde and mass culture (fig. 15.2). Though the escapism of many Hollywood films constituted a problem for many New York intellectuals, *New Theater* critic Robert Gessner argued that "all revolutionary artists . . . must, in order to be at this time effectively

Figure 15.1. *Liberty* (1929). Shooting Los Angeles as if it were a city—actually, as if it were New York! Stan Laurel and Oliver Hardy in Leo McCarey's *Liberty*. Photo courtesy of Photofest.

heard, consider seriously the question of working through Hollywood" (1934).

On other occasions, Robert Gessner did voice some despair about the possibilities for a progressive artist to achieve anything in Hollywood. In the June 1935 issue of *New Theater,* for instance, he argued that progressive filmmakers should fashion their own movies outside of the Hollywood studios (Gessner 1935). But in that same issue, Louis Norden also extolled John Ford's *The Informer* (1935), a story of revolution and betrayal in British-occupied Ireland. The film, Norden concluded, was "a really great picture," marked by a "realistic" style embodied in the characters and the photography through which Ford has been able to give "the feeling of depth to a scene" (1935).

If opinions about Hollywood cinema varied over time among intellectually and politically progressive New York circles, what did not

Figure 15.2. The Garden of Allah. New Yorkers once congregated around the famous swimming pool of the Garden of Allah in West Los Angeles. "What a gathering of literati it was," wrote Budd Schulberg in *Writers in America.* "It was almost as if the Algonquin Round Table had moved cross country into the garden and under the palm trees" (1983, 17). Photo courtesy of Photofest.

change was these circles' conviction that art could arise in Hollywood out of the hybridization of mass culture and modernism. In this context, working in the Hollywood film industry could mean not so much the abandonment of modernism as the way to bring modernist art and progressive politics to the masses or, to use Stanley Aronowitz's words, to achieve that "hibridity of left wing art" that characterizes so much of the cultural production of the thirties (1993, 145–46).

To battle the poisonous escapism of Hollywood films, progressive Hollywood pioneers should inject the antidote in the form of American reality, inserted in the themes, in the characters, and in the techniques employed by the Hollywood film. A good Hollywood film could, in fact, promote social engagement in its audience by tackling the issues of the day and proposing progressive solutions. In the first issue of another short-lived but quite influential New York magazine *Films,* Philip Sterling noted that this was possible and that it had actually been done since the beginning of Hollywood cinema. "We can assume," he wrote "that, from the invention of the Kinetoscope to the last Academy dinner, there has also existed a tradition of protest, of the urge of social change. Not only can this assumption be made; it can be documented and designated as the democratic tradition on the screen." In its first forty years, Hollywood had produced not only "a fond, uncritical defense of the status quo" but also a "democratic tradition" that progressive filmmakers would expand. As examples of this tradition, Sterling (1940, 7) pointed to D. W. Griffith's *A Corner in Wheat* (1909), Ernst Lubitsch's *Broken Lullaby* (1932), and William Wellman's *Wild Boys of the Road* (1933).

In what was a marked change from the previous decade, throughout the thirties New York progressive film intellectuals often looked with much interest to the Hollywood narrative style. In the twenties, American intellectuals' veneration for German expressionist imports had prompted the American Legion to boycott *Das Kabinett des Doktor Caligari* in New York City as well as in Los Angeles (Petrie 1985; Elsaesser 2000, 363). In 1924, comedian Will Rogers threatened to "put on a beard and say it was made in Germany" if his latest film, *The Ropin' Fool,* failed at the box office. Then, he told New York critics, "you'll call it art" (Jacobs 1939, 307). By the beginning of the 1930s, according to cultural historian Richard Pells, "the search for personal freedom and an abstract international culture was giving way to a spirit of commitment and a willingness to write about 'America'" (Pells [1974] 1984, 158). Ten years after Rogers's caustic remarks about New York film critics, some of them had become more interested in the Hollywood product, and *New Republic*'s critic Otis Ferguson argued that one of Warner's films, *Black Fury* (1935), for all its problems and the obvious, studio-imposed softening of the film's anticapitalist message, was "nearer to our life" than the German-made, Wilhelm Pabst–directed, *Kameradschaft* (1931) because its characters "were so cleverly worked into a pattern of cause and result, environment and hopes, that they were neither block symbols nor foreigners, but people you knew and hoped the best of" (1940).

Beyond the flaws of the Hollywood narrative and mode of film production, what many New York modernists saw in Hollywood was the possibility of overcoming the "shrinkage and fragmentation" that increasingly characterized American culture. For these New Yorkers, Hollywood offered options not available in the Greenwich Village theaters or in the literary journals of Manhattan. The major studios and national theater chains promised the opportunity to re-create a national audience for modernist and progressive art beyond the boundaries of cultural classes and rigidly separated spheres of filmmaking (Bender 1987, 249–55). That American art needed reform was quite clear to these artists and intellectuals. At the end of the 1920s, some of modernism's most successful practitioners (T. S. Eliot, Ezra Pound) had tied their work to elitism and, often, to reactionary politics. More important, in the late twenties the modernist project seemed floundering on an increasingly fragmented audience and what Thomas Bender calls the "diffusion of literary life into particular locales and coteries" (Bender 1987, 251). Their engagement of Hollywood cinema promised to yield the reconstruction of a modern, universal language able to reactivate the dialogue between artists, democracy, and audience.

As the thirties went on, the threat and reality of fascist dictatorships engulfing most of Europe lent an increased urgency to Americans' interest in Hollywood. Hollywood stood for the possibility to construct an antifascist modernism that could move the masses into the struggle against dictators. It is in this intellectual context that the migration of many stage and screen New York vanguardists ought to be cast as opposed to the popular explanation that usually relies exclusively on the lures of technology and big salaries. "I don't think it is realized," Howard Koch reminisced in the late seventies, "that perhaps what Greenwich Village was in the late teens . . . that same vitality was transferred in this period, the New Deal period, to Hollywood" (Koch 1974, 28).

In perceiving these Hollywood New Yorkers as intellectual mercenaries, the dominant interpretation follows the standard dichotomy between high and low brow, culture and mass culture, modernism and Hollywood. Going Hollywood, according to this narrative is the equivalent of selling out, and cultural critic James Morrison correctly notes that "the exclusion of film from the domain of cultural modernism is an inevitable consequence of the theoretical bifurcation between modernism and mass culture as cultural forms" (Morrison 1998, 17–18). Yet judging from the behavior of many of these writers during the McCarthyist blacklist of the late forties and early fifties, quite a few of them were ready to abandon Hollywood when the political or intellectual situation made impossible the pursuit of their political and aesthetic goals. Referring to the American radicals who went Hollywood in the thirties, Abraham Polonsky argues that "you can't possibly explain the Hollywood communists away by saying 'they came to Hollywood for the money.' . . . If they had come only for the money and glamour, a lot of them would have become stool pigeons—to hold their jobs, to continue making money and doing pictures. But only a small percentage of them [did so]" (Buhle and McGilligan 1997, 492).

By the end of the thirties the effects of this migration were visible both in Hollywood and in a few Hollywood films. Far from considering themselves "New York writers" stranded in Hollywood, some of the new Hollywoodians were developing professional identities that demonstrated no shame for their Hollywood activities. In his 1932 play *Bi-*

ography, New York writer, turned Hollywood screenwriter, S. N. Behrman vented the standard anti-Hollywood view.[1] Yet, in 1934, Behrman published an article in the *New Yorker* in which he turned the tables on the New Yorkers and argued that the down-with-Hollywood spirit (as embodied in Moss Hart and Stanley Kaufman's play *Once in a Life Time*) was not necessarily less commercial than Hollywood: "The satirizing of Hollywood is now firmly entrenched as one of the most thriving branches of the national literary industry." Nor was it inherently better. Hart's Hollywood work (*As Thousands Cheer*) was both "subtler and truer" than his New York work. Hollywood was still a "mob art," and New York had the upper hand, but things could change. "Charlie Chaplin was brought to world fame by Hollywood. . . . There is no reason [why] someone should not come along who might use this extraordinary medium with Shakespearean fullness."

Behrman was not alone. New York–born Columbia graduate and future blacklistee Sidney Buchman had arrived in Hollywood in 1932 and was a member of the Screen Writers' Guild from its inception. As the thirties went on, his regard for Hollywood grew. "I'm one of the few guys who think Hollywood is a training school for writers," he told the *Post,* "but that's the way it worked out for me. . . . The discipline has its value" (*New York Post,* November 27, 1939). Once a writer moved to Hollywood, the world might forget that she or he was an author, concluded Norman Reilly Raine, the creator of *Tugboat Annie* for the *Saturday Evening Post,* who had gone to Hollywood in 1933 and was by 1937 a stalwart supporter of the Screen Writers' Guild. Still, Hollywood could be regenerating. After awhile the writer "begins to feel more at home, and, curiously enough, recaptures some of that fine energy and ambition to make the grade that characterized his early efforts in fiction. It's like life backward" (*New York World Telegram,* October 23, 1937). Even the quintessential New York wit, Dorothy Parker, somewhat agreed. "I have been writing for motion pictures for two years," Parker wrote in 1936, "[and] I do not feel that I am participating in a soft racket." Screenwriting was hard work, certainly well paid, but money and good writing were not mutually exclusive. "I can look my God and my producer—whom I do not, as do many, confuse with each other—in the face and say that I have earned every cent of it."

These defenses of Hollywood also arose from the actual success of some of the efforts of the New York intellectuals in Hollywood. By the end of 1934, recently arrived urban writers had founded the Screen Writers' Guild, the presidents of which, from 1933 to 1940, with the partial exception of Ralph Block, had all come from the New York scene.[2] New Yorkers were also affecting the cultural institutions of Hollywood and Los Angeles. The Los Angeles Theater Alliance was founded in 1939 by a coalition of New Yorkers who, according to Henry Myers, "would like to put on a show, because they missed it" (Myers 1959, 110; Buhle and McGilligan 1997, 240–41). Their first production, *Meet the People,* premiering Christmas day 1939, was successful enough to invert the traditional itinerary of American theater. *Meet the People* was the first West Coast production profitable enough to travel to Broadway from Los Angeles rather than vice versa. Developed from an idea by former Broadway talents Henry Myers, Edward Eliscu, and Jay Gorney, *Meet the People* was a celebration of the New Hollywood and its hybridized, politicized modernism. The show did not obscure the difficulties within the Hollywood studios, but it did stress the progress of the community. It made fun of the Hollywood producers (in the skit "How Movies Are Made" by Milt Gross), but opened with a piece in which Hollywood—represented as the "Sleeping Beauty"—is awakened by progressive artists and finally comes in touch with the real people ("The Legend of the Sleeping Beauty" by New Yorkers Ben and Sol Barzman).

Hollywood seemed to emerge from its being a "state of mind" to acquire a historical and political body. "The world no longer eyes Hollywood as the home of the movies and Symphonies Under the Stars," read an ad for *Meet the People.* "On the one hand, it sees the greatest concentration of literary and artistic talent, and on the other, progressive, spirited people bending their energy toward defeating bigotry and upholding the best in American tradition. Now these two groups join hands in an enterprise inevitably determined by their outlook and experience—a democratic theater. . . . A democratic theater is a community function. To permit it to be usurped for private profit and self exploitation is to acquiesce to a commercial dictatorship." [3]

According to Carey McWilliams, Hollywood discovered its physical and geographical body as the community began to invest heavily in politics. Indeed the writer dates "the beginning of a conscious rapprochement between Hollywood and Los Angeles" from the founding of the Hollywood Anti-Nazi League (HANL) in 1936 (McWilliams [1946] 1983, 348). And New Yorkers—along with European refugee filmmakers—dominated the HANL chaired by New York wit Donald Ogden Stewart. In tune with the hybridizationism of the New Yorkers, the goal of the league was to use Hollywood to bring the antifascist message to the world. When in April 1939, thanks to the concerted efforts of the league, Warner released the first openly anti-Nazi film produced by a major studio, *Confessions of a Nazi Spy* (1939), *New Masses* noted how this film showed the official arrival of New York avant-garde in Hollywood: "The fruitful experiments of men like Joris Ivens and Herbert

Kline, and neglected bands like Frontier Films have at last reached Hollywood" (Dugan 1939). Symptomatically, in 1955 Cold War liberal critic Robert Warshow argued that *Confessions of a Nazi Spy* was as much an epitome of the intellectual culture of the thirties (and of what was wrong with it) as the novel *The Grapes of Wrath* and the song "Ballad for Americans" (Warshow [1962] 1975, 34).

Now largely forgotten, in 1939 *Confessions* made a profound impression on American intellectuals. The absence of initial screen credits, the interspersion of newsreel in the film, the use of real exteriors, and the collective flair of the acting ("a group's job" commented *Variety*, noting the limited screen time of the star of the film, Edward J. Robinson) pointed to the productive miscegenation of the Hollywood genre film (the spy melodrama) with the thirties avant-gardes—especially the New York tradition of radical theater and the New Dealish practice of the Living Newspapers with their emphasis on topicality and collective, rather than individual, performances (*Variety*, May 3, 1939, 16). Referring to *Confessions* and to other Hollywood films, in 1940, the progressive film critic of the *New York Times*, Bosley Crowther, noted that in the previous year Hollywood had shown more and more signs of the "documentary influence," and Manfred George, the editor of the New York–based refugee magazine *Aufbau*, reviewing *Confessions* in 1939, remarked that "Hollywood is now a more important center of the intellectual struggle against the dictatorships" (my translation from the German). Through politics and New Yorkers, Hollywood seemed to have found its body.

A DISREPUTABLE OCCUPATION: NEW YORK–HOLLYWOOD, 1948–60

The late thirties had seen an intellectual rebirth of the Hollywood community but doubts about the possibility of remaking Hollywood into an instrument of a democratic form of modernism already emerged during World War Two.[4] While paraded by many as an example of politically and intellectually engaged filmmaking, *Confessions* had remained a rather isolated case, even though the government's Office of War Information (OWI)—created in June 1942 and staffed with many progressive intellectuals from New York and from the film industry—had tried to promote the production of a socially responsible Hollywood cinema (U.S. Office of War Information 1942; War Activities Committee 1945; Black and Koppes 1987). Because of the timidity of the upper echelons of OWI and the profit-driven choices of the Hollywood producers, however, the hybridization of Hollywood films with progressive politics and art had been only moderately successful, and Hollywood cinema had failed to tackle the political and social problems of the nation—in particular, its racist social order.

By the end of the war, some New York intellectuals had changed their minds about the possibility of turning Hollywood cinema into an instrument for democracy. In 1937, *New Masses* editor Mike Gold had celebrated the "proletarian pioneers" who had chosen to go to Hollywood and make mass movies with a progressive message (Gold 1937). By 1946, however, Gold was unable to see any hope in the "luxury and phony atmosphere of Hollywood" (Gold 1946). For a few others, including the intellectuals who gathered around the *Partisan Review* in the second half of the thirties, Hollywood had never constituted a serious prospect for the action of the engaged intellectual. When in 1939 Clement Greenberg stressed the superiority of avant-garde to the kitsch-infected mass art, there was little doubt about the category into which Hollywood film culture would fall (1961, 3–21). Rapidly this position became the dominant one among American intelligentsia. Indeed by the early fifties, even the most movie-conscious of the New York intellectuals, Robert Warshow, firmly emphasized the cultural fence that separated high art and films and, not so implicitly, Hollywood from New York. In his 1954 application for a Guggenheim fellowship (now the preface to his *Immediate Experience*) Warshow wrote: "I have had enough serious interest in the product of the 'higher arts' to be very sharply aware that the impulse which leads me to a Humphrey Bogart movie has little in common with the impulse which leads me to the novels of Henry James or the poetry of T. S. Eliot" (Warshow [1962] 1975, 27).[5]

That the years from 1946 to 1960 witnessed a reconfiguration of the intellectuals' position toward American mass-marketed production is certain. In a 1959 interview, Edward Dmytryk recounted how Hollywood was first "painted as a special community of geniuses . . . then in the last ten years they have gone to the opposite extreme" (32). The Communist Party was among the first to change its mind about Hollywood and take its distance from the film community. After looking with some benevolence to Hollywood and its product, in the aftermath of the abandonment of Earl Browder's Popular Front and his plan to create the American Communist Political Association in April 1945, the cultural cadres of the party changed their minds about Hollywood. In the days and months following the famous controversy over Albert Maltz's essay "What Shall We Ask of Writers?" in *New Masses*, the main cultural organizer of the party, Mike Gold, wondered whether Maltz had "let the luxury and phony atmosphere of Hollywood at last poison him" (Gold 1946; Maltz 1946; Aaron 1961, 386–39). In the mid-thirties, the New York playwright John Howard Lawson had gone to Hollywood, where he had become a successful screenwriter as well as the most respected doctrinaire among the Hollywood Communists. In his 1949 *Theory and Techniques of Playwriting and Screenwriting,* Lawson still showed that he had some hope in Hollywood's potential. In 1953, however, when he reedited and reprinted his book, he was convinced by party ideologue Victor J. Jerome (1950) to change his argument and state that the motion picture "is neither creative nor in the hands of the artist. It is destructive and in the hands of the monopolists" (Lawson, 1953, 21).

By 1947 the party had been joined by almost the entire American intelligentsia, with the "vital center" of Arthur Schlesinger, Jr., in the forefront. Eager to differentiate themselves from the McCarthyists, Cold War liberals denounced the "Hollywood Ten" not only as Stalinists but as producers of bad culture as well (Andersen 1985, 176–89). For example, the March–April 1953 issue of the *Partisan Review* contained an essay by Arthur Schlesinger, Jr., in which he expressed his dislike both for Joseph McCarthy and for the Communists and spurred the "highbrow" to participate in American politics as a counterforce against both Communism and reactionary anti-intellectualism (Schlesinger 1949, 125–26; 1953). The same issue featured an essay by Harvey Swados lambasting popular taste in general and "social significance" movies specifically. As an expression of popular taste, social significance movies "reinforc[ed] conservative moral concepts and strengthen[ed] a traditional distrust and envy of the intellectuals and dissidents" (Swados 1953).

Following Greenberg, American intellectuals Lionel Trilling, and Dwight Macdonald declared the death of Hollywood. Some of them found inspiration in the work done on the "culture industry" by the Frankfurt School, and a few delved into Max Horkheimer and Theodor W. Adorno's *The Dialectic of the Enlightenment* published in 1947 in Amsterdam.[6] For Horkheimer and Adorno (1947), Hollywood was an integral part of the "culture industry," and, as such, it was instrumental in the elimination of critical and independent thinking from modern capitalist society (Riesman 1950, 239; Mills 1956; Macdonald [1960] 1983). In 1991, historian Steven J. Ross noted how the legacy of the Frankfurt School was still dictating the terms of the debates about mass culture in disparate fields such as sociology, communication studies, and history (1991, 334–35).

New York intellectuals abandoned their optimism about American popular culture, constructing a sort of "sanitary cordon" around the citadel of cinema. Those who compromised and remained in Hollywood experienced the ill-disguised contempt of American intellectuals. In 1953, the Jewish, liberal magazine *Commentary* nonchalantly summed up the new interpretation: "The Jews who journeyed West to make movies," wrote Morris Freedman, "might have remained in New York to make dresses" (Freedman 1953, 392). As they came to internalize this attitude, those Hollywoodians who had not completely relinquished their identity as artist or intellectuals developed a personal schizophrenia that put their ideals at odds with their source of income. Ironically, they spun Hollywood-made, anti-Hollywood tales like *Sunset Boulevard* (1950; written and produced by former *New Yorker* staff writer Charles Brackett along with European refugee Billy Wilder). *Sunset Boulevard* told the tale of a cruel Hollywood system that ate its own children once age had made them useless for the camera. Hollywood and its ruthless studio system were also the target of *The Bad and the Beautiful* (1952; directed by former Broadway star Vincente Minnelli and written by Charles Schnee) and, especially, of *The Big Knife* (1955), written by former Hollywoodian Clifford Odets. Odets had come back to New York in 1948 and declared to the *New York Times* that he had first "found much of interest" in Hollywood when he had settled there in the thirties and forties but had lately become convinced that the film industry was a "celluloid dragon scorching to death every human fact in his path." In contrast to the public dimension and accessibility of Hollywood films, playwrights now exalted a privatized dimension of art and a limited audience composed of "a few, serious, responsible friends" that "find more enjoyment in the personally felt and written play than in Miss Grable's legs" (Odets 1948).

The growing schism between Hollywood and "serious filmmaking" fueled interest for a New York–based avant-garde while it subtracted intellectual energies from the Hollywood community. By 1947, even the *Hollywood Quarterly* began to take into account alternatives to Hollywood. Reviewing the career of Josef von Sternberg, avant-garde filmmaker Curtis Harrington appreciated the reasons for the director's move from Hollywood to New York and deemed his approach to cinema "of unparalleled historical importance" (Harrington 1947–48, 405). By 1947, Lewis Jacobs, the keen, New York–based critic of Hollywood cinema and the author of one of the first scholarly histories of Hollywood cinema, *The Rise of American Film* (1939), was himself writing an essay on "experimental cinema" (Jacobs 1947–48, 111–24, 278–93).

With the centripetal power of Hollywood on the wane, avant-garde film was coming back in full force in New York. In October 1947, Amos

Vogel, a Viennese-born refugee, leased the Provincetown Theater in the Greenwich Village for the first program of Cinema 16, an enterprise dedicated to noncommercial filmmaking (MacDonald 1997, 8). In *Theater Arts,* German refugee and film theorist Siegfried Kracauer argued that "there seems to be a new avant-garde movement in the making. In all likelihood, it owes something to the widespread discontent with the current Hollywood product." New York, Kracauer continued, was again an avant-garde center, well represented by the new films by Alexander Hammid, Maya Deren, and Hans Richter (1948).

Vogel indeed advocated a rigid demarcation of the cinematic spheres, opposing avant-garde to the "empty tinsel of Hollywood" (MacDonald 1997, 70). His polemical target was less the blatantly commercial Hollywood cinema, than the good Hollywood cinema. He extolled the films of Maya Deren's insofar as they showed "something there, that to me was far more important than the so-called best Hollywood films" (MacDonald 1997, 9). A refugee and a progressive antifascist, Vogel separated the politics of a film from its artistic or cultural value. Cinema 16, for instance, programmed the Nazi film *The Eternal Jew* (1940) for its historical interest in the face of the protests of New York leftists and refugees (MacDonald 1997, 61). The polemic with Hollywood was evident in *Dreams That Money Can Buy* (1948) by Hans Richter, a Leftist German refugee who was a favorite of Vogel and his circle (Richter [1976] 1986). Framed in a parody-like, noirish narrative about "Joe" (Jack Bittner), an unemployed veteran who becomes a seller of dreams, *Dreams* "mixes dreams with reality" in its six episodes, each of them designed by a nonrealist artist.[7] The third of these episodes ("Ruth, Roses, and Revolvers"), from an idea by Man Ray, explicitly targeted the Hollywood narrative. At a picture show, spectators are asked to behave exactly as the character on screen, which they sheepishly do. Taking its distance from Hollywood and its mass audience, Richter's film was playing out a crucial aspect of the new avant-garde cinema and rejected mass culture as corrupting.

A few New York intellectuals took a softer stance on Hollywood. On his way to Hollywood ten years after the main wave of migration, *Time*'s film critic James Agee disagreed both with the antirealism of the new avant-garde and with its anti-Hollywood attitude. Agee had been the most critical among the 1930s partisans of Hollywood, yet he saw Richter's and Deren's films as lacking in originality—a simple reiteration of the 1920s elitist modernism. As for Hollywood, it certainly had limits, but the new avant-garde had a clear liability: the "self deceit in the direction of arrogance and artiness—the loss of, and contempt for, audience, which can be just as corrupting as its nominal opposite" (Agee 1946, 269).

What Agee meant was that the hybridization between high and low art and Hollywood that had been the centerpiece of the New York avant-garde of the thirties was still the way to go. While rapidly loosing ground among New York filmmakers and intellectuals, this stance possibly found its last incarnation in *The Quiet One* (1948), a film directed by the *New Theater* and Frontier Film veteran Sidney Meyers for which Agee wrote the commentary. *The Quiet One,* the winner of the Critics' Award at the Venice Film Festival, is the story of Donald, a mentally disturbed child from Harlem who is cured thanks to the care of the Wiltwyck School for Boys. The film is seen by many scholars as one of the models for the New American Cinema of the early sixties. In my opinion, *The Quiet One* seems rather to reflect the permanence of the hybridized ideals of the thirties in the New York film circles of the late forties as it sure-handedly singles out the social causes of Donald's problems and negotiates a middle ground between fiction and documentary, between Hollywood's love for narrative and avant-garde's emphasis on noncommercialism, real-life exteriors, and social significance.

The film's reception confirms this point. *The Quiet One* was praised by the older generation of progressive filmmakers, including the vanguardist New York exhibitor, Arthur Mayer, who showcased it at the Little Carnegie in Manhattan, and old-time progressive *New York Times* film critic Bosley Crowther, who termed it an "excellent little picture . . . pictorially authentic, filmed in actual locales, and played by a 'pick-up' cast of actors, professional and amateurs" (1949).[8] The reception of the film by the new political and aesthetic avant-garde was, however, lukewarm. The newly selected Eastern cadres of the Communist Party disliked it (while the old guard of the California communists liked it) and a "character from the Museum of Modern Art" took exception to the authors' rejection of the "pure" documentary approach and their use of professional actors in the major roles (e.g., the boy is played by a professional child actor, Donald Thompson), a choice the authors defended as warranted to ensure the intelligibility and the efficacy of the film (Gilliard and Levitt 1977, 135).

That *The Quiet One* was still tied to the older tradition becomes clearer if we compare it to the following New York art film to capture the national and international critical attention. The winner of the Best Film Award at the Venice Festival, *Little Fugitive* (1952) was collectively directed by Morris Engel, Ray Ashley, and Ruth Orkin and tells the story of Joey (Richie Andrusco), a little boy who escapes from his Brooklyn neighborhood to the Coney Island amusement park after he comes to believe that he has caused his older brother's death. The film has a happy ending: the older brother, Lennie (Ricky Brewster), has only faked death to get rid of Joey; Lennie finds Joey unharmed on the Coney Island beach in time to take him home and catch the cowboy show on television. But the end does not obscure the main, and more innovative, section of the film that focuses on Joey's aimless wanderings in the amusement park. A veritable film in the film, this central chapter of *Little Fugitive* really anticipates the themes of the new American cinema, with its long, handheld camera shots, often taken from the child's point of view, and its bleak take on American mass society as represented by the Coney Island customers, so absorbed by their obsessive consumerism that they don't notice a small child lost in their midst.

Indeed by the mid-1950s the anti-Hollywood efforts of the New York avant-garde and film intellectuals multiplied. In New York City, Cinema 16 offered its aficionados a weekly dosage of Maya Deren, Stan Brakage, and Alexander Hammid (MacDonald 1997). From 1956 to 1961, together with Maya Deren, Vogel handed out to independent filmmakers the "Creative Cinema Awards." Also in Greenwich Village, Jonas Mekas —a refugee from Lithuania who had arrived in New York in 1949 along with his brother the filmmaker Adolphas—was actively championing "art over commerce," "the responsible filmmaker," and foreign films through the important magazine *Film Culture,* founded in 1955 (Taylor 1999, 85; James 1992). A veritable catholic film lover throughout his career, Mekas was, in the beginning, quite open to Hollywood films, but by 1958 his columns in the *Village Voice* were becoming increasingly critical of Hollywood product. "My next review of a big Hollywood movie," Mekas wrote in August 1959, "will consist of adjectives only, such as bad, horrible, boring, disgusting, stupid, ridiculous, etc., etc., interspersed with few four-letter words. Our old generation of filmmakers is so boringly bad and so outdated that all their current films, all unanimously acclaimed by New York reviewers, could be perfectly described by such a collection of adjectives" (1959).

By 1957, the author of *The Quiet One,* Sidney Meyers, directed (along with Ben Maddow and Joseph Strick) *The Savage Eye* (1957), a film that repudiated the West Coast in a variety of ways (fig. 15.3). The story of Judith McGuire—a middle-aged divorced woman, interpreted by Broadway actress Barbara Baxley—the film rejects linear narrative to present a whirlwind of Los Angeles images (from bingo parlors to the Santa Monica Piers, religious healers, and department stores), framing what the authors perceive as the miserable existence of this single woman.

Figure 15.3. *The Savage Eye* (1957). Los Angeles anomie: Broadway actress Barbara Baxley as Judith McGuire, a lonely woman in the grip of Los Angeles mass culture. Photo courtesy of Photofest.

The filmmakers also make clear that Judith is the victim of mass society, of which Los Angeles is the ultimate production and consumption center. No wonder the film was shot in Los Angeles, gloated the *New Yorker*, taking for granted an implicit difference between New York City and the West Coast metropolis: Los Angeles is "where an old friend is somebody you met a week ago Friday" (McCarten 1960, 108).

It was in this climate that Jonas Mekas announced the birth of a new cinema movement heralded by the independent films of New Yorkers John Cassavetes (*Shadows*, 1959), Morris Engel (*Weddings and Babies*, 1958), Jerome Hill (*The Sand Castle*, 1961), and Alfred Leslie and Robert Frank (*Pull My Daisy*, 1959). All of these films, Mekas wrote, reject hybridization with Hollywood and "mistrust and loathe the official cinema and its thematic and formal stiffness. . . . Hollywood films (and we mean Hollywood all over the world) reach us beautiful and dead" (Mekas 1959). With several other filmmakers, including Peter Bogdanovich, Mekas gathered at 165 West 46 Street in Manhattan on September 28, 1960, to declare the birth of the New American Cinema Group. The Filmmakers' Cooperative (founded in 1962) and the Filmmakers

Cinematheque (founded in 1964) were soon to follow in an attempt to supply the new avant-garde with distribution and exhibition outlets.

TO THE RESCUE: THE IMPORTANCE OF ANDREW SARRIS

By 1955, Hollywood films were hardly popular among New York intellectuals.[9] In the mid-fifties, Andrew Sarris remembers, "there were very few people teaching film in New York. There was Robert Gessner at NYU and not too many others" (Gunning 1992, 62). By 1960, Gessner, a *New Theater* veteran, was complaining that in the United States film criticism was underdeveloped especially in comparison with the French and Italian critics. In the United States, "'movies and scholarship' are words which sound strange when heard in juxtaposition. The two [are] not . . . even accorded the respectable status of a sad but legal *mésalliance*" (Curry 1986, 46). A few years later, Jerzy Toeplitz suggested that the establishment of serious film criticism in the United States was delayed and noted that to be successful American film intellectuals had to "overcome many prejudices and . . . enter by force the University area. So long as this remains undone, . . . film scholarship will be relegated to the very bottom and will not be treated seriously [remaining] . . . an area of operation for amateurs and pseudoscholars" (Toeplitz 1963, 31). In 1966, only sixteen people showed up for the annual meeting of the Society of Cinematology—later the Society of Cinema Studies—founded in 1959 (Curry 1986, 45). Three years earlier Colin Young had noted that "the gap between the professional film industry and the academic film world may be growing. The universities produce critics more enamored of foreign products than of Hollywood" (1963, 31).

Dying at an early age in 1953, James Agee did not have the time to mend the separation between New York's avant-garde and Hollywood. This role was going to be played by a young New York film critic, Andrew Sarris. By refocusing American highbrow film criticism on Hollywood, Sarris indeed reestablished Hollywood films at the center of the New York and national film criticism after the *pars destruens* performed by Cold War film criticism. Until he jumped on the auteurist wagon, Sarris's career had been rather obscure. Before Jonas invited him to collaborate on *Film Culture,* he had not published anything and was being supported by his mother, a small business owner. With a few exceptions, none of the essays Sarris had published in *Film Culture* from 1955 to 1961 had been more substantial than a review of a single film. Nor was his thinking particularly original. In these early efforts, Sarris wrote as an American highbrow critic deriving quite a bit from the sociological film criticism of Siegfried Kracauer and John Grierson (Sarris 1970, 1978, 51; Giovacchini 2001a). In one of his few substantial essays from this period, Sarris showed an early awareness of the French debates about auteurism and its cult of a selected group of film directors, along with his trademark passion for hierarchies and ranking and for collapsing film history into bio-filmographies. In his 1955 essay "The Trouble with Hitchcock," Sarris castigated the British director for being too enamored of "touches and highlights," far from what the critic calls the "the top rank of directors" (Carol Reed, David Lean, George Stevens, John Huston, Carl Dreyer, Roberto Rossellini, and Jean Renoir), and even "the second layer" of filmmakers (William Wyler, Elia Kazan, Billy Wilder, and Claude Autant-Lara [Sarris 1955, 31]).

In his 1961 article "The Director's Game," Sarris definitively switched to auteurism. In this essay, the critic asked whether it is "possible to predict in any degree which of these [films, by all the directors listed in *Variety* of January 18, 1961] will ultimately materialize as the worthiest artistically." His answer was that it was indeed possible to make such a prediction, if one were to listen to the suggestions coming from the Parisian film circles and, therefore, if "one stipulates that the director is king and the past offers [some] guide to the future" (Sarris 1961, 68–81).

Two years later, *Film Culture* published Sarris's most important article, later developed into the introductory chapter to his 1968 book *The American Cinema:* "Notes on the Auteur Theory in 1962" (Sarris 1973, 38–52). The magazine followed suit and built on Sarris's take devoting the entire following issue to "the American directors" (Mekas 1963). For the volume, Sarris wrote "The American Cinema," a very long essay that collapsed Hollywood cinema onto its directors who were then ranked into five classes: "Pantheon Directors," "Second Line," "Third Line," "Esoterica," and "Beyond the Fringe." By the time he wrote this essay, Sarris had become the official American translator of André Bazin and the *politique des auteurs.* By then, Hitchcock—celebrated by the *Cahiers du Cinéma*—was no longer a wannabe but a full member of the pantheon. Demoted from the "top rank," instead, was a former favorite, John Huston.

In the following thirty years, Sarris tightly fastened his writings to the *politique des auteurs.* In 1973 he dedicated his volume of collected essays, *The Primal Screen,* "to all the auteurists in creation" (7). *You Ain't Heard Nothing Yet,* his latest book, continues André Bazin's project of establishing the importance of sound in film, and Bazin is the film theorist most frequently cited in that text: his name is invoked eleven times in the body of the text—not a surprise in a book written by "a registered New York based auteurist." The very organization of the volume is framed by the centrality of the idea of the director/auteur, with the "Director" section—once again divided into bio-filmographies of the Hollywood worthies—accounting for three-fourths of the book's pages (Sarris 1998).

Sarris's loyalty to auteurism did not necessarily make for theoretically sound work, and Greg Taylor has recently called the critic's theories "embarrassingly weak." Devoid of Bazin's aesthetic and moral accents, Sarris's obsession with the personal "touch" of the individual director was simply "a model of vanguard provocation masquerading as aesthetic theory" (Taylor 1999, 88). The logical loopholes of Sarris's theory were easily exploited by his fellow critics. Manny Farber, the vanguard critic of the *Nation* and the *New Republic,* noted that Sarris was unable to explain the collective, and at times centrifugal, community that originated a film. "The massive attempt in the 1960s to bring some order and shape into film history—creating a Louvre of great films and detailing the one genius responsible for each film," Farber pointedly wrote in 1966, "is doomed to failure because of the subversive nature of the medium: the flash bomb vitality that one scene, actor, or technician injects across the grain of a film" ([1966] 1971, 184–87.) For Pauline Kael, Sarris's focus on personality did not work. Why should personality be a criterion to establish the worth of a director? "The smell of a skunk," she famously wrote in 1963, "is more distinguishable than the perfume of a rose; does this make it better?" (Kael 1965, 292–319).

At the same time, it would be a mistake to repudiate the importance of Sarris's work solely on the basis of its obvious theoretical fallacies. A closer look at Sarris's work reveals that, in translating Bazin, Sarris was refashioning the theories of the French critic to jumpstart an American intellectual debate about Hollywood after it was abruptly stopped because of the reconfiguration of the 1950s. Sarris's criticism is not an example of the faddism of American culture, although as adopted by some of his followers it may have been made slightly pathetic by the fact that by the 1960s French critics had already taken some distance from the *politique des auteurs,* questioning its theoretical value or abandoning it altogether (Bazin 1957; Comolli et al. 1965). Already in 1963, Sarris uses auteurism not in defense of cinema generally but almost exclusively in defense of Hollywood cinema, ironically constructing a nationalist discourse from a critical intervention meant to open national French culture to a more cosmopolitan approach to cinema. For Bazin, cinema and Hollywood cinema had always remained distinct, and in his rare ventures outside of the terrain of a filmic text, the French critic had remained quite skeptical about American values. Sarris is interested in establishing the supremacy of Hollywood cinema, almost at the risk of compromising his claim about the necessity to focus on individual authors. "The American cinema," he argued in "Notes on the Auteur Theory in 1962," "has been consistently superior to that of the rest of the world from 1915 through 1962" (Sarris 1973, 48).

Sarris's translation of Bazin was eminently fit for the American debate about cinema in the early sixties. His criticism targeted the sociological criticism of the 1930s while overcoming the roadblock that the anti-Hollywood consensus of the 1950s had created in the way of any critical discourse focusing on Hollywood. The critic made clear that he did not want to go back to the criticism of *Films* and argued against the "politically oriented" (read, "Marxist") critics who despised Hollywood for being taken over by "capitalists" (Sarris 1968, 21). At the same time, from the first pages of "Notes on the Auteur Theory," expanded into the introduction to *The American Cinema,* the critic made clear that his intent was to fill the gap opened within American film criticism by the 1950s. "Many alleged authorities on film," he wrote, "disguise their ignorance of [Hollywood] cinema as a form of intellectual superiority" (Sarris 1968, 17) to focus on "foreign," "documentary" or "avant-garde" films. On the contrary, Sarris wanted to reestablish Hollywood cinema as the focus of his work, and *The American Cinema* "pointedly" —and polemically—excluded "the vast realms of documentary, animated, and experimental filmmaking" (Sarris 1968, 16). In May 1976, he concluded belligerently that "avant-garde films are more boring than ever" (Sarris 1978).

Sarris's criticism still emphasized a certain contempt for the Hollywood studios—a dark "backdrop" against which the shine of the individual genius could be better highlighted. But as opposed to the vanguardist film critics of the fifties and early sixties, such as Parker Tyler or Jonas Mekas, who preferred the avant-garde to Hollywood, his work was both accessible to the mainstream and interested in the Hollywood products. The pret-a-porter structure of Sarris's theories and his emphasis on lists and hierarchies proved particularly fruitful in reopening the discourse about American mass-marketed cinema to that growing middle-class audience that had been the (partly uninvited) reader of much 1950s criticism à la Dwight Macdonald or à la Lionel Trilling.

Indeed, Sarris often stressed that his conclusions were "tentative" and almost invited his audience to construct their own auteurist kit by often revising his own lists. In a 1966 essay, the critic informed his readers that he had changed his mind on some of the conclusions he had come to in his 1963 "Notes on the Auteur Theory": "Of my top people, I am higher on Chaplin, Ford, Griffith, Hitchcock, Murnau, Ophuls,

Renoir, Sternberg, Fuller, Keaton, Lang, Lubitsch, Sirk, Losey, lower on Flaherty, Hawks, Stroheim, Welles, Cukor, Ray, Walsh" (Sarris 1966, 22). "Best director" lists were easy to build and to revise, and Sarris's criticism was as liberating as it was simple to imitate and easy to challenge. "Come," Sarris seemed to tell the new generations of filmmakers, intellectuals, and college graduates, "Hollywood is again safe, interesting, and intellectually legit."

HOLLYWOOD WITHOUT HOLLYWOOD

One of the themes of Woody Allen's Academy Award–winning *Annie Hall* (1977) is an invidious intellectual comparison between New York and Los Angeles. The film takes place in New York City, where Alvin Singer (Woody Allen) is a successful stand-up comedian and humorist. In the course of the film, Allen/Singer establishes the essence of New York via a savagely biased comparison with Los Angeles, where Annie Hall (Diane Keaton) has temporarily moved in pursuit of a singing career. New York—gloriously photographed by Gordon Willis—is *the* city experience par excellence: ethnically diverse, culturally alive, architecturally intriguing. Los Angeles is dead-brain-ville. The city is devoid of crime but has no real people. It is crowded with cars, full of obnoxious policemen, and run by health food buffs and "sun-burned Santa Clauses." Compelled to go to Los Angeles to present a television award, Alvin feels out of place. He cannot drive a car and gets in trouble with a cop (fig. 15.4). The "coast," he concludes, is "garbage." Abandoned by Annie, he goes back to his beloved Manhattan. Apparently he was not the only one: *Annie Hall* "was the film that drove me back to New York," wrote *New Yorker*'s Terence Rafferty. When the critic saw it in Santa Cruz, "most of the people in the audience were transplanted New Yorkers and it was like pouring water on people crawling through the desert" (Fox 1996, 97).

The film reflects quite well the conundrum and the contradictions of contemporary New York filmmakers. While it is anti–Los Angeles, *Annie Hall* is not avant-garde, at least in the sense intended by the New American Cinema manifesto of 1960. The winner of the 1977 Academy Award for best film, *Annie Hall* shares less with *Pull My Daisy* than with the Hollywood comedies of Preston Sturges. Allen, in fact, along with the rest of his generation of New York filmmakers—a generation that includes Martin Scorsese, Spike Lee, Brian De Palma, Susan Seidelman, and Peter Bogdanovich, to name a few influential names—is far from rejecting Hollywood narrative, though like his predecessors of the 1930s, he aspires to be considered an artist and an intellectual.

Figure 15.4. *Annie Hall* (1977). The destiny of a New Yorker in Los Angeles: Woody Allen is thrown in jail by the LAPD. Photo courtesy of Photofest.

Indeed, the work of these filmmakers shows the cultural importance of the reorientation engineered by Andrew Sarris. By translating Bazin for the American context, Sarris made the study of Hollywood permissible once again, in turn making possible the rise of the Hollywood-saturated "movie brat" generation of the late sixties and early seventies. "In my first years at film school it really wasn't so terrific if you went around liking Nicholas Ray movies or John Wayne," Martin Scorsese notes reminiscing about his first years at New York University at the beginning of the sixties (Thompson and Christie 1996, 8). By the time he had graduated and begun to teach at the end of the decade, the situation had reversed. "There was a film criticism class in which the teacher would give the students films like *Wild Strawberries* (1957) or *Nights of Cabiria* (1957) and a book to read that complemented it. The students got angry with the teacher and there was a kind of uprising, so we revamped the schedule and said, 'Now look at these American films by Ford and Hawks, they're wonderful!'" (Thompson and Christie 1996, 21).

By the mid-seventies, it was possible to do as Woody Allen had done—to "go Hollywood linguistically" while maintaining a Manhattan address. Better cameras and better film stock made it possible to shoot outside sound stages in the colorful New York streets, and the 1976 reopening of the Paramount studios in Astoria (now Kaufman Astoria Studios) after thirty years of army control (from 1941 to 1971) gave New York filmmakers the opportunity to use Hollywood technologies, along with New York ideas and Broadway talent. Because of the decentralization of studio production structures it was no longer necessary to move to Hollywood. And New York films, New York actors, and especially New York streets, as Richard Koszarsky has recently noted, have dominated American cinema, winning six of the thirteen Academy Awards for best film between 1968 and 1980 (Koszarsky 2000, 1377–95).[10]

Like the first generation of New York filmmakers who had moved to Hollywood in the early thirties, this new generation created a new hybridized cinema that blended a strong attraction for narrative Hollywood films with some of the New York avant-garde vernacular. In this vein, Woody Allen mixed Brechtian in-camera addresses with screwball comedy situations in *Annie Hall.* Martin Scorsese did sinuously mobile, handheld camera work, and in *Mean Streets* (1973) joined the Hollywood genre of the gangster film with the New York exteriors celebrated by the New American Cinema of fifteen years earlier. While they seemed overall uninterested by the structural cinema of the "purest" of the New York vanguardists such as Stan Brakhage and Gregory Markopolous, the movie brats often admired and referred to the cinema of John Cassavetes. And not surprisingly, since Cassavetes ("an unresolved talent not entirely happy with the Establishment or against it," according to the famous judgment by Andrew Sarris) had always attempted to find a middle ground between Hollywood and the New York avant-garde—famously receiving the first Independent Film Award from Jonas Mekas in 1959 for his first version of *Shadows,* then recutting the film according to United Artists suggestions, declaring this version superior to the earlier one, and finally refusing to sign the 1960 New American Cinema manifesto (Sarris 1968, 209).[11]

Unlike for the thirties generation, the lure of Hollywood no longer necessarily prompted physical migration but was instead revealed by concerns for narrative cinema, the fundamental lexicon of classical Hollywood films. Scorsese could, therefore, confess his love for many commercial classical Hollywood filmmakers and yet lament his 1970–71 stay in Hollywood (to film *Boxcar Bertha* [1972], among other reasons) as "a very, very unpleasant time for me because of the adjustment between New York and California" (Scorsese 1998; see also Thompson and Christie 1996, 30–31).

"I think my journey West, so to speak, has really been one that I think of as the pursuit of the Narrative," California-born and Columbia University–educated filmmaker Kathryn Bigelow suggests (Smith 1995,

60). Bigelow started out as an avant-garde artist working with Richard Serra and Vito Acconci, but soon moved on to cinema, debuting with *The Loveless* (1982), a sui generis biker movie that she codirected with Monty Montgomery in 1982. And all her films are vanguardist interrogations of the icons of mass culture: the bikers in *The Loveless,* the vampires in *After Dark* (1989), the surfers in *Point Break* (1991), and finally Los Angeles itself, as the center of the mass culture industry, in the perverse sci-fi of *Strange Days* (1996), which Bigelow terms "the synthesis of all the different tracks I've been exploring, either deliberately or unconsciously, ever since I started making art." In the tradition of 1930s hybrid art, Bigelow's is, in the director's own words, a "frighteningly accessible" work that "can operate on several levels simultaneously . . . able to satisfy a lot of literary and conceptual impulses for yourself as an artist but at the same time, tell a very populist story" (Bigelow 1991).

Again unlike the thirties generation, the new hybridizationists feel the lure of Hollywood less for political than for linguistic reasons. As opposed to their predecessors, they have only a moderate concern for an openly political cinema able to address directly the issues of the day. "It is hard to find a present day topic that doesn't date immediately," said New York film scholar turned director Peter Bogdanovich (Harris 1990, 79). A statement of love for the classical Hollywood cinema of the studio era, Bogdanovich's *The Last Picture Show* (1971) is meant to focus on the end of the studio system at the beginning of the fifties rather than any decline of American society. *The Last Picture Show* is the story of a group of teenagers (interpreted by Jeff Bridges, Cybill Shepherd, and Timothy Bottoms) growing up in Anarene, Texas, in 1951. There is nothing to do in Anarene but make awkward and publicly scrutinized love and go to the movies at the old Royal Theater, run by old Sam (interpreted by Ben Johnson, a famous character actor in John Ford's movies). Bogdanovich uses long sequences from Hollywood classical films (Vincent Minnelli's *Father of the Bride* [1950] and Howard Hawks's *Red River* [1948]) as a counterpoint for the desolate off-screen life of his characters. Between the characters in the theater and those on the screen, there is no doubt about who's accomplishing more. With the possible exception of the movie theater, Anarene seems to have no connection with the outside world. When Duane (Bridges) leaves to fight in Korea nobody in town seems to care. Nor does the director, for whom the real tragedy is the end of the Hollywood studio system epitomized in the film by the closing of the Royal after Sam's death.

For this new generation of filmmakers, objects and words at times lose any reference to history and reality. In his seminal *Pulp Fiction* (1994), Quentin Tarantino liberally uses the word "nigger" and seems unconcerned with its historical genealogy. The Italian Fascist song about the conquest of Ethiopia, "Faccetta nera" (Little black face), would have possibly reminded the members of the thirties generation of Italian soldiers attacking Ethiopian villages. Martin Scorsese had no concerns about such associations in 1973 and used the tune in a deceptively neutral fashion, as source music for *Mean Streets*. Generalizations are, of course, dangerous: Spike Lee's film *Bamboozled* (2000) deals very passionately and provocatively with the problems arising from any separation between signs (words, objects, films themselves) and their historical meaning. Lee's cinema often uses New York, and especially Brooklyn, as the microcosm of national struggles and debates (Giovacchini 1995) yet, by and large, one would be hard-pressed to find a sense of direct political urgency in this post-Sarris generation of filmmakers—at least in terms comparable with their thirties predecessors. Even here the example of Andrew Sarris is important, as the critic himself emptied all political connotations of Bazin's criticism by making the *politique des auteurs* equidistant between the anti-Hollywood aesthetes of the fifties and the politically oriented radicals of the thirties (Hess 1974, 20–22; Gozlan 1968, 52–71). One indeed has the impression that, by carefully eschewing direct political themes and rejecting physical contact with Hollywood while painstakingly exploring all the mythopoetic possibilities of the Hollywood film and of the Hollywood genres, these filmmakers have perhaps returned Hollywood to an imaginary place—a state of film history, if not of mind.

Conclusion

David Halle

NEW YORK AND LOS ANGELES SCHOOLS

The "Los Angeles school" is shorthand for a fascination with the periphery of the traditional urban core and especially with its dynamism. The "New York school" refers to a passionate interest in the central city as a desirable place where all social classes can reside, though not necessarily in the same neighborhoods. One of the tenets of this volume has been that the best aspects of the Los Angeles school perspective can be fruitfully applied to New York and vice-versa, which is why this book has, within the constraints of a single volume, tried to produce a coherent picture of each city and region, especially drawing on the new 2000 census data.

The perspectives associated with each of these schools are clearly appropriate for studying any major metropolitan region, and every other metro region offers fruitful examples of this over the past few decades. But Los Angeles and New York are arguably the sites where these center-periphery perspectives have been applied most energetically and creatively in recent decades, and so it makes sense to label them accordingly and to pay special attention to these two regions, especially since they also contain the nation's two most populous cities.

It might be cautioned, with some justification, that metropolitan regions, because of differences of structure or local culture, vary somewhat in the degree to which the Los Angeles school or the New York school perspective can be plausibly advocated. For example it is not entirely accidental that a series of secession attempts—Hollywood, the port of San Pedro, and the largest serious secession attempt in the history of American cities, the San Fernando Valley—were recently seriously considered in the city of Los Angeles. In a November 2000 ballot, residents of San Fernando Valley (but not Hollywood or the port of San Pedro) did vote, albeit by a tiny majority, to secede. But the measure failed because, by large majorities, the rest of the city of Los Angeles opposed secession of the San Fernando Valley. With about 1.35 million people, an independent San Fernando Valley would be the sixth-largest city in the United States, taking with it about 36 percent of the population of the city of Los Angeles. New York City, too, faced a serious secession movement, that of Staten Island, the possible secession of which was on the 1993 mayoral election ballot. But a central weakness of that movement was major doubt about the economic viability of Staten Island, given that Manhattan had a disproportionate share of the city's productive wealth. By contrast, the economic viability of the San Fernando Valley, though a serious issue, was not as daunting since the city of Los Angeles was already far more economically decentralized than was New York City. In that sense, the fissuring and decentralizing tendencies that the Los Angeles school loves to study are very much local issues, though they resonate through every metropolitan region.

But it is a mistake to lapse into a determinism that holds that the perspectives of the Los Angeles school and the New York school are each appropriate for their respective geographic areas, and it could for example be argued that in some areas of life in New York a touch of the "Los Angeles perspective" may be salutary and a way of redressing the imbalance between Manhattan and the other boroughs. The debate over rebuilding the World Trade Center after the September 11, 2001, attack is illustrative. Much of the rebuilding debate, for almost a year after the attack, was not just Manhattancentric but focused on only that part of Manhattan south of Sixtieth Street. On the one hand were those who wished more or less to rebuild fully what had been the World Trade Center area of downtown and, further, to correct, at least partially, its major flaw: the absence of a direct link to the surface rail system that funnels suburban commuters straight into Penn Station and Grand Central Station. On the other hand were those who wished to direct some development to the current (east) midtown Manhattan central business district and/or to construct a new midtown central business district on the far west side of Manhattan, from about Twentieth Street to Fiftieth Street. (Until September 11, 2001, downtown Manhattan was the largest central business district in the United States, followed by Chicago and then the current midtown Manhattan, but it had been losing ground for decades to those and other central business districts.)

However, beyond these Manhattancentric plans, radical proposals to distribute growth more evenly through the city slowly began to surface.

These proposals to "disaggregate growth" involved bolstering other center business districts within New York City, including Harlem, Flushing and Jamaica in Queens County, Sunnyside in Brooklyn, a section of the Bronx around Yankee Stadium, and the Saint George section of Staten Island. Indeed, the idea that major cities should recognize and encourage "multiple downtowns" is now being seriously debated (e.g., Sorkin 2002; Taylor 2002). This reflects both traditional economic pressures (for more space, lower rents, easier auto access) and the current, terrorist attack–related fear of being overconcentrated in one highly visible location, itself a revival of the Cold War era fear of nuclear attack on major cities, a fear that helped drive the suburbanization of that time.[1]

These proposals for multiple downtowns suggest a certain natural convergence here between the New York and Los Angeles school perspectives. The limits of this convergence are also underscored by the fact that, in New York City, the "multiple downtowns" proposals do not typically envisage going beyond the city borders—to do so tends to be seen as an unfortunate drain on the vitality of the city. Still, further net employment disaggregation beyond the borders of New York City seems likely if not inevitable. For example, in March 2002, Morgan Stanley, the largest securities company in Manhattan, spent $42 million to buy a former Texaco headquarters in Westchester County as a second locus for its operations, a move driven by a combination of long-standing economic reasons and new security concerns.

Likewise, the debates in the arts sphere over the location of Disney Hall in Los Angeles and the implications of the temporary movement of the Museum of Modern Art from Manhattan to Queens illustrate both the propensity for Los Angeles type and New York type approaches to find fertile ground in their respective regions and the inadvisability of lapsing into a determinism here. On the one hand, criticism of the decision to locate Disney Hall (the new home of the Los Angeles Philharmonic Orchestra) in downtown Los Angeles resonates in the reality of the city of Los Angeles. The view that a stellar cultural institution such as Disney Hall should be located outside the urban core is not implausible there, given such precedents as the long-established Norton Simon Museum in Pasadena or the recent Getty Center on the Westside and given the continued uncertainly about the viability of downtown Los Angeles as an economic and cultural center. András Szántó's chapter in this volume on art galleries and museums makes this clear. Moves to aggrandize downtown Los Angeles culturally will continue to risk the scorn of the extremist wing of the Los Angeles school as in the charge that Disney Hall is just the latest example of the "Manhattan penis envy" exhibited by "an ever-diminishing downtown-oriented Los Angeles elite that is vainly striving to create a New York model of what a city should be, with its economic and cultural focus in the center, even though LA's strength is as a polycentric city" (Joel Kotkin, quoted in Russell 1997). By contrast, to argue in New York City that a major cultural institution should be located beyond the central core would be harder, as it would be less in accord with existing practice.

Yet the very dearth of stellar cultural institutions beyond the core in New York (the Brooklyn Museum of Art is one of a very few examples) is a prima facie argument for placing others there now, as some people are realizing. Consider the movement in July 2002 of the Museum of Modern Art (MoMA) to temporary quarters in Long Island City, Queens, just a short distance across the East River, while MoMA renovates its Manhattan quarters. To try to inject some glamour into the move, MoMA organized a grand procession carrying some of its cherished art pieces from Manhattan to Queens. The borough of Queens seized the opportunity of MoMA's temporary relocation to foreground its other cultural institutions with a map and brochure (Queens Council on the Arts 2001).[2] And although there is, at present, no plan for MoMA to relocate its prime buildings in Queens on a permanent basis (MoMA actually would have preferred to locate its temporary quarters in Manhattan but it was unable to find suitable space that was affordable), MoMA has already established other permanent links in Queens, for example, P.S. 1 in Long Island City. This underlines the acceptability of moving at least second-level cultural institutions beyond Manhattan. How far these traces of the Los Angelization of the New York art world will go is unclear.[3]

Further, while social science can argue that researchers need to apply the Los Angeles and New York school perspectives even-handedly to metro regions, debates will continue because at stake are not just empirical issues and not just political struggles between, for example, competing cities and states but also central values such as what really constitutes civilized (city-like) life and whether it can be created in areas beyond the classic urban core. For example those in the Los Angeles school mode are more likely to stress the importance throughout metropolitan America of edge cities—the conglomerates of office, commercial or retail, and residential spaces that have sprung up on the periphery in the past thirty years. Those in the New York school mode are more likely to question the credentials of these conglomerates and to suggest that they may not merit the "city" part of the designation, often constituting instead lesser entities such as "subcities" or, in some cases, just "basically giant shopping and entertainment malls" with lots of office space (Gans 1991, 35) or, more dismissively, "nonplace urban realms" that are the "antithesis of a traditional sense of place" (Sorkin 2002, 199).

A central aim of this book, then, has been to lay out some of the issues —empirical, political, social, and values-related—in these ongoing and important tussles between the Los Angeles and New York perspectives.

THE DECLINE OF THE BLACK GHETTO IN LOS ANGELES, THE "NEW WHITES," AND LATINOS IN THE INLAND EMPIRE

Beyond these center and periphery issues, which are arguably the framework for everything else, the chapters in this volume have suggested new ways of thinking about other critical issues. Among these are, for example, those relating to the black and Latino populations of these cities. In the past century, America's urban regions were epicenters for some of the central debates about race and ethnicity in the United States, and this book's findings suggest that New York and Los Angeles will continue as such.

For example, the black population dropped in relative and absolute terms in both cities between 1990 and 2000, but did so far more dramatically in Los Angeles, by about 69,427 or 14 percent of the total black population, to about 425,000 people. In New York City, largely because of continuing immigration from the Caribbean, the black population dropped only slightly, by 14,720 persons or just 0.7 percent of the total black population, and remains substantial at 2,152,000. Indeed, the rather different cases of the black populations of the cities of Los Angeles and New York in some respects come close to representing two extremes among the many likely futures of inner-city black ghettos.

End of the Black Ghetto in Los Angeles?

In Los Angeles, the marked thinning of the central city black population, clearly depicted in the year 2000 census maps in chapters 1 and 5, raises the real possibility of the end of the black ghetto, not in the next decade but as a foreseeable, though not inevitable, eventual scenario. Further, movement of blacks to the suburbs, a major cause of this thinning out of the black ghetto, may also continue to occur in the Los Angeles region in somewhat dispersed and integrated mode, though the possibility of the eventual emergence of substantial black concentrations there ("black suburbs," New York–region style) cannot be ruled out either.

By contrast, black ghettos and concentrations seem more likely to persist in New York City although a degree of thinning out in some cases, for example, Harlem, is apparent. Further, black concentrations continue to be exported beyond the city borders as black suburbs, although for sure there are also blacks in the New York region's suburbs who live in integrated settings. Black ghettos and residential concentrations have a long history in New York City and its suburbs and are now supported or, at least are not usually attacked, by black politicians who benefit at the polls from the existence of heavily black voting constituencies.

What is new and different in New York City's black ghettos is not so much the thinning out of black concentrations as the economic and sociopolitical impact of the growing proportion of foreign-born blacks there, beyond the already-mentioned substantial demographic impact in preventing the kind of numerical decline seen in Los Angeles. For example, relations between native-born and foreign-born blacks, already the subject of several studies (Kasinitz 1992, Waters 1999, Waldinger 2001), will constitute a major motif in coming decades, as Sabagh and Bozorgmehr stressed in chapter 3.

Latinos in the Suburbs of Los Angeles

If the demographic decline of the black population in the city of Los Angeles raises the possibility of the eventual end of the black ghetto in that city, the demographic vitality of the Latino population in the city and surrounding region of Los Angeles also underpins a startling outcome for Latinos there. Latinos have moved into new suburban housing, especially in the eastern part of Los Angeles County and further east in San Bernardino and Riverside Counties (the "Inland Empire") in numbers that make them already a third or more of these areas and will surely lead them to become a majority in the next decades. So extensive is the Latino spread in Los Angeles that there are usually no identifiable boundaries that clearly separate them from nonminority-dominated areas, as the 2000 census maps in chapters 1 and 5 show. These dense settlements of Latinos are not ghettos, in the normal sense of that term. Although the large-scale movement of Latinos to the suburbs, either directly on first immigrating or after a period in the inner city, is occurring in many parts of the United States (for a study based on 2000 census data, see Pew Hispanic Center 2002), the numbers involved are most striking in the Los Angeles region. Never in the history of suburbanization has a new immigrant group moved to the suburbs in such numbers so quickly, which is one reason why these areas constitute such a dramatic stage and yet another reason to justify the Los Angeles school's fascination with the periphery of the Los Angeles region.

The New Whites: Cities That Are Both Multicultural and Predominantly White

Analysis of the cities of New York and Los Angeles should also force us to rethink, and perhaps retire, the "dwindling whites" stereotype that has dominated our understanding of the residential composition of these and many other cities for much of the post–World War II period. According to this stereotype, the proportion of minorities—blacks, Hispanics, and Asians—is rising while the proportion of "whites" is rapidly declining. One problem with this perspective is the recent fall in the proportion of blacks in both cities between 1990 and 2000, substantial in Los Angeles, slight in New York. The second problem is that a significant number of the Hispanics/Latinos (about half and perhaps far more, depending on how the census question is worded) in Los Angeles and New York classify themselves as white when asked by the census. When we include as "whites" these Latinos (the "new whites," if you wish), then the cities of New York and Los Angeles are either 45 percent and 47 percent white, respectively or 60 percent and 81 percent white, respectively, depending on which census question wording we accept. In short, the populations of cities like New York and Los Angeles are nowadays both highly multicultural (as New York has been for most of its history) and quite substantially white.

If this idea that in the year 2000 the population of the city of Los Angeles might plausibly be said to be 81 percent white at the same time as it is 47 percent Latino does not fit our usual way of thinking about that city, then so much the worse for our usual way of thinking. Only by ignoring this self-classification, the "new whites," can the stereotype of a dwindling band of whites in these cities be maintained. It is well known that other groups in their early histories in the United States, for example, the Irish, Italians, and Jews, were first classified by many others as nonwhites, a classification that is now widely viewed in retrospect as socially and politically retrograde. It is time to recognize that the same is happening to Latinos and to correct the practice.

As a corollary, we should cease the scandalously illogical habit of referring in the same data discussion to the nonmutually exclusive categories of "Latinos" and "whites." Just one example, from among those pervasive in the media and even in academic discourse, is the following from a *New York Times* article about the possible secession of the San Fernando Valley: "Many suburbs in the region that were once predominantly white are now heavily Latino" (Sterngold 2002). Although the practice is sometimes saved from illogic by specifying that the "whites" are actually a subset of whites, the "non-Latino whites," often there is no such clarification. In any case, the practice is unnecessary. One can refer to, and advocate on behalf of, Latinos (and Asians) by comparison with the rest of the population with the latter simply referred to as the rest of the overall group or by another designation that is logically sound, rather than as "whites." There is no other area of social life for which data using nonmutually exclusive categories are so routinely presented for serious consideration. Alas, so widespread is the practice that it will likely take a long time to eradicate, even if the will to do so develops, of which there is little sign so far.

URBAN ISSUES

Sociopolitical Stability

These two cities will continue as laboratories for the study of major urban problems and issues. Of these, sociopolitical stability is central. As a by-product of the high levels of immigration that resulted from the 1965 Immigration Act, each city saw in the past decade a partial return to the older, nineteenth-century forms of riots involving ethnic or racial groups attacking one another. Examples were the Crown Heights riot in New York in 1991, involving black-Jewish conflict, and that part of the 1992 Los Angeles riots where blacks and Latinos turned on Koreans.

These kinds of interethnic or interracial riots were not uncommon in U.S. cities in the nineteenth century and up to World War II, but they had by the 1960s become less frequent and, as it then appeared, had been largely replaced by what seemed to be a new era of rioting. This new era involved, above all, blacks destroying property amid symbolic protests, often triggered by incidents of police brutality, about perceived inequalities such as residential segregation. Watts in 1965 and Newark in 1967—both mega riots—were notorious examples from each region. The potential for these kinds of property or symbolic riots still remains, for while the composition of the inner-city ghetto is changing, ghetto life (Latino or black) remains a marked feature of each city, as does a certain amount of police brutality toward minorities. Recent examples are the 2002 city of Inglewood incident, where a bystander videotaped the beating of a handcuffed black sixteen-year-old boy by at least two white policemen (the city of Inglewood is surrounded by the city of Los Angeles and is ecologically part of the latter's black ghetto) and the continued repercussions of the Louima case in New York City, where the third retrial of one of the officers accused of torturing Louima in 1997 continued to make headlines in 2002.

Indeed, each city now has the ingredients for both types of riots—

interethnic riots and 1960s style "property riots"—and for a mixing of the two in a new, hybrid, and rather complex upheaval. The 1992 riots in Los Angeles, triggered by the repercussions of police brutality toward a black man but also involving attacks by Latinos and blacks on Korean stores, had major components of both types, as Sears points out in his chapter in this volume. And while neither city or region has had a major or mega riot since 1992, social stability remains a question mark in both, with large-scale immigration having added the possibility of interethnic conflict to police brutality and grievances related to ghetto life as precipitating causes. Indeed, a widespread reaction in Los Angeles to the 2002 Inglewood brutality was concern that this might trigger another 1992 Rodney King riot (Merl 2002).

Education

Neither New York City nor the city of Los Angeles has been able noticeably to improve its public school system despite a decade or more of effort. Each system continues to lurch from one desperate reform attempt to another, as Julia Wrigley stressed, with periodic setbacks continuing to threaten to cancel out advances. For example, in 2002 the New York State legislature agreed to give the mayor the power to appoint the schools chancellor. This was hailed as a huge political and organizational advance that would let the mayor focus attention on this critically important area. Yet shortly thereafter, in June 2002, the New York City school system received a major financial reverse when the Appellate Division of New York State's Supreme Court overturned Judge Leland DeGrasse's landmark January 2001 decision that New York State could not continue to spend less than the statewide per-student average on schools in New York City. The new 2002 ruling allowed the funding disparity to continue on the grounds that New York State was not obliged to fund its schools equally or even to provide a good education to its students. Its obligation to New York City schools, the Court ruled, was just to ensure that they provided a "minimally adequate," eighth grade–level education that would enable students to enter "low-level" jobs, such as messenger and hamburger flipper. Sounding, in its class bias, remarkably like nineteenth-century England as Julia Wrigley pointed out, the Court pronounced that "society needs workers in all levels of jobs, the majority of which may very well be low level."

Crime

In retrospect, dealing with crime in the decade from 1992 to 2002—at least crime of the conventional kind not related to terrorism—was much easier than dealing with public school education. In part this is because police departments, as quasi-military units, are susceptible to the introduction of drastic reforms while school systems are far more complex and harder to change. Also in part it's because increased funds for spending on crime reduction seem politically easier to secure than funds for public school improvement. Another part of this, as Jack Katz stressed (chap. 6), is that we simply do not understand why conventional crime levels declined in this decade. At any rate, there is no sign of a return in either city to the crime levels of the late 1980s and early 1990s, even though in the city of Los Angeles there is concern about a modest rise in some levels of crime and much public wrestling with problems associated with the leadership of the police department.

Fascinating here is the 2002 choice by Mayor Hahn, with the approval of the city council, of former New York City police commissioner Bill Bratton as chief of the Los Angeles Police Department. Bratton has a clear mandate to reform the LAPD and to reduce crime. Whether he can achieve these goals is highly relevant to the still raging debate as to whether it was changes in police practices introduced by Bratton from 1993 to 1996, and by his predecessor Raymond Kelly, or other factors such as demographics that produced the dramatic decline in crime in New York City in the 1990s.

Also after September 11, 2001, the police departments of both cities have the daunting problem of defending against weapons of mass destruction used by terrorists, with each city's harbor area especially vulnerable. This new era of crime fighting will certainly tax police resources for years to come.

Welfare Reform and Urban Poverty

Finally, the two chapters on welfare reform in New York City and Los Angeles County (chaps. 8 and 9) provided an admirably clear outline of four factors that converge to make for a complex present and an uncertain future. First, by 2001 and stemming from the 1996 federal welfare reform legislation, the welfare rolls had been cut drastically in both cities. Second, there had been a striking rise in the proportion of the "working poor"—families with at least one person working who were nevertheless at income levels classified as poverty. This supported the view that the commonest kinds of jobs being created in the economies of the two cities were jobs that sometimes paid too little to support a family and underlined the concern that forcing welfare recipients back into the workforce might not provide sufficient means to meet their basic economic needs. Third, the rapid expansion of the economies of both cities, which had provided a propitious backdrop for welfare reform, slowed after 2001 to the point of cessation. Fourth, it became clear that continued high levels of immigration were a major causal factor underlining many of the labor market and poverty trends in both New York City and Los Angeles, which complicated the effort to monitor and assess the impact of welfare reform. For example, the much-noted fall in median incomes in certain neighborhoods during the period 1990–2000, was likely primarily a result of immigration, with welfare reform an important but secondary causal factor. In short, trying to meet the needs of, and understand what is happening to, the poor of each place will continue to present a major challenge.

Finally, the authors of this volume are committed to updating their analyses in the light of new data and developments. These updates, and the new data, are available on the University of California, Los Angeles, LeRoy Neiman Center Web site and also on a CD.

NOTES

INTRODUCTION

1. The "rediscovery" of the central city by the public and others has been discussed since about the mid-1960s, but charting with any precision these public attitudes (such as declining or rising interest in New York City and in cities in general) is hard since there are no survey data that measure public opinion over time on these topics. Absent of survey data, the depiction of the city in hit movies (defined as the five top-grossing movies for each year) is not a bad indicator of popular attitudes. This evidence, and common sense, suggest that more favorable attitudes to New York City and other cities from 1960 on have been punctuated by periods of pessimism, too, associated with times of high crime and economic recession and, recently, urban terrorism. During the post–World War II suburbanization wave, the status of, and interest in, city living seemed to decline considerably. While in the 1930s there were eleven hit movies that focused on New York City (occurring in the years 1930, 1933, 1934, and 1936), there were only three such movies from 1950 to 1965. Further, two of them mostly depicted the city as a place of cramped tenements inhabited by people too poor to leave (*Rear Window,* which was number three in 1954, and *West Side Story,* which was number two in 1961). Then from 1968 to 1999 the movies suggest a growing interest in New York City. New York City failed to figure prominently in a top-five grossing movies in only two consecutive years during this period, though for roughly the last half of this period (1985–96), years that coincide with the dramatic rise and fall in the city's murder rate, the city is often depicted negatively, overrun by crime. (e.g., *Batman,* which was number one in 1989, and *Batman Forever,* which was number one in 1995, depict New York City as a dangerous place whose citizens need to be rescued from criminals by superhumans.) This attitude changed sharply in the late 1990s as the city's crime rate plummeted.

Intellectuals have picked various years as key in the changing, and often more favorable, attitude to New York City after the initial period of post–World War II suburbanization. Robert Stern stresses 1960, when the city's postwar building boom got under way in earnest. Radical changes in the city's zoning facilitated the replacement of many of the traditional buildings with skyscraper tower slabs, implying a certain kind of revitalization. Conversely, these changes, spearheaded by the real estate industry, threatened the city's traditional neighborhood life. At this time, neighborhood activists such as Jane Jacobs concluded that "the city, with its neighborhoods, its parks, its landmarks, and its cohesiveness, was a great resource, which could be saved; there might even be some fun to be had in saving it" (Stern et al. 1960, 9–10). William Whyte saw this movement gaining ground in 1988. He wrote: "The rediscovery of the pleasures of downtown has been made in city after city" (1988, 1). Ten years later Gratz and Mintz concurred: "Positive change and sustainable growth are occurring in many American downtowns, neighborhood commercial streets, Main Streets, and big city business districts. From New York's Corning to Michigan's Holland, to California's Pasadena, and beyond, rebirth is clear" (1998, 1).

2. These three counties have population densities of 395, 204, and 81 persons per square mile, respectively. When adjusted to refer only to usable land, the densities are 790, 612, and 648 persons per square mile.

3. The embryo of an explicit Los Angeles school consisted of a series of meetings and publications during the late 1980s (Dear 1998, 52). An article in 2000 celebrating the "Los Angeles school" in the *Chronicle of Higher Education* underlined its now established presence in the intellectual world (Miller 2000). The term "school" here refers to a group that shares certain perspectives and ideas. However there is also considerable intellectual, and also locational, diversity. For example, two of the school's most cited current writers, Garreau and Fishman, are based in the areas of Washington, D.C., and New Jersey, respectively, and the school's founding thinker, Fogelman, was based in Boston. There are also, naturally, current divisions, e.g., between those with a postmodern bent (e.g.Dear, Soja) and those who stress industrial studies (Scott).

4. For a longer account of the ideas of the classic Chicago school, see n. 17 in the introduction.

5. He defines "substantial leasable office space" as more than 5 million square feet—larger than downtown Memphis—and substantial leasable retail space as more than 600,000 square feet—the equivalent of a fair-sized mall.

6. These are based on Garreau's 1988 maps, updated with the following sources: *America's Top-Rated Smaller Cities* (Garoogian 2000), *America's Top-Rated Cities* (Garoogian 2001a, vols. 1–4), and *Comparative Guide to American Suburbs* (Garoogian 2001b); and Urban Land Institute (2000).

7. *The Edge City News: Tools for the New Frontier* (dkc.mse.jhu.edu/City/Mockup/History/news.html). Here, in addition to the above criteria, "edge cities" are defined as having a minimum of 24,000 jobs. An emerging edge city has between 14,000 and 24,000 jobs.

8. Fishman (1987, 16), too, sees Los Angeles as having pioneered the technoburbs.

9. The title of Davis's second book on Los Angeles, *Ecology of Fear: Los Angeles and the Imagination of Disaster* (1998), succinctly conveys his "noir" outlook. A tendency to exaggerate the seriousness of Los Angeles's two mega riots

of the past fifty years—huge and catastrophic though they were—is part of this noir outlook. For example, Soja (1996, 426) called the 1992 riot the "most violent urban insurrection in American history," although the 119 people killed in New York City's draft riot of 1863 exceeds the forty-five people killed in 1992. Michael Dear's (2000, 3) claim that the 1992 riot was the worst civil unrest "experienced in twentieth-century urban America" (rather than in America's entire history) is reasonable, although Detroit's 1967 riot looks almost as bad. (See tables 12.1–12.3 in this volume for these comparisons.) On a tendency of some members of the Los Angeles school to hyperbole when discussing Los Angeles, see Ethington (2001).

10. A sociologist who proposed "Los Angeles school" ideas early on is Scott Greer (1962).

11. Scott and Soja (1996, 1) express a similar uncertainty: it is "still an open question whether to view Los Angeles as an exceptional case, a persistently peculiar type of city, or as an exemplary, if not paradigmatic, illustration of the essential and generalizable features of late-twentieth-century urbanization."

12. As can be seen in the following, very schematic, key to these and related terms, Dear and Flusty's (1998) approach has the flavor of the "Frankfurt school" of sociology, which portrayed social life as dominated by large corporations that imposed their vision and ideology on the subordinate masses. Thus "global latifundia" refers to the way large corporations have taken control of the environment to exploit it; "privatopia" refers to the private housing developments, administered by homeowners' associations, where the rich and powerful (the "cybergeoisie") who run the system live; "holsteinization" is the process whereby the masses ("protosurps") are manipulated to desire the corporations' products; and "praedatorianism" is the process whereby the forces of control prevent resistance.

13. A set of essays that examined these ideas for New York City in the 1980s is Mollenkopf and Castells (1991).

14. The most comprehensive study to date of post-1965 immigration to Los Angles is Waldinger and Bozorgmehr (1996a).

15. See n. 3 above, in the introduction.

16. There are many others. A brief, and very incomplete, list would include Robert Caro's (1984) study of the impact on New York City's neighborhoods of Robert Moses's highways and other massive projects, William Kornblum (e.g., on Times Square), Neil Smith's study of gentrification in New York City (1996), Susan and Norman Fainstein's studies of urban political economy (e.g., 1983), and John Mollenkopf, Phil Kasinitz, and Mary Waters, especially their forthcoming study of the second generation of immigrants.

17. The Chicago school's classic model, developed in the 1920s, was E. W. Burgess's "concentric ring" theory of how various sectors of the city evolved. At the center of this model was the central business district, which was also where the homeless of those days ("hobos") lived; this zone was surrounded by a zone of transition into which business and light manufacturing and new immigrants were moving and where the city's "slums" and vice were concentrated. The next zone out was inhabited by workers, often second-generation immigrants, who wanted to live within easy access of work, albeit in modest homes.

Still, the inhabitants of this zone looked to move out to the "promised land" of the next two zones. Thus the next zone out was high-class apartment buildings or somewhat exclusive areas of single family housing for the middle class. The furthest out zone contained the commuter suburbs (Burgess 1925, 47–62). The dynamic terms of the model were "invasion," "succession," and "segregation," which, encapsulating the belief that moving outward was the preferred goal, indicated the struggles through which social groups attempted to move from inner to outer rings.

After Word War II, members of the Chicago school of urban studies, reformulated by scholars such as Morris Janowitz and Gerald Suttles, abandoned the concentric rings model and were more likely to see the central city as a place for the middle class and well-to-do, thus somewhat converging with the perspective of the New York school (William Kornblum, personal conversation, 2001). For accounts of the Chicago school, see Bulmer (1984), Wiley (1986), Lal (1990), Abbott (1999), Soja (2000), and Dear (2001, 2002). Several of these accounts argue that it is a style of research focused on urban ethnography, rather than the concentric circles model, that is the main characteristic of the Chicago school.

18. The classic, and highly critical, account of urban renewal in New York City and the region is Robert Caro's (1984) biography of Robert Moses. The classic sociological protest over urban renewal is Herbert Gans's (1962b) study of the West End of Boston, discussed later in this chapter.

19. Zukin's later work has been far ranging, but much of it remains stimulated by an immersion in the ongoing drama of urban development in New York City, especially Manhattan. For example, in an essay titled "Space and Symbols in an Age of Decline" (1996), Zukin draws on such New York City material as the history of Times Square, the history of art museums and galleries, and business improvement districts to produce a theory of the relationship between a "symbolic economy" (i.e., the way social groups and the physical structure of the city are represented) and a "political economy" (i.e., investment and changing land uses) in the city.

20. Recently, Jackson turned an essay about his hometown, Memphis, into a eulogy for "Main Street" America in general, repeating his belief in the superiority of the central city over the suburbs. When he was growing up, Jackson writes, "Main Street" Memphis was a treasure, for it was about the only place in Memphis where racial groups and social classes came together. He concludes with a lament for what has been lost:

> In recent years, many once sleepy downtown areas around the United States have begun to wake up, attracting single people, young couples, and empty nesters no longer worried about deteriorating schools. Together, they are turning old Main Streets into thriving entertainment and business centers. . . . In most places, however, Americans have come to realize almost too late that without a central business district a city has no soul. For that reason, the loss of Main Street . . . is a national tragedy. *(Jackson 2000, 183)*

21. It is the revised version that takes the story up to 1976.

22. In 1992, New York State hired Stern and other "star designers" to come

up with an interim plan for Times Square. Stern's plan, which was basically implemented, eschewed major new building and instead called for an updated version of Forty-second Street in its heyday, with a blaze of colorful, multilayered signage revamping second-story shops and bars. Paul Goldberger, the architecture critic, wrote that: "Disney came to 42nd Street not so much because Disney was ready to become like New York as because New York was ready to become like Disney" (Goldberger 1996; see also Slatin, 1994).

23. In his path-breaking study of sidewalk vendors on Sixth Avenue in Manhattan, Duneier writes: "New York City and Greenwich Village are unique in many ways. . . . I cannot hope to show how the sidewalk works in low-income neighborhoods where the majority of dense sidewalk interactions occur among members of the same class or social group. . . . I must leave it to my readers to test my observations against their own, and hope that the concepts I have developed to make sense of this neighborhood will prove useful in other venues" (1999, 11).

24. Gans, unlike Jacobs, was against urban high rises not just on principle but, rather, only if they unjustly displaced working-class residents.

25. Robert Putnam, in his recent and influential study *Bowling Alone,* does want to argue that suburban life is fragmented and lacks community. He recognizes that Gans's study of Levittown suggests the contrary but then explains the discrepancy by arguing that the lack of community appeared in American suburban life after Gans wrote his study (Putnam 2000, 209–10). Whether Gans would agree is unclear.

26. Although only one of the contributors, Jennifer Wolch, can be said to be a recognized member of either school.

27. Neil Smith has written some of the most interesting studies of gentrification in Manhattan, especially the East Village and Harlem. Actually Smith's view and Beveridge's can both be true, since they are talking about different things. Smith is focusing on changes over time in the class composition and building stock of certain Manhattan neighborhoods. By "gentrification," he means the process by which "poor and working-class neighborhoods in the inner city are refurbished via an influx of private capital and middle-class homebuyers and renters" and also the sheer rehabilitation or redevelopment from scratch of existing buildings (Smith 1996, 32, 39). Beveridge is comparing current income levels in New York City with current income levels beyond the city.

28. The political balkanization of the region surrounding New York City was stressed as long ago as 1961 by Robert Wood and Vladimir Almendinger, who titled their study *1400 Governments: The Political Economy of the New York Metropolitan Region.*

29. The view that more than two to three generations of immigrants will assimilate is often called "straight-line theory." The contrary view was stated with great drama many years ago by Nathan Glazer and Daniel Moynihan ([1963] 1970) in *Beyond the Melting Pot.* Actually, contemporary advocates of both positions often occupy a common, middle ground, each conceding that there is much unevenness and delay in integration, while differing on the likely eventual outcome. For a range of positions, see Alba and Nee (1997), Gans (1997), Perelman and Waldinger (1997), and Portes (1997).

30. From 1990 to 2000, the black population fell in the Northeast by 387,019, in the Midwest by 149,674, and in the West by 42,798. It rose in the South by 579,491. See Frey (2001).

31. Levitan focuses on poverty rates for families with children, a group that comprises roughly 60 percent of all the poor individuals in New York City and that is the object of much of the recent policy debate.

32. Mayor Giuliani became jealous at how much media attention Bratton had received over the drop in crime, culminating in his picture on the cover of *Time* magazine in 1995, and forced his resignation in 1996. Bratton outlined his innovative strategies for fighting crime in a memoir (Bratton and Knobler 1998).

33. Thirty-six of the top-five grossing movies for each year during the period 1968–99 depict New York City in a central way, and these movies are spread fairly evenly over the period. For the way the image of the city that these audiences have enjoyed seeing has changed during this time see n. 1 above.

34. Recent studies of one or more of these cities that have organized their material around a single theme include Abu-Lughod (1999), whose masterful account links the histories of New York, Chicago, and Los Angeles to the global economy; Fainstein et al. (1992), who organize their study of New York and London around a critique of the oversimplified idea that these cities are developing into "dual cities," with a top and bottom (but a thin middle) organized into two economies, two segregated neighborhoods and two social systems; and Fred Siegel (1997), who argues that New York, Washington D.C., and Los Angeles were brought to social and financial ruin by a new "dependent liberalism," installed after, and in many ways as a result of, the 1960s urban riots and centering on an urban welfare system that gave recipients the idea that they were entitled to government support.

35. Thus Sassen ([1991] 2001), in an early classic account of "global cities" such as New York, London, Paris, São Paulo, and Miami, discusses such varied topics as the dispersal of manufacturing to the urban periphery, the concentration of management functions in city centers, the bifurcated labor force, immigration, and the location of cultural activities in the city center. A recent study of globalization that likewise covers a wide range of subtopics is Scott (2001). For an interim summary of the vast and growing literature on "globalization," see the collection of articles in Therbörn (2000). "Globalization" is discussed in chaps. 2 and 4 of this volume.

CHAPTER ONE

1. There have been other comparisons of New York to Los Angeles. Most recently, of course, there is Janet Abu-Lughod's work (1999). Though such analyses are very interesting and look at many important factors, the effort here is to compare explicitly, using the same sorts of data, the development of these two important regions from 1940 until the eve of the millennium. We have imposed our own geographic classification on both regions, which allow for explicit comparison. Obviously, there are many nuanced differences in the pattern of development of both metropolises, but here we are seeing the extent to which the same trends are affecting both regions to make them more "alike."

2. The changing manner in which the census defined metropolitan areas is discussed in the published volumes that accompany each census. Metropolitan areas were defined in terms of commuting and other patterns. Except for New England, whole county units were used beginning in 1950. The areas do seem to be arbitrary, especially when looked at over time. The discussion in this section is drawn from numerous published volumes. These shifting definitions make it important that, for the sort of historical comparison being presented here, the same areas are used throughout all the decades under consideration.

3. Exact population and other information are contained in the appendix table on which each figure is based. Thus, figure 1.1 is based upon table 1.A1.

4. All these comparisons use counties for New York and use counties and the Los Angeles Minor Civil Division and the balance of Los Angeles County for Los Angeles. Using a finer-grained comparison would probably increase the differences within the area.

5. See Massey and Denton (1989) for a definition of "hypersegregated."

6. Recently, the New York legislature enacted a repeal of the commuter tax, which taxes those who earn an income in New York City, even if they do not live there. This repeal was to apply only to those who live in New York State. The courts found this plan unconstitutional and invalidated the commuter tax altogether.

7. All these analyses are based on the public use samples from the 1990 census. Comparable data for the 2000 census will not be available until 2003. It is unlikely that patterns found will have changed in any radical ways.

CHAPTER TWO

1. Information on firms drawn from the census does not differentiate between those primarily serving other businesses and those serving consumers. In fact, most serve both, although different branches may specialize in one or the other customer group. Only a few types of firms, e.g., advertising agencies, have only business customers.

2. New York's job losses were concentrated in the city's banking, securities, insurance, and business-services industries.

3. While we feel that Markusen and Gwiada's definition of a world city is too broad (e.g., Detroit ranks as a world city according to their definition), we also find Sassen's focus on producer services industries overly restrictive (e.g., Los Angeles is definitely not a global city according to Sassen's definition). We have therefore drawn from both definitions in assessing the global city characteristics of New York and Los Angeles.

4. Markusen and Gwiasda (1994) also claim that New York "lacks the layering of urban functions—political, industrial, financial, educational—that is the essence of primate cities and their ability to contribute as seedbeds of innovation and generators of new types of employment" (168). As we will discuss later, New York's dependence on a small number of industries, and particularly the securities and commodities industry, leaves the city more vulnerable to economic downturns than the more balanced Los Angeles economy.

5. Markusen and Gwiasda (1994, 167) define the "gunbelt" as "that broad

perimeter of the United States that has hosted higher than average defense spending receipts since the 1950s—from New England down through the South Atlantic states through Texas, Colorado, and the intermountain west to the west coast from San Diego to Seattle, with Los Angeles as its centre of gravity."

6. Markusen and Gwiasda (1994, 171) point out that "in 1960, the New York region led the nation in total numbers of jobs yet mirrored the nation's economic structure: New York's manufacturing shares of all jobs exactly matched the national average of 31 percent." By the New York region, Markusen and Gwiada are referring to the New York metropolitan region.

7. Between 1977 and 1989, Los Angeles' manufacturing employment actually grew by 8.5 percent, with manufacturing firms adding more than 70,000 manufacturing jobs. In stark contrast, New York's manufacturing firms shed more than 200,000 jobs during the same period, a decline of more than 34 percent.

8. Nevertheless, not all tourism jobs in New York and Los Angeles are low paying. Income and occupational polarization is evident even within the tourism industry itself, with some industries and occupational groupings characterized by low wages and others by much higher wages. Amusement and recreation services and eating and drinking establishments are among the fastest growing components of the tourism industry in New York and Los Angeles, yet they stand at opposite ends of the spectrum with respect to average wage and salary income of their employees. Workers in both the New York and Los Angeles amusement and entertainment industry earn nearly three times as much on average as workers in the cities' restaurant industry. In Los Angeles, the average wages in amusement and recreation services and eating and drinking places are $46,606 and $10,317, respectively. In Manhattan, they are $43,304 and $15,893.

9. In 1980, the national labor force participation rate for men sixteen and older was 77.4 percent, and for women sixteen and older, it was 51.5 percent. In New York City, the corresponding labor force participation rates for men and women were 69 percent and 47 percent, respectively—significantly lower than the national averages. In 1990, national labor force participation rates for men and women were 76.4 percent and 57.5 percent, respectively; and although the New York City labor force participation rates for men and women still lagged behind the national average, at 71 percent and 54 percent, respectively, the gap had diminished substantially.

10. McMahon et al. (1998) define the middle class as all households that fall between 80 percent and 200 percent of the city median in terms of total income.

11. Household incomes are in 1996 dollars. The data presented here pertain to the city of Los Angeles.

12. The much faster rate of growth for the top is largely attributable to the small size of the base.

13. The 2001 economic downturn was affecting both cities before September 11. The Los Angeles Economic Development Commission (2001) predicted moderate employment growth of 1.4 percent for 2001, an increase of 59,200 jobs. Some of Los Angeles's key industries, including apparel/textile manufacturing, international trade, and motion pictures were already suffering. In New

York, heavy dependence on the securities and commodities industry meant that the sharp decline in stock market capitalization that had already occurred did not bode well for the city, at least in the medium term.

14. The title of John Mollenkopf's (1992) book on New York City politics in the 1980s is *A Phoenix in the Ashes;* along with the city's penchant for generating new political coalitions is its capacity for spawning new industries and transformed neighborhoods.

CHAPTER THREE

We thank David Halle, Roger Waldinger, Peter Lobo, and Madeleine Tress for providing material and helpful comments on earlier drafts of this chapter. Grants from the Academic Senate of the University of California, Los Angeles, the Professional Staff Congress of the City University of New York, and Wegman Brothers provided partial support for this research.

CHAPTER FOUR

The study was partially supported by a research grant from the Asian American Studies Center at the University of California, Los Angeles. Part of the research on Flushing was a collaboration with Christopher Smith. We thank John Logan and David Halle for their helpful comments and Amy Chai, Robert Gedeon, and Gihong Yi for their research assistance.

1. Throughout the text, the term "metropolican area" refers to "principal metropolitan statistical area" (PMSA), and the term "region" refers to "consolidated metropolitan statistical area" (CMSA). The New York PMSA includes the five counties of New York City plus Putnam, Rockland, and Westchester Counties. The Los Angeles–Long Beach PMSA consists of Los Angeles County. The New York and Los Angeles CMSAs are defined in fig. i.1.

2. The Chinese-American population was 3.5 percent of the total population in the Los Angeles–Long Beach PMSA (Los Angeles County) and 4.1 in the New York–New York PMSA in 2000. In the Los Angeles region (CMSA), there are eleven suburban municipalities with a high concentration of Chinese-American population.

3. Flushing in this chapter refers to the core area in central or downtown Flushing, which is officially defined by the Queen's Community Board number 7 as an area including eleven contiguous census tracts in the 1980, 1990, and 2000 censuses: 797, 845, 851, 853, 855, 857, 859, 865, 867, 871, and 875. California's Monterey Park in 1980 includes eleven tracts: 5304, 4817.01, 4817.02, 4820.01, 4820.02, 4821.01, 4821.02, 4822, 4826, 4827, and 4828; in 1990, thirteen tracts: 4817.02, 4817.11, 4817.12, 4820.01, 4820.02, 4821.01, 4821.02, 4822.01, 4822.02, 4826, 4827, 4828, and 5304; and in 2000, fifteen tracts: 4817.11, 4817.12, 4817.13, 4817.14, 4820.01, 4820.02, 4821.01, 4821.02, 4822.01, 4822.02, 4826, 4827.01, 4827.02, 4828, and 5304. New York's Chinatown in 1980, 1990, and 2000 includes fourteen tracts—seven in the core area (6, 8, 16, 18, 27 29, and 41) and seven in the extended area (2.01, 2.02, 14.02, 22.01, 43, 15.01, and 25 [Zhou 1992]). Los Angeles's Chinatown in 2000 includes six tracts—two in the core area (1977 and 2071) and four in the extended area (1971.10, 1972, 1975, and 1976 [census tract number 1971.10 was number 1971 in 1990, and tract number 2072

was part of Chinatown in 1980]). Flushing and Monterey Park differ drastically in area but are similar in population size (55,139 vs. 62,237 in 2000), whereas New York's Chinatown is both larger in area and nearly four times as populous as Los Angeles's Chinatown (95,330 vs. 25,082 in 2000).

4. Interview by Min Zhou, Flushing, N.Y., May 1993.

5. Mayors are not elected in Monterey Park. Instead, council members become mayors for nine months on a rotating basis. Thus, Lily Lee Chen was not only the mayor but also the one Chinese-American member of the council.

6. The Forty-ninth District is a southern California electoral district that includes Monterey Park, Alhambra, Rosemead, San Gabriel, El Sereno, and City Terrace parts of East Los Angeles.

7. Interview with a Chinese immigrant by Min Zhou at a real estate agency in Temple City, Calif., March 1999.

8. Interview with two elderly white homeowners by Min Zhou, Flushing, N.Y., May 1993.

CHAPTER FIVE

1. The report, e.g., considered Norwegian a race. The report did use five overriding categories, namely, the Caucasian, Ethiopian, Mongolian, Malay, and American or, as familiarly called, the white, black, yellow, brown and red races (Dillingham Commission 1911).

2. For an excellent analysis of these "ethnic communities" in Los Angeles and New York using 1990 census data, see Logan et al. (2002). They define an "ethnic community" (1) as "a neighborhood selected as a living environment by those who have wider options, based on their market resources"—the contrast here is with minority ghettos, where residents are ensnared, and also with "immigrant enclaves" into which first-generation immigrants move but only temporarily—and (2) as consisting of contiguous census tracts where the ethnic group in question constitutes 40 percent or more of one tract and at least 35 percent of the other tract(s).

3. Here, and throughout this book, we use the terms "Hispanic" and "Latino" interchangeably, following the new guidelines adopted by the Office of Management and Budget (OMB) and applied to the 2000 census (Office of Management and Budget 2000) These guidelines became binding on all government agencies and all agencies public or private that receive federal funds.

4. The major innovation in the 2000 census was the accommodation to reporting more than one "race," so that respondents were allowed, for the first time, to select more than one of the categories offered on the race question. (For a study of the entire issue, see Perlmann and Waters 2002.) The race question on the 1990 decennial census had read: "Race Fill ONE circle for the race that the person considers himself/herself to be." The race question on the 2000 census read: "What is Person 1's race? Mark x one or more races to indicate what this person considers himself/herself to be." This innovation was intended to capture the fact that the population, via immigration and a certain amount of intermarriage, was, many people felt, becoming more racially blurred. (An alternative method suggested to achieve the same end, but that was rejected, was

to offer the category "multiracial" as an option on the race question.) Actually, in some ways the 2000 innovation just returned the census to the days before 1930 when it also expended much effort in trying to capture multiracialism, using at that time the blood-content terminology (Beveridge 2001). For example in 1890 the Census Bureau's instructions to its enumerators read: "Be particularly careful to distinguish between blacks, mulattos, quadroons, and octoroons. The word 'black' should be used to describe those persons who have three-fourths or more black blood; 'mulatto,' those persons who have from three-eighths to five-eighths black blood; 'quadroon,' those persons who have one-fourth black blood; and 'octoroon,' those persons who have one-eighth or any trace of black blood." Beginning in 1930 people in the United States could only officially be of one race. The 1930 census instructions to its enumerators clearly defined the so-called one-drop rule, to wit: "A person of mixed white and Negro blood should be returned as a Negro, no matter how small the percentage of Negro blood. Both black and mulatto persons are to be returned as Negroes, without distinction." Before 1890, the census had enumerated people based on skin color not on the biological race concept.

Some experts predicted that the 2000 change to allow respondents to select more than one race would produce major results. The head of the Census Bureau, Kenneth Prewitt, saw it as "one of the most exciting demographic dramas in world history" (Beveridge 2001). In fact, the results were strikingly minor. Nationwide, only 2.4 percent of the population chose more than one race (U.S. Bureau of the Census 2001). In the entire state of California, in the city of Los Angeles, and in New York City, only 5 percent selected more than one race. In the state of New York, the percentage selecting more than one race was even lower, 3.1 percent. Among those who chose more than one race, many chose "Some other race" as one of their races. As discussed, "some other race" is not an "official" category.

At any rate, when using data on the race question from the 2000 census, it is necessary to decide, from the various possible solutions suggested, how to analyze the roughly 5 percent of respondents who selected more than one race. In this study, that group is ignored since it is so small and since the various methods produce very similar outcomes. For example, the percentage black for New York City for just one race is 26.6 compared with 26.9 using the OMB/U.S. Department of Justice method (see below). The percentage white is 44.7 compared with 44.7 (i.e., identical), while Asian is 9.8 compared with 10.2. The percentage black for the city of Los Angeles for just one race is 11.2 compared with 11.5 using the OMB/U.S. Department of Justice method. The percentage white is identical at 46.9, while Asian is 10.0 compared with 10.7. The percentage black for the county of Los Angeles for just one race is 9.8 compared with 10.0 using the OMB/U.S. Department of Justice method. The percentage white is identical at 48.7, while Asian is 11.9 compared with 12.9. When data are presented here on racial groups, the data are for those persons who selected one group only. There are other strategies for dealing with the multiple responses issue. For example, some researchers assign fractional scores to the group's total. Thus, if a respondent selected "black" and "white," half of the respondent (.5) would be assigned to each of those group's totals.

For redistricting and other governmental purposes that require comparing with earlier censuses, the U.S. Department of Justice promulgated a method that, in effect, reinstituted the one-drop rule. In this method, the only "whites" are those who only report white without any other race. If white is reported with another race, then the total is applied to that race. If white is reported with two other races or two other (minority) races are reported, then the total is assigned to a new category "other multiracial." This category is tiny in most jurisdictions. There is a certain logic to this method, since the Justice Department is concerned to limit "retrogression," which is having fewer minority political seats in a jurisdiction that has the same or greater proportion of minorities as before (U.S. Department of Justice 2001).

5. The federal government requires the Census Bureau to collect data on race and Hispanic origin but not to collect it using two separate questions. Thus the Census Bureau explains: "The race and Hispanic origin categories used by the Census Bureau are mandated by the Office of Management and Budget Directive No.15, which requires all federal record keeping and data presentation to use four race categories (White, Black, American Indian and Alaska Native, Asian and Pacific Islander) and two ethnicity categories (Hispanic, non-Hispanic). These classifications are not intended to be scientific in nature, but are designed to promote consistency in federal record keeping and data presentation" (U.S. Bureau of the Census 1999). In 1995 the Census Bureau tested combining the two questions and several other reasonable alternative ways of wording the race question, in specially worded questions on its Current Population Surveys "Race and Ethnicity Supplement" survey (U.S. Bureau of the Census 1997). For discussion of this and other question wording changes, see Office of Management and Budget (2000).

6. Nationwide in 2000, 48 percent of Hispanics/Latinos classified themselves as (only) white, and 42 percent as "some other race." This higher percent selecting "white" than in New York or Los Angeles likely partly reflects the lower proportion of new immigrants in this group.

7. Actually, the full CPS questionnaire, which, unlike the decennial census, is administered by an interviewer, does contain the option "other-specify," but this is not shown to respondents. The interviewer fills it in should the respondent volunteer a response other than those offered (Clyde Tucker, Bureau of Labor Statistics, e-mail, June 18, 2001).

8. Of the 17 percent of Hispanics/Latinos in New York City who did not classify themselves as "white" on the race question, 14 percent classified themselves as black, and the remainder as either Asian or Indian/Eskimo. Among the various categories of Hispanics in New York City, the propensity to identify as "white" is very strong among Mexicans (100 percent). It is somewhat lower among Puerto Ricans (89 percent; of the remaining Puerto Ricans almost all, 9 percent, chose "black"), Cubans (87 percent; all of the rest chose black); Central and South Americans (82 percent; of the rest, the largest group by far, 13 percent, chose black), and among those who classify themselves as "other Spanish/Hispanic/Latino" (51 percent; of the rest, 36 percent chose black and 13 percent chose Asian).

Among the various categories of Hispanics in the city of Los Angeles, the propensity to identify as "white" on the race question (2000 CPS data) is very strong among Mexicans and Chicanos (99 percent), Puerto Ricans (100 percent), and Central and South Americans (97 percent). It is less strong among Cubans (77 percent; of the rest, 6 percent classified themselves as black and 18 percent as Asian), and among "other Spanish/Hispanic/Latino" (62 percent; of the rest, 20 percent chose black and 18 percent chose Asian).

There are many complexities here. For example, in the Dominican Republic, "black" is equated with Haitian and is therefore shunned by all as a category because of the long history of border conflicts between the two countries. Dominican passports have three racial categories: Blanco, Indio Claro, and Indio Oscuro, but not black. This would discourage Dominicans from classifying themselves as black on the race question. Still, Dominicans have settled in proximity to blacks in Manhattan, just northwest of Harlem, which is probably not insignificant (Torres-Saillant 1998; Sagás 2000).

9. For other official reporting purposes, use is made of what are called the MARS data (Modified Age, Race/Sex and Hispanic Origin data). The race data here have been modified to make reporting categories comparable to those used by state and local agencies for whom "other race" is usually an acceptable reporting category. Thus the 1990 census included 9,804,847 persons who checked the "other race" category rather than one of the fifteen racial categories listed on the census form. The Census Bureau reassigned each such person to the specified race reported by another person who was geographically close and had an identical response to the Hispanic-origin question. Hispanic origin was used because more than 95 percent of the "other race" persons were of Hispanic origin. See U.S. Bureau of the Census 1992. Because of this procedure, the modified proportion of whites, and of Latinos who classify themselves as white, actually ends up resembling the proportions obtained by using the CPS data that omits "some other race" from the options presented to respondents. Also, because of OMB's skepticism about the "some other race" category, no other entity (e.g., school districts) is allowed to report "some other race" when they collect race data.

10. Rodríguez and Cordero-Guzmán (1992) make this argument for Puerto Ricans in the United States. For an interesting overview of recent research on the racial identity of Latinos, with special reference to New York City, see Itzigson and Dore-Cabral (2001). For example, the authors argue that Dominican immigrants reserve the term "black" for Haitians, who do the most menial work in the Dominican Republic.

11. For example, an April 2001 New York Times story (front page) summarized recently released 2000 census data with the headline: "Whites in Minority in Largest Cities, the Census Shows." The article began: "For the first time, nearly half of the nation's largest cities are home to more blacks, Hispanics, Asians and other minorities than whites, an analysis of the latest census figures shows" (Schmitt 2001a, A1). A week later, another front-page *New York Times* article argued, in similar fashion, that the 2000 census showed that in recent decades "even as whites fled cities, they were replaced in many instances by immigrants, mainly Hispanics" (Schmitt 2001b, A1). Likewise, the *Los Angeles Times* (2001a,U1–3) proclaimed that the just released census data showed "the shrink-

ing white population in Los Angeles County" and that "Latinos have replaced whites as the largest ethnic group in both the city and county of Los Angeles."

12. Examples of the view that Hispanics/Latinos are not white are everywhere in the popular and serious press. In May 2001, Bob Herbert, the liberal Op-Ed writer for the *New York Times,* criticized the mayoral campaign of Puerto Rican Fernando Ferrer, the Bronx borough president: "The Ferrer campaign has focused so intently on appealing to Latino and black voters that it has given the impression to large numbers of New Yorkers that it is not sufficiently concerned about issues that are important to Whites" (2001). In November 1999, as the superintendent of the Los Angeles Unified School District was ousted, the *Los Angeles Times* complained about an "all-white" school board making decisions in a school system populated primarily by minorities, especially Latinos. Likewise, a February 14, 2000, *New York Times* article on New York City's new schools chancellor, Harold Levy, opined, "Unlike all but one of the previous seven chancellors, who were Black or Hispanic, Mr. Levy is White" (*New York Times* 2000). The important sociopolitical points that many of these writers are making about the secondary status accorded to Latinos could be made just as effectively by highlighting the position of Latinos (and blacks and Asians, if appropriate) without misleadingly implying that Latinos are nonwhite. For example, the *New York Times* could simply have said that Mr. Levy, unlike six of the past seven school chancellors, is neither black nor Hispanic.

Serious researchers too sometimes imply that Hispanics/Latinos are not whites. For example, an article in an American Sociological Association publication proclaims, without anywhere a qualification, that "Whites Will Soon Be a Minority in Orange County " even though the data refer only to non-Hispanic whites (*Footnotes* 2001). One of the rare protests over this practice is by Patterson (2001).

Actually many Asians would probably also classify themselves as both white and Asian, but, unlike Hispanics, they are not given the opportunity to do so by the census. On the race question, they must select *either* Asian *or* white. Were Asians able to choose both classifications, then the cities of New York and Los Angeles would appear to have an even larger proportion of whites.

13. Analyzing trends in the Los Angeles CMSA from 1970 to 1990, Clark found that levels of residential separation between blacks and non-Hispanic whites were generally declining but were rising between Hispanics and non-Hispanic whites (Clark 1996).

14. The formula is: $D = .5 \times \Sigma\, |(x^i/X) - (y^i/Y)|$ where X and Y are the metropolitan area (e.g., county) populations of the two groups being compared (e.g., whites vs. blacks) and x^i and y^i are their respective populations in census tract i. The dissimilarity index began to be heavily used after the 1940 and 1950 census when data were reported at the tract level. Another segregation measure, exposure and isolation, is often used as well. This measures the probability that one group will have another group as a neighbor.

15. Although tracts without a single black are rare, tracts where blacks are present but constitute less than 1 percent of the population are not uncommon in either region.

16. Of the other eight tracts without a single black in the New York CMSA,

two are in Middle Village, Queens (discussed in the text). A third is also in Queens in a small section of Astoria (119 people) that is an enclave bounded on one side by the East River. A fourth tract is in Manhattan (from Forty-ninth Street to Fifty-seventh Street and Fifth Avenue to Park Avenue, with 269 people). Two tracts (with 2,166 and 2,100 people) are in Suffolk County, and two are in New Jersey (one in Interlaken, Monmouth County, the other just south of Mantoloking, Ocean County).

17. Based on interviews collected by Beveridge.

18. In one of the first analyses of Los Angeles County using 2000 census data, Ethington et al. (2001) stressed the fact that "levels of segregation remain high among the four principal race-ethnic groups: Whites, Blacks, Hispanics and Asians." This is compatible with the findings of this chapter for Los Angeles County, although Ethington et al. use a different segregation index (the exposure index) to highlight their findings. It is, however, important to consider developments in the rest of the Los Angeles CMSA, especially in San Bernardino and Riverside Counties, which, this chapter argues, are not just replicating those of Los Angeles County.

19. Accounts of these areas are of great interest. See Roberts (1994) for a discussion of middle-class blacks in Queens; see Haynes (2001) for an account of Runyon Heights in Yonkers since its founding. The interplay of class and race for the black middle class is dealt with by Mary Pattillo-McCoy (2000). Research on the rising black middle class in Laurelton is from Beveridge's students studying the area.

20. Gans (1967) wrote about an early example of a racially integrated suburb in the New York CMSA, Levittown, N.J. Racial integration there, which seems to have been successful, did not occur naturally but by court order. Levitt, the builder, originally (1958) refused to sell houses there to blacks. Because of its enormous size Levittown drew public attention and Levitt was required by the courts to reverse policy.

21. In the early 1990s, Yonkers, an area in Westchester just north of the Bronx, underwent a long desegregation struggle, with the entry of blacks bitterly resisted by several residents.

22. Thus Orange County, N.Y., which is also toward the periphery of the New York CMSA, has a much higher percent of blacks—8 percent—and a much higher *D* score.

23. In an early assessment of 2000 census data for U.S. metropolitan regions, John Logan and colleagues argued that significant decreases in segregation from 1990 to 2000 between blacks and non-Hispanic whites and between Hispanics and non-Hispanic whites were only found where blacks or Hispanics were 3 percent or less of the population (Mumford Center 2001).

24. For a more optimistic view, see Allen and Turner (1997, 77–79).

25. Logan et al. (2002) notes the tendency of Dominicans to concentrate residentially. Dominicans and Afro-Caribbeans are the only two ethnic groups in the New York CMSA to have a majority of its members live in ethnic neighborhoods.

26. In Los Angeles County and Orange County from 1970 to 1990 separation, between Hispanics and non-Hispanic whites increased continually, but in

San Bernardino County from 1970 to 1990, separation between Hispanics and non-Hispanic whites fell continually. In Riverside County, it was more or less unchanged from 1970 to 1980 and then declined from 1980 to 1990, while in Ventura County it rose from 1970 to 1980 and then leveled off from 1980 to 1990.

27. Logan et al. (2002) notes that there are far more middle-class ethnic communities in the Los Angeles suburbs than in the New York suburbs. But the reverse is true for blacks.

28. See n. 5 above, this chapter.

CHAPTER SIX

The germ of this chapter was presented at the University of California, Los Angeles (UCLA), Neiman conference of 1999; to the Criminal Justice Reading Group at UCLA; at the Oñati Institute for the Sociology of Law in 1997; and as the Fortunoff lecture at New York University Law School in 1998. One outgrowth was *The Gang Myth* (Katz 2000), from which a few passages are duplicated here. A version closer to the present mutation was discussed at the Law and Society Center at University of California, Berkeley, in 2001. Suggestions at various points along the way from Jeffery Fagan, Malcolm Feeley, Joan Howarth, Robert Kagan, Mark Kleiman, Eric Monkkonen, Harry Scheiber, David Sklansky, Jonathan Zasloff, and Franklin Zimring were particularly helpful. Curtis Jackson-Jacobs, Zachary Katz, and Sal Zerilli provided essential and creative research assistance. This chapter was prepared while I was a fellow at the Center for Advanced Study in Behavioral Sciences. I thank the center for its support.

1. We are most familiar with myths as described by classicists and by anthropologists. In those contexts, myths explain troublesome events and patterns in a people's contemporary life by reference to cosmological and primordial causes. But we should also recognize that science itself is a myth system, at least on its theoretical side. Theory does not simply summarize empirical findings; it also, and more important, explains how the current state of knowledge became what it is and shapes the path of inquiry by grounding the bets that are inevitable in research. This chapter is a not a general brief against myths. Indeed, elsewhere I have argued that we should exploit religious myth as a source for social-psychological theory (Katz 1996). Troublesome problems arise with myths only when they cannot be acknowledged as the basis of social policies.

2. If I were following colloquial usage, I would have written "New York" and "LA," as that usage truncates the West Coast name to create a two-syllable parity. No one says "NY," an awkward formula to execute that offers no syllabic economy, but even Los Angeles residents who otherwise are disgusted with the area find the familiar shorthand irresistibly charming. The masses appear to agree with an Armenian acquaintance of mine who once commented, when complaining about the lack of community in the area, "In LA, only name o.k." There is a small and hopeless campaign, carried on by some Anglos who would claim old-family status or mark their awareness of the Spanish origins of the city's name, to use the full form, which offers a speaker the opportunity to give the *g* a hard pronunciation that, if it does not sound like a Spanish *g*, at least still evokes a time when an Anglo pronunciation of the city's name was emerging.

3. Also left open in this essay is the explanation of why crime first rose dramatically and then significantly declined in the two cities under consideration here and elsewhere in the United States. Andrew Karmen (2000) offers the most elaborated and even-handed answer to date. Through a close and frequently ingenious examination of New York crime data, and by interpreting parallel trends around the United States, he grants a minor contribution to crime rate declines from policing but emphasizes the contributions of changes in drug consumption and other high-risk behaviors in minority poverty-stricken youth communities, immigration effects, and the reduction of the at-risk population in the 1990s due to the events of the 1980s, including AIDS deaths, deportation, imprisonment, drug overdose, and murder.

4. In Los Angeles, the association of crime, ethnic minority youth, and gang organization dates from the 1940s and the "Sleepy Lagoon" murder case. For a brief report on this infamously racist prosecution of Mexican-origin young men, see Verge (1993).

5. The figures reported in table 6.1 were produced by excluding articles that did not meet any one of three criteria. First, "gang" had to be used as a noun or adjective. Stories about "ganging up" on someone were excluded. Included were stories that mentioned a gang problem, gang crime, gangs, a gang member, a gang beating, gang attack, gang shooting, gang rape, or antigang organizations in law enforcement, communities, or schools. Second, an article was excluded if it lacked an indication that a persistent or organized group was responsible (e.g., stories with phrasing such as "a gang of youth attacked"). Still included under this criterion were stories about antigang law enforcement or antigang community organizations or activities; organized crime gangs and drug gangs; gang shootings and gang retaliation. Third, the story had to indicate that the gang was local to the newspaper's home area. This criterion was necessary to exclude counting as New York stories the many articles that were published in the *New York Times* about gangs outside of New York, e.g., in Los Angeles. For the *New York Times,* the article had to be relevant to New York City; for the *Los Angeles Times,* to Los Angeles County. These are areas of roughly similar population size. The story had to refer to a gang event or member in the area or, if it was a national or state story, mention some relevance to local issues. The initial, presifted figures were Los Angeles, 3,080 articles, New York, 1,517.

The two *Times* papers hold similar positions in the local media framework. It is possible that other local newspapers, such as the *New York Daily News* and the *Los Angeles Daily News,* use "gang" more often. A check of *New York Daily News* stories for 1998, however, did not show a pattern different from that in the *New York Times.* (There were about 20 percent more gang stories than the *New York Times* but still many of the *Daily News* gang stories, about one-third, were about drug gangs, mafia gangs, or a gang of corrupt city workers/sanitation supervisors). In any case, the newspaper counts are offered as indicators of local culture. Even if the *New York Times* has shied from using "gang" as a sensational term, city differences in editorial style would not explain why "gang" has been a rallying cry in political discourse in Los Angeles but not in New York over the past fifteen years. I mention—both to disclose bias and as supportive evidence

—that, in the early 1990s I published *Los Angeles Times* Op-Ed pieces critical of the gang focus in local culture and law enforcement and that, fortunately at least for the current argument, they apparently had no effect (Katz 1991, 1992a, 1992b).

6. My awareness of this appreciation was developed in part through extensive interviews that I conducted with the U.S. attorney in Brooklyn in the late 1970s. Warren Christopher, who served as head of the commission investigating the Los Angeles Police Department after the Rodney King riots, fits this model; the exceptional nature of his professional career in Los Angeles proves the rule.

7. Carter described the attack on Louima as "'the most depraved act that's ever been reported or committed by a police officer or police officers against another human being'" and "said that the court system is making 'some progress toward getting police officers—at least in this extreme circumstance—to testify against the police officers who were responsible.'" Giuliani "praised the verdict . . . as a shining example of police officers who were willing to testify so that justice could be done" (Fried and Harden 1999, M1).

8. Other logically useful data are produced in ways that make them too problematic for confident interpretation. Conviction data, which would be useful to compare with arrests to assess overcharging practices, are generated by other agencies (courts, prosecutors) and, as a practical matter, are not easily meshed with police generated reports. "Offense" data are primarily constituted by arrests, but other, less systematic factors are added to produce figures differing from arrest, which we have in any case; and different agencies, city and state, produce different offense figures. Supplemental homicide reports, which provide a richer array of data on given cases, are not produced by systematically similar processes across police departments. And data on robberies, assaults, and so on or statistics that summarize the rate of commission of all types of crime are too subject to victim and police interpretations, which are close to the very matters we wish to investigate.

9. California's attorney general's office found almost a doubling of gang-related homicides in the period 1978–87. The proportion of homicides in which the contributing circumstance was gang-related increased from 6.0 percent in 1978 to 11.4 percent in 1987 (Van de Kamp 1987). From about 1988 to 1992, "LAPDs Gang Tracking System (GTS) [grew] . . . more than 50 percent per year, from 12,000 records to 65,000 in only four years" (Reiner 1992, xxvii).

10. For a similar finding about the decline of nongun homicides from 1985 to 1997 in New York City, see Zimring and Fagan (2000).

Zimring and Fagan suggest that the decline in gun homicides after 1994 is substantially explained by regression to the mean (what I discuss below as the unusual high point reached in New York in 1990), but might in part be credited to police policies. The timing, however, indicates that if policing had an effect, it was by the substantial increase in the size of the New York force from 1991 to 1994, not necessarily because of changes in management strategy or administration philosophy. See also Fagan et al. (1998), which compares New York's declines with the largest decline experienced in any five-year period, from 1950 to 1996, in the twelve other largest U.S. cities and finds New York among the top five and Los Angeles among the bottom two. They conclude: "How much of the decline [in gun deaths] can be claimed by law enforcement alone simply cannot be determined. . . . The trend in nongun homicide for more than a decade remains a pleasant mystery that shrouds the whole explanation of variations in New York homicide in fog" (1322–23). The comparative picture I am presenting is tailored to factors relevant to the current argument (the sixteen-to-nineteen-year-old age group; the fifteen years from 1984 to 1998, which roughly capture a distinctive period in popular and political cultures in Los Angeles and New York) and will therefore differ from comparisons made for other purposes.

11. After the 1992 riots, LAPD officers were openly contemptuous of expectations that they should try to bring crime down through arrests. One sergeant was quoted in the *Los Angeles Times* as saying: "An officer can go down an alley where gangsters hang out or he can go down a main street where nothing is happening. Why would you choose to go down the alley when the public doesn't seem to support you for your efforts?" (Cannon 1997, 25). I suggest we read this as evidence about how the Los Angeles public was blocked from crediting the police for the subsequent decline in crime, not as demonstrating what the Los Angeles police actually did or, more precisely, did not do.

12. For assessing gang influence, male figures are more telling than are combined sex figures. Of the adolescents arrested for homicides, about 95 percent are male, and among adolescent homicide victims, about 90 percent are male. For New York, for the four years in question, the percentage of sixteen-to-nineteen-year-old homicide victims that was male ranged from 87 percent in 1984 to 93 percent in 1994. In Los Angeles, the range was between 91 and 92 percent for these four years. Population rates that combine male and female figures would unnecessarily dilute and obscure what is going on in contemporary American urban youth violence.

13. As to the lack of opposition from community groups, this story went on to cite Paul Hoffman, legal director of the southern California chapter of the American Civil Liberties Union (ACLU), as saying they were looking into the possibility that police had acted improperly. Six months later, "black leaders, including frequent critics of the Los Angeles Police Department, said Wednesday that a panel created last year by Chief Daryl F. Gates has improved communication and crime-fighting efforts in the city's black communities." These black leaders included Joseph Duff, president of the Los Angeles chapter of the NAACP; a spokesman for the Nation of Islam; Mark Ridley-Scott of the Southern Christian Leadership Conference of Greater Los Angeles; and Urban League president John Mack (*Los Angeles Times* 1990, B3).

14. Miller writes that "the *Times* maintained what was essentially a moratorium on the use of the term 'gang' to refer to regularly congregating youth groups for a period of approximately six years between 1966 and 1972. . . . In late 1971, the moratorium was lifted as suddenly as the *Times* had claimed that gangs had vanished. . . . A year prior to the *Times* report of one hundred gangs in the Bronx and many more in other boroughs, police and Youth Authority officials stated conclusively [to Miller in interviews] that the last gang had disappeared from the streets of the city and that there was *no* gang problem in New York" (1976, 96–97).

15. Parker loved the show. In his words, "*Dragnet* was one of the great instruments to give the people of the United States a picture of the policeman as he really is. It was most authentic. We participated in the editing of the scripts and in their filming. . . . This program showed the true portrait of the policeman as a hard-working, selfless man, willing to go out and brave all sorts of hazards and work long hours to protect the community" (Cannon 1997, 23).

16. The connections between Hollywood and the Los Angeles policies on gangs were not indirect. I draw here on comments over the years from acquaintances who have been in high positions in the music and film industry. "Industry" executives, some of whom were leaders of the southern California branch of the ACLU, were personally intimidated by "thug-like" minority vendors of gang culture who would regularly bring armed associates to business meetings. Through sometimes bitter internal struggles, they pressed the civil liberties organization to lay low while they encouraged law enforcement to conduct Operation Hammer.

17. And the U.S. attorney's office in Los Angeles has never taken initiative in overseeing official misconduct in law enforcement. For law graduates with bright career prospects, the federal prosecution office in Los Angeles offers unrivaled possibilities for obtaining trial experience, especially in large narcotics cases, that is invaluable in the market for civil litigation jobs in large law firms. For personal career advancement, there is no need to take risks in opening controversial cases against the police or, for that matter, against any target. Unless the Justice Department or public outcry creates the initiative, Los Angeles's federal prosecution office never takes responsibility for overseeing the LAPD or any other significant part of the area's governmental life.

18. My understanding of the different cultures in prosecution offices in Los Angeles and New York is based on interviews I have conducted with federal and county prosecutors on scattered occasions and, in particular, on an observational and interview study in the U.S. attorney's office located in Brooklyn in the late 1970s and interviews with assistant U.S. attorneys in Los Angeles in 1980. In one memorable case, the federal district attorney in Brooklyn successfully prosecuted then-Queens district attorney Gold for corruption (the charges included embezzling money by falsely claiming expenses for a trip to a national district attorneys' conference in Las Vegas). Gold, whose defense included the claim that exculpating documents were in a briefcase that was stolen while he was urinating in a public restroom, had himself risen to prominence years before by prosecuting an NYPD brutality case.

19. As noted earlier, Walter Miller in the early 1970s found that the *New York Times* and other newspapers changed their use of the gang metaphor in abrupt fashion not grounded in street realities. The *Times* and the *Daily News* have recently been running an increasing number of gang stories. We may be on the cusp of another sea change in New York crime coverage

20. Such relationships are common. Usually, however, the dialectic is that of a city that, as an economic powerhouse, pits itself against what is seen as a corrupt ceremonial and political capital, for example Milan, with its anticorruption crusading magistrates, and Rome; manufacturing elites in Lyon rebelling against corrupt royal Paris in the late eighteenth century; Monterrey, Mexico, a base of

the anticorruption Partido Acción National (PAN party) that promoted Vincente Fox, and Mexico City; and, at the start of U.S. history, financing and marketing New York vs. ceremonial Washington. In the United States, the lack of a city that is both a political and economic center enables these collective tensions to play out culturally in less constant directions. In the current juxtaposition of coastal cities, Los Angeles, despite its politically neutered status, is cast in the role of a frivolous, ceremonial, superficial cultural capital by the presence of "Hollywood," while New York plays the role of the professionally righteous, managerially elite city.

CHAPTER EIGHT

Many thanks to Liza Weinstein for her superb research assistance and to David Halle, David Howell, and Pamela Frendt for their helpful comments.

1. The family poverty rate is the percentage of families who live below an income threshold adjusted for family size and composition. This method of measuring poverty, which was adopted by the federal government in the 1960s, has been criticized from all quarters. Those who believe that it overstates poverty point out that the definition of "income" excludes important cash, near cash, and in-kind resources such as earned income tax credit refunds, food stamps, and housing assistance. Those who believe that the poverty measure understates poverty focus on the low level of the income thresholds in light of the cost of living. The poverty threshold for a family of one adult and two children in 2000, e.g., was $13,874.

This chapter focuses on poverty rates for families with children, the object of much of the recent policy debate. This group comprises roughly 60 percent of all the poor individuals in New York City.

2. The divergence between the New York City and U.S. poverty rates occurred between the late 1960s, when the two rates were nearly identical, and the early 1980s, when the city poverty rate was roughly twice that for the nation.

3. Working families are defined as families with children that include at least one person who work at any time during the course of the year prior to the survey.

4. New York City's Human Resources Commission has done little, e.g., to track the fate of welfare leavers. To date it has issued only one report, *Leaving Welfare: Findings from a Survey of Former New York City Welfare Recipients* (Bush et al. 1998).

5. The National Bureau for Economic Research dates the national recession from July 1990 to March 1991. In this chapter, we take 1989 as the peak year of the prior boom.

The discussion in this section rests on a more detailed analysis provided in the Working Group on New York City's Low-Wage Labor Market (2000).

6. The figures on payroll growth are tabulated from U.S. Bureau of Labor Statistics, Current Employment Survey data (various years).

7. The $30,000 threshold is roughly midway between 200 percent of the poverty line for a family of three and a family of four.

8. I tabulated declines in goods-producing industries from *Covered Employment and Wages* data provided by the New York State Department of Labor

(2001). This data set is derived from quarterly employer unemployment insurance filings. It provides employment and average wages for detailed (three-digit SIC code) industries. Because the data are for workers covered by the unemployment insurance system they differ from the Current Employment Survey data reported above. The "low-wage service sector" comprised 23 percent of total New York City private-sector employment in 2000.

9. Estimates of adult public assistance leavers are derived from New York City Human Resources Administration caseload data provided by the New York City Independent Budget Office. The number of working-age immigrants seeking work in the low-wage labor market is estimated from New York City Department of Planning (1996) and U.S. Immigration and Naturalization Service (1999). The number of high school leavers coming into the low-wage labor market is estimated from New York City Board of Education data provided in July 2000 by Lori Mei, Deputy Director, Division of Assessment and Accountability.

10. These administrative data are not directly comparable to the Bureau of Labor Force labor force data described above. The growth of the labor force is a net year-to-year change. The administrative data are net changes in the number of adult public assistance recipients. Every welfare leaver is not necessarily a labor force entrant.

11. These data, it should be noted, are significantly different from the by-industry earnings data, discussed in the previous section, that suggest that real earnings have been rising in most industries. Several factors may account for this discrepancy. First, the industry-level data provide average wage rates; these are more highly influenced by the high earnings at the top of the industry job ladder than the median wages reported in this section. Second, many of the high-wage earners captured in the industry data (which measures employment located in the city) are commuters and are not included in the wage data for New York residents.

12. This section follows and updates "More Work, More School . . . More Poverty? The New Poor in New York City" (Community Service Society of New York 2000).

CHAPTER TEN

1. The research for this chapter is based on archival materials from charter reform, newspaper accounts of the process and my own front-row seat as executive director of the city of Los Angeles (Appointed) Charter Reform Commission, 1997–99.

CHAPTER ELEVEN

1. Past research on group conflict has focused on the relationship between intergroup competition and racial prejudice. Specifically, research by sociologist Larry Bobo (1983, 1988, 1996) points to the causal influence of interracial group conflict on racial attitudes such as ethnocentrism and intergroup discrimination. The group-interest approach applies the notion of group conflict to the study of political behavior. Unlike Bobo's research, however, this perspective does not attempt to link perceived conflict to underlying racial attitudes but, rather, suggests that a conflictual decision context makes these attitudes salient

to political choices. Group conflict then is important to political behavior as it influences the relative weights that voters apply to these sets of attitudes in the context of electoral politics.

2. All of the data used in this project come from computer-assisted random digit-dialed citywide telephone surveys. The 1993 New York City preelection poll was conducted in May by WCBS TV and the *New York Times* and includes 1,273 respondents. The 1993 New York City exit poll was conducted by Voter Research and includes 1,788 respondents. The 1997 New York City preelection poll was conducted by ABC News and includes 1,179 respondents. The 1997 New York City exit poll was conducted by Voter News Service and includes 1,951 respondents. The Los Angeles 1993 preelection poll was conducted in May by the *Los Angeles Times* and includes 1,503 respondents (1993b). The Los Angeles 1993 exit poll was also conducted by the *Los Angeles Times* and includes 3,402 respondents (1993c). The 1997 *Los Angeles Times* exit poll includes 3,035 respondents.

3. The logistic regression analyses for 1993 are conducted on preelection polls as the variety of questions necessary to conduct these analyses were not available in the exit polling. The logistic regression technique used here can be somewhat problematic from an interpretive point of view. Regression coefficients represent the increase in a probable Giuliani vote associated with a one-unit increase in the score on any of the relevant measures. Unlike the coefficients in linear regression analysis, however, the impact of any given factor is not constant across values and cannot be interpreted independently of other factor scores. In order to accommodate the difficulty in interpreting these coefficients, I standardized all of the independent variables by uniformly scaling them from 0 to 1. Thus, the regression coefficients for all of the variables represent the relative increase in the probability of a Giuliani vote when an individual moves from the lowest to the highest value in the measure. All of the variables were scaled from most liberal to most conservative or from low to high. Thus a positive and significant regression coefficient means that higher levels of conservatism, education, racial animus, satisfaction with the current status of race relations, or Republican identification are associated with higher probabilities of a Giuliani vote. The uniform scaling of the variables further allows judgments regarding the relative size of the variable's impact on the vote within regression equations.

4. All of the independent variables are scaled from 0 to 1. Thus the regression coefficient represents the relative increase in the probability of a Giuliani vote when an individual moves from the lowest to the highest score on each measure, all else being equal. I report reduced-fit models. Education and income variables were included in earlier versions but failed to attract robust coefficients.

5. Unlike New York, Los Angeles has nonpartisan elections and an at-large primary system. Any candidate who garners more than 50 percent of the vote in the primary is the winner, otherwise the top two candidates vie for the mayoralty in a runoff.

6. For a discussion of black and Latino voting behavior in this election, see Kaufmann (1994).

7. Partisan identification and ideology measures are scaled from 0 to 1;

Democrat to Republican and liberal to conservative. Retrospective evaluations of Bradley are scaled positive to negative. Income is scaled from low to high.

8. The turnout analysis conducted for New York City voting in 1997 employs data from the 1997 annual report of the board of elections. The analysis uses the demographic data for each assembly district to assess its racial composition. Districts with more than 60 percent of any group are categorized as predominantly black, Latino, or white. Districts where no racial or ethnic group comprises 60 percent are categorized as mixed. The reported racial and ethnic turnout rates reflect the aggregate turnout in predominantly white, black, and Latino assembly districts.

CHAPTER TWELVE

1. See, e.g., Engh (2000, 1676) and Coquery-Vidrovitch (2000, 1685).

2. Miami in 1980 and Los Angeles in 1992 are the two riots in the United States in the past two decades in which most people died, eighteen and forty-five, respectively.

3. On Watts, see Fogelson (1969), Cohen (1970), Sears and McConahay (1973), Oberschall (1968), and Horne (1995). On 1992 in Los Angeles, see Morrison and Lowry, Sonenshein, Bobo, Hirosi, Petersilia, Tierney, Frer, Regalado and Sears, all in Baldassare (1994).

4. The other account of the Newark riots is by the executive director of the Department of Urban Works in the Episcopal Diocese of Newark (Wright 1968). Underlining the Newark riot's status as understudied by academics in the New York region, it was left to the Kerner Commission to organize a special survey of the Newark rioters, the only systematic survey on that topic (National Advisory Commission on Civil Disorders 1968, 170–96).

The governor's report on the Crown Heights riots is excellent (Report to the Governor 1993). But there are no studies of Crown Heights by academics. There is an account by the Reverend Herbert Daughtry (1977), pastor of the House of the Lord Pentecostal Church in Brooklyn, which is focused on defending the author from charges that what he did and wrote about Crown Heights and other incidents was anti-Semitic. Daughtry had been very active in New York in opposing injustice toward blacks. There is also a play about Crown Heights (Smith 1993).

5. There are two studies of the 1977 black-out-related riots in New York City, neither by academics. One was prepared for the Defense Civil Preparedness Agency (Stein 1978), and the other for the Ford Foundation by a journalist and by a community organizer (Curvin and Porter 1979). (Porter, the journalist, later became director of the journalism program at Brooklyn College and wrote a study of the 1980 Miami riot [Porter and Dunn 1984].) We do not want to suggest that these studies, or those of the Newark riots, are inadequate, just that the absence of studies by academics is significant.

6. Even the Kerner Commission, e.g., does not formally define a "riot" or "civil disorder" (terms it uses synonymously), though the commission does have a set of criteria for ranking the level of seriousness of riots vs. civil disorders (National Advisory Commission on Civil Disorders 1968, 112–13, 158–64).

7. In this, era labor conflicts also commonly turned to violent riots. For a

comprehensive analysis of deadly ethnic riots, with a focus on those occurring outside the United States, see Horowitz (2001).

8. Examples of other notorious riots in this era are that of 1817, when an anti-Chinese crowd of more than 5,000 ransacked and burned much of San Francisco's Chinatown, and Chicago's 1919 race riot in which thirty-eight people died when whites became angry because a black youth crossed the color line at a public beach.

9. Academic discussions of riots tend to focus on two related questions. First, what are the causes of riots? Second, what kind of people riot? For a summary, see Feagin and Hahn (1973) and Rule (1988). The most reasonable approaches suggest that the answers to both questions are often complex. Most riots are typically the result of many causes, including long and deep-seated grievances, more recent grievances, a triggering event, plus such facilitating phenomena as media coverage, and, in some cases, false and aggravating rumors. The demographic composition of most riots is also typically varied, including people motivated by political and social grievances, the curious, those out to grab loot, criminals, and so on. Indeed, Sears's comment on the complexity of the 1992 Los Angeles riots ("It may in fact have been multiple riots at once" [1994, 251]) seems more broadly applicable.

10. Other definitions of riots are not as useful for our purposes as this one. For example, Spilerman makes the involvement of blacks a necessary criterion for counting as a riot (1976, 772n. 4). This probably made sense for the 1960s riots that he is analyzing but is too restrictive here since it would, e.g., rule out Latino riots as well as police riots. Button defines a riot as "an incident of collective action involving one or more of the following: rock or bottle throwing, fighting, looting, burning and killing" (Button 1978, 182). This definition is consistent with the one used in this chapter, but our stress on the illegal invasion of public space allows for groups being so out of hand as to constitute a "riot" without major violence necessarily occurring. Gilje defines a riot as "any group of twelve or more people attempting to assert their will immediately through the use of force outside the normal bounds of law." Our stress on the lack of concealment enables the routine activities of organized crime (e.g., Mafia) to be excluded from consideration as riots, which solves a problem Gilje concedes that his definition could not solve. On the many issues involved in defining riots, see Marx (1972) and Gilje (1996, 4).

11. The data are in Jacobson (1985, 22–26). The number of buildings burned refer to fires deemed "suspicious" in origin. The number of fires dropped drastically after Lloyds of London, the main underwriter, stopped this type of fire insurance in the Bronx.

12. Giuliani, campaigning for mayor, was one of the speakers addressing the rally.

13. These criteria are consistent with major indices of riot severity used by other authors. For example, Spilerman (1976, 774) and Button (1978, 183) also focus on the number of arrests, number of injuries, number of deaths and amount of property damage. The Kerner Commission (National Advisory Commission on Civil Disorders 1968, 113) includes the length of time the riot lasted, which is clearly important too. It was one of the most widely mentioned fea-

tures of the Crown Heights and Rodney King riots. Hence it is included in the definition used in the text.

14. Using the number of stores damaged rather than a monetary estimate of the amount of damage avoids the need to adjust for inflation. Also, monetary estimates of financial damage from riots are notoriously hard to make with much accuracy.

15. As mentioned above, it is impractical here to cover every riot during the period. Below are two examples of riots, one from each region, that did not qualify as major or mega.

Tompkins Square Park, Manhattan, August 1988. This was both a civilian riot and a police riot. The neighborhood was a mixture of poor residents, counterculture youngsters, nightclubs, and gentrifiers. The park was a gathering place until late into the night for rock fans, the homeless, and others. In June, prodded by the local block association, the Community Board imposed a 1 A.M. curfew for Tompkins Park, which, over the next few weeks, the police enforced to the growing ire of many of those who were accustomed to late night gathering in the park. On the evening of Saturday, August 6, around 11:30, about 150–200 protestors marched into the park waving banners proclaiming "Gentrification is Class War." The protest was boisterous, with firecrackers, but not out of hand. At that point, several of the eighty-six police officers on foot and the eleven officers on horseback removed or covered their badges. Stung by bottles thrown from the crowd the police, numbering now about 450 including reinforcements, waded into the protestors and ran amok through the neighborhood beating protestors and nonprotestors with nightsticks. The turmoil lasted until 6 A.M. Six people were arrested and fifty-two were injured. See Smith (1996) for detail.

Ramona Gardens, East Los Angeles, August 3, 1991. At about 1:30 A.M. on Saturday evening two sheriffs deputies chased a car that they said was speeding into the Ramona Gardens public housing project in East Los Angeles. Their car was hit by a beer bottle thrown from a group partying nearby. The deputies left their car to investigate and got into a dispute with a youth who grabbed the sheriff's flashlight. When the youth ignored an order to drop the flashlight, the deputy shot him dead. A melee broke out involving about 300 people who were protesting the shooting, and for a few hours police officers with shotguns surrounded the 500-unit complex, blocking all traffic in and out. They arrested six people.

16. When Lindsay died in December 2000, most of the obituaries mentioned his visits to Harlem during the period as among his crowning achievements. For example, "Gordon Davis, who was a Lindsay special assistant and is the incoming president of Lincoln Center, remembers, 'I will never forget the night Martin Luther King was killed, because of what John Lindsay did that night. While other cities across America went up in flames, New York did not.' . . . Mr. Lindsay walked through the streets of Harlem that night in 1968. David Garth, his political consultant was with him, along with two aides. 'There was a wall of people coming across 125th Street, going from west to east,' Mr. Garth said, 'I thought we were dead. John raised his hand, said he was sorry. It was very quiet. . . . That gave him credibility when it hit the fan'" (Purnick 2000).

17. The two studies that do discuss the 1977 black-out-related riots, neither by academics, are Stein (1978) and Curvin and Porter (1979).

18. A famous example took place in Boston in 1919 when two-thirds of the police struck. The response from the governor, Calvin Coolidge, and the police commissioner was tepid, and for two days the city was enveloped in riots. A 1969 strike by Montreal police was also accompanied by major riots. Marx (1972) identifies a second type of "issueless riot," consisting of "expressive outbursts which occasionally accompany victory celebrations or ritualized festivals." An example is the joyous rioting that broke out in San Francisco in August 1945 following the news of the Japanese surrender.

19. In a typology of collective disturbances Ted Gurr (1970, 22–58) uses the term "welfare disturbance" to refer to cases in which the violence is aimed at getting more goods, money, or housing.

20. "Most civil disturbances throughout the turbulent 1960s involved some form of protest against police or other forms of authority. The inter group nature of the disturbance in Crown Heights was reminiscent of the racial disturbances occurring in various cities between the 1920s and 1940s" (Report to the Governor 1993, 133). In his concluding chapter, Horowitz (2001, 561) gives reasons why, since 1950, deadly ethnic riots no longer occur in the United States and implies they are unlikely to occur again. These reasons concern the decline of nationalism and of the legitimacy of attributing negative value judgments to certain ethnic groups. In a footnote, Horowitz does acknowledge that Miami in 1980 and Los Angeles in 1992 had some of the features of deadly ethnic riots. He might have added Crown Heights and then might have wondered why there has been a recent partial return to ethnic riots in the three U.S. cities most affected by post-1965 immigration.

21. This riot lasted five days, during which there were eighteen deaths and 1,100 arrests.

22. On rapid changes in the power structure as a critical cause of collective violence in European history, see Tilly (1979).

23. As Gilje (1996, 10) commented about nineteenth-century interethnic or racial relations: "Americans could kill each other because they did not identify with each other."

24. The Kerner Commission argued that the riots of the 1960s were precipitated by a causal chain consisting of three links: first, a reservoir of deep underlying grievances (such as racial discrimination in jobs and housing, high black unemployment, and perceptions of police bias against blacks); second, in the months just before the riot, a pattern of several "incidents" in the neighborhood revolving around particular examples of perceived bias against blacks; followed by, third, a final incident that was usually no different from the previous incidents but in this case "triggered" the riot. The Kerner Commission argued that plausibly the entire chain was the "precipitant" of disorder (National Advisory Commission on Civil Disorders 1968, 118). Spilerman (1971, 1976) has argued that the degree of black deprivation in particular urban neighborhoods had no statistical relation to whether a riot or disturbance would break out or to how severe it would be if it did break out. He argued, on this basis, that the wide availability, nationally, of televised accounts of the riots and

of the underlying grievances was an additional critical causal factor behind the riots.

25. This interpretation of the causes of the 1992 riots was first suggested to us by Jack Katz.

CHAPTER THIRTEEN

1. Washington, D.C.–Baltimore (25 percent), Chicago (19 percent), Philadelphia (18 percent), and even New York (18 percent) had many more blacks. Only Boston (5 percent) and the San Francisco Bay Area (9 percent) were comparable to Los Angeles (Russell 1996).

2. Some have argued that such measures of symbolic racism do not measure racial prejudice at all because they are "confounded" with ideology (Sniderman and Tetlock, 1986). However, numerous studies that have shown that the effects of symbolic racism on candidate and policy preferences typically hold up virtually unchanged when ideology is controlled, as in table 13.2 (e.g., Sears et al. 1997).

3. Gilens (1999) makes a compelling case that welfare, in particular, became strongly racialized in the nation as a whole beginning in the late 1960s and remains quite racialized today.

4. Of the twenty largest cities, those with black mayors that had larger black populations than Los Angeles were Washington, D.C. (66 percent), Baltimore (59 percent), Memphis (55 percent), Philadelphia (40 percent), and Chicago (38 percent).

5. The 2000 presidential voting in Florida created a particularly vehement protest from blacks when it seemed to have violated norms of procedural justice.

6. Such civil disorders inevitably reflect a mixture of group animosities and "rioting for fun and profit," as analyses of the 1960s ghetto rioting indicated (cf. Banfield [1970] with Sears and McConahay [1973]).

7. The University of California, Los Angeles, has a highly diverse student body—almost 40 percent Asian and 15 percent Latino. Its undergraduates are predominantly from California (94 percent) and, especially, from Los Angeles County (47 percent). The university admits from the top one-eighth of California high school graduates. This selectivity is likely, if anything, to underrepresent first-generation immigrants. For a preliminary report of these data, see Sears et al. (2001).

8. Strength of ethnic identity was measured by the sum of three items: "How important is your ethnicity to your identity?" "How often do you think of yourself as a member of your ethnic group?" "How close do you feel to other members of your ethnic group?"

CHAPTER FOURTEEN

I gratefully acknowledge the help of Jordan Fischbach, who conducted research and compiled the gallery and museum maps, Peggy Chapman, who assisted with graphic design, and Jeremy Simon, who provided editorial assistance. Research for this chapter was completed in the fall of the year 2000 and therefore does not reflect some significant changes that have taken place since that time.

1. In 1935 1,129 artists, teachers, potters, photographers, and scholars received Works Projects Administration support in New York (Sandler 1979, 5–8).

2. "I remember," John Baldessari recently recalled, "in the late 1960s at Max's Kansas City—a famous New York bar—a conversation with a lot of well-known artists, brainstorming. I came out with some sort of strange idea. And you could hear a pin drop, and someone said: 'But how would that fit into art history?' You would never hear that question in L.A." (Gopnik 2002).

3. The $2.5 billion figure is from an article in the *New York Times* (September 20, 1964) referenced by Rosenberg and Fliegel (1965). Indicative of the optimism, the *Times* projected that the art market's combined volume would reach $7 billion by 1970.

4. During the oil crisis, art sales in New York attained $1 billion (Mayor's Committee on Cultural Policy 1974, 8).

5. Among the sixties' milestones were the creation of CalArts (1961), a new art department at the University of California, Irvine (1964), the rising influence of UCLA, and the decision to relocate Art Center to a 175-acre campus in Pasadena (1969).

6. Hap Tivey in Wortz1983, 72-75. "Because the Los Angeles gallery system is still fairly weak, the artists here just can't afford, by and large, to become dependent on selling work. As a result you have a situation in which neither fashion nor economics necessarily dictates artistic direction" (Mark Lere quoted in Cotter 1987, 173).

7. There were seventy-five openings in Los Angeles in September 1990, up from fifty-five a year earlier (Clothier 1990).

8. The maps for this article were compiled from multiple sources. The online *ArtScene* guide (www.artscenecal.com) contains a comprehensive listing of galleries and museums in southern California. This information was compared to the *Art in America* annual gallery guide (2000). The May 2000 *Art Now Gallery Guide New York* coupled with the *Art in America* listings and the *Elsewhere: Williamsburg* map yielded addresses for New York. The locations were plotted with *Delorme* XMAP Business Software. Each source had its definition of art galleries, and some borderline institutions did not make the lists. Temporary exhibition spaces and galleries designated by *Art in America* as commercial or print dealerships were excluded (borderline listings were generally accepted). The maps record gallery and museum locations as of July 2000 (Williamsburg locations are updated as of September 2000).

9. Some popular Chelsea-area galleries, in addition to those mentioned, are 303, I-20, D'Amelio Terras, Marianne Boesky, Gorney Bravin and Lee, Greene Naftali, Casey Kaplan, Paul Kasmin, Friedrich Petzel, Postmasters, Max Protech, Holly Solomon, and John Weber.

CHAPTER FIFTEEN

1. In Behrman's play *Biography,* a brash, honest, young, editor tells a writer that "in the new state men like you won't have to prostitute themselves in Hollywood" (1933, 14).

2. The Screen Writers' Guild's presidents from 1933 to 1940 were John Howard Lawson (1933–34), Ernest Pascal (1935–36), Dudley Nichols (1937–38),

Charles Brackett (1938–39), and Sheridan Gibney (1939–41). Ralph Block, the only non–New Yorker among the guild's presidents, had written for both the New York *Herald Tribune* and the *New Republic* before working his way up the hierarchy of the New York offices of the studios, first as director of advertising and publicity for Goldwyn Pictures, then in 1926 working for the Paramount offices. See his obituary in *Variety* (January 16, 1974, 95).

3. Program for the play *Meet the People* (n.d.), *Meet the People* File, Billy Rose Collection, New York Public Library.

4. An exhaustive analysis of this change would exceed the scope of this chapter. Suffice it to say that beyond and before the well-known elements relating to the economic uncertainties of the industry, the beginning of the House Un-American Activities investigations, and the rise of television, the scholar of the Hollywood community ought to consider the reversal of American intelligentsia's attitude toward Hollywood in the postwar period. The democratic possibilities of Hollywood had been advertised at the UCLA Writers' Congress of 1943, which witnessed the collaboration of Hollywoodians and New York film intellectuals like Leo Hurwitz and progressive distributor Arthur Mayer. As the debates at the UCLA Congress show, however, by 1943 several American intellectuals were aware that many of these possibilities had failed to materialize. In the end, while paraded by many as an example, *Confessions* had remained a rather isolated case. The hybridization of Hollywood films with politics and art had been only moderately successful, and Hollywood cinema had also failed to tackle the political and social problems of this country, in particular its racist social order. See Harry Hoijer, "Statement of the Problem," Box 1, "Minority Groups" Folder, Writers Congress Papers, University of California Los Angeles—Special Collections. I extensively examine this transitional period in the final two chapters of Giovacchini (2001b).

5. In this intellectual framework, those New York filmmakers who decided to go to Hollywood in the early thirties have often been seen as cultural sellouts or, as in Richard Pells's *Radical Visions,* as antimodernist intellectuals ([1974] 1984).

6. Martin Jay persuasively writes that the institute did not gather much popularity during its stay in the United States from 1934, when Horkheimer arrived from Geneva at Columbia University, to 1950, when he moved the Frankfurt school back to Bonn. "There was however an area in which Critical Theory did have an influence in the fifties, the debate over mass culture, which reached its crescendo in the middle of the decade" (Jay 1986, 46).

7. The six episodes of *Dreams,* and the nonrealist artists that designed them, are ordered in the following way: (1) Max Ernst, (2) Fernand Léger, (3) Man Ray, (4) Marcel Duchamp, (5) Alexander Calder, and (6) Hans Richter.

8. Mayer's positive evaluation is reported in Otis L. Guernsey, Jr., unidentified clipping, February 20, 1949, *The Quiet One* Clipping File, Billy Rose Collection, New York Public Library.

9. I have based this section of my chapter on a more extensive analysis of the cultural importance of Sarris's criticism, which I have published in Giovacchini (2001a).

10. The six Academy Award winners for best film between 1968 and 1980

with strong New York ties are *Urban Cowboy* (John Schlesinger, 1969), *The French Connection* (William Friedkin, 1971), *The Godfather* (Francis Ford Coppola, 1972), *The Godfather II* (Francis Ford Coppola, 1974), *Annie Hall* (Woody Allen, 1977), *Kramer vs. Kramer* (Robert Benton, 1979).

11. Nor does the most recent generation of independent filmmakers seem particularly interested in resurrecting the rather stern postures of the New American Cinema. On the contrary, as film historian Emanuel Levy has noted, the new generation of independent New York filmmakers, while often taking Scorsese and Allen as models, is characterized by "the absence of prominent followers of an earlier American avant-garde—Stan Brakhage, Robert Frank, Shirley Clarke, Ed Pincus, Jonas Mekas, Rick Leacock, and Andy Warhol to mention a few" (Levy 1999, 54–55).

CONCLUSION

1. A fair example of this distribution of foci in the rebuilding debate were the papers presented at the Evolve New York Conference, Urban Planning Program, Columbia University (May 9, 2002). The proposal for disaggregating growth was presented by the Michael Sorkin Studio, "Rebuilding through Disaggregation" (Sorkin Studio 2002). In August 2002, the New York Stock Exchange, partly for economic reasons and partly driven by concerns to diversify in case of future terrorist attacks, announced it would not build its long-mooted second trading floor across the street from its current Wall Street site but would, instead, either build elsewhere in New York City or beyond the city borders in New York State. Reflecting the new willingness to disaggregate economic development within New York City, as well as the recognition that major economic institutions felt concentration in one location left them too vulnerable to terrorist attacks, the mayor of New York City argued that "Brooklyn or Queens make an awful lot more sense" than Westchester for a new site (Wyatt 2002, B3).

2. Among the other arts-related institutions that the brochure stressed were Socrates Sculpture Park, the Isamu Noguchi Garden Museum, the Kaufman Astoria film and television studios, and the American Museum of the Moving Image.

3. For a skeptical view, see R. C. Baker (2002). A Queens artist, Baker had doubts that the Manhattan-centeredness of many in New York's elite art world was actually breaking down—doubts that were supported by a MoMA employee's comment that the two-mile journey across the East River felt like "being on an adventure" (Baker 2002, A19).

BIBLIOGRAPHY

Aaron, Daniel. 1961. *Writers on the Left*. New York: Harcourt & Brace.

Abbott, Andrew. 1999. *Department and Discipline: Chicago Sociology at One Hundred*. Chicago: University of Chicago Press.

Abrahams, Marvin. 1967. "Functioning of Boards and Commissions in the Los Angeles City Government." Ph.D. diss., University of California, Los Angeles.

Abu-Lughod, Janet L. 1999. *New York, Chicago, Los Angeles: America's Global Cities*. Minneapolis: University of Minnesota Press.

Adrian, Charles R. 1959. "A Typology of Non-Partisan Elections." *Western Political Quarterly* 12:449–58.

Agee, James. 1946. "Films." *Nation* 162 (March 2): 269–70.

Aiken, Michael, and Robert Alford. "Community Structure and Innovation: The Case of Urban Renewal." *American Sociological Review* 35:650–65.

Alba, Richard 1990. *Ethnic Identity: The Transformation of White America*. New Haven, Conn.: Yale University Press.

Alba, Richard, and Victor Nee. 1997. "Rethinking Assimilation Theory for a New Era of Immigration." *International Migration Review* 31:826–74.

Allen, James P., and Eugene Turner. 1997. *The Ethnic Quilt: Population Diversity in Southern California*. Northridge: Center for Geographical Studies, California State University, Northridge.

Alvarez, R. M., and Tara Butterfield. 2000. "The Resurgence of Nativism in California? The Case of Proposition 187 and Illegal Immigration." *Social Science Quarterly* 81:167–80.

Ancess, Jacqueline, and Suzanna Wichterle Ort. 1999. "How the Coalition Campus Schools Have Re-Imagined High School: Seven Years Later." National Center for Restructuring Education, Schools, and Teaching, Teachers College, Columbia University, New York.

Andersen, Thom. 1985. "Red Hollywood." In *Literature and the Visual Arts in Contemporary Society*, edited by S. Ferguson and B. Groseclose. Columbus: Ohio State University Press.

Anderson, Brian C. 1999. "How 211 Nobodies Strangle New York City." *City Journal* 9:54–57.

Appointed Los Angeles Charter Reform Commission. 1998a. "Report on Public Outreach, November 4." City of Los Angeles.

———. 1998b. "Governing Body: Staff Report to the Joint Conference Committee. November 20." City of Los Angeles.

Arax, Mark. 1987. "Monterey Park: The Nation's First Suburban Chinatown." *Los Angeles Times,* April 6, A1.

Arian, A., A. S. Golberg, J. H. Mollenkopf, and E. T. Rogowsky. 1991. *Changing New York Politics.* New York. Routledge.

Aronowitz, Stanley. 1993. "Cultural Politics of the Popular Front." In *Roll Over Beethoven,* edited by S. Aronowitz. Hanover, Conn.: Wesleyan University Press.

Art in America. 2000. "2000 Guide to Galleries, Museums, Artists." Special issue of *Art in America,* no. 8.

Ashton, Dore. 1979. *The New York School: A Cultural Reckoning.* New York: Penguin.

Assembly Select Committee on the California Middle Class. 1998. *The Distribution of Income in California and Los Angeles: A Look at Recent Current Population Survey and State Taxpayer Data.* Sacramento: California State Legislature.

Baker, R. C. 2002. "Take the 7 Train." *New York Times,* April 8, A19.

Baldassare, Mark, ed. 1994. *The Los Angeles Riots: Lessons for the Urban Future.* Boulder, Colo.: Westview Press.

———. 1999. *PPIC Statewide Survey: The Changing Political Landscape of California.* San Francisco: Public Policy Institute of California.

Baldassare, Mark, M. A. Shires, C. Hoene, and A. Koffman. 2000. "The Organizational and Fiscal Challenges of Providing Public Services in Los Angeles County." *Research Brief: Public Policy Institute of California,* vol. 33.

Ballou, Dale. 1996. "The Condition of Urban School Finance: Efficient Resource Allocation in Urban Schools." National Center for Education Statistics, Papers in School Finance. Washington: U.S. Government Printing Office.

———. 1999. "City Students Finally Get Their Day in Court." *Educational Priorities Panel Monitor* 3 (fall): 3, 10–11.

Banfield, Edward C. 1970. *The Unheavenly City.* Boston: Little, Brown.

Baxandall, Michael. 1972. *Painting in Florence in Fifteenth-Century Italy: A Primer in the Social History of Pictorial Style.* Oxford and New York: Oxford University Press.

Bazin, André. 1957. "De la politique des auteurs." *Cahiers du Cinéma* 12, no. 70 (April): 2–11.

Behn, Richard, and Douglas Muzzio. 1993. *Empire State Survey: New Yorkers on Immigration.* New York: Empire Foundation and Lehman Institute.

Behrman, S.N. 1933. *Biography.* New York: Farrar & Rinehart.

———. 1934. "In Defence of Hollywood." *New Yorker* (January 20), 38–43.

Bender, Thomas. 1987. *New York Intellect.* Baltimore: John Hopkins University Press.

Berger, Joseph. 2002. "The Odd Circle of School Control: 'Power to the People' in 1960's Is Now Seen as 'Amateur Hour.'" *New York Times,* June 16, 25.

Bernstein, Iver. 1990. *The New York Riots: Their Significance for American Society and Politics in the Age of the Civil War.* New York: Oxford University Press.

Bernstein, Jared. 1997. "Welfare Reform and the Low-Wage Labor Market: Employment, Wages, and Wage Politics." Technical Paper 226. Economic Policy Institute, Washington, D.C.

Berry, Jeffrey M., Kent E. Portnoy, and Ken Thomson. 1993. *The Rebirth of Urban Democracy.* Washington, D.C.: Brookings Institution.

Betts, Julian R., Kim S. Rueben, and Anne Danenberg. 2000. *Equal Resources, Equal Outcomes: The Distribution of School Resources and Student Achievement in California.* San Francisco: Public Policy Institute of California.

Beveridge, Andrew. 2001. "Redefining Race." *GothamGazette.com,* February (http://www.gothamgazette.com/demographics/feb.01.shtml).

Bigelow, Kathryn. 1991. "One on One: James Cameron and Kathryn Bigelow." *American Film* 16 (7): 40–43.

Black, Gregory D., and Clayton R. Koppes. 1987. *Hollywood Goes to War: How Politics, Profits, and Propaganda Shaped World War Two Movies.* New York: Free Press.

Bloch, H. A., and A. Niederhoffer. 1958. *The Gang.* New York: Philosophical Library.

Bobo, Lawrence. 1983. "Whites' Opposition to School Busing: Symbolic Racism or Realistic Group Conflict?" *Journal of Personality and Social Psychology* 45:1196–1210.

———. 1988. "Group Conflict, Prejudice, and the Paradox of Contemporary Racial Attitudes." In *Eliminating Racism: Profiles in Controversy,* edited by P. A. Katz and D. A. Taylor. New York: Plenum Press.

———. 1999. "Prejudice as Group Position: Micro-Foundation of a Sociological Approach to Racism and Race Relations." *Journal of Social Issues* 55:445–72.

Bobo, Lawrence, and V. L. Hutchings. 1996. "Perceptions of Racial Group Competition: Extending Blumer's Theory of Group Position to a Multiracial Context." *American Sociological Review* 61:951–72.

Bobo, Lawrence, and Devon Johnson. 2001. "Racial Attitudes in Prismatic Metropolis: Mapping Identity, Stereotypes, Competition, and Views on Affirmative Action." In *Prismatic Metropolis: Inequality in Los Angeles,* edited by L. Bobo, M. L. Oliver, J. H. Johnson, Jr., and A. Valenzuela, Jr. New York: Russell Sage Foundation.

Bobo, Lawrence, and Michael P. Massagli. 2001. "Stereotyping and Urban Inequality." In *Urban Inequality: Evidence from Four Cities,* edited by A. O'Connor, C. Tilly, and L. Bobo. New York: Russell Sage.

Bozorgmehr, Mehdi, Claudia Der-Martirosian, and Georges Sabagh. 1996a. "Middle Easterners: A New Kind of Immigrant." In *Ethnic Los Angeles,* edited by R. Waldinger and M. Bozorgmehr. New York: Russell Sage Foundation.

Bozorgmehr, Mehdi, Georges Sabagh, and Ivan Light. 1996b. "Los Angeles: Explosive Diversity." In *Origins and Destinies: Immigration, Race and Eth-*

nicity in America, edited by S. Pedraza and R. Rumbaut. Belmont, Calif.: Wadsworth.

Bratton, W., and W. P. Knobler. 1998. *Turnaround: How America's Top Cop Reversed the Crime Epidemic.* New York: Random House.

Braunder, Sarah, and Pamela Loprest. 1999. "Where Are They Now? What States' Studies of People Who Have Left Welfare Tell Us." New Federalism Series Working Paper A-32. Urban Institute, Washington D.C.

Brennan, Barry. 1977. "The Sinking of the Art World." *Journal: A Contemporary Art Magazine* (January–February), 22–25.

Bridges, Amy. 1997. *Morning Glories: Municipal Reform in the Southwest.* Princeton, N.J.: Princeton University Press.

Brodkin, Karen. 1998. *How Jews Became White Folks and What That Says about America.* New Brunswick, N.J.: Rutgers University Press.

Buhle, Paul, and Patrick McGilligan. 1997. *Tender Comrades.* New York: St. Martin's Press.

Bulmer, Martin. 1984. *The Chicago School of Sociology: Institutionalization, Diversity, and the Rise of Social Research.* Chicago: University of Chicago Press.

Burgess, Ernest W. 1925. "The Growth of the City." In *The City,* edited by R. E. Park, E. W. Burgess, and R. D. McKenzie. Chicago: University of Chicago Press.

Burr, Elizabeth, Gerald C. Hayward, Bruce Fuller, and Michael W. Kirst. 2002. "Crucial Issues in California Education 2000: Are the Reform Pieces Fitting Together?" Policy Analysis for California Education, University of California, Berkeley.

Burrows, Edwin, and Mike Wallace. 1999. *Gotham: A History of New York City to 1898.* New York: Oxford University Press.

Burtless, Gary. 2000. "Can the Labor Market Absorb Three Million Welfare Recipients?" In *The Low-Wage Labor Market: Challenges and Opportunities for Economic Self-Sufficiency,* edited by K. Kaye and D. S. Nightingale. Washington D.C.: U.S. Department of Health and Human Services.

Button, James. 1978. *Black Violence: Political Impact of the 1960s Riots.* Princeton, N.J.: Princeton University Press.

Bush, Andrew S., Swati Desai, and Lawrence M. Mead. 1998. *Leaving Welfare: Findings from a Survey of Former New York City Welfare Recipients.* New York: Office of Policy and Program Analysis, Human Resources Administration.

Campaign for Fiscal Equity. 1999. "Plaintiff's Witnesses: Dr. Hamilton Lankford." Testimony given November 16 and 19. (www.cfequity.org.)

———. 2000. "Reforming New York State's Flawed School Finance System." *In Evidence: Policy Reports from the CFE Trial,* vol. 2 (November).

———. 2001. "Teacher Quality Matters." *In Evidence: Policy Reports from the CFE Trial,* vol. 4 (December).

Campbell, A., P. Converse, W. Miller, and D. Stokes. 1960. *The American Voter.* Chicago: University of Chicago Press.

Cancian, Marie, R. Haveman, T. Kaplan, D. Meyer, and B. Wolfe. 1998. *Work, Earnings and Well-Being after Welfare: What Do We Know?* Madison: Institute for Research on Poverty.

Cannon, L. 1997. "The Blue Line." *California Journal* 28 (July): 22–26.

———. 2000. "LAPD Confidential: America's Most Infamous Police Department Is in Trouble Again Devastated by This Cop's Confession." *New York Times Magazine,* October 1.

Capeci, Dominic. 1977. *The Harlem Riot of 1943.* Philadelphia: Temple University Press.

Carlos, Lisa, and Penny Howell. 1999. *Class Size Reduction in California 1996–98: Early Findings Signal Promise and Concerns.* Report Summary. [Sacramento, Calif.]: CSR Research Consortium.

Carlson, Virginia, and Nikolas C. Theodore. 1995. *Are There Enough Jobs? Welfare Reform and Labor Market Reality.* Dekalb, Ill.: Office for Social Policy Research, Northern Illinois University.

Carmines, E. G., and James A. Stimson. 1989. *Issue Evolution: Race and the Transformation of American Politics.* Princeton, N.J.: Princeton University Press.

Carney, Francis M. 1964. "The Decentralized Politics of Los Angeles." *Annals of the American Academy of Political and Social Science* 353:107–21.

Caro, Robert. 1984. The Power Broker: Robert Moses and the Fall of New York. New York: Knopf.

Castells, Manuel. 1989. *The Informational City: Information Technology, Economic Restructuring, and the Urban-Regional Process.* Oxford and Cambridge, Mass.: Basil Blackwell.

Chan, Sucheng. 1991. *Asian Americans: An Interpretive History.* New York: Twayne Publishers.

Charles, Camille Zubrinsky. 2001. "Residential Segregation in Los Angles." In *Prismatic Metropolis,* edited by L. Bobo, M. L. Oliver, J. H. Johnson, Jr., and A. Valenzuela, Jr. New York: Russell Sage Foundation.

Cheleden, S. V., C. van Laar, and D. O. Sears. 1996. "Becoming an American: The Political Socialization of Latinos." Paper presented at the meeting of the American Political Science Association, San Francisco, Calif., August 29–September 1.

Chemerinsky, E. 2000. "An Independent Analysis of the Los Angeles Police Department's Board of Inquiry Report on the Rampart Scandal." Police Protective League, Los Angeles.

Chin, G. J., ed. 1997. *New York City Police Corruption Investigation Commission, 1894–1994.* Buffalo, N.Y.: William S. Hein & Co.

Christopher, W., and Independent Commission on the Los Angeles Police Department. 1991. *Report of the Independent Commission on the Los Angeles Police Department.* Los Angeles: The Commission.

Chua-Eoan, H. 2000. "Black and Blue." *Time* (March 6), 24–28.

Citrin, J., D. P. Green, and D. O. Sears. 1990. "White Reactions to Black Candidates: When Does Race Matter?" *Public Opinion Quarterly* 54:74–96.

Clare, Henry. 1987. "Los Angeles Art Boom." *Studio International* (May), 38–41.

Clark, G., and M. J. Dear. 1984. *State Apparatus: Structures and Language of Legitimacy.* Boston: Allen & Unwin.

Clark, William. 1996. "Residential Patterns: Avoidance, Assimilation and Succession." In *Ethnic Los Angeles,* edited by R. Waldinger and M. Bozorgmehr. New York: Russell Sage Foundation.

———. 1998. *The California Cauldron: Immigration and the Fortunes of Local Communities.* New York: Guilford Press.

Class Size Reduction Research Consortium. "Class Size Reduction in California, 1996–98: Early Findings Signal Promise and Concerns." Report Summary. June. CSR Research Consortium, California Department of Education.

———. 2002. "Class Size Reduction in California: Summary of Findings from 1999–00 and 2000–01." Edited by Brian M. Stecher and George W. Bohrnstedt. CSR Research Consortium, California Department of Education.

Clothier, Peter. 1989a. "Smoggy Euphoria." *ARTnews* (May), 50–53.

———. 1989b. "L.A.: Outward Bound." *ARTnews* (December), 126–31.

———. 1990. "The Next Wave." *ARTnews* (December), 112–17.

Cohen, Nathan, ed. 1970. *The Los Angeles Riots: A Socio-Psychological Study.* New York: Praeger Publishers.

Colpitt, Frances. 1983. "History Repeats Itself, Parts I, II." *Journal: A Contemporary Art Magazine* (September–October), 39.

Colvin, Richard Lee. 1999. "News Analysis: How L.A. Unified Got into This Fix." *Los Angeles Times,* October 17, A1.

Community Service Society of New York. 2000. "More Work, More School . . . More Poverty?" CSS Data Brief 2. Community Service Society of New York, New York.

Comolli, Jean-Louis, J.-A. Fieschi, G. Guégan, M. Mardore, C. Ollier, and A. Téchiné. 1965. "Vingt ans après: Le cinéma américain et la politique des auteurs." *Cahiers du Cinéma,* no. 172 (November), 18–30.

Cook, Adrian. 1974. *The Armies of the Streets: The New York City Draft Riots of 1863.* Lexington: University Press of Kentucky.

Cope, M. 1997. "Responsibility, Regulation, and Retrenchment: The End of Welfare?" In *State Devolution in America,* edited by L. Staeheli et.al. Thousand Oaks, Calif.: Sage Publications.

Coquery-Vidrovitch, Catherine. 2000. "Is L.A. a Model or a Mess?" *American Historical Review* 105 (5): 1682–90.

Cotter, Holland. 1987. "Eight Artists Interviewed." *Art in America* 75, no. 5 (May): 169.

Council of Economic Advisors. 2001. *Economic Report of the President.* Washington, D.C.: U.S. Government Printing Office.

Crain's New York Business. 2000. *Book of Lists.* New York: Crain's New York Business.

———. 2001. "Economic Spotlight." *Crain's New York Business* (October 15–21), 2.

Crane, Diana. 1987. *The Transformation of the Avant Garde: The New York Art World, 1940–1985.* Chicago: University of Chicago Press.

Crowther, Bosley. 1940. "Realistic Stepchild of the Movies." *New York Times Magazine,* August 25, 12–13.

———. 1949. "The Quiet One." *New York Times,* February 20, 2:1.

Curry, Ramona. 1986. "Twenty-five Years of SCS: A Sociopolitical History." *Journal of Film and Video* 38 (2):90–97.

Curvin, Robert, and Bruce Porter. 1979. *Blackout Looting! New York City, July 13, 1977*. New York: Gardner Press.

Dalaker, Joseph, and Mary Naifeh. 1998. *Poverty in the United States, 1997*. Current Population Reports, ser. P-60: Consumer Income, no. 201. Washington, D.C.: Department of Commerce, Bureau of the Census.

Dalaker, Joseph. 2001. *Poverty in the United States, 2000*. Current Population Reports, ser. P-60: Consumer Income, no. 214. Washington, D.C.: Department of Commerce, Census Bureau.

Darling-Hammond, Linda. 2000. "Teacher Quality and Student Achievement: A Review of State Policy Evidence." *Education Policy Analysis Archives*, vol. 8 (January).

Daughtry, Herbert. 1997. *No Monopoly on Suffering: Blacks and Jews in Crown Heights (and Elsewhere)*. Trenton, N.J.: Africa World Press.

Davidson, Abraham A. 1994. *Early American Modernist Painting, 1910–1935*. New York: Da Capo Press.

Davis, Mike. 1990. *City of Quartz: Excavating the Future in Los Angeles*. New York: Verso.

———. 1998. *Ecology of Fear: Los Angeles and the Imagination of Disaster*. New York: Metropolitan Books.

Dawsey, Darrell. 1989. "Hammering Gangs: Angry Residents in South L.A. Want Police to Hit Harder." *Los Angeles Times*, July 4, 26.

Dear, Michael. 2000. *The Postmodern Urban Condition*. Oxford: Blackwell.

———, ed. 2001. *From Chicago to LA; Making Sense of Urban Theory*. Thousand Oaks, Calif.: Sage Publications.

———. 2002. "Los Angeles and the Chicago School: Invitation to a Debate." *City and Community*, vol. 1.

Dear, Michael, and Steven Flusty. 1998. "Postmodern Urbanism." *Annals of the Association of American Geographers* 88 (1): 50–72.

Denton, Nancy, and Douglas Massey. 1991. "Patterns of Neighborhood Transition in a Multi-Ethnic World: U.S. Metropolitan Areas 1970–1980." *Demography* 28:41–63.

Department of Public and Social Services, Los Angeles County. 1997a. *DPSS Caseload Characteristics, Los Angeles County Totals: Report Month of August 1997*. City of Industry, Calif.: Bureau of Administrative Services, Research and Statistics Section.

———. 1997b. *Welfare Caseloads and Labor Market January 1976–December 1997*. City of Industry, Calif.: Bureau of Administrative Services, Research and Statistics Section.

———.1998a. *Caseload Characteristics, Los Angeles County Totals: Report Month of August 1998*. City of Industry, Calif.: Bureau of Administrative Services, Research and Statistics Section.

———. 1998b. *Caseload Characteristics, Los Angeles County Totals: Report Month of December 1998*. City of Industry, Calif.: Bureau of Administrative Services, Research and Statistics Section.

———. 1998c. *GR Report on Discontinuance of Cash Grant: Report Month of December 1998*. City of Industry, Calif.: Bureau of Administrative Services, Research and Statistics Section.

———. 1998d. *Number of Penalties in Effect—December 1998*. City of Industry, Calif.: Bureau of Administrative Services, Research and Statistics Section.

———. 1998e. *Number of Sanctions in Effect—December 1998*. City of Industry, Calif.: Bureau of Administrative Services, Research and Statistics Section.

———. 1999a. "Caseload Data January 1990–August 1999" (http://www.ladpss.org/dpss/r_and_s). Bureau of Administrative Services, Research and Statistics Section, City of Industry, Calif.

———. 1999b. *GAIN Sanction Report—4/98 to 12/98*. City of Industry, Calif.: Bureau of Administrative Services, Research and Statistics Section.

———. 2002. *Statistical Report, April 2002*. City of Industry, Calif.: Research, Evaluation and Quality Assurance Division.

DeVerteuil, G., W. Lee, and J. Wolch. 2002. "New Spaces for the Local State? The Case of General Relief in Los Angeles County." *Journal of Social and Cultural Geography* 3 (3):229–46.

Devine, John. 1996. *Maximum Security: The Culture of Violence in Inner-City Schools.* Chicago: University of Chicago Press.

DiCamillo, M., and M. Field. 1996. *Post-Election Survey: Synopsis of the Findings.* San Francisco: Field Institute.

Dillingham Commission. 1911. Reports of the Immigration Commission. Washington, D.C.: Government Printing Office.

Dmytryk, Edward. 1959. *Oral History.* New York: Columbia University Oral History Project.

Drayse, M., D. Flaming, and P. Force. 2000. *The Cage of Poverty.* Los Angeles: Economic Roundtable.

Dugan, James. 1939. "Hollywood's Greatest Films." *New Masses,* May 9, 27–29.

Dugger, Celia W. 1996. "Queens Old-Timers Uneasy as Asian Influence Grows." *New York Times,* March 31, A1.

Duneier, Mitch. 1999. *Sidewalk.* New York: Farrar, Straus & Giroux.

Dykstra, Clarence A. 1925. "Los Angeles Returns to the Ward System." *National Municipal Review* 14 (May): 210–12.

Economic Alliance of the San Fernando Valley. 2000. *San Fernando Valley Almanac.* Woodland Hills, Calif.: Civic Center, Project Strategies Group.

Economic Policy Institute. 2000. *State Income Inequality Continued to Grow in Most States in the 1990s, Despite Economic Growth and Tight Labor Markets.* Washington, D.C.: Center on Budget and Policy Priorities.

Edison Media Research. 2001. *New York City Mayoral Election Exit Poll, November 6.* Somerville, N.J.: Edison Media Research.

Education Week on the Web. 2002. "Quality Counts 2002: California Report Card." (http://www.edweek.com/sreports/qc02/rc/rcard_frameset.htm.)

Edwards, Richard C. 1979. *Contested Terrain: The Transformation of the Workplace in the Twentieth Century.* New York: Harper Torchbooks.

Ellis, V. 1998. "Dispute Delays Benefits for Elderly Immigrants." *Los Angeles Times,* November 29, B1.

———. 1999. "State Fails to Meet US Welfare-to-Work Goal; Officials Say the Standards for Two-Parent Families Are Too High: Penalties Could Reach $28 Million." *Los Angeles Times,* January 25, A1.

Elsaesser, Thomas. 2000. *Weimar Cinema and After: Germany's Historical Imaginary.* New York: Routledge.

Engh, Michael. 2000. "At Home in the Hetropolis: Understanding Postmodern L.A." *American Historical Review* 105 (5): 1676–82.

EPP Monitor. 1998. "Class Size Matters." *Educational Priorities Panel Monitor* 3:3.

Erie, Steven P. 1992. "How the Urban West Was Won: The Local State and Economic Growth, 1880–1932." *Urban Affairs Quarterly* 27 (June): 519–54.

Espenshade, Thomas, and Charles A. Calhoun. 1993. "An Analysis of Public Opinion toward Undocumented Immigration." *Population Research and Policy Review* 12:189–224.

Espenshade, Thomas, and Karen Hempstead. 1996. "Contemporary American Attitudes toward U.S. Immigration." *International Immigration Review* 30:535–70.

Ethington, Philip. 2001 "Waiting for the 'LA School.'" *Southern California Quarterly,* vol. 80.

Ethington, Philip, William Frey, and Dowell Myers. 2001. "The Racial Resegregation of Los Angeles County, 1940–2000." Race Contours 2000 Project, Public Research Report no. 2001-04 (http://www.usc.edu/schools/sppd/research/census2000/race_census/research_reports/Contours_PRR_2001-04e.pdf).

Evans, H., and F. Rose. 1993. "GOP's New York Win, Echoing Los Angeles Vote, Gives Party Chance to Provide Cures for Urban Ills." *Wall Street Journal,* November 4, A16.

Fagan, J., F. E. Zimring, and J. Kim. 1998. "Declining Homicide in New York: A Tale of Two Trends." *Journal of Criminal Law and Criminology* 88 (4): 1277–1324.

Failing, Patricia. 1986. "Los Angeles Gets a New Temple of Art." *ARTnews* (November), 88–94.

Fainstein, Norman, and Susan Fainstein. 1983. *Restructuring the City: The Political Economy of Urban Redevelopment.* New York: Longman.

Fainstein, Susan S. 2001. "Inequality in Global City-Regions." In *Global City-Regions,* edited by A. J. Scott. New York: Oxford University Press.

Fainstein, Susan S., Ian Gordon, and Michael Harloe, eds. 1992. *Divided Cities: New York and London in the Contemporary World.* Oxford: Blackwell.

Farber, Manny. [1966] 1971. *The Subverters.* Reprinted in *Negative Space: Manny Farber and Criticism.* New York: Praeger Publishers.

Farley, Reynolds. 2001. "Metropolises of the Multi-City Study of Urban Inequality: Social, Economic, Demographic, and Racial Issues in Atlanta, Boston, Detroit, and Los Angeles." In *Urban Inequality: Evidence from Four Cities,* edited by A. O'Connor, C. Tilly, and L. Bobo. New York: Russell Sage.

Farley, Reynolds, and William H. Frey. 1994. "Change in the Segregation of Whites from Blacks during the 1980s: Small Steps toward a More Integrated Society." *American Sociological Review* 59:23–45.

Feagin, Joe, and Harlan Hahn. 1973. *Ghetto Revolts: The Politics of Violence in American Cities.* New York: Macmillan.

Ferguson, Otis. 1940. "Life Goes to the Pictures." *Films* 1 (spring): 24–25.

Ferman, Barbara. 1997. *Challenging the Growth Machine: Neighborhood Politics in Chicago and Pittsburgh.* Lawrence: University Press of Kansas.

Ferraro, John. 1998. Letter to Elected Charter Reform Commissioners. December 4. City Archives, Los Angeles.

Finegold, Kenneth. 1995a. *Experts and Politicians: Reform Challenges to Machine Politics in New York, Cleveland, and Chicago.* Princeton, N.J.: Princeton University Press.

———. 1995b. "Traditional Reform, Municipal Populism, and Progressivism: Challenges to Machine Politics in Early-Twentieth-Century New York City." *Urban Affairs Review* 31 (September): 20–42.

Fiorina, Morris. 1981. *Retrospective Voting in American National Elections.* New Haven, Conn.: Yale University Press.

Fishman, Robert. 1987. *Bourgeois Utopias: The Rise and Fall of Suburbia.* New York: Basic Books.

Fliegel, Seymour. 1993. *Miracle in East Harlem: The Fight for Choice in Public Education.* New York: Times Books.

Flynn, Kevin. 1999. "Revisiting a Killing: Many Details, but a Mystery Remains." *New York Times,* February 14.

Fogelson, Robert. 1967. *The Fragmented Metropolis: Los Angeles, 1850–1930.* Cambridge, Mass.: Harvard University Press.

———. 1969. *Mass Violence in America: The Los Angeles Riots.* New York: Arno Press.

Fong, Timothy P. 1994. *The First Suburban Chinatown: The Remaking of Monterey Park, California.* Philadelphia: Temple University Press.

Footnotes. 2001. "Orange County: What Better Place to Go to Study Social Change?" *Footnotes* (March 1).

Force, P., M. Drayse, and J. Henly. 1998. *By The Sweat of Their Brow: Welfare to Work in Los Angeles.* Los Angeles: Economic Roundtable.

Fox, J. A. 2000. *Demographics and U.S. Homicide: The Crime Drop in America.* New York: Cambridge University Press.

Fox, Julian. 1996. *Woody: Movies from Manhattan.* London: B. T. Bratsford.

Frank, Peter. 1978. "Patterns in the Support Structure for California Art." *Journal: A Contemporary Art Magazine* (June–July), 42.

Fredrickson, George M. 1999. "Models of American Ethnic Relations: A Historical Perspective." In *Cultural Divides: Understanding and Overcoming Group Conflict,* edited by D. A. Prentice and D. T. Miller. New York: Russell Sage.

Fredrickson, Tom. 2000. "NYC Economy to Slow after Near-Record Year." *Crain's New York Business* 16, no. 50 (December 11–17): 1, 42.

Freedman, Morris. 1953. "New England and Hollywood." *Commentary* 16 (October): 392.

Freese, P. 1997. "Mugging People Who Have Nothing." *Los Angeles Times,* January 17, B9.

Frendt, Pamela, and Marc Levine. 1996. "Welfare Reform and the Metropolitan Milwaukee Labor Market." Briefing Paper 6. Center for Economic Development, University of Wisconsin—Milwaukee, Milwaukee.

Frey, William H. 1991. "Are Two Americas Emerging?" *Population Today* 19: 6–8.

———. 1994. "The New White Flight." *American Demographics* (April).

———. 1996. "Immigration, Domestic Migration, and Demographic Balkanization in America: New Evidence for the 1990s." *Population and Development Review,* vol. 22, no. 4.

———. 2001. "Coming Full Circle." *Milken Institute Review,* vol. 3, no. 4.

Fried, Joseph P., and Blaine Harden. 1999. "The Louima Case: The Overview." *New York Times,* June 9, M1.

Friedman, David. 2000. "Education: A System Rigged for the Wealthy." Los Angeles Times, November 5, M:1.

Friedmann, Johnathan. 1986. "The World City Hypothesis." *Development and Change* 17 (1): 69–83.

Friis-Hansen, Dana, et al., eds. 1987. *LA, Hot and Cool, the Eighties: MIT List Visual Arts Center, December 19 1987–February 7, 1988.* Cambridge, Mass.: The Center.

Fruchter, Norm. 2000. "Millennial Prospects: Educating All New Yorkers." Paper presented at Rethinking the Urban Agenda, a series presented by the Century Foundation and the Graduate Center of the City University of New York, New York, November 2.

Fulton, William. 1997. *The Reluctant Metropolis: The Politics of Urban Growth in Los Angeles.* Point Arena, Calif.: Solano Press Books.

Gabler, Neal. 1988. *An Empire of Their Own: How the Jews Invented Hollywood.* New York: Doubleday Anchor.

Gallagher, J., et al. 1998. *One Year after Federal Welfare Reform: A Description of State Temporary Assistance for Needy Families (TANF) Decisions as of October 1997.* Occasional Paper no. 6. Washington, D.C.: Urban Institute.

Gans, Herbert. 1962a. "City Planning and Urban Realities." *Commentary* (February).

———. 1962b. *The Urban Villagers: Group and Class in the Life of Italian-Americans.* New York: Free Press.

———. 1967. *The Levittowners: Ways of Life and Politics in a New Suburban Community.* New York: Pantheon.

———. 1991. "Life on the Edge of the City's Limits." *Washington Post National Weekly Edition, Book World* (September 9–15).

———. 1997. "Towards a Reconciliation of 'Assimilation' and 'Pluralism': The Interplay of Acculturation and Ethnic Retention." *International Migration Review* (winter).

Garoogian, Andrew, ed. 2000 *America's Top-Rated Smaller Cities: A Statistical Profile.* 3d ed. Lakeville, Conn.: Grey House Publishing.

Garoogian, David, ed. 2001a. *America's Top-Rated Cities: A Statistical Handbook.* Vols 1–4. 8th ed. Millerton, N.Y.: Grey House Publishing.

———, ed. 2001b *The Comparative Guide to American Suburbs.* 2d ed. Millerton, N.Y.: Grey House Publishing.

Garreau, Joel. 1988. *Edge City: Life on the New Frontier.* New York: Doubleday.

George, Manfred. 1939. "Was geht in Hollywood an." *Aufbau* (May 1), 16.

Gerber, Elizabeth R. 1998. *Interest Group Influence in the California Initiative Process (May).* San Francisco: Public Policy Institute of California.

Gessner, Robert. 1934. "Massacre in Hollywood." *New Theater* 1 (March): 17.

———. 1935. "Movies about Us." *New Theater* 2 (June): 12.

Gilens, Martin. 1999. *Why Americans Hate Welfare: Race, Media, and the Politics of Antipoverty Policy.* Chicago: University of Chicago Press.

Giles, M. W. 1977. "Percent Black and Racial Hostility: An Old Assumption Revisited." *Social Science Quarterly* 58:412–17.

Gilje, Paul. 1996. *Rioting in America.* Bloomington: Indiana University Press.

Gilliam, F. D. Jr. 1996. "Exploring Minority Empowerment: Symbolic Politics, Governing Coalitions, and Traces of Political Style in Los Angeles." *American Journal of Political Science* 40 (1): 56–81.

Gilliam, F. D., Jr., and K. F. Kaufmann. 1998. "Is There an Empowerment Life-cycle? Long-Term Black Empowerment and Its Impact on Voter Participation." *Urban Affairs Review* 33 (6): 741–66.

Gilliard, Barry Linn, and Victoria Levitt. 1977. "The Quiet One: A Conversation with Helen Levitt, Janice Loeb, and Bill Levitt." *Film Culture,* 63–64.

Giovacchini, Saverio. 1995. "Shoot the Right Thing: African American Filmmakers and the Contemporary American Public Discourse." In *Towards a New American Nation,* edited by A. M. Martellone. Bodmin: Keele University Press.

———. 1998. "In the Land of Milk and Honey: European Anti-Fascist Exiles in Hollywood." *Historical Journal of Film, Radio, and Television* 18 (August): 437–43.

———. 2001a. "The Gap: How André Bazin Became Captain America." In *Across the Atlantic: Representations and Cultural Exchanges, 1800–2000,* edited by L. Passerini. Brussels: Presses Interuniversitaires Européennes PIE-Peter Lang.

———. 2001b. *Hollywood Modernism. Film and Politics in the Age of the New Deal.* Philadelphia: Temple University Press.

Gittell, Marilyn. 1973. *School Boards and School Policy: An Evaluation of Decentralization in New York City.* New York: Irvington Publishers.

———. 1994. "School Reform in New York and Chicago: Revisiting the Ecology of Local Games." *Urban Affairs Quarterly* 30 (September): 136–51.

Gladstone, David L., and Susan S. Fainstein. 2001. "Tourism in US Global Cities: A Comparison of New York and Los Angeles." *Journal of Urban Affairs* 23 (1): 23–41.

Glaser, J. 1994. "Back to the Black Belt: Racial Environment and the White Racial Attitudes in the South." *Journal of Politics* 56 (1): 21–41.

Glazer, Nathan. 1997. *We Are All Multiculturalists Now.* Cambridge, Mass.: Harvard University Press.

Glazer, N., and D. Moynihan. [1963] 1970. *Beyond the Melting Pot: The Negroes, Puerto Ricans, Jews, Italians, and Irish of New York City.* Cambridge, Mass.: MIT Press.

Gold, Matea. 2001. "Grass Roots Politics Hints at Cracks in L.A.'s 'Ethnic Walls'." *Los Angeles Times,* January 14.

Gold, Mike. 1937. "Notes on the Cultural Front." *New Masses* (December 7), 1–5.

———. 1946. "The Road to Retreat." *Daily Worker,* February 12.

Goldberger, Paul. 1996. "The New Times Square: Magic That Surprised the Magicians." *New York Times,* October 15, C11.

Goldin, Greg. 2002. "Urbanites: Frank O. Gehry Has Gripe." *LA Weekly*, April 5–11.

Goodnough, Abby. 1999. "For School Districts Sullied by Corrupt Past, New Doubt." *New York Times*, December 13, B1.

Goodwin, M., S. Duncan, and S. Halford. 1993. "Regulation Theory, the Local State, and the Transition of Urban Politics." *Society and Space* 11:67–88.

Gorman, Paul. 1996. *Left Intellectuals and Popular Culture in Twentieth-Century America*. Chapel Hill: University of North Carolina Press.

Government Accounting Office (GAO). 1998. *Welfare Reform: Many States Continue Some Federal or State Benefits for Immigrants*. Report to the Ranking Minority Member, Subcommittee on Children and Families, Committee on Labor and Human Resource, U.S. Senate. Washington, D.C.: Government Accounting Office.

Governor's Commission on the Los Angeles Riots [McCone Commission]. 1965. Violence in the City—an End or a Beginning? Los Angeles.

Gozlan, Gérard. 1968. "In Praise of André Bazin." *Positif* 47. English Translation and reprint in *The New Wave*, edited by Peter Graham52–71. New York: Doubleday.

Gratz, Roberta, and Norman Mintz. 1998. *Cities Back from the Edge: New Life for Downtown*. New York: John Wiley.

Greenberg, Clement. 1961. "Avant Garde and Kitsch." In *Art and Culture: Critical Essays*, edited by Clement Greenberg. Boston: Beacon Press.

Greene, David A. 1996. "LA Story." *Art Monthly*, no. 193 (May), 8–10.

Greene, Robert. 1998a. "Charterama: The Powerlessness of the Mayor." *Civic Center NEWSource* (July 27).

———. 1998b. "Charter Commissioners Trim CAO in Favor of Mayor, City Controller." *Metropolitan News-Enterprise* (August 31).

Greer, Scott. 1962. *The Emerging City*. New York: Free Press.

Groneman, Carol, and David Reimers. 1995. "Immigration." In *The Encyclopedia of New York*, edited by Kenneth T. Jackson. New Haven, Conn.: Yale University Press.

Guilbaut, Serge. 1983. *How New York Stole the Idea of Modern Art: Abstract Expressionism, Freedom and the Cold War*. Chicago: University of Chicago Press.

Gunning, Tom. 1992. "'Loved Him, Hated Him': An Interview with Andrew Sarris." In *To Free the Cinema: Jonas Mekas and the New York Underground*, edited by D. E. James. Princeton, N.J.: Princeton University Press.

Gurin, Patricia, Shirley Hatchett, and J. S. Jackson. 1989. *Hope and Independence: Blacks' Response to Electoral and Party Politics*. New York: Russell Sage Foundation.

Gurr, Ted. 1970. *Why Men Rebel*. Princeton, N.J.: Princeton University Press.

Halle, David. 1984. *America's Working Man: Work, Home and Politics among Blue-Collar Property Owners*. Chicago: University of Chicago Press.

———. 1993. *Inside Culture: Art and Class in the American Home*. Chicago: Chicago University Press.

Harrington, Curtis. 1947–48. "The Dangerous Compromise." *Hollywood Quarterly* 3: 405.

Harris, Thomas J. 1990. *Bogdanovich's Picture Shows.* Metuchen, N.J.: Scarecrow Press.

Harrison, R. J. and D. H. Weinberg. 1992. "Racial and Ethnic Residential Segregation in 1990." Paper presented at the annual meeting of the Population Association of America, Denver, Colo., April 13.

Hatocollis, Anemona. 1999. "A Dogged Investigator, Often Attacked." *New York Times,* December 8, B8.

Hayden, Tom. 1967. *Rebellion in Newark.* New York: Random House.

Haynes, Bruce. 2001. *Red Lines, Black Spaces.* New Haven, Conn.: Yale University Press.

Hendrie, Caroline. 1997. "Second Thoughts about LEARN Surface in L.A." *Education Week* (May 28).

———. 1998. "Philadelphia Restructuring Would Be a First for Big U.S. Districts." *Education Week* (January 14).

Henig, Jeffrey R., Richard C. Hula, MMarion Orr, and DDesiree S. Pedescleaux. 1999. *The Color of School Reform: Race, Politics, and the Challenge of Urban Education.* Princeton, N.J.: Princeton University Press.

Herbert, Bob. 2001. "Mr. Ferrer's Dilemma." *New York Times,* May 10, A29.

Hess, Frederick M. 1999. *Spinning Wheels: The Politics of Urban School Reform.* Washington, D.C.: Brookings Institution Press.

Hess, John. 1974. "*La Politique des Auteurs:* World View as Aesthetics." *Jump Cut,* no. 2 (July–August), 20–22.

Higgins, Winifred Haines. 1963. "Art Collecting in the Los Angeles Area, 1910–1960." Ph.D. diss., University of California, Los Angeles.

Hinckley, Barbara. 1981. *Coalitions and Politics.* New York: Harcourt Brace Jovanovich.

Hochschild, Jennifer L. 1995. *Facing Up to the American Dream.* Princeton, N.J.: Princeton University Press.

Horkheimer, Max, and Theodor W. Adorno. 1947. *Dialektik der Aufklärung.* Amsterdam: Querido.

Horne, Gerald. 1995. *Fire This Time: The Watts Uprising and the 1960s.* Charlottesville: University of Virginia Press.

Horowitz, Donald. 2001. *The Deadly Ethnic Riot.* Berkeley: University of California Press.

Horton, John. 1995. *The Politics of Diversity: Immigration, Resistance, and Change in Monterey Park, California.* Philadelphia: Temple University Press.

Huyssen, Andreas. 1986. *After the Great Divide: Modernism, Mass Culture, Postmodernism.* Bloomington: Indiana University Press.

Hymowitz, Kay. 2000. "Confusing Poverty and Immigration." *New York Post,* July 25.

Institute for Education and Social Policy. 1997. *Who We Are: Students and Schools in the NYNSR Project, 1995–96.* A Report of the New York Networks for School Renewal (NYNSR) Research Collaborative. July. New York: New York University.

International Trade Administration. 2001. "Oversees Visitors to Select U.S. Cities/Hawaiian Islands, 2000–1999." (http://tinet.ita.doc.gov/view/f-2000-45-561.)

Itzigsohn, Jose, and Carlo Dore-Cabral. 2001. "The Manifold Character of Panethnicity: Latino Identities and Practices among Dominicans in New York City." In *Mambo Montage: The Latinization of New York,* edited by Agustin Laó-Montes and Arlene Dávila. New York: Columbia University Press.

Ivins, Molly. 1998. "California Politics Is Nutty Way of Operating." *Fresno Bee,* May 31, F3.

Jackson, B. O., and M. B. Preston. 1994. "Race and Ethnicity in Los Angeles Politics." In *Big City Politics, Governance, and Fiscal Constraints,* edited by G. E. Peterson. Washington, D.C.: Urban Institute Press.

Jackson, Kenneth T. 1985. *Crabgrass Frontier: The Suburbanization of the United States.* New York: Oxford University Press.

———, ed. 1995. *The Encyclopedia of New York.* New Haven, Conn.: Yale University Press.

———. 1996. "All the World's a Mall: Reflections on the Social and Economic Consequences of the American Shopping Center." *American Historical Review,* vol. 101, no. 4.

———. 2000. "Memphis Tennessee." In *American Places: Encounters with History,* edited by W. Leuchtenberg. New York: Oxford University Press.

Jacobs, Jane. 1961. *The Death and Life of Great American Cities.* New York: Random House.

Jacobs, John. 1999. "At Education Helm, Eastin Battles to Turn Schools." *Sacramento Bee,* May 6, B7.

Jacobs, Lewis. 1939. *The Rise of American Film.* New York: Harcourt & Brace.

———. 1947–48. "Experimental Cinema in America." *Hollywood Quarterly* 3: 111–24, 278–93.

Jacobson, Michael. 1985. "The Enigmatic Crime: A Study of Arson in New York City." Ph.D. diss., City University of New York.

Jacobson, Michael, and Philip Kasinitz. 1986. "Burning the Bronx for Profit: Why Arson Pays." *Nation* (November 15).

Jacoby, Tamar. 1998. *Someone Else's House: America's Unfinished Struggle for Integration.* New York: Basic Books.

James, David E., ed. 1992. *To Free the Cinema: Jonas Mekas and the New York Underground.* Princeton, N.J.: Princeton University Press.

James, George. 1992. "Police Department Report Assails Officers in New York Rally." *New York Times,* September 29, A1.

Janowitz, Morris. 1969. "Patterns of Collective Racial Violence." In *The History of Violence in America: Historical and Comparative Perspectives,* edited by H. Graham and T. Gurr. Beverly Hills, Calif.: Sage Publications.

Jaret, Charles. 1999. "Troubled by Newcomers: Anti-Immigrant Attitude and Action during Two Eras of Mass Immigration to the United States." *Journal of American Ethnic History* 18:9–39.

Jay, Martin. 1986. "The Frankfurt School in Exile." In *Permanent Exiles,* edited by M. Jay. New York: Columbia University Press.

Jencks, Christopher, and Meredith Phillips, eds. 1998. *The Black-White Test Score Gap.* Washington, D.C.: Brookings Institution Press.

Jepsen, Christopher, and Steven Rivkin. 2002. *Class Size Reduction, Teacher*

Quality, and Academic Achievement in California Public Elementary Schools. San Francisco: Public Policy Institute of California.
Jerome, Victor J. 1950. *The Negro in Hollywood Films.* New York: Mass & Mainstream.
Jessop, B. 1994. "The Transition to Post-Fordism and the Schumpeterian Workfare State." In *Toward a Post-Fordist Welfare State,* edited by R. Burrows and B. Loader. London: Routledge.
Johnson, Jean, Steve Farkas, and Ann Duffett, with Joanna McHugh. 1998. "Some Gains, but No Guarantees: How New York City's Employers Rate the Public Schools." Opinion Research Report from Public Agenda Conducted for the New York City Partnership and Chamber of Commerce. July (http://www.publicagenda.org/aboutpa/aboutpa30.htm).
Johnston, Robert C. 1998. "California Poll Finds Support for State Action on Schools." *Education Week* (March 11).
———. 2000. "Settlement Ends Crew's Tenure as N.Y.C. Chief." *Education Week* (January 12).
Johnston, Robert C., and Jessica L. Sandham. 1999. "States Increasingly Flexing Their Policy Muscle." *Education Week* (April 14).
Kadetsky, Elizabeth. 1994. "Bashing Illegals in California: 'Save Our State' Initiative." *Nation* 259:416–19.
Kael, Pauline. 1965. *I Lost It at the Movies.* Boston: Little, Brown.
Kaprow, Allan. 1964. "Should the Artist Be a Man of the World?" *Art News* (October), 34–37.
Karlstrom, Paul J. 2000. "Art School Sketches: Notes on the Central Role of Schools in California Art and Culture." In *Reading California: Art, Image and Identity, 1900–2000,* edited by S. Barron, S. Bernstein, and I. S. Fort. Berkeley: University of California Press.
Karmen, Andy. 2000. *New York Murder Mystery: The True Story behind the Crime Crash of the 1990s.* New York: New York University Press.
Kasinitz, Philip. 1992. *Caribbean New York: Black Immigrants and the Politics of Race.* Ithaca, N.Y.: Cornell University Press.
Kassin, Saul. 2002. "False Confessions and the Jogger Case." *New York Times,* November 1, A31.
Katz, Jack. 1987. "What Makes Crime 'News'?" *Media, Culture and Society* 9 (January): 47–75.
———. 1988. *Seductions of Crime: Moral and Sensual Attractions in Doing Evil.* New York: Basic Books.
———. 1991. "The Only Way Los Angeles Can Clear Its Name of Police Brutality." *Los Angeles Times,* March 10.
———. 1992a. "The DA's Failure Is Fully Revealed." *Los Angeles Times,* May 4.
———. 1992b. "Gangs Aren't the Cause of Crime." *Los Angeles Times,* May 31.
———. 1996. "The Social Psychology of Adam and Eve." *Theory and Society* 25 (4): 545–82.
———. 2000. "The Gang Myth." In *Social Dynamics of Crime and Control: New Theories for a World in Transition,* edited by S. Karstedt and K. D. Bussmann, 171–87. Portland, Oreg.: Hart.
Kaufmann, K. M. 1994. "Us versus Them: A Group Conflict Analysis of the 1993

Los Angeles Mayoral Election." Paper presented at the annual meeting of the Western Political Science Association, Albuquerque, March.

———. 1996. "Riots and Rebellion: The Impact of Civil Unrest on the voting Behavior of Whites." Paper presented at the annual meeting of the Midwest Political Science Association, Chicago, April.

———. 1998a. "Racial Conflict and Political Choice: A Study of Voting Behavior in Los Angeles and New York." *Urban Affairs Review* 33 (5): 655–85.

———. 1998b. "Voting in American Cities: The Group Interest Theory of Local Voting Behavior." Ph.D. diss., University of California, Los Angeles.

Kieffer, George. 1998. "A Stronger Mayor, but Not a CEO." *Los Angeles Times,* November 18.

Kiewiet, D. Roderick. 1999. "Californians Can't Blame Everything on Proposition 13." *Institute of Governmental Studies and Public Affairs Report,* vol. 40 (November).

Kinder, D. R., and Lynn M. Sanders. 1996. *Divided by Color: Racial Politics and Democratic Ideals.* Chicago: University of Chicago Press.

Kinder, D. R., and D. O. Sears. 1981. "Prejudice and Politics." *Journal of Personality and Social Psychology* 40 (3): 414–31.

Kino, Carol. 1996. "Living Room Galleries. *Atlantic Monthly* (July).

Kirby, A. 1990. "A Smoking Gun: Relations between the State and the Local State in the Case of Firearms Control." *Policy Studies Journal* 18 (3): 739–52.

Kleppner, Paul, and Nikolas Theodore. 1997. *Work after Welfare: Is the Midwest's Booming Economy Creating Enough Jobs?* Midwest Job Gap Project. Dekalb, Ill.: Office for Social Policy Research, Northern Illinois University.

Kling, Rob, Spencer Olin, and Mark Poster, eds. 1995. *Beyond the Edge: The Dynamism of Postsuburban Regions.* Berkeley: University of California Press.

Koch, Howard. 1974. Interview by Eric Sherman. Oral History Transcripts, Louis B. Mayer Library, American Film Institute, Los Angeles.

Kodras, J. 1997. "Restructuring the State: Devolution, Privatization, and the Geographic Redistribution of Power and Capacity in Governance." In *State Devolution in America,* edited by L. Staeheli et. al. Thousand Oaks, Calif.: Sage Publications.

Kohn, Michael. 1985. "Report from Los Angeles." *Flash Art* (summer), 37–39.

Kontorovich, E. V. 1998. "Why New York Can't Build Schools." *City Journal* 8:27–35.

Kornblum, William. 2002. *At Sea in the City.* Chapel Hill, N.C.: Algonquin Books.

Koszarsky, Richard. 2000. "New York, New York: Il centro di produzione della costa orientale." In *Storia del cinema mondiale,* vol. 2, *Gli Stati Uniti,* edited by Gian Piero Brunetta. Turin: Einaudi.

Kracauer, Siegfried. 1948. "Filming the Subconscious." *Theater Arts* 32 (February): 37–38.

Krugman, Paul. 2002. "For Richer." *New York Times,* October 20, magazine.

Krull, Craig. 1996. *Photographing the L.A. Art Scene, 1955–1975.* Santa Monica, Calif.: Smart Art Press.

Lake, R. 1997. "State Restructuring, Political Opportunism, and Capital Mobility." In *State Devolution in America,* edited by Lynn A. Staeheli; Janet E. Kodras; and Colin Flint. Thousand Oaks, Calif.: Sage Publications.

Lal, Barbara Ballis, 1990. The *Romance of Culture in an Urban Civilization.* New York: Routledge.

Lambert, B. 1997. "At Fifty, Levittown Contends with Its Legacy of Bias." *New York Times,* December 28, 23.

Lamont, Michèle. 2000. *The Dignity of Working Men: Morality and the Boundaries of Race, Class, and Immigration.* Cambridge, Mass.: Harvard University Press.

Lankford, Hamilton, Susanna Loeb, and James Wyckoff. 2002. "Teacher Sorting and the Plight of Urban Schools: A Descriptive Analysis." *Educational Evaluation and Policy Analysis* 24:37–62.

Lapinski, John S., P. Peltola, G. Shaw, and A. Yang. 1997. "The Polls—Trends: Immigrants and Immigration." *Public Opinion Quarterly* 63:356–93.

Laslett, John H. M. 1996. "Historical Perspectives: Immigration and the Rise of a Distinctive Urban Region, 1900–1970." In *Ethnic Los Angeles,* edited by R. Waldinger and M. Bozorgmehr. New York: Russell Sage Foundation.

Lauria, M. 1997. "Introduction: Reconstructing Urban Regime Theory." In *Reconstructing Urban Regime Theory: Regulating Urban Politics in a Global Economy,* edited by M. Lauria. Thousand Oaks, Calif.: Sage Publications.

Laws, G. 1989. "Privatization and Dependency on the Local Welfare State." In *the Power of Geography: How Territory Shapes Social Life,* edited by J. Wolch and M. Dear. Boston: Unwin Hyman.

Lawson, John Howard. 1953. *The Film in the Battle of the Ideas.* New York: Masses & Mainstream.

Lee, Barrett, and Peter Wood. 1991. "Is Neighborhood Racial Succession Place Specific?" *Demography* 28:21–40.

Lee, Felicia. 1990. "Loose-Knit Type of Youth Gangs Troubling Police." *New York Times,* December 11, B3.

Lee, Jaekyun. 1997. "State Activism in Education Reform: Applying the Rasch Model to Measure Trends and Examine Policy Coherence." *Educational Evaluation and Policy Analysis* 19:29–43.

Lee, W. 1994. "Restructuring the Local Welfare State: A Case Study of Los Angeles." Ph.D. diss., University of Southern California.

Legislative Analyst's Office. 1996. *Federal Welfare Reform (H.R. 3734): Fiscal Effect on California.* Sacramento: Legislative Analyst Office.

———. 1999. *A K–12 Master Plan: Starting the Process.* May. Sacramento: Legislative Analyst Office.

Levin, Kim. 1988. *Beyond Modernism: Essays on Art from the '70s and 80s.* New York: Harper & Row.

Levy, Emanuel. 1999. *Cinema of Outsiders.* New York: New York University Press.

Li, Wei. 1997. "Spatial Transformation of an Urban Ethnic Community from Chinatown to Chinese Ethnoburb in Los Angeles." Ph.D. diss., University of Southern California.

Lieberson, Stanley, and Arnold R. Silverman. 1965. "The Precipitants and Underlying Conditions of Race Riots." *American Sociological Review* 30:887–98.

Lii, Jane H. 1996. "Neighborhood Report: Northern Queens: Common Heritage, but No Common Ground." *New York Times,* April 21, 11:1.

Little Hoover Commission. 1999. *Recommendations for Improving the School Facility Program in Los Angeles Unified School District.* Sacramento, Calif.: The Commission.

Lobo, Peter, Joseph Salvo, and, Vicky Virgin. 1996. *The Newest New Yorkers: 1990–1994.* New York: Department of City Planning.

Loewen, James W. 1971. *The Mississippi Chinese: Between Black and White.* Cambridge, Mass.: Harvard University Press.

Logan, John, Richard D. Alba, and Wenquan Zhang, 2002. "Immigrant Enclaves and Ethnic Communities in New York and Los Angeles." *American Sociological Review,* vol. 67, no. 2.

Lopez, David E., Eric Popkin, and Edward Telles. 1996. "Central Americans: At the Bottom, Struggling to Get Ahead." In *Ethnic Los Angeles,* edited by R. Waldinger and M. Bozorgmehr. New York: Russell Sage Foundation.

Lopez, Ian Haney. 1994. "The Social Construction of Race: Some Observations on Illusion, Fabrication, and Choice." *Harvard Civil Rights–Civil Liberties Law Review* 29, no. 1 (winter).

Loprest, Pamela. 1999. "Families Who Left Welfare: Who Are They and How Are They Doing?" New Federalism Series Discussion Paper 99-02. Urban Institute, Washington, D.C.

Los Angeles Business Journal. 1999. *The Book of Lists.* Los Angeles: Los Angeles Business Journal.

———. 2000. *The Book of Lists.* Los Angeles: Los Angeles Business Journal.

Los Angeles Convention and Visitors Bureau. 2002. "La Travel Review: A Review of Travel and Tourism in L.A." March (http://www.lacvb.com/poe02/poe02fst_vs.html).

Los Angeles County Economic Development Corporation (LAEDC). 2001. "LAEDC Releases Mid-2001 Economic Forecast—Southern California and California to Narrowly Avoid a Recession." July 30 press release (http://laedc.org/Press/PR42.shtml).

Los Angeles Police Department. 2001. *Crime Statistics Summary.* (http://www.lapdonline.com/general_information/crime_statistics/2001_crime_summary.htm.)

Los Angeles Times. 1990. "Gates' Forum Credited for LAPD-Black Dialogue," *Los Angeles Times,* January 18, B3.

———. 1993a. "Schools and Immigration." Poll 306. *Los Angeles Times,* 8.

———. 1993b. "Los Angeles Times Poll: Mayoral Runoff Election." Poll 314, May. Computer file. *Los Angeles Times;* distributed by Roper Center for Public Opinion Research, Storrs, Conn.

———. 1993c. "Los Angeles Times Poll: Mayoral Runoff Election." Exit Poll 316, June. Computer file. *Los Angeles Times;* distributed by Roper Center for Public Opinion Research, Storrs, Conn.

———. 1993d. "Orange County Immigration and Race Relations." Poll 319. *Los Angeles Times,* 9.

———. 1997. "Los Angeles Times Poll: Primary Mayoral Election." Exit Poll

394, April 8. Computer file. *Los Angeles Times;* distributed by Roper Center for Public Opinion Research, Storrs, Conn.

———. 1998. "Supervisors OK Plan to Link Aid, Job Training." *Los Angeles Times,* December 16, B14.

———. 1999a. "The State: There Republicans Go Again: Son of Prop. 187 a Possibility." *Los Angeles Times,* November 14.

———. 1999b. "Prop. 187 Backers Pushing New Initiative." *Los Angeles Times,* December 3, B1.

———. 1999c. "Two Ways of Looking at Latino Vote: Republicans Can't Agree on Plan to Shed Anti-immigrant Perception and Win Converts While Democrats Worry That They Might Lose Hold." *Los Angeles Times,* December 26, B1.

———. 2000. "Successor Plan to Prop. 187 Won't Be on Ballot: Backers of Proposed State Initiative to Deny Services to Illegal Immigrants Didn't Get Enough Signatures or Gain Republican Support." *Los Angeles Times,* April 22, Orange County ed., B3.

———. 2001a. "Census 2000." *Los Angeles Times,* March 30.

———. 2001b. "Latinos Recover Optimism Lost in '90s." *Los Angeles Times,* March 11, B1, 8.

———. 2001c. "Los Angeles Times Poll: Los Angeles City General Election." Exit Poll 460, June 2001. Computer file. *Los Angeles Times;* distributed by Roper Center for Public Opinion Research, Storrs, Conn.

Louisiana Museum of Modern Art. 1997. *Sunshine and Noir: Art in L.A., 1960–1997.* Humbelaek, Denmark: Louisiana Museum of Modern Art.

Loukaitou-Sideris, Anastasia, and Tridib Banerjee. 1998. *Urban Design Downtown.* Berkeley: University of California Press.

Macdonald, Dwight. [1960] 1983. "Masscult and Midcult." *Partisan Review* (spring). Reprinted in *Against the American Grain.* New York: Da Capo, 3–75.

MacDonald, Heather. 1999. "How Gotham's Elite High Schools Escaped the Leveller's Ax." *City Journal* 9 (spring): 68–79.

MacDonald, Scott. 1997. "An Interview with Amos Vogel." *Wide Angle* 19: 49–83.

MaCurdy, T., and M. O'Brien-Strain. 1997. *Who Will Be Affected by Welfare Reform in California.* San Francisco: Public Policy Institute of California.

Maltz, Albert. 1946. "What Shall We Ask of Writers?" *New Masses,* February 12, 19–22.

Mamiya, Christin. 1992. *Pop Art and Consumer Culture: American Super Market.* Austin: University of Texas Press.

Marcuse, Peter. 1989. "Dual City: A Muddy Metaphor for a Quartered City." *International Journal of Urban and Regional Research* 13 (4): 697–708.

Marcuse, Peter, and Ronald van Kempen. 2000. Introduction to *Globalizing Cities: A New Spatial Order?* edited by Peter Marcuse and Ronald van Kempen. Oxford: Blackwell.

Markowitz, Ruth Jacknow. 1993. *My Daughter, the Teacher: Jewish Teachers in the New York City Schools.* New Brunswick, N.J.: Rutgers University Press.

Markusen, Ann, and Vicky Gwiasda. 1994. "Multipolarity and the Layering of Functions in World Cities: New York City's Struggle to Stay on Top." *International Journal of Urban and Regional Research* 18 (2): 167–93.

Markusen, Ann, P. Hall, S. Campbell, and S. Deitrick. 1991. *The Rise of the Gunbelt.* New York: Oxford University Press.

Marx, Gary. 1972. "Issueless Riots." In *Collective Violence,* edited by James Short and Marvin Wolfgang. New York: Aldine.

Massey, Douglas. 1996. "The Age of Extremes: Concentrated Affluence and Poverty in the 21st Century." *Demography* 33:395–412.

Massey, Douglas, R. Alarcon, J. Duran, and H. Gonzolez. 1987. *Return to Aztlan: The Social Process of International Migration from Western Mexico.* Berkeley and Los Angeles: University of California Press.

Massey, Douglas, and Nancy Denton. 1988. "The Dimensions of Racial Segregation." *Social Forces* 67, no. 2 (December): 281–315.

———. 1989. "Hypersegregation in US Metropolitan Areas: Black and Hispanic Segregation along Five Dimensions." *Demography* 26:373–93.

———. 1993. *American Apartheid: Segregation and the Meaning of the Underclass.* Cambridge, Mass.: Harvard University Press.

Massey, Douglas, and A. B. Gross. 1991. "Explaining Trends in Residential Segregation, 1970–1980" *Urban Affairs Quarterly* 27:13–25.

Mauro, Frank, and Gerald Benjamin, eds. 1989. *Restructuring the New York City Government: The Reemergence of Municipal Reform.* New York: Academy of Political Science.

Mayor LaGuardia's Commission on the Harlem Riot of March 19, 1935. 1969. *The Complete Report of Mayor LaGuardia's Commission on the Harlem Riot of March 19, 1935.* New York: Arno Press.

Mayor's Committee on Cultural Policy. 1974. *Report of the Mayor's Committee on Cultural Policy, October 15, 1974.* New York: The Committee.

Mazón, Mauricio. 1984. *The Psychology of Symbolic Annihilation: The Zoot-Suit Riots.* Austin: University of Texas Press.

McCall, Carl H. 2000. "Getting It Right on How School Aid Is Distributed." *New York Post,* January 11, 38.

McCarten, John. 1960. "No Rose Colored Glasses?" *New Yorker* (June 18), 108–10.

McCarthy, Kevin, Steven Erie, and Robert E. Reichardt. 1998. "Comparing Los Angeles' Governance System with Those of Other Cities." In *Meeting the Challenge of Charter Reform,* edited by K. McCarthy, S. Erie, and R. E. Reichardt. Santa Monica, Calif.: Rand Corporation.

McDonald, Joseph. 1999. "The Trouble with Policy-Minded School Reform." *Education Week* (September 8).

McGreevy, Patrick. 1998. "Labor Leaders Key on Mayor's Role." *Los Angeles Daily News,* July 28.

McKenna, Kristine. 1996. "A Tale of Three Cities." *Art and Antiques* (summer), 45–59.

McKinley, James. 1992. "Dinkins Denounces Police Protest as Furthering an Image of Racism." *New York Times,* September 18.

McMahon, Thomas L., L. Angelo, T. A. Ross, and R. P. Ryan. 1998. *New York City's Middle Class: The Need for a New Urban Agenda*. New York: New York Council.

McPhail, Clark. 1971. "Civil Disorder Participation: A Critical Examination of Recent Research." *American Sociological Review* 36:1058–73.

McWilliams, Carey. [1946] 1983. *Southern California Country: An Island on the Land*. Edited by Gibbs M. Smith. Salt Lake City: Peregrine Books.

———. 1949. *North from Mexico: the Spanish-Speaking People of the United States*. Philadelphia: J. B. Lippincott Co.

Meier, Deborah. 1996. *The Power of Their Ideas: Lessons for American from a Small School in Harlem*. Boston: Beacon Press.

Mekas, Jonas. [1959] 1970. "A Call for a New Generation of Film-Makers." *Film Culture,* vol. 19. Reprinted in *Film Culture Reader,* edited by P. A. Stitney. New York: Praeger Publishers.

———. 1959. "Movie Journal." *Village Voice,* August 5, 6.

———, ed. 1963. "American Directors." Special issue of *Film Culture,* no. 28 (spring).

Mendel, Ed. 1999. "Political Feud Scuttled 1980s School Reform." *San Diego Union-Tribune,* March 21, A1.

Merl, Jean. 1998. "Quiet Force at City Hall Wades into Charter Fray Politics." *Los Angeles Times,* September 14.

———. 2002. "Inglewood Leaders Strive to Prevent Post-Trial Violence." *Los Angeles Times,* October 14, B1.

Myers, Henry. 1959. *Oral History.* New York: Columbia University Oral History Project.

Miller, D. W. 2000. "The New Urban Studies." *Chronicle of Higher Education* (August 18), A15.

Miller, Matthew. 1998. "Watching the California Dream Fade." *San Diego Union-Tribune,* April 2, B-11.

Miller, W. B. 1976. "Youth Gangs in the Urban Crisis Era." In *Delinquency, Crime, and Society.* edited by James F. Short, Jr, 91–128. Chicago: University of Chicago Press.

Mills, C. Wright. 1956. *White Collar.* New York: Oxford University Press.

Min, Pyong Gap. 1996. *Caught in the Middle: Korean Communities in New York and Los Angeles.* Berkeley: University of California Press.

Mishel, Lawrence, John Bernstein, and John Schmitt. 2001. *The State of Working America: 2000–2001.* Ithaca, N.Y.: Cornell University Press.

Mishel, Lawrence, and John Schmitt. 1995. "Cutting Wages by Cutting Welfare: The Impact of Reform on the Low-Wage Labor Market." Briefing Paper 58. Economic Policy Institute, Washington, D.C.

Mollenkopf, John Hull. 1992. *A Phoenix in the Ashes.* Princeton, N.J.: Princeton University Press.

———. 1995. "New York: The Great Anomaly." Paper delivered at the annual meeting of the American Political Science Association, Chicago, September.

———. 1999. "Urban Political Conflicts and Alliances: New York and Los Angeles Compared." In *The Handbook of International Migration: The Ameri-*

can Experience, edited by C. Hirschman, P. Kasinitz, and J. DeWind. New York: Russell Sage.

Mollenkopf, John Hull, and Manuel Castells, 1991. *Dual City: Restructuring New York.* New York: Russell Sage.

Mollenkopf, John, David Olson, and Timothy Ross. 2001. "Immigrant Political Participation in New York and Los Angeles." In *Governing American Cities: Interethnic Coalitions, Competitions, and Conflict,* edited by Michael Jones-Correa. New York: Russell Sage Foundation.

Monkkonen, Eric. 2001. *Murder in New York City.* Berkeley: University of California Press.

Moore, Charles, Peter Becker, and Regula Campbell. 1984. *The City Observed, Los Angeles: A Guide to Its Architecture and Landscapes.* New York: Vintage Books.

Morgenthau, T. 1999. "Justice for Louima." *Newsweek* (June 7), 42.

Morris, Richard T., and Vincent Jeffries. 1970. "The White Reaction Study." In *The Los Angeles Riots: A Socio-Psychological Study,* edited by Nathan Cohen. New York: Praeger Publishers.

Morrison, James. 1998. *Passport to Hollywood: Hollywood Films, European Directors.* Albany, N.Y.: SUNY Press.

Morrison, Peter and Ira Lowry. 1994. "A Riot of Color: The Demographic Setting." In *The Los Angeles Riots,* edited by Mark Baldassare. Boulder, Colo.: Westview Press.

Moure, Nancy Dustin Wall. 1993. *Loners, Mavericks and Dreamers: Art in Los Angeles before 1990.* Laguna Beach, Calif.: Laguna Beach Art Museum.

Mozingo, Joe. 2000. "New Urban Oases." *Los Angeles Times,* November 7, B-1.

Muchnic, Suzanne. 1995. "Los Angeles: Innovations and Optimism." *ARTnews* (March), 104–5.

Muller, Thomas. 1993. *Immigrants and the American City.* New York: New York University Press.

Mumford Center. 2001. "Ethnic Diversity Grows, Neighborhood Integration Is at Standstill." (http://mumford1.dyndns.org/cen2000/report.html.)

Murray, Charles. 1984. *Losing Ground: American Social Policy, 1950–1980.* New York: Basic Books.

Murray, R., and A. Vedlitz. 1978. "Racial Voting Patterns in the South: An Analysis of Major Elections from 1960 to 1977 in Five Cities." *American Academy of Political and Social Science Annals* 439:29–39.

Myres, John W. 1999. "Why Reforms Won't Work in California." *Education Week* (June 9).

Myres, Terry R. 1995. "Call My Agent." *New Art Examiner* (May), 23–25.

Nash, Gerald. 1985. *The American West Transformed: The Impact of the Second World War.* Bloomington: Indiana University Press.

National Advisory Commission on Civil Disorders [Kerner Commission]. 1968. *Report of the National Advisory Commission on Civil Disorder.* Washington, D.C.: Government Printing Office.

Newman, Amy. 2000. *Challenging Art: Artform, 1962–1974.* New York: SoHo Press.

Newsweek. 1989. "A Racist Ambush in New York." *Newsweek* (September 4), 25.

Newton, Jim. 1998a. "Labor Attacks Charter Reforms." *Los Angeles Times*, July 28.

———. 1998b. "Top City Official Declares War on Charter Reforms." *Los Angeles Times*, September 11.

———. 1999a. "Charter Panel Rejects Plan to Compromise." *Los Angeles Times*, January 6.

———. 1999b. "City Charter Panel Seeks to Accelerate Reform Plan Politics." *Los Angeles Times*, February 18.

New Visions for Public Schools. 1999. "Crisis in Leadership: Finding and Keeping Leaders for New York City's Public Schools." February. New Visions for Public Schools, New York.

New York City. 1998. "Mayor's Office of Immigrant Affairs and Language Services: Mission Statement." (http://www.nyc.gov/html/imm/html/missionx.html.)

———. 1999. "Mayor's Office of Immigrant Affairs and Language Services." (http://www.nyc.gov/html/imm/html/missionx.html).

New York City Department of City Planning. 1999. *The Newest New Yorkers, 1995–1996*. New York: New York City Department of City Planning.

———. 2002. *NYC 2000: Results from the 2000 Census, Socioeconomic Characteristics*. New York: New York City Department of City Planning.

New York City Police Department. 2002. "Compstat Citywide Calendar Year Historical Comparisons 2001 through 1993." (http://www.nyc.gov/html/nypd/pdf/chfdept/cscity.pdf.)

New York Observer. 1999. "Are the Poor Getting Poorer?" *New York Observer*, October 18.

New York State Department of Labor. 2001. "Covered Employment and Wages Program (ES-202)." Data provided electronically by James Brown, Division of Research and Statistics, New York State Department of Labor, Albany, N.Y.

New York State Education Department. 2001. *New York, the State of Learning: Statewide Profile of the Educational System*. Albany, N.Y.: State Education Department.

New York Times. 2000. "Race Declines in Importance in Board Search for Chancellor." *New York Times*, February 14, sec. B.

Norden, Louis. 1935. "Two Scoundrel Die Hard." *New Theater* 2 (June): 12.

NYC and Company. 2002. "Visitor Statistics." (http://www.nycvisit.com/content/index.cfm?pagePkey=598.)

Oberschall, Anthony. 1968. "The Los Angeles Riot of August 1965." *Social Forces* 15:322–41.

Odets, Clifford 1948. "On Coming Home," *New York Times*, July 25, 2:1.

Office of Management and Budget. 2000. "Revisions to the Standards for the Classification of Federal Data on Race and Ethnicity." February 10. (http://www.whitehouse.gov/omb/fedreg/ombdir15.html.)

Office of the State Comptroller. 1998. "New York City's Economic and Fiscal Dependence on Wall Street." Report 5–99, August 13. New York: Office of the State Comptroller.

Ogawa, Rodney T., Deborah Huston, and Deborah E. Stine. 1999. "California's

Class-Size Reduction Initiative: Differences in Teacher Experience and Qualifications across Schools." *Educational Policy* 13:659–73.

Olson, Lynn. 1997. "'Annenberg Challenge' Proves to Be Just That." *Education Week* (June 25).

Ong, Paul. 2001. "Residential Segregation in United States Metropolitan Areas." Center for Regional and Policy Studies, University of California, Los Angeles.

Orfield, Gary, and Susan E. Eaton. 1996. *Dismantling Desegregation: The Quiet Reversal of Brown v. Board of Education.* New York: New Press.

Ortiz, Vilma. 1996. "The Mexican-Origin Population: Permanent Working Class or Emerging Middle Class?" In *Ethnic Los Angeles,* edited by R. Waldinger and M. Bozorgmehr. New York: Russell Sage Foundation.

Parker, Dorothy. 1936. "To Richard with Love." *Screen Guilds' Magazine* 3 (May): 8.

Parker, Laura. 1989. "Police Officer Is Convicted of Slayings: Verdict Reached Amid High Tension in Miami." *Washington Post,* December 8.

Parks, B. C. 2000. "Rampart Area Corruption Inquiry." Los Angeles Police Department, Los Angeles.

Parvin, Jean. 1991. "Immigrants Migrate to International City." *Crain's New York Business* 7, no. 27 (July): 8.

Patterson, Orlando. 2001. "Race by the Numbers." *New York Times,* May 8, A31.

Pattillo-McCoy, Mary. 2000. *Blue Picket Fences.* Chicago: University of Chicago Press.

Peck, J. 2001. *Workfare States.* London: Guilford Press.

Pecora, Vincent. 2002. "The Culture of Surveillance." *Qualitative Sociology* (spring).

Pells, Richard H. [1974] 1984. *Radical Visions and American Dreams: Culture and Social Thought in the Depression Years.* New York: Harper. Reprinted, Middletown, Conn.: Wesleyan University Press.

Perelman, Joel, and Roger Waldinger. 1997. "Second Generation Decline? Children of Immigrants, Past and Present—a Reconsideration." *International Migration Review* (winter).

Perelman, Joel, and Mary C. Waters. 2002. *The New Race Question: How the Census Counts Multiracial Individuals.* New York: Russell Sage Foundation.

Petersilia, Joan, and Allan Abrahamse. 1994. "A Profile of Those Arrested." In *The Los Angeles Riots: Lessons for the Urban Future,* edited by Mark Baldassare. Boulder, Colo.: Westview Press.

Peterson, P. 1981. *City Limits.* Chicago: University of Chicago Press.

Petrie, Graham. 1985. *Hollywood Destinies.* London: Routledge.

Pettigrew, T.F. 1971. "When a Black Candidate Runs for Mayor: Race and Voting Behavior." In *People and Politics in Urban Society,* edited by H. Hahn. Beverly Hills, Calif.: Sage Publications.

Pettigrew, Thomas F., and D. A. Alston. 1988. *Tom Bradley's Campaigns for Governor.* Washington, D.C.: Joint Center for Political Studies.

Pew Historic Center. 2002. "Latino Growth in Metropolitan America." Washington, D.C.: Brookings Institution.

Pinch, P. 1992. "Ordinary Places? The Social Relations of the Local State in Two 'M4-Corridor' Towns." *Political Geography* 11 (5): 485–500.

Pitt, Leonard, and Dale Pitt. 1977. *Los Angeles A to Z: An Encyclopedia of the City and County.* Berkeley: University of California Press.

Plagens, Peter. 1974. *Sunshine Muse, Art on the West Coast, 1945–1970*. New York: Praeger Publishers.

———. 1981. "Schjeldahl Demystified by Plagens." *Journal: A Contemporary Art Magazine* (winter), 26.

Pogodzinsky, J. M. 2000. "The Teacher Shortage: Causes and Recommendations for Change." Department of Economics, San Jose State University, San Jose, Calif.

Port Authority of New York and New Jersey. 2000. *Regional Economy: Review and Outlook for the New York–New Jersey Metropolitan Region.* New York: Port Authority of New York and New Jersey.

Porter, Bruce, and Marvin Dunn. 1984. *The Miami Riot of 1980: Crossing the Bounds.* Lexington, Mass.: D. C. Heath.

Portes, Alejandro. 1997. "Immigration Theory for a New Century: Some Problems and Opportunities." *International Migration Review* (winter).

Portes, Alejandro, and Ruben G. Rumbaut. 1996. *Immigrant America.* 2d ed. Berkeley and Los Angeles: University of California Press.

Portes, Alejandro, and Alex Stepick. 1993. *City on the Edge: The Transformation of Miami.* Berkeley: University of California Press.

Principe, Francis J. 1997. "The Dyer Avenue Express (Reverend's Observation of Religious Practices of People Taking the Same Subway Train)(The Last Word)." *Commonweal* 124:31.

Purnick, Joyce. 2000. "Remembering a Mayor, Faults and All." *New York Times,* December 21, B1.

Putnam, Robert. 2000. *Bowling Alone: The Collapse and Revival of American Community.* New York: Simon & Schuster.

Queens Council on the Arts. 2001. *The Art Loop: Western Queens.* Woodhaven, N.Y.: Queens Council on the Arts.

Quinnipiac College Polling Institute. 1999. "New York City Trends." *Trend Archives.*

Quinnipiac University Polling Institute. 2002. "New York City Poll Release, March 27." Quinnipiac University Polling Institute, Hamden, Conn.

Raab, Selwyn. 1997. "Experts Say Gigante Had Reduced Role, So Conviction Won't Hurt Crime Family." *New York Times,* July 26, sec. 1, 25.

Rabinovitz, Lauren. 1997. "Experimental and Avant-Garde Cinema in the 1940s." In *Boom and Bust: The American Cinema in the 1940s,* edited by Thomas Schatz. New York: Scribner's.

Rathod, Janet, et al. In press. "New York City Politics versus Federal Politics: The Formation of Immigration Policy Executive Order 124." *Wagner Review.*

Ravitch, Diane, and Joseph P. Viteritti. 1997. "New York: The Obsolete Factory." In *New Schools for a New Century: The Redesign of Urban Education,* edited by Diane Ravitch and Joseph P. Viteritti. New Haven, Conn.: Yale University Press.

Reiff, David. 1991. *Los Angeles: Capital of the Third World.* New York: Simon & Schuster.

Reiner, I. 1992. "Gangs, Crime and Violence in Los Angeles." Office of the District Attorney, County of Los Angeles, Los Angeles.

Report to the Governor on the Disturbance in Crown Heights [Girgenti Report]. 1993. "Report to the Governor on the Disturbance in Crown Heights." New York State Division of Criminal Justice Services, Albany.

Richter, Hans. [1976] 1986. *The Struggle for the Film.* New York: St. Martin's Press.

Riesman, David, with Reuel Denney and Nathan Glazer. 1950. *The Lonely Crowd.* New Haven, Conn.: Yale University Press.

Roane, Kit R. 1998. "Thirty-nine Charged in Crackdown on Lower East Side Drug Gang." *New York Times,* May 16, B3.

Robins, Corinne. 1984. *The Pluralist Era: American Art, 1968–1981.* New York: Harper & Row.

Rodriguez, Clara. 1992. "Race, Culture, and Latino 'Otherness' in the 1980 Census." *Social Science Quarterly* 73:931–37.

Rodriguez Clara, and Hector Cordero-Guzman. 1992. "Placing Race in Context." *Ethnic and Racial Studies* 15 (October): 523–41.

Roediger, David R. 1968. *The Wages of Whiteness: Race and the Making of the American Working Class.* New York: Verso.

Rogers, David. 1968. *110 Livingston Street: Politics and Bureaucracy in the New York City School System.* New York: Vintage.

Rohrlich, Ted. 1997a. "LA Officials Join Protest of Cuts in Immigrants 'Aid'." *Los Angeles Times,* June 11, B3.

———. 1997b. "Riordan Plan Would Add to Mayor's Clout." *Los Angeles Times,* October 15.

———. 1998. "Charter Panel Compares Big Orange to Big Apple." *Los Angeles Times,* April 2.

Romano Jay. 2002. "Lawmakers to Co-ops: Justify Bans." *New York Times,* November 17, 11.7.

Romo, Richard. 1983. *East Los Angeles: A History of a Barrio.* Austin: University of Texas Press.

Rosenberg, Bernard, and Norris Fliegel. 1965. *The Vanguard Artist.* New York: Amsterdam Books.

Ross, Steven J. 1991. "Struggles for the Screen." *American Historical Review* 96 (April): 334–35.

Rosten, Leo C. 1941. *Hollywood: The Movie Colony, the Movie Makers.* New York: Harcourt, Brace & Co.

Rothstein, Richard. 1999. "For Schools Chiefs, Impossible Juggle." *New York Times,* December 29, B9.

Rousmaniere, Kate. 1997. *City Teachers: Teaching and School Reform in Historical Perspective.* New York: Teachers College Press.

Ruenzel, David. 2002. "California's Ambitious Education Reform Agenda: Will It Energize Schools and Teachers? In *Crucial Issues in California Education 2000: Are the Reform Pieces Fitting Together?* edited by Elizabeth Burr, Gerald C. Hayward, Bruce Fuller, and Michael W. Kirst. Berkeley, Calif.: Policy Analysis for California Education.

Ruggles, Steven, Matthew Sobek, Catherine A. Fitch, Patricia Kelly Hall, and Chad Ronnander. 1997. *Integrated Used Microdata Series: Version 2.0*. 3 vols. Minneapolis: Historical Census Projects, University of Minnesota.

Rugoff, Ralph. 1989. "Liberal Arts." *Vogue* (August), 331.

Rule, James. 1988. *Theories of Civil Violence*. Berkeley: University of California Press.

Rumbaut, Ruben G. 1998. "Transformations: The Post-Immigrant Generation in an Age of Diversity." Paper presented at the annual meeting of the Eastern Sociological Society, Philadelphia, March 19–22.

Russell, Cheryl. 1996. *The Official Guide to Racial and Ethnic Diversity*. New York: New Strategist Publications.

Russell, John. 1997. "Buddy, Can You Spare $150 Million?" *New Times LA*, April 10.

Sabagh, Georges. 1993. "Los Angeles, a World of New Immigrants: An Image of Things to Come?" in *Migration Policies in Europe and the United States*, edited by G. Luciani. Dordrecht: Kluwer Academic Publishers.

Sabagh, Georges, and Mehdi Bozorgmehr. 1996. "Population Change: Immigration and Ethnic Transformation." In *Ethnic Los Angeles*, edited by R. Waldinger and M. Bozorgmehr. New York: Russell Sage.

Sack, Kevin. 2001. "Despite Report after Report, Unrest Endures in Cincinnati." *New York Times*, April 16.

Sagás, Ernesto. 2000. *Race and Politics in the Dominican Republic*. Gainesville: University Press of Florida.

Sahagun, Louis. 1999. "Zacarias Fights Legality of Naming Miller CEO." *Los Angeles Times*, October 15, A1.

Saito, Leland. 1998. *Race and Politics. Asian and Latino and White in Los Angeles Suburbs*. Urbana: University of Illinois Press.

Salvo, Joseph, and Peter Lobo. 1992. *The Newest New Yorkers: An Analysis of Immigration into New York City during the 1980s*. New York: Department of City Planning.

———. 1997. "Immigration and Changing Demographic Profile in New York." In *The City and the World: New York's Global Future*. New York: Council of Foreign Relations Press.

Sandler, Irving. 1978. *The New York School: The Painters and Sculptors of the Fifties*. New York: Harper & Row.

———. 1979. *The Triumph of American Painting: A History of Abstract Expressionism*. New York: Harper & Row.

———. 1988. *American Art of the 1960s*. New York: Harper & Row.

———. 1996. *Art in the Postmodern Era: From the Late 1960s to the Early 1990s*. New York: Harper Collins.

Sarris, Andrew. 1955. "The Trouble with Hitchcock." *Film Culture* 5–6 (winter): 31.

———. 1961. "The Director's Game." *Film Culture* 22–23 (summer): 68–81.

———. 1966. "Random Reflections—II." *Film Culture* 40 (spring): 22.

———. 1968. *The American Cinema.* New York: Dutton.
———. 1970. *Confessions of a Cultist.* New York: Simon & Schuster.
———. 1973. *The Primal Screen.* New York: Simon & Schuster.
———. 1978. "Avant-Garde Films Are More Boring than Ever." In *Politics and Cinema,* edited by Andrew Sarris. New York: Columbia University Press.
———. 1998. *You Ain't Heard Nothing Yet: The American Talking Film, History and Memory, 1927–1949.* New York: Oxford University Press.
Sassen, Saskia. [1994] 2001. *The Global City.* 2d ed. Princeton, N.J.: Princeton University Press.
———. 2000. *Cities in a World Economy.* 2d ed. Thousand Oaks, Calif.: Pine Forge.
Sassen, Saskia, and Frank Roost. 1999. "The City: Strategic Site for the Global Entertainment Industry." In *The Tourist City,* edited by Dennis R. Judd and Susan S. Fainstein. New Haven, Conn.: Yale University Press.
Sauerwein, Kristina. 2000. "Push Comes to Shove at Crowded L.A. School." *Los Angeles Times,* September 25, Valley ed., B:1.
Savitch, H. V. 1994. "Reorganization in Three Cities: Explaining the Disparity between Intended Actions and Unanticipated Consequences." *Urban Affairs Quarterly* 29 (June): 565–95.
Sayre, Wallace S., and Herbert Kaufman. 1960. *Governing New York City: Politics in the Metropolis.* New York: Russell Sage Foundation.
Scarborough, James. 1993. "Los Angeles Prophet and Loss." *Art Press* (October), E11.
Schemo, D. J. 1994. "Suburban Taxes Are Higher for Blacks, Analysis Shows." *New York Times,* August 17, A1.
Schjeldahl, Peter. 1981. "L.A. Demystified! Art and Life in the Eternal Present." *Journal: A Contemporary Art Magazine* (winter), 21–28.
Schlesinger, Arthur, Jr. 1949. *The Vital Center: The Politics of Freedom.* Boston: Houghton Mifflin.
———. 1953. "The Highbrow in American Politics." *Partisan Review* 19 (March–April): 157–65.
Schmalz, Jeffrey. 1989. "More than 200 Arrested in Miami in Second Night of Racial Disturbance." *New York Times,* January 18.
Schmidley, Dianne. 2001. *Profile of the Foreign-Born Population in the United States: 2000.* Washington, D.C.: U.S. Department of Commerce, Economics and Statistics Administration, Bureau of the Census. (http://www.census.gov/population/www/socdemo/foreign.html.)
Schmitt, Eric. 2001a. "Whites in Minority in Largest Cities, the Census Shows." *New York Times,* April 30, A1.
———. 2001b. "Most Cities in US Expanded Rapidly over Last Decade." *New York Times,* May 7.
Schmidt, Peter. 1995. "L.A. Breakup Plans Gather Head of Steam." *Education Week* (October 25).
Schneider, Robert. 2000. "The Postmodern City from an Early Modern Perspective." *American Historical Review* (December), 1668–75.
Schockman, H. Eric. 1996. "Is Los Angeles Governable? Revisiting the City

Charter." In *Rethinking Los Angeles,* edited by M. J. Dear, H. E. Schockman, and G. Hise. Beverly Hills, Calif.: Sage Publications.

Schrag, Peter. 1998. "Not a Good Choice on State Schools." *San Diego Union-Tribune,* October 22, B15.

———. 1999. *Paradise Lost: California's Experience, America's Future.* Berkeley: University of California Press.

Schulberg, Budd. 1983. *Writers in America: Four Seasons of Success.* New York: Stein & Day.

Schuman, Howard, C. Steeh, L. Bobo, and M. Krysan. 1997. *Racial Attitudes in America: Trends and Interpretations.* Rev. ed. Cambridge, Mass.: Harvard University Press.

Schwartz, Frederick A. O., and Eric Lane. 1998. "The Policy and Politics of Charter Making: The Story of New York City's 1989 Charter." *New York Law School Law Review* nos. 3–4: 729–1015.

Scorsese, Martin. 1998. "Guilty Pleasures." *Film Comment* 34 (May–June): 46–48.

Scott, Allen. 1996. "High Technology Industrial Development in the San Fernando Valley and Ventura County." In *The City: Los Angeles and Urban Theory at the End of the Twentieth Century,* edited by Allen Scott and Edward Soja. Berkeley: University of California Press.

———, ed. 2001. *Global City—Regions; Trends, Theory, Policy.* New York: Oxford University Press.

Scott, Allen, and Edward Soja, eds. 1996. *The City: Los Angeles and Urban Theory at the End of the Twentieth Century.* Berkeley: University of California Press.

Sears, David O. 1988. "Symbolic Racism." In *Eliminating Racism: Profiles in Controversy,* edited by P. A. Katz and D. A. Taylor. New York: Plenum Press.

———. 1994. "Urban Rioting in Los Angeles: A Comparison of 1965 with 1992." In *The Los Angeles Riots,* edited by Mark Baldassare. Boulder, Colo.: Westview Press.

Sears, David O., and Harris M. Allen, Jr. 1984. "The Trajectory of Local Desegregation Controversies and Whites' Opposition to Busing." In *Groups in Contact: The Psychology of Desegregation,* edited by N. Miller and M. B. Brewer. New York: Academic Press.

Sears, David O., and J. Citrin. 1985. *Tax Revolt: Something for Nothing in California.* Enlarged ed. Cambridge, Mass.: Harvard University Press.

Sears, David O., J. Citrin, S. V. Cheleden, and C. van Laar. 1999. "Cultural Diversity and Multicultural Politics: Is Ethnic Balkanization Psychologically Inevitable? In *Cultural Divides: Understanding and Overcoming Group Conflict,* edited by D. A. Prentice and D. T. Miller. New York: Russell Sage Foundation.

Sears, David O., P. J. Henry, Ming-Ying Fu, and Kerra Bui. 2001. "The Origins and Persistence of Ethnic Identity among Contemporary American University Students." Paper presented at the annual meeting of the International Society for Political Psychology, Cuernavaca, July 16.

Sears, David O., and D. R. Kinder. 1970. "The Good Life, 'White Racism,' and the Los Angeles Voter." Paper presented at the fiftieth annual meeting of the Western Psychological Association, Los Angeles, April 15.

———. 1971. "Racial Tensions and Voting in Los Angeles." In *Los Angeles: Viability and Prospects for Metropolitan Leadership,* edited by W. Z. Hirsch. New York: Praeger Publishers.

Sears, David O., and John McConahay. 1973. *The Politics of Violence: The New Urban Blacks and the Watts Riot.* Boston: Houghton Mifflin.

Sears, David O., and C. van Laar. 1999. "Black Exceptionalism in a Culturally Diverse Society." Psychology Department, University of California, Los Angeles.

Sears, David O., C. van Laar, M. Carillo, and R. Kosterman. 1997. "Is It Really Racism? The Origins of White Americans' Opposition to Race-Targeted Policies." *Public Opinion Quarterly* 61:16–53.

Sennett, Richard. 1990. *The Conscience of the Eye.* New York: Alfred Knopf.

Service Employees International Union. 1998. "Mayor's Authority to Fire General Managers: Los Angeles City 'High Propensity' Voters." December. Report of poll conducted by Fairbank, Maslin, Maullin, and Associates, Santa Monica, Calif.

Setlow, Carolyn E. and Renae Cohen. 1993. *1992 New York City Intergroup Relations Survey.* New York: American Jewish Committee.

Sexton, J. 1997. "Welfare Neighborhood: A Pastor's Dilemma." *New York Times,* August 24, 27.

Shefter, Martin. 1983. "Regional Receptivity to Reform." *Political Science Quarterly* 98 (fall): 459–84.

Shields, Patrick M., Camille E. Esch, Daniel C. Humphrey, Viki M. Young, Margaret Gaston, and Harvey Hunt. 1999. *The Status of the Teaching Profession: Research Findings and Policy Recommendations, a Report to the Teaching and California's Future Task Force.* Santa Cruz, Calif.: Center for Future Teaching and Learning.

Shipps, Dorothy. 1997. "The Invisible Hand: Big Business and Chicago School Reform. *Teachers College Record* 99:73–116.

Sidanius, J., and F. Pratto. 1999. *Social Dominance: An Intergroup Theory of Social Hierarchy and Oppression.* New York: Cambridge University Press.

Siegel, Fred. 1997. *The Future Once Happened Here: New York, D.C., L.A., and the Fate of America's Big Cities.* San Francisco: Encounter Books.

Siegal, Nina. 2000. "Landmark Status for Harlem Buildings." *New York Times,* June 15.

Silverman, E. B. 1999. *NYPD Battles Crime: Innovative Strategies in Policing.* Boston: Northeastern University Press.

Simon, Rita J., and James P. Lynch. 1999. "A Comparative Assessment of Public Opinion toward Immigrants and Immigration Policies." *International Migration Review* 33:455–67.

Simpson, Charles R. 1981. *SoHo: The Artist in the City.* Chicago: University of Chicago Press.

Singerman, Howard. 2000. *Art Subjects: Making Artists in the American University.* Los Angeles: UCLA Press.

Singerman, Howard, and Christopher Knight. 1987. "A Conversation between

Two Los Angeles Art Critics." In *LA, Hot and Cool, the Eighties: MIT List Visual Arts Center, December 19 1987–February 7, 1988,* edited by Dana Friis-Hansen et al. Cambridge, Mass.: The Center.

Singleton, Gregory. 1979. *Religion in the City of Angels: American Protestant Culture and Urbanization, Los Angeles, 1850–1930*. Ann Arbor, Mich.: UMI Research Press.

Skelton, George. 1999. "Paying the Price for Embarrassing Wrong Candidate." *Los Angeles Times,* January 28, A3.

Skocpol, T. 1992. *Protecting Soldiers and Mothers: The Political Origins of Social Policy in the United States.* Cambridge, Mass.: Belknap Press, Harvard University Press.

Slatin, Peter. 1994. "Disney to the Rescue in Times Square." *New York Times,* April 16.

Sleeper, J. 1990. *The Closest of Strangers: Liberalism and the Politics of Race in New York.* New York: W. W. Norton.

Sleeper, J. 1993. "The End of the Rainbow? The Changing Politics of America's Cities." *New Republic* (November 20).

Smith, Anna Deavers. 1993. *Fires in the Mirror: Crown Heights, Brooklyn and Other Identities.* New York: Anchor Books.

Smith, Dan. 1999. "Changes Urged in Running of Schools." *Sacramento Bee,* May 12, A6.

Smith, Gavin. 1995. "Momentum and Design: Kathryn Bigelow Interviewed by Gavin Smith." *Film Comment* 31 (September–October): 46–50, 55–60.

Smith, Neil. 1996. *The New Urban Frontier: Gentrification and the Revanchist City.* New York: Routledge.

———. 1998. "Giuliani Time: The Revanchist 1990s." *Social Text* 16 (4): 1–20.

Smith, Robert. 2001. "Mexicans: Social, Educational, Economic, and Political Problems and Prospects in New York." In *New Immigrants in New York,* edited by Nancy Foner, 275–300. New York: Columbia University Press.

Sniderman, P. M., and Phillip E. Tetlock. 1986. "Reflections on American Racism." *Journal of Social Issues* 42:173–87.

Soja, Edward. 1989. *Postmodern Geographies.* New York: Verso.

———. 1996. "Los Angeles, 1965–1992: From Crises Generated Restructuring to Restructuring-Generated Crisis." In *The City: Los Angeles and Urban Theory at the End of the Twentieth Century,* edited by A. Scott and E. Soja. Berkeley: University of California Press.

———. 2000 Postmetropolis: Critical Studies of Cities and Regions. Oxford: Blackwell.

Sommer, H. 1998. "Welfare Reform." In *Atlas of Southern California.* Vol. 2, edited by M. J. Dear and H. Sommer. Los Angeles: Southern California Study Center, University of Southern California.

Sonenshein, Raphael J. 1993. *Politics in Black and White: Race and Power in Los Angeles.* Princeton, N.J.: Princeton University Press.

Sonenshein, Raphael J., H. Eric Schockman, and Richard DeLeon. 1995. "Urban Conservatism in an Age of Diversity: A Comparison of the Mayoralties of Rudolph Giuliani, Richard Riordan, and Frank Jordan." Paper presented at the annual meeting of the Western Political Science Association, Pasadena, Calif., March.

Sonenshein, Raphael J., and N. Valentino. 1995. "Minority Politics at the Crossroads: Voting Patterns in the 1993 Los Angeles Mayoral Election." Paper presented at the annual meeting of the Western Political Science Association, Pasadena, Calif., March.

Sonstelie, Jon, Eric Brunner, and Kenneth Ardon. 2000. *For Better of for Worse? School Finance Reform in California*. San Francisco: Public Policy Institute of California.

Sorkin, Michael. 2002. "The Center Cannot Hold." In *After the World Trade Center: Rethinking New York City,* edited by Michael Sorkin and Sharon Zukin. New York: Routledge.

Sorkin Studio, Michael. 2002. "Rebuilding through Disaggregation." Paper presented at the Evolve New York Conference, Urban Planning Program, Columbia University, New York, May 9.

Sorkin, Michael, and Sharon Zukin, eds. 2002. *After the World Trade Center: Rethinking New York City*. New York: Routledge.

South Asian American Leaders of Tomorrow (SAALT). 2001. "American Backlash: Terrorists Bring War Home in More Ways than One." Special Report of South Asian American Leaders of Tomorrow (SAALT), Washington, D.C.

Spilerman, Seymour. 1971. "The Causes of Racial Disturbances: A Comparison of Alternative Explanations." *American Sociological Review* 35:627–49.

———. 1976. "Structural Characteristics of Cities and the Severity of Racial Disorders." *American Sociological Review* 41:771–93.

Spitzer, E. 1999. "The New York City Police Department's 'Stop and Frisk' Practices." Attorney General of the State of New York, Civil Rights Bureau, New York.

Stein, John. 1978. *The Lightless Night of Looting: Lessons from the 1977 New York City Blackout*. New York: Defense Civil Preparedness Agency.

Steinberg, Jacques. 1999. "Most School Boards Oversee Their Own Projects." *New York Times,* July 27, B6.

Sterling, Philip. 1940. "A Channel for Democratic Thought." *Films* 1 (spring): 7.

Stern, Robert, Thomas Mellins, and David Fisman. [1960] 1997. *Architecture and Urbanism between the Second World War and the Bicentennial*. 2d ed. New York: Monacelli Press.

Sterngold, James. 2002. "Move to Secede Splits Latinos in the Valley." *New York Times,* June 10, A14.

Swados, Harvey. 1953. "Popular Taste and 'The Caine Mutiny'." *Partisan Review* 19 (March–April): 248–56.

Swertlow, Frank. 1999. "Out of the Spotlight." In *The Book of Lists*. Los Angeles: Los Angeles Business Journal.

Szántó, András. 1996. "Gallery: Transformations in the New York Art World in the 1980s." Ph.D. diss., Columbia University.

Tajfel, Henri, and John C. Turner. 1986. "The Social Identity Theory of Intergroup Behavior." In *Psychology of Intergroup Relations,* edited by Stephen Worchel and William G. Austin. 2d ed. Chicago: Nelson-Hall.

Tang, Angelica O., and Madeleine Tress. 1999. "Immigrants and the Economic

Revitalization of New York City." City of New York Mayor's Office of Immigrant Affairs and Language Services, New York.

Taylor, Greg. 1999. *Artists in the Audience.* Princeton, N.J.: Princeton University Press.

Taylor, Tess. 2002. "Multicentered Cities." *Metropolis* (August–September).

Tedin, K. L. 1994. "Self-Interest, Symbolic Values, and the Financial Equalization of the Public Schools." *Journal of Politics* 56 (3): 628–49.

Therbörn, Goran, ed. 2000. "Globalizations Are Plural." *International Sociology* 15, no. 2 (June): 149–408.

Thompson, David, and Ian Christie, eds. 1996. *Scorsese on Scorsese.* London: Faber & Faber.

Thrasher, F. M. 1963. *The Gang: A Study of 1,313 Gangs in Chicago.* Chicago: University of Chicago Press.

Tierney, Kathleen J. 1994. "Property Damage and Violence: A Collective Behavior Analysis." In *The Los Angeles Riots: Lessons for the Urban Future,* edited by Mark Baldassare. Boulder, Colo.: Westview Press.

Tilly, Charles. 1979. "Collective Violence in European Perspective." In *Violence in America,* edited by Graham Gurr. Beverly Hills, Calif.: Sage Publications.

Toeplitz, Jerzy. 1963. "Film Scholarship: Present and Prospective." *Film Quarterly,* vol. 16, no. 3 (spring).

Tolbert, Charles, Patrick M. Horan, and E. M. Beck. 1980. "The Structure of Economic Segmentation: A Dual Economy Approach." *American Journal of Sociology* 85:1095–1116.

Tomasky, Michael. 2002. "The City Politic: Winner Take All." *New York Magazine,* June 17.

Tomkins, Calvin. 1980. *Off the Wall: Robert Rauschenberg and the Art World of Our Time.* New York: Penguin.

———. 1988. *From Post to Neo: The Art World of the 1980s.* New York: Penguin.

Torres-Saillant, Silvio. 1998. "The Tribulations of Blackness: Stages in Dominican Racial Identity." *Latin American Perspectives* 25, no. 3 (May): 126–46.

Tseng, Yenfeng. 1994. "Suburban Ethnic Economy: Chinese Business Communities in Los Angeles." Ph.D. diss., University of California, Los Angeles.

Tyack, David. 1990. *The One Best System: A History of American Urban Education.* Cambridge, Mass.: Harvard University Press.

Tyack, David, and Elisabeth Hansot. 1990. *Managers of Virtue: Public School Leadership in America, 1820–1980.* New York: Basic Books.

Tyler, Tom R., R. J. Boekmann, H. J. Smith, and Y. J. Huo. 1997. *Social Justice in a Diverse Society.* Boulder, Colo.: Westview Press.

U.S. Bureau of the Census. 1960. *Census of Population and Housing: Characteristics for Census Tracts and Block Numbering Areas.* Washington, D.C.: Government Printing Office.

———. 1970. *Census of Population and Housing: Characteristics for Census Tracts and Block Numbering Areas.* Washington, D.C.: Government Printing Office.

———. 1977–97. *County Business Patterns.* Washington, D.C.: Government Printing Office.

———. 1980a. *Census of Population and Housing: Characteristics for Census*

Tracts and Block Numbering Areas. Washington, D.C.: Government Printing Office.

———. 1980b. "Census of Population and Housing, 1980." CD-ROM Summary Tape File 1A. Department of Commerce, Economics and Statistics Administration, Bureau of the Census, Washington, D.C.

———. 1982. *1980 Census of Population.* Vol. 1, *Characteristics of the Population.* Chap. B, *General Population Characteristics.* Pt. 6, *California.* Washington, D.C.: Department of Commerce, Bureau of the Census.

———. 1990a. *Census of Population and Housing: Characteristics for Census Tracts and Block Numbering Areas.* Washington, D.C.: Government Printing Office.

———. 1990b. "Census of Population and Housing, 1990." CD-ROM Summary Tape File 1A. Department of Commerce, Economics and Statistics Administration, Bureau of the Census, Washington, D.C.

———. 1992. *1990 Census of Population.* Vol. 1, *Characteristics of the Population.* Chap. B, *General Population Characteristics.* Pt. 34, *New York.* Washington, D.C.: Department of Commerce, Bureau of the Census.

———. 1993. *Census of the Population and Housing, 1990: Public Use Microdata Sample (PUMS), 5-Percent Sample.* Washington, D.C.: Government Printing Office.

———. 1994. *Statistical Abstract of the United States, 1994.* 114th ed. Washington, D.C.: Government Printing Office.

———. 1996. "Voting Registration in the Election of November 1994 by States." (http://www.census.gov/population/www/socdemo/voting.html.)

———. 1997. "CPS Methodology and Documentation." July. (http://www.bls.census.gov/cps/racethn/1995/sspecs2.htm.)

———. 1998. "Voting and Registration in the Election of November 1996 by States." (http://www.census.gov/population/www/socdemo/voting.html.)

———. 1999. "Explanation of Race and Hispanic Origin Categories." September 15. (http://www.census.gov/population/estimates/rho.txt.)

———. 2000a. "State and County Quick Facts." (http://quickfacts.census.gov/qfd/.)

———. 2000b. "U.S. Census 2000: Summary Files 1 and 2." (http://www.census.gov/population/www/censusdata/c2kproducts.html.)

———. 2000c. "2000 Summary File 1." (http://factfinder.census.gov/servlet/BasicFactsServlet.)

———. 2001a. *Current Population Surveys, March 1961–2001.* Santa Monica, Calif.: Unicon Research Corporation [producer and distributor of CPS Utlities].

———. 2001b. "Overview of Race and Hispanic Origin." (http://www.census.gov/prod/2001pubs/c2kbr01-1.pdf.)

———. Various years a. *Current Population Survey.* Department of Commerce, Bureau of the Census, Washington, D.C. (http://www.nber.org/cps.)

———. Various years b. *Current Population Survey, Annual Demographic File.* Department of Commerce, Bureau of the Census, Washington, D.C. (http://www.nber.org/cps.)

U.S. Bureau of Labor Statistics. Various years. *Nonagricultural Wage and Salary Employment from the Current Employment Statistics Program*. Department of Labor, Bureau of Labor Statistics, Washington, D.C. (http://stats.bls.gov/sae/home.htm.)

U.S. Department of Justice, Federal Bureau of Investigation. 2001 (and other annual reports). *Crime in the United States*. Uniform Crime Reports. Washington, D.C.: Government Printing Office.

U.S. House of Representatives. 1996. *Green Book*. Washington, D.C.: Committee on Ways and Means,

U.S. Immigration and Naturalization Service. 2001. *2000 Statistical Yearbook of the Immigration and Naturalization Service*. Washington, D.C.: Government Printing Office.

———. 1997. *1996 Statistical Yearbook of the Immigration and Naturalization Services*. Washington, D.C.: Government Printing Office.

———. 1999. *Annual Report: Legal Immigration, Fiscal Year 1998*. Washington, D.C.: Government Printing Office.

———. 2000a. "Table 3: Immigrants Admitted by State and Metropolitan Area of Intended Residence." (http://www.ins.gov/graphics/aboutins/statistics/annual/fy96/997.htm.)

———. 2000b. "Table 10: Immigrants Aged 16 to 64 Admitted by Occupation: Fiscal Years 1994–96." (http://www.ins.gov/graphics/aboutins/statistics/annual/fy96/1014.htm.)

U.S. Office of War Information, Bureau of Motion Pictures. 1942. *Government Information Manual for the Motion Picture Industry*. Washington, D.C.: Office of War Information.

Urban Land Institute. 2000. Urban Land Institute Metropolitan Area Market Profiles: North America. Washington, D.C.: Urban Land Institute.

Van de Kamp, John K. 1987. *Homicide in California*. Sacramento, Calif.: Office of the Attorney General, Bureau of Criminal Statistics and Special Services.

Vanderleeuw, J. 1990. "A City in Transition: The Impact of Changing Racial Composition on Voting Behavior." *Social Science Quarterly* 71:326–38.

Verge, Arthur. 1993. *Paradise Transformed: Los Angeles during the Second World War*. Dubuque, Iowa: Kendall Hunt.

Viteritti, Joseph P. 1989. "The Tradition of Municipal Reform: Charter Revision in Historical Context." In *Restructuring New York City Government: The Reemergence of Municipal Reform*, edited by Frank Mauro and Gerald Benjamin. New York: Academy of Political Science.

Voorsanger, Catherine, and John K. Howat. 2000. *Art and the Empire City*. New York: Metropolitan Museum of Art; New Haven, Conn.: Yale University Press.

Voter News Service. 1998. *Voter News Service New York City Mayoral Election Exit Poll, November 1997*. Computer file. New York City: Voter News Service; distributed by Inter-University Consortium for Political and Social Research, Ann Arbor, Mich.

Voter Research and Surveys. 1993. *Voter Research and Surveys New York City Mayoral Election Exit Poll, 1993*. Computer file. New York City: Voter Research and Surveys; distributed by Inter-University Consortium for Political and Social Research, Ann Arbor, Mich.

WABC-TV/*New York Daily News*. 1991. *WABC-TV/New York Daily News New York City Mayoral Election Polls, January–November 1989, no. 9*. Computer file. Radnor, Pa.: Chilton Research Services; distributed by Inter-University Consortium for Political and Social Research, Ann Arbor, Mich.

Waldinger, Roger. 1996a. "Ethnicity and Opportunity in the Plural City." In *Ethnic Los Angeles,* edited by R. Waldinger and M. Bozorgmehr. New York: Russell Sage Foundation.

———. 1996b. "From Ellis Island to LAX: Immigrant Prospects in the American City." *International Migration Review* 30:1078–86.

———. 1996c. *Still the Promised City?* Cambridge, Mass.: Harvard University Press.

———. 2001. "Strangers at the Gates." In *Strangers at the Gates: New Immigrants in Urban America,* edited by Roger Waldinger. Berkeley: University of California Press.

Waldinger, Roger, and Mehdi Bozorgmehr, eds. 1996a. *Ethnic Los Angeles.* New York: Russell Sage Foundation.

———. 1996b. "The Making of a Multicultural Metropolis." In *Ethnic Los Angeles,* edited by Roger Waldinger and Mehdi Bozorgmehr. New York: Russell Sage Foundation.

Waldinger, Roger, and Michael Lichter. 2003. *How the Other Half Works: Immigration and the Social Organization of Labor.* Berkeley and Los Angeles: University of California Press.

Waldinger, Roger, and Yenfen Tseng. 1992. "Divergent Diasporas: The Chinese Communities of New York and Los Angeles Compared." *Revue Europeenne des Migrations Internationales* 8 (3): 91–115.

Wall Street Journal. 2001. "No Escape: Could Helicopters Have Saved People from Trade Center? Police Choppers Hovered, But Roof Was Locked: Rescuers Feuded in Past." *Wall Street Journal,* October 23, A1.

War Activities Committee 1945 Report. 1945. *Movies at War: Report of the WAC of the Motion Picture Industry.* Washington, D.C.: War Activities Committee.

Warshow, Robert. [1962] 1975. *The Immediate Experience: Movies, Comics, Theatre and Other Aspects of Popular Culture.* New York: Atheneum.

Waters, Mary. 1999. *Black Identities: West Indian Immigrant Dreams and American Realities.* Cambridge, Mass.: Harvard University Press.

WCBS-TV News/*New York Times*. 1994. *WCBS-TV News/The New York Times New York City Poll, May 1993*. Computer file. New York: WCBS-TV News; distributed by Inter-University Consortium for Political and Social Research, Ann Arbor, Mich.

Weisman, Jonathan. 1991. "Los Angeles Reform Coalition Faces Early Roadblocks." *Education Week* (May 15).

Welch, Susan, and Timothy Bledsoe. 1988. *Urban Reform and Its Consequences.* Chicago: University of Chicago Press.

Weschler, Lawrence. 1982. *Seeing Is Forgetting the Name of the Thing One Sees.* Los Angeles: University of California Press.

White, Kerry A. 1998. "Los Angeles Mayor Seeks to Unseat Four on Board." *Education Week* (September 30).

Whyte, William H. 1956. *The Organization Man.* New York: Simon & Schuster.

———. 1988. *City: Rediscovering the Center.* New York: Doubleday.

Wiley, Norbert. 1986. "Early American Sociology and the Polish Peasant" *Sociological Theory* 4 (spring): 20–40.

Willensky, Elliott, and Norval White. 2000. *A.I.A. Guide to New York City.* New York: Three Rivers Press.

Williams, Richard. 1990. *Hierarchical Structures and Social Value: The Creation of Black and Irish Identities in the United States.* Cambridge: Cambridge University Press.

Willman, Martha L. 1999. "Study Cites Schoolroom Toxin Risks: Health Report Says Students in Prefabricated Buildings May Have Increased Exposure to Cancer-Causing Agents." *Los Angeles Times,* May 28, B:1.

Wilson, J. Q., and G. L. Kelling. 1982. "Broken Windows: The Police and Neighborhood Safety." *Atlantic* 249 (March 3): 29–38.

Winnick, Louis. 1990. *New People in Old Neighborhoods: The Role of New Immigrants in Rejuvenating New York's Communities.* New York: Russell Sage Foundation.

Wolch, Jennifer. 1990. *The Shadow State: Government and Voluntary Sector in Transition.* New York: Foundation Center.

Wolch, Jennifer, and Michael Dear. 1993. *Malign Neglect: Homelessness in an American City.* San Francisco: Jossey-Bass.

Wolch, Jennifer, and G. DeVerteuil. 2001. "New Landscapes of Urban Poverty Management." In *TimeSpace,* edited by N. Thrift and J. May, 149–68. London: Routledge.

Wolch, Jennifer, and H. Sommer. 1997. *Los Angeles in an Era of Welfare Reform: Implications for Poor People and Community Well-Being.* Los Angeles: Southern California Inter-University Consortium of Homelessness and Poverty.

Wolfinger, R. E. and F. I. Greenstein. 1968. "The Repeal of Fair Housing in California: An Analysis of Referendum Voting." *American Political Science Review* 62:753–69.

Wood, Robert, with Vladimir V. Almendinger. 1961. *1400 Governments: The Political Economy of the New York Region.* Cambridge, Mass.: Harvard University Press.

Woods, Joseph. 1973. "The Progressives and the Police: Urban Reform and the Professionalization of the Los Angeles Police." Ph.D. diss., University of California, Los Angeles.

Working Group on New York City's Low-Wage Labor Market. 2000. *Building a Ladder to Jobs and Higher Wages.* New York: Community Service Society of New York.

Wortz, Melinda. 1980. "Is Los Angeles Ready for Two Museums of Modern Art?" *ARTnews* (January), 114–15.

———. 1983. "The L.A./N.Y. Shift." *ARTnews* (January), 72–75.

Wright, Nathan. 1968. *Ready to Riot.* New York: Holt, Rinehart & Winston.

Wrigley, Julia. 1982. *Class Politics and Public Schools: Chicago, 1900–1950.* New Brunswick, N.J.: Rutgers University Press.

Wyatt, Edward. 2002. "Stock Exchange Abandons Plans for a New Headquarters Building across the Street," *New York Times,* August 2, B3.

Young, Beth Aronstamm. 1999. "Characteristics of the 100 Largest Public Elementary and Secondary School Districts in the United States: 1997–1998."

Education Statistics Quarterly: Elementary and Secondary Education. NCES no. 1999318. U.S. Department of Education, National Center for Education Statistics, Washington, D.C. (http://nces.ed.gov/pubs2001/quarterly/fall/elem_100largest.html.)

———. 2002. "Characteristics of the 100 Largest Public Elementary and Secondary School Districts in the United States: 2000–01." NCES 2002-351. U.S. Department of Education, National Center for Education Statistics, Washington, D.C. (http://nces.ed.gov/pubs2002/100_largest/.)

Young, Colin. 1963. "University Film Teaching in the United States." *Film Quarterly,* vol. 16, no. 3 (spring).

Zelevansky, Lynn. 2000. "A Place in the Sun: The Los Angeles Art World and the New Global Context." In *Reading California: Art, Image and Identity, 1900–2000,* edited by S. Barron, S. Bernstein, and I. S. Fort. Berkeley: University of California Press.

Zhou, Min. 1992. *Chinatown: The Socioeconomic Potential of an Urban Enclave.* Philadelphia: Temple University Press.

———. 1998. " 'Parachute Kids' in Southern California: The Educational Experience of Chinese Children in Transnational Families." *Educational Policy* 12 (6): 682–704.

Zhou, Min, and John R. Logan. 1991. "In and Out of Chinatown: Residential Mobility and Segregation of New York City's Chinese." *Social Forces* 70 (2): 387–407.

Zhou, Yu. 1996. "Ethnic Networks as Transactional Networks: Chinese Networks in the Producer Service Sectors of Los Angeles." Ph.D. diss., University of Minnesota.

———. 1998. "How Do Places Matter? A Comparative Study of Chinese Ethnic Economies in Los Angeles and New York City." *Urban Geography* 19 (6): 531–52.

Zimring, F. E., and J. Fagan. 2000. "The Search for Causes in an Era of Crime Declines: Some Lessons From the Study of New York City Homicides." *Crime and Delinquency* 46 (4): 446–56.

Zirkzee, Jacqueline. 1995. "Getty Megalomania." *Tableau* (Amsterdam) (December), 62–65.

Zukin, Sharon. 1982. *Loft Living: Culture and Capital in Urban Change.* New Brunswick, N.J.: Rutgers University Press.

———. 1995. *The Culture of Cities.* Oxford: Blackwell.

———. 1996. "Space and Symbols in an Age of Decline." In *Re-Presenting the City: Ethnicity, Capital, and Culture in the Twenty-first Century Metropolis,* edited by Anthony King. New York: New York University Press.

CONTRIBUTORS

Andrew A. Beveridge is professor of sociology at Queens College and the Graduate Center of the City University of New York.

Mehdi Bozorgmehr is associate professor of sociology at City College and the Graduate Center and founding codirector of the Middle East and Middle Eastern American Center at the Graduate Center of the City University of New York.

Geoffrey DeVerteuil is on the faculty of the University of Manitoba, Department of Geography.

Susan S. Fainstein is professor of urban planning at the Graduate School of Architecture, Planning and Preservation, Columbia University.

Robert Gedeon is a graduate student in the Department of Sociology, University of California, Los Angeles.

David F. Gladstone is visiting assistant professor at the College of Urban and Public Affairs, University of New Orleans.

Saverio Giovacchini is associate professor in the history department at the University of Maryland, College Park.

David Halle is director of the University of California, Los Angeles, LeRoy Neiman Center for the Study of American Society and Culture, and professor of sociology at UCLA.

Jack Katz is professor of sociology at University of California, Los Angeles.

Karen Kaufman is assistant professor in the department of government and politics at the University of Maryland.

Rebecca Kim is assistant professor in the Department of Sociology at the University of California, Los Angeles.

Mark Levitan is senior policy analyst, Community Service Society of New York.

Kevin Rafter is a doctoral candidate in the Department of Environmental Psychology at the Graduate Center of the City University of New York.

Georges Sabagh, who passed away in November 2002, was emeritus professor of sociology and former director of the Center for Near Eastern Studies at the University of California, Los Angeles.

David O. Sears is professor of psychology and political science and director of the Institute for Social Science Research at the University of California, Los Angeles.

Heidi Sommer is a doctoral student at the Goldman School of Public Policy at the University of California, Berkeley.

Raphael J. Sonenshein is professor of political science at California State University, Fullerton.

András Szántó is deputy director of the National Arts Journalism Program at Columbia University.

Lois M. Takahashi is associate professor in the Department of Urban Planning at the University of California, Los Angeles.

Susan Weber is an honors graduate of State University of New York at Old Westbury and an M.A. graduate from Queens College of the City University of New York in applied social research.

Jennifer Wolch is professor in the Department of Geography, University of Southern California.

Julia Wrigley is professor of sociology at the Graduate Center of the City University of New York.

Min Zhou is professor of sociology and Asian American studies at the University of California, Los Angeles.

INDEX

Locators in boldface refer to pages with figures or tables.